A History of Indian Buddhism

Asian Studies at Hawaii, No. 36

A History of Indian Buddhism

From Śākyamuni to Early Mahāyāna

Hirakawa Akira
Translated and Edited by Paul Groner

ASIAN STUDIES AT HAWAII
UNIVERSITY OF HAWAII
UNIVERSITY OF HAWAII PRESS

Printed in the United States of America
97 98 99 00 01 02 8 7 6 5 4

Library of Congress Cataloging-in-Publication Data
Hirakawa, Akira, 1915–
[Indo Bukkyō shi. English]
A history of Indian Buddhism : from Śākyamuni to Early Mahāyāna /
Hirakawa Akira ; translated and edited by Paul Groner.
p. cm. — (Asian studies at Hawaii ; no. 36)
Translation of: Indo Bukkyō shi.
Includes bibliographical references.
ISBN 0–8248–1203–4
1. Buddhism—India—History. I. Groner, Paul. II. Title.
III. Series.
DS.A2A82 no. 36
[BQ336]
950 s—dc20
[294.3'0954] 89–20647
CIP

University of Hawai'i Press books are printed
on acid-free paper and meet the guidelines
for permanence and durability of the Council
on Library Resources

CONTENTS

PART THREE: EARLY MAHĀYĀNA BUDDHISM

TRANSLATOR'S PREFACE

THE JAPANESE VERSION of this book, *Indo Bukkyōshi,* volume 1, was published by Shunjūsha of Tokyo in 1974; volume 2, not included here, was published in 1979. When Hirakawa began work on it, he intended to write a handbook for students interested in the development of Buddhism across Asia that would serve as a useful guide to the basic issues in Buddhist doctrine, history, and bibliography. Although the project soon became much longer and had a narrower focus than he had originally planned, it benefited in at least two ways from Hirakawa's original intention. First, it is an exceptionally comprehensive discussion of Indian Buddhism, treating its history, doctrine, and bibliography with an admirable degree of completeness. Most of the significant topics in Indian Buddhism are discussed in some detail. Second, it is a very clearly written text. Because Hirakawa wrote it with students as the intended audience, he composed it in a style that could be readily understood by students and informed general readers.

The present volume is a translation of the first of Hirakawa's two-volume history. It covers the period from Śākyamuni Buddha to Early Mahāyāna just before Nāgārjuna and includes the periods on which Hirakawa did most of his own earlier research. From 1960 to 1968, he published three important studies on Buddhist institutions: *Ritsuzō no kenkyū* (A study of the *Vinaya-piṭaka*), *Genshi Bukkyō no kenkyū* (A study of Early Buddhism), and *Shoki Daijō Bukkyō no kenkyū* (Studies in Early Mahāyāna Buddhism). These studies, all coming out of his interest in the *vinaya,* demonstrated his mastery of Indian Buddhist institutional history. This research was particularly important in his formulation of a new theory of the rise of Mahāyāna. By focusing on the need to identify an institutional base from which Mahāyāna arose, Hirakawa argued that *stūpa* worship and the formulation of Mahāyāna sets of precepts provided important evidence for the development of Mahāyāna Buddhism.

Besides these book-length studies, Hirakawa has written over 240 articles on various aspects of Buddhism. These cover a wide variety of issues, such as the usage of fundamental terms or the roles particular figures played in the Indian Buddhist tradition. The ideas advanced in many of these articles and the background research that went into them have been incorporated into this history.

Hirakawa has also been aware of the need for improved reference tools for scholars. He is currently supervising the compilation of a Chinese-Sanskrit Buddhist dictionary, a tool that will assist scholars in making better use of Chinese translations of Indian texts. He has also been an advocate of the use of computers in Buddhist studies. One of the earliest results of this interest was the publication of a detailed and computerized index of the articles in *Indogaku Bukkyōgaku kenkyū* (Journal of Indian and Buddhist Studies), one of the leading publications on Buddhism in Japan. His interest in reference tools also led to his supervision of a concordance of the Sanskrit, Tibetan, and Chinese versions of Vasubandhu's *Abhidharmakośa (Kusharon sakuin)*. Because the *Abhidharmakośa* is one of the most systematic expositions of Buddhist doctrine ever composed, it has been an influential text across Asia, even among those who did not accept many of its positions. The doctrinal exposition of *abhidharma* thought in Hirakawa's *History of Indian Buddhism* is based primarily on the *Abhidharmakośa*.

This volume thus incorporates Hirakawa's mature views on subjects that he has studied in depth for several decades. It is published here as an independent work, giving an overall view of the first half of Indian Buddhist history. The second volume of Hirakawa's history covers Indian Buddhism from Nāgārjuna through Tantric Buddhism and the decline of Buddhism in India.

As Hirakawa notes in his preface, the understanding of the history of Indian Buddhism is an ongoing process that must be continually elaborated and revised as our knowledge of the subject expands. He thus sees his own work as being improved upon by subsequent histories of Indian Buddhism by both Japanese and Western scholars. Hirakawa's historical interpretation is representative of Indian Buddhism as it is viewed by many, but certainly not all, Japanese scholars. It also differs from the perspective of many Western authors who have written histories of Indian Buddhism. Three ways in which Hirakawa's treatment differs from most of the histories of Indian Buddhism written in English are elaborated below: (1) use of primary sources, (2) secondary scholarship consulted, and (3) comprehensive coverage.

First, English-language surveys of Indian Buddhism have relied predominantly upon Sanskrit and Pāli primary source materials, often ignoring important primary source materials available in Chinese and Tibetan translation. In contrast, Hirakawa has utilized materials from Chinese and Tibetan as well as Sanskrit and Pāli. For example, English-language surveys have usually depended upon Pāli materials for their presentation of Early Buddhism, mainly because these sources have been extensively studied by British, Indian, and Sri Lankan scholars as a result of Britain's historical ties with South Asia. For similar reasons, *abhidharma* studies in English have usually concentrated on the Theravāda tradition. Hirakawa has been able to use Chinese translations of early Buddhist texts such as the *āgamas* and *abhidharma* texts to better place the Pāli material in the context of Indian Buddhism as a whole. For example, in the field of *abhidharma,* Hirakawa places his emphasis on the development of the Sarvāstivāda tradition rather than on Theravāda, primarily because the Sarvāstivāda material helps elucidate later Mahāyāna developments. However, far from ignoring the Pāli material, Hirakawa describes its place in the development of Indian Buddhism and uses it to provide a contrast with the Sarvāstivāda interpretations. In addition, Hirakawa has used the scant source material concerning the Mahāsaṅghika and other schools to elucidate the role that these traditions played in the evolution of Indian Buddhism.

Many English-language surveys of Indian Buddhism rely primarily on undated Sanskrit materials for much of their presentation of Mahāyāna; Hirakawa has used these sources, but also has employed dated Chinese translations of Mahāyāna sources as well as inscriptions from archeological sites to present a much fuller description of the origin, development, and social setting of Mahāyāna. His treatment of later Mahāyāna developments in the second volume has benefited from the increasing use of Tibetan materials by Japanese scholars. The importance of Chinese and Tibetan materials is reflected in the chapters of Hirakawa's work that discuss sources for the study of each period of Buddhism.

Second, Hirakawa has utilized secondary studies that have been ignored by many scholars who wrote in English. Modern Japanese scholars have published more on Buddhism than the rest of the world combined. A bibliography of journal articles on Buddhism published by Japanese authors between 1970 and 1983 includes almost four thousand entries on Indian Buddhism (Ryūkoku daigaku Bukkyōgaku kenkyūshitsu [ed.], *Bukkyōgaku kankei zasshi ronbun bunrui mokuroku* [Kyoto: Nagata Bunshōdō, 1986], vol. 4). Unfortunately, few of these studies are known to Western scholars working on Indian Buddhism. Hirakawa's extensive reading of Japanese secondary scholarship is summarized in the *History of Indian Buddhism.* This work thus serves as more than a record of Hirakawa's own views of Buddhism; along with Nakamura Hajime's *Indian Buddhism,* it introduces the Western audience to the issues that Japanese scholars have considered important and to some of their conclusions.

At times the subjects that attracted Japanese attention have differed from those upon which Western scholars concentrated. For example, topics such as Pure Land, Buddha-nature *(tathāgatagarbha),* and the early development of Esoteric Buddhism receive much more emphasis in Hirakawa's history than they have in English-language surveys, partly because these traditions played major roles in the development of Chinese and Japanese Buddhism. Western scholars often have underestimated the importance of these traditions as they focused their attention on the traditions that interested them. The numbers of Chinese translations of *tathāgatagarbha* or Pure Land texts suggest that these topics may have played a more significant role in the development of Early Mahāyāna than some Western scholars have thought. In his discussion of Early Mahāyāna, Hirakawa traces these and other doctrinal themes back to early sources whenever possible, demonstrating the gradual evolution of many Mahāyāna positions.

Third, Hirakawa's history maintains a better balance and is more comprehensive than many English-language histories. Earlier surveys of Indian Buddhism have generally emphasized either one aspect of Buddhism, such as Theravāda, or one approach, such as Buddhist philosophy. Hirakawa's history includes three types of discussions: historical, bibliographical, and doctrinal. It also gives ample space to a number of subjects that have not been adequately treated in most earlier surveys, particularly in the areas of *abhidharma* traditions other than Theravāda and Sarvāstivāda, Mahāyāna devotionalism, and Esoteric Buddhist elements in Early Mahāyāna. Balance and comprehensiveness are especially important in a survey because the author should discuss connections between events and ideas that might be ignored in narrower, more specialized studies. Hirakawa examines the relations between movements in Buddhism, often tracing developments back to their origins in Early Buddhism.

In the past decade, English-language scholarship on Indian Buddhism has been evolving in ways that will remedy many of the problems indicated above. The study of Tibetan sources and the use of inscriptions from archeological sites appear in increasing numbers of scholarly articles. Younger scholars are using Chinese and Tibetan primary sources, as well as French and Japanese secondary scholarship. The recent publication of an English translation of Étienne Lamotte's *Histoire du Bouddhisme Indien des origines à l'ère Śaka* will add immensely to the information available in English. If this translation of Hirakawa's history is useful in the evolution of Buddhist studies in the West, it will have served its purpose.

Finally, a few comments about the translation are necessary. This translation follows Hirakawa's text closely with several minor deviations. Hirakawa's introduction has been adapted to fit the needs of a Western audience. The first two chapters have been combined, and several minor changes in the text have been made after discussions with Hirakawa.

Since Hirakawa's history was originally intended as a general reference for Japanese students, it is not as heavily annotated as the Western reader might normally expect of this type of book. The chapter notes, all of which have been included in a notes section following the text, generally refer to secondary studies in Japanese. Occasionally a note has been added to clarify some aspect of the translation or to refer to a significant Japanese discussion of an issue. The text references refer to primary sources. Because Hirakawa included few references to primary sources in his original text, I have augmented these so that sources for direct quotations or references to specific passages have been indicated to make the text conform to Western styles of scholarship. Many of the added references have been included after consulting Hirakawa's other writings and the studies to which he refers.

I have elected not to add extensive editorial notes discussing variant views on such subjects as the biography of the Buddha, the rise of Mahāyāna, or the role that *tathāgatagarbha* teachings played in Early Mahāyāna. Because the translation was intended to present Hirakawa's views, adding extensive annotation would have been tantamount to writing a new book. However, to help the reader find discussions of some of these problems in Western languages, bibliographical notes for each chapter have been included in a bibliographical essay preceding the bibliography at the end of the book.

Hirakawa included a full bibliography of Japanese secondary works and mentioned a number of works in Western languages in the Japanese version of this book. I have translated the titles of the Japanese works in the Japanese bibliography at the end of the book. The number of Western-language works in the bibliography of related readings has been substantially augmented. I have also added to the bibliographical essay short bibliographical comments for each chapter consisting of notes about both primary and secondary sources the reader might consult for additional information or other views. For additional references, the reader should refer to Frank Reynolds' *Guide to the Buddhist Religion* for English-language sources or to Nakamura Hajime's *Indian Buddhism: A Survey with Bibliographical Notes* for Japanese sources.

The titles of primary source texts have generally been given in both their Chinese and Sanskrit pronunciation at their first appearance; this choice was made to emphasize the importance of Chinese sources in the history. However, after the first occurrence, I have usually only given the Sanskrit title to keep the text from becoming too cumbersome. I have also added the *Taishō* number, a reference to the Chinese canon, to texts available in Chinese to aid the reader in identifying the text and as a reminder that many of the texts are available in dated Chinese translations. Because the Sanskrit titles of works preserved in Chinese are sometimes problematic, I have adopted the convention used in the *Hōbōgirin: Répertoire du Canon bouddhique sino-japonaise* of placing an asterisk (*) after the Sanskrit title if it is based on a Sanskrit or Pāli work, a number sign (#) if it is based on a reconstruction from Tibetan, and a question mark (?) if the reconstruction is doubtful. When a Sanskrit or Pāli work is being referred to, no annotation is given after the title.

In discussions of Early Buddhism, most authors are faced with the problem of whether to use Pāli or Sanskrit terms. Because a completely satisfactory solution was difficult to arrive at, I have adopted the following convention. Sanskrit has been the preferred language, partly because its use was also applicable to Sarvāstivāda and Mahāyāna sources. However, because the Pāli sources are so valuable in any discussion of Early Buddhism as well as indispensable for a discussion of Theravāda *abhidhamma* and history, I have used Pāli at certain times. The most common occurrences have been either when a primary source in Pāli is being referred to or in discussions of Theravāda *abhidhamma*. In addition, some terms are known primarily in Chinese translation. In particular, some of the terms used in Nikāya Buddhism in schools other than the Theravāda and Sarvāstivāda or in early Mahāyāna are known only from Chinese translations. A Sanskrit reconstruction of such terms would be difficult and lead to questionable results. In addition, terms have also been developed within East Asia that reflect or sum up the Indian situation well. In such cases, the term has been given in Chinese rather than a questionable Sanskrit reconstruction. In all cases where I have rendered Chinese and Japanese terms into Sanskrit, I have striven to use the concordances and reference works for the texts under discussion.

This translation could not have been completed without the encouragement of a number of people, only a few of whom I can mention here. Hirakawa Akira repeatedly answered my questions concerning certain passages or about the Sanskrit equivalents to Chinese terms. Stanley Weinstein of Yale encouraged me to undertake the project and reassured me of its value when I felt discouraged. My wife Cindy helped with the style through her careful reading. Patricia Crosby and the editorial staff at the University of Hawaii Press have improved the text with their careful editorial questions.

I dedicate the translation to Professor Hirakawa, who read *vinaya* texts with me and introduced me to the world of Japanese scholarship when I was a graduate student in Tokyo from 1971 to 1974. The clarity of his explanations, his concern for Buddhist scholarship, and his interest in his students have served as a constant inspiration to me.

AUTHOR'S PREFACE

Indian culture is often said to lack historical consciousness. Because virtually no materials with accurate dates for India's ancient history exist, writing a history of Indian Buddhism may seem like a futile undertaking. However, an accurate historical account of Buddhism in India is vital to our knowledge of the overall development of Buddhism.

During the last century, both Western and Japanese scholars have made great strides in the study of the history of Indian Buddhism. On the basis of their research, books have been published in Japan and the West with titles such as *The History of Indian Buddhism* or *The History of Indian Philosophy.* The present volume follows the pattern established by such studies. It reflects the current state of research and follows established opinions and theories as far as possible. In many cases, however, scholars have not arrived at a consensus. Such basic issues as the date of the historical Buddha's death, or *parinirvāṇa,* are still being disputed. According to sources such as the Sri Lankan chronicle *Dīpavaṃsa,* almost all the schisms of Sectarian (Nikāya or Hīnayāna) Buddhism had occurred before the reign of King Aśoka. In contrast, according to the sources of the Northern Buddhist tradition, the schisms occurred after Aśoka's reign. This issue not only affects our evaluation of Aśoka's rule but our account of the entire development of Early Buddhism and the emergence of Nikāya Buddhism. In this study, a chronology that permits the most reasonable account of the historical development of Buddhism has been adopted, but since this chronology has not yet been proven to be correct, other chronologies and accounts may prove to be more accurate.

Many other scholarly problems remain in Indian Buddhism, making the compilation of a definitive history impossible. Although I could have explained and contrasted the various views of each topic, such an approach would have made the study too cumbersome. Nor has all the evidence for each position been presented. Instead, in most cases only the most reasonable position has been introduced to produce a unified and consistent narrative.

Some of the relevant primary sources for positions are cited in parentheses within the text. In this volume, sources are usually from either the *Taishō shinshū daizōkyō* (Chinese version of the canon, cited hereafter as *T*) or Pāli texts published by the Pāli Text Society. Studies by modern (usually Japanese) scholars analyzing these materials are listed in the endnotes. Research by Westerners is discussed in the bibliographical essay compiled by the translator. The bibliographies are compilations of sources that a student undertaking serious research on Buddhism might consult, rather than exhaustive lists of studies.

When I first began this book, I intended to write a one-volume survey of the development of Buddhism from India to Japan that could be used as a reference. Because Tokyo University was the site of student disturbances at the time, I found it difficult to allot my time as I had originally intended and eventually had to abandon my original plan for the book. I finally decided to concentrate on the history of Indian Buddhism and to divide the book into two parts. The current translation is the first volume of this project.

In most narratives of Indian Buddhism, a number of gaps and inconsistencies are evident. I have striven to make this book more accessible to the reader than previous histories by stressing the connections between different periods and types of Indian Buddhism and by eliminating the gaps between periods and varieties of Buddhism. For this reason, special attention has been paid to such topics as the transition from Early to Sectarian Buddhism, the emergence of Mahāyāna Buddhism, and the contents of early Mahāyāna Buddhist scriptures. When several accounts of these topics exist in primary sources, they are compared in detail. I have also striven to clearly describe the doctrinal positions of major forms of Buddhism such as *abhidharma* in simple language unencumbered by technical jargon.

This book owes much to the research of other scholars. Because I have been able to read and assimilate only a small part of the vast research on Indian Buddhism, errors may be present in the text. Criticisms and suggestions will be gratefully received and used to improve any future editions.

ABBREVIATIONS

AN	*Aṅguttara-nikāya*
Ch.	Chinese
DN	*Dīgha-nikāya*
IBK	*Indogaku Bukkyōgaku kenkyū*
KN	*Khuddaka-nikāya*
MN	*Majjhima-nikāya*
P.	Pāli
-PP	*-Prajñāpāramitāsūtra*
S.	Sanskrit
SN	*Saṃyutta-nikāya*
T	*Taishō shinshū Daizōkyō*
Tib.	Tibetan
VP	*Vinaya-piṭaka*
*	edited Sanskrit version of the text is extant
#	Sanskrit title based on Tibetan sources
?	Sanskrit title uncertain

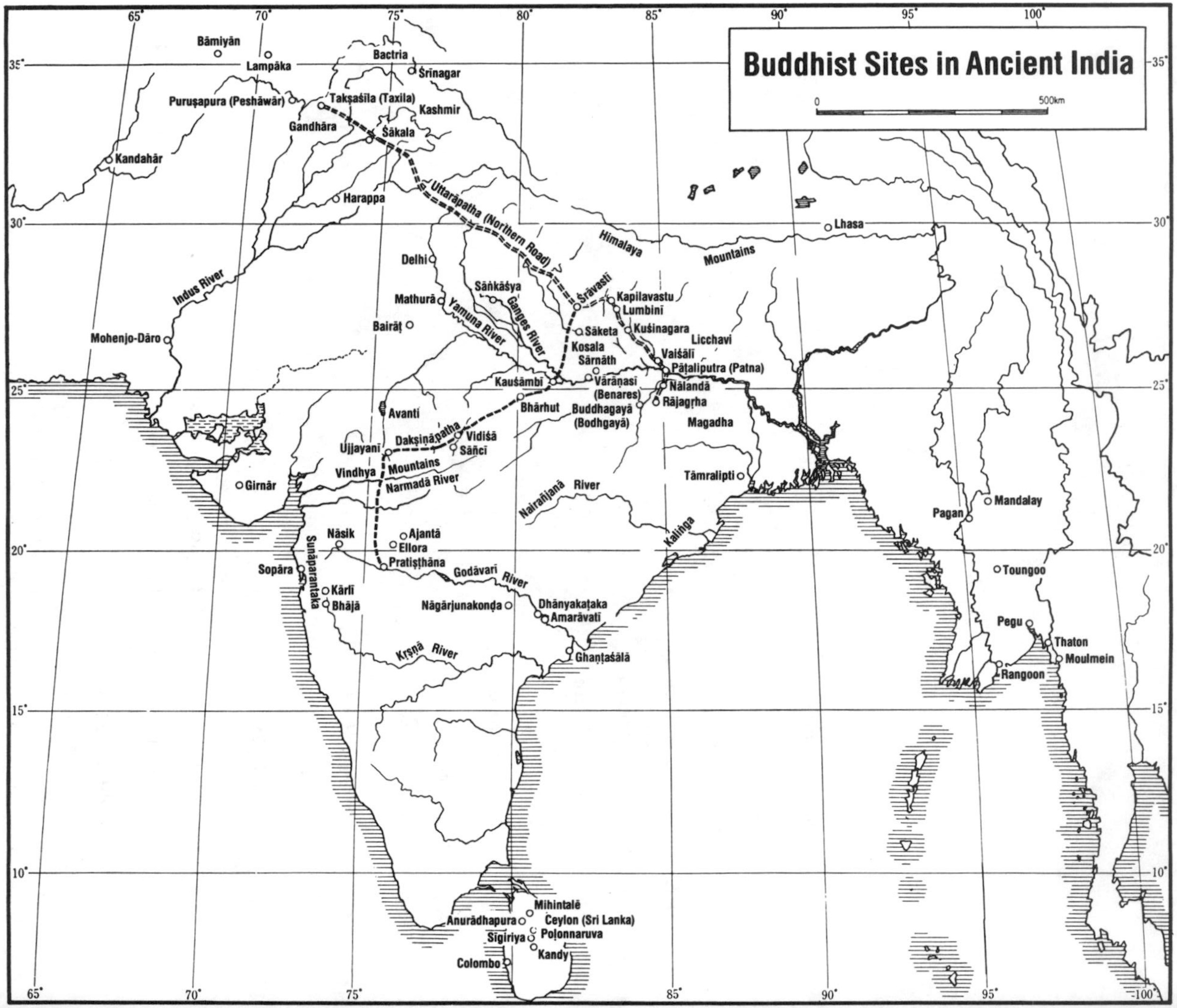
Buddhist Sites in Ancient India
0
500km
Bāmiyān
Lampāka
Bactria
Śrīnagar
Puruṣapura (Peshāwār)
Takṣaśila (Taxila)
Kashmir
Gandhāra
Śākala
Kandahār
Harappa
Uttarāpatha (Northern Road)
Himalaya
Mountains
Lhasa
Delhi
Indus River
Sāṅkāśya
Śrāvastī
Kapilavastu
Lumbinī
Mathurā
Yamuna River
Ganges River
Bairāṭ
Sāketa
Kuśinagara
Licchavi
Mohenjo-Dāro
Kosala
Vaiśālī
Sārnāth
Pāṭaliputra (Patna)
Kauśāmbī
Vārāṇasī
(Benares)
Nālandā
Rājagṛha
Bhārhut
Buddhagayā
(Bodhgayā)
Magadha
Avantī
Dakṣiṇāpatha
Vidiśā
Ujjayanī
Sāñcī
Vindhya
Mountains
Narmadā River
Tāmralipti
Girnār
Nairañjanā
River
Pagan
Mandalay
Kaliṅga
Nāsik
Ajantā
Ellora
Pratiṣṭhāna
Sunāparantaka
Sopāra
Godāvarī
River
Toungoo
Kārlī
Bhājā
Nāgārjunakoṇḍa
Dhānyakaṭaka
Amarāvatī
Pegu
Thaton
Moulmein
Kṛṣṇā
River
Ghaṇṭaśālā
Rangoon
Mihintalē
Anurādhapura
Ceylon (Sri Lanka)
Sigiriya
Poḷonnaruva
Kandy
Colombo
65°
70°
75°
80°
85°
90°
95°
100°
35°
30°
25°
20°
15°
10°

Introduction

The Special Characteristics of Indian Buddhism

BECAUSE BUDDHISM originated and developed in India, using the adjective "Indian" to describe it may seem unnecessary. When Buddhism spread beyond India to Southeast Asia, Tibet, China, Japan, and other lands, certain aspects of Buddhism were emphasized in each locale, generating a wide variety of interpretations and practices. Buddhism was adapted to meet the requirements of the people of each area, resulting in a wide variation of interpretations. Indian Buddhism, too, had unique characteristics not emphasized in other regions. Thus, the term "Indian Buddhism" is often used today to distinguish it from the Buddhism of other countries.

When Indian Buddhism is compared to Chinese and Japanese Buddhism, differences in climate and geography are seen to affect religious practice; those adaptations in practice brought about changes in doctrine. In contrast, the countries where Theravāda Buddhism is practiced—such as Sri Lanka, Burma, Thailand—have climates and geographies resembling those of India more than those of China and Japan. As a result, Theravāda religious practice is much closer to Indian Buddhism than to East Asian Buddhism.

A brief survey of the development and geographical spread of Indian Buddhism reveals much about the universal qualities and the distinctive characteristics of Indian Buddhism, as well as providing an overview of its development. Buddhism was founded in the fifth century B.C.E. by

Śākyamuni, who was born in a region of northern India and Nepal controlled by the Śākya tribe. After he decided to become a religious mendicant, he traveled to the country of Magadha in central India, south of the Ganges River, where he performed religious austerities. When he was approximately thirty-five years old, Śākyamuni realized enlightenment. This experience, central to Buddhism, was described as "being enlightened to the undying" and "discovering the path to freedom from suffering." Although humankind is afflicted by various types of suffering, the fear of death is the most basic, leading Śākyamuni to describe his experience in terms of the "undying." Although Śākyamuni ceased to exist physically when he was eighty years old, his declaration of enlightenment expressed his confidence that his mind had realized eternal truths. The suffering present in all human existence has been a constant concern of mankind. Śākyamuni's discovery of an answer to this problem, a path of liberation from suffering, has been the most universally appealing characteristic of Buddhism. More than any other feature, it has enabled Buddhism to survive until the present.

In India, however, Buddhism disappeared. By briefly surveying the history of Indian Buddhism, some of its special characteristics as well as several reasons for its disappearance can be ascertained. At the time of Śākyamuni Buddha's death in the fifth century B.C.E., the Buddhist order consisted of small groups of mendicants in central India. Through the efforts of Śākyamuni's disciples, Buddhism spread to the south and west. In the third century B.C.E., after the conversion of King Aśoka, Buddhism was soon promulgated throughout India. With the growth of the order and increases in the numbers of monks, disputes arose over the observance of monastic discipline and the interpretation of doctrine. The early order eventually divided into two schools: the progressive Mahāsaṅghika and the conservative Sthaviravāda (P. Theravāda). Additional schisms occurred until many schools existed and Buddhism entered its sectarian (Nikāya or Hīnayāna) period.

The terms "eighteen schools" or "twenty schools" are found in many traditional sources that refer to Sectarian Buddhism, but the names of many more than twenty schools are known from inscriptions. Of these schools, the Theravāda, Sarvāstivāda, Sautrāntika, Sammatīya (all of Sthaviravāda lineage), and the Mahāsaṅghika schools were the most important. By the beginning of the common era, Mahāyāna Buddhism had also begun to develop. Mahāyāna (great vehicle) Buddhists criticized the adherents of Nikāya Buddhism by calling them "Hīnayāna" (inferior vehicle) Buddhists, a deprecatory term applied especially to Sarvāstivādins.

Although a number of schools had arisen and had criticized each other, all of them were recognized as Buddhist. This toleration for a wide variety of interpretations was based on the Buddhist emphasis on the importance of the individual's enlightenment and his freedom to contemplate and interpret doctrine. According to the *Wen-shu-shih-li wen ching* (*T* 14:501a–b, *Mañjuśrīparipṛcchā?*), the schisms within Buddhism resulted from the differing explanations of Śākyamuni's teaching by twenty of his followers. Each adherent, however, was said to have received and transmitted the Buddha's true teaching. In the travel diary of I-ching (635–713), a Chinese monk who journeyed through India and Southeast Asia, the Buddha's teaching was said to be like a golden cane that had been broken into eighteen pieces. Just as each piece of the cane was part of the original staff, so did the essence of the Buddha's teachings remain unchanged even though the early order had been fragmented into eighteen schools (*Nan-hai chi-kuei nei-fa chuan, T* 54:205c). Similar discussions are found in Buddhist scriptures. Buddhist schools could recognize each other as Buddhist because their teachings were not established on blind faith. Although this tolerance for doctrinal differences is one of Buddhism's finest features, it permitted the appearance of such a variety of differing opinions in the order that it led to a weakening of the doctrinal stances that differentiated Buddhism from the other Indian religions of that time.

The rise of Mahāyāna Buddhism approximately five hundred years after the Buddha's death is an example of how Buddhism responded to the demands of a new time. Mahāyāna Buddhism included many elements not found in early Buddhism. Despite these innovations, the original spirit of the Buddha's teaching was not lost in early Mahāyāna. In fact, early Mahāyānists revived the spirit of the Buddha's teaching by adapting it for a new age. However, these innovative elements brought hidden dangers with them. As time passed, many Buddhists became more interested in the new additions than in the original message of the Buddha.

Magical elements played an important role in Mahāyāna Buddhism from the beginning, probably because they were a response to the religious needs of the common people. Perfection of wisdom *sūtras* contained claims that the text could protect those who followed it. In addition, perfection of wisdom *sūtras* were sometimes called "great wisdom *mantras*" *(mahā-vidyā-mantra)* or "great mantras" *(mahā-mantra).* According to the *Fa-hua ching (T* 9:56c–58b, *Saddharmapuṇḍarīkasūtra),* faith in the bodhisattva Avalokiteśvara would protect a person from all disasters. Advocacy of the efficacy of *dhāraṇī* (magical incantations) was found in many Mahāyāna scriptures. Over the centuries, these magical formulas came to play an increasingly important role in Mahāyāna

Buddhism until, by the sixth century, Esoteric Buddhism had emerged as a distinct movement and begun to develop in India.

Although Esoteric Buddhism clearly belongs within the Buddhist fold, its rituals are virtually indistinguishable from those of Hinduism. Eventually much of the doctrinal basis for Esoteric Buddhism was ignored and only its ritual emphasized, contributing to the eventual absorption of Esoteric Buddhism by Hinduism. In contrast, Chinese, Japanese, and Southeast Asian Buddhism developed in areas and cultures that differed from India. As a result, many elements of Indian Buddhism were not easily assimilated by the indigenous cultures. In fact, many of the distinguishing characteristics of Indian Buddhism were preserved because they were so conspicuous in other countries. For example, because Buddhist teachings of nonsubstantiality provided the doctrinal basis for the "Hindu" ceremonies in the Chinese and Japanese Esoteric Buddhist traditions, these traditions never lost their Buddhist character. In India, however, as Buddhism became more Esoteric, it was increasingly assimilated into Hinduism, until it finally lost its Buddhist character.

Early Mahāyāna Buddhism was a religion of many facets; it included Amitābha worship, as well as such scriptures as the *Prajñāpāramitā, Lotus (Saddharmapuṇḍarīka),* and *Avataṃsaka sūtras.* From the second century of the common era onward, theoretical works based on these scriptures were composed. The Mādhyamika School was based on teachings concerning nonsubstantiality. At first, the appellation "Mādhyamika" was not used to designate the school because an opposing Mahāyāna tradition was not present. Only after the Yogācāra tradition arose about one century after Mādhyamika did the term "Mādhyamika" come to be used. Yogācāra was based on the systematic investigation of ideation-only doctrines. For the next several centuries the two traditions coexisted.

Even before Yogācāra emerged as a distinct tradition, early Mahāyāna texts had been compiled concerning ideation-only *(vijñaptimātratā)* and Buddha-nature (*tathāgatagarbha,* the potential to realize Buddhahood). Among them were the *Tathāgatagarbhasūtra* (*T* 666–667), *Śrīmālādevīsiṃhanādasūtra* (*T* 310.48, 353) and the *Mahāparinirvāṇasūtra* (*T* 374–375). As time passed, the Mādhyamika and Yogācāra schools developed and influenced each other, as well as Esoteric Buddhism.

Even during the period when Mahāyāna Buddhism was most influential, Nikāya Buddhism was still flourishing. In fact, Nikāya Buddhism was always the stronger of the two movements, as is demonstrated in the travel diaries of such Chinese pilgrims to India as Fa-hsien (in India 399–414), Hsüan-tsang (602–664), and I-ching (635–713). By I-ching's time, the differences between Nikāya and Mahāyāna Buddhism had become less pronounced and the two traditions had begun to blend together. Esoteric Buddhism subsequently became popular and powerful, influencing both the Nikāya and Mahāyāna traditions. Finally, as Hinduism became stronger and the Muslims invaded India, Buddhism lost much of its vigor. At the end of the twelfth century, the Vikramaśīla Monastery was burned by Muslim troops, an event that symbolized the disappearance of Buddhist institutions from most of India. Buddhism did survive, however, in eastern Bengal, where a small number of people have carried on the Buddhist tradition until the present.

Even after the Muslim invasions, Hinduism remained strong. Jainism also managed to survive although with only a small number of adherents; Buddhism, however, disappeared, even though it had once spread across and dominated India. A consideration of several of the reasons for the different destinies of the religions helps elucidate some of the characteristics of Indian Buddhism.

Indian Buddhism did not establish a fixed orthodox doctrinal position and then firmly reject any deviations from it as heterodoxy. Consequently, Buddhist doctrine gradually changed in a variety of ways. One reason for Buddhism's disappearance from India may lie in its liberal attitude toward different interpretations of doctrine. This argument does not imply that the Buddhist tolerance of doctrinal diversity was mistaken. Because people's abilities to understand Buddhism differed and historical circumstances changed, it was appropriate that Buddhist doctrine reflect the needs of its audience. However, if Buddhism could evolve freely, then the possibility that Buddhism could disappear also had to be considered. Theories concerning the decline or disappearance of "True" Buddhism circulated very early in Buddhist history. One of the most influential theories in East Asia divided Buddhist history into three periods: True Dharma, Counterfeit Dharma, and the End of the Dharma.

Buddhism is not the only religion that does not stress strict adherence to a certain set of doctrines. Hinduism also adopted this flexible attitude. For example, the *Bhagavad-gītā,* one of the best known Hindu scriptures, permits a variety of doctrinal positions. The demand for uncompromising fidelity to doctrine is rarely, if ever, found in Hinduism. Thus, a liberal attitude toward doctrine by itself cannot explain the disappearance of Buddhism from India.

Buddhism's rejection of an eternal and substantial Self *(ātman),* a position maintained since Early Buddhism, may have been an important factor. Buddhism competed with Hinduism, Jainism, and other religious traditions that all argued for the existence of a substantial Self.

In addition, theories advocating the existence of *ātman* were closely tied to teachings about rebirth. Because the belief in rebirth is one of the most important tenets of Indian religion, Buddhists also had to develop theories to explain it. However, rebirth is not a necessary tenet of Śākyamuni's teachings. Although he did not reject rebirth, Śākyamuni was primarily concerned with liberation from the suffering of existence. If existence consisted of cycles of birth and death, then deliverance from those cycles was his goal. Thus Early Buddhists did not need to dismiss rebirth. Instead, theories concerning rebirth were incorporated into Buddhism, and the ultimate goal of the Buddhist practitioner was interpreted as freedom from the cycles of birth and death.

If rebirth were accepted as a religious teaching, then something must account for continuity from existence to existence. Although Buddhists did not recognize the existence of *ātman,* they eventually had to recognize the existence of some entity or force that passed through the cycles of rebirths and performed at least some of the functions of an *ātman*. The Mahāyāna concepts of Buddha-nature *(tathāgatagarbha)* and store-consciousness *(ālaya-vijñāna)* were similar in some of their functions to *ātman*. Within Nikāya Buddhism, the Sarvāstivāda School developed a systematic and mechanical explanation of human existence to demonstrate that no *ātman* existed. However, the Sarvāstivāda School lost much of its strength. In contrast, the Sammatīya School gained strength in later times, in part because of the appealing quality of their argument that a lasting *pudgala* (Person) was present in each individual. The travel diaries of both Hsüan-tsang and I-ching reveal that by the seventh and eighth centuries the Sammatīya School was more powerful than the Sarvāstivāda.

Buddhism arose at a time of much suffering. The teachings of nonsubstantiality and the nonexistence of a substantial Self were emphasized by the historical Buddha. As time passed, however, Buddhist teaching changed and doctrines developed that were similar to the views on *ātman* maintained by other Indian religions. Even as these teachings developed, Buddhism was already losing influence in India. Thus, Buddhism's original rejection of the *ātman* was probably one of several factors that led to its decline in India.

Teachings and theories about rebirth played a key role in the development of Indian Buddhist thought. In contrast, when Indian Buddhism was introduced to China and Japan, although rebirth was accepted as a part of Buddhism, it did not play a central role in the development of East Asian Buddhism. This difference arose because traditional Chinese and Japanese beliefs in spirits and souls were not based on rebirth. In conclusion, the following two points are two of the main themes that can be traced through Indian Buddhism. First, Buddhism's fundamental aim, the deliverance of people from suffering, was one of its most attractive features. Second, the history of Indian Buddhism is inextricably concerned with the formulation of doctrines that explain the mechanisms of rebirth.

The Periods of Indian Buddhism

Indian Buddhism may be divided into the following five periods: (1) Early Buddhism, (2) Nikāya or Sectarian (often called Hīnayāna) Buddhism, (3) early Mahāyāna Buddhism, (4) later Mahāyāna Buddhism, and (5) Esoteric Buddhism. Although the five periods are arranged in the chronological order in which the traditions arose, they are also based on a categorization of types of Buddhism as much as historical criteria. This book covers the first three periods.

The discussion of the first period is focused around a clear description of the Buddha's teaching. The portrait of Early Buddhism is completed with a discussion of the Buddha's biography and an account of the establishment of the early Buddhist order. The order continued to develop after the Buddha's death. Although the historical sources for this period are meager, the history of the order through the time of King Aśoka is chronicled. Aśoka's view of Buddhism is included in this section because it was similar in many ways to Early Buddhism.

Approximately one century after the Buddha's death, the early order split into the Mahāsaṅghika and Sthaviravāda schools. Later, further schisms occurred, resulting in a number of additional schools. The second period of Buddhist history is concerned with the development of Sectarian (Nikāya) Buddhism. Buddhist doctrine at that time was typified by the development of scholastic *abhidharma* philosophy. Because the tradition differed from Early Buddhism in many ways, most scholars distinguish between Early and Sectarian Buddhism. Sectarian Buddhism was a major force in India for over one thousand years, but most of its important doctrinal development occurred during its first three centuries, between 150 B.C.E. and 150 C.E.

Of the more than twenty sects, the doctrines of only the Sarvāstivāda and Theravāda schools are understood in any detail today. Only a little is known about the doctrines of other schools because of the paucity of information concerning them. The Sautrāntika and Sammitīya schools flourished after the beginning of the common era. Although both probably had highly developed systems of doctrine, detailed information about them has not survived. When I-ching departed from Canton for

India in 671, the Theravāda, Sarvāstivāda, Sammatīya, and Mahāsaṅghika schools were still thriving. Later, they gradually blended with Mahāyāna Buddhism. In addition, both Sectarian and Mahāyāna Buddhism were influenced by Esoteric Buddhism. Unfortunately, little is known about the later phases of Sectarian Buddhism.

Mahāyāna scriptures were already in existence by the first century B.C.E., indicating that Mahāyāna Buddhism must have arisen around the beginning of the common era while Sectarian Buddhism was still developing. Early Mahāyāna practitioners were especially interested in teachings on nonsubstantiality or emptiness. Although mentions of nonsubstantiality can be found in Early Buddhist scriptures, Mahāyānists stressed and developed this theme far beyond anything found in either Early or Nikāya Buddhism.

Mahāyāna Buddhists strove to emulate the Buddha, following the same path and achieving the same status as he did by realizing Buddhahood and saving all sentient beings. Mahāyānists denigrated Sectarian Buddhists, claiming that Sectarian Buddhists were content to remain disciples of the Buddha instead of striving to equal his achievement. Mahāyāna Buddhists referred to Sectarian Buddhism as *"śrāvakayāna"* (vehicle for disciples or hearers), a term that implied that Sectarian Buddhists were more passive and had lower aspirations than Mahāyānists. Sectarian Buddhists were criticized as being content to study for their own benefit while Mahāyānists strove to teach others and bring them salvation. Mahāyāna Buddhists referred to themselves as "bodhisattvas" (beings who aspired to realize supreme enlightenment) and to their teachings as the *"bodhisattvayāna"* (vehicle for bodhisattvas). Although the term *"bodhisattva"* had been used earlier by Sectarian Buddhists to refer to the historical Buddha when he was still practicing to realize enlightenment, the Mahāyāna usage extended this appellation to many others. Later, the terms *"śrāvakayāna"* and *"bodhisattvayāna"* were often replaced by the terms "Hīnayāna" (small or inferior vehicle) and "Mahāyāna" (great vehicle). From approximately 100 B.C.E. to 100 C.E., large numbers of Mahāyāna scriptures were composed by nameless bodhisattvas.

In the third part of this study, early Mahāyāna Buddhism, the origins of Mahāyāna and the contents of early Mahāyāna scriptures are examined.

The last two periods of Indian Buddhism are not discussed in this volume, but a brief summary of later developments will help place the themes discussed above in perspective. During the fourth period, later Mahāyāna Buddhism, four major types of thought developed: (1) Mādhyamika, which arose after the second century C.E.; (2) Yogācāra teachings of ideation-only, which appeared one century after Mādhyamika; (3) Tathāgatagarbha doctrines that developed in parallel with Yogācāra thought; and (4) Buddhist logic, which arose after the above three traditions. The Mādhyamika tradition eventually split into two schools of thought: the Svātantrika and the Prāsaṅgika. Later, some Mādhyamika and Yogācāra groups joined to produce a Yogācāra-Mādhyamika tradition. By the sixth and seventh centuries, Esoteric Buddhism had arisen and attracted the attention of some advocates of Mādhyamika and Yogācāra. However, many aspects of the relationship between Mahāyāna and Esoteric Buddhism remain unclear.

The fifth period of Indian Buddhism concerns Esoteric Buddhism. The serious academic study of this tradition is still in its early stages because of a number of problems that make research difficult. Although a large number of Esoteric Buddhist scriptures are extant, they have not been put into any kind of order. In addition, because Esoteric Buddhism was influenced by Hinduism, further research into Hinduism is necessary. Finally, ritual as well as doctrine must be examined if Esoteric Buddhism is to be fully understood. In Esoteric Buddhist texts, teachings are sometimes referred to as "Esoteric" and differentiated from "exoteric" Mahāyāna teachings, thereby indicating that the compilers of Esoteric works believed that it had features not found in the Mahāyāna tradition. Consequently, Esoteric Buddhism is assigned to a separate period of Indian Buddhism.

In this study, the categorization of periods has been based on the development of Indian Buddhism because its purpose is to describe the development of Indian Buddhist doctrine; but the study could also have focused on other models and have been arranged according to Indian dynastic history.

Although Buddhism was a major force in India from the fifth century B.C.E. until after the tenth century C.E., this period covers only about one-half of Indian history. Most Indian historians consider the invasion of India by Muslims of Turkish ancestry in the eleventh century to mark the division between ancient and medieval history. Modern Indian history begins in the eighteenth century with British control of India. Thus the story of "Buddhist India" belongs to ancient history. During that period, it was one of a number of Indian religions. Thus the reader must remember that this survey of Indian Buddhism covers only part of the history of Indian thought.

PART ONE

EARLY BUDDHISM

CHAPTER 1

Indian Religion at the Time of the Buddha

India Before Buddhism

BUDDHISM WAS INFLUENCED by the social and religious environment in which it developed. In approximately 1500 B.C.E., the Aryans crossed the mountains of the Hindu Kush and invaded India. When they arrived, they found aboriginal peoples such as the Mundas and Dravidians. The Dravidians had a highly developed culture and constituted a large proportion of the population. Although they were subjugated by the Aryans and integrated into society as slave classes, the Dravidians influenced later Indian culture in many ways. Elements of their religion such as the worship of goddesses, snake gods, and tree spirits played a particularly important role in the Hinduism of later centuries.

Another people, too, lived in India before the arrival of the Aryans. They are the people who founded the Indus civilization, a highly developed culture that was situated on the Indus River and is thought to have flourished from approximately 2500 to 1500 B.C.E. Two of its cities, Harappā and Mohenjo-dāro, are particularly well known as archeological sites. Archeological investigations have revealed that this culture covered an extensive area, worked with bronze, and constructed well-organized cities. Many of the objects found suggest that Indus civilization substantially influenced Hinduism; but the sudden decline of the Indus civilization has left unanswered questions about how its people contributed to the development of later Indian civilization.

The Aryans entered India from the northwest; by 1200 B.C.E., they had settled along the upper reaches of the Ganges River in the Punjab. Their religion, based on the *Ṛg-veda,* was a form of polytheism in which forces of nature, such as the sky, rain, wind, and thunder, were deified. From 1000 B.C.E. on, they continued their advance eastward, gradually settling the fertile area between the Ganges and the Jumna rivers. Because the area was blessed with natural resources and free from external enemies, the Aryans developed a rich culture from 1000 to 500 B.C.E., and many of the developments that characterized later Indian civilization can be traced back to this period. By 1000 B.C.E., three texts that were successors to the *Ṛg-veda*—the *Sāma-veda, Yajur-veda,* and *Atharva-veda*—had been compiled. The *Brāhmaṇas,* which explain the proper procedures for performing Vedic sacrifices, were composed around 800 B.C.E., and the philosophical texts of the early *Upaniṣads* were compiled around 500 B.C.E.

During this period, the Aryans were a tribal people primarily engaged in farming and herding. Merchant and artisan classes had begun to appear, although large cities had not yet developed. Labor was becoming more specialized. Society was divided into four classes, called *varṇa* (colors). At the top were two classes: the priestly class *(brāhmaṇa),* composed of those who sacrificed to the gods, and the ruling caste *(kṣatriya),* composed of rulers and warriors. Below them was the *vaiśya* class, composed of farmers, herders, merchants, and artisans. The duty of the slave class *(śūdra)* was to serve the other three classes. Eventually the system became more specialized and produced the many divisions that make up the caste system today. A member of one class was usually not allowed to marry or even eat with someone from another class.

Monarchies ruled by kings *(rājan)* with dictatorial powers arose, and alliances and rivalries developed. The Indian epic the *Mahābhārata* concerns the effects of a war between the tribes, that between the Bharatas and the Pūrus. Among the famous kings of this period was Janaka from Videha, a country to the east of the central lands *(madhyadeśa)* of Brahmanism, which were situated between the Ganges and Jumna rivers. In Videha, culture and thought revolved around powerful kings, while in the central lands, the priests were the center of society. As the Aryans advanced eastward and conquered the central areas drained by the Ganges, they expanded their territory and strengthened their kingdoms. Relations with the conquered population were closer than in the central lands because the culture and social system were not as influenced by Aryan culture. It was during this time of political and social change in areas similar to Videha that the founder of Buddhism was born.

Indian Religion at the Time of the Buddha

The Buddha was born during a period when important social and religious changes were occurring in central India. These changes later played a significant role in enabling Buddhism to spread throughout India. Although Vedic religion and its priestly class were influential and powerful in northern India, they had only begun to spread to the recently conquered lands of central India, which were dominated by the warrior classes.

As the Aryans gradually advanced from northern India down into central India, small tribes united to form monarchies. Sixteen countries existed in central India at the time of the Buddha, but the weaker ones were gradually being conquered by the more powerful monarchies. The most important of these large countries were Kauśala, in the northwestern part of central India with its capital at Śrāvastī, and Magadha, south of the central part of the Ganges River with its capital at Rājagṛha. Magadha would eventually unify India, relying on its rich farm areas for its power. At the time of the Buddha, powerful kings were already beginning to emerge.

The Gangetic plain with its hot climate and plentiful rainfall is a rich farm area. At first, farmers and a landlord class dominated the area; but with the development of wealthy classes, merchants and craftsmen appeared on the Gangetic plain, and cities developed. The merchants and the craftsmen organized into guilds and trade organizations. Later, a class of very wealthy merchants *(śreṣṭhin)* developed. Thus at the time of the Buddha, major political and economic changes were occurring in central India, and the old system of social classes was disintegrating.

The Brahman priestly class had lost much of its prestige, suggesting that the religion of the *Vedas* with its worship of natural phenomena no longer had as much appeal as in earlier times. The intellectual classes of the period were interested in the Upanishadic philosophy, which identified *ātman* (individual soul) with *brahman* (cosmic principle). They could no longer be satisfied with seemingly primitive religious beliefs that deified natural phenomena. In addition, the Aryans had come into contact with Dravidian religion and had been influenced by it. All of these factors helped create an environment conducive to the development of new religious beliefs.

Central India at that time was an agriculturally rich area that produced abundant food and thus could support leisured classes as well as large numbers of monks. People with religious interests often left their homes and became wandering mendicants *(parivrājaka),* living off alms from householders while they immersed themselves into a search for truth. Although people could usually be confident of their livelihood during this time, it was also a period with few diversions or amusements. As a result, young people in particular seem to have been beset by anxieties and boredom and to have turned away from the everyday world to seek truth in religion. Many men and women of good families joined religious orders.

At the time of the Buddha, there were two primary classes of religious practitioners in India: the *brāhmaṇas* and the *śramaṇas*. The *brāhmaṇas,* representatives of the more traditional type of practitioner, were followers of Vedic religion who officiated at sacrifices. At the same time, they devoted themselves to seeking the Absolute through the study of a philosophy that identified *ātman* with *brahman.* A *brāhmaṇa*'s life ideally was divided into four stages. When young, he was accepted as a disciple by a teacher and devoted himself to the study of the *Vedas.* When his studies were completed, he returned home to marry and became a householder. When he grew old, he let his son take over the household and retired to the forest to live and perform religious practices. Finally, he abandoned even his abode in the forest to live a life of wandering and died while wandering.

The second type of religious practitioner, the *śramaṇa* or "person who strives," was a new type of figure not mentioned in the older *Upaniṣads.* He abandoned his home to lead a life of wandering and begging. Often he entered this way of life while young; there was no requirement that he pass through the other stages of life before becoming a *śramaṇa.* He devoted himself to controlling and limiting his desires, practicing yoga, and performing severe religious austerities in the forest to experience the Absolute or to escape death.

Six famous *śramaṇas* who lived around the time of the Buddha are mentioned in Buddhist scriptures. They are called the Six Heterodox Teachers. Each was the leader *(gaṇin)* of a group of disciples. The six are called Pūraṇa Kāśyapa, Maskarin Gośālīputra, Ajita Keśakambala, Kakuda Kātyāyana, Sañjayin Vairaṭṭīputra, and Nirgrantha Jñātīputra.

One of the primary concerns of these *śramaṇas* was whether moral actions would have any effect on the person who performed them. The first heterodox teacher, Pūraṇa, argued that good and bad actions had no particular effect on the person who performed them. He denied morality, arguing that even if a person murdered and stole, his actions could not necessarily be considered bad since they resulted in no moral effects.

The second heterodox teacher, Maskarin Gośālīputra, denied causality. According to Gośālīputra, a person's rise or fall in the world was determined by fate, not by his actions. His followers were called the Ājīvakas (Ājīvikas). The term "Ājīvika" is translated in Chinese Buddhist texts as "a heterodox religion (whose members lead) an evil life" *(hsieh-ming wai-tao);* however, the Indian term probably meant "those who follow a strict mode of life," referring to the severe austerities performed by the Ājīvika followers. The group is mentioned in the edicts of Aśoka and in the *Artha-śāstra.* Along with the Buddhists and Jainas, the Ājīvikas remained an important group in India during the following centuries. Gośālīputra is said to have practiced austerities with one of the founders of Jainism, Mahāvīra, and apparently believed that he could attain salvation through those austerities.

The third heterodox teacher, Ajita Keśakambala, took a materialist position and argued that everything was composed of only four elements: earth, water, fire, and wind. Consequently, moral acts were meaningless. The materialist position was later maintained by the Lokāyata or Cārvāka tradition.

The fourth heterodox teacher, Kakuda Kātyāyana, recognized seven elements: earth, water, fire, wind, pain, pleasure, and life. Because the seven elements were unchanging, Kakuda argued that when a man was killed with a knife, the knife only entered the spaces between the elements. Because the elements, the only real entities, were unharmed, the killing was of no consequence. Kakuda's theory of the elements was a forerunner of Vaiśeṣika theories.

The fifth heterodox teacher, Sañjayin Vairaṭṭīputra, was a skeptic. He refused to give definite answers to questions, relying instead on evasive statements. The skeptics' position was apparently based on serious doubts about the nature of knowledge and on their investigations of logic. Two of the Buddha's most important disciples, Śāriputra and Mahāmaudgalyāyana, came from this school.

The sixth heterodox teacher, Nirgrantha Jñatīputra, is also known as Mahāvīra, one of the founders of Jainism. The term "Nirgrantha" refers to being freed of fetters. Mahāvīra originally belonged to the Nirgrantha School, a group of ascetics who attempted to free themselves of physical and mental fetters through the practice of austerities. Through assiduous practice, Mahāvīra attained enlightenment and realized that he was a Jina (a victor or one who had conquered ignorance). After Mahāvīra's death, his school called itself the Jaina order. The Nirgrantha School claims to have had a long history before Mahāvīra's time. In fact Pārśva (or Pāsa), Mahāvīra's predecessor in the largely mythological lineage of the twenty-four founders of Jainism, was a historical figure.

Jainism and Buddhism were among the strongest of the non-Brahmanical religions, and they share many of the same doctrines and technical terms. The goal of the Jainas is to free the soul by overcoming the instincts and desires that arise from the physical body. The Jainas thus perform austerities to weaken the body's strength. The Jaina practitioner is also expected to make five great vows, which form the basis of his moral discipline. The prohibition against killing is particularly strict. The rule against possessions is carried to such an extreme by one group, the Digambara, that even clothes are discarded, and male followers practice their austerities in the nude. Jaina doctrine and epistemology were highly developed. The Jainas compiled a canon that has survived until today. Their oldest scriptures are written in the Ardhamāgadhī language.

The period around the fifth century B.C.E. in central India was a time of ferment in the history of Indian thought, as the above list of heterodox teachers indicates. As we have seen, one of the most important questions discussed by religious thinkers at this time was whether or not moral actions affected the person who had performed them (in other words, the existence and functioning of karmic cause and effect). If moral actions did have effects, then the religious practitioner had to investigate how he might break his karmic bonds and free his mind or soul. This question was closely related to teachings concerning rebirth. Although doctrines concerning rebirth are not found in the *Vedas,* by the time of the *Upaniṣads* teachings on rebirth had begun to appear. The term *"saṃsāra"* for rebirth does not appear in the oldest *Upaniṣads,* but it is used frequently in *Upaniṣads* composed after the time of the Buddha. It thus appears that the concept of repeated cycles of birth and death was being given its classical formulation at the same time that Buddhism was being established. Once the concept of rebirth was established, people naturally began to speculate about whether some entity or soul might travel through the cycles of birth and death.

People were discussing karma before the time of the Buddha, of course. The idea of karmic fruits, however, was not generally recognized at that time. These vague ideas of karma were incorporated into Buddhism and systematically interpreted in a uniquely Buddhist manner as a law of cause and effect. The Jainas too recognized karmic causes and effects, but for them the results of actions were usually characterized as "punishments" *(daṇḍa).*

A large number of theories were advanced concerning the Self or entity *(ātman, jīva;* P. *attan),* which transmigrated through births and deaths, and the realm *(loka)* in which the Self existed. In the Pāli *Brahmajālasutta,* no less than sixty-two different positions on these subjects are described. A particularly important issue concerned the manner in which a constantly changing mind could grasp or perceive the unchanging *ātman* thought to exist behind it. According to Jaina sources, there were 363 different contending schools that could be classified into four basic groups: those who recognized karma, those who did not recognize karma, the skeptics, and the moralists.

In Buddhist texts, the non-Buddhist schools of thought are divided into three main groups: those who believe that everything occurs through the will of god (P. *issaranimmāna-vāda*), those who maintain that every event is predetermined by past karma (P. *pubbekatahetu*), and those who believe that everything occurs by chance (P. *ahetu, apaccaya*). The Buddha rejected all three of these alternatives because they denied free will and the efficacy of human efforts; instead, he preached a moral law of cause and effect that transcended these three positions.

Non-Buddhist positions were categorized in other ways. One of the most important is a classification into two philosophical positions. The first, the *pariṇāma-vāda* position, was maintained by the orthodox Brahmanical thinkers, who argued that both the Self and the world evolved and developed from the unitary Brahman. The second was maintained by thinkers such as Kakuda Kātyāyana, who did not recognize a single Absolute, but instead argued that people and the world were composed of collections of eternal elements. Their position is called *ārambha-vāda*. Both of these positions were being formulated at the time of the Buddha.

Religious practices at this time were also classified into two major groups: meditation and ascetic practices. Those who advocated meditation tried to realize deliverance through contemplation and quieting the mind. The ascetics tried to attain salvation by using ascetic practices to cut off the delusions that controlled the mind.

In conclusion, by the time of the Buddha, Vedic religion had already lost most of its power to attract people, but no new religious authority had replaced it. In this age of religious ferment, many thinkers appeared, each seeking the Absolute within himself.

CHAPTER 2

The Life of the Buddha

Terminology

THE FOUNDER OF BUDDHISM is called the "Buddha" by both the Buddhist and non-Buddhist religious traditions of India; his followers were sometimes referred to as Bauddhas by the adherents of other schools.[1] The term "Buddha" means "enlightened one." Thus Buddhism might be called "the religion of enlightenment." Although the term "Buddha" eventually was used to refer to the founder of Buddhism, it originally was a common noun often used by the Jainas. For example, according to the Jaina text the *Isibhāsiyāiṃ,* the forty-five sages *(ṛṣi)* are "all *buddhas* who will not return to this world."[2] The Jainas usually used the term "Jina" (spiritual victor) to refer to their de facto founder Mahāvīra. Consequently, their religion is known as Jainism. The term "Jina" is also found in Buddhist texts, especially in those from the Mahāyāna tradition. Another term used by both Jainas and Buddhists was *"arhat"* or *"arahant"* (worthy). This term was especially important in Jainism because followers of Jainism were known as *ārhata.*[3] In Buddhism it came to refer to those followers of the Buddha who had attained enlightenment, while the term "Buddha" was used to refer only to Śākyamuni Buddha. Because Śākyamuni's followers often used the term "Buddha," their religion took its name from that term. Jainism and Buddhism also shared many other terms such as *muni* (sage) and *bhagavat* (lord).[4]

Birth of the Buddha

The historical Buddha is often referred to as Śākyamuni (the sage of the Śākya or Sakiya people). He was born into the Gautama (P. Gotama) clan. According to traditional accounts, his personal name before he left home to live a religious life was Siddhārtha (P. Siddhattha). The Śākyas were a small *kṣatriya* (warrior caste) tribe who lived on the border of India and Nepal; their capital was at Kapilavastu. The Śākyas were primarily engaged in rice farming. Although Śākyamuni was said to be from a *kṣatriya* family, the Śākya tribe does not appear to have been divided into four castes. Consequently, no evidence exists to indicate whether Śākyamuni was of Aryan or Oriental racial stock. The government was an oligarchy with the leaders alternating as head *(rājan)* of the tribe. Although the Śākya tribe governed itself, it was not completely independent since it was dominated by Kauśala to the south.

Modern scholars often refer to the historical Buddha as Gautama Buddha. Since Gautama is the clan name of the Buddha, the title may have significance when contrasted with Buddhas such as Kāśyapa and Maitreya, who were from different clans. However, since both Kāśyapa and Maitreya are only legendary figures, there are no historical Buddhas who come from any clan other than the Gautama clan. The epithet "Śākyamuni" (Sage of the Śākyas) refers to the historical Buddha in terms of a social group that was larger than the Gautama clan. Moreover, Śākyamuni is the title that has traditionally been used to refer to the historical Buddha.

The Buddha's father, Śuddhodana, was one of the leaders of the Śākyas. The Buddha's mother was named Māyā. Because she died seven days after the birth of the future Buddha, he was raised by her younger sister, Mahāprajāpatī Gautamī. Nanda was his younger half-brother.

As the time approached for Māyā to give birth to the future Buddha, she set out to return to her native village of Devadaha. She gave birth during the journey in a grove at Lumbinī. One or two centuries later, when King Aśoka was on a pilgrimage of the sites associated with the Buddha's life, he traveled to Lumbinī and had a *stūpa* (memorial monument) and a pillar erected there. Approximately eight centuries later, the Chinese pilgrim Hsüan-tsang visited the site. The pillar was discovered in 1896 and the inscription on it deciphered, identifying a site in the modern village of Rummindei as the birthplace of the Buddha.

According to legend, when the Buddha was born a sage named Asita came down from the Himalayas. After looking at the physical features of the baby, he predicted: "This child has only two paths open to him. If he remains a householder, he will become king and unite the world as a universal ruler. If he leaves home (to become a religious mendicant), he will become a Buddha."

Birthdate of the Buddha

A number of different theories have been advanced concerning the birthdate of the Buddha. The Buddha is said to have died at eighty years of age. Thus, most theories are based on determining the date of his death and then calculating backward to arrive at the date of his birth. One of the most widely accepted theories is based on the Sri Lankan historical chronicles, the *Dīpavaṃsa* and the *Mahāvaṃsa.* On the basis of these sources, Wilhelm Geiger calculated that the Buddha died in 483 B.C.E. and consequently had been born in 563 B.C.E.[5] Hermann Jacobi, using the same method and sources, maintained that the Buddha died in 484 B.C.E.[6] The Japanese scholar Kanakura Enshō has arrived at the same date.[7] The "dotted record" transmitted along with the Chinese translation of the Theravāda commentary on the *Vinaya,* the *Samantapāsādikā* (*T* 1462), also indicates a similar date. At the conclusion of each rainy season retreat after the Buddha's death, a dot was added to this text. This "dotted record" was cited by Fei Ch'ang-fang, who finished compiling a Buddhist bibliography and history, the *Li-tai san-pao chi,* in 597 C.E. Fei noted that 975 dots had been added to the text as of the year 489 C.E. An error by Fei changes the date to 490 C.E. The death of the Buddha would thus have occurred 975 years prior to 490 C.E., in 485 B.C.E., according to the dotted record.[8]

The above theories were based primarily on the Sri Lankan historical chronicles. Although some discrepancies are found in the theories, most modern scholars agree that the Buddha died within a few years of 480 B.C.E. Around the end of the nineteenth century, Max Müller argued that the Buddha had died in 477 B.C.E. and maintained that the Sri Lankan chronicles should be corrected to conform to evidence found in Brahmanical and Jaina works. However, many variant theories are found in the Hindu *Purāṇas* and Jaina texts. Müller unscientifically selected only those texts that approximated the material found in the Sri Lankan chronicles. Consequently, Müller's theory has few, if any, modern supporters.

The prominent modern Japanese scholar Ui Hakuju (1882–1963) has criticized the above theories. Basing his argument on materials from the Northern tradition of Buddhism, Ui argued that only 116 years had passed between the death of the Buddha and Aśoka's accession to the throne. The Buddha's dates were thus 466–386 B.C.E.[9] Ui noted that the Sri Lankan chronicles stated that 218 years had elapsed between the Buddha's death and Aśoka's reign and that five kings had ruled during that period. However, 218 years was too long a period for only five kings to have ruled; Ui thus rejected the date of the Buddha's death based on the Sri Lankan tradition. Ui arrived at his revised date of 386 B.C.E. for the Buddha's death by taking 271 B.C.E. as the date of Aśoka's accession and then counting backward 116 years on the basis of evidence from the Northern tradition. More recently, Nakamura Hajime has accepted most of Ui's calculations but revised the date of Aśoka's accession to 268 B.C.E., thus arguing that the death of the Buddha occurred in 383 B.C.E.[10]

A difference of approximately one century remains between the position maintained by Ui and the positions held by most Western scholars (who have generally based their calculations on Sri Lankan sources). At present, it seems impossible to arrive at a convincing theory to explain the differences between the two positions. Initially, the Sri Lankan chronicles would seem to be the superior source because of their detailed lists of kings and the number of years each reigned. The sources of the Northern tradition seem weaker because they state only that more than one hundred years elapsed between the death of the Buddha and the accession of Aśoka, without listing the names of kings and the number of years they reigned. However, the Sri Lankan tradition lists only five kings as reigning for a period of more than two centuries. It also includes a lineage of five masters of the *vinaya* between the time of Śākyamuni and Aśoka: Upāli, Dāsaka, Sonaka, Siggava, and Moggaliputta Tissa. (The Northern tradition also maintains that five monks assumed important leadership roles in the order between the time of the Buddha and Aśoka: Mahākāśyapa, Ānanda, Madhyāntika, Śāṇakavāsī, and Upagupta.)

According to the Sri Lankan chronicles, Buddhism had divided into a large number of schools by the time of Aśoka. However, little evidence indicating that so many divisions had already occurred is found in Aśoka's edicts, although edicts from Sāñcī, Sārnāth, and Kauśambī, all important Buddhist sites during Aśoka's reign, admonished the order against permitting schisms. Such edicts indicate that conflicts were arising in Buddhist orders in a number of areas. These disagreements probably occurred after the debate at the Second Buddhist Council over the ten points of monastic discipline. If the fragmentation of Buddhism into many schools had not advanced very far by the time of Aśoka, then Nakamura's dates of 463–383 B.C.E. for the Buddha would be appropriate; they fit in well with the subsequent history of the development of the Buddhist order (see chapter six). The adoption of Nakamura's dates in this history, however, should not be interpreted as a rejection of the Sri Lankan chronicles as sources. Rather, the problem of the Buddha's dates needs to be studied further, particularly in relation to the development of Jainism and Brahmanism.

Renunciation of Lay Life

According to traditional accounts, Śākyamuni lived a life of luxury as a child. When he grew to be a young man, he married Yaśodharā; they had a son, Rāhula. Śākyamuni was deeply disturbed, however, by existential problems concerning the meaning of life. When he was twenty-nine years old (according to variant accounts, he was nineteen or thirty-one), he left his family to become a wandering mendicant.

Śākyamuni seems to have had a contemplative nature. Even before he left his family, he had once begun to meditate without any effort or preparation and had attained the First Trance as he was sitting under a tree watching his father, the king, plowing a nearby field as part of a religious ceremony. Śākyamuni is also said to have noticed the birds eating the worms turned up by the plowing and to have been profoundly moved by the way in which living creatures all harmed each other. He realized that although people may be repelled by seeing an old man, everyone ages. Although people do not want to suffer from illness or to come in contact with sick people, no one can escape illness. Although people fear death and do not wish to die, no one can escape death.

Śākyamuni's concern over the existential problems of life and death was dramatized in later biographies through descriptions of his encounters with four men while on four sightseeing journeys outside his father's palace. First he encountered an old man, then a sick man, and finally a dead man. Deeply disturbed, he returned home each time. On his fourth outing he saw a wandering mendicant and resolved to leave home and become a religious mendicant.

Śākyamuni left home against his parents' will. In the middle of the night, he mounted his favorite horse, Kaṇṭhaka, and with his charioteer, Chanda, left the palace secretly. According to the *Mahāparinibbānasuttanta* (*DN,* vol. 2, p. 151), he "left home to seek the good *(kusala).*"

Religious Austerities

Śākyamuni left home, shaved his head, put on robes, and set out for the country of Magadha to the south, the home of many groups of mendicants. At that time, the public road known as the Northern Route (Uttarāpatha) began at Śrāvastī, ran east past Kapilavastu, and then turned south to Kuśinagara, Vaiśālī, and the Ganges River. The road then crossed the Ganges, entered Magadha, and ended in Rājagṛha.

Śākyamuni probably traveled to the city of Rājagṛha on this road. According to traditional sources, King Bimbisāra saw Śākyamuni begging one day and decided to invite him to become a minister in the government. Bimbisāra dispatched a retainer to persuade Śākyamuni to abandon his religious quest, but Śākyamuni refused.

Śākyamuni eventually began practicing religious austerities under the guidance of one of the most famous religious leaders of that time, Ārāḍa Kālāma (P. Āḷāra Kālāma), a master of meditation. He taught Śākyamuni how to attain a State of Nothingness through meditation. Śākyamuni, however, was not satisfied with the results of the meditation and went to practice under a different teacher, Udraka Rāmaputra (P. Uddaka Rāmaputta), who had attained a trance state of Neither Perception nor Nonperception. This trance was more subtle than the State of Nothingness and was said to completely quiet the mind, perhaps by uniting it with some form of the Absolute. However, Śākyamuni realized that when he emerged from the trance, his mind was still buffeted by everyday problems. Thus simply quieting the mind through meditation was not equivalent to realizing the Absolute. Meditation was useful in disciplining the mind; but the Absolute also had a rational quality, which could be realized only through wisdom. And so Śākyamuni left Udraka Rāmaputra.

The Trance of Nothingness and the Trance of Neither Perception nor Nonperception are both included in the early Buddhist list of Four Formless Trances. Although some scholars have questioned whether these trances were actually contrived by Ārāḍa and Udraka, meditation *(dhyāna)* was certainly used to quiet the mind before the time of the Buddha. Relics from the Indus civilization indicate that the Indus people probably practiced meditation. Ārāḍa and Udraka were certainly practitioners of meditation. When the Buddha described the Threefold Teaching of morality, meditation, and wisdom, however, he placed wisdom above meditation. In this way he indicated his belief that meditation by itself would not allow a practitioner to discover the truth. Meditation was a necessary tool for training the mind, but only when it was combined with wisdom could the truth be realized.

Śākyamuni then sought the solitude of the forest to practice austerities. He chose a spot near the village at Uruvilvā-senāni on the Nairañjanā River where he underwent disciplines such as constantly clenching his teeth and pressing his tongue against his palate. Only through a strong act of will could he overcome the pain such practices entailed. Once he entered a trance and stopped all breath from passing through his mouth and nose, but then is said to have begun breathing through his ears. Finally he stopped even this type of breathing. Bearing the pain and suffering that accompanied these practices required much effort; but in this way, religious practitioners tried to establish correct mindfulness and to develop a state of mind that would not be subject to suffering. By stopping his breath, Śākyamuni is said to have fallen into a state close to death.

At other times Śākyamuni fasted, living without food for several days. He also used the technique of gradually reducing his food intake until he had completely stopped eating. Because of these long periods of fasting, he became emaciated, his skin hung loose, his hair fell out, and his body was wracked with pain. Through these ascetic practices and by overcoming his pain, Śākyamuni strengthened his resolve and tried to free his mind from all suffering.

During the time a practitioner is in the forest performing his austerities and learning to bear pain, various wrong views may arise because he clings to life. Or he may be tempted by the desires and pleasures of the householder's life. Doubts may arise concerning whether he is following the correct religious path. He may fear harm from the animals of the forest at night. For Śākyamuni, these doubts, fears, and wrong views were personified as Māra the evil one (Māra-Pāpimant), who tried to persuade the future Buddha to abandon his austerities. Māra followed Śākyamuni for seven years, but never succeeded in persuading Śākyamuni to abandon his quest. (In later biographies, the Buddha's austerities are usually said to have lasted six years, a figure that may be interpreted as "six full years" or almost seven years. According to some later accounts, the future Buddha spent this period at Mount Daṇḍaka in Gandhāra.)

A strong will was necessary to overcome the fears, doubts, and suffering that ascetic practices entailed. The future Buddha had strengthened his will to the point where his mind was probably free from any suffering. Although he had partially attained the freedom he sought, he realized that strong resolve is not the same as correct knowledge. The future Buddha had undergone suffering and pain greater than that borne by any other man. During this time, he had developed and maintained correct mindfulness but still had not realized any religious knowledge surpassing that of ordinary people. At that point, he remembered the time from his youth when, accompanying his father to an agricultural festival, he had sat under a tree and easily attained the First Trance. After thinking about this incident from his youth, Śākyamuni abandoned austerities and decided that meditative practices were indeed the path to enlightenment *(bodhi)*.

Enlightenment

Although Śākyamuni had ceased his ascetic practices, his body was so emaciated that he thought it would be difficult to attain the bliss of even the First Trance. He finally decided to eat solid food to restore his strength. Milk and rice were offered by a young woman named Sujātā. After eating, Śākyamuni bathed in the Nairañjanā River and drank some water. When the mendicants who had been accompanying him saw him abandoning his austerities, they said, "The *śramaṇa* Gautama has fallen into luxurious ways and abandoned his spiritual efforts" and left him.

With the renewed strength from the food, Śākyamuni built a seat under an *aśvattha* tree, commenced meditating, and finally attained supreme enlightenment *(abhisambodhi),* thereby becoming a Buddha (enlightened being). The *aśvattha* tree, a type of fig tree, later became known as the *bodhi* (enlightenment)-tree. The site was called Buddhagayā; a *stūpa* was later erected there and it became a major pilgrimage site for Buddhists.

According to the Theravāda tradition, the Buddha attained enlightenment on the night of the full moon of the month of Vaiśākha (Visākhā), which falls in April or May of the Western calendar. In Japan, the eighth day of the twelfth month is said to be the day of the Buddha's enlightenment. According to traditional accounts, the Buddha left home when he was twenty-nine, attained enlightenment when he was thirty-five, taught others for forty-five years, and died at eighty. According to a variant tradition, however, he left home when he was nineteen, attained enlightenment at thirty, and preached for fifty years.

In traditional biographies, the Buddha's enlightenment is described as occurring after a battle with Māra, the god of death and desire. With enlightenment, the Buddha overcame his fear of death and cut off his desires. Hence the battle with Māra may represent some of the psychological conflicts that religious practitioners encounter. In later accounts, Māra is said to have actually appeared in front of the Buddha. Māra also appeared after the Buddha's enlightenment to tempt the Buddha and to indicate that even an enlightened being cannot escape desires such as those for food and sleep or pains such as illness and death. The Buddha, however, never succumbed to Māra's temptations.

Determining the exact content of the Buddha's enlightenment poses several major scholarly problems. The *Āgamas* include a number of statements concerning the Buddha's enlightenment. The Japanese scholar Ui Hakuju has compiled a list of fifteen explanations from early sources.[11] Three of these are particularly noteworthy. According to these explanations, the Buddha attained enlightenment either by understanding the Four Noble Truths, realizing the twelve links of Dependent Origination, or mastering the Four Trances and attaining the Three Superhuman Powers. (These teachings are explained in chapter three.) The Four Noble Truths, however, are designed to be used in instructing others and do not seem to represent the content of the Buddha's enlightenment in its earliest form. Simpler versions of the theory of Dependent Origination can be found in early sources, indicating that the twelve-link version of the theory was formulated later. However, the twelve-link version of Dependent Origination may be a systematized explanation based on Śākyamuni's meditations when he realized enlightenment. The third theory, that the Buddha attained the Four Trances and Three Superhuman Powers when he attained enlightenment, was also a relatively late theory, according to Ui.

The last element of the Three Superhuman Powers, the knowledge that all one's defilements have been eradicated, is similar in many ways to the Four Noble Truths and the theory of Dependent Origination. According to another tradition, the Buddha understood the Dharma (Teaching) when he was enlightened. When he was sitting under a tree in meditation after his enlightenment, he is said to have thought, "It is ill to live without paying honor and obedience to a superior. But I do not see anyone in the world who has perfected morality, meditation, wisdom, emancipation, or the knowledge of emancipation more than I. Thus I will live by paying honor and obedience to the Dharma through which I am enlightened" (*SN,* vol. 1, p. 139). In this sense, both the Four Noble Truths and the doctrine of Dependent Origination are the Dharma. The Dharma that the Buddha realized through his enlightenment can be understood by examining the most basic elements of the Buddhist doctrines contained in the early scriptures.

Some modern scholars of Buddhism have emphasized in their interpretations of the Buddha's enlightenment the Buddha's origins as a member of the Gautama clan of the Śākya tribe. Although the Buddha did come from a particular tribe, he had followers from a variety of states of central India. When he died and was cremated, eight of the countries of central India divided his ashes and erected *stūpas.* Thus Buddhism was at first a religion practiced by a limited group of people in a small area, but later it spread to all of India and to many other parts of Asia. In contrast, Jainism, which arose at the same time as Buddhism and had similar doctrines, never spread outside India. Hinduism, which was much stronger than Jainism, only spread to a few parts of South and Southeast Asia. It seems, then, that Buddhism had qualities that enabled it to become a world religion and make it significant to more than just a limited number of tribes or peoples. Those qualities were already present in the Buddha's enlightenment. If that enlightenment had been a phenomenon that could be explained as a function of his membership in a certain tribe, then the transformation of Buddhism into a world religion would have required some major figure as a spokesman. But no such figure appears in the history of Buddhism. The religion founded by the Buddha included a teaching, the elimination of suffering, that transcended the concerns of any particular tribe.

Through meditation the Buddha realized the wisdom that accompanies enlightenment. Traditionally, he is said to have realized enlightenment through the cultivation of the Four Trances and the Threefold Studies. Enlightenment, however, is not equivalent to the Four Trances. Trance (*dhyāna;* Ch. *ching lu* 'quiet contemplation') is only one type of meditation. It was called a comfortable way to attain enlightenment because the practitioner sits in a full-lotus position with the body in a comfortable position. Severe austerities are not required. The practitioner concentrates his spiritual energy and enters the first trance and then gradually deepens it, going into the second, third, and fourth trances. Through this practice the mind is quieted. Other forms of meditation—*yoga,* for example—were also practiced in India. Through these practices the mind could be concentrated and focused until it had become quiet or thought had ceased. Advocates of the various schools of *yoga* claimed that a form of mystical wisdom could be realized through such practices. Buddhist *dhyāna* differed from yogic trance in that it was much more dynamic; it was a form of mental concentration that permitted the free activity of wisdom.

The definition of Buddhist enlightenment as "seeing things as they actually are" suggests the dynamic nature of Buddhist meditation. The mind was considered to have an innate wisdom. Because its basic nature involved thought, when the mind was quieted and focused and concentration strengthened, then a superior form of wisdom would naturally be manifested. Both Buddhist meditation and *yoga* were means of producing wisdom, but since they employed different methods of concentration, the resultant wisdom probably differed. The wisdom produced when enlightenment was realized through Buddhist meditation was described as "seeing the Dharma."

The Buddha progressed through more profound meditative states as he passed through the Four Trances. These were probably the natural result of his many years of training, a temperament that seems to have been suited to meditation from the time he was young, and the training he received from his early teachers Ārāḍa and Udraka. The term *dhyāna* has been used since the early *Upaniṣads* with the meaning of "meditation" (*Chāndogya Upaniṣad* 7.6.1), but the Four Trances should probably be regarded as a new meditation system developed by Buddhists. The Four Trances were a dynamic way of focusing the mind. The wisdom produced through them was not a mystical form of intuition. Rather, it allowed a person to see things as they actually are in a rational and free manner. With that wisdom, the practitioner could know truth and firmly adhere to that truth. When he could not be shaken or moved from that truth by fear, pain, or passions, he had realized enlightenment. Because the mind had been freed from the fetters of the defilements and passions, this state was called "emancipation" or "salvation" *(mokṣa, vimokṣa, vimukti).* The truth that he realized through his enlightenment was called *nirvāṇa* (P. *nibbāna*). Some scholars have explained salvation as referring to the freedom of the mind from afflictions and *nirvāṇa* as referring to peace.[12]

The First Sermon

After the Buddha had attained enlightenment, he remained under the *bodhi*-tree and entered a deep state of meditative concentration *(samādhi)* that lasted for seven days. When he emerged from his meditation, he went and sat under another tree to contemplate the bliss that had resulted from his enlightenment. While he was sitting under this second tree, two merchants, Trapuśa and Bhallika, saw the Buddha, offered him cakes sweetened with honey, and thus became the first lay Buddhists. The Buddha did not leave the tree for five weeks. During this time, he began to doubt whether he should teach the contents of his enlightenment to others. Because his teaching (Dharma) was subtle and profound, he feared that others would not understand it even if he preached it to them. The Buddha's doubts may also have arisen from his temporary difficulty in discovering a purpose in life once he had attained enlightenment, the highest goal for a religious man. The Buddha overcame his doubts by turning away from the self-centered quest for his own enlightenment, deciding instead to preach to others and help them toward salvation. The resolution of the Buddha's doubts is portrayed in a myth that relates that during the five weeks when the Buddha was quietly contemplating his enlightenment he began to feel hesitant about preaching. Only when the god Brahmā intervened and encouraged him to preach did the Buddha agree to do so.

Some modern scholars have argued that deep religious significance can be found in Śākyamuni Buddha's hesitation to preach.[13] But the hesitation could have sprung from many sources. Someone who has himself accomplished a major undertaking can perhaps understand that nihilistic feelings may beset a person after success. Many of the Buddha's disciples probably experienced such feelings after they had realized enlightenment. The legends about Śākyamuni's hesitation to preach may have arisen because the Buddha was tempted simply to enter complete *nirvāṇa* after his enlightenment, thereby avoiding the difficulties that the propagation of his teaching would entail. Buddhists came to believe that some Buddhas in the past had decided, in fact, not to preach. Some modern scholars argue that the *pratyekabuddha* (P. *paccekabuddha*) originated from such stories. The *pratyekabuddha* was a *buddha* who had attained enlightenment but died (entered complete *nirvāṇa*) without ever deciding to preach to others. The *pratyekabuddha* was said by later Buddhists to have a separate vehicle *(yāna)* to enlightenment. Other modern scholars have argued that the concept of the *pratyekabuddha* did not arise from stories about Śākyamuni Buddha's hesitancy to preach but from the examples of sages *(ṛṣi)* who lived and practiced alone.[14]

Once the Buddha decided to preach, he had to determine who his first audience would be. He eventually decided to preach to the five monks who had helped him when he was undergoing austerities because he thought they would be able to understand the truths he had discovered. He traveled west to the Deer Park (Mṛgadāva) at Benares. Today the Deer Park is known as Sārnāth and is the site of ruins commemorating the Buddha's first sermon. Among the ruins is a pillar erected by King Aśoka. On the capital of the pillar are some exquisitely carved lions and the wheel of the teaching (Dharmacakra).

The Buddha's preaching is called the "turning of the wheel of the teaching." When the Buddha preached his first sermon to the five monks at Benares, he told them to avoid the two extremes of asceticism or luxurious living; instead, they were to follow the Middle Way *(madhyamā-pratipad).* He also told them about the Four Noble Truths, which consisted of the truths of suffering, the cause of suffering, the cessation of suffering, and the way to end suffering. The first of the five men to become enlightened through the Buddha's teaching was Ājñātakauṇḍinya, who became Śākyamuni's first disciple. Later the other four attained enlightenment and also became disciples, thus establishing the Buddhist order *(saṅgha).* The Buddha then explained that people had no eternal soul and were composed of the five aggregates, whereupon the five disciples realized the enlightenment of *arhats* (an *arhat* is defined as someone who had completely eliminated all defilements). Because the Buddha had eliminated all his defilements he was also called an *arhat.*

However, since the wisdom of the Buddha attained through enlightenment surpassed that of his disciples, the disciples were not called *buddhas*. The men who became monks were called mendicants *(bhikṣu)* because they lived by begging their food while devoting themselves to religious practice.

Growth of the Buddhist Order

The Buddha's first disciples were the five monks to whom he preached at Sārnāth. According to the earlier biographies of the Buddha, he next converted Yaśas, the son of a wealthy elder *(śreṣṭhin)* of Benares. Yaśas' parents and wife became Buddhist laymen *(upāsaka)* and laywomen *(upāsikā)*. Fifty-four of Yaśas' friends entered the order and were ordained as monks. All of them are said to have become *arhats*. The Buddha sent them out to spread his teachings, saying: "Go out and preach, monks, out of compassion for sentient beings, and out of concern for the world. Bring benefits, happiness, and caring to gods and men. No two of you should go to the same place. Preach the Dharma with reason and eloquence so that it will be good at the beginning, middle, and end" (*Vinaya,* vol. 1, p. 20). Out of compassion, the Buddha wished to convey to common people at least some of the truths he had realized.

The Buddha subsequently returned to Magadha, where he converted many people. The Buddha's victory over a noted religious teacher, Uruvilvā Kāśyapa, through a demonstration of superhuman powers, resulted in the conversion to Buddhism of Uruvilvā Kāśyapa, his two younger brothers, and their disciples. The Buddha's fame spread as a result of these and other conversions. When he led his retinue to Rājagṛha, King Śrenika Bimbisāra became a lay disciple and gave the Buddha a bamboo grove, which was used as quarters for monks. Bimbisāra thus became the first head of state to protect the order, and the bamboo grove became the base for the order's activities.

Two disciples of the skeptic Sañjayin, Mahāmaudgalyāyana and Śāriputra, became the Buddha's disciples. Śāriputra was converted when he heard one of the Buddha's first five monastic converts, Aśvajit, recite, "Of all things that arise from cause, the Tathāgatha has explained their causes and their cessations. Thus has the great *śramaṇa* taught" (*Vinaya,* vol. 1, p. 41). Śāriputra then persuaded Mahāmaudgalyāyana also to become the Buddha's disciple. The Buddha is said to have predicted that the two men would become leaders of the order; and, in fact, they played major roles in spreading the Buddha's teachings.

Around the same time, Mahākāśyapa converted to Buddhism when he saw the Buddha near the Bahuputraka Caitya (*Mahāvastu,* vol. 3, p. 50). He is said to have practiced religious austerities assiduously. After the Buddha's death, he assembled the order and supervised recitation of the Buddha's teachings at the First Council.

Among the Buddha's major female lay disciples was Viśākhā Mṛgāramātṛ, a native of Śrāvastī and a generous donor to the order. Much later, the king of the city, Prasenajit, was converted to Buddhism by his wife, Mallikā.

The most important of the Buddha's lay disciples was Sudatta, a wealthy merchant from Śrāvastī known by the epithet Anāthapiṇḍada or "the giver of food to the unprotected" because of the many alms he gave to orphans. He first heard that "a Buddha had appeared" when he was on a business trip to Rājagṛha. Before the night was over, he had visited the Buddha at Śītavana. After Sudatta became the Buddha's disciple, he invited the Buddha to come to Śrāvastī. To provide Buddhist monks with residences, Sudatta purchased a park from Prince Jeta of Śrāvastī, had quarters for the monks built in it, and presented it to the order. This monastery was known as Jetavana. Its first buildings were erected in just three months, indicating that they were probably simple wood structures.

A number of years after his enlightenment, the Buddha returned to Kapilavastu to see his father, the king, and his foster mother, the queen. At that time he initiated his son Rāhula, who was still a child, as a novice *(śrāmaṇera)* and assigned Śāriputra to instruct Rāhula. The Buddha subsequently initiated many other young men including his cousins Devadatta and Ānanda, his half-brother Nanda, and a barber named Upāli, who had served the Śākya nobility. Upāli eventually became an expert in monastic discipline and played an important role in the early Buddhist order.

During the forty-five years between the Buddha's enlightenment and death, he traveled and preached in central India, staying primarily in Magadha and Kauśala. On a typical journey, the Buddha might have set out from Rājagṛha in the southeast and traveled north, passing through Nālandā and arriving in the small village of Pāṭaliputra (at the site of the modern city of Patna). The Buddha would then cross the Ganges River and go to Vaiśālī on the north bank, entering the country of the Licchavis. He would continue north through Kuśinagara and then turn west to Kapilavastu and southwest to Śrāvastī. From there he might go south through Āḷavī to Kauśāmbī, then east to Benares, and from there back to Rājagṛha.

Many of these sites became shrines or important Buddhist centers. One of the Buddha's favorite places to stop near Rājagṛha was

Gṛdhrakūṭa Hill. He sometimes stayed at the Āmrayaṣṭikā and Yaṣṭivana groves near Rājagṛha. The First Council was held in the Saptaparṇaguhā, a cave near Rājagṛha. In Vaiśālī, he would often stay at the large Mahāvana lecture hall. In Kauśāmbī, the capital of Vatsa, King Udayana of Vatsa became an important patron of Buddhism after he was converted by his wife, Queen Śyāmāvatī. A small monastery in Kauśāmbī, the Ghositārāma, was given to the Buddhist order by a devout layman, Ghosita; after the Buddha's death it developed into a large monastery.

During the Buddha's lifetime, the monasteries were built of wood. Passages in the *Vinaya* as well as archeological excavations of Pāṭaliputra have indicated that many of its oldest sections, even the palaces of kings, were constructed of wood, and the fences around the earliest *stūpas* were also wooden. As timber became scarcer, however, stone was increasingly used. The Buddhist *stūpas* and other monuments that have survived until the present day were constructed of stone.

After many of the young men of the Śākyas had become monks, the Buddha's foster mother and aunt, Mahāprajāpatī Gautamī, expressed her desire to become a nun. She went before the Buddha together with a number of young women to ask permission to become nuns, but the Buddha refused her request even after she had repeated it several times. Only after Ānanda interceded with the Buddha was the establishment of an order of nuns *(bhikṣuṇī)* reluctantly permitted. To govern the relations between monks and nuns and to prevent sexual activity, the Buddha established stringent restrictions concerning the interactions between them. In addition, nuns were required to observe "eight weighty rules" *(gurudharma)* that made them subordinate to the order of monks. Despite such restrictions on their activities, many able nuns were active during the lifetime of the Buddha. Kṣemā and Dharmadinnā were famous for their knowledge and frequently lectured to men. Utpalavarṇā was skilled in the use of superhuman abilities, and Kṛśāgautamī attained a remarkably profound level of enlightenment. The names of many other nuns are recorded in early Buddhist literature.

Details about many of the Buddha's lay disciples are known. Citra was well versed in Buddhist doctrine, and Ugra of Vaiśālī and Mahānāma of the Śākyas were famed for their almsgiving.

The names of many of the Buddha's monastic disciples are known, as are details about them. The bandit Aṅgulimālya was taught by the Buddha and became his disciple. Kṣullapanthaka could not memorize even one verse of the Buddha's teaching, but he still attained a deep level of enlightenment through the Buddha's guidance. Pūrṇa Maitrāyaṇīputra was an able preacher. Mahākātyāyana and Mahākauṣṭhila were skilled at explaining the Dharma. Mahākātyāyana spread Buddhism to Avanti, south of central India. Pūrṇa was responsible for spreading Buddhism to Sunāparantaka on the west coast of India. According to a story that probably dates from the period after Buddhism had already spread to South India, a Brahman named Bāvarī from the Deccan in South India sent sixteen of his disciples to central India to hear the Buddha's teachings ("Pārāyanavagga" chapter of the *Suttanipāta*). The sixteen disciples journeyed along the old trade route known as the Southern Road (Dakṣiṇāpatha) from Pratiṣṭhāna in the Deccan through Ujjayinī in the country of Avanti, on to Vidiśā, Kauśāmbī, and Sāketa, finally arriving in Śrāvastī. Because the Buddha was no longer in Śrāvastī, they continued traveling up the Northern Road (Uttarāpatha) to Rājagṛha, where they met the Buddha and became his disciples. Among their number were Ajita and Tissa-Metteya, two men who later may have been somehow identified with Maitreya (P. Metteya), the future Buddha.

Death of the Buddha

The Buddha's teachings continued to spread through central India. During this time, Buddhism competed with other religious groups in India. The most noteworthy of these were the Jainas and Ājīvikas. Both Aśoka and his grandson Daśaratha donated caves in the Barabar Hills to the Ājīvikas, indicating that the Ājīvikas were still influential in central India during the centuries after the Buddha's death.

During the last years of the Buddha's life, Devadatta plotted to cause a schism in the Buddhist order. He joined forces with Ajātaśatru, who had killed his father, King Bimbisāra of Magadha, in order to inherit the throne. Together they made plans that would bring them fame and power. Devadatta went to Śākyamuni to ask for permission to lead the Buddhist order, but Śākyamuni refused his request. Devadatta is then said to have attempted to kill the Buddha by releasing a mad elephant that tried to charge the Buddha. Later he pushed a rock off a mountaintop down toward the Buddha, a fragment of which cut the Buddha's foot. When these attempts to kill the Buddha failed, Devadatta attempted to cause a schism in the order by proposing five new rules that required greater austerities for monks. He thus tried to attract to his cause many of those who had only recently joined the order. However, two of the Buddha's leading disciples, Śāriputra and Mahāmaudgalyāyana, managed to thwart his plans. Among Devadatta's followers were Kokālika and Katamorakatiṣyaka. Ajātaśatru later repented the murder of his father, Bimbisāra, and became a follower of the Buddha.

King Prasenajit of Kauśala died and was succeeded by his son Viḍūḍabha. Because the Buddha's tribe, the Śākyas, had insulted Viḍūḍabha earlier, one of the new king's first acts was to attack and destroy them. This occurred late in Śākyamuni's lifetime. Later, Kauśala was destroyed by Ajātaśatru, who then turned his attention toward the Vṛji people, who lived north of the Ganges.

Around that time, Śākyamuni was leaving Rājagṛha on the last journey before his death. He crossed the Ganges and entered Vaiśālī, where he converted the courtesan Āmrapālī, who gave her gardens to the Buddhist order. While he was passing the rainy season retreat alone at Vaiśālī, the Buddha became very ill. According to later traditions, Māra appeared before him and urged him to die. The Buddha then predicted that he would die in three months.

Śākyamuni continued his journey, leaving Vaiśālī, passing through many villages, and eventually arriving at Pāvā. There he was fed by a blacksmith named Cunda and became violently ill with diarrhea and hemorrhaging. The food Śākyamuni had been served was called *sūkaramaddava* in Pāli; modern scholars have identified it as either a soft type of pork or a variety of mushroom. The Buddha continued to travel despite his illness, arriving in Kuśinagara (Kusinārā), where he died (or entered *parinirvāṇa*) in a grove of *śāla* trees.

According to the *Mahāparinibbāna suttanta,* Śākyamuni left a number of instructions for the order before he died. For example, when he was asked about the future of the order, he answered, "What does the order expect of me? I have preached without distinguishing between esoteric and exoteric doctrines. In the teachings of the Buddha there is no such thing as the closed fist of a teacher hiding things from his disciples" (chap. 2, v. 32). He thus explained that the Buddha was not to be thought of as the head of the order; rather, the order was to be a cooperative community without a specified leader. After the Buddha's death, his teachings are said to have been passed from Mahākāśyapa to Ānanda, and then to Madhyāntika and so forth. Yet even this lineage refers only to the maintenance of the Buddha's teachings, not to the leadership of the order. The Buddha's attitude is expressed well in his words: "Be a lamp unto yourselves. Be refuges unto yourselves. Let the Dharma be your lamp. Let the Dharma be your refuge" (chap. 2, v. 35).

The Buddha instructed his followers who had become mendicants not to honor his remains *(śarīra).* Rather they were to strive after the highest good (P. *sadattha*). He told them, "You should not think that your teacher's words have ceased and that you no longer have a teacher. Rather you should let the teachings (Dharma) and rules *(vinaya)* that I have set forth be your teacher after I have died" (chap. 6, v. 1). Shortly before his death he asked his assembled disciples three times "Have you any questions?" When they remained silent all three times, he told them, "All things must decay. Be diligent in striving for salvation" (chap. 6, vv. 5–10). Then he entered a trance and died (entered complete *nirvāṇa*).

After the Buddha's death, the Mallas of Kuśinagara took his body, honored it with flowers, scents, and music, and then cremated it. The remains were divided among eight of the peoples of central India, who took their shares and constructed *stūpas* for them. *Stūpas* were also build by individuals for the urn that had held the Buddha's remains and for the ashes from the cremation. In 1898 Peppé excavated an old *stūpa* at Piprāhwā, a site connected with the Śākyas. In it he discovered an urn with an inscription written in characters that indicated it might have been composed at the time of King Aśoka or earlier. According to the inscription, the urn contained the remains of Śākyamuni, which had been enshrined by the Śākyas. After the contents of the urn had been identified as Śākyamuni's remains, part of them were presented to Thailand. Thailand, in turn, divided its portion and sent part of the remains to Japan, where they were enshrined at the Nittaiji Temple in Nagoya. The urn is in the collection of the Calcutta Museum.

In 1958 an urn containing the remains from a cremation was found at the site of Vaiśālī. Although the urn had no inscription, it was similar to the one Peppé had discovered and identified as containing the Buddha's remains. The account in the *Mahāparinibbāna suttanta* of the division of the Buddha's relics into eight parts thus seems to be based on historical fact. These *stūpas* were the forerunners of other *stūpas* that were later erected throughout India and served as centers for Buddhist devotees.

CHAPTER 3

Early Buddhist Doctrine

Introduction to Doctrine

THE TEACHINGS the Buddha had preached during the last forty-five years of his life were recited at the First Council *(saṅgīti).* (Although writing existed at this time, the scriptures were transmitted orally.) The Dharma and *Vinaya* traditionally are said to have been collected at the council. The doctrines (Dharma) were organized into scriptures *(sūtras)* and the *sūtras* were eventually collected to form a *Sūtra-piṭaka* (basket of *sūtras*). The rules and regulations of monastic discipline *(vinaya)* were collected and organized into a *Vinaya-piṭaka* (basket of *Vinaya*). The *Sūtra-piṭaka* is also called the *Āgama* or transmitted (teachings), a term indicating that the *sūtras* consisted of teachings handed down from the past.

As the teachings were committed to memory and passed down from one generation to the next, explanations reflecting the understanding and interpretations of later generations were incorporated into the scriptures. The *sūtras* were expanded and changes were inevitably introduced into the original teachings. Although the teachings found in the *Āgamas* (or *sūtras*) include much more than the teachings of the historical Buddha, many of the *Āgamas* are closely related to the historical Buddha's teachings. Any attempt to ascertain the original teachings of the historical Buddha must be based on this literature. As shall be discussed subsequently, earlier and later passages in the *Āgamas* have been distinguished by modern scholars. In this chapter, the basic teachings of the Buddha and his disciples found in the *Āgamas* are considered together as

"Early Buddhist doctrine." Scholars have been unable to distinguish the teachings of the Buddha from those of his immediate disciples.[1]

Modern scholars have often commented on the basic rationality of Early Buddhist doctrine. Many of the sayings included in an early popular collection of verses, the *Dhammapada,* are ethical and rational; they provide a strong contrast to the superstition that characterized some of the other religions in India at this time. For example, according to the *Dhammapada* (v. 5): "Enmity is not eliminated by enmity. Only when enmity is abandoned, is it eliminated. This is an unchanging and eternal truth." The following verse from the *Dhammapada* (v. 60) is typical of the rational attitude underlying much of the Buddha's teaching: "The night is long for a person who cannot sleep. A *yojana* [approximately nine miles] is a long way for a person who is tired. The cycles of birth and death are long for a foolish person who does not know the True Dharma." Because he believed that moral actions would make men happy and lead to a rich, productive life, the Buddha constantly urged people to act ethically, to love each other, and not to kill. He preached that almsgiving led to happiness but stealing did not, and that speaking the truth led to contentment but lying did not. The Buddha's teachings did not stop with morality. He taught people how to live rationally, how to free themselves from the contradictions and problems of everyday life.

Buddhism strives to raise the moral standards of society and to teach people to live rationally. From the time of early Buddhism onward, Buddhist monasteries have been noted for their hygienic conditions and their high level of culture. Within the simple structure of monastic life, people found the freedom to develop spiritually and culturally. Architectural and artistic techniques developed around monasteries and *stūpas.* Discourses on agricultural methods and on the investment of merchants' assets are found in the *Āgamas,* and discussions on medicines and medical practices are included in the *Vinaya.* But Buddhism does more than teach people how to live rational and sensible lives. It contains insights into the existential and spiritual problems that people encounter and guides them as they seek to escape from their suffering. Buddhist practice focuses on the resolution of the problem of human suffering.

The Four Noble Truths

The suffering *(duḥkha)* that characterizes human existence is often categorized into four types: birth, old age, illness, and death. An additional four types are sometimes added: separation from loved ones, association with people one hates, inability to obtain what one desires, and clinging to the five aggregates (*skandha,* discussed later in this chapter). The periods of happiness that occur in a person's life invariably end when he is confronted with the suffering of illness and death. The basic cause of such suffering lies in man's clinging to his existence. When birth, old age, illness, and death are considered as natural phenomena, they are not suffering. They are characterized as suffering only when considered from the point of view of the individual. Because birth, old age, illness, and death are inescapable facts of human existence, suffering is called the First Noble Truth *(duḥkha-āryasatya).* The full extent to which human existence is characterized by suffering can only be understood by a sage *(ārya).*

The Second Noble Truth concerns the cause of suffering *(duḥkhasamudaya-āryasatya).* Existence entails suffering for the individual because of the very basic mental attribute of "thirst" *(tṛṣṇā),* which lies at the bottom of all of his desires. This thirst is never satisfied; it is the desire that lies at the heart of man's discontent. It is called "thirst" because in intensity it resembles the fervent longing for water of a man with a parched throat. Man is reborn because of this thirst; it is therefore called "the cause of rebirth." Suffering and rebirth are difficult to escape because man seeks unceasingly to satisfy his thirsts, lusts, and longing for happiness.

Three basic types of desire or thirst *(tṛṣṇā)* are distinguished: the desire for sensual objects *(kāma-tṛṣṇā),* the desire for continued existence *(bhava-tṛṣṇā),* and the desire for nonexistence *(vibhava-tṛṣṇā). Kāma-tṛṣṇā* includes the desire for objects of the senses and objects of sexual lust. *Bhava-tṛṣṇā* is the desire for eternal existence, and *vibhava-tṛṣṇā* is the desire to terminate existence. A fourth type of desire, the wish for good fortune, is sometimes added to the above three. These specific types of desires must be distinguished from thirst *(tṛṣṇā)* because thirst can never be satisfied and is the basis of all desires. It is sometimes identified with ignorance *(avidyā).* The various defilements all arise and taint the mind because of thirst and ignorance. Thus the Second Noble Truth concerns the cause of suffering, the way in which thirst is the basis of all defilements *(kleśa).*

The Third Noble Truth, the extinction of suffering *(duḥkhanirodha-āryasatya),* concerns the eradication of thirst. This state is called *"nirvāṇa"* (P. *nibbāna*). Because the mind is freed from all the fetters of thirst, *nirvāṇa* is also called emancipation *(vimukti, vimokṣa, mokṣa).* A person is first partially freed through wisdom, a stage called "emancipation through understanding" *(prajñā-vimukti).* Next, all the defilements are eradicated and the entire mind is freed, a stage called "emancipation of the mind" *(ceto-vimukti).* In this state the mind operates in complete freedom, unaffected by thirst. Because true bliss *(sukha)* is experienced, *nirvāṇa* is sometimes said to be the bliss of extinction. Because the term *"nirvāṇa"* may be translated as "extinction," some people have considered *nirvāṇa* to be a nihilistic state. However, only thirst is extinguished, not the mind itself. Through the extinction of thirst, correct wisdom is manifested, and with that wisdom the unchanging truth of *nirvāṇa* is realized. Thus *nirvāṇa* would seem to be a state of existence that can be logically posited. However, *nirvāṇa* can also be understood as "perfect peace," the tranquility of the mind that has realized *nirvāṇa.* Some scholars prefer to interpret *nirvāṇa* as perfect peace.[2]

The Fourth Noble Truth is the way that leads to the cessation of suffering *(duḥkhanirodhagāminī pratipad).* It is explained through the Eightfold Noble Path *(āryāṣṭāṅga-mārga),* which consists of cultivating the following attitudes and practices: right views, right thought, right speech, right conduct, right livelihood, right effort, right mindfulness, and right concentration. The first element of the path, right views, refers to "seeing things as they actually are." The person who sees the world and himself as they actually are comes to know the truth of Dependent Origination. On the basis of right views, right thought arises, and is followed by right speech, right actions, right livelihood, and right effort. If the Buddhist's everyday life is based on right views, his life is in accord with religious truth. The seventh element of the eightfold path, right mindfulness, has two aspects, right awareness and right memory. Together they are the mental powers necessary to maintain a correct state of mind. The last element of the eightfold path is right concentration. On the basis of right views and right mindfulness, the Buddhist practitioner unifies and controls his mind, and thereby practices right concentration or meditation. Of the eight elements of the path, right views and right concentration are the most important. Wisdom arises out of meditation. By practicing the Eightfold Noble Path, the Buddhist can realize *nirvāṇa* or deliverance.

In Sanskrit the Four Noble Truths are called *ārya-satya.* The term *"ārya"* is translated as "noble" or "sage." The Buddha may have decided to describe some of his most basic doctrines with the word *"ārya"* because he was confident that the truth he had realized was in fact a truth for the Aryan people. (At that time, the Aryan people might have constituted the world as he knew it.)

The Four Noble Truths were the subject of the Buddha's first sermon, delivered to the five monks at the Deer Park. When the five monks had heard the sermon they obtained "eyes of wisdom" *(dharma-*

cakra) and realized that "everything which arises *(samudaye-dharma)* will cease *(nirodhe-dharma).*" They are also said to "have seen the Dharma, known the Dharma, and become enlightened to the Dharma." Thus was the world of the Dharma opened to them.

The Middle Path and Unanswered Questions

The Eightfold Noble Path is also called the Middle Path or Way *(madhyamā-pratipad).* A life devoted to the pursuit of one's desires is vulgar and base. Indulging in sensual pleasure does not lead to spiritual progress. However, the alternative of performing painful austerities does not bring benefits. The Buddha rejected both of these extremes and attained enlightenment by following the Middle Path. The Middle Path consists of such elements as right views, right thought, and right concentration. The significance of the term "right" is not completely explained in the discourses on the Eightfold Noble Path. Rather, it is found in the explanations of the Middle Path.

All people hope that their experiences will be pleasant, but a life devoted singlemindedly to pleasure leads to degradation, not to spiritual progress. The practice of austerities requires a strong will and serious effort; and although such effort is admirable, physical suffering by itself will not result in enlightenment. Austerities alone do not improve the practitioner's ability to reason. The significance of the term "right" in the elements of the Eightfold Noble Path lies in the wisdom to discover the Middle Path between two extremes. The formula of the Middle Path is applied to a variety of situations. Besides its use in regard to pleasure and suffering (*VP,* vol. 1, p. 10), it is applied to such extreme opposite points of view as annihilationism and eternalism (*SN,* vol. 2, p. 38) or the positions that everything exists and nothing exists (*SN,* vol. 2, p. 17). While the Middle Path between suffering and pleasure refers to religious practice, the Middle Path between annihilationism and eternalism or between the views that everything exists and nothing exists refers to religious doctrines. The religious practitioner should strive to perceive things as they actually are, and not speculate or hold prejudices. If he is to follow the Middle Path, then he must avoid fixed and extreme positions.[3]

Viewing things as they actually are led the Buddha to adopt a position of refusing to answer certain questions *(avyākṛta).* When the Buddha was asked whether the universe was eternal or not or whether the universe extended forever, he remained silent and did not answer. He also remained silent when he was asked whether the soul was the same as the body or distinct from it and when he was questioned about whether the Tathāgata (One who has thus come or Buddha) existed after death or not. The Buddha thus knew the limits of knowledge and did not answer questions concerning metaphysical subjects about which man could not have knowledge.

Maintaining silence is difficult when a person is being challenged to respond. Most religious thinkers during the Buddha's time argued that only they knew the absolute truth and that any divergent views were false. They indulged themselves in arguments, each maintaining that his position was correct and attacking the views of others. These men were proud and egoistic. Even if they had discovered religious truths, those truths were sullied by the blind way in which people clung to and defended them. Because the Buddha rejected any type of clinging, he viewed these debates as futile and did not participate in them. He was rational and self-controlled. He believed that even though each of the heterodox thinkers insisted that his position presented absolute truth, their positions were all relative. This situation is illustrated in Buddhist texts by an ancient tale in which King Ādarśamukha had a number of blind men feel an elephant and then explain what an elephant is (*Udāna,* chap. 6, sec. 4). Their descriptions of the elephant differed in accordance with the part of the animal they had felt: for example, the man who felt the tail said the elephant was like a rope; the one who felt the side compared the elephant to a wall.

The Buddha's ability to see things as they actually are and to rise above prejudices and preconceptions is demonstrated by his statement that the four castes are equal.[4] "Men are not born vile. They become vile through their actions. Do not ask about their birth. Only ask about their actions" (*Suttanipāta,* chap. 3, v. 462). Thus did the Buddha insist that a man's worth be determined through his actions.

The Five Aggregates and the Teaching of No-Self

The Buddhist doctrine of no-Self *(anātman;* P. *anattan)* is one of the most basic teachings in Buddhism. It refers to the Buddhist position that no person has a real, permanent, and substantial Self. It does not deny, however, that people have selves or identities in the conventional sense of the word. (In this study, when the word "self" is used in the sense of an eternal entity, it is capitalized; when it is used in the sense of changing entities or personalities, it is not capitalized.) When these selves are viewed correctly they will be seen to develop and change. The ordinary person, however, views at least part of himself as unchanging and thus posits the existence of a permanent Self and clings to this imagined Self. Because he clings to this Self, he suffers in various ways. Yet, if the ordinary person viewed phenomena correctly, he would find no permanent Self.

In Early Buddhism, the body and mind are analyzed into five groups or aggregates *(skandha;* P. *khandha)* to demonstrate the teaching of no-Self. The five aggregates are form *(rūpa),* sensation *(vedanā),* perception *(saṃjñā;* P. *saññā),* mental formations *(saṃskāra;* P. *saṅkhārā),* and consciousness *(vijñāna;* P. *viññāṇa). Rūpa* (form) refers to things with form and color, particularly the body. *Vedanā,* sensations or sense-impressions, are classified into three groups: pleasant, unpleasant, and neither pleasant nor unpleasant. *Saṃjñā* are perceptions, the forming of mental images or representations. *Saṃskāra* refers to the power of mental formation. In this case, it refers especially to the functioning of volition or the will. *Vijñāna* or consciousness refers to the functions of recognition and judgment.

Because a person is composed of these five constantly changing aggregates, his self is impermanent *(anitya).* If a person clings to the false view of an unchanging Self, he will inevitably suffer. Thus impermanent things are said to be or lead to suffering *(duḥkha).* If a permanent Self did exist, it would not be something that suffered or led to suffering, since permanent entities exist in complete freedom and thus have nothing to do with suffering. Thus the very fact of suffering indicates that a person does not have a Self. (If the Self or *ātman* existed, according to Buddhism, it would have the characteristics of being eternal, independent, the central element in the personality, and the controller of actions.) The Buddhist scriptures include statements such as: "A particular thing is not one's Self (when it can be said that) this thing is not mine *(mama),* I *(aham)* am not this thing, or this thing is not my Self. Things should be viewed with correct wisdom, just as they are."[5] According to the doctrine of no-Self, the personality is in a state of flux. However, the teaching of no-Self is not nihilistic. According to the *Suttanipāta* (vv. 858, 919), both clinging to the idea of the absence of Self *(nirattan)* and clinging to the idea of a permanent Self *(attan)* are errors.

Eventually, the first aggregate, form (or *rūpa*), was interpreted as including all material things. Consequently, all impermanent phenomena were encompassed within the doctrine of the five aggregates. Such impermanent phenomena were called conditioned *dharmas (saṃskṛta dharma;* P. *saṅkhata dhamma)* and were contrasted with unchanging or eternal existents, which were called unconditioned *dharmas (asaṃskṛta dharma;* P. *assaṅkhata-dhamma).* Both *nirvāṇa* and space were considered to be unconditioned *dharmas.* This fundamental classification of *dharmas* into conditioned and unconditioned categories is found in the *Āgamas.*

At a later date, a distinction was made between the view that no permanent Self could be found within the five aggregates *(pudgala-nairātmya)* and the more inclusive position that no permanent entity could be found within the *dharmas (dharma-nairātmya),* but this distinction is not found in the *Āgamas.*

The Dharma and Dependent Origination

"Seeing the Dharma" was an important religious aspect of the Buddha's enlightenment. When the five monks heard the Buddha preach his first sermon and heard about the Four Noble Truths, they saw the Dharma and realized the Dharma. Their pure Dharma-eyes (P. *dhamma cakkhuṃ udapādi*) were opened. The term Dharma (P. Dhamma) comes from the root *"dhṛ,"* which means "to hold or keep." From that root, the term came to mean "that which does not change." It thus was applied to the ideas and norms that maintained the social and moral order. Besides good, virtue, and truth, from ancient times in India the term *"dharma"* was used to refer to the customs and duties observed by people—in other words, to the social order. In Buddhism the term is used with all these meanings. For example, in v. 5 of the *Dhammapada,* the term is found with the meaning of truth: "Enmity is not eliminated by enmity. Only when enmity is abandoned, is it eliminated. This is an unchanging and eternal truth (P. *dhamma sanantano*)." In this way, Buddhism adopted uses of the term Dharma that dated from before the time of the Buddha.

Buddhists also broadened the meaning of the term *dharma.* Before the Buddha, the term was used to refer to the Good and the Truth. That which was bad and not good was called *"adharma"* in Sanskrit to indicate that it was not included within the Dharma. However, Buddhists classified even defilements *(kleśa-dharma)* and evils *(pāpakā-akuśalā-dharmāḥ)* as *dharmas.* Thus a new and broader explanation of *dharma* as an element of existence *(bhava)* was developed.[6] (In this study, when the term *"dharma"* is used to refer to unchanging truths, it is capitalized; when it refers to constantly changing elements of existence, it is not capitalized.)

The great commentator Buddhaghosa lived during the fifth century C.E. Born in South India, he later went to Sri Lanka, where he collected and organized the doctrinal studies of Sri Lankan Theravāda Buddhists. On the basis of these studies, he wrote commentaries on almost all of the *Nikāyas,* as well as independent works such as the *Visuddhimagga* (Path of Purification). According to Buddhaghosa (*Sumaṅgalavilāsinī,* vol. 1, p. 99), the term *dhamma* has four meanings: *guṇa* (characteristic), *desanā* (teaching), *pariyatti* (scripture), and *nissatta* (thing). Elsewhere (*Atthasālinī,* chap. 2, l. 9; also see *The Expositor,* vol. 1, p. 49), Buddhaghosa deletes *desanā* from the list of four meanings and adds *hetu* (cause).

First, within the context of the Three Jewels (Buddha, Dharma, and *saṅgha*), Dharma means "the Teaching." At the same time it refers to the truth or to *nirvāṇa* that is shown through the Teaching. Second, when *dharma* (Ch. *fa-tsang*) is used to refer to the ninefold classification of the Teaching *(navāṅga-śāsana),* it is used in the sense of scripture. The ninefold classification of the Teaching was a system of organizing the material in the *Āgamas* on the basis of content. This division was made before the material was compiled into a *Sūtra-piṭaka.* The third meaning of *dharma* occurs when the term is used in the sense of cause *(hetu),* as in good or evil *dharmas.* Such *dharmas* produce effects. For example, a good *dharma* has the power to produce good. When *dharma* refers to something neither good nor evil *(avyākṛta),* it is not used in the sense of cause since such an event does not have the power to cause a good or bad effect. In the same way, something that was not a real entity might be called an "expedient *dharma*" *(prajñapti-dharma),* but it would not be a *dharma* in the sense of cause. The fourth meaning of *dharma* is "characteristic" *(guṇa).* This meaning is found in the list of the eighteen characteristics possessed only by the Buddha *(aṣṭādaśa āveṇikā buddhadharmāḥ).*

Finally, the use of *dharma* as meaning "thing" (P. *nissatta, nijjīva*) is peculiar to Buddhism. This use of the term does not occur in the *Vedas* or in the early *Upaniṣads.* The *dharmas* that the Buddha realized in his enlightenment are included in this usage. When the Buddha realized enlightenment, he "understood" *nirvāṇa. Nirvāṇa* is truth and real existence. In the sense that it really exists, *nirvāṇa* is included as a *dharma.*

In other words, *dharma* is used to refer to that aspect of phenomena that has the quality of truth—that is, of having an enduring quality. A practitioner "sees the Dharma" when he discovers in what sense phenomena endure. For example, the self can be considered to be an impermanent phenomenon like many others. But when a practitioner has uncovered the truth about the self he is said to have understood the "self as *dharmas*" or "the self made up of *dharmas.*" This use of the term *dharma* appears in phrases such as "all *dharmas* are nonsubstantial" *(sarve dharmā anātmānaḥ)* or in discussions on how *dharmas* function according to the laws of Dependent Origination.

In Early Buddhism, objects and individuals as they appear to us are not considered *dharmas.* Rather, *dharmas* are the fundamental existents of which phenomena (such as objects and individuals) are composed. For example, the five aggregates *(skandha)* of which a person is com-

two events was only one hundred years. If the above account of the political situation in India is correct, one hundred years would seem to be too short for the time span between the Buddha's death and Aśoka's succession. In the *A-yü-wang chuan* (*T* 50:99c, *Aśokarājāvadāna**), a work belonging to the Northern tradition of Buddhism, the names of twelve kings of Magadha are listed, beginning with Bimbisāra and concluding with Susīma, a contemporary of Aśoka. The durations of their reigns, however, are not listed, making it difficult to determine whether the figure of 100 years or 218 years is more trustworthy. The many points in which the various accounts disagree prevent any of them from being considered an infallible source. Although the dates in the Sri Lankan chronicles would seem to be more trustworthy than those in other accounts, even the Sri Lankan histories present many difficult problems when they are used to reconstruct a history of the early Buddhist order. Consequently, the problem of determining what period elapsed between the Buddha and Aśoka must remain unsolved for the present. The following account of the development of the Buddhist order relies upon both the Sri Lankan chronicles and the Northern sources.[3]

The Second Council and the First Major Schism in the Order

After the Buddha's death, missionaries spread Buddhism from central India to the southwest along the Southern Route. Buddhism was also transmitted to western India, where it flourished in Mathurā (Madhurā), a city on the banks of the Jamuna to the southeast of modern Delhi. Mathurā is a considerable distance from central India. Because it is the location where Krishna worship arose, it is a sacred place to Hindus. At one time, however, Buddhism flourished there, and it was a stronghold of the Sarvāstivādin School. According to scriptures, Mahākātyāyana preached in Mathurā. No *sūtras* record the Buddha as preaching there. In fact, he stated that Mathurā had five major problems that made it unpleasant to live in (such as being dusty and having many mad dogs), and he therefore avoided it. Since Mathurā was far from central India, it would take some time before Buddhism reached it.

One hundred years after the Buddha's death, at the time of the Second Council, Buddhism was still not strong in Mathurā. The Second Council was held because the monks of Vaiśālī were said to have adopted ten practices that violated the precepts. When a dispute arose over these practices, seven hundred monks assembled in Vaiśālī and determined that the monks of Vaiśālī were in error. Although deciding the status of the ten practices in question was the main reason for the meeting, the *Dīpavaṃsa,* a Sri Lankan chronicle, refers to the meeting as the "Second Council" because the canon was chanted after the other business had been completed.[4] However, the "Chapter on the Council of the Seven Hundred" in the *Vinaya* states only that the meeting concerned the ten practices and does not consider it to be the Second Council.

According to Pāli sources the ten disputed practices and the rules they violated were as follows:

1. Carrying salt in an animal horn—violated a rule against the storing of food
2. Taking food when the shadow on the sundial is two fingers past noon—violated a rule against eating after noon
3. After eating, traveling to another village to eat another meal the same day—violating the rule against overeating
4. Holding several fortnightly assemblies within the same boundaries *(sīmā)*—violated procedures requiring all monks within the *sīmā* to attend the same fortnightly assembly
5. Confirming an ecclesiastical act in an incomplete assembly and obtaining approval from absent monks afterward—violated the rules of procedure at monastic meetings
6. Citing habitual practice as the authority for violations of monastic procedures—violated the rules of procedure
7. Drinking milk whey after meals—violated the rule against eating special food when one was not sick
8. Drinking unfermented wine—violated the rule against drinking intoxicating beverages
9. Using a mat with fringes—violated the rule concerning the measurements of rugs
10. Accepting gold and silver—violated the rule prohibiting monks from receiving gold and silver

All of these practices were banned in the full sets of precepts for monks.[5] Because observing the full precepts would have required special efforts by the monks, the advocates of the ten practices were attempting to liberalize monastic practice. The argument concerning the tenth practice, whether monks could touch gold and silver, was especially bitter. In the following discussion, the story of the Second Council is summarized in accordance with the "Chapter on the Council of Seven Hundred" from the Pāli *Vinaya.*

Approximately one century after the Buddha's death, a monk named Yaśas (P. Yasa-kākāṇḍakaputta) was traveling in Vaiśālī when he noticed that the monks of that area were receiving alms of gold and silver directly from lay believers. When he pointed out to them that their activity was in violation of the rules in the *vinaya,* the monks of Vaiśālī expelled him from the order. Yaśas then traveled west to seek assistance.

Yaśas appealed to monks from Avanti, Pāvā (Pāṭheyyakā), and areas along the Southern Route. Avanti and other areas along the Southern Route had already been opened up to Buddhism by Mahākātyāyana and Pūrṇa and thus must have been the sites of well-established orders by this time. The monks of Pāvā were probably from the western part of Kauśala. This area was to the far west of Śrāvastī, and included Sāṅkāśya and Kanyākubja. A little further to the west was Mathurā. Pāvā was the site of a very strong Buddhist order at this time. Thus, a century after the Buddha's death, Buddhism had spread beyond central India and was becoming an important force in western India.

Among the influential monks in the west was an elder named Saṃbhūta Sāṇavāsī, who lived on Mount Ahogaṅga. Another important elder was Revata, who was from Soreyya, a town on the upper reaches of the Ganges River near Sāṅkāśya, the center of the area around Pāvā. Because Yaśas sought help in the west, the argument over the ten points of *vinaya* is often thought of as a dispute between the monks of the east and the west. However, because some monks in the east (Magadha and Vaiśālī) joined with those in the west in opposing the adoption of the ten points, the dispute should be viewed as one between a conservative group, which advocated a strict interpretation of the precepts, and a more liberal group, which wished to permit certain exceptions to the observance of the precepts.

The dissemination of Buddhism during the century after the Buddha's death led to an increase in the numbers of monks and its diffusion over a broader geographical area. Ample opportunities existed for differences of interpretation to lead to controversies involving the order. The conservative position prevailed at the council, probably because most of the elders favored a conservative approach. Eventually, a decision was reached to appoint four monks from the west and four from the east to consider the ten points and judge their orthodoxy. The elders chosen as representatives ruled that all ten points should be rejected. Many monks, however, refused to accept their ruling, and their dissatisfaction contributed to a schism in the order.

The schism, often called the basic schism (Ch. *ken-pen fen-lieh*), resulted in the formation of two schools: the Mahāsaṅghika, whose monks refused to accept the conservative ruling of the committee of eight monks, and the Sthaviravāda (P. Theravāda), whose monks agreed with the conservative ruling. The name Mahāsaṅghika means "great assembly" and suggests that many monks belonged to the liberal faction.

According to the *I-pu-tsung-lun-lun* (*T* 2031, *Samayabhedoparacanacakra**; hereafter cited as *Samaya*), a work by Vasumitra from the Northern tradition concerning the formation of the schools of Hīnayāna Buddhism and their doctrines, the cause of the basic schism was five teachings promulgated by Mahādeva. However, many modern scholars believe that Mahādeva's five points were in fact the cause of a later schism and that they mistakenly were considered by Vasumitra to have been the cause of the basic schism.

According to the *vinayas* of various schools and other sources, the controversy over the ten points of practice occurred a century after the Buddha's death. Moreover, the Sri Lankan chronicles and the *Samaya* of the Northern tradition both date the basic schism to the same time. Still other stories concerning schisms in the order are recorded in Tibetan sources; however, both Northern and Southern (Pāli) sources are in agreement that a schism that resulted in the formation of the Mahāsaṅghika and Sthavira schools occurred one century after the Buddha's death. Since the *vinayas* of the Theravāda, Sarvāstivādin, Mahīśāsaka, and Dharmaguptaka schools all record that the controversy over the ten points of *vinaya* occurred one century after the Buddha's death, this dispute must be considered to be the cause of the basic schism.

The five points of doctrine advanced by Mahādeva may have added to the controversy surrounding the first schism. Mahādeva taught that (1) *arhats* may be sexually tempted, (2) *arhats* have a residue of ignorance, (3) *arhats* may have doubts, (4) *arhats* may attain enlightenment through the help of others, and (5) the path is attained with an exclamatory remark. The five points indicate that Mahādeva had a low opinion of the enlightenment of *arhats*. Mahādeva's five points of doctrine are included in the Sarvāstivādin School's *Samaya* (*T* 49:15a, 18a, 20a) and *Mahāvibhāṣā* (*T* 27:511a–c), as well as the Theravāda work, the *Kathāvatthu* (bk. 2, parts 1–5). Mahādeva's five points of doctrine thus are representative of the issues debated by the schools of Hīnayāna Buddhism.

In discussing the basic schism, the extent of Buddhism's spread in India and the difficulties in communication between areas of India must be taken into account. The schism probably did not occur over a period of days or months. Consequently, scholars cannot determine exactly when it occurred or at what point it was completed. However, the schism clearly did occur a little more than a century after the Buddha's death. As the dissension gradually spread and involved many of the orders in various parts of India, arguments over a number of different points arose. According to the *Samaya,* Mahāsaṅghika doctrine included certain views on the bodies of the Buddha and the concept of the bodhisattva that might have drawn opposition from more conservative monks. However, these doctrines were probably developed by later Mahāsaṅghika monks and do not represent Mahāsaṅghika doctrine at the time of the basic schism.

Sāṇavāsī and Monastic Lineages

The chapters on the Second Council contained in the various *vinayas* are in agreement about the identities of the senior monks of the Buddhist order approximately a century after the Buddha's death. In the east Sarvakāmin was an important elder, and in the west Revata and Saṃbhūta Sāṇavāsī were influential. The roles of these three men are stressed in the Sri Lankan sources and are related to the accounts of a monk named Śāṇakavāsī in Northern sources.

In such Northern sources as the *Divyāvadāna, A-yü-wang chuan* (*T* 2042, *Aśokarājāvadāna**), *A-yü-wang ching* (*T* 2043, *Aśokarājasūtra*?), and *Ken-pen yu-pu lü tsa-shih* (*T* 1451, *Mūlasarvāstivāda vinayakṣudrakavastu#*), the following patriarchal lineage is given: Mahākāśyapa, Ānanda, Śāṇakavāsī, and Upagupta. The monk Madhyāntika must also be mentioned. Madhyāntika was a fellow student with Śāṇakavāsī under Ānanda; however, since Madhyāntika became a disciple of Ānanda just before Ānanda died, Madhyāntika should probably be considered a contemporary of Upagupta. Śāṇakavāsī, Madhyāntika, Upagupta, and others mentioned in these lineages are also discussed in Sri Lankan sources. In the following paragraphs, the roles of these men and the relation between the Northern and Sri Lankan accounts of them are analyzed.

Saṃbhūta Sāṇavāsī is mentioned in the chapter on the Second Council in the Pāli *Vinaya*. He was a disciple of Ānanda, as was Śāṇakavāsī, who is mentioned in Northern sources. Both lived about one century after the Buddha's death. According to the Pāli *Vinaya,* Sāṇavāsī lived on Mount Ahogaṅga. Śāṇakavāsī is said to have resided on Mount Urumuṇḍa in Mathurā (*Divyāvadāna,* p. 349). Although the names of the two mountains were different, both mountains are said to have been reached by boat. (The name of Mount Ahogaṅga indicates that it was probably on the Ganges River.)

The name "Sāṇavāsī" does not appear in the following list of patriarchs found in Sri Lankan sources: Upāli, Dāsaka, Sonaka, Siggava, and Moggaliputta Tissa. Aśoka's teacher Moggaliputta Tissa is said to have resided on Mount Ahogaṅga (*Samantapāsādikā,* p. 53). King Aśoka sent a boat to the mountain to bring Moggaliputta back to the capital. In contrast, Northern sources state both that Śāṇakavāsī's disciple Upagupta was Aśoka's teacher and that Upagupta succeeded his teacher on Mount Urumuṇḍa. Moreover, according to Northern sources, Aśoka sent for Upagupta with a boat and the boat then returned to Pāṭaliputra. In conclusion, although the names of the two mountains are different, the accounts resemble each other in many ways. Śāṇakavāsī of Northern sources is not called "Saṃbhūta" as is Sāṇavāsī of the Sri Lankan tradition. Although Śāṇakavāsī and Saṃbhūta Sāṇavāsī cannot be proven to be identical, since they were both Ānanda's disciples and lived at the same time and in similar places, they probably were, in fact, the same person.

In Sri Lankan sources such as the *Dīpavaṃsa, Mahāvaṃsa,* and the *Samantapāsādikā,* the following lineage of *vinaya* masters is recorded: Upāli, Dāsaka, Sonaka, Siggava, and Moggaliputta Tissa. Since, according to Sri Lankan sources, Moggaliputta Tissa is said to have been Aśoka's teacher, five generations of teachers would have served between the death of the Buddha and the accession of Aśoka to the throne. In Northern sources, Aśoka's teacher is said to have been Upagupta; thus, according to Northern sources, four generations of teachers would have passed between the death of the Buddha and Aśoka. Saṃbhūta Sāṇavāsī does not appear in the lineage in the Northern sources because, as a disciple of Ānanda, Sāṇavāsī belonged to a different lineage. In contrast, the Sri Lankan lineage of *vinaya* masters was based on the fact that Moggaliputta's preceptor was Siggava and Siggava's preceptor was Sonaka and so forth back to Upāli. Consequently, there was no place in the Sri Lankan lineage to add Ānanda.

According to the lineages found in Northern sources, Upagupta's preceptor was Śāṇakavāsī, Śāṇakavāsī's preceptor was Ānanda, and Ānanda's preceptor was Mahākāśyapa. However, doubt exists about whether Ānanda's preceptor was Mahākāśyapa. According to the Pāli *Vinaya,* Ānanda's preceptor was named Belaṭṭhasīsa, indicating that Ānanda's preceptor probably was not Mahākāśyapa (*Vinaya,* vol. 4, p. 86). Why Mahākāśyapa was listed as Ānanda's preceptor must be considered further.

After the Buddha's death Mahākāśyapa was probably the Buddha's most powerful disciple. Mahākāśyapa presided over the First Council. Moreover, a number of stories in the *Āgamas* demonstrate the respect held for Mahākāśyapa. For example, in one story the Buddha shared his seat with Mahākāśyapa and then had him preach. In another story, the Buddha exchanged his tattered robes for Mahākāśyapa's large hempen robe *(saṅghāṭī).* Since Śāriputra and Maudgalyāyana had predeceased the Buddha, Mahākāśyapa was recognized by everyone as the most influential figure in the Buddhist order after the Buddha's death. Consequently, later, when those in Ānanda's lineage traced their spiritual ancestry, they did not mention Ānanda's actual preceptor since he was almost completely unknown and did nothing to bolster Ānanda's authority. Instead, they devised a legend in which Mahākāśyapa bestowed the teaching on Ānanda.

One of the major objections to the tradition that Mahākāśyapa was Ānanda's preceptor is that many legends suggesting that serious discord existed between Mahākāśyapa and Ānanda are found in the *Āgamas* and *vinayas*. For example, according to the chapter on the First Council in the *Vinaya,* after the First Council, Mahākāśyapa described several serious errors made by Ānanda and urged Ānanda to confess them. Other stories concern criticisms that Ānanda's followers made against Mahākāśyapa when he was older. Mahākāśyapa was influential immediately after the Buddha's death, but later Ānanda's followers gained in strength until they became the stronger faction.

Ānanda had many strong connections with the orders in the west. In many episodes in the *Āgamas,* he is described as staying and preaching to people at the Ghositārāma in Kauśāmbī, in the western part of central India.[6] Since Ānanda liked to proselytize in the west, he probably had many disciples there. When a committee of eight monks was chosen to investigate the points at issue at the Second Council, six of the eight were Ānanda's disciples. Because Ānanda had lived longer than most of the Buddha's other immediate disciples, his disciples were among the eldest members of the order approximately one century after the Buddha's death.

The above account agrees with other information about Ānanda's age. At the time of the Buddha's death, Ānanda served as his personal attendant, a position probably not held by an elderly monk. According to the *Ta-chih-tu lun* (*T* 25:68a, *Mahāprajñāpāramitopadeśa*) and the commentary on the *Theragāthā,* Ānanda was the Buddha's attendant for twenty-five years. If Ānanda had become the Buddha's attendant immediately after he was ordained, then he was probably forty-five years old at the Buddha's death and might well have lived for another thirty to forty years.

Ānanda's disciple Śāṇakavāsī was a native of Rājagṛha according to Northern sources such as the *A-yü-wang ching* (*T* 2043, *Aśokarājasūtra*?). He introduced Buddhism to Mathurā in the west. Mount Urumuṇḍa, mentioned earlier, was in Mathurā, and Śāṇakavāsī's disciple Upagupta was a native of Mathurā (*A-yü-wang chuan, T* 50:114b, 117b). Thus by the time of Śāṇakavāsī, Buddhism was spreading to Mathurā.

According to Sri Lankan sources, most of the elders chosen to serve on the committee to decide the issues that arose at the time of the Second Council traced their lineages back to Upāli even while acknowledging that they were Ānanda's disciples. This discrepancy probably occurs because Mahinda, the monk who transmitted Buddhism to Sri Lanka, was in Upāli's lineage (Upāli, Dāsaka, Sonaka, Siggava, Moggaliputta, Mahinda). Mahinda's lineage was probably emphasized in Sri Lankan sources because Mahinda was one of the most important figures in Sri Lankan Buddhism. Lineages were a sacred issue for monks, and tracing a lineage back through a series of preceptors and disciples was an acknowledged way of proving the orthodoxy of a person's ordination. Consequently, monks would not have forgotten or fabricated the lineage of Mahinda and his preceptor. The fact that monks such as Sonaka and Siggava, who are included in the lineage between Upāli and Moggaliputta Tissa, do not appear as major figures in the history of the Buddhist order suggests that such lineages are probably authentic. The lineage should be understood as referring to the relationship between preceptor and disciples, not as indicating that figures such as Sonaka and Siggava were part of a lineage of monks who supervised the order.

According to Sri Lankan sources, there were five generations of *vinaya* masters between the death of the Buddha and the time of Aśoka. According to Northern sources such as the *A-yü-wang chuan* (*T* 2042, *Aśokarājāvadāna**), because Ānanda's disciple Śāṇakavāsī was long-lived, Aśoka's teacher Upagupta was in the fourth generation after the Buddha. The lineage in the Northern sources from Ānanda to Śāṇakavāsī to Upagupta was based on the relationship of preceptor to disciple, reflecting the importance of ordinations, but the relationship between Mahākāśyapa and Ānanda was not one of preceptor to disciple. To explain this discrepancy, the lineage in Northern sources had to assume the format of being a transmission of the teaching rather than an ordination lineage. According to Northern sources, Aśoka's teacher was Upagupta of Mount Urumuṇḍa; in Sri Lankan sources, Aśoka's teacher was Moggaliputta Tissa of Mount Ahogaṅga. Although the two teachers resemble each other in certain ways, they cannot reasonably be identified as the same person. Questions concerning whether only one monk or both monks were Aśoka's teachers remain unanswered at present.

Evidence from the lineages thus indicates that the Sri Lankan figure of 218 years for the period between the Buddha's death and Aśoka's succession is simply too long. The figure of 116 years found in Northern sources is much more reasonable.

Madhyāntika and the Dispatch of Missionaries

The Northern and Southern (Sri Lankan) traditions agree on a number of points concerning Madhyāntika. According to the Northern tradition, he was Ānanda's last disciple. Approximately a hundred years after the Buddha's death, he went to Kashmir, where he built a place to meditate and live. Stories about him describe how he converted some evil dragons (Nāga) in Kashmir to Buddhism, spread Buddhism among the people, and taught the people how to grow tulips to make their living.

According to the Sri Lankan tradition, missionaries from the Buddhist order were sent to various lands during the reign of Aśoka at the recommendation of Moggaliputta Tissa. Eminent monks were dispatched to nine areas, with Majjhantika going to Kashmir and Gandhāra. Majjhantika took five monks with him to Kashmir and converted evil dragons there by using his superhuman powers and the people by teaching the *Āsīvisopama-sutta.* Majjhantika is probably the same person as the Madhyāntika mentioned in the Northern sources. Since the Madhyāntika mentioned in the Northern sources was said to be the last disciple of Ānanda, he could have been a contemporary of Upagupta. And if Upagupta lived during Aśoka's reign, then the missionary activities of both men would have been assisted by Aśoka's support of Buddhism. Since Buddhism had spread to Mathurā during this time, then Madhyāntika might very well have taken it farther north to Kashmir.

According to Sri Lankan chronicles, at the same time Majjhantika was proselytizing in Kashmir, other eminent monks from the order in Magadha were spreading Buddhism to other parts of India. Each eminent monk was sent with a group of five monks, since five was the minimum number required to perform full ordinations. A list of these eminent monks, the areas in which they proselytized, and the *sūtras* that they preached follows.

Mahādeva went to Mahisamaṇḍala and preached the *Devadūtasutta*
Rakkhita went to Vanavāsī and preached the *Anamattagīvasutta*
Dhammarakkhita went to Aparantaka and preached the *Agghikhandupamasutta*
Mahādhammarakkhita went to Mahāraṭṭha and preached the *Mahānāradakassapa-jātaka*
Mahārakkhita went to Yonaloka and preached the *Kālakārāmasuttanta*
Majjhima went to Himavantapadesa and preached the *Dhammacakkapavattanasutta*

Sonaka and Uttara went to Suvaṇṇabhūmi and preached the *Brahmajālasutta*

Mahinda went to Laṅkādīpa (Sri Lanka) and preached the *Culahatthipadopamasutta* and other *sūtras*

Mahisamaṇḍala, where Mahādeva was sent, seems to be to the south of the Narmadā River, but it has also been identified with Mysore. According to the *Shan-chien lü* (*T* 24:681c–82a), the Chinese translation of Buddhaghosa's *Samantapāsādikā,* Mahādeva and Majjhantika were teachers *(ācārya)* at Mahinda's full ordination. Episodes concerning two figures named Mahādeva are included in Sarvāstivādin sources. Mahādeva is said to be both a monk who caused the schism between the Sthavira and Mahāsaṅghika schools by preaching his "five points" and a Mahāsaṅghika monk who lived at Mount Caitika and caused the schism that led to the formation of the Caitika School (which is related to the Mahāsaṅghika School) by proclaiming the "five points." The former figure, the monk responsible for the basic schism, is probably a fictional character. The latter lived approximately two centuries after the Buddha's death at Mount Caitika, along the middle part of the Kṛṣṇā River in Āndhra. It is unclear whether this Mahādeva should be identified with the monk of the same name who was dispatched as a missionary by Moggaliputta Tissa.

The place called "Aparantaka" has been identified with a site on the west coast of India, an area previously opened to Buddhism by Pūrṇa. Mahāraṭṭha is near Bombay in Mahārāṣṭra; Yonaloka was in the north in the area where a number of Greeks lived. Himavantapadesa was in the Himalayan region, and Suvaṇṇabhūmi was in eastern India near Burma.

Besides Majjhima, four other monks—Kassapagotta, Alakadeva, Dundubhissara, and Sahadeva—helped propagate Buddhism in the Himalayan area. Among the funerary urns found at the second *stūpa* at Sāñcī were one for "Kāsapagota" [*sic*], a teacher in the Himalayan area, and another for the sage "Majhima" [*sic*]. These archeological finds provide additional evidence concerning Majjhima's activities in Himalayan areas.

Mahinda equipped himself for his journey to Sri Lanka at the Vidiśā monastery (P. Vedisagiri) near Sāñcī, bade farewell to his mother, and departed with five monks. From Vidiśā he probably traveled to the west coast of India, boarded a ship going south, rounded the tip of the Indian subcontinent, and landed in Sri Lanka. Because the dispatch of missionaries to various parts of India is proven in part by inscriptions, the scriptural account of the missionaries may be regarded as essentially factual.

To summarize, Ānanda opened Kauśāmbī to Buddhism. One hundred years after the Buddha's death, Buddhism had spread to Sāṅkāśya, Kanyākubja, Avanti, and along the Southern Route. Buddhism was subsequently introduced to Mathurā by Śāṇakavāsī and Upagupta. Missionaries were then dispatched to Kashmir, southern India, and the Himalayan region. Stories concerning the territory exposed to Buddhism during the lifetimes of Śāṇakavāsī and Upagupta agree with the account of the dispatch of missionaries in the next period. Thus the missionaries were probably sent out between 100 and 150 years after the Buddha's death. If the Sri Lankan version of Buddhist history is followed in which 218 years elapsed between the Buddha's death and Aśoka's succession, then there would be a hundred-year gap between Śāṇakavāsī and Moggaliputta during which the order would have been virtually moribund.

The Third Council

As the above discussion indicates, a number of differences exist between the Northern and Southern accounts of the early Buddhist order. There are also important points of agreement between the different accounts. By the time of King Aśoka, there had been four or five generations of leaders of the *saṅgha,* and the propagation of Buddhism in Kashmir had begun. In the south, Buddhism had spread to the Deccan plateau.

According to the Sri Lankan tradition, during Aśoka's reign missionaries were sent to various parts of India. However, a project of this magnitude probably could not have involved just one school of Nikāya (Hīnayāna) Buddhism, the Theravāda. Moreover, according to the fifth chapter of the *Dīpavaṃsa,* a Sri Lankan chronicle, many schisms occurred during the second century after the Buddha's death. These schisms eventually led to the eighteen schools of Nikāya Buddhism. Thus according to the Sri Lankan account, the Caitika School of the Mahāsaṅghika lineage (founded by Mahādeva) would already have been established in Andhra by the time of Aśoka's succession to the throne. The Dharmaguptaka and the Kāśyapīya schools would have already split away from the Sarvāstivādin School, and the Kashmiri Sarvāstivādin School would already have had a strong base. In addition, according to the Sri Lankan tradition, other schools had been established by Aśoka's time, such as the Mahīśāsakas, Dharmaguptakas, Sammatīyas, and Vātsīputrīyas, and had probably spread beyond central India. Thus, according to Sri Lankan sources, by the time of Aśoka, Buddhism had probably already spread throughout India and most of the schisms of Nikāya Buddhism had already occurred. It is doubtful whether missionaries would have been dispatched to these areas when Buddhism was already so firmly established in them. The accounts in the Sri Lankan chronicles of the schisms and the dispatch of the missionaries by Aśoka are clearly difficult to reconcile with each other.

If both the schisms and the dispatch of missionaries are historical events, then the Northern tradition's account is more reasonable. According to this account, the missionaries were dispatched before the schisms of Nikāya Buddhism. (The Sri Lankan claim that many of the schisms occurred before Aśoka's reign is discussed in chapter 8.)

According to the Sri Lankan chronicles, bitter dissension was evident in the order during Aśoka's time. However, such discord would probably have been resolved by a series of schisms that gave monks a choice of orders. A more natural order of events would place the dissension before the schisms. The Sri Lankan chronicles describe discord in the order at Pāṭaliputra during Aśoka's reign, indicating that discord had broken out in the orders of central India. To resolve the situation, Moggaliputta Tissa was summoned from Mount Ahogaṅga. The edicts of Aśoka from Kauśāmbī, Sāñcī, and Sārnāth strongly warned against schisms in the order, stating that monks who caused schisms were to be expelled and laicized. (The fact that the edicts were carved in stone suggests that the discord probably had been occurring for a long period.) The carved edicts warning against schisms were located at the strongholds of the western monks of Avanti and the Southern Route at the time of the Second Council, and thus reflect the situation in Indian Buddhism after the dispute over the "ten points" of *vinaya* had occurred.

According to the Sri Lankan tradition, Moggaliputta Tissa was invited to Pāṭaliputra, where he defrocked heretics and purified the order so that those remaining adhered to Vibhajjhavāda doctrine. Later he assembled one thousand monks and convened the Third Council. To specify orthodox doctrinal positions, he compiled the *Kathāvatthu* (Points of Controversy). These events occurred in approximately the eighteenth year of Aśoka's reign. However, if most of the schisms of Nikāya Buddhism had already occurred, as is stated in the Sri Lankan sources, it is unlikely that the various orders could have been purified and forced to conform to Vibhajjhavāda doctrine. Moggaliputta Tissa probably would not have been able to stop the arguments between the monks of

Kauśāmbī, Sāñcī, and Sārnāth. Moreover, if Moggaliputta Tissa did assemble one thousand monks and convene a council, he probably would not have selected monks from other schools. Consequently, the Third Council cannot be recognized as an event involving the Buddhist orders of all of India.

Since the *Kathāvatthu* was compiled within the Theravāda order, some sort of council must have been convened. However, the council was held not during Aśoka's reign, but approximately a century after Aśoka. Since the doctrines of the various schools of Nikāya Buddhism are examined and criticized in the *Kathāvatthu,* this text must have been compiled after these schools arose, probably during the last half of the second century B.C.E. Thus if the Third Council is considered to be a historical event, it was a council held only within the Theravāda School during the latter part of the second century B.C.E.

The Dates of the Buddha

The above discussion clearly demonstrates the difficulties of accepting the traditional Sri Lankan account of the early Buddhist order. Sri Lankan statements that the Buddha died 218 years before Aśoka's succession to the throne and that most of the schisms in the orders had occurred by Aśoka's time are difficult to reconcile with other aspects of Buddhist institutional history. Since both the Northern and Southern traditions agree that only four or five generations passed between the Buddha's death and the time of Aśoka, a figure of approximately one century for this period seems reasonable. Moreover, a survey of other primary source materials reveals that only the Sri Lankan tradition has maintained the longer period; the "218 years" figure does not appear in materials from India proper. Moreover, the absence of the figure of 218 years in India is not due to any lack of communication between Sri Lanka and India. A Sri Lankan king had the Mahābodhi-saṅghārāma built at Buddhagayā as a residence for Sri Lankan monks (*Ta-t'ang hsi-yu chi, T* 51:918b), and a Sri Lankan temple existed at Nāgārjunakoṇḍa (see chapter 14). Despite such ties, no mention of a figure of 218 years is made in Indian sources.

Sources from India proper generally state that Aśoka became king around one hundred years after the Buddha's *nirvāṇa.* Furthermore, the figure of 218 years is not the only one found in Sri Lanka. Fa-hsien was a Chinese Buddhist pilgrim who traveled to India and Sri Lanka and then returned to China in 416. He spent two years at the Abhayagiri monastery in Sri Lanka. In his travel diary, Fa-hsien noted that at the time of his arrival in Sri Lanka, monks there claimed that 1,497 years had elapsed since the Buddha's *nirvāṇa* (*T* 51:865a). Calculations based on this figure indicate that the Buddha's *nirvāṇa* would have occurred sometime before 1000 B.C.E., a date not even close to one based on a period of 218 years between the Buddha's death and Aśoka's succession. The figure of 218 years was thus not even accepted by all Sri Lankan monks.

A survey of other primary source materials from India reveals that in most cases Aśoka's reign is dated one hundred years or slightly more after the Buddha's *nirvāṇa.* Among the texts with a figure of one hundred years are the *Ta chuan-yen lun ching* (*T* 4:309c, *Kalpanāmaṇḍitikā**), *Seng-ch'ieh-lo-ch'a so-chi ching* (*T* 4:145a), *Hsien yü ching* (*T* 4:368c, *Damamūkanidānasūtra*), *Tsa pi-yü ching* (*T* 4:503b), *Chung-ching chuan tsa-p'i-yü* (*T* 4:541c), *Tsa a-han ching* (*T* 2:162a, *Saṃyuktāgama*), *Divyāvadāna* (p. 368; Vaidya ed., p. 232), *A-yü-wang chuan* (*T* 50:99c, *Aśokarājāvadāna**), *A-yü-wang ching* (*T* 50:132a, *Aśokarājasūtra*?), *Ta-chih-tu lun* (*T* 25:70a, *Mahāprajñāpāramitopadeśa*), and the *Fen-pieh kung-te lun* (*T* 25:39a). In Hsüan-tsang's travel diary (*T* 51:911a), the period is one hundred years long, and in I-ching's travel diary (*T* 54:205c) it is only somewhat longer, thus indicating that the figure of approximately one hundred years was accepted in India at the time of their travels.

In the Tibetan translation of the *Samayabhedoparacanacakra* (Peking no. 5639), Aśoka's succession is said to have occurred one hundred years after the Buddha's *nirvāṇa,* while in Hsüan-tsang's Chinese translation (*T* 49:15a) the period is said to be more than one hundred years. Paramārtha's Chinese translation, the *Pu chih-i lun,* and another Chinese translation, the *Shih-pa-pu lun,* both have a figure of 116 years (*T* 49:18a, 20a); however, in the Yüan and Ming dynasty editions of Paramārtha's translation, the figure is changed to 160 years. According to the *Ta-fang-teng wu-hsiang ching* (*T* 12:1097c; *Mahāmeghasūtra#*), 120 years elapsed between the Buddha's *nirvāṇa* and Aśoka's succession. In the *Mo-ho mo-yeh ching* (*T* 12:1013c, *Mahāmāyāsūtra*?), the period is stated to be less than 200 years. According to Bhavya's *Sde-pa tha-dad-par byed-pa daṅ rnam-par bśad-pa* (*Nikāyabhedavibhaṅga-vyākhyāna,* Peking no. 5640), a Theravāda tradition dated the first major schism between the Sthaviras and Mahāsaṅghikas as occurring 160 years after the Buddha's *nirvāṇa,* during Aśoka's reign.

Some scholars have relied heavily on Bhavya's figure of 160 years after the Buddha's death for the first schism. On the basis of the figure of 160 years, which occurs in the Yüan and Ming dynasty editions of the *Pu chih-i lun,* they have argued that the figures of 116 years or "slightly more than one hundred years" found in other translations should be amended to 160 years. However, the Sung dynasty and the Korean editions of the *Pu chih-i lun,* both older than either the Yüan or the Ming dynasty editions of the text, have figures of 116 years. Since the evidence for the figure of 160 years is comparatively late and since no other materials with a figure of 160 years have been found, the figures of 116 years or "slightly more than one hundred years" must be accepted as more trustworthy. Moreover, Bhavya presents the figure of 160 years as only one of a number of theories. Finally, the 160-year figure must still be reconciled with the Theravāda figure of 218 years. Thus, the evidence for the figure of 160 years is highly questionable.

On the basis of the development of the Buddhist order and Buddhist historical materials, then, a figure of about one hundred years has been shown to be the most reasonable figure for the period between the death of the Buddha and the succession of Aśoka to the throne. However, an investigation of the reigns of the kings of Magadha indicates that 116 years is too short, and thus many scholars favor a period of 218 years or advocate a compromise figure of 160 years. However, the three figures cannot all be adopted at the same time. For the purpose of discussing the history of the Buddhist order, since the 218-year figure presents many problems, the 116-year figure will be followed in this account.

In summary, after the death of the Buddha, the Buddhist order spread to the west and southwest. The Buddha's long-lived disciple Ānanda was influential during this period. Later, Ānanda's disciple Śāṇakavāsī was preeminent in the western order; however, Buddhism had still not spread as far as Mathurā at this time. Still later, Sarvakāmin (P. Sabbakāmin) was preeminent in the eastern order while Revata was influential in the west. At this time, the controversy over the ten points of *vinaya* arose, and the elders met in Vaiśālī to deliberate over the disputes and resolve them. Many monks did not submit to the council's decision, however, and the dispute later became a cause for the schism that resulted in the Sthavira and Mahāsaṅghika schools. Thus, approximately one hundred years after the Buddha's death, there were already frequent disputes in the Buddhist orders in the various parts of India.

During Śāṇakavāsī's later years, Buddhism spread to Mathurā. A little more than one century after the Buddha's death, Aśoka came to the throne. Śāṇakavāsī had already died, and Upagupta and Moggaliputta were the preeminent monks in the order. When Aśoka converted to Buddhism, he invited the two teachers to his capital at Pāṭaliputra. According to Northern sources, at Upagupta's urging, Aśoka traveled to Buddhist pilgrimage sites with Upagupta and erected *stūpas* at various places. Aśoka's pilgrimages are mentioned, in fact, in his inscriptions. According to Sri Lankan sources, Moggaliputta put an end to the disputes among the monks in Pāṭaliputra and advocated the dispatch of missionaries to various lands. Majjhantika was sent to bring the teachings of Buddhism to Kashmir, Majjhima and Kassapagotta to the Himalayan region, and Mahādeva to southern India. Buddhism thus spread to all of India with Aśoka's conversion and assistance. During Aśoka's reign, the disputes within the order became more evident, but still not severe enough to cause a schism. Only after Aśoka's death did the actual schism of the order into the Sthavira and Mahāsaṅghika schools occur, probably in part because of the decline of the Mauryan empire. Thus serious disputes arose within the early Buddhist order's ranks before Aśoka's reign, but the order did not actually split into schools until after Aśoka's death. The spread of Buddhism to all of India meant that regional differences were added to doctrinal differences with the result that further schisms occurred rapidly during the century after Aśoka's death.

CHAPTER 7

The Buddhism of King Aśoka

The Edicts

THE BUDDHISM of King Aśoka is presented here in conjunction with Early Buddhism, since Aśoka's ideas are closer to Early Buddhism than to Nikāya Buddhism. The dates of King Aśoka's reign, usually given as 268–232 B.C.E., are based on Rock Edict XIII, which listed the names of five kings to the west of India to whom King Aśoka sent missionaries to spread Buddhism. Included were the kings of Syria, Egypt, and Macedonia. The dates of King Aśoka's reign, with a possible error of two to ten years, were calculated by comparing the dates of these five kings. Because Indians had little interest in history, we have few Indian historical records; these dates provide a benchmark upon which many other dates of ancient Indian history are based. According to the Sri Lankan historical chronicle the *Mahāvaṃsa* (chap. 20, v. 6), Aśoka reigned for thirty-seven years; according to the *Purāṇas,* he ruled for thirty-six years. The inscriptions that survive from Aśoka's reign provide the most reliable source for discussing his times. Besides the edicts, Sri Lankan sources such as the *Mahāvaṃsa, Dīpavaṃsa,* and *Samantapāsādikā* should also be consulted. The Northern tradition includes such sources as the *A-yü-wang chuan* (*T* 2042, *Aśokarājāvadāna**), the *A-yü-wang ching* (*T* 2043, *Aśokarājasūtra?*), and the *Divyāvadāna.*

According to legendary biographies, Aśoka led a violent life as a youth and was responsible for the deaths of many people. Later, however, he converted to Buddhism and ruled benevolently. Consequently, he was called Dharmāśoka (Aśoka of the Teaching). Aśoka's edicts are a more reliable source for information about his life. They state that Aśoka converted to Buddhism and became a Buddhist layman in the seventh year of his reign, but was not particularly pious for the following two and one-half years. In the eighth year of his reign he conquered the country of Kaliṅga after a campaign in which he saw many innocent people killed. Prisoners were deported to other lands, children were separated from parents, and husbands from wives. The king was greatly saddened by these scenes and came to believe that war was wrong, that the only real victory was one based on the truths of Buddhist teachings *(dharma-vijaya),* not one based on force and violence.

For more than a year, Aśoka lived near a Buddhist order and performed religious austerities. In the tenth year of his reign, he "went to *saṃbodhi*" (Rock Edict VIII). The term "*saṃbodhi*" means enlightenment and can be interpreted as meaning either that the king was enlightened or that he journeyed to Buddhagayā, the place of the Buddha's enlightenment. From that time on, Aśoka embarked on a series of pilgrimages to sites connected with the Buddha's life. According to one edict, some time after the twentieth year of his reign, he visited Lumbinī, the site of the Buddha's birth (Rummindei Pillar Edict). Aśoka assiduously practiced his religion and strove to establish and extend the Dharma in the lands he ruled or influenced. Under his reign, the people were taught with pictures depicting heavenly palaces. Thus, according to the inscriptions, the people who formerly had no relations with the gods now had such relations (Brahmagiri Rock Edict).

From the twelfth year of his reign until the twenty-seventh year, King Aśoka worked to spread Buddhist teachings as he understood them by having stone inscriptions carved. Many of these have been discovered. Some, carved on polished stone slabs, are known as Rock Edicts, while others, carved on large sandstone pillars, are called Pillar Edicts. There are two types of Rock Edicts. Fourteen Major Rock Edicts have been discovered at seven places along the borders of the territory that Aśoka controlled, including Girnār. They generally have long texts and are the most representative of the edicts. Minor Rock Edicts have been discovered at seven places in central and southern India. These edicts generally concern Buddhism, but some concern Aśoka's practices. The inscription concerning the seven *sūtras* that Aśoka recommended (see below) was found at Bairāṭ, one of the sites of the Minor Rock Edicts.

Both Major and Minor Pillar Edicts have survived. Six or seven Major Pillar Edicts have been discovered at six sites, primarily in central India. Like the Rock Edicts, they generally concern the content of the Dharma. They were erected after the twenty-sixth year of Aśoka's reign. The Minor Pillar Edicts were usually situated at Buddhist pilgrimage sites such as Sārnāth and Sāñcī. The subjects covered by them concern the Buddhist order *(saṅgha)* and include warnings against schisms. These pillars were generally capped with carvings of animals. The pillar discovered at Sārnāth is capped by four lions facing outward. Beneath them are four wheels of the teaching. This exquisite carving has been adopted as a national symbol, appearing on modern India's seal; the wheel appears on its flag.

Aśoka's inscriptions were first discovered by modern scholars in the nineteenth century. These discoveries have continued in recent years. In 1949 an inscription in Aramaic was discovered at Lampāka in Afghanistan. An inscription written in both Greek and Aramaic was found at Kandahār in 1958, and the discovery of a Rock Edict within the city limits of Delhi was reported in 1966. More than thirty edicts have been identified. Although great progress has been made in understanding the inscriptions since the first one was deciphered in 1873 by James Prinsep, many unsolved problems concerning the inscriptions remain.

The Dharma Preached by King Aśoka

The king believed the Buddhist teaching that all men were essentially equal. Hence, all men, including himself, were to observe the Buddha's Teaching (Dharma). People were to follow a moral code of compassion and sincerity. Among the recommended activities were having compassion for living beings, speaking the truth, acting with forbearance and patience, and helping the needy. Although these prescriptions are simple, Aśoka believed that they were immutable truths that all should follow. To transmit them to future generations, he had his edicts carved in stone.

The importance of respect for the lives of sentient beings was repeatedly stated in Aśoka's edicts. Needless killing was prohibited. If animals were to be killed, pregnant and nursing animals were to be spared. Two types of hospitals were built in the country, one for animals and one for people. Medicinal plants were cultivated, trees planted alongside the roads, and wells dug. Places to rest and obtain drinking water were built for travelers (Rock Edict III). In these ways, Aśoka eased the lives of both men and animals and demonstrated his love and affection *(dayā)* for all sentient beings.

In Aśoka's edicts, the importance of obedience to parents, teachers, and superiors was repeatedly stressed. Elders were to be treated with courtesy. Friends, scholars, brahmans, *śramaṇas,* poor people, servants, and slaves were to be treated properly, and the dignity of each person respected. In addition, alms were to be given to brahmans, *śramaṇas,* and the poor. The king himself gave up the sport of hunting and embarked on Dharma tours *(dharma-yātrā)* around the country (Rock Edict VIII). On these tours, he visited religious authorities and scholars, gave alms, held interviews with the common people, and taught and admonished the people about the Dharma. These Dharma tours were Aśoka's greatest pleasure. For Aśoka, teaching or giving the Dharma *(dharma-dāna)* to others constituted the most excellent form of almsgiving and resulted in friendships based on the Dharma. By preaching the Dharma to others, a person would receive rewards in this life, and countless merits would be produced for his later lives. Along with the emphasis on giving the Dharma to others, Aśoka urged people to consume less and accumulate little, and thus control their desires.

Aśoka was especially diligent in his conduct of government affairs. He ordered that governmental problems be reported to him at any and all times, even when he was eating, in the women's quarters, or in his gardens. For Aśoka, conducting good government was the king's chief responsibility to the people of the country. Benefiting all the beings of the world and then increasing those benefits was the noblest task in the world. All the king's efforts to rule were thus expressions of his desire to repay his debts to other sentient beings. He wished to make people happy in this world and help them attain heaven in their future lives. He considered all sentient beings to be his children (Rock Edict VI).

In the edicts, the Dharma was defined in a variety of ways, as goodness *(sādhu),* few passions *(alpāsrava),* many good acts *(bahukalyāṇa),* affection *(dayā),* almsgiving *(dāna),* truth *(satya),* and purity of action *(śauca).* The realization of Dharma *(dharma-pratipatti)* was said to consist of affection, generosity in giving, truth, purity, gentleness *(mārdava),* and goodness: if a person engaged in almsgiving, but had not learned to control his senses *(saṃyama)* or lacked gratitude *(kṛtajñatā)* or was without steadfast sincerity *(dṛdhabhakitā),* he was a base person. Aśoka warned that brutality, inhumanity, anger, pride, and jealousy all led to even more defilements. "Good is not easy to accomplish. Anyone just beginning to do good will find it difficult," he stated. But then Aśoka noted that he had "accomplished many good deeds" (Rock Edicts IV–V).

Aśoka spread his views on the Dharma in two ways, through regulations concerning the Dharma *(dharma-niyama)* and quiet contemplation of the Dharma *(dharma-nidhyāti).* Regulations concerning the Dharma were promulgated by the king. These laws were directed in particular against killing. Thus, through the force of law the people were made to observe Aśoka's views on taking life.

Contemplation of the Dharma involved quieting the mind and meditating on the Dharma. Through such contemplation the people would attain a deeper understanding of the prohibition on taking life and then apply it to their other actions. Quiet contemplation of the Dharma was considered to be superior to regulations enforcing the Dharma (Pillar Edict VII).

Aśoka emphasized the importance of not killing, of valuing all life, and of respecting people. Even a person sentenced to death was given a respite of three days for relatives to appeal or for the condemned to prepare for the next life. By the twenty-sixth year of his reign, Aśoka had already declared amnesties for prisoners twenty-five times (Pillar Edict V). The main teaching of Aśoka's Dharma, respect for life, was based on the realization that other beings were also alive and had feelings. The other virtues stressed by Aśoka—kindness, giving, truthfulness, purity of action, obedience to parents, just treatment of others, gratitude to society—all arose out of that basic realization. The contents of Aśoka's Dharma were rich indeed.

In order that the Dharma might always be practiced throughout the area he ruled, Aśoka appointed ministers of Dharma *(dharma-mahāmātra)* who were to travel throughout the country every five years and ascertain that the Dharma was being preached (Separate Rock Edict I: Dhauli).

Because the longest edict, Rock Edict XIV, does not specifically state that Aśoka's Dharma was derived from Buddhism, some scholars have questioned whether it was Buddhist. However, the Dharma preached by Aśoka was not based upon any non-Buddhist tradition. For example, the term *"dharma"* was discussed in such Hindu *Dharmaśāstra* works as the *Laws of Manu,* where it was used to mean law as in criminal and civil law. The term was also used in Nyāya thought, and both *dharma* and *adharma* were terms in Jaina philosophy. But in each case, the term was used in completely different ways from Aśoka's edicts. The term *"dharma"* was used in Vedic and Upaniṣadic literature with a meaning close but not identical to Aśoka's use. The central idea of the *Upaniṣads,* however, was the identity of Brahman and *ātman;* the term *"dharma"* did not occupy the central position in Upaniṣadic thought as it did in Aśoka's thought.

In the *Bhagavad-gītā, dharma* was an element in the important term *"svadharma"* (one's own duty), which was used in the Karmayoga (Way of Action) system. A variety of moral virtues was listed in the *Bhagavad-*

gītā, many of them identical to those in Aśoka's edicts. However, war was commended in the *Bhagavad-gītā,* whereas Aśoka disapproved of it.

In contrast to non-Buddhist religion, the term "Dharma" occupied a central place in Buddhist thought. It is one of the Three Jewels *(triratna):* the Buddha, his Teaching (Dharma), and the order *(saṅgha).* The Minor Rock and Pillar Edicts reveal that Aśoka was a devoted Buddhist. Thus Aśoka's Dharma was clearly derived from Buddhism.

Aśoka's Support of the Buddhist Order

Although Aśoka had converted to Buddhism, he treated other religions fairly. Rock Edict XII states that he "gave alms *(dāna)* and honored *(pūjā)* both members of religious orders and the laity of all religious groups *(pārṣada).*" In Rock Edict VII, he declared that he "wished members of all religions to live everywhere in his kingdom." In Pillar Edict VII, Aśoka noted that he had appointed ministers of Dharma to be responsible for affairs related to the Buddhist order. Other ministers of Dharma were responsible for the affairs of Brahmans, Ājīvikas, or Jainas (Nirgranthas).

Aśoka was fair in his treatment of all religions, but he was particularly devoted to Buddhism, as is illustrated by the inscriptions concerning his own life. Aśoka converted to Buddhism around the seventh year of his reign. According to the Minor Rock Edict from Rūpnāth, for the next two years he was not very devout in his practice, but then for a period of more than a year he "drew near to the order" *(saṅghaḥ upetaḥ)* and practiced assiduously. The phrase "drew near to the order" probably indicated that Aśoka was affiliated with the Buddhist order and performed the same practices as a monk. According to Rock Edict VIII, Aśoka went to *"saṃbodhi"* (probably the *bodhi*-tree at Buddhagayā) in the tenth year of his reign. The Nigālīsāgar Pillar Edict recorded that in the fourteenth year of his reign, Aśoka had a *stūpa* dedicated to the past Buddha Konākamana repaired and then personally made offerings at it. The Lumbinī Pillar Edict recorded that sometime after the twentieth year of his reign, Aśoka traveled to the Buddha's birthplace and personally made offerings there. He then had a stone pillar set up and reduced the taxes of the people in that area. The edicts at Sāñcī, Sārnāth, and Kauśāmbī all warned against schisms in the order and declared that any monk or nun who tried to cause a schism would be defrocked. Warnings against schisms were included in the Minor Rock Edicts as well.

In the Bairāṭ Edict, Aśoka paid honor to the order and then declared that he respected *(gaurava)* and put his faith *(prasāda)* in the Three Jewels. He then stated that all of the Buddha's teachings were good, but that certain doctrines *(dharmaparyāya)* were particularly useful in ensuring that Buddhism would endure for a long time. The names of the following seven texts were then listed.

1. *Vinayasamukase* (The Superior Teaching of the *Vinaya; Vinaya,* vol. 1, p. 7ff.)
2. *Aliyavasāṇi* (Noble Lineage; *AN,* IV:28, vol. 2, p. 27)
3. *Anāgata-bhayāni* (Dangers of the Future; *AN,* V, vol. 3, p. 100f.)
4. *Munigāthā* (Verses on Recluses; *Suttanipāta,* vv. 207–221)
5. *Moneyasūte* (*Sūtra* on the Practice of Silence, *Suttanipāta,* vv. 679–723)
6. *Upatisapasine* (Upatissa's Question, *Suttanipāta,* vv. 955–975)
7. *Lāghulovāda* (The Exhortation to Rāhula, *MN,* no. 61)

In order that the correct teaching might long endure, monks, nuns, laymen, and laywomen were to listen to these works frequently and reflect on their contents.

The only edict concerning *stūpas* relates how Aśoka repaired a *stūpa* belonging to the past Buddha Konākamana (Konakamuni). However, in literary sources such as the *A-yü-wang ching* (*T* 2043, *Aśokarājasūtra*?) descriptions are found of how Aśoka made offerings to the Buddha's relics. In addition, Aśoka is said to have ordered 84,000 *stūpas* built throughout the realm and to have benefited many people. At the urging of Upagupta, Aśoka embarked on a series of pilgrimages to pay homage at Buddhist sites, including Lumbinī, the Deer Park at Sārnāth, Buddhagayā, and Kuśinagara. At many of these sites he had *stūpas* constructed. *Stūpas* were also built for two of the Buddha's most important disciples, Śāriputra and Maudgalyāyana. Later, when the Chinese pilgrims Fa-hsien and Hsüan-tsang traveled through India, they reported that many of these *stūpas* still remained. In more recent times, archeologists have excavated and studied many *stūpas* and discovered that the oldest parts of the *stūpas* often date back to Aśoka's time, indicating the accuracy of these records.

Because Aśoka was a fervent convert to Buddhism and strove to propagate it, he was praised and called "Dharma Aśoka." The ideology of Dharma propagated by Aśoka included many lofty ideals. Unfortunately, how extensively it spread among the people and how deeply it was understood by them remains unclear. Aśoka greatly aided the Buddhist order, recognizing that it contained people who put the Dharma into practice. However, as the order became wealthy, the discipline of those in it may well have begun to decline. Large gifts to the order became burdensome to the nation's economy.

According to the *A-yü-wang ching* and other sources, when Aśoka was old, his ministers and the prince acted against Aśoka and forbade any gifts to the order. In the end, Aśoka was allowed to give the order only half a myrobalan *(āmalaka)* fruit, which he held in the palm of his hand. This legend indicates that Aśoka's career probably declined at the end of his life. In fact, the Mauryan empire lost much of its power and disappeared shortly after Aśoka's death. Yet Aśoka's Dharma cannot be judged as being without value because of the fate of his empire. Rather, his Dharma must be judged on its own merits.

PART TWO

NIKĀYA BUDDHISM

CHAPTER 8

The Development of Nikāya Buddhism

THE TERM "Nikāya Buddhism"[1] refers to monastic Buddhism after the initial schism into the Mahāsaṅghika and Sthavira schools had occurred. It must be remembered, however, that other groups of Buddhists existed at this time. For example, Buddhist laymen were not included in the Buddhist *saṅgha,* but were very active during and after the Buddha's life. Immediately after the Buddha's death, laymen divided his remains *(śarīra)* into eight parts and constructed burial mounds *(stūpas)* for them. These *stūpas* were constructed at the intersections of major roads (*DN,* vol. 2, p. 142) where large groups of people could assemble, not at the monasteries where monks lived. *Stūpas* were administered by laymen who were autonomous from the order of monks, and most of the devotees were also laymen. According to the *A-yü-wang ching* (*T* 2043, *Aśokarājasūtra*?), a biography of King Aśoka, the king ordered that the eight *stūpas* be opened and the relics divided and distributed throughout the country, where they were to be the basis of new *stūpas*. In part, Aśoka was responding to the growing popularity of *stūpa* worship. In addition to the sites of the old *stūpas,* four great pilgrimage sites had been established and were frequently visited by believers: the Buddha's birthplace, the tree under which he attained enlightenment, the park where he preached his first sermon, and the place where he died. Unfortunately, however, literary sources do not describe in any detail the beliefs or doctrines held by these groups of lay believers, although they obviously congregated around *stūpas* to praise the Buddha and strengthen their faith in him.

Although the activities of these groups of lay believers later came to play an important role in the rise of Mahāyāna Buddhism, the mainstream of Early Buddhism was continued not by such lay groups, but by the schools of Nikāya Buddhism. The Buddha's main teachings were transmitted by his immediate disciples such as Mahākāśyapa and Ānanda (Śāriputra and Maudgalyāyana had predeceased the Buddha) to their disciples, and then were eventually passed on to the monks of Nikāya Buddhism.

Nikāya Buddhism was often called "Buddhism for disciples" or "Buddhism of those who studied." It did not stress the importance of teaching others. Because Nikāya Buddhism seemed so passive to Mahāyāna Buddhists, they called it Śrāvakayāna (the vehicle of the *śrāvakas*). The term *"śrāvaka"* meant "those who listened to the Buddha's words," and thus referred to his disciples. Originally, lay people were also called *śrāvakas,* but by the time of Nikāya Buddhism the term seems to have been limited to those who had been ordained.

Nikāya Buddhist doctrine was a monastic teaching for those who were willing to leave their homes to become monks or nuns, strictly observe the precepts, and perform religious practices. Both doctrinal study and religious practice presupposed the abandonment of a person's life as a householder. A strict line separated those who had been ordained from lay people. In addition, Nikāya Buddhism was for those who were secluded in their monasteries. While in retreat, they led ascetic lives and devoted themselves to scholarship and religious practices. It was not a Buddhism of the streets, dedicated to saving others; rather, the emphasis was on the completion of a person's own practice. Consequently, Mahāyāna Buddhists deprecated Nikāya Buddhism by calling it Hīnayāna (small vehicle), meaning it had a narrow or inferior teaching.

Since their monasteries were often wealthy, Nikāya Buddhists did not have to trouble themselves about living expenses and were able to devote most of their time to religious practices. Their orders often received the devotion and financial help of kings, queens, and merchants, who gave large estates to the monasteries. King Kaniṣka was particularly famous for his support of the Sarvāstivādin School; but according to inscriptions, even before Kaniṣka, a North Indian governor-general *(mahākṣatrapa)* named Kusuluka and a governor *(kṣatrapa)* named Patika gave land to the order. In South India, the queens and royal families of the Āndhran dynasty supported the Buddhist orders. Many inscriptions survive recording their gifts of land. Many other inscriptions dating from the second century B.C.E. to the fifth century C.E. record gifts of cave-temples and land to *stūpas* and to the Buddhist order as a whole. According to these inscriptions, orders belonging to more than twenty schools existed during this period.

In addition to receiving support from royalty, Buddhist orders were aided by the merchant classes. Merchants traded with foreign countries and distant cities, traveling across deserts and through dark forests in caravans or crossing the sea to reach their destination. To overcome the difficulties and dangers that they encountered on their travels, merchants had to be brave, patient, and capable of making calm and rational decisions. The rational qualities of Buddhism matched the needs of such people. In addition, when merchants traveled to foreign countries, they had to be able to associate freely with peoples of different nationalities and social classes. The strict caste system of Hinduism made it an inappropriate religion for such merchants. (Farmers, in contrast, were strongly tied to Hinduism.) Since Buddhism did not recognize the caste system, it was especially attractive to merchants.

Merchants were interested not only in the schools of Nikāya Buddhism, but also in the Mahāyāna orders. Among the rich merchants and leaders of merchant classes *(śreṣṭhin)* were Ugra and Sudatta, a convert of the Buddha who was known for the alms he gave to orphans and the needy. The names of many other merchant leaders who were early Buddhist believers are known from early Buddhist sources. Merchant leaders were often portrayed as being in the audiences in Mahāyāna scriptures. Such people probably also gave alms to the Nikāya Buddhist orders. With aid from both kings and merchant leaders, the members of the Nikāya Buddhist orders could devote themselves to their scholarship and practice. The analytical and highly detailed *abhidharma* systems of Buddhist doctrine were formulated in such monasteries.

The Second and Third Councils

In chapter six we analyzed the story of how a dispute over ten items of monastic discipline led to an assembly of elders at Vaiśālī. According to the Chapter on the Council of Seven Hundred of the Pāli *Vinaya,* seven hundred elders discussed the ten items in accordance with the *vinaya.* Thus, their meeting is called a council on *vinaya (vinayasaṅgīti).* No mention is made in the Pāli *Vinaya* of the compilation of the *Sutra-piṭaka* or *Vinaya-piṭaka* after the investigation of the ten points was concluded. The Chinese translations of the full *vinayas* agree with this account. Although the chapter titles of the Chinese *vinayas* on the council suggest that the *vinaya* was recited and compiled again, within the chapters themselves no mention is made of a reorganization of the *Vinaya-* or *Sūtra-piṭaka.* In contrast, according to the Sri Lankan chronicles, the *Dīpavaṃsa* and *Mahāvaṃsa,* after the dispute over the ten items was concluded, the seven hundred elders with Revata as their leader held a council on doctrine *(dhamma-saṅgaha)* that required eight months to complete. This is called the Second Council *(dutiya-saṅgaha)* in the Theravāda tradition.

The *Dīpavaṃsa* account continues, adding that the dissenting monks who were expelled from the order then gathered ten thousand supporters and held their own council to compile the Buddha's teachings. This was called the Great Council *(Mahāsaṅgīti).* These monks were said to have compiled false teachings, rejected the canon agreed upon at the First Council, and compiled their own canon. They moved *sūtras* from one part of the canon to another, thereby distorting the doctrines of the five *Nikāyas.* They confused orthodox and heterodox teachings and did not distinguish between teachings to be taken literally and those requiring interpretations. They discarded parts of the *sūtras* and the *vinaya* and composed false scriptures, which they substituted for the rejected texts.

According to the *Dīpavaṃsa* account, the monks of the Great Assembly compiled new versions of the *sūtras* and *vinaya* quite different from those of the Sthaviras. This group is called "the monks of the Great Council" (Mahāsaṅgītika) in the *Dīpavaṃsa* and "the Great Assembly" (Mahāsaṅghika) in the *Mahāvaṃsa.* The name "Mahāsaṅghika" meant that these monks constituted the majority of monks at the initial schism. Thus, according to the Sri Lankan tradition, after the initial schism the Theravāda and Mahāsaṅghika schools each held a separate council.

No mention of a council is found in the *I pu tsung lun lun* (*T* 2031, *Samayabhedoparacanacakra#*, hereafter referred to as *Samaya*), a history and discussion of the schools of Nikāya Buddhism according to Northern Buddhist traditions. According to the *Samaya,* a hundred years after the Buddha's death, during the reign of King Aśoka, "four groups could not reach agreement in discussions about the five points of doctrine proposed by Mahādeva" (*T* 49:15a). Consequently, the Buddhist order was divided into two schools, the Sthavira and the Mahāsaṅghika. The four groups were the Nāga group (Tib. Gnas-bstan-klu), the group from the border area (Tib. Śar-phogs-pa), the learned group (Tib. Maṅ-du-thos-pa), and the venerable group. (Only three groups are mentioned in the Tibetan translation, but four groups are mentioned in a Chinese translation, *T* 49:20a.)

Vinayas from both the Mahāsaṅghika and the Sthavira lineages agreed that a council of seven hundred monks was convened to discuss ten points of controversy. (However, the ten points are not specifically mentioned in the *Mo-ho-seng-ch'i lü, T* 1425, *Mahāsaṅghikavinaya*?.) Thus, there is agreement that a council was convened, but only Theravāda sources such as the *Dīpavaṃsa* include statements that the

Sūtra-piṭaka was recited and examined after the council. This series of events is generally referred to as the Second Council, but sources do not agree about whether the *Vinaya-* and *Sūtra-piṭakas* were reorganized at this time. Since sources do agree that seven hundred monks did assemble and convene a council, at least this aspect of the tradition must be recognized as a historical fact.

The story of the Third Council is found only in Sri Lankan sources such as the *Dīpavaṃsa, Mahāvaṃsa,* and *Samantapāsādikā.* According to these sources, the Second Council was held a hundred years after the Buddha's death during the reign of King Kālāśoka; the Third Council *(tatiya-saṅgaha)* was held during the reign of King Aśoka, who was crowned 218 years after the Buddha's death. The Third Council is said to have been presided over by Moggaliputta Tissa, and the doctrines discussed at the council to have been recorded in the *Kathāvatthu* (Points of Controversy). The Sri Lankan tradition thus distinguishes between the reigns of Kālāśoka (P. Kālāsoka) and Aśoka (P. Asoka) and relates the story of two councils. In contrast, in the *Samaya* (*T* 49:18a), a work in the Northern tradition, King Aśoka's reign is said to have occurred a little more than a century after the Buddha's death. This latter time scale does not allow sufficient time for a Third Council to have been convened. Moreover, the work in which the disputes of the Third Council are said to have been collected, the *Kathāvatthu,* is found only in the Theravāda tradition. The Third Council is not mentioned in the literature of the other schools. Thus, if it was held, it apparently involved only the Theravāda School.

The Sri Lankan account of the Third Council follows. During the reign of King Aśoka, the Buddhist order flourished because of the king's financial support, but many people became monks only because monasteries offered an easy way of life *(theyyasaṃvāsaka).* Monastic rules were not closely observed and religious practice was neglected. Disputes arose in the order. Not even the fortnightly assembly was held. To correct such abuses, Moggaliputta Tissa with the support of King Aśoka purged the order. Those who agreed that Buddhism was *vibhajjavāda* (the teaching of discrimination) were accepted as Buddhist monks; those who disagreed were expelled from the order. Moggaliputta Tissa then compiled the *Kathāvatthu* to explain the orthodox position, assembled a thousand *arhats,* and held a council to compile the Dharma. This was the Third Council.

The Sri Lankan Theravāda School understood Buddhism as the "teaching of discrimination" *(vibhajjavāda).* Nothing was to be adhered to in a one-sided manner. If people single-mindedly insisted that they understood the truth, arguments would inevitably ensue. Thus, reality was to be understood by "discriminating" between one-sided negative and positive positions. The Theravāda School was also called the Vibhajjavādin (those who discriminate) School. The Third Council was probably held at some point within the Theravāda School and focused on this tradition of discriminating between extremes. Thus, the historicity of the Third Council cannot be completely denied.

The contents of the *Kathāvatthu* are based on points of controversy that arose among the various schools of Nikāya Buddhism. The text thus presupposes the completion of the various schisms of the schools. The present text of the *Kathāvatthu* must be dated at least one hundred years after Aśoka, perhaps during the last half of the second century B.C.E. If the text of the *Kathāvatthu* accurately reflects the issues of the Third Council, then that council must have occurred in the second century B.C.E.

Later Schisms

After the initial split that resulted in the Sthavira and Mahāsaṅghika schools, further divisions occurred that led to a proliferation of schools. The Mahāsaṅghika School was the first to experience a schism, probably because it had more members and had adopted a more liberal attitude toward doctrinal issues. As a result, it was more difficult to administer than the Sthavira School. According to the *Samaya* (*T* 2031), three additional schools—the Ekakvyavahārika, Lokottaravādin, and Kaukuṭika—split off from the Mahāsaṅghika during the second century after the Buddha's death. Two more schisms, which occurred during the second century after the Buddha's death, resulted in the Bahuśrutīya and the Prajñaptivādin schools. At the end of that century, Mahādeva proclaimed his five points at a *caitya* (reliquary) in southern India. The arguments that arose concerning the five points resulted in a fourth schism and three new schools: the Caitika, Aparaśaila, and Uttaraśaila. Thus, a total of eight new schools arose out of the Mahāsaṅghika School during the second century after the Buddha's death.

According to the *Samaya,* the Sthaviras maintained their unity during the century when the schools of the Mahāsaṅghika lineage were undergoing schisms. However, divisions in the Sthavira lineage began occurring during the third century after the Buddha's death. First, the Sarvāstivādin (also known as the Hetuvāda) School split away from the Sthavira (or Haimavata) School. Next, the Vātsīputrīya School broke away from the Sarvāstivādin School. The Vātsīputrīya School subsequently gave rise to four more schools: the Dharmottarīya, Bhadrayānīya, Sammatīya, and Ṣaṇṇagarika. In a fourth schism, the Sarvāstivādin School gave rise to the Mahīśāsaka School, which in turn, in a fifth schism, led to the formation of the Dharmaguptaka School. The Dharmaguptaka School claimed that its teachings had been received from the Buddha's disciple Maudgalyāyana. In a sixth schism, the Kāśyapīya (or Suvarṣaka) School broke away from the Sarvāstivādin School. The above six schisms occurred during the third century after the Buddha's death. The seventh, in which the Sautrāntika (or Saṅkrāntika) School broke away from the Sarvāstivādin School, occurred during the fourth century after the Buddha's death. The Sautrāntika School emphasized the importance of *sūtras* over *śāstras* and claimed that its teachings originated with Ānanda, the monk who had chanted the *sūtras* at the First Council.

The Sthavira lineage underwent seven schisms that resulted in eleven schools, while the Mahāsaṅghika School divided into a total of nine schools. The schisms in the two original schools thus resulted in a total of twenty schools. The phrase "the schisms into the eighteen schools," which is found in a number of Buddhist texts, refers to the eighteen schools produced by these later schisms, but not to the two original schools.

The Mahāsaṅghika School continued to exist as a separate entity despite undergoing four schisms. The fate of the original school of the Sthaviras is not so clear. The first schism in the Sthavira lineage resulted in the Sarvāstivādin and Haimavata schools. Although the Haimavata School is called the "original Sthavira School" in the *Samaya,* the Haimavata School was influential only in an area in the north and was far from central India, where most of the important events in very early Buddhist history occurred. Moreover, the school does not seem to have been very powerful. The other schools in the Sthavira lineage split off from the Sarvāstivādin School. Consequently, the account found in the *Samaya* seems questionable. Vasumitra, the author, was a Sarvāstivādin monk, and may have written this account to demonstrate that the Sarvāstivādin School was the most important school among those in the Sarvāstivādin lineage. Vasumitra's overall position thus would seem to conflict with his statement that the Haimavata was the original Sthavira School.

The early schisms of the Sthavira lineage occurred during the third century after the Buddha's death. According to Ui Hakuju's theory, the Buddha died in 386 B.C.E. (or 383 B.C.E. according to Nakamura Hajime), 116 years before Aśoka's coronation. If Ui's dates are used, then the Mahāsaṅghika schisms would have occurred during the third century B.C.E. and the Sthavira schisms during the second and first cen-

Figure 2. The Schools of Nikāya Buddhism according to the *Samaya*

Schools of the Mahāsaṅghika lineage
(total of nine schools; eight according to the Ch'en dynasty translation of the *Samaya*)

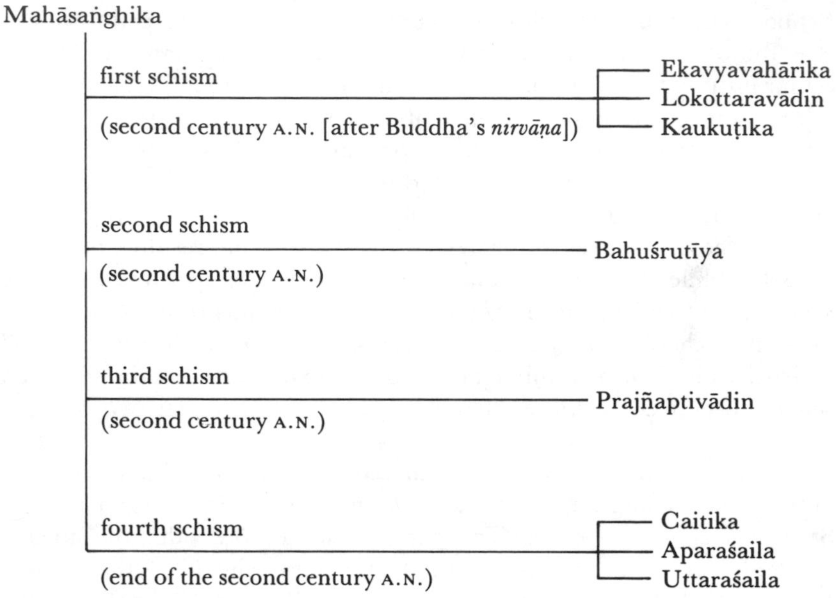

turies B.C.E. The Sautrāntika School would have come into existence by the first century B.C.E.[2]

If the Sri Lankan chronicles are followed, however, then the Buddha's death is placed in 484 B.C.E. (according to Jacobi and Kanakura Enshō), 218 years before Aśoka's coronation. Thus the Mahāsaṅghika schisms would have occurred before Aśoka's time and the Sthavira schisms during the century after Aśoka. Figure 2 illustrates the schisms according to Hsüan-tsang's translation of the *Samaya* (*T* 2031).

The account of the schisms presented in the Sri Lankan chronicles, the *Dīpavaṃsa* and *Mahāvaṃsa,* differs substantially from the description found in the *Samaya.* According to the Sri Lankan chronicles, the schisms in both the Mahāsaṅghika and Theravāda (Sthavira) lineages all occurred during the second century after the Buddha's death. Since the Sri Lankan chronicles state that Aśoka became king 218 years after the Buddha's death, the schisms presumably would have been com-

Schools of the Sthavira lineage
(total of eleven schools; the original Sthavira and Haimavata schools are distinguished in the Ch'in translation, making a total of twelve)

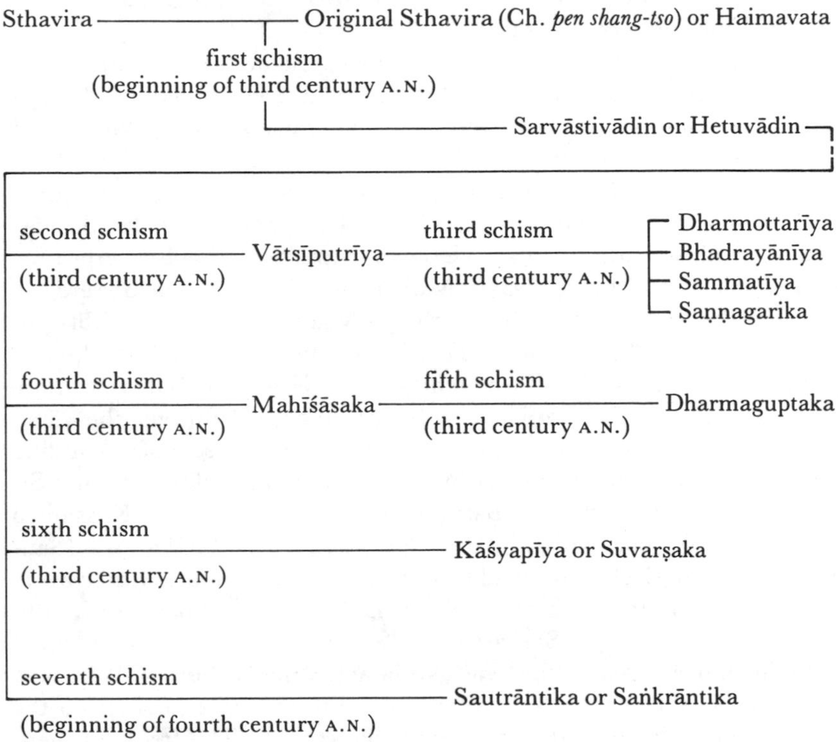

pleted before Aśoka ascended the throne. Aśoka would thus have reigned during the height of sectarian Buddhism. The Aśokan edicts, however, give little evidence that Aśoka ruled during a period when Buddhism was fiercely sectarian.

According to the *Dīpavaṃsa* and *Mahāvaṃsa,* the first schism occurred when the Mahāsaṅghika (Mahāsaṇgītika or Mahāsaṅghika Vajjiputtaka) School gave rise to the Gokulika (called the Kaukuṭika in the *Samaya;* the *Samaya* equivalent is given in parentheses for the next few paragraphs) and the Ekavyohārika (Ekavyavahārika) schools. In a second schism, the Paññati (Prajñaptivādin) and Bahussutaka (Bahuśrutīya) schools broke away from the Gokulika School. (According to the *Samaya,* all four of the above schools split away from the Mahāsaṅghika School.) Next, the Cetiyavāda (Caitika) School arose. According to the *Dīpavaṃsa,* it broke away from the Mahāsaṅghika School; but in the *Mahāvaṃsa,* it is said to have arisen from the Paññati and Bahussutaka schools. A total of six schools (including the Mahāsaṅghika) is mentioned in this series of schisms.

The later schisms in the schools of the Theravāda (Sthavira) lineage begin with the formation of the Mahiṃsāsaka (Mahīśāsaka) and Vajjiputtaka (Vātsīputrīya) schools out of the Theravāda School. Next, four schools—the Dhammutariya (Dharmottarīya), Bhadrayānika (Bhadrayānīya), Chandāgārika (Ṣaṇṇagarika), and Saṃmitīya (Sammatīya)—arose out of the Vajjiputtaka School. The Sabbatthavāda (Sarvāstivāda) and Dhammaguttika (Dharmaguptaka) schools were then formed out of the Mahiṃsāsaka (Mahīśāsaka) School. (The *Samaya,* on the other hand, maintains that both the Mahīśāsaka and the Vātsīputrīya arose from the Sarvāstivāda.) Thus, the Sarvāstivādin School is portrayed as one of the oldest schools in the *Samaya,* but as a more recent school in the Sri Lankan chronicles. In both traditions, the Vātsīputrīya is said to have been the source for four later schools including the Sammatīya and Dharmottarīya. Finally, according to the Sri Lankan chronicles, the Sabbatthavāda gave rise to the Kassapiya (Kāśyapīya) School, which in turn gave rise to the Saṅkantika (Saṅkrāntika) School. The Suttavāda (Sautrāntika) School later broke away from the Saṅkrāntika. (In the *Samaya* the last three schools are said to have split away from the Sarvāstivādin School.)

In the above account, the Theravāda and other schools of its lineage total twelve. When these twelve are added to the six schools from the Mahāsaṅghika lineage, they total eighteen schools. The frequent mention of "eighteen schools" in various sources probably indicates that at one time eighteen schools did, in fact, exist. According to the Sri Lankan chronicles, the eighteen schools were formed during the second century after the Buddha's death. Other schools appeared later, however. The *Dīpavaṃsa* lists the following six schools without identifying the schools from which they arose: Hemavatika (Haimavata), Rājagiriya, Siddhatthaka, Pubbaseliya, Aparaseliya (Aparaśaila), and Aparārājagirika. In the *Samaya,* the Haimavata is identified with the Sthavira School formed at the time of the initial schism, and is thus one of the oldest schools. In the *Mahāvaṃsa,* in contrast, it is listed as a later school. The Aparaseliya School is included in the schools that developed out of the Mahāsaṅghika School, according to the *Samaya.* In Buddhaghosa's commentary on the *Kathavātthu,* four schools are called "Andhaka schools": the Pubbaseliya, Aparaseliya, Rājagiriya, and Siddhatthaka. They seem to have been related to the Mahāsaṅghika School.

In the *Mahāvaṃsa*'s list of the six later schools, the Apararājagirika School is replaced by the Vājiriya School. In addition, the Dhammaruci and Sāgaliya schools, which broke away from the Sri Lankan Theravāda School, are also mentioned. The schisms according to the Sri Lankan chronicles are diagramed in Figure 3.

As has been noted, the preceding two accounts of the schisms in the Buddhist orders differ in several important ways. The account of the origins of the Sarvāstivādin School found in the Sri Lankan chronicles is probably correct. The areas of agreement in the accounts presented by the two traditions provide us with at least a general view of the order of the schisms.

The names of a number of schools not found in the above two accounts are known. André Bareau has compiled the names of thirty-four schools from literary sources and from inscriptions recording gifts made to various orders. Below is a list of schools that follows the spelling given by Bareau.[3]

1. Mahāsāṅghika
2. Lokottaravādin
3. Ekavyāvahārika
4. Gokulika or Kukkuṭika
5. Bahuśrutīya
6. Prajñaptivādin
7. Caitīya or Caitika
8. Andhaka
9. Pūrvaśaila or Uttaraśaila
10. Aparaśaila
11. Rājagirīya
12. Siddhārthika
13. Sthavira
14. Haimavata
15. Vātsīputrīya
16. Sammatīya
17. Dharmottarīya
18. Bhadrayānīya
19. Ṣaṇṇagarika or Ṣaṇḍagiriya
20. Sarvāstivādin Vaibhāṣika
21. Mūlasarvāstivādin
22. Sautrāntika or Saṅkrāntivādin
23. Dārṣṭāntika
24. Vibhajyavādin (Sri Lankan Theravāda School)
25. Mahīśāsaka
26. Dharmaguptaka
27. Kāśyapīya or Suvarṣaka
28. Tāmraśātīya (Sri Lankan School)
29. Mahāvihāra Sect of the Theravādin School
30. Abhayagirivāsin or Dhammarucika
31. Jetavanīya or Sāgalika
32. Hetuvādin
33. Uttarāpathaka
34. Vetullaka

Figure 3. Schools of Nikāya Buddhism according to Theravāda Sources

Schools of the Mahāsaṅghika lineage

(relation of traditional six schools indicated by solid lines; dotted lines indicate additional schisms)

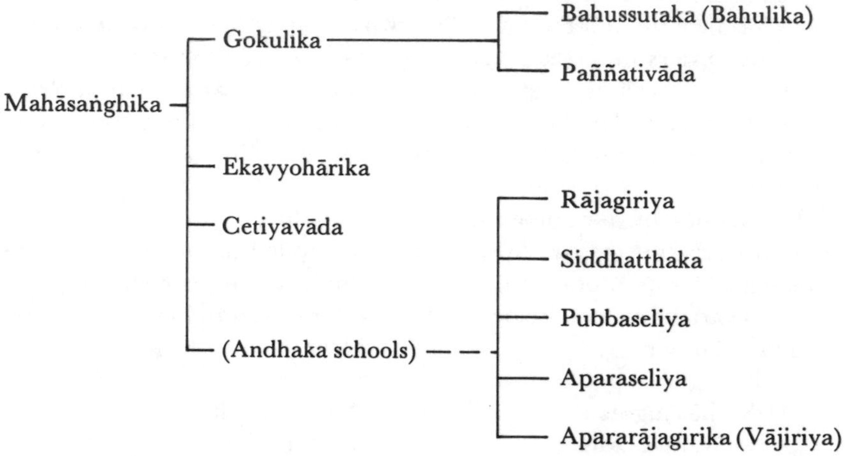

Schools of the Theravāda lineage

(relation of traditional twelve schools indicated by solid lines; dotted lines indicate additional schisms)

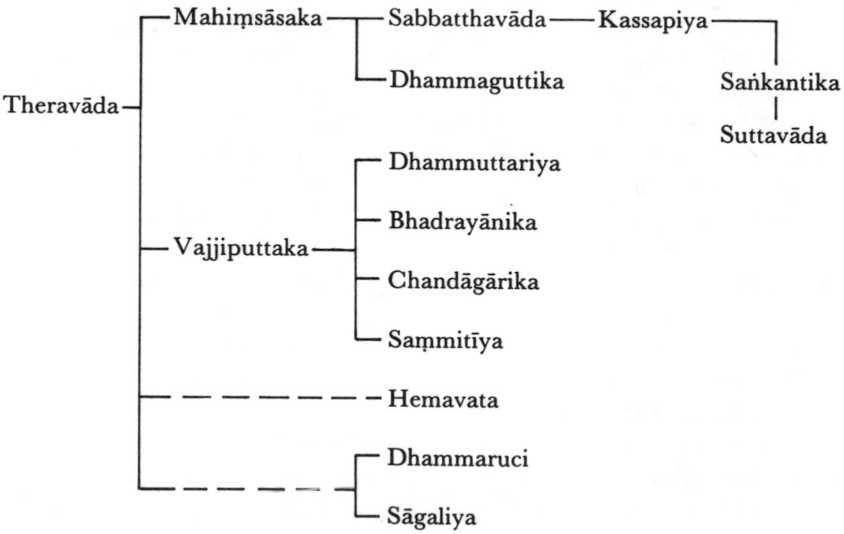

Sources for the Study of the Schisms

In the Sri Lankan tradition, the major sources for the study of the schisms are such works as the *Dīpavaṃsa,* the *Mahāvaṃsa,* and Buddhaghosa's *Kathāvatthu-aṭṭhakathā.* A key source in the Sarvāstivādin tradition, Vasumitra's *Samayabhedoparacanacakra* (cited as *Samaya*), survives in three Chinese translations (*T* 2031–2033) and a Tibetan translation (Peking no. 5639). The above works are the most important sources for the study of the schisms of Nikāya Buddhism. In addition, two Chinese translations of Indian texts, the *Wen-shu-shih-li wen ching* (*T* 468, *Mañjuśrīparipṛcchā*?) and the *She-li-fu wen ching* (*T* 1465, *Śāriputraparipṛcchā*?), are useful. The sixth part of the third fascicle of Seng-yu's *Ch'u san-ts'ang-chi chi* (*T* 2145) includes a valuable discussion of the schisms that focuses on the positions of the five schools whose full *vinayas* were translated into Chinese. This account was influential in Chinese Buddhism.

The following sources in Tibetan are also important: Bhavya's *Sde-pa tha-dad-par byed-pa daṅ rnam-par bśad-pa* (Peking no. 5640, *Nikāyabhedavibhaṅga-vyākhyāna*), Vinītadeva's *Gshuṅ tha-dad-pa rim-par klag-paḥi ḥkhor-lo-las sde-pa tha-dad-pa bstan-pa bsdus-pa* (Peking no. 5641, *Samayabhedoparacanacakre nikāya-bhedopadeśana-saṅgraha*), and the *Dge-tshul-gyi daṅ-poḥi lo dri-ba* (Peking no. 5634, *Śrāmaṇera-varṣāgra-pṛccha*).

In Bhavya's *Nikāyabhedavibhaṅga-vyākhyāna* various theories concerning the schisms of Nikāya Buddhism are presented, including accounts from the Sthavira, Mahāsaṅghika, and Sammatīya schools. According to a Sthavira legend, Aśoka ascended the throne 160 years after the Buddha's death. Sammatīya traditions maintained that the initial schism between the Sthavira and Mahāsaṅghika schools occurred 137 years after the Buddha's death. Dissension continued for the next sixty-three years, with the first schisms in the Mahāsaṅghika School occurring during that time. Some modern scholars regard the date of 137 years after the Buddha's death for the initial schism as reliable. Bareau has argued that the account in Vinītadeva's work represents the Mūlasarvāstivādin position. A number of theories are also presented in Tāranātha's history of Indian Buddhism. However, since the works by Bhavya and others that have survived in the Tibetan tradition were compiled during or after the sixth century, long after the schisms had occurred, their value as historical sources for the schisms is diminished. Other later sources with information on the schisms are the *Mahāvyutpatti* (entry no. 275) and I-ching's *Nan-hai chi-kuei nei-fa chuan* (*T* 2125, *A Record of the Buddhist Religion as Practiced in India and the Malay Archipelago*).[4]

In most of these works, the initial schism is said to have resulted in the formation of two schools. However, theories also exist that maintain that the initial schism resulted in three (Sthavira, Mahāsaṅghika, and Vibhajyavādin) or four schools (either the Mahāsaṅghika, Sarvāstivādin, Vātsīputrīya, and Haimavata schools or the Mahāsaṅghika, Sarvāstivādin, Theravāda, and Sammatīya schools). In the *Mahāvyutpatti* the four basic schools are listed as the Sarvāstivādin, Sammatīya, Mahāsaṅghika, and Theravāda. I-ching listed the Mahāsaṅghika, Theravāda, Mūlasarvāstivādin, and Sammatīya schools as the four basic schools (*T* 54:205b). However, in some *sūtras* and *śāstras*, a *vinaya* tradition singling out the following five schools for special emphasis is mentioned: Dharmaguptaka, Sarvāstivādin, Kāśyapīya, Mahīśāsaka, and Vātsīputrīya (in some lists, the Mahāsaṅghika School replaces the Vātsīputrīya). Hsüan-tsang mentioned such a *vinaya* tradition in his travel diary (*T* 51:882b).

To summarize, the first or initial schism resulted in two schools: the Sthavira and the Mahāsaṅghika. After a number of further schisms, four schools emerged as the most powerful ones of their time: the Mahāsaṅghika, Theravāda, Sarvāstivādin, and Sammatīya. Later, the Sammatīya School became particularly strong, as is indicated by the entries in the travel records of Fa-hsien and Hsüan-tsang.

In the discussions of Buddhism found in Brahmanical philosophical texts, the Mahāyāna Mādhyamika and Yogācāra schools and the Nikāya Buddhist Vaibhāṣika (Sarvāstivādin) and Sautrāntika schools are often mentioned. Later, in Śaṅkara's (eighth century) *Brahmasūtrabhāṣya* (II. 2. 18), three schools are discussed: Sarvāstitvavādin (Sarvāstivādin), Vijñānāstitvavādin (Yogācāra), and Sarvaśūnyatvavādin (Mādhyamika). According to scholars, the Sautrāntika School was included in the Sarvāstitvavādin category by Śaṅkara. Later Vedanta thinkers regarded Śaṅkara's philosophy as the high point of Indian philosophy and ranked other schools of thought below it in a hierarchical fashion. For example, in works such as the *Sarvamata-saṅgraha, Sarvasiddhanta-saṅgraha* (attributed to Śaṅkara), Mādhava's (fourteenth century) *Sarvadarśana-saṅgraha,* and Madhusūdana Sarasvatī's (fifteenth or sixteenth century) *Prasthānabheda,* the materialist Lokāyata tradition is ranked the lowest. Directly above it is Buddhism (Bauddha) and then Jainism. Four traditions are listed under Buddhism: the Mādhyamika, Yogācāra, Sautrāntika, and Vaibhāṣika. Thus the Sautrāntika and Sarvāstivādin schools were viewed as being representative of Hīnayāna Buddhism.

Vedanta scholars probably chose these four schools of Buddhism because they represented a variety of positions and could be presented in a diagrammatic fashion. The Sarvāstivādins were said to regard the external world as real *(bāhyārtha-pratyakṣatva)*. The Sautrāntikas were said to regard the external world as having only an instantaneous existence and thus to have argued that its existence could be recognized only through inference *(bāhyārthānumeyatva)*. The Yogācārins were said to recognize only consciousness as existing and to deny the existence of the external world *(bāhyārthaśūnyatva)*. Finally, the Mādhyamikas claimed that both subject and object were nonsubstantial *(sarvaśūnyatva)*.

Later Developments in Nikāya Buddhism

Once Buddhism had spread through India during King Aśoka's reign, it continued to develop. In the initial schism between Mahāsaṅghikas and Sthaviras, most of the monks who supported the adoption of the ten items of monastic discipline in dispute had been associated with the Vṛjis (Vajjiputtaka) of Vaiśālī in central India; they had constituted the nucleus of the Mahāsaṅghika order. Consequently, after the schism, the Mahāsaṅghikas became particularly influential in central India.

In contrast, the monks who opposed the ten items had been from Avanti in western India and from along the Southern Route. Consequently, the Sthavira order was more influential in western India. Aśoka's son Mahinda is traditionally credited with introducing Theravāda Buddhism to Sri Lanka. Mahinda's mother was from Vidiśā in Ujjayinī along the Southern Route. Mahinda assembled the materials for his journey in western India and set out from the west coast by ship. The Pāli language closely resembles the language found on inscriptions at Girnār. All of this evidence suggests that the Sthavira order was centered in western India.

Sarvāstivādin works lead to similar conclusions concerning the geographical distribution of the two schools. According to fascicle 99 of the *Mahāvibhāṣā* (*T* 27:510a–512a), the dispute over the five issues that Mahādeva raised occurred during Aśoka's reign. After the Sthavira monks were defeated in the debate by the greater number of Mahāsaṅghika monks and expelled from the Kukkuṭārāma monastery (established in Pāṭaliputra by Aśoka), they went to Kashmir. According to the *A-yü-wang ching* (*T* 50:155c–156a, *Aśokarājasūtra*?), Upagupta established Buddhism in Mathurā, and Madhyāntika established it in Kashmir. These traditions agree with the fact that Kashmir later became a stronghold of the Sarvāstivādin School. The great wealth the Sarvāstivādins accumulated in Kashmir enabled the school to develop a detailed *abhidharma* philosophy.

Thus, the Sthavira School was influential in the western and northern parts of India, while the Mahāsaṅghika School was dominant in the central and southern parts of India. Many inscriptions concerning the Mahāsaṅghika School have been discovered in southern India. In general, however, the Mahāsaṅghika tradition was weaker than the Sthavira tradition. The names of many schools belonging to the Sthavira tradition, such as the Sarvāstivādin, Theravāda, and Sammatīya, are well known. In contrast, outside of the Mahāsaṅghika School itself, the names of relatively few schools from the Mahāsaṅghika lineage are well known. In addition, many works belonging to schools of the Sthavira tradition have survived, but only the *Mahāvastu,* a biography of the Buddha from the Lokottaravādin School, and two or three other works from schools in the Mahāsaṅghika tradition are extant.

Many of the later schisms in Nikāya Buddhism occurred during the second century B.C.E. The reasons for the schisms are not clear. Nor is it known where most of the "eighteen schools" were located. Although Mahāyāna Buddhism had arisen by the first century B.C.E., Nikāya Buddhism did not decline. Instead, both Nikāya and Mahāyāna Buddhism flourished during the next few centuries. In fact, Nikāya Buddhism was the larger of the two movements.

Many scholars have argued that Mahāyāna Buddhism arose from the Mahāsaṅghika School. The Mahāsaṅghika School was not, however, absorbed by Mahāyāna Buddhism; it continued to exist long after Mahāyāna Buddhism developed. Even during I-ching's (635–713) travels, it was counted among the four most powerful Buddhist orders in India.

There are relatively few materials extant regarding the later development of Nikāya Buddhism. The travel records of Chinese pilgrims to India are particularly valuable in this respect. Fa-hsien left China in 399. In his travel record, the *Fo-kuo chi* (*T* 2085), he mentioned three classifications of monasteries: Hīnayāna monasteries, Mahāyāna monasteries, and monasteries in which both Hīnayāna and Mahāyāna teachings were studied. For example, according to Fa-hsien's diary, three thousand monks in the country of Lo-i (Rohī or Lakki) in North India studied both Hīnayāna and Mahāyāna teachings, and three thousand monks in Pa-na (Bannu or Bannū) studied Hīnayāna teachings. Because Fa-hsien's diary is only one fascicle long, the entries are not detailed, but he does indicate that nine countries were Hīnayānist, three were Mahāyānist, and three were both Hīnayānist and Mahāyānist. In addition, he mentioned more than twenty other countries where Buddhism was practiced (although he did not identify the type of Buddhism followed). While Fa-hsien gives us some idea of Buddhism in fifth-century India, he did not record the names of the schools in the various parts of India he visited. Many aspects of our view of Indian Buddhism at that time must therefore remain vague.

The next significant travel diary was written by Hsüan-tsang (602–664), who left China for India in 629. His travel record, the *Hsi-yu chi* (*T* 2087, *Buddhist Records of the Western World*), is a detailed report of Indian Buddhism in the seventh century. The doctrinal affiliations of ninety-nine areas were recorded. Of these, sixty were Hīnayāna, twenty-four Mahāyāna, and fifteen were places in which both Hīnayāna and Mahāyāna teachings were followed. Of the sixty areas where Hīnayāna teachings were followed, fourteen were Sarvāstivādin, nineteen were Sammatīya, two were Theravāda, three were Mahāsaṅghika, one was Lokkotaravādin, five were Mahāyāna-Theravāda, and sixteen were only said to by Hīnayānist with no further information supplied.

The above numbers suggest that in the first half of the seventh century, the Hīnayāna orders were very influential in India. The Sarvāstivādin and Sammatīya schools were especially powerful. The only mentions of schools of the Mahāsaṅghika lineage were the three locations where the Mahāsaṅghika School itself was followed and the single place identified as Lokottaravādin.

When Hsüan-tsang mentioned five places that followed the Mahāyāna-Theravāda School, he was probably referring to a branch of the Sri Lankan Theravāda School that had adopted many elements of Mahāyāna thought (*T* 51:918b, 929a, 934a, 935c, 936c). In the seventh century, there were two main branches of Sri Lankan Buddhism: the Mahāvihāra-vāsin, which represented the orthodox Theravāda School, traditionally said to have been brought to Sri Lanka by Mahinda; and the Abhayagiri-vihāra-vāsin, which adopted many elements of the Vetulyaka branch of Mahāyāna teachings. When Fa-hsien traveled to Sri Lanka in 410, he reported that five thousand monks belonged to the Abhayagiri-vihāra-vāsin, three thousand to the Mahāvihāra-vāsin, and two thousand to the Cetiyapabbatavihāra. While he was in Sri Lanka, Fa-hsien obtained a number of texts of the Mahīśāsaka School, including its *Vinaya, Ch'ang a-han* (corresponding to the Pāli *Dīgha-nikāya*), *Tsa a-han* (corresponding to the Pāli *Khuddaka-nikāya*), and the *Tsa-tsang* (*T* 745, *Kṣudrakasūtra*). Hsüan-tsang was unable to go to Sri Lanka because of wars on the island during the time he was in India. However, he did note that "the Mahāvihāra-vāsin reject the Mahāyāna and practice the Hīnayāna, while the Abhayagiri-vihāra-vāsin study both Hīnayāna and Mahāyāna teachings and propagate the *Tripiṭaka*" (*T* 51:934b). Thus Hsüan-tsang probably called the Abhayagiri-vihāra-vāsin a Mahāyāna-Theravāda group because they followed some Mahāyāna teachings while relying primarily on Theravāda teachings.

By the time of Hsüan-tsang, Indian Buddhism was already beginning to decline. Hsüan-tsang described the general state of Buddhism at Gandhāra when he wrote that its *stūpas* were largely "overgrown ruins." Also, "although there were over one thousand monasteries, they were dilapidated and deserted ruins, overgrown with weeds. There were also many temples belonging to non-Buddhist religions" (*T* 51:879c). His description reveals further that Hinduism was gradually gaining in strength.

Although the Sarvāstivādin School had been the strongest school of Nikāya Buddhism, by Hsüan-tsang's time the Sammatīya School had become the most influential. For example, inscriptions from Sārnāth reveal that although the monastery at the Deer Park had belonged to the Sarvāstivādin School during the Kuṣāṇa dynasty, by the fourth century it was controlled by the Sammatīya School. One of the main reasons for this change may have been that the Sammatīya School's affirmation of a "person" *(pudgala)* was closer to the Hindu doctrine of Self *(ātman)* than it was to the *dharma* theory of the Sarvāstivādin School.

When I-ching traveled to India in 671, he spent most of his time studying at the great Buddhist university at Nālandā. According to his travel diary, *Nan-hai chi-kuei nei-fa chuan* (*T* 2125, *A Record of the Buddhist Religion as Practiced in India and the Malay Archipelago*), the distinction between Hīnayāna and Mahāyāna monks was not very clear. Both observed the 250 "Hīnayāna" precepts and practiced in accordance with the Four Noble Truths. Those who read Mahāyāna texts and worshipped bodhisattvas were Mahāyānists, while those who did not do either were Hīnayānists (*T* 54:205c). Among the Mahāyānists, only the Mādhyamika and Yogācāra schools were mentioned. I-ching generally emphasized the way Mahāyāna and Hīnayāna practices were mixed.

I-ching described Hīnayāna Buddhism as being dominated by the Mahāsaṅghika, Theravāda, Mūlasarvāstivādin, and Sammatīya schools. In Magadha all four schools were practiced, although the Sarvāstivādin School was particularly strong. In Sindh and Lo-ch'a (Sanskrit name unknown) in western India, the Sammatīya School was dominant, although the other three were present to a lesser extent. In southern India, the Theravāda School was powerful and the other schools had only a minor presence. Sri Lanka was completely dominated by the Theravāda School, and the Mahāsaṅghika School had withdrawn from the island. In eastern India, all four schools were present. Southeast Asia was dominated by the Mūlasarvāstivādin School, with the Sammatīya School maintaining a small presence. Only Mo-lo-yu (the Malay peninsula?) exhibited Mahāyāna influence.

The travel records cited above indicate that Indian Buddhism in the sixth and seventh centuries was dominated by the Sarvāstivādin, Sammatīya, and Theravāda schools. When Hsüan-tsang visited India, he noted the existence of Sarvāstivādins, but made no mention of the Mūlasārvastivādins. Fifty years later, I-ching noted the existence of the Mūlasarvāstivādins, but did not mention the Sarvāstivādins. The term "Mūlasarvāstivādin" occurs primarily in sources from the Tibetan tradition, such as the works of Bhavya and Tāranātha and the *Mahāvyutpatti*. The differences between the two terms and the reasons they came to be used are not completely clear. However, the distinction was probably made when the Sarvāstivādin School in central India dramatized its differences with the school in Kashmir by calling itself the Mūlasarvāstivādin School.

Sarvāstivādin teachings are said to have been passed along a lineage consisting of Mahākāśyapa, Ānanda, Śāṇakavāsī, Upagupta, and so forth. Both Śāṇakavāsī and Upagupta lived in Mathurā. Upagupta received King Aśoka's patronage; Madhyāntika, an able disciple of Śāṇakavāsī, established the school in Kashmir. However, Madhyāntika was not listed in the lineages of the school. For example, a biography of Aśoka (*A-yü-wang chuan; T* 50:121a, 126a) includes the following lineage: Mahākāśyapa, Ānanda, Śāṇakavāsī, Upagupta, and Dhītika. The same lineage is found in the fortieth fascicle of the *Ken-pen-shuo-i-ch'ieh-yu-pu p'i-na-yeh tsa-shih* (*T* 24:411b), a work containing miscellaneous information on the Mūlasarvāstivādin *vinaya,* indicating that the lineage was accepted by the Mūlasarvāstivādins. In contrast, in another work on Aśoka, the seventh fascicle of the *A-yü-wang ching* (*T* 50:152c), the following lineage was included: Mahākāśyapa, Ānanda, Madhyāntika, Śāṇakavāsī, and Upagupta. Madhyāntika was probably inserted in the lineage at the insistence of the Sarvāstivādins of Kashmir. The central Indian Sarvāstivādins did not accept the lineage, however. Later, when the power of the Kashmir school declined, the central Indian school asserted its claims to preeminence by calling itself the Mūlasarvāstivādin School.

The Theravāda Tradition of Sri Lanka

The island of Sri Lanka, off the southern tip of India, has an area of approximately 25,000 square miles and a population of thirteen million people. In the past, it has been called Tambapaṇṇī, Siṃhala, Laṅkādīpa, and Ceylon. Theravāda Buddhism is practiced by many of the inhabitants, a tradition that is also followed in Thailand, Burma, Laos, and Cambodia.

Buddhism was first brought to Sri Lanka by Aśoka's son Mahinda, four other monks, and Mahinda's servants. The king of Sri Lanka, Devānampiya Tissa, had a temple constructed in the capital city of Anurādhapura for Mahinda and his followers to practice in. The temple was later called the Mahāvihāra and became the base for the Mahāvihāravāsin sect in Sri Lanka. The Cetiyapabbatavihāra monastery was built in Mihintalē, the port at which Mahinda had arrived. Mahinda's younger sister, the nun Saṅghamittā, also went to Sri Lanka. She brought a cutting from the *bodhi*-tree and established the order of nuns on the island. Buddhism subsequently flourished on Sri Lanka, with many monks and nuns joining the order and with imperial support contributing to the construction of monasteries.

The construction of the Abhayagiri-vihāra in the first century B.C.E. is especially noteworthy, since this monastery became the base for a second major sect of Theravāda Buddhism in Sri Lanka. The struggle between the monks of the Abhayagiri-vihāra and the monks of the Mahāvihāra continued to influence Sri Lankan religious history for the next several centuries. In 44 B.C.E., Vaṭṭagāmaṇi Abhaya became king of Sri Lanka; however, he was forced to flee shortly thereafter by the Tamils. Fifteen years later he regained the throne and ruled for twelve years (29–17 B.C.E.). In 29 B.C.E. he had the Abhayagiri monastery built and presented it to the elder Mahātissa—whom the Mahāvihāra monks had previously expelled from their monastery. When Mahātissa went to reside in the Abhayagiri monastery, he was accompanied by a number of monks from the Mahāvihāra, thus leading to a split between the two groups.

During the reign of Vaṭṭagāmaṇi Abhaya, the Buddhist canon, which had traditionally been transmitted through memorization and recitation, was finally written down. Five hundred monks from the Mahāvihāra sect participated in the copying sessions. They did not receive any assistance from the king since he supported the Abhayagiri sect. The monks would recite the works they had memorized and other monks would then verify their accuracy. Next, the recitations were edited and written down. At this time, the canon consisted of the *Tripiṭaka (sutra, vinaya,* and *abhidharma)* and commentaries. The decision to put the canon into written form was a major step in arriving at a definite formulation of its contents.

Meanwhile, the Abhayagiri sect had welcomed an elder of the Vajjiputtaka School in India named Dhammaruci and his disciples to their monastery. The Abhayagiri sect is consequently sometimes known as the Dhammaruci sect. During subsequent years, the Abhayagiri sect maintained close relations with Indian Buddhists and adopted many new teachings from India. In contrast, the Mahāvihāra sect has carefully maintained the Vibhajjavāda tradition of Theravāda Buddhism until the present day.

During the reign of Vohārika Tissa (269–291), a number of Indian adherents of the Vetullavāda sect of Mahāyāna Buddhism came to Sri Lanka and were allowed to stay at the Abhayagiri-vihāra by the monks; but the king quickly expelled the Indian monks from Sri Lanka. The Vetullavāda monks later reasserted their influence at the Abhayagiri-vihāra. In protest, a group of monks from Abhayagiri left the monastery and established a third sect at Dakkhiṇāgiri during the reign of Goṭhābhaya (309–322). This group, known as the Sāgaliya sect, was associated with the Jetavana monastery. King Goṭhābhaya had sixty of the Vetullavāda monks arrested, expelled from the order, and deported to India. Later, King Mahāsena (r. 334–361) suppressed the Mahāvihāra sect, which then entered a long period of decline. The Abhayagiri sect, in contrast, prospered. During the reign of Siri Meghavaṇṇa (362–409) a relic of the Buddha, one of his teeth, was brought to Sri Lanka from Kaliṅga in India and enshrined in the Abhayagiri monastery.

In the fifth century during the reign of Mahānāma (409–431), the great commentator Buddhaghosa came to Sri Lanka. He lived at the Mahāvihāra monastery, where he wrote commentaries on the *Tripiṭaka* and general expositions on Buddhist doctrine and practice. According to the *Cūlavaṃsa* (37:215–246), Buddhaghosa was a Brahman who had come from the vicinity where the Buddha had attained enlightenment in central India. According to Burmese sources, he was a native of Thaton, Burma, who traveled to Sri Lanka 943 years after the Buddha's death in the reign of King Mahānāma. Recent scholarship has revealed that Buddhaghosa was probably a native of South India. Whatever the case may be, it is certain that Buddhaghosa did come to Sri Lanka from a foreign country, resided at the Mahāvihāra, and supported the Mahāvihāra tradition. In addition, he wrote the *Visuddhimagga* (Path of Purification) and a series of detailed commentaries on the Buddhist canon based on older works in the Theravāda tradition. According to some sources, he translated the old Sinhalese commentaries into Pāli. After he completed his writings, he returned to his native country. Buddhaghosa's formulation of Theravāda doctrines has remained the standard one until the present time.

The rivalry between the Mahāvihāra and Abhayagiri sects continued through the centuries. In general, more rulers seem to have supported the Abhayagiri sect. The Mahāvihāra sect, however, successfully endured its many hardships and preserved a purer form of Theravāda doctrine and monastic discipline. During the first half of the eighth century, Mahāyāna and Esoteric Buddhism were practiced in Sri Lanka.

Two of the monks responsible for promulgating Esoteric Buddhism in China, Vajrabodhi and Amoghavajra, visited the island.

In the first half of the eleventh century during the reign of Mahinda V, when Sri Lanka was invaded by the Śaivite Chola dynasty of South India, the capital city and the Buddhist monasteries were reduced to ruins. After a half century of fighting, the Sri Lankan king Vijayabāhu I (1059–1113) forced the Cholas to leave the island, restored the monarchy, and invited Buddhist elders from Burma to restore Buddhism in Sri Lanka.

In the twelfth century, King Parakkamabāhu I (1153–1186) defrocked the decadent monks in the Mahāvihāra, Abhayagiri, and Jetavana sects and purified the Buddhist orders in Sri Lanka. The orthodox Theravāda Buddhism of the Mahāvihāra sect subsequently received government support, and the Abhayagiri sect was completely banned, never to regain influence. This marked the end of the ten centuries of rivalry between the sects. The Mahāvihāra sect and its orthodox Theravāda tradition have continued to dominate Sri Lankan Buddhism until the present day.

In subsequent centuries, the island was invaded by the Cholas, Portuguese, Dutch, and British. In the eighteenth century, King Kittisiri Rājasiṃha invited ten monks from Thailand to help restore the Buddhist order. Afterward, Southeast Asian monks were periodically invited to Sri Lanka to strengthen the order. Today Sri Lankan Buddhism is divided into a number of fraternities tracing their origins to these missions from Southeast Asia. The major fraternities are the Siyam, Kalyāṇi, Amarapura, and Rāmañña.

CHAPTER 9

Abhidharma *Literature*

The Establishment of the *Abhidharma-Piṭaka*

THE LITERATURE by which the schools of Nikāya Buddhism are differentiated is called the *abhidharma*. The term *"abhidharma"* (P. *abhidhamma*) means "the study of the *dharma*." The term *"dharma"* refers to the doctrines preached by the Buddha; it may also refer to the truths revealed by those teachings. Consequently, *abhidharma* may be interpreted as meaning studies of the Buddha's teachings or research into the truths revealed by the Buddha.

Even before the contents of the *Sūtra-piṭaka* had been finalized, the Buddha's disciples were analyzing his teachings with methods similar to those employed later in *abhidharma*. These early analyses were often incorporated into *sūtras*. After the *Sūtra-piṭaka* had been established and its contents determined, *abhidharma* investigations were considered to be a separate branch of literature. *Abhidharma* studies were later compiled into a collection called the *Abhidharma-piṭaka,* which was combined with the *Sūtra-piṭaka* and *Vinaya-piṭaka* to make up the "Three Baskets" or *Tripiṭaka* (P. *Tipiṭaka*) of the early Buddhist canon. The canon was limited to these three baskets or collections. In the Theravāda School, the term "Pāli" (or Pāḷi) is used with the meaning of "scripture" to refer to the *Tripiṭaka,* but not to refer to the commentaries on the *Tripiṭaka.*[1]

The Sarvāstivādin School argued that the *abhidharma* was preached by the Buddha. Sarvāstivādins thus believed that the entire *Tripiṭaka* was, in a broad sense, the Buddha's preaching.[2] However, the similarities in the texts of the *Sūtra-piṭakas* and *Vinaya-piṭakas* followed by the various schools reveal that the basic contents of these two collections were determined before the divisions of Nikāya Buddhism had occurred. In contrast, the contents of *abhidharma* literature varies with each of the schools, indicating that this class of literature was compiled after the basic divisions of the schools had occurred. The *Abhidharma-piṭakas* of most of the schools were probably compiled during a period beginning in 250 B.C.E. (after the first major schism) and ending around the start of the common era.

From *Sūtra-piṭaka* to *Abhidharma-piṭaka*

With the increase in the volume of *abhidharma* literature, a special division of the canon, an *Abhidharma-piṭaka,* was established. Before this, the canon went through a transitional phase in which material was placed in a "mixed basket" *(Kṣudraka-piṭaka)* of the canon.[3] The *Kṣudraka-piṭaka* was the repository for materials that had been left out of the four *Āgamas* (the *Dīrghāgama, Madhyamāgama, Saṃyuktāgama,* and *Ekottarāgama*) and thus included both early and later texts. The Mahīśāsaka, Dharmaguptaka, and Mahāsaṅghika were among those schools that included the *Kṣudraka-piṭaka* in their canon.

The only extant example of such a division of the canon is found in the Theravāda *Tipiṭaka,* where it is called the *Khuddaka-nikāya* rather than the *Kṣudraka-piṭaka.* The term *"kṣudraka"* (P. *khuddaka*) means "small" or "mixed"; but the meaning "mixed" is more appropriate. However, a "mixed *āgama*" (*Tsa a-han ching,* or literally, *kṣudrakāgama;* cf. *Abhidharmakośabhāṣya,* p. 466) is included in the Chinese canon (*T* 99 and 101). Since this work corresponds roughly to the Pāli *Saṃyutta-nikāya* and not to the *Khuddaka-nikāya,* the term *"Khuddaka-nikāya"* is translated into Chinese for convenience as *hsiao-pu* or "small section." The *Khuddaka-nikāya* is not small, however, as it is the largest of the five *Nikāyas.*

Fifteen works are included in the Pāli *Khuddaka-nikāya.* Among them are very old writings such as the *Dhammapada* (Words of the Doctrine), *Suttanipāta* (Collections of Suttas), *Theragāthā* (Verses of the Elder Monks), and *Therīgāthā* (Verses of the Elder Nuns). Other texts included in the *Khuddaka-nikāya* were composed at a later date; among these are the *Niddesa* (Exposition) and the *Paṭisambhidāmagga* (Way of Analysis). In both style and content the latter two works are similar to fully developed *abhidhamma* literature, and thus represent a literary stage between the *Nikāyas* and the works of the *Abhidhamma-piṭaka.*[4] Both texts were compiled around 250 B.C.E., a date that would make them forerunners of *abhidhamma* literature.

The *Niddesa* is divided into two parts: the "Mahāniddesa" and the "Cullaniddesa." The first part is a commentary on the "Aṭṭhaka," the fourth chapter of the *Suttanipāta.* The second part consists of commentaries on two parts of the *Suttanipāta:* on the fifth chapter ("Pārāyana") and on the *Khaggavisāṇa-sutta,* which is contained in the first chapter. Since the five chapters of the *Suttanipāta* are not explained in the order in which they are found today in the Pāli canon, the *Suttanipāta* was obviously not edited into its modern format of five chapters until after the *Niddesa* was compiled. Many elements of the *Niddesa,* such as its method of defining doctrines and its technical terms, are similar to those found in *abhidhamma* texts.

The *Paṭisambhidāmagga* (Path of Discrimination) contains discussions of the practical applications of many of the topics found in *abhidhamma* literature. At the beginning of the text is a list of fifty-five topics that are discussed in the work. These topics are called *mātikā,* a term characteristically used in Theravāda *abhidhamma* texts. The list of *mātikā* in the *Paṭisambhidāmagga* is not as refined or as well organized as those in later Theravāda *abhidhamma* texts.

The *Niddesa* and *Paṭisambhidāmagga* are found only in the Theravāda canon. No texts representing this transitional phase from *sūtra* to *abhidharma* are found in extant Sarvāstivādin literature.

The Theravāda *Abhidhamma-piṭaka*

The Theravāda *Abhidhamma-piṭaka* is composed of seven treatises compiled successively between 250 and 50 B.C.E. The oldest of these is the *Puggalapaññati* (Designation of Human Types). The next oldest text is the first part of the *Dhammasaṅgaṇi,* which consists of lists of 122 *mātikā* (matrices or topics) in the "Abhidhamma-mātikā" and 42 in the "Sutta-mātikā." These lists function as tables of contents for the work. The previously mentioned *Puggalapaññati* has its own list of *mātikā,* while most of the other treatises of the Pāli *Abhidhamma-piṭaka* are based on the lists in the *Dhammasaṅgaṇi* (Buddhist Psychological Ethics). The various *dhammas* are differentiated on the basis of these lists. The *Vibhaṅga,* however, contains its own list of topics, the "Sutta-bhājaniya"; this list appears to be early. Thus the *Puggalapaññati* and the lists at the beginning of the *Dhammasaṅgaṇi* and *Vibhaṅga* (Book of Analysis) constitute the oldest parts of the Pāli *Abhidhamma-piṭaka.* Before the *abhidhamma* texts were compiled, the determination of lists of *mātikā* was an important issuc among early Buddhist scholars. The analysis of *dhammas* in the seven treatises of the *Abhidhamma-piṭaka* therefore primarily focuses on the 122 elements of the *"Abhidhamma-mātikā"* of the *Dhammasaṅgaṇi*. The men who memorized the *mātikā* were known as *mātikā-dhara*.

The remaining portions of the *Dhammasaṅgaṇi* and *Vibhaṅga* were compiled next. This literature consisted of analyses of Buddhist doctrine through the examination of *dhammas* from various perspectives. The last works of the *Abhidhamma-piṭaka* to be compiled were the *Dhātukathā* (Discourse on Elements), *Yamaka* (Book of Pairs), and *Paṭṭhāna* (Conditional Relations). These three treatises contain more detailed analyses of doctrines, including the dynamics of the relations and interactions of the various *dhammas*. The *Kathāvatthu* (Points of Controversy), a work containing criticisms of the heretical teachings of other schools, also was compiled during this later period.

The works of the Pāli *Abhidhamma-piṭaka* are not arranged in the order of their composition. Rather, they are found in the following sequence, which was determined by Buddhaghosa.

1. *Dhammasaṅgaṇi* (Enumeration of *Dhammas* or Buddhist Psychological Ethics)
2. *Vibhaṅga* (The Book of Analysis)
3. *Kathāvatthu* (Points of Controversy)
4. *Puggalapaññati* (Description of Human Types)
5. *Dhātukathā* (Discourse on Elements)
6. *Yamaka* (Book of Pairs)
7. *Paṭṭhāna* (Conditional Relations).

Many other *abhidhamma* works exist in Pāli, but they are considered to be extracanonical and are not included in the *Abhidhamma-piṭaka*.

The contents of the three major sections of the Theravāda canon—the *Sutta-*, *Vinaya-*, and *Abhidhamma-piṭakas*—were finally determined around the first century B.C.E. As the study of Buddhist doctrine and practice continued, commentaries *(aṭṭhakathā)* were written. A number of texts survive that are representative of the transitional period between works included in the *Abhidhamma-piṭaka* and full commentaries. They are the *Milindapañha* (Questions of King Milinda), the *Nettipakaraṇa* (The Guide), and the *Peṭakopadesa* (Piṭaka-Disclosure).[5] (These three works are included in the *Khuddaka-nikāya* of the Burmese version of the Theravāda canon.) The *Peṭaka* was also probably of this genre, but unfortunately it has not survived. These works were written in approximately the first century C.E., after the contents of the *Abhidhamma-piṭaka* had already been established.

The *Milindapañha* is based on discussions of Buddhist doctrine between a Greek king Milinda (or Menandros, r. ca. 150 B.C.E.), who ruled in northern India, and a Buddhist monk named Nāgasena. The text exists in both Pāli and Chinese (*Na-hsien pi-ch'iu ching; T* 1670). Several schools besides the Theravāda used the text. The *Peṭaka* also seems to have been studied in a number of schools. (The term *"p'i-le"* referred to in the second fascicle of the *Ta-chih-tu lun* [*T* 25:70b, *Mahāprajñāpāramitopadeśa*] may refer to the *Peṭaka.*)

The *Abhidharma-piṭaka* of the Sarvāstivādin School

The *Abhidharma-piṭaka* of the Sarvāstivādin School is composed of seven treatises. The major treatise is the *Jñānaprasthāna* (Source of Knowledge) by Katyāyanīputra; it was compiled approximately three hundred years after the death of the Buddha in the first or second century B.C.E. Since this work systematized Sarvāstivādin doctrine in an authoritative way, it was highly regarded by Sarvāstivādin thinkers. Consequently, the other six treatises were called "feet" *(pāda)* or auxiliary texts while the *Jñānaprasthāna* was known as the "body" *(śarīra)* or main text. (The terms "body" and "legs" were applied by later monks.) Although the *Jñānaprasthāna* was the most important of the seven texts, it was not the earliest.

The six "feet" texts do not all date from the same time. The earliest is the *Saṅgītiparyāya,* followed by the *Dharmaskandha.* These two treatises reflect the same stage of development as Pāli texts dating from the early to the middle of the period when the *Abhidhamma-piṭaka* was being compiled. The *Vijñānakāya, Dhātukāya, Prajñaptiśāstra,* and *Prakaraṇapāda* all display more advanced doctrines and are similar in development to the later texts of the Pāli *Abhidhamma-piṭaka.* (The first chapter of the *Prakaraṇapāda,* on doctrines expressed as sets of five elements, apparently circulated as an independent text at an early date. The fourth chapter, on sets of seven, also seems to have been an independent text, suggesting that the *Prakaraṇapāda* may have been a collection of independent texts.) The *Prajñaptiśāstra* and *Jñānaprasthāna* both include more advanced doctrines than the texts of the Pāli *Abhidhamma-piṭaka.* Such doctrinal treatments as the classification of *dharmas* into five major types (Ch. *wu-wei*), the systematization of the mental faculties, the teaching that *dharmas* exist in all three time periods (past, present, and future), the four (or sometimes three) aspects of *dharmas* (origination, subsistence, decay, and extinction), and the classification of the four conditions and six causes are all unique to the Sarvāstivāda School.

With the exception of the *Prajñaptiśāstra,* the "body and six feet" of the Sarvāstivādin *Abhidharma-piṭaka* are all extant in complete Chinese translations. The Chinese version of the *Prajñaptiśāstra* is a partial translation, containing only the section on causes; but a seemingly complete Tibetan translation (Peking nos. 5587–5589) exists with sections on the cosmos, causes, and karma. The other five "feet" and the *Jñānaprasthāna* were not translated into Tibetan. The *Jñānaprasthāna,* its six "feet," and the authors to whom the texts are attributed are listed below.

1. *Jñānaprasthāna* (*T* 1543–1544)	Katyāyanīputra
2. *Prakaraṇapāda* (*T* 1541–1542)	Vasumitra
3. *Vijñānakāya* (*T* 1539)	Devaśarman
4. *Dharmaskandha* (*T* 1537)	Śāriputra
5. *Prajñaptiśāstra* (*T* 1538)	Maudgalyāyana
6. *Dhātukāya* (*T* 1540)	Pūrṇa
7. *Saṅgītiparyāya* (*T* 1536)	Mahākauṣṭhila

The names of the authors of the seven treatises listed above are from Yaśomitra's *Sphuṭārthā Abhidharmakośavyākhyā* (p. 11), where the classification of the seven treatises as "body" and "feet" is also found (p. 9). The Chinese translations have a slightly different list of authors.

Many other Sarvāstivādin *abhidharma* treatises exist. Some Sarvāstivādins seem to have believed that the *Abhidharma-piṭaka* should not have been limited to the above seven texts. However, since the above list has traditionally been highly regarded by Buddhists (for example, see the *Abhidharmakośavyākhyā*), these seven works should probably be considered as the Sarvāstivādin *Abhidharma-piṭaka.*

Besides the Chinese and Tibetan translations mentioned above, a number of fragments of Sanskrit *abhidharma* texts discovered in Central Asia are extant. Fragments of texts such as the *Saṅgītiparyāya* and the *Prakaraṇapāda* have been published by Waldschmidt and others.[6] The existence of a fragment of the *Dharmaskandha* has also been announced.[7]

Abhidharma-piṭaka from Other Schools

The Sarvāstivādin and Pāli *Abhidharma-piṭakas* are extant in their complete forms. In addition, several *abhidharma* works falling outside these two traditions should also be mentioned. The *She-li-fu a-p'i-t'an lun* (*T* 1548, *Śāriputrābhidharmaśāstra*?) in thirty fascicles, which probably belonged to the Dharmaguptaka School, is particularly important.[8] Although it does not display the advanced doctrinal development of the Pāli and Sarvāstivādin traditions, it is valuable because it is one of the few extant longer *abhidharma* works from another tradition. A short, three-fascicle, incomplete translation of a Saṃmitīya work also survives, the *San-mi-ti-pu lun* (*T* 1649, *Sāṃmitīya-śāstra*?). The *pudgalavādin* (personalist) position is presented in this work. The date of composition of the text has not been clearly determined.

The *Ch'eng-shih lun* (*T* 1646, *Tattvasiddhiśāstra*?) by Harivarman was probably composed between 250 and 350, and thus was compiled too late to be included in an *Abhidharma-piṭaka*. The text, which seems to reflect a Sautrāntika point of view, was translated into Chinese by Kumārajīva and studied widely in China during the fifth and sixth centuries.

When the Chinese pilgrim Hsüan-tsang returned from India, he brought both Hīnayāna and Mahāyāna *sūtras* and *śāstras* with him. According to his travel diary, among the Hīnayāna texts were sixty-seven works from the Sarvāstivādin School, fourteen Theravāda works, fifteen Mahāsaṅghika works, fifteen Sammatīya works, twenty-two Mahīśāsaka works, seventeen Kāśyapīya works, and forty-two Dharmaguptaka works. Hsüan-tsang's figures indicate that the canons of these schools included *Abhidharma-piṭakas*. However, since Hsüan-tsang translated only the Sarvāstivādin texts, the works from the other schools are no longer extant. I-ching, in his travel diary, notes that the Sarvāstivādin, Sammatīya, Theravāda, and Mahāsaṅghika schools each had a canon of approximately 300,000 verses.

Commentarial Literature

Only the commentaries on the *Abhidharma-piṭakas* of the Sarvāstivāda and Theravāda schools are extant. A number of commentaries were composed in Sinhalese in the first and second centuries C.E. by monks of the Sri Lankan Theravāda School. Among these commentaries were *Mahāṭṭhakathā, Andhakaṭṭhakathā, Mahāpaccarī, Kurundaṭṭhakathā, Saṅkhepaṭṭhakathā,* and *Uttaravihāraṭṭhakathā.* In the fifth century a new group of commentators appeared, which included Buddhaghosa, Buddhadatta, and Dhammapāla. They produced new commentaries based on the ones composed several centuries earlier. Since their new commentaries supplanted the older ones, the earlier commentaries were subsequently lost. The *Uttaravihāraṭṭhakathā* is a work of the Abhayagiri-vihāra sect of the Theravāda School. The Chinese translation of Upatissa's (fl. second century) *Vimuttimagga,* the *Chieh-t'o-tao lun* (*T* 1648), also expounds the positions of the sect.

The most important commentator in the Theravāda tradition was

Buddhaghosa (fl. fifth century). One of his major works, the *Vissudhimagga* (Path of Purification), explains the doctrines of the Mahāvihāra sect of the Theravāda School. Buddhaghosa also extensively utilized the old Sinhalese commentaries to write new commentaries *(aṭṭhakathā)* in Pāli on the Theravāda canon. Buddhaghosa's voluminous commentaries are considered to be the culmination of three centuries of Sri Lankan scholarship. The most famous of his commentaries are as follows:

Samantapāsādikā—commentary on the *Vinaya*
Sumaṅgalavilāsinī—commentary on the *Dīgha-nikāya*
Papañcasūdani—commentary on the *Majjhima-nikāya*
Sāratthappakāsinī—commentary on the *Saṃyutta-nikāya*
Manorathapūraṇī—commentary on the *Aṅguttara-nikāya*
Atthasālinī—commentary on the *Dhammasaṅgaṇi*

In addition, Buddhaghosa wrote the *Dhammapadaṭṭhakathā,* which is a commentary on the *Dhammapada,* and the *Paramatthajotikā,* which includes commentaries on the *Suttanipāta* and the *Khuddakapāṭha.* Buddhaghosa managed to write commentaries on virtually the entire Theravāda canon. His *Atthasālinī* and *Visuddhimagga* are among the most important expositions of Theravāda doctrine. His commentary on the *Kathāvatthu,* the *Kathāvatthuppakaraṇaṭṭhakathā,* is important because it identifies the positions held by the Hīnayāna schools in doctrinal controversies. Elements of Mahāyāna doctrine are also found in these commentaries and would make a fruitful subject for further research.

The Sri Lankan chronicles must also be mentioned here, although they are not canonical commentaries. The *Dīpavaṃsa* relates the story of the Buddha's birth, the history of central India, the transmission of Buddhism to Sri Lanka, and the subsequent history of Sri Lanka until the reign of Mahāsena (r. 325–352). The identity of the author is not known; however, since Buddhaghosa was familiar with the *Dīpavaṃsa,* it was apparently compiled during the first half of the fifth century. The chronicle is a valuable source, for it relates secular political history as well as Buddhist history. Because the literary style of the *Dīpavaṃsa* was awkward, it was rewritten as the *Mahāvaṃsa* by Mahānāma during the reign of Dhātusena (r. 460–478). Although the subject matter of the *Mahāvaṃsa* is the same as that of the *Dīpavaṃsa,* the *Mahāvaṃsa* is more detailed. The *Cūlavaṃsa* is a long chronicle, based on the *Mahāvaṃsa,* that relates Sri Lankan history up to the eighteenth century. The *Sāsanavaṃsa,* composed in Burma by Paññasāmin, is also an important historical source. It traces the history of central India until the time of the Third Council and then relates the missionary activities of monks in various lands. The section concerning Burma (known in the chronicle as Aparantaraṭṭha) in the sixth chapter is especially valuable. Although the *Sāsanavaṃsa,* compiled in 1861, is a relatively recent work, it is based on much older sources.

After the time of Buddhaghosa, Sri Lankan Buddhism declined for several centuries. In the eleventh century, the Mahāvihāra sect reasserted itself, and many scholarly monks appeared. Among them was Anuruddha, author of the *Abhidhammatthasaṅgaha,* an outline of Theravāda Buddhist doctrine.

In India the Sarvāstivādin School flourished in both Gandhāra and Kashmir. The two groups, however, differed on certain points of doctrine. The Gandhāra group was the more progressive, and eventually the Sautrāntika School arose out of it. Since the Kashmir group was more conservative, Kashmir remained a Sarvāstivādin stronghold. After the *Jñānaprasthāna* and its six auxiliary treatises were composed, a school of commentators *(vaibhāṣika)* arose. The results of two hundred years of scholarship by these commentators was compiled into the *A-p'i-ta-mo ta-p'i-p'o-sha lun* (*T* 1545, *Abhidharma-mahāvibhāṣā-śāstra*?; hereafter cited as the *Mahāvibhāṣā*). This work was compiled as a commentary on the *Jñānaprasthāna,* but it is much more than a commentary. It contains discussions of new developments in Sarvāstivādin doctrine and harsh criticisms of the doctrines of other groups of monks, including the Mahāsaṅghikas, Dārṣṭāntikas, and Discriminators. Heterodox doctrines held by some Sarvāstivādin monks are also criticized.

The *Mahāvibhāṣā* is extant only in Chinese. A two-hundred-fascicle translation of the text was done by Hsüan-tsang (*T* 1545). (Earlier, during the Northern Liang dynasty [397–439], a hundred-fascicle translation was completed by Buddhavarman and others, but part of it was burned in a fire during the frequent wars of that period so that only the first sixty fascicles of that translation are extant [*A-p'i-t'an p'i-p'o-sha lun, T* 1546].) According to an afterword by Hsüan-tsang, four hundred years after the Buddha's death King Kaniṣka (r. 132–152) assembled five hundred *arhats* and had them compile the canon (*T* 27:1004a). The Sarvāstivādin *Abhidharma-piṭaka* is said to date from that time. Modern scholars call this the Fourth Council. (According to Hsüan-tsang's travel diary, the *Hsi-yu chi* [*T* 51:882a], Pārśva presided over the meeting.) Since Kaniṣka's activities are mentioned in the *Mahāvibhāṣā,* some scholars believe it should be dated after Kaniṣka's reign. The work is enormous, however, and is certainly a compilation of several centuries of scholarship. Thus, it was probably compiled into its final form as a *śāstra* sometime in the third century, while the essential parts of the work date back to the second century C.E., before the time of Nāgārjuna.

In the *Mahāvibhāṣā,* the positions of many Sarvāstivādin scholars are quoted and criticized. Particularly important are the comments and criticisms of four scholars known as "the four critics of the *Vibhāṣā*" (*Abhidharmakośabhāṣya,* p. 296; *Abhidharmadīpa,* p. 259): Ghoṣaka, Dharmatrāta, Vasumitra, and Buddhadeva. They represent the orthodox Sarvāstivādin position, but even their views are sometimes criticized in the *Mahāvibhāṣā.* Ghoṣaka is credited with the authorship of the *Abhidharmāmṛtarasaśāstra* (*T* 1553), a handbook of *abhidharma;* but it is not clear whether the author of the handbook is identical with the person mentioned so often in the *Mahāvibhāṣā.* A number of figures named Dharmatrāta are known: the one mentioned in the *Mahāvibhāṣā,* the compiler of the *Udānavarga,* the author of the *Wu-shih p'i-p'o-sha lun* (*T* 1555, *Pañcavastukavibhāṣāśāstra*?), and the author of the *Tsa a-p'i-t'an-hsin lun* (*T* 1552, *Abhidharmasārapratikirnakaśāstra*?). The author of this last work lived in the fourth century and thus cannot be identified with the Dharmatrāta of the *Mahāvibhāṣā.*

Figures named Vasumitra are mentioned frequently in *abhidharma* literature, including the scholar referred to often in the *Mahāvibhāṣā* and the author(s) of the *Prakaraṇapāda*(*T* 1541–1542), *Samayabhedoparacanacakra* (*T* 2031–2033), and *Tsun p'o-hsü-mi p'u-sa so-chi lun* (*T* 1549). Determining whether all of these figures are identical or not is extremely difficult; there were probably at least two people named Vasumitra.

Buddhadeva was a Dārṣṭāntika thinker. The name "Buddhadeva" appears in an inscription on a pillar with a lion-capital (Konow, *Kharoṣṭhī Inscriptions,* p. 48). Some scholars have argued that the inscription refers to the same man named in the *Mahāvibhāṣā.* Pārśva was another influential Vaibhāṣika.

The compilation of the *Mahāvibhāṣā* was a major achievement and marked the end of one phase of Sarvāstivādin *abhidharma* studies. Because the work was so large, it did not offer a systematic view of *abhidharma* theory. Consequently, during the period when the *Mahāvibhāṣā* was being completed, Sarvāstivādin scholars began writing shorter works outlining *abhidharma* theory. Among these are the *Pi-p'o-sha lun* (*T* 1547, *Vibhāṣāśāstra*?) by Sitapāṇi(?), the *A-p'i-t'an hsin lun* (*T* 1550, *Abhidharmahṛdayaśāstra*?) by Dharmaśrī(?), the *Tsa a-p'i-t'an hsin lun* (*T* 1552, *Saṃyuktābhidharmahṛdayaśāstra*?) by Dharmatrāta, and the *Ju a-p'i-t'a-mo lun* (*T* 1554, *Abhidharmāvatāraśāstra#*) by Skandhila. Later, Vasubandhu compiled his monumental work, the *Abhidharmakośabhāṣya.* Two Chinese translations (*T* 1558 by Hsüan-tsang and *T* 1559 by Paramārtha) and one Tibetan translation of this work exist. In addition, the Sanskrit text of the verses was published by V. V. Gokhale in 1953 as the *Abhidharmakośakārikā.* The Sanskrit text of both the verses and prose commentary by Vasubandhu was published in 1967 by P. Pradhan as the *Abhidharmakośabhāṣya.*

Some scholars place Vasubandhu's life from ca. 320 to 400, but a date of around 450 seems more reasonable. To explain the various problems concerning Vasubandhu's dates, Erich Frauwallner has suggested that two men named Vasubandhu might have played key roles in Buddhist history. The earlier Vasubandhu would have lived around 320–380 and been the younger brother of Asaṅga, while the latter would have been the author of the *Abidharmakośa* with dates of 400–480. However, Frauwallner's argument has not gained wide acceptance. It is more reasonable to view Vasubandhu as a single figure with dates of around 400–480.[9]

Vasubandhu's *Abhidharmakośa* is a skillful and systematic presentation of the Sarvāstivādin position. However, because Vasubandhu sometimes criticized Sarvāstivādin doctrines from the Sautrāntika point of view, Saṅghabhadra wrote a treatise, the *A-p'i-ta-mo shun-cheng-li lun* (*T* 1562 [*Abhidharma*] *Nyāyānusāraśāstra*?), presenting the position of the Kashmiri Sarvāstivādin School. In his work, Saṅghabhadra refuted the teachings of the *Abhidharmakośa* and defended orthodox Sarvāstivādin doctrines; but even Saṅghabhadra was influenced by the *Abhidharmakośa* and advanced some new doctrines that differed from the traditional positions maintained by Sarvāstivādins. Consequently, his teachings are referred to as doctrines of "the new Sarvāstivādin (School)." Saṅghabhadra also wrote the *A-p'i-ta-mo-tsang hsien-tsung lun* (*T* 1563, *Abhidharmakośaśāstrakārikāvibhāṣya#*).

The *Abhidharmakośa* profoundly influenced subsequent Buddhism. After it was written, the study of the *Abhidharmakośa* became the major activity of later *abhidharma* researchers, and a number of commentaries on it were written. Guṇamati (480–540) and Vasumitra are both credited with commentaries on the *Abhidharmakośa,* but neither commentary is extant. Sthiramati's (510–570) commentary, the *Tattvārtha,* survives in a complete Tibetan translation (Peking no. 5875) and in fragments in a Chinese translation (*T* 1561). Later, Yaśomitra wrote the *Sphuṭārthā Abhidharmakośavyākhyā,* which exists in Sanskrit and Tibetan (Peking no. 5593). A commentary by Śamathadeva is also extant in Tibetan. Recently the Sanskrit (no Chinese or Tibetan translation exists) text of the *Abhidharmadīpa,* an *abhidharma* work that follows the *Abhidharmakośa,* was published. In addition, subcommentaries by Pūrṇavardhana and others exist in Tibetan.

The basic Sarvāstivādin *abhidharma* literature is completely extant in Chinese translation and includes the seven treatises of the *Abhidharma-piṭaka,* the *Mahāvibhāṣā,* the *Abhidharmakośa,* and many other texts. Tibetan translations of *abhidharma* material are primarily concerned with the *Abhidharmakośa* and its commentaries. In recent years, Sanskrit texts of such works as the *Abhidharmakośa, Sphuṭārthā Abhidharmakośavyākhyā,* and *Abhidharmadīpa* have been found, adding to our understanding of the *abhidharma* tradition. Among the texts discovered by a German expedition to Central Asia were some on *abhidharma.* Several of these have been mentioned earlier.[10]

Abhidharma Texts from Other Schools

Few texts from schools other than the Theravāda and Sarvāstivāda are extant. Texts such as the *She-li-fu a-p'i-t'an lun* (*T* 1548, *Śāriputrābhidharmaśāstra*?), *San-mi-ti-pu lun* (*T* 1649), and *Ch'eng-shih lun* (*T* 1646, *Tattvasiddhiśāstra*?) have already been discussed. Other *abhidharma* texts should also be mentioned. The *Ssu-ti lun* (*T* 1647, *Catuḥsatyaśāstra*?) in four fascicles contains citations from a text called the *A-p'i-t'an-tsang lun* or *Tsang lun* (*Peṭaka*?) and from Sautrāntika sources. Although it is clearly a text compiled by the monks of one of the schools of Nikāya Buddhism, scholars have not determined which school produced the *Ssu-ti lun.* The *P'i-chih-fo yin-yüan lun* (*T* 1650) in two fascicles is a commentary on the verses on the rhinoceros in the *Suttanipāta.* The *Fen-pieh kung-te lun* (*T* 1507) in five fascicles is a commentary on the *Ekottarāgama* (*T* 125). These texts, too, were composed by monks from the Nikāya schools.

The *Mahāvibhāṣā* (*T* 1545), *Kathāvatthu,* and Buddhaghosa's commentary on the *Kathāvatthu* also contain numerous references to the doctrines of Nikāya Buddhism. The best systematic account of Nikāya doctrine in a primary source is Vasumitra's *Samayabhedoparacanacakra* (*T* 2031–2033 and Tibetan translation, Peking no. 5639). This text has long been a subject of research in East Asia and is usually read with K'uei-chi's (632–682) commentary, the *I-pu-tsung-lun-lun shu-chi* (*Zokuzōkyō* part 1, vol. 83, fasc. 3). (The *Ibushūrinron jukki hotsujin* edited by Ōyama Ken'ei is a valuable reference.) Chi-tsang's (549–623) *San-lun hsüan-i* also contains useful information on Nikāya doctrine, as do the *Ch'eng-yeh lun* (*T* 1609, *Karmasiddhiprakaraṇa*#), *Wu-yun lun* (*T* 1612, *Pañcaskandhaprakaraṇa*#), and *Vyākhyā-yukti,* all by Vasubandhu.[11] In addition, Mahāyāna sources contain passages critical of the schools of Nikāya Buddhism, which sometimes yield information about doctrine. However, even when all of these sources are consulted, a comprehensive view of Nikāya doctrine is still difficult to formulate.

CHAPTER 10

The Organization of the Dharmas *in the* Abhidharma

Abhidharma and *Mātṛkā*

UNLIKE THE TERM *"dharma,"* which was in use before the time of the Buddha, the term *"abhidharma"* (P. *abhidhamma*), is peculiar to Buddhism. In the *Āgamas* it is used in the sense of "referring to the *dharma.*" Later it also came to have the meaning of "research into the *dharma.*" The element *"abhi"* in the word *abhidharma* has the meaning of "referring to," but it can also mean "superior." Consequently, *abhidharma* is sometimes interpreted as meaning "superior *dharma.*" In Sarvāstivādin texts, it is usually found with the sense of "referring to the *dharma,*" while in Pāli texts it is most often used with the meaning of "superior *dharma.*"[1]

The early stages of the analysis of the Dharma (the Teachings of the Buddha) can be found in the *Āgamas.* In these passages, often called *abhidharma-kathā* (discussions of *abhidharma*), the Buddha's words were collected and classified. In analyses called *vibhaṅga,* his Teachings were explained in simpler words or examined and applied to other situations. The critical analysis of teachings was an important aspect of the Buddha's enlightenment. Thus some of the texts in the *Āgamas* are devoted to detailed analyses of doctrine. For example, the Middle Path consisted of an analytical process of choosing the Middle Way from a synthesis of two extreme positions. In other texts the teaching is arranged according to the number of elements in the doctrine or the subject matter under discussion.

Once the contents of the *Sūtra-piṭaka* had been firmly determined, *abhidharma* studies could no longer be included in it, and a new way of organizing the results of these analyses was needed. Studies of the *dharma* were compiled into the *Abhidharma-piṭakas*. Among the important aspects of studying *abhidharma* were the selection of topics for research and the subsequent analysis of those topics *(dharma-pravicaya)*. These topics were called *mātṛkā* (P. *mātikā*), which may be translated as "matrices" or "lists."[2] The people who devoted themselves to these studies were called *mātikādhara* in Pāli. *Mātṛkā* are not clearly listed in the Sarvāstivādin *abhidharma* texts, but such lists of topics played a central role in the development of the Pāli *abhidhamma* texts. In the beginning of the earliest Pāli *abhidhamma* treatise, the *Puggalapaññatti* (Human Types), is a table of contents called the *mātikā-uddesa,* which lists the following six topics *(paññatti)* that correspond to *mātikā: khandha* (aggregates), *āyatana* (sense organs and their objects), *dhātu* (sense organs, sense objects, and sense-consciousnesses), *sacca* (truths), *indriya* (faculties), and *puggala* (human types). The last category is subdivided into sections that extend from one person to ten persons. Many additional *mātikā* are contained within these divisions. The main subject of the *Puggalapaññatti* is the analysis of these numerical groups of human types.

The contents of the *Śāriputrābhidharmaśāstra* (*T* 1548) are arranged in the following order: *āyatana, dhātu, skandha,* the Four Noble Truths, and *indriya.* It thus includes most of the same *mātṛkā* listed in the Pāli *Puggalapaññatti.* However, the topics of the *Śāriputrābhidharmaśāstra* are not called *mātṛkā* even though they would seem to correspond to *mātṛkā.* Moreover, a variety of other topics has been inserted between the end of fascicle five, where the discussion of *indriya* (bases of cognition) ends, and the beginning of fascicle eight, where the discussion of *pudgala* (persons) begins.

At the beginning of the Pāli *abhidhamma* work entitled the *Dhammasaṅgaṇi* (Compendium of *Dhammas*) is a section called the *"Abhidhamma-mātikā"* where twenty-two threefold doctrinal topics and one hundred twofold topics are listed. (A threefold doctrinal topic is a teaching divided into three parts, such as the Three Jewels: the Buddha, his Teaching, and the Buddhist order.) These lists are followed by a supplementary list of forty-two twofold topics entitled the *"Suttantika-mātikā."* The explanations of the *mātikā* that constitute the main part of the text of the *Dhammasaṅgaṇi* are placed after the lists of topics. The process by which these *mātikā* were chosen and collected by members of the Theravāda School is not clear, but of the forty-two twofold topics listed in the *"Suttantika-abhidhamma,"* thirty-one are also included in a list of thirty-three twofold topics found in a *sutta,* the *Saṅgītisuttanta* (*DN,* no. 33). Since the order of the designations listed in the two works is very close, the list of *dhammas* in the *Saṅgītisuttanta* apparently provided the basis for the *mātikā*. The Pāli *Saṅgītisuttanta* corresponds to two works in the Chinese canon: the *Chung-chi ching* in the *Ch'ang a-han ching* (*T* 1, *Dīrghāgama*) and the *Ta-chi-fa-men ching* (*T* 12, *Saṅgītisūtra**). This *sūtra* eventually influenced the Sarvāstivādin *abhidharma* treatise the *Saṅgītiparyāya* (*T* 1536).

Mātikā are explained in two other works of the Pāli *Abhidhamma-piṭaka,* the *Vibhaṅga* and the *Paṭṭhāna,* indicating that the term *mātikā* was used often in Theravāda Buddhism. In the *Śāriputrābhidharmaśāstra* (*T* 1548), topics identical to *mātṛkā* are discussed, but are not referred to as *mātṛkā*. *Mātṛkā* are not mentioned in the seven treatises of the Sarvāstivādin *Abhidharma-piṭaka;* however, some of these Sarvāstivādin treatises, such as the *Saṅgītiparyāya* (*T* 1536) and the *Dharmaskandha* (*T* 1537), are commentaries based on *mātṛkā*. Consequently, in the Sarvāstivādin treatise *Shun-cheng-li lun* (*T* 1562, *Nyāyānusāraśāstra*?), the term "*mātṛkā*" is explained (*T* 29:330b), and a number of examples of *mātṛkā* are listed. Among the examples are elements of the thirty-seven acquisitions that lead to enlightenment *(saptatriṃśad-bodhipakṣikā-dharmāḥ)* such as the four mindfulnesses *(catvari smṛtyupāsthānani)* and the four right efforts *(catvari samyakprāḥānani)*. According to the text, "Beginning with the *Saṅgītiparyāya, Dharmaskandha,* and *Prajñaptiśāstra,* all such works are called *mātṛkā*" (*T* 29:330b). Thus the texts themselves were considered to be *mātṛkā*. Elsewhere in the *Shun-cheng-li lun* (*T* 29:595b), the term "*upadeśa,*" one of the twelve divisions of the teaching, is explained as being equivalent to *mātṛkā* and *abhidharma*.

In the *A-yü-wang chuan* (*T* 2042, *Aśokarājāvadāna**) a division of the canon called the *Mātṛkā-piṭaka* (Ch. *mo-te-le-ch'ieh tsang*) is mentioned instead of an *Abhidharma-piṭaka* (*T* 50:113c). Its contents are said to begin with the four types of mindfulness, the four right efforts, and other elements of the thirty-seven acquisitions that lead to enlightenment, and are thus close to the explanation in the *Shun-cheng-li lun*. Similar explanations are found in such works as the *A-yü-wang ching* (*T* 50:152a, *Aśokarājasūtra*?) and the *Ken-pen yu-pu-lü tsa-shih* (*T* 24:408b, *Mūlasarvāstivāda vinayakṣudrakavastu#*). Thus *mātṛkā* were known within the Sarvāstivādin and Mūlasarvāstivādin schools. The thirty-seven acquisitions leading to enlightenment were a particularly important example of *mātṛkā* for these schools. However, the term "*mātṛkā*" is not found in the seven treatises of the Sarvāstivādin *Abhidharma-piṭaka;* instead, the term "*abhidharma*" is used. Consequently, the compilers of the *Mahāvibhāṣāśāstra* and the *Abhidharmakośa* did not discuss the term *mātṛkā*.

Mātṛkā were not only used for the classification of *dharmas;* they were also employed in *vinaya* texts. Although *mātṛkā* are not found in the Pāli *Vinaya,* they are used in Sarvāstivādin *vinaya* texts. The title of the *Sa-p'o-to-pu p'i-ni mo-te-lo ch'ieh* (*T* 1441, *Sarvāstivādavinayamātṛkā*?) suggests that it is a collection of *mātṛkā* from the *Vinaya.* A commentary on the Dharmaguptaka *vinaya,* the *P'i-ni mu ching* (*T* 1463, *Vinayamātṛkāsūtra*?) has a similar title.

As the *mātṛkā* used to explain the Dharma developed, they were gradually incorporated into the various *Abhidharma-piṭakas.* The term *"mātṛkā"* is still preserved in the treatises of the Theravāda *Abhidhamma-piṭaka,* but it has been expunged from the Sarvāstivādin *Abhidharma-piṭaka* and the *Śāriputrābhidharmaśāstra* and replaced with the term *"abhidharma."* As the *mātṛkā* system was elaborated, explanations and commentaries concerning the meanings of key words were developed and doctrines were explicated in detail. Gradually, a branch of Buddhist studies arose that was primarily concerned with the explanation of doctrine. This tradition was called "studies of the Dharma" or *abhidharma.*

One meaning of the word *"abhi"* is "facing." If this definition is used, then *abhidharma* can be interpreted as "facing or viewing the Dharma" and was thus occasionally translated into Chinese as *"tui-fa."* However, as noted earlier, *"abhi"* also has the meaning of "superior," and *abhidharma* may also be interpreted as meaning "superior or incomparable Dharma" (*Atthasālinī,* I. 2; *The Expositor,* vol. 1, p. 4; *dhammātireka, dhammavisesaṭṭha; Mahāvibhāṣā, T* 1545, fasc. 1, intro.). The latter interpretation suggests that the *abhidharma* tradition is superior to and transcends the earlier, unanalyzed Dharma. In the *Mo-ho-seng-chi lü* (*T* 22:475c, *Mahāsaṅghikavinaya*?), *abhidharma* is said to be the ninefold teaching *(navaṅga-śāsana),* and it is interpreted as meaning "superior Dharma." The Buddha's teaching was thus sometimes seen as *abhidharma.*

The major characteristic of *abhidharma* is its emphasis on analysis *(vibhaṅga).* Problems are examined from a variety of perspectives to arrive at a comprehensive understanding of issues. In Buddhaghosa's *Atthasālinī* (I. 3; *The Expositor,* vol. 2, p. 4) these investigations are called analysis of *sūtras (suttanta-bhājaniya),* analysis of *abhidharma (abhidhamma-bhājaniya),* and analysis through questions and answers *(pañhā-pucchaka-naya).* In the Sarvāstivādin School analyses of *dharmas* involved a variety of perspectives such as whether the *dharma* is visible *(sanidarśana)* or not, impenetrable *(pratigha)* or not, influenced *(sāsrava)* by the defilements or not; whether scrutiny *(vicāra)* and investigation *(vitarka)* can be applied to it or not; which of the three realms (desire, form, and formless) it exists in; and whether it is morally good, bad, or neutral. These categories were called the "gates of analysis."

Dharma and *Abhidharma*

The term "Dharma" refers to the Teachings preached by the Buddha.[3] Since the Buddha's Teachings concerned the facts of human existence, Dharma can be interpreted as referring to the true nature of human existence. Human existence is made up of constantly changing phenomena and of the basic entities that constitute phenomena. Examples of phenomenal existence are the body, the mind, and the external world. However, phenomenal existence can be analyzed further. For example, within the body are elements such as the visual, auditory, and gustatory faculties. Since the visual and auditory faculties perform different functions, they have different qualities. The various types of perception and the organs that are the bases of those perceptions are called *indriya.* The body is analyzed into visual, auditory, olfactory, gustatory, and tactile organs. The "tactile organ" refers to the skin, flesh, muscles and other parts of the body without the other four sense organs.

The mind, too, is analyzed into components such as judgments, memories, and emotions. These components are analyzed further, revealing many mental faculties. For example, a list of defilements *(kleśa)* might include lust *(rāga),* hatred *(dveṣa* or *pratigha),* pride *(māna),* doubt *(vicikitsā),* and wrong views *(dṛṣṭi).* Other mental faculties were also included in such lists. Some pairs of mental faculties or qualities seem to be mutually exclusive. Such pairs include love and dislike, lust and hatred, and good and bad. Consequently, some *abhidharma* thinkers argued that it was unreasonable to believe that all such mental faculties were attributes of a single entity called the mind. Rather, the mind was composed of many mental faculties acting in concert. Mental faculties such as doubt, faith, lust, and hatred were considered to be independent entities, and the activities and changes of the mind were understood in terms of their interactions. The elemental entities of which phenomenal existence was composed were called *"dharmas,"* a usage of this term that is particularly important in Nikāya Buddhism. When the term *"dharma"* is used in the *abhidharma* tradition, it often refers to the entities that make up phenomena.

Ultimate Existence *(Paramārtha-sat)* and Conventional Existence *(Saṃvṛti-sat)*

In the *Abhidharmakośa* (*T* 29:166b; *Abhidharmakośabhāṣya,* p. 334, ll. 1–2), existence is divided into two categories: ultimate existence *(paramārtha-sat)* and conventional existence *(saṃvṛti-sat). Dharmas* are classified as *paramārtha-sat.*[4] The difference between the two categories can be illustrated with the following examples. A vase can be destroyed by smashing it and is therefore said to exist in a conventional sense. A piece of cloth would be classified in the same manner. A human being, a conglomeration of various physical and mental elements, exists in a conventional sense *(saṃvṛti-sat).* However, if the vase had been green, then that green color would continue to exist even though the vase had been smashed. Even if the vase were reduced to the smallest elements, to atoms *(paramāṇu),* the green color would still exist. Items that do not depend on other items for their existence, which exist in and of themselves (or have self-nature *[svabhāva]*) are said to be ultimately existent and are called *dharmas.* Mental functions, such as lust, may also be called *dharmas* since they cannot be analyzed into more basic elements. *Dharmas* are also analyzed in terms of their powers. Thus the *dharma* called "lust" has the power of causing lust to arise in the mind.

Any element that cannot be analyzed further is ultimately existent. It is a *dharma* and has its own self-nature *(sa-svabhāva).* It is a real existent (*dravyataḥ sat, Abhidharmakośavyākhyā,* p. 524, l. 29). In the *Mūlamadhyamakakārikā,* self-nature *(svabhāva)* is defined as "that which exists in and of itself" *(svobhāvaḥ),* "something that is not made" *(akṛtrima),* and "something not dependent on other things for its existence" *(nir-āpekṣā, Prasannapadā,* p. 262, ll. 11–12).

A *dharma* is also defined as something that has its own distinctive mark (*svalakṣanadhāraṇād dharmaḥ, Chü-she lun, T* 29:1b; *Abhidharmakośabhāṣya,* p. 2, l. 9; *atthano lakkhaṇaṃ dhārentīti dhamma, Visuddhimagga,* chap. 15, par. 3; Harvard Oriental Series, vol. 41, p. 48, l. 17). The color green of a *dharma* of green would be the distinctive mark *(svalakṣana)* of that *dharma.* In contrast, self-nature *(svabhāva)* would refer to the existent called green, which is made up of atoms. Strictly speaking, since self-nature itself is equivalent to being a *dharma,* it is not correct to say that something having self-nature is a *dharma.* Something that has a self-nature and is made up of *dharmas* has conventional existence. Thus self-nature—in other words, that which has a distinctive mark—is a *dharma.* However, the terms "self-nature" and "distinctive mark" are sometimes used interchangeably without the above distinction.

Conditioned *Dharmas (Saṃskṛta Dharma)* and Unconditioned *Dharmas (Asaṃskṛta Dharma)*

As was explained above, *dharmas* have a real existence as elements. However, phenomena are constantly changing, so that although *dhar-*

mas are real existents, they are not necessarily eternal real existents. Consequently, *dharmas* were classified as either conditioned (transitory) or unconditioned (eternal) *dharmas*. This classification of *dharmas* is found in the *Āgamas,* but was not systematically explained until the rise of Nikāya Buddhism.

Nirvāṇa is an example of an unconditioned *(asaṃskṛta) dharma.* It is a real existent, transcending time. When the Buddha attained enlightenment, he was one with *nirvāṇa.* In the Sarvāstivādin *abhidharma* system, *nirvāṇa* is called analytical cessation *(pratisaṅkhyā-nirodha)*—the cessation attained through the analytical power of wisdom. In other words, through the power of wisdom, the defilements are cut off and will never arise again. The Sarvāstivādin *abhidharma* system also recognized nonanalytical cessation *(apratisaṅkhyā-nirodha)* and space *(ākāśa)* as unconditioned *dharmas,* making a total of three types of *dharma* in this category. Nonanalytical cessation *(apratisaṅkhyā-nirodha)* refers to cessation that occurs because the necessary conditions for the production (of defilements and so forth) are not present and will not be present in the future. This type of *dharma* of cessation does not rely on the analytical power of wisdom to arise. *Nirvāṇa* is recognized by the Sarvāstivādins as being the supreme *dharma.* In the *Abhidharmakośa* (*Chü-she lun,* fasc. 1), only *nirvāṇa* is referred to as a *dharma* in the ultimate sense *(paramārthadharma).*

In certain cases, even the characteristics of *dharmas (dharmalakṣanaḥ)* are considered to be *dharmas* (*Abhidharmakośabhāṣya,* p. 2, l. 5). A *dharma* is something with its own distinctive mark or characteristic. *Nirvāṇa* is thus considered a *dharma.* Conditioned *dharmas* also have their own marks even though they are impermanent. Both the Theravāda and Sarvāstivādin schools explain the impermanence of conditioned *dharmas* by noting that although each *dharma* has its own mark, the mark exists for only a very short period in the present. According to the *Abhidharmakośabhāṣya* (p. 193, l. 1), "Conditioned *dharmas* cease each instant *(saṃskṛtaṃ kṣaṇikaṃ).*" According to the *Visuddhimagga* (chap. 11, par. 41; Harvard Oriental Series 41, p. 308, l. 29), "They are *dhammas* because they each have their own characteristic and maintain it for an appropriate length of time *(khaṇānurūpadhāraṇena).*" Conditioned *dharmas* are real existents, but because they cease in an instant, they cannot be clung to or grasped. If this point had been pursued, it might have led to the position that *dharmas* were nonsubstantial; however, the existence of the *dharmas* was emphasized by the schools of Nikāya Buddhism. The problem of the nonsubstantiality of *dharmas* was eventually taken up by Mahāyāna Buddhists.

If the phrase "everything is impermanent" (*sabbe saṅkhārā anicca,*

Dhammapada, v. 277) is interpreted literally, it would mean that conditioned *dharmas* cease instantaneously. This position was held by the Sarvāstivādin School. Although mental faculties clearly do seem to cease instantaneously, some schools noted that the *dharmas* that constituted the phenomena of the outside world such as mountains, earth, and our bodies seemed to last for a longer time. The Vātsīputrīyas and Sammatīyas recognized the principle that *dharmas* cease instantaneously but insisted that the *dharmas* that constituted the outside world persisted for a time (S. *kalantara-vasa*?). According to the *I pu-tsung lun lun* (*T* 49:16c, 17b, *Samayabhedoparacanacakra#*, hereafter *Samaya*), besides the Sarvāstivādins, the Mahīśāsakas and the Kāśyapīyas maintained the position that *dharmas* arose and ceased instantaneously.

Abhidharma as Absolute Truth and Conventional Truth

As was explained above, *nirvāṇa* was considered to be the highest of the various *dharmas.* Since the study of these *dharmas* is called *abhidharma,* the wisdom *(prajñā)* that arises along with an understanding of the *dharmas* may also be called *abhidharma.* The wisdom that knows *nirvāṇa* is one with *nirvāṇa;* it is the wisdom of enlightenment. Thus according to the *Abhidharmakośa,* "Pure wisdom and its accompaniments are called *abhidharma.*" Thus the pure wisdom of enlightenment and the various physical and mental *dharmas* that function in concert with that wisdom are all called *"abhidharma"* or "*abhidharma* as absolute truth" (*paramārthiko 'bhidharmaḥ, Abhidharmakośabhāṣya,* p. 2, l. 5; *T* 19:1b).

The term *"abhidharma"* also refers both to the texts that enable the practitioner to realize the absolute truth and to the knowledge still influenced *(sāsrava)* by the defilements through which the practitioner studies the *abhidharma* texts. These definitions of the term are sometimes referred to as "*abhidharma* as conventional truth" *(sāṅketiko 'bhidharmaḥ).*

When *abhidharma* refers to the wisdom with which *nirvāṇa* is known, monks stressed that *abhidharma* was the Buddha's preaching. If the term was used to mean superior or incomparable Dharma, the texts usually referred to *abhidharma* as absolute truth. *Abhidharma* texts thus employed the term *"abhidharma"* in two senses that corresponded to absolute and conventional truth.

Unconditioned *Dharmas* and the Body of the Buddha

One of the most basic ways to classify *dharmas* is according to whether they are conditioned or unconditioned. In the Sarvāstivādin tradition since the compilation of the *Dharmaskandha* (*T* 26:505a), three unconditioned *dharmas* have been recognized: analytical cessation *(pratisaṅkhyā-nirodha),* nonanalytical cessation *(apratisaṅkhyā-nirodha),* and space *(ākāśa).* In the Theravāda tradition, only one unconditioned *dharma, nirvāṇa,* is recognized (*Dhammasaṅgaṇi,* p. 244), a position also maintained in the *Āgamas* and by the Vātsīputrīya School. According to the *Samaya* (*T* 49:15c), the Mahāsaṅghika, Ekavyavahārika, Lokottaravādin, and Kaukuṭika schools all recognized the following nine unconditioned *dharmas:* (1) analytical cessation, (2) nonanalytical cessation, (3) space, (4) the realm of the infinity of space *(ākāśānantyāyatana),* (5) the realm of the infinity of consciousness *(vijñānānantyāyatana),* (6) the realm of nothingness *(akiṃcanyāyatana),* (7) the realm of neither consciousness nor unconsciousness *(naivasaṃjñā-nasaṃjñāyatana),* (8) the law of Dependent Origination (Ch. *yüan-chi chih-hsing*), and (9) the law of the noble path (Ch. *sheng-tao chih-hsing*).[5] The Mahīśāsaka School also recognized nine unconditioned *dharmas;* but its list differed somewhat from that of the Mahāsaṅghika School and included such items as immovability (Ch. *pu-tung*), the eternal law of good *dharma* (Ch. *shan-fa chen-ju*), the eternal law of bad *dharma* (Ch. *e-fa chen-ju*), the eternal law of indeterminate *dharma* (Ch. *wu-chi chen-ju*), the eternal law of the path (Ch. *tao-chih chen-ju*), and the eternal law of Dependent Origination (Ch. *yüan-chi chen-ju*). The law of Dependent Origination was included in the list of unconditioned *dharmas* because it was regarded as an unchanging principle. The Sarvāstivādins disagreed with this position and did not recognize the existence of a principle of Dependent Origination separate from conditioned *dharmas.* For the Sarvāstivādins, the law of Dependent Origination itself was conditioned.

For the Mahīśāsakas, the path to *nirvāṇa* was recognized as an unconditioned *dharma* because the practices established by the Buddha were considered to be eternal truths. The Sarvāstivādins opposed this position by maintaining that although *nirvāṇa* was unconditioned, the wisdom the Buddha had realized was conditioned and not eternal. This issue was closely related to the debate about whether the Buddha's body is eternal or not. According to the Sarvāstivādin and Theravādin positions, the Buddha had entered *parinirvāṇa* in Kuśinagara when he was eighty years old. Thus both the body of the Buddha and his wisdom were not eternal. The Buddha was considered to be a conditioned entity, existing only in the form of a normal human being. According to the *Samaya,* the Mahāsaṅghika and related schools disagreed with this interpretation. They maintained that "Buddhas are all supermundane. . . . The physical bodies [Ch. *shih-shen;* S. *rūpakāya*] of the Buddhas are limitless. . . . The knowledge that he has already mastered the Four Noble Truths and that there is nothing more that he must accomplish is always present in a Buddha until the time of his *parinirvāṇa*" (*T* 49:15b–c). The Buddha's existence, consequently, extended beyond the eighty years of life of the historical Buddha, Śākyamuni. Although this conception of the Buddha was not as developed as Mahāyāna ideals of the *saṃbhogakāya* (body of bliss), it still recognized the eternal aspect of the historical Buddha. Consequently, the adherents of these schools recognized the noble path to salvation as unconditioned.

In terms of the Four Noble Truths, the Sarvāstivādins and Theravādins viewed only the Third Noble Truth—the truth of *nirvāṇa* or the extinction of suffering—as unconditioned. In contrast, followers of the Mahāsaṅghika, Mahīśāsaka, and related schools considered both the Third *(nirvāṇa)* and the Fourth Truth (the path) to be unconditioned. Furthermore, by considering the law of Dependent Origination to be unconditioned, they argued that an unchanging truth could be found in the world of delusion represented by the first two Noble Truths (suffering and its cause). These theories later developed into the concept that delusion and enlightenment were fundamentally the same since both were nonsubstantial. It was also close to the position that the mind was inherently pure, but had been tainted with impurities. According to the *Samaya,* the Mahāsaṅghikas had argued, in fact, that the mind was essentially pure (*T* 49:15c). According to the *Śāriputrābhidharmaśāstra,* which may be a Dharmaguptaka text, the mind had a pure nature, but was tainted by external defilements (*T* 28:697b). Implicit in such a position were the beliefs that the basic nature of the mind was eternal and unconditioned and that the essential nature of conditioned *dharmas* was, in fact, unconditioned. These positions had much in common with the doctrine that the law of Dependent Origination was unconditioned.

According to the *Śāriputrābhidharmaśāstra* (*T* 28:526c), there were nine unconditioned *dharmas* that were objects of the mind *(dharmāyatana):*

1. Cessation through wisdom *(pratisaṅkhyā-nirodha),* which permanently eliminates the defilements
2. Cessation through factors other than wisdom *(apratisaṅkhyā-nirodha)* by which *dharmas* lose the possibility of being produced because the necessary conditions for production are not present
3. Determination *(niyāma* or *niyata)* of the family *(gotra)* of practitioners to which a person belongs (once a person's family has been determined to be that of *śrāvakas, pratyekabuddhas,* or bodhisattvas, it cannot be changed.)
4. Dependent Origination seen as an eternal truth *(dharma-sthiti)*
5. The unchanging quality of mutual dependence or conditioning *(pratyaya;* the text lists ten types of *pratyaya)*

6. Knowledge of the infinity of space *(ākāśānantyāyatana-jñāna)*
7. Knowledge of the infinity of consciousness *(vijñānānantyāyatana-jñāna)*
8. Knowledge of the realm of nothingness *(ākiṃcanyāyatana-jñāna)*
9. Knowledge of the realm of neither perception nor nonperception *(naivasaṃjñā-nasaṃjñāyatana-jñāna)*

Of the nine, only the first and the third were unconditioned *dharmas* pertaining to the realization of *nirvāṇa.* All nine were included in the category of mental objects. It is significant that *pratyaya* is considered to be an unconditioned *dharma* since this position is consistent with maintaining that Dependent Origination is unconditioned.

According to the *Mahāvibhāṣā* (*T* 27:116c), the Discriminators *(fen-pieh-lun che)* also argued that Dependent Origination was unconditioned. The views on unconditioned *dharmas* of many of the schools of Nikāya Buddhism are introduced and discussed in the *Mahāvibhāṣā* and the *Kathāvatthu,* indicating that unconditioned *dharmas* were clearly one of the most controversial subjects in Nikāya Buddhism.

Impure *(Sāsrava)* and Pure *(Anāsrava) Dharmas*

Impure *dharmas* are those tainted with defilements *(kleśa;* P. *kilesa).* Pure *dharmas* are untainted. Because Buddhas and *arhats* have eliminated the defilements through the wisdom obtained in enlightenment, such wisdom is called pure. Since unconditioned *dharmas* do not combine with defilements, they too are pure. In the *Abhidharmakośa* (*T* 29:1b), the term *"sāsrava"* (impure) is defined as "all that is conditioned except the path to salvation." Both the cause of this world of illusion (desire, the Second Noble Truth) and the effect (suffering, the First Noble Truth) are said to be impure.

When defilements taint other *dharmas,* the *dharmas* harmonize with each other and increase the strength of the defilements *(anuśāyita).* This occurs in two ways. The first way occurs when *dharmas* associate and taint each other *(samprayogato 'nuśāyita).* For example, if lust and wisdom function simultaneously, then wisdom will be tainted or colored by lust. The second way occurs when defilements influence events through objects of cognition *(ālambana 'nuśāyita).* For example, when a beautiful object is seen, defilements or passions arise and taint the object of cognition. A Buddhist story relates how a Brahman woman's passions were aroused when she saw the Buddha. Through this story, Sarvāstivādins argued that even the Buddha's physical body could become an object of defilement. For the Sarvāstivādins, since all of the *dharmas* that can cause the defilements to arise are impure *dharmas,* all physical bodies, including that of the Buddha, are impure.

The adherents of the Mahāsaṅghika School criticized this view by arguing that all Buddhas are free of any impure *dharmas*. When a person looks at the Buddha's beautiful body, since the flames of his passions are quieted, the body of the Buddha cannot be an object of defilement. This debate was related to a more general problem in Nikāya Buddhism of whether physical elements were necessarily impure or whether some of them might be pure.

The Varieties of *Dharmas*

The Sarvāstivādin system described above is sometimes characterized by the phrase "the first fifteen elements *(dhātu)* are all influenced by the defilements." In other words, out of the eighteen elements, the five sense organs (eye, ear, nose, tongue, body), the five sense objects (forms, sounds, smells, tastes, and tangible objects), and the five corresponding sense-consciousnesses are all tainted. These fifteen elements would be tainted even for a Buddha. Only the mind, mental objects, and mental consciousness may be untainted, that is, free of any influence from the defilements.

Three major classifications of *dharmas* are found in the *Āgamas:* the five aggregates *(pañca-skandhāḥ),* the twelve bases of cognition *(dvadaśa-āyatanāni),* and the eighteen elements *(aṣṭādaśa-dhātavaḥ).* Their relationships are diagrammed in Figure 1 in chapter three.

Matter

The Sanskrit term for matter, *rūpa,* is used in two senses in Buddhist texts. When it is included in lists such as the five *skandhas* (aggregates), it is used in a broad sense. In such cases, it refers to ten of the twelve bases of cognition *(āyatana):* the five sense organs (*indriya:* eye, ear, nose, tongue, and body) and the five sense objects (*viṣaya:* forms, sounds, smells, tastes, and tangible objects). In its narrow sense, the term *"rūpa"* refers only to form *(saṃsthāna)* and color *(varṇa),* the objects of vision. Besides classifying the five sense organs and sense objects in the aggregate of matter *(rūpa-skandha),* the Sarvāstivādin School classified unmanifested matter *(avijñapti-rūpa)* as a form of matter, making a total of eleven types of matter.

When the Buddhist notion of matter is reconciled with the eighteen elements *(dhātu),* the five sense organs and five sense objects are classified as matter. Since unmanifested matter is classified as a mental object, part of the base of cognition *(āyatana)* or element *(dhātu)* of mental objects is included in the aggregate of matter. When matter is considered in light of the twelve bases of cognition, only the mind and some mental objects are not classified as matter. In the classification of the eighteen elements, the mind, mental objects except unmanifested matter, and the six consciousnesses are not matter. But in the Sarvāstivādin list of seventy-five *dharmas,* only eleven *dharmas* are matter.

The varieties of matter can be classified into more precise categories. Although the five sense organs are not analyzed further, the sense objects are examined in detail. For example, visual objects are classified into four basic colors (blue, yellow, red, and white) and eight basic shapes (long, short, square, round, high, low, even, and uneven). Other categories such as clouds and smoke are added to make a total of twenty-one visual categories. In addition, there are eight types of sounds (including pleasant and unpleasant), three (or sometimes four) types of smells (good, bad, excessive, and not excessive), and six types of tastes (sweet, sour, salty, pungent, bitter, and astringent). There are eleven tactile objects, including such qualities as heaviness, lightness, and coldness. The four elements *(mahābhūta)*—earth, water, fire, and wind—are also listed as tactile objects because they can be perceived only with the body. Thus, when a person looks at fire or water, he may see red or blue, but the essence of the element, such as the heat of fire and the wetness of water, can be perceived only with his body. The essence of earth is hardness and the essence of wind is movement.

All matter other than the four elements is called *bhautika* or "that which is composed of the four elements." The five sense organs, five sense objects (except that part of the category of tangible objects that includes the four elements), and unmanifested matter are all *bhautika.* In contrast the four elements are called "that which makes up form."

Although the five sense organs and five sense objects are composed of atoms *(paramāṇu), bhautika* matter is not directly constituted of atoms of the elements. Rather, the elements and *bhautika* matter are each formed from different atoms. All of the basic types of *bhautika* matter necessary for the formation of "molecules" (forms, smells, tastes, and tangible objects) must arise simultaneously and be accompanied by the elements in various combinations. In fluids the water element is dominant, in solids the earth element predominates, and in hot objects the fire element is prevalent. The minimum state in which material objects exist is a "molecule" of at least eight atoms that arise concomitantly. These eight atoms are the four elements and four *bhautika* atoms of form, smell, taste, and touch. If any one of these varieties of atoms is absent, the "molecule" cannot exist. For sound, nine varieties of atoms are present. In the "molecules" of the sense organs, the number of varieties of atoms increases.

Sense organs, such as the eyes, are said to be different from other parts of the body because they are delicate organs, having the function of cognition. They are made of a subtle or pure form of matter *(rūpa-prasāda).* Unmanifested matter *(avijñapti-rūpa),* although classified as matter, is not composed of atoms and is thus called a mental object. As the term "unmanifested" implies, it is a type of matter that cannot be seen. Unmanifested matter is discussed in chapter twelve.

Correspondences between Different Systems of *Dharmas*

Matter is given special attention in most of the early classification systems of *dharmas* such as the twelve bases of cognition or the eighteen elements. In the twelve bases only the mind and mental objects are not matter. Of the eighteen elements only the mind, mental objects, and the six consciousnesses are not matter. However, the mind and its functions were analyzed further by early Buddhists. For example, four of the five aggregates (sensation, perception, mental formations, and consciousness) are not matter. Sensations and perceptions are each considered to be psychological functions. Sensations *(vedanā)* refer to the sensations received by the sense organs. Perception *(saṃjñā)* is the mental process of forming images or notions in the mind.

In the Sarvāstivādin tradition, the various mental or psychological functions are regarded as real entities or *dharmas.* They are called concomitant mental faculties *(caitasika-dharma),* a term also found in Pāli Theravāda *abhidhamma* texts *(cetasika-dhamma).*[6] In Sarvāstivādin texts, all of the concomitant faculties except sensation and perception are included in the fourth aggregate, namely mental formations *(saṃskāra).* Those *dharmas* called "forces that are neither mental nor material" *(citta-viprayuktā-saṃskārā dharmāḥ)* are also included in the fourth aggregate. In the systems of twelve bases *(āyatana)* and eighteen elements *(dhātu),* the aggregates of sensations, perceptions, and mental formations are included in the category of mental objects.

The fifth aggregate, consciousness *(vijñāna),* is the subjective aspect of cognition. Sometimes the consciousness or mind *(citta)* is compared to a king (Ch. *hsin-wang*) and the concomitant mental faculties (Ch. *hsin-so*) are compared to the retainers dependent upon the king. In the classification of the twelve bases, the mind corresponds to the *mana-āyatana* or mental base. In the classification of the eighteen elements, the mind corresponds to the element of the mind *(manovijñānadhātu)* and the six consciousnesses. The three unconditioned *(asaṃskṛta) dharmas* are not included in the five aggregates. Only conditioned *dharmas* correspond to the aggregates. However, in the classifications of the twelve bases and eighteen elements, unconditioned *dharmas* are included in the category of mental objects.

Since the correspondences between the various classification systems are complex, a brief review may be helpful. Matter corresponds to the form aggregate. In the twelve bases it corresponds to the five internal and five external bases of sense cognition and to part of the base of mental objects. In the eighteen elements, it corresponds to the five sense organs, the five sense objects, and part of the category of mental objects. The mind corresponds to the consciousness aggregate. In the twelve bases, it corresponds to the mental base. In the eighteen elements it corresponds to the mind and to the six consciousnesses. Thus the various *dharmas* considered to be the objects of the mind are not analyzed to a high degree in the *Āgamas*. In the *abhidharma* literature, however, they are analyzed extensively. Consequently, much of *abhidharma* philosophy focuses on the concomitant mental faculties, the forces that are neither mental nor material, and the unconditioned *dharmas*.

Defilements *(Kleśa)*

Many of the defilements mentioned in *abhidharma* literature as concomitant mental faculties were originally found in the *Āgamas*. Among the lists in the *Āgamas* are the three poisons of lust *(rāga),* hatred *(dveṣa),* and delusion *(moha);* the four violent outflows *(ogha)* of desire, wrong views, ignorance, and attachment to existence; the five hindrances *(nīvaraṇa)* of lust, hatred *(pratigha),* sloth and torpor *(styāna-middha),* restlessness and worry *(auddhatya-kaukṛtya),* and doubt *(vicikitsā);* the five fetters *(saṃyojana)* that bind a person to the desire realm, namely, belief in a Self, doubt, the belief that rituals will lead to salvation, lust, and anger; the five fetters that bind a person to the form and formless realms, namely, attachment to form, attachment to the formless, pride, restlessness, and ignorance; and the seven fetters of desire, hatred, wrong views, doubt, pride, attachment to existence in the form and formless realms, and ignorance. In addition, the *Āgamas* include mentions of individual defilements such as being unashamed of one's wrong actions *(āhrīkya)* or lack of any embarrassment over one's wrong actions in front of others *(anapatrāpya)*. (For examples of such lists see the *Saṅgītisutta,* no. 33 of the *Dīghanikāya.*) Most of the major defilements discussed in the *abhidharma* literature are found in the above lists.

In the Sarvāstivādin *abhidharma* treatise the *Dhātukāya* (*T* 26:614b) defilements are categorized into such groups as the ten general functions of defilement, the ten minor functions of defilement, the five defilements, and the five wrong views. In later texts these groups are organized further. Finally, in the *Abhidharmakośa* (*T* 29:19c), eighteen defilements are listed and divided into the following three groups.

General functions of defilement *(kleśamahābhūmikā dharmāḥ)*

1. Delusion *(moha)*
2. Negligence *(pramāda)*
3. Indolence *(kauśīdya)*
4. Disbelief *(āśraddhya)*
5. Torpor *(styāna)*
6. Restlessness *(auddhatya)*

Minor functions of defilement *(parīttakleśabhūmikā dharmāḥ)*

1. Anger *(krodha)*
2. Resentment *(upanāha)*
3. Flattery *(śāṭhya)*
4. Jealousy *(īrṣyā)*
5. Rejection of criticism *(pradāsa)*
6. Concealment of wrongdoing *(mrakṣa)*
7. Parsimony *(mātsarya)*
8. Deceit *(māyā)*
9. Conceit *(mada)*
10. Causing injury *(vihiṃsā)*

General functions of evil *(akuśalamahābhūmikā dharmāḥ)*

1. Absence of shame *(āhrīkya)*
2. Absence of embarrassment *(anapatrāpya)*

In addition to the above defilements, eight *dharmas* are said to be indeterminate functions *(aniyata)*. They are as follows:

1. Remorse *(kaukṛtya)*
2. Drowsiness *(middha)*
3. Investigation *(vitarka)*

4. Scrutiny *(vicāra)*
5. Lust *(rāga)*
6. Hatred *(pratigha)*
7. Pride *(māna)*
8. Doubt *(vicikitsā)*

With the exception of investigation and scrutiny, all of the indeterminate *dharmas* can be considered defilements. Moreover, lust, hatred, and doubt can be considered grave defilements. Consequently, the *Abhidharmakośa*'s system of classification of indeterminate *dharmas* is not completely satisfactory.

In the *Abhidharmakośa* (*T* 29:98b) the defilements are called proclivities *(anuśaya),* and a chapter is devoted to these proclivities. Six of them are listed: lust, hatred, pride, ignorance, wrong views, and doubt. The category of wrong views is sometimes expanded to a list of five proclivities: belief in a Self, clinging to extreme positions such as annihilationism or eternalism, disbelief in causation, clinging to wrong views, and the belief that rituals will lead to salvation. When the category of wrong views is replaced by these five beliefs, a list of ten proclivities is the result. These ten proclivities are analyzed according to criteria of which of the three realms (desire, form, and formless) they occur in and which of the Four Noble Truths or meditation may be used to eliminate them. A list of ninety-eight defilements is thereby produced. The purpose of religious practice is to cut off these defilements.

In addition to the ninety-eight defilements, the following list of ten bonds *(paryavasthāna)* is included in the "Chapter on Proclivities" in the *Abhidharmakośa:* lack of shame over one's own wrongdoing *(āhrīkya),* lack of embarrassment before others over wrongdoing *(anapatrāpya),* jealousy *(īrṣyā),* parsimony *(mātsarya),* distraction *(auddhatya),* remorse *(kaukṛtya),* torpor *(styāna),* drowsiness *(middha),* anger *(krodha),* and concealment of wrongdoing *(mrakṣa).* When these ten are added to the ninety-eight proclivities, the resulting list is called the "108 defilements."

The categorization of defilements in the *Abhidharmakośa* has not been completely systematized since their treatment varies in different chapters. The defilements listed under such categories as the six general functions of defilement, ten minor functions of defilement, two general functions of evil, and six of the eight indeterminate functions are not completely consistent, particularly in the case of indeterminate functions.

In the Theravāda *abhidhamma* text the *Dhammasaṅgaṇi* (p. 76), a number of mental functions are discussed. The mind is classified under three categories: good, bad, and neutral types of consciousness. Thirty types of mental faculties contribute to the production of a bad type of consciousness, including wrong views, wrong intention, lack of shame, lack of embarrassment before others, lust, ignorance, and dullness. However, the Theravāda view on defilements was still not completely systematized in the seven canonical *abhidhamma* treatises since no category for defilements alone was established. A later noncanonical *abhidhamma* text, the *Abhidhammatthasaṅgaha,* lists the following fourteen mental functions of evil: ignorance *(avijjā),* lack of shame over one's wrongdoings *(ahirika),* lack of embarrassment before others over one's wrongdoings *(anottappa),* brooding *(kukkucca),* craving *(lobha),* wrong views *(diṭṭhi),* pride *(māna),* hatred *(paṭigha),* jealousy *(issā),* parsimony *(macchariya),* restlessness *(uddhacca),* torpor *(thīna),* drowsiness *(middha),* and doubt *(vicikicchā).* When these mental functions of evil act concomitantly with the mind and other mental faculties, the result is a defiled or evil type of consciousness.

The Analysis of the Mind: Concomitant Mental Faculties *(Citta-samprayukta-saṃskāra)*

Because a major objective of Buddhist practice was to cut off the defilements *(kleśa),* a wide variety of passions was discussed in the *Āgamas.* But only the most basic mental functions other than the defilements were mentioned in the *Āgamas.* Among the mental functions mentioned in these early texts were sensation *(vedanā),* perception *(saṃjñā),* volition *(cetanā),* attention *(manaskāra),* contact (between the sense organ, object, and consciousness [*sparśa*]), mindfulness *(smṛti),* investigation *(vitarka),* scrutiny *(vicāra),* and desire *(chanda).* With the development of *abhidharma* literature, other mental functions were added, giving a much more detailed view of the activity of the mind. To cut off the passions, the relationship of the defilements to the other mental functions had to be investigated and described.

In the Sarvāstivādin tradition, the process of categorizing and describing the mental functions began with the *abhidharma* work the *Dhātukāya* (*T* 1540). The culmination of these efforts is found in the *Abhidharmakośa*'s list of forty-six *dharmas* classified into the following six categories (*T* 29:19a; *Abhidharmakośabhāṣya,* p. 55, l. 13):

1. General functions *(mahābhūmika),* ten *dharmas*
2. General functions of good *(kuśalamahābhūmika),* ten *dharmas*
3. General functions of defilement *(kleśamahābhūmika),* six *dharmas*

4. General functions of evil *(akuśalamahābhūmika),* two *dharmas*
5. Minor functions of defilement *(parittakleśabhūmika),* ten *dharmas*
6. Indeterminate functions *(aniyata),* eight *dharmas*

In the Sarvāstivādin system, the mind is called *citta-bhūmi* or the mind-ground, a term that appears in the *Dhātukāya* (*T* 26:41b). The use of the term *"bhūmi"* suggests that the mind is viewed as the base upon which the mental faculties are manifested. The *citta-bhūmi* also has the power to produce the mental faculties. The mind may also be thought of as the base for the functioning of the mental faculties. However, since a good mind cannot function with a base that is not good, the existence of five types of grounds *(bhūmi)* or bases, each with its own particular mental qualities, is postulated. (Although six types of mental faculties are said to exist, indeterminate functions are not considered to be a *bhūmi.*) For example, the *kleśabhūmi* is considered to be the base from which the defilements arise. Defilements such as lust and anger are not always present in the mind; they arise when circumstances are favorable to the production of defilements. Consequently, a ground or base where they exist in a latent form is thought to be present. Other states of mind, such as a good mind, have their own bases. The base for mental functions such as embarrassment before others over one's wrong actions *(apatrāpya),* shame over one's actions *(hrī),* and assiduous striving *(vīrya)* is called the "good ground" *(kuśalabhūmi).* This type of speculation eventually led to the Sarvāstivādin School's division of mental faculties into five types of mental grounds: general functions, general functions of good, general functions of defilement, general functions of evil, and minor functions of defilement. A sixth category of indeterminate functions included those mental functions not limited to any particular ground(s).

The forty-six mental functions are listed below.

A. The ten general functions are those that arise in mental states, whether they are good, evil, or indeterminate, and in the mental states of the three realms (desire, form, and formless):

1. Sensation *(vedanā)*
2. Intention *(cetanā)*
3. Perception *saṃjñā)*
4. Desire *(chanda)*
5. Contact *(sparśa)*
6. Wisdom *(prajñā)*
7. Mindfulness *(smṛti)*

8. Mental application *(manaskāra)*
9. Ascertainment *(adhimokṣa)*
10. Concentration *(samādhi)*

B. The ten general functions of good are always present in good mental states. When the following ten mental functions are present in the mind, a "good mental state" exists:

1. Belief *(śraddhā)*
2. Earnestness *(apramāda)*
3. Suppleness *(praśrabdhi)*
4. Equanimity *(upekṣā)*
5. Shame *(hrī)*
6. Embarrassment *(apatrāpya)*
7. Refraining from craving *(alobha)*
8. Refraining from hatred *(adveṣa)*
9. Refraining from causing injury *(avihiṃsā)*
10. Assiduous striving *(vīrya)*

C. The six general functions of defilement are always present in defiled minds. They are listed along with the *dharmas* in the following three categories in the section on defilements in this chapter:

D. The two general functions of evil
E. The ten minor functions of defilement
F. The eight indeterminate functions.

The *Abhidharmakośa* states only that "investigation, scrutiny, remorse, drowsiness, and so forth" are indeterminate functions, and does not list eight *dharmas*. However, since the *dharmas* of lust, hatred, pride, and doubt are not included in any other categories, the Chinese commentator P'u-kuang added them to the list of indeterminate functions to make a total of eight (*Chü-she-lun chi, T* 41:78b). The Indian commentator Yaśomitra also states that there are eight *dharmas* in the category of indeterminate functions, suggesting that the tradition of including eight *dharmas* in this category originated in India (*Abhidharmakośabhāṣya,* p. 132, ll. 21–22). However, Yaśomitra added four other defilements to the four already found in the *Abhidharmakośa*. Regardless of which list is followed, sources are in agreement that eight *dharmas* are included in this category, making a total of forty-six mental functions.

The Concomitant Arising of the Mind and Mental Functions

As was discussed earlier, the Sarvāstivādins maintained that mental faculties were independent entities. Such faculties as lust and hatred seemed to perform such directly opposed functions that they had to be distinct *dharmas*. However, even though many faculties were contained in the mind, each person appeared to have a certain unity that marked him as an individual. The Sarvāstivādins had to explain that unity. If the mental faculties were all completely independent entities, then that unity would be difficult to account for. The Sarvāstivādins solved this problem by arguing that the mind (*citta,* in other words, consciousness and judgment) and mental faculties arise at the same time and work cooperatively. For example, when a good mind arises in the desire realm, it involves the mind as well as the ten general mental faculties *(mahābhūmika),* the ten general faculties of good *(kuśala-mahābhūmika),* investigation *(vitarka),* and scrutiny *(vicāra).* Thus the mind and twenty-two faculties would simultaneously arise. In the case of an unvirtuous mind, the mind, the ten general faculties, the six general faculties of defilement *(kleśa-mahābhūmika),* the two general faculties of evil *(akuśala-mahābhūmika),* investigation, and scrutiny, a total of twenty mental faculties, all would arise simultaneously. For a mind morally neutral and obscured (that is, one that does not perceive religious truth [*nivṛta-avyākṛta*]), the mind, the ten general faculties, the six general faculties of defilement, investigation, and scrutiny, a total of eighteen faculties, would all arise simultaneously. For a mind neutral and not obscured, the six general functions of defilement would not arise; thus, only the mind and twelve mental faculties would arise simultaneously. In more specific cases, such as when lust, anger, or repentance occur, the number of concomitant mental faculties would vary.

In the form and formless realms, the mind is in a meditative state. From the second *dhyāna* (trance) upward, both investigation and scrutiny cease. In addition, anger does not arise in these higher realms. As a person progresses in these meditative states, the number of concomitant mental faculties decreases.

The Sarvāstivādins explained the unity of the activity of the mind by using a theory of the concomitant arising of mind and mental faculties. This cooperative functioning is called *saṃprayukta* (concomitance). According to the *Abhidharmakośa* (*T* 29:22a), the mind and mental faculties arise concomitantly in five ways: both depend on the same base *(āśraya)* or sense organ, both have the same object *(ālambana),* the way in which the object is perceived is the same for both *(ākāra),* both function at the same time *(kāla),* and both maintain their own identities as substances *(dravya).*

The Theravāda School also has developed a theory of the concomitance of the mind and mental faculties, but its contents differ slightly from that of the Sarvāstivādin School (*Visuddhimagga,* chap. 17, par. 94).

In the Sarvāstivādin School, the term *saṃprayukta* has the meaning *saṃprayuktaka-hetu* (concomitant cause). For example, according to the *Abhidharmakośa,* a good mind in the desire realm requires the concomitant arising of the mind and at least twenty-two mental faculties. None of the required mental faculties may be absent. If one of them is lacking, then the other twenty-one mental faculties cannot arise; thus, that one *dharma* is necessary for the remaining twenty-one to arise. It is because of this type of interdependence that the mind and the various mental faculties are described as being concomitant causes for each other. A similar relationship is found among form *(rūpa) dharmas. Dharmas* of the four elements and secondary matter *(bhautika)* arise simultaneously to constitute matter. However, the relationship of the various *dharmas* of *rūpa* that arise at the same time is not called "concomitant cause," but "simultaneous cause" *(sahabhū-hetu).* The four elements of earth, water, fire, and air always arise simultaneously. If one element is missing, the other three cannot arise independently. Thus, each element acts as a cause for others. This type of relationship is called "simultaneous and mutual cause and effect." The term "concomitant cause" refers only to psychological phenomena and is a special type of simultaneous cause.

The Mental Faculties According to Theravāda Buddhism

In the Theravāda tradition, consciousness is classified into eighty-nine types on the basis of its qualities. Eighty-one are varieties of mundane consciousness, distributed among the three realms as follows: fifty-four types for the desire realm, fifteen for the form realm, and twelve for the formless realm. The remaining eight types of consciousness are supramundane, making a total of eighty-nine varieties.

According to another Theravāda classification system, the eight types of supramundane consciousness can each exist in any of the first five trances *(jhāna),* making a total of forty types of supramundane consciousness. When these are added to the eighty-one types of mundane consciousness, the result is a list of 121 types of consciousness. However, the list of eighty-nine varieties is the most common.

An early example of this style of classification is found in the *Paṭisambhidāmagga.* The system was fully formulated in the *Dhammasaṅgaṇi* and was accepted as established doctrine during the period when commentaries on the *Abhidhamma-piṭaka* were being compiled. The classification of consciousness into good, bad, and neutral types is found in the *Āgamas.* Other schools of Nikāya Buddhism further classified the types of consciousness into lists of ten and twelve according to whether they were mundane or supramundane and according to which of the three realms (desire, form, and formless) they belonged. However, the detail found in the Theravāda list of eighty-nine types of consciousness is not found in the doctrines of other schools.

The term *"cetasika"* (mental functions) has long been used in Theravāda Buddhism. For example, in the *Dhammasaṅgaṇi* (p. 9ff.), the mental faculties that arise in each of the eighty-nine types of consciousness are specified. In the discussion of the first type of good consciousness of the desire realm, fifty-six mental faculties are mentioned. However, the repetitions are frequent, and when the mental faculties are enumerated, a total of only twenty-nine actually come into play in the various types of consciousness. The mental faculties in different types of consciousness are also discussed in the *Kathāvatthu,* but only eighteen mental faculties are mentioned, indicating that the number of mental faculties had still not been determined in a definitive way when the treatises of the Theravāda *Abhidhamma-piṭaka* were being compiled. Finally, Buddhadatta, a contemporary of Buddhaghosa, listed fifty-two mental faculties in his *Abhidhammāvatāra.* The fifty-two mental faculties were accepted as the orthodox number in the Theravāda School, though later works do not always agree completely on which should be included. According to the *Abhidhammatthasaṅgaha* there are:

Thirteen neutral mental faculties
1. Seven universal faculties (found in every consciousness)
2. Six particular faculties (found only in some states of consciousness)

Fourteen mental faculties of evil
1. Four universal faculties (found in every evil consciousness)
2. Ten particular faculties

Twenty-five mental faculties of good and purity
1. Nineteen universal faculties of good
2. Three faculties of abstinence
3. Two faculties of unlimitedness
4. One faculty of wisdom

The universal neutral mental faculties *(sabbacittasādhāranā)* arise in all types of consciousness. They correspond to the general faculties *(mahābhūmika)* of the Sarvāstivādin School. The Theravādins, with fifty-two mental faculties, have a longer list than the forty-six mental faculties of the Sarvāstivādins. The difference arises because the Theravādins classify as mental faculties some *dhammas* that the Sarvāstivādins did not recognize as mental faculties. Among these are life force (*jīvitindriya;* a similar *dharma* is classified as a force not concomitant with the mind by the Sarvāstivādins), tranquility of mental faculties (*kāyapasaddhi,* opposes restlessness), lightness of mental faculties (*kāyalahutā,* opposes drowsiness and torpor), pliancy of mental faculties (*kāyamudutā,* opposes pride and wrong views), adaptability of mental faculties (*kāyakammaññatā,* produces serenity in propitious things), proficiency of mental factors (*kāyapāguññatā,* opposes disbelief), and rectitude of mental factors (*kāyujjukatā,* opposes deception). In addition, right speech *(sammāvācā),* right action *(sammākammanta),* and right livelihood *(sammāājīva)* are considered to be mental factors by the Theravādins, but are not included in Sarvāstivādin lists of *dharmas.* There are also other differences between the Theravādin and Sarvāstivādin views of mental faculties.

The Concomitant Mental Faculties as Presented in Other Schools

The *She-li-fu a-p'i-t'an lun* (*T* 1548, *Śāriputrābhidharmaśāstra*?) belongs to neither a Theravādin nor a Sarvāstivādin lineage. Concomitant mental faculties are mentioned in various places throughout the text. When these faculties are systematically collected, a list of thirty-three is produced. Mentions of concomitant mental faculties are found scattered throughout the text of Harivarman's *Ch'eng-shih lun* (*T* 1646, *Tattvasiddhiśāstra*?). When these are systematically collected, they total thirty-six *dharmas* according to some authorities and forty-nine *dharmas* according to others. Although concomitant mental faculties are discussed in the *Ch'eng-shih lun,* they are not considered to be distinct and real entities.

The Sautrāntika School is famous for its refusal to recognize the independent existence of concomitant mental faculties. According to the *A-p'i-ta-mo shun-cheng-li lun* (*T* 29:284b, *Nyāyānusāraśāstra*?) by Saṅghabhadra, the Sautrāntikas recognized only sensation, perception, and volition as concomitant mental faculties. The Dārṣṭāntikas, who belonged to the same lineage as the Sautrāntikas, also did not recognize concomitant mental faculties. According to the *Kathāvatthu* (bk. 7, sec.

3), neither did the Rājagiriya and Siddhattaka schools, both of the Mahāsaṅghika lineage. The adherents of these schools emphasize the unitary nature of the mind. When sensation is occurring, the entire mind is sensation. When perception is occurring, the whole mind is perception. The varieties of psychological phenomena are thus viewed as manifestations of a unitary mind.

The Unity and Continuity of the Personality

The Sarvāstivādins explained the no-Self theory in a mechanical fashion, considering each of the mental functions to be separate entities. But this type of interpretation did not sufficiently explain the organic unity of the mind. Consequently, the Sarvāstivādins advanced the theory of the concomitant arising of the mind and mental functions. Since the mind and mental functions arose and ceased in an instant, the theory of concomitance still did not sufficiently explain the unity of the mind. To solve this problem, the Sarvāstivādins described the mind as a ground or base *(citta-bhūmi).* The Yogācārin branch of Mahāyāna Buddhism explained the unity of the mind by postulating a realm of the unconscious, the *ālaya-vijñāna,* from which both the conscious mind and its objects arose. The Sarvāstivādins did not acknowledge this type of consciousness, but did recognize five types of *citta-bhūmi* from which psychological phenomena arose.

The defilements *(kleśa)* are also called *anuśaya.* The Sarvāstivādins interpreted *anuśaya* as meaning "something that gradually becomes stronger," while the Sautrāntikas interpreted it as "something sleeping" or dormant. The word *"anuśaya"* may be translated as meaning "proclivity to do wrong." Even when hatred and lust are not manifest in the conscious mind, they are still believed to be present in the conscious mind in a dormant state. Although the *citta-bhūmi* was said to be the locus of these proclivities, the doctrine of *citta-bhūmi* still did not enable the Sarvāstivādins to describe the continuity of the mind adequately. To this end, they argued for the presence of a *dharma* of life-force *(jīvitendriya),* which would explain the obvious continuities of a person during his lifespan. In addition, the Sarvāstivādins discussed the continuum of mind *(citta-saṃtāna),* the way in which former and latter instants of mind constituted a stream of consciousness. In the end, because the Sarvāstivādin view of mental faculties was insufficient to provide a convincing explanation of the continuity of the mind, the Sarvāstivādins were still faced with solving problems such as how memory could function when the mind was arising and ceasing each instant.

Other schools did not recognize the mind-ground doctrine and thus had to find different ways to explain the continuity and unity of the personality. For example, the Theravāda School used the idea of a subconscious dimension of mind *(bhavaṅga-viññāṇa* or *bhavaṅga-citta)* to explain these problems. The term *"bhavaṅga"* is found in the Pāli *abhidhamma* text *Paṭṭhāna* (vol. 1, p. 163f.) and in the *Milindapañha* (bk. 4, chap. 8, sec. 36). When no mental functions are present in consciousness (that is, when a person is unconscious), *bhavaṅga-viññāṇa* is still present. When stimuli from the outside world or from within the mind activate the consciousness, however, the mind changes from its subconscious state to a consciousness directed toward sense objects. This process is called "adverting the mind" *(āvajjana)*. Cognition is explained as consisting of twelve processes, including reception *(sampaṭicchana),* judging an impression *(santīraṇa),* and determination *(voṭṭhappana)*. In addition, the Theravāda School developed a list of fifty-two mental faculties, a detailed analysis of the mind comparable to that found in Sarvāstivādin texts. The list of twelve processes that occur during cognition is a theory peculiar to the Theravāda School. Although Buddhism generally paid more attention to psychological analysis than other religious traditions, the Theravāda School carried such analyses farther than the other schools within Buddhism. The Theravāda treatment of the *bhavaṅga* (which served as both a subconscious and a life-force) is similar to positions adopted in the Yogācāra tradition.

The Sautrāntika School explained the continuity of the mind by using the concept of mental seeds *(bīja)*. Seeds were the mental experiences of the past preserved in the mind in a latent state. The continuities and changes of psychological phenomena were described by referring to the changes that seeds went through with terms such as continuity *(santati),* transformation *(pariṇāma),* and distinction (*viśeṣa,* the last in the series of changes the seeds underwent). To elucidate the continuity or identity of each individual, the Sautrāntikas used the concept of a true person or *pudgala (paramārtha-pudgala)*. The Sautrāntikas also recognized the existence of a subtle form of the mental *skandhas (ekarasa-skandha)* that would continue from earlier rebirths to later ones, a position so distinctive that the Sautrāntikas were consequently sometimes called by another name, Saṅkrāntivādin (the school that maintains the transmigration of the *skandhas*). This special form of the *skandhas* was similar to a subtle consciousness *(sūkṣma-manovijñāna)* that continually existed and was not cut off by death, but continued on to the next life. Perception continued to exist in this subtle consciousness, but only to a minute degree, thus making subtle consciousness similar to the unconscious. The subtle consciousness was said to continue to function behind man's grosser, everyday consciousness.

The Vātsīputrīyas and Sammatīyas are famous for maintaining that a *pudgala* (person) existed that transmigrated from one existence to another. The *pudgala* was criticized by other Buddhist schools as being equivalent to an eternal soul *(ātman).* However, the Vātsīputrīyas argued that the *pudgala* was neither identical to nor separate from the *skandhas.* If it were identical to the *skandhas,* then the Buddha's teaching that no eternal Self could be found in the *skandhas* would have been violated. If the *pudgala* were separate from the *skandhas,* then it would have been impossible to recognize it. The *pudgala* was thus a metaphysical entity, somewhat similar to the *ātman* or eternal Self, which Buddhists generally did not recognize. However, the Vātsīputrīyas acknowledged the existence of an *ātman* or Self in a different sense than that advocated by many of the non-Buddhist traditions. The *pudgala* was an entity that provided the continuity in a person's existences, but was neither identical to nor separate from the *skandhas.* The Vātsīputrīyas suggested a new category of phenomena to which this Self belonged, the inexplicable (Ch. *pu-k'o-shuo tsang*). This category was added to four other categories recognized by the Sarvāstivādins (conditioned *dharmas* in the past, present, and future and unconditioned *dharmas*), making a total of five categories of existence recognized by the Vātsīputrīyas. The Vātsīputrīya view of a Self was vehemently criticized in the ninth chapter of the *Abhidharmakośa.*

Various views of a "self" that would explain the continuity between births and rebirths were proposed by other schools. According to the first fascicle of the *She ta-sheng lun* (*T* 31:134a, *Mahāyānasaṅgraha#*), the Mahāsaṅghikas postulated the existence of a "basic consciousness" (Ch. *ken-pen shih*), and the Mahīśāsakas maintained that a *skandha* in a subtle way persisted through births and deaths (Ch. *ch'iung sheng-ssu yün*). According to the *Mahāvibhāṣā* (*T* 27:772c, 774a), the Dārṣṭāntikas and Discriminators recognized the existence of a subtle (Ch. *hsi-hsin*) or continuing subconscious mind. These ideas served as the basis for the development of Mahāyāna doctrines of *ālaya-vijñāna.* Finally, the doctrine that the mind is originally pure, which was maintained by the Mahāsaṅghikas and the authors of the *Śāriputrābhidharmaśāstra* (*T* 28: 697b), was based on the position that there was a continuing pure mental substratum.[7]

Forces Not Concomitant with the Mind
(Citta-viprayuktāḥ Saṃskārāḥ)

Functions that do not arise concomitantly with the mind are nevertheless classified as part of the aggregate of mental formations *(saṃskāra-*

skandha). As was explained above, mental faculties are *dharmas* that arise concomitantly with the mind and are part of the *saṃskāra-skandha.* In the classifications of *āyatanas* (bases) and *dhātus* (elements), they are included as part of the *dharma-āyatana* or *dharma-dhātu* (mental objects). However, other forces *(saṃskāra),* which do not arise concomitantly with the mind, are also included in the *saṃskāra-skandha.* The Sarvāstivādins established a group of fourteen *dharmas* that fit into this group. They are neither physical nor mental. Some of them have a physiological aspect, but others do not.

The fourteen forces that do not arise concomitantly with the mind are as follows:

1. Possession *(prāpti)*
2. Dispossession *(aprāpti)*
3. Similarity of being *(nikāya-sabhāga)*
4. Birth and existence in a heaven without perception *(āsaṃjñika)*
5. Absorption without perception *(asaṃjñisamāpatti)*
6. Absorption of cessation *(nirodhasamāpatti)*
7. Life-force *(jīvitendriya)*
8. Origination *(jāti)*
9. Subsistence *(sthiti)*
10. Decay *(jarā)*
11. Extinction *(anityatā)*
12. Words *(nāmakāya)*
13. Sentences *(padakāya)*
14. Syllables *(vyañjanakāya)*

Life-force is the lifespan viewed as a *dharma.* Absorption without perception is a meditation in which the mental functions up to and including perception cease. The absorption of cessation is an even deeper meditation in which the mental functions up to and including sensation cease. Because both are unconscious states, they are included in the category of forces neither mental nor material. The above three *dharmas* are objectifications of certain aspects of living or existence. When a person who has entered an absorption without perception dies, he is reborn in a realm of no perception. Because this realm is devoid of perception, the *dharmas* of which it is composed are included among the forces that are not concomitant with the mind.

Similarity, the *dharma* used to explain how sentient beings are distinguished into groups, is present in all sentient beings. A being exists as a horse or a cow because it possesses a horse or cow *dharma* of similarity.

The *dharmas* of possession *(prāpti)* and dispossession *(aprāpti)* are related to the process of eliminating defilements. Although defilements may not actually be arising in the mind of an ordinary person at a particular moment, the defilements are still present in a latent form and still have not been eliminated. *Prāpti* is the force that links the defilements to a person. Thus a person's continuum (which is constantly changing) is said to "possess" defilements. Even though the defilements themselves may not be manifest, the *prāpti* of the defilements is present within the continuum. In contrast, because an *arhat* has eliminated his passions, even if a worldly mind should arise in him, the *prāpti* of the defilements would not become a part of his continuum. Thus, if the same ordinary thought were to arise both in an ordinary man and in an *arhat,* the results would be very different in terms of the arousal of the defilements. When the defilements are cut off, the *dharma* of *aprāpti* or dispossession keeps the defilements away. The *dharmas* of *prāpti* and *aprāpti* are required as part of the Sarvāstivādin explanation of a continually changing person. But even the *dharmas* of *prāpti* and *aprāpti* themselves arise and cease each instant and are dependent on other *dharmas* and a part of the continuum that makes up a personality.

Other *dharmas* considered not concomitant with the mind were the forces that give significance to words *(nāmakāya),* sentences *(padakāya),* and syllables *(vyañjanakāya).* These forces are viewed as real entities.

The four characteristics—origination *(jāti),* subsistence *(sthiti),* decay *(jarā),* and extinction *(anityatā)*—are particularly controversial categories among the *dharmas* not concomitant with the mind.[8] In the Sarvāstivādin system, they are the forces behind the instantaneous nature of phenomena, the forces that cause the impermanence of everything. These four forces were considered to be separate entities from the phenomena they affected. Because all of the instantaneously appearing *dharmas* originated, subsisted, decayed, and became extinct at the same instant, the forces behind impermanence came to be considered as real existences in and of themselves, as forces neither mental nor material.

Forces not concomitant with the mind *(citta-viprayuktāḥ saṃskārāḥ)* are also discussed in the *Śāriputrābhidharmaśāstra* (*T* 28:547b), indicating that such *dharmas* must have been recognized by the school that produced that text. A chapter devoted to the subject is included in the *Tattvasiddhiśāstra* (*T* 32:289a), discussing approximately the same group of *dharmas* found in Sarvāstivādin sources. An important difference exists, however, in the manner in which *citta-viprayuktāḥ saṃskārāḥ* are treated in these traditions. Although the Sarvāstivādins considered these *dharmas* to be real entities *(dravya),* the author of the *Tattvasiddhiśāstra* considered them to be only expediently posited entities. According to Buddhaghosa's commentary on the *Kathāvatthu* (bk. 11, chap. 1; bk. 14, chap. 6), the Sammatīyas and the Pūrvaśailas recognized forces not concomitant with the mind. In Vasumitra's *Samaya* (*T* 49:15c, 16c), the Mahīśāsakas are said to maintain that the "nature of the proclivities *(anuśaya)* is that they are not concomitant with the mind." The Mahāsaṅghikas are said to hold the position that "the *anuśayas* are neither the mind *(citta)* nor mental faculties *(caitasika-dharma)*." Dormant passions were thus considered to be *dharmas* not concomitant with the mind by the Mahāsaṅghikas and Mahīśāsakas.

Many of the schools of Nikāya Buddhism recognized the existence of *dharmas* not concomitant with the mind. The Theravāda School, however, does not recognize them, but does include a number of *dharmas* that concern such issues as lifespan or physical qualities in their list of fifty-two mental states or faculties *(cetasika)*. Consequently, the Theravādins do not use the term "*dharmas* not concomitant with the mind." The relationship between physiology and psychology is subtle. For example, because the heartbeat is a physiological function but is easily influenced by psychological factors, the Theravādins could consider lifespan to be a mental function.

The Seventy-five *Dharmas* in Five Groups

Various types of *dharmas* or elements of existence discussed within the *abhidharma* tradition have been reviewed above. The Sarvāstivādin School classified these *dharmas* into five groups: form *(rūpa)*, mind *(citta)*, mental faculties *(caitasika)*, forces not concomitant with the mind *(citta-viprayuktāḥ-saṃskārāḥ)*, and unconditioned *dharmas (asamskṛta)*. This classification system first appears in the *Prakaraṇapāda* (*T* 26:692b). In this text, form *dharmas* are presented first. Next, the mind that takes form as an object is discussed. Third, the mental faculties that arise concomitantly with the mind are described. Fourth, the forces not concomitant with the mind are presented. These four groups are all conditioned *dharmas*. The fifth group, unconditioned *dharmas*, is contrasted with the first four. When the *Prakaraṇapāda* was compiled, this classification of the elements of existence was the clearest exposition available of the types of *dharmas*. Later, the contents of each group of *dharmas* were definitively determined in the *Abhidharmakośa* in the following manner:

1. Form: eleven *dharmas* (the five sense organs, five sense objects, and unmanifested matter)
2. The mind: one *dharma*
3. Mental functions: forty-six *dharmas* (listed earlier in the discussion of the analysis of the mind)

4. Forces not concomitant with the mind: fourteen *dharmas* (listed earlier in the discussion of this topic)
5. Unconditioned *dharmas:* three *dharmas* (analytical cessation, non-analytical cessation, space)

The classification of *dharmas* into five groups was used in India only by the Sarvāstivādins. Later in China, the Ch'eng-shih *(Tattvasiddhiśāstra)* School adopted a list of eighty-four *dharmas* divided into the same five groups (fourteen form *dharmas,* one mind, forty-nine mental faculties, seventeen forces not concomitant with the mind, and three unconditioned *dharmas*). (See the *Yuimakyōgisho anraki, Dainihon Bukkyō zensho,* vol. 5.) Chinese monks organized the *dharmas* of the *Tattvasiddhiśāstra* into a system similar to that of Sarvāstivādin texts; but nothing corresponding to this arrangement is found in the text of the *Tattvasiddhiśāstra* (*T* 1646).

No attempt to make a comprehensive list of all the *dharmas* is found in Theravāda Buddhism. In the *Abhidhammatthasaṅgaha,* lists of 89 and 121 types of consciousness, fifty-two mental faculties, and eleven and twenty-eight types of form are found; but no comprehensive list of all the *dharmas* is included. Thus, a comprehensive list of all *dharmas* would seem to be unique to the Sarvāstivādin School.

In Early Buddhism, the elements of existence were classified into groups such as the five aggregates, twelve bases, and eighteen elements, but these early classifications fell short of the needs of *abhidharma* scholars in a variety of ways. Unconditioned *dharmas* were not included in the five aggregates *(skandha).* Moreover, from the point of view of the *abhidharma* specialist, the two aggregates of sensation *(vedanā)* and perception *(saṃjñā)* could be included in the aggregate of mental formations *(saṃskāra).* Thus, the five aggregates did not provide a good model for the classification of *dharmas.* In many passages in the *Āgamas,* all existence is said to be encompassed by the twelve bases *(āyatana)* of cognition. Both conditioned and unconditioned *dharmas* are included in the twelve bases and eighteen elements *(dhātu).* However, a large number of *dharmas* such as the mental functions, forces not concomitant with the mind, and unconditioned *dharmas* are included in the one base or element of mental objects. In contrast, ten bases and ten elements are devoted to form *(rūpa).* This type of analysis is clearly out of balance and not suitable for the classification of *dharmas.* Thus, the Sarvāstivādin classification of five groups was a significant new departure in the analysis of *dharmas.*

CHAPTER 11

Buddhist Cosmology and the Theory of Karma

The Three Realms

BUDDHIST COSMOLOGY[1] has played an important role in China, Japan, and other Buddhist countries. For example, it was influential in Japan until the Meiji period (1866–1912). Modern geography and astronomy have invalidated the view of the universe drawn in traditional Buddhist works. However, since many Buddhist doctrines are illustrated through cosmology, it cannot be dismissed as irrelevant simply because its view of the physical universe is not supported by modern scholarly disciplines. The description of Buddhist cosmology in the following pages is based on the "Chapter on the World" from the *Abhidharmakośa.*

Buddhist cosmology shares many of its elements with other Indian traditions. In Vedic India, people believed that hell (Naraka, Niraya) was located beneath the earth and that the god of death, Yama, resided there. Yama was said to have originally resided in heaven but to have moved underground to hell. Buddhist thinkers adopted and systematized such views. According to Buddhist sources, there were sixteen hells, eight hot ones and eight cold ones. The surface of the earth was dominated by a huge mountain in the center called Sumeru (also known as Meru or Neru). Around Mount Sumeru were four continents—Jambudvīpa in the south (where human beings were thought to reside), Pūrvavideha in the east, Avaragodānīya in the west, and Uttarakuru in the north—surrounded by an ocean. A range of mountains around the edge of the world kept the water from spilling out. In addition, Mount Sumeru was surrounded by other mountain ranges and oceans. Altogether there were a total of eight oceans and nine mountain ranges. The last mountain range marked the outer boundaries of the world and was called the Great Iron Mountains. This system was described as a "container-world" *(bhājana-loka)* for sentient beings.

Above the world were heavens inhabited by gods and other heavenly beings. The heavens were divided into two groups: the Desire Heavens and the Form Heavens. There were six Desire Heavens. The lowest was situated on a platform on the top of Mount Sumeru and was inhabited by four heavenly kings responsible for guarding the four directions. The next heaven, in the middle of the platform, was the abode of the thirty-three Vedic gods. The four remaining heavens floated above the top of Mount Sumeru. Beginning with the lowest they were as follows:

1. Yāmānāṃ sthānam—heaven of Yama
2. Tuṣita—Heaven where future Buddhas reside before their final birth
3. Nirmāṇa-rataya—Heaven where beings create their own objects of pleasure
4. Para-nirmita-vaśa-vartin—Highest Desire Heaven (The pleasures of all the other Desire Heavens can be enjoyed from this heaven.)

The heavens of the form realm were divided into Four Meditation *(dhyāna)* Heavens, with the Fourth Meditation Heaven occupying the highest place. The Four Meditation Heavens were, in turn, subdivided into seventeen heavens as follows:

First Meditation Heavens
1. Brahmakāyika—Heaven of Brahmā's followers
2. Brahmapurohita—Heaven of Brahmā's retainers
3. Mahābrahman—Heaven of Brahmā himself

Second Meditation Heavens
1. Parīttābhā—Heaven of lesser light
2. Apramāṇābha—Heaven of unlimited light
3. Ābhāsvara—Heaven of universal light

Third Meditation Heavens
1. Parīttaśubha—Heaven of lesser purity
2. Apramāṇaśubha—Heaven of unlimited purity
3. Śubhakṛtsna—Heaven of universal purity

Fourth Meditation Heavens

1. Anabhraka—The cloudless heaven
2. Puṇyaprasava—Heaven where the fortunate are born
3. Bṛhatphala—Heaven where worldlings with great deeds are born
4. Avṛha—Heaven for the rebirth of the sage without passions
5. Atapa—Heaven without the heat of passion
6. Sudṛśa—Heaven of perfect manifestation
7. Sudarśana—Heaven of perfect vision
8. Akaniṣṭha—Highest (form) heaven

Variations in the list of heavens exist. The Sarvāstivādin School of Kashmir maintained that the heaven of Brahmā's ministers and the heaven of Brahmā himself should be combined since the ministers were Brahmā's retainers, thus making sixteen heavens. The Sarvāstivādin teachers in the west argued in favor of the list of seventeen Form Heavens. The Sautrāntika School claimed that there were eighteen Form Heavens. In the *Shih-chi ching* of the *Ch'ang a-han ching* (*T* 1, *Dīrghāgama*), a text that was probably used in the Dharmaguptaka School, the names of twenty-two heavens in the form realm are listed. The twenty-two Form Heavens are also mentioned in the *Śāriputrābhidharmaśāstra* (*T* 28:601c). Although differences existed between the positions held by various schools, all of them agreed that the highest heaven of the form realm was called Akaniṣṭha. In the Mahāyāna tradition, the heaven was also known as the peak or *bhavāgra* (Ogihara, *Bonwa daijiten,* s.v. *akaniṣṭha*).

The formless realm *(ārūpya-dhātu)* was a world without bodies or places, a spiritual realm consisting of four levels: unlimited space, unlimited consciousness, nothingness, and neither perception nor nonperception.

The desire, form, and formless realms collectively were called the three realms. They made up the world where sentient beings were reborn. In the desire realm, sexual differences were present. Consequently, it was a realm with sexual and other desires. Struggles over material objects led to desire, anger, and fights. Since Vedic times the gods have been considered to be differentiated sexually, and stories have been told of their jealousies and battles. The Buddhists incorporated these gods into their cosmology and placed them in such places as the Heaven of the Thirty-three (Trāyāstriṃśa), one of the six Desire Heavens. Of the gods, only Brahmā resided in a heaven of the form realm, the First Meditation Heaven. Brahmā received this honor because the meditations on the four unlimited minds *(catvāry apramāṇāni)*—amity, compassion, sympathetic joy, and equanimity—were also called the four *brahma-vihāras* (abodes of Brahmā). They were considered to be practices that might result in rebirth in Brahmā's heaven. Because Brahmā's heaven was so closely connected with these meditations, Brahmā was said to reside in the First Meditation Heaven.

The Four Meditation Heavens were worlds modeled after meditations. If a practitioner meditated and attained one of the four meditations, but died without attaining enlightenment, then he could not enter *nirvāṇa;* he would, however, be reborn in a heaven that corresponded to the meditation he had attained, not in a bad destiny. Because a person experienced physical happiness or bliss in meditation, his rebirth was said to be in the form realm, where he would have a body with which to experience bliss. However, while he was deep in meditation, he would experience neither hunger nor sexual desire and would not perceive the outside world. No conflicts or any other type of interaction with other people would occur. Consequently, in the form realm no sexual distinctions existed. Food was unnecessary and anger unknown. Buddhist descriptions of the inhabitants of the Meditation Heavens thus reflected the experiences of people in deep meditation. As an individual rose to higher levels in the form realm, his body became larger and his lifespan longer.

A complex system of hot and cold hells was located under the earth. The hells, the four great continents, the sun and moon, the six Desire Heavens, and Brahmā's heaven together made up one world. The world itself floated in space, where it was supported by circles of various substances. Directly beneath the world was a circle of metal. This circle rested on a circle of water that, in turn, rested on a circle of wind *(vāyu-maṇḍala),* a whirlwind of air that kept the system floating in space. Countless numbers of such worlds existed floating in space. One thousand worlds made up one small chiliocosm. One thousand small chiliocosms made up one middle chiliocosm, and one thousand middle chiliocosms made up one great chiliocosm. A Buddha could preach through one great chiliocosm. Sārvastivādins believed that two or more Buddhas would never appear at the same time in the same great chiliocosm. Since the Buddhas had finite lifespans and their teachings lasted only a limited time, past Buddhas had appeared before Śākyamuni Buddha, and in the future, Maitreya Buddha was expected to appear.

Since many great chiliocosms existed simultaneously throughout the universe, monks began to consider the problem of whether a number of Buddhas could appear at the same time. The Sārvastivādins denied that many Buddhas could appear at the same time, but the Mahāsaṅghikas argued that many Buddhas might appear at the same time in different regions of the universe. This issue is discussed in the *Kathāvatthu.* In the *Mahāvastu,* the position is maintained that many Buddhas might appear at the same time in various parts of the universe.

A description of the universe similar to the above account is found in several *sūtras,* including the *Shih-chi ching* in the *Ch'ang a-han ching* (*T* 1, *Dīrghāgama*), the *Ta lou-t'an ching* (*T* 23, *Lokasthāna*?), and the *Ch'i-shih yin-pen ching* (*T* 25). Cosmological theory was developed further in *abhidharma* works such as the *Li shih a-p'i-t'an lun* (*T* 1644, *Lokaprajñaptyabhidharma*?). These theories were systematized in Sarvāstivādin texts such as the *Mahāvibhāṣā* (*T* 1545) and the *Abhidharmakośa* (*T* 1558). In addition, a number of doctrinal differences were found in the cosmological theories of the various schools of Nikāya Buddhism.

The Jainas presented a view of the universe that differed in many ways from Buddhism. Hindu theories about the universe were developed further in the *Purāṇas.* These sources can be compared with those from the Buddhist tradition.

The Destruction and Formation of the World

Since even the world is impermanent, it eventually must decay. All the worlds in a great chiliocosm are produced at the same time. Likewise, the destruction of all the worlds of a great chiliocosm occurs at the same time. The destructive process begins with the development of morally good minds in sentient beings. After a long time, the sentient beings in the hells are all reborn in higher realms. The hells, emptied of all sentient beings, would serve no purpose. The destruction of a world thus begins with the hells. After a time, animals and then men are reborn in the heavens and the earth is emptied. The three calamities (disasters brought about by wind, fire, and water) begin to destroy the world through storms, fires, and floods. Eventually the world and heavens up to and including Brahmā's heaven are destroyed.

The physical world is called the "container-world" because it contains sentient beings and depends upon the collective karma of those sentient beings for its maintenance. If those sentient beings cease to exist in the container-world, the karmic forces that hold matter together vanish, and the world decays into atoms that float in space. The period from beginning to end during which the world is destroyed is called the Period of Destruction; it lasts twenty eons *(kalpas).* Next is a Period of Emptiness, in which matter floats in space as atoms; it, too, lasts twenty eons. Finally, the sentient beings reborn in the Second Meditation Heaven and above begin exhausting the good karma that led to their rebirths in heaven. Their karma matures, causing their rebirth in the First Meditation Heaven (Brahmā-heaven) and below. This karma causes a great wind that becomes the circle of wind on which the world will rest. The container-world is progressively formed during the Period of Formation, which lasts twenty eons. It is followed by a Period of Maintenance that also lasts twenty eons, during which the world is maintained. Then the world decays again. The universe continues in this fashion forever, repeating the stages of formation, maintenance, destruction, and emptiness.

Rebirth

Sentient beings repeat the cycles of life and death *(saṃsāra)* within the world described above. The following five destinies *(gati)* or births are open to a sentient being: denizen of hell *(naraka, niraya),* hungry ghost *(preta),* animal *(tiryañc),* human being *(manuṣya),* or god *(deva).* Needless to say, rebirth in hell would involve the most suffering and rebirth in heaven would be the most pleasant. Some schools of Buddhism recognize a sixth destiny, the *asuras* or demons who constantly fight with the gods for control of heaven. According to the *Mahāvibhāṣā* (*T* 27:868b), the Sarvāstivādin School recognized only five destinies and criticized the positions of schools that maintained that there were six destinies as contradicting the *sūtras.* According to the *Kathāvatthu* (bk. 8, sec. 1), the Theravāda School also recognized only five destinies. In his commentary on the *Kathāvatthu,* Buddhaghosa identified the schools that recognized six destinies as the Andhakas and the Uttarāpathakas, both of Mahāsaṅghika lineage. In the *Ta-chih-tu lun* (*T* 25:135c, *Mahāprajñāpāramitopadeśa*), the Vātsīputrīya School is said to maintain that there are six destinies. Because the *Ta-chih-tu lun* also follows the six-destiny doctrine, the six-destiny doctrine is generally held to be the orthodox position in China and Japan although most of Nikāya Buddhism adopted the five-destiny theory.

Sentient beings may be born in four different ways. Birds and reptiles are born from eggs, animals from wombs, insects from moisture, and the gods through transformation. A sentient being's life cycle is divided into four stages: birth, the time between birth and death, death, and the time between death and the next birth *(antarābhava).* During the period between death and the next birth, a being is said to exist as a spirit composed of subtle types of the five *skandhas* (aggregates). It is called a *gandharva* and must wander and search for the place of its next birth.

The Sarvāstivādin School recognized the existence of the *antarābhava;*

however, the majority of the schools of Nikāya Buddhism argued against the recognition of a state between lives. The *antarābhava* is rejected in the *Kathāvatthu* (bk. 8, sec. 2). In his commentary on the *Kathāvatthu,* Buddhaghosa stated that the Saṃmitīya and the Pubbaseliya schools accepted the existence of the *gandharva.* According to the *Mahāvibhāṣā* (*T* 27:356c), the Discriminators rejected it. The Mahīśāsakas are also said to have rejected it. The *Samayabhedoparacanacakra* (*T* 2013) lists the Mahāsaṅghika, Ekavyavahārika, Lokottaravādin, and Kaukuṭika as schools that do not recognize *gandharvas.* In the *Śāriputrābhidharmaśāstra* (*T* 28:608a), the existence of the *antarābhava* is denied. In the *Tattvasiddhiśāstra* (*T* 32:256b–c), arguments both for and against the doctrine are presented. The status of the *antarābhava* apparently inspired considerable controversy among the schools of Nikāya Buddhism.

The instant when the *antarābhava* enters the mother's womb is called *pratisaṃdhi.* It corresponds to the third link, namely consciousness, in the twelve-link doctrine of Dependent Origination. Five stages in the development of the fetus in the mother's womb *(pañca garbha-avasthāḥ)* are enumerated: *kalala* (first week of development), *arbuda* (second week), *peśin* (third week), *ghana* (fourth week), and *praśākhā* (the thirty-four weeks extending from the fifth week until birth). Five stages of development after birth *(pañca jāta-avasthāḥ)* are also enumerated: infant or toddler (birth to five years old), childhood (six to fourteen years), youth (fifteen to twenty-nine years), mature adulthood (thirty to thirty-nine years), old age (above forty years until death). In this manner, cycles of birth, life, death, and *antarābhava* repeat. No beginning of the cycles exists.

Rebirth and Karma Interpreted through the Twelve Links of Dependent Origination

The function of karma in rebirth can be explained using the twelve links of Dependent Origination. The first two links, ignorance *(avidyā)* and mental formations *(saṃskāra),* relate how the past actions in a person's previous lives affect his present situation. Ignorance concerns the defilements that a person had in the past *(pūrva-kleśa).* Mental formations represent the karma resulting from the good and bad actions of a person in the past *(pūrva-karman)* that determine many aspects of his present life. The third link, consciousness *(vijñāna),* represents the consciousness that enters a mother's womb at the beginning of a person's present life. The other aggregates are also present in very subtle forms at this moment, but since consciousness is the dominant aggregate, it is used to represent this stage in a person's life. This method of explanation of Dependent Origination in which the links are classified according to a time or stage in a person's life is called the *āvasthika* interpretation. In this type of exegesis, the dominant aggregate during a particular stage is sometimes singled out for emphasis.

The fourth link, name and form *(nāmarūpa),* corresponds to the fetus growing in the mother's womb and the development of its body and mind. The completion of the fetus's sense organs corresponds to the fifth link, the six sense organs *(ṣaḍāyatana).* The child from birth until one or two years of age is equated with the sixth link, contact *(sparśa)* between sense organ and object. The sense organs, objects, and consciousness are all present, but the infant still cannot properly discriminate between suffering and pleasure. The stage at which a child is able to differentiate between suffering and pleasure but does not yet have any sexual desires corresponds to the seventh link, sensation *(vedanā).* The emergence of sexual lust corresponds to the eighth link, desire *(tṛṣṇā).* Striving for fame and fortune is represented by the ninth link, grasping *(upādāna).* A person thus accumulates karma that will bear fruit in the future. This stage corresponds to the tenth link, becoming *(bhava).*

The links of desire and grasping in the present are similar to the link of ignorance of the past, since all result in the formation of karma. In a similar way, the link of becoming in the present is similar to the link of mental formations in the past, since both can be equated with karma. The third through the tenth links are all explained as referring to a person's present life. The five links from consciousness to sensation are called the five fruits of the present, which were caused by actions of the past. The three links of desire, grasping, and becoming are called the three present causes, which will bear fruit in the future.

A person's future birth is determined by the three present causes. Future births are represented by the eleventh link, birth *(jāti).* Thus, *jāti* is similar to consciousness at the moment of conception in the present life, in other words to the third link, consciousness. The result of future birth is old age and death *(jarāmaraṇa),* the twelfth link. It corresponds to the links of name and form through sensation in the present life.

When the twelve links are distributed among three lifetimes, two links concern past causes, five links present effects, three links present causes, and two links future effects. The cycle of cause and effect is repeated twice. Consequently this explanation is referred to as "the two cycles of cause and effect over the three time periods."

Ignorance, desire, and clinging are all defilements *(kleśa).* The karma arising from these defilements is represented by the links of mental formations and becoming. The phenomena *(vastu)* arising from karma are represented by the remaining links, from consciousness to sensation and birth, old age, and death. Thus phenomena arise from karma. Later, those same phenomena serve as the basis for additional karma. The twelve links of Dependent Origination thus illustrate how existence can be characterized as endless cycles of defilement, karma, and phenomena. Moreover, since phenomena are characterized by suffering, these cycles may also be characterized as defilement, karma, and suffering. In this manner, the twelve links may be explained as an illustration of karmic cause and effect.

The above description has been called an "embryological interpretation" by some modern scholars because of its emphasis on the physical development of an individual. Although this explanation probably departed from the original intent of the teaching of the twelve links, it eventually became very influential because it linked rebirth with Dependent Origination. The Sarvāstivādin School stressed it (*Abhidharmakośa, T* 29:48a). It also appears in Theravāda texts. Buddhaghosa explained it along with a number of other interpretations of Dependent Origination (*Visuddhimagga,* chap. 17, sec. 284; Harvard Oriental Series, vol. 41, p. 495).

The Four Interpretations of Dependent Origination

Sarvāstivādins used the twelve links of Dependent Origination to explain rebirth and karma. However, they did not ignore other types of explanations. Four interpretations are discussed in the *Chü-she lun* (*T* 29:48c; *Abhidharmakośabhāṣya,* p. 132, ll. 24ff.): instantaneous *(kṣaṇika),* prolonged *(prākarṣika),* serial *(sāṃbandhika),* and a set of stages *(āvasthika).* According to the interpretation of Dependent Origination as instantaneous, all twelve links are present in the five aggregates at the same instant. This explanation stresses the interdependence and simultaneous existence of the twelve links.

The second explanation, the interpretation of Dependent Origination over a prolonged period of time, concerns the causal relationships between *dharmas,* which arise at different and sometimes widely separate times. The third interpretation, serial, concerns the manner in which the twelve links instantaneously arise and cease in continuous series. In the fourth interpretation, Dependent Origination as a set of stages, each link is considered to represent a stage in the processes of rebirth and karma.

The Six Causes *(Hetu)*, Four Conditions *(Pratyaya)*, and Five Effects *(Phala)*

In their discussions of Dependent Origination *(pratītyasamutpāda),* the Sarvāstivādins analyzed causation into six causes, four conditions, and five fruits (or effects). The four conditions are said to have been first preached by the Buddha and to have appeared in the *Āgamas,* but are not found in the extant versions of the *Āgamas.* A list of ten conditions appears in the *Śāriputrābhidharmaśāstra* (*T* 28:679b–c), in which the Sarvāstivādin four conditions are included. The four conditions are also included in the list of twenty-four conditions found in the Theravāda *abhidhamma* text the *Paṭṭhāna* (p. 1ff., section on Conditional relations). Thus it appears that the Sarvāstivādin doctrine of the four conditions probably arose out of the early studies of conditions *(pratyaya)* conducted by the schools of Nikāya Buddhism. In the Sarvāstivādin tradition, the four conditions are first mentioned in the *Vijñānakāyapādaśāstra* (*T* 26: 547b) and later in the *Mahāvibhāṣā* (*T* 1545) and the *Abhidharmakośa* (*T* 1558).

In contrast, the doctrine of six root causes *(hetu)* appeared later and was discussed for the first time in the *Jñānaprasthāna* (*T* 26:920b). Consequently the six root causes are unique to the Sarvāstivādin School. These doctrines are explained below in accordance with the *Abhidharmakośa* (*T* 29:30a).

The Sarvāstivādins explained existence by classifying it into seventy-five *dharmas.* Cause and effect were discussed mainly in terms of the seventy-two conditioned *dharmas* that function as causes. Thus, the Sarvāstivādins considered Dependent Origination itself to be conditioned (in contrast to some other schools in which it was considered to be an unconditioned *dharma*). The causal characteristics of *dharmas* have been compared to water behind a dam. The water has the potential to produce electricity as it flows over the dam, but once it flows over the dam it loses that potential. In the same way existents *(dharmas)* will have different potentials depending upon their position. For the Sarvāstivādins, root causes describe the potential or power of *dharmas,* not the relations between *dharmas.* The Sarvāstivādins classified the causal potential of *dharmas* (which is different from the intrinsic nature of *dharmas*) into six categories: cause that serves as the reason of being *(kāraṇahetu),* simultaneous cause *(sahabhūhetu),* homogeneous cause *(sabhāgahetu),* concomitant cause *(saṃprayuktakahetu),* universal cause *(sarvatragahetu),* and cause of fruition *(vipākahetu).*

The first category, *kāraṇahetu* (cause as the reason of being), refers to cause in its broadest sense. For any single *dharma,* all other *dharmas* serve as *kāraṇahetu.* In other words, all other *dharmas* assist in the production of any given *dharma.* Even if they do not function in a positive way, they are said to help because they do not prevent the arising of the *dharma* in question; this type of root cause is called a powerless *kāraṇahetu.* Even unconditioned *dharmas* have this characteristic, since they do not prevent the arising of conditioned *dharmas. Dharmas* that have the positive potential to produce other *dharmas* are said to be "empowered" *kāraṇahetu.*

The second category, *sahabhūhetu* (simultaneous cause), refers to *dharmas* that simultaneously serve as the cause and effect of each other. They are interdependent. For example, the four elements (earth, water, fire, and wind) must all arise simultaneously in a molecule. If one is missing, the others cannot arise. Thus they serve as auxiliary causes for each other. Two explanations of simultaneous cause were advanced in which the concept was explained by using the model of a tripod. In the first explanation, the term refers to the relationship among the three legs. Each leg is a simultaneous cause for the other two (Ch. *chü-yu-yin hu-i-kuo*). According to the second explanation, the three legs are called simultaneous causes because they cooperate in supporting something separate from themselves, the effect (Ch. *chü-yu-yin t'ung-i-kuo*).

The third category, *sabhāgahetu* (homogeneous cause), refers to the manner in which a good cause leads to a good result or a bad cause leads to a bad result. In this case, *dharmas* of a particular type would be the cause for the arising of other *dharmas* of that same type. A homogeneous cause gives rise to a concordant effect *(niṣyanda-phala).*

The fourth category, *saṃprayuktakahetu* (concomitant cause), is descriptive of the concomitant relationship between the mind *(citta)* and mental faculties *(caitasika).* It is not used to describe the relationship between *dharmas* of matter or material objects. Concomitance refers to five ways in which the mind and mental faculties correspond: they depend on the same sense organs, they have the same sense object, they take the same aspect of that object, they function at the same time, and they harmoniously act to produce one type of thought (that is, they have the same essence). Because the concomitant cause describes the simultaneous and mutual relationship between the mind and mental functions, it is considered to be a special instance of cause as the reason of being *(kāraṇahetu).*

The fifth category, *sarvatragahetu* (universal cause), is descriptive of a special instance of homogeneous cause. In this case, a particularly powerful type of defilement, universal proclivity *(sarvatragānuśaya),* influences the mind and the mental defilements in its own sphere *(bhūmi),* including all the defilements, regardless of which of the Four Noble Truths or meditation might be used to eliminate them. Universal causes thus taint both the mind and mental faculties. Eleven types of such defilements exist. The *sarvatragahetu* concerns causes and effects that arise at different times.

The sixth category, *vipākahetu* (cause of fruition), refers to the case in which cause and effect are of different types. For example, a good cause may produce a pleasant effect. A bad cause may produce suffering or unhappiness. Thus a good or bad fruitional cause leads to a fruit of retribution *(vipākaphala)* that is pleasant, unpleasant, or neutral. The cause of fruition differs from the homogeneous cause *(sabhāgahetu),* in which the cause and effect are similar. Through these two categories of cause, the moral law of cause and effect is explained. For example, a good *dharma* would have the potential to give rise to another good *dharma* and thus act as a homogeneous cause or to give rise to pleasure and thus act as a cause of fruition. In the latter case, pleasure (or suffering) is not considered to be good (or bad) and thus the cause is said to differ from the effect.

Five effects or fruits *(phala)* relating to the six causes are described: fruit of retribution *(vipākaphala),* dominant effect *(adhipatiphala),* concordant effect *(niṣyandaphala),* anthropomorphic effect *(puruṣakāraphala),* and separative effect *(visaṃyogaphala).* The fruit of retribution is the result of the cause of retribution. The dominant effect is the result of the aggregate of causes as reasons of being *(kāraṇahetu).* Homogeneous *(sabhāgahetu)* and universal causes *(sarvatragahetu)* both result in concordant effects *(niṣyandaphala).* In other words, the cause and effect are similar. Simultaneous *(sahabhūhetu)* and concomitant causes *(saṃprayuktakahetu)* both result in anthropomorphic effects *(puruṣakāraphala).* The term "*puruṣakāra*" literally means "human activity," but in this case, it is interpreted as referring to the way in which *dharmas* can simultaneously be both causes and effects of each other. However, if the term *puruṣakāraphala* is interpreted literally as the "effects of human activity," then dominant and concordant effects could also be said to be varieties of *puruṣakāraphala.*

The above four effects can be matched up with all of the six causes. However, the Sarvāstivādins recognized a fifth effect, a separative effect *(visaṃyogaphala).* This effect is identified with enlightenment, that is, with cessation through analysis *(pratisaṅkhyā-nirodha)* and *nirvāṇa.* It is realized through religious practice. However, since *pratisaṅkhyā-nirodha* is an unconditioned *dharma,* it cannot be produced by conditioned *dharmas.* Yet because *nirvāṇa* is realized through practice, *pratisaṅkhyā-nirodha* is categorized as an effect without a cause. Religious practice could be classified as a cause in the sense of functioning as a reason for being *(kāraṇahetu),* but the Sarvāstivādins did not recognize the possibility of a conditioned *dharma* serving as the cause of an unconditioned *dharma.* Consequently, separative effect was said to have no cause.

In addition to the list of six types of cause, the Sarvāstivādins had another list of five aspects of cause, which described the relationship between the four elements and secondary matter *(bhautika).* The elements were said to be the causes of the origin, transformation, support, duration, and development of *bhautika* matter. In the previously discussed system of six causes, these five aspects would all be classified under the category of cause as a reason for being *(kāraṇahetu).*

The Sarvāstivādins sometimes added four more effects to the five discussed earlier, making a total of nine. The four additional effects are effect depending on a base, as trees depend on the earth *(pratiṣṭhāphala);* effect arising from the religious practices of a worldling *(prayogaphala);* effect arising from the harmonious activity of a number of causes *(sāmagrīphala);* and effect arising from meditation while on the path for nobles *(bhāvanāphala).*

The four conditions *(pratyaya)* are causal condition *(hetupratyaya),* immediately preceding condition *(samanantarapratyaya),* condition of the observed object *(ālambanapratyaya),* and predominant condition *(adhipatipratyaya).* The category of causal condition encompasses all of the six causes except cause as a reason of being. Immediately preceding conditions refer only to the mind and mental functions, not to material things. In the stream of continually arising *dharmas* of mind and mental functions, the *dharmas* of one instant must cease before the *dharmas* of the next moment can arise. Only after a "place" exists for these *dharmas* can they appear. Thus the *dharmas* of the preceding instant are called the "immediately preceding condition." The third category, the condition of the observed object, refers to objects of perception. For example, for eye-consciousness and its concomitant mental faculties, all forms function as conditions of the observed object. In a similar manner, for ear-consciousness and its concomitant mental faculties, all sounds serve as conditions of the observed object. The fourth category, predominant condition, is identical to cause as a reason for being.

The relationships among the six causes, four conditions and five effects are diagrammed in Figure 4.

Only the causal and predominant conditions are concompassed by the six causes. Consequently, the four conditions cover a broader range than the six causes. In the *Śāriputrābhidharmaśāstra* (*T* 28:679), the following ten types of conditions are enumerated.

Figure 4. Relationships among the Six Causes, Four Conditions, and Five Effects

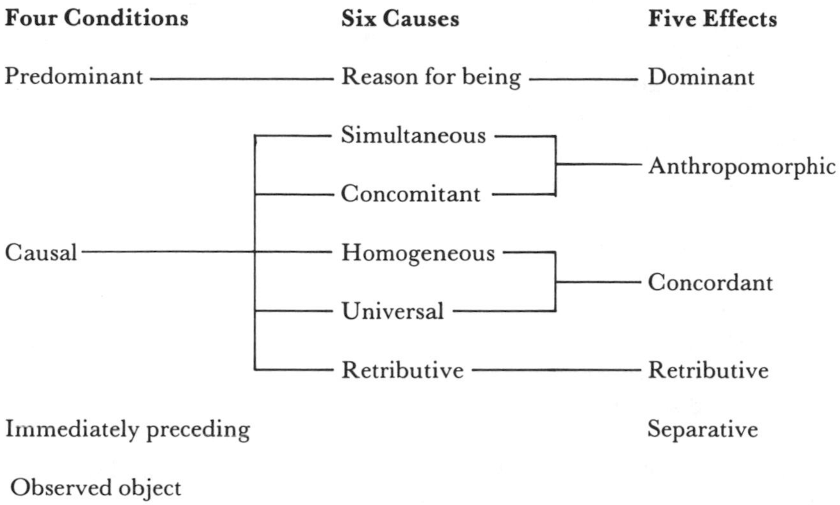

1. Causal *(hetu-pratyaya)*
2. Proximity *(anantara-pratyaya)*
3. Object of cognition *(ālambana-pratyaya)*
4. Dependence *(niśraya-pratyaya)*
5. Karmic *(karma-pratyaya)*
6. Retribution or fruition *(vipāka-pratyaya)*
7. Conascence *(sahajāta-pratyaya)*
8. Differentiation *(anyonya-pratyaya)*
9. Repetition *(āsevana-pratyaya)*
10. Predominance *(adhipati-pratyaya)*

In the Theravāda *abhidhamma* text *Paṭṭhāna* (p. 1f., Conditional relations), the following twenty-four types of conditions are enumerated.

1. Cause *(hetu)*
2. Object *(ārammaṇa)*
3. Predominance *(adhipati)*
4. Proximity *(anantara)*
5. Contiguity *(samanantara)*
6. Conascence *(sahajāta)*
7. Mutuality *(aññamañña)*
8. Dependence *(nissaya)*

9. Strong dependence *(upanissaya)*
10. Prenascence *(purejāta)*
11. Postnascence *(pacchājāta)*
12. Repetition *(āsevana)*
13. Karma *(kamma)*
14. Retribution *(vipāka)*
15. Nutriment *(āhāra)*
16. Faculty *(indriya)*
17. Meditation *(jhāna)*
18. Path *(magga)*
19. Association *(sampayutta)*
20. Dissociation *(vippayutta)*
21. Presence *(atthi)*
22. Absence *(natthi)*
23. Disappearance *(vigata)*
24. Nondisappearance *(avigata)*

The lists of four, ten, and twenty-four types of conditions and the list of six types of causes have many elements in common.

In conclusion, in order to use the twelve links of Dependent Origination to explain the circumstances of rebirth, the schools of Nikāya Buddhism devised an explanation that distributed the twelve links over the past, present, and future in two cycles of cause and effect. In addition, they analyzed the various conditions that might affect Dependent Origination and compiled lists like those above. But they may have become so engrossed in analysis that they lost sight of the overall significance of the doctrine of Dependent Origination.

CHAPTER 12

Karma and Avijñapti-rūpa

Dharmas and Karma

To a large extent, *abhidharma* thought is a systematization of the doctrine of karma (S. *karman;* P. *kamma*).[1] Since Buddhism does not recognize the existence of a creator god, Buddhist thinkers often employ the doctrine of karma to explain the creation of the world. However, it should be noted that *dharma,* not karma, is the most basic concept in Buddhism. The Buddha (the enlightened one) attained enlightenment by understanding *dharmas.* The world and its inhabitants are composed of *dharmas.* Moreover, since individual existences can be explained by referring to *dharmas,* people are said to have no real and substantive identity apart from *dharmas.* Consequently, Buddhists advocate a no-Self *(anātman)* doctrine. Once a person has understood *dharma* theory, the view that he is a substantive entity separate from other existences vanishes. The world of *dharmas* is a world of causal connections where everything is interrelated. The self is only a provisionally recognized, constantly changing entity, dependent upon other existences.

Since the world is composed of *dharmas,* even gods are composed of *dharmas.* Consequently, Buddhism has no place for a creator god who transcends *dharmas.* Although all existence is composed of *dharmas,* the ordinary person *(pṛthagjana)* mistakenly clings to the view that he is an independent, substantive entity. He believes that he is separate from others and bases his actions on that wrong view. He grows attached to those things that he perceives as his own and develops rivalries with other people. Arguments arise as he becomes proud of himself and jealous of others. He covets more and more material things. These defilements *(kleśa)* are all based upon a fundamental ignorance *(moha)* of *dharmas* and causation.

Although a person does not have a permanent and real Self, he still clings to the idea of a Self. The ordinary person's actions are profoundly influenced by this misconception. Although no Self actually exists, the psychological attitudes based on clinging to the idea of a Self are real. Theft and murder are committed because of such attitudes. If a person commits murder, he may then fear retaliation or punishment, and his psychological attitudes such as fear and guilt will also be real. Thus, the psychological states based on the concept of a Self, such as coveting things, fearing retaliation, or feeling guilty, all bring about results that are somehow appropriate to those attitudes. Even though no real Self exists, the relationship between actions and their consequences is established as if there were a Self. The world of *dharmas* is transformed into a world of karma.

From the point of view of absolute truth no Self exists, yet a world governed by karmic cause and effect based on misconceptions about such Selves is established. With enlightenment, however, that world vanishes. Consequently, the Dārṣṭāntikas argued that even the karma that would plunge one into deepest hell could be transformed. In other words, the karmic consequences of even the most heinous acts, such as patricide or matricide, could be obviated. Such a belief was based on the understanding that karma was essentially nonsubstantial. However, the ordinary person could not completely deny the effects of karma just as he could not readily eliminate his tendency to cling to the idea of a Self even though he tried to do so. For the ordinary person, a denial of karma would be tantamount to nihilism.

The Three Types of Action

The original meaning of "karma" is "action." In the *Mahāvibhāṣā* (*T* 27:587b), three definitions of karma are distinguished. The first is "action," karma in its broadest sense. The second meaning is "ritual." Included in this usage are the administrative procedures of the Buddhist order. If a part of an administrative procedure is omitted or if the proper order is not followed, an administrative action or ritual is rendered invalid. Since rituals and administrative action are particularly important types of actions, they are chosen for special treatment in Buddhist thought. East Asian Buddhist texts distinguish between these two uses of the term karma by using different characters to write them even though the original Sanskrit term in both cases is the same. Karma as ritual action is transliterated into Chinese as *chieh-mo* and read in Japanese as either *katsuma* or *konma.* The Chinese character *yeh* (Japanese reading *gō*) is used to refer to karma in its broader sense as action.

The third meaning concerns the results of actions. Good and bad actions entail results or fruits. In this case karma refers to those fruits. A force that cannot be perceived remains after a good or bad action has been completed. That force is also called karma. For example, the words of even the most solemn promise vanish after an instant. When a person is killed, the act of killing quickly ends. Although various pieces of evidence of the killing may remain, that evidence is different from the act itself. And the evidence will also vanish eventually. Yet even after the action has ended, a force that cannot be perceived remains. Although the moment it takes to make a promise quickly passes, a person may still feel responsible for fulfilling that promise even after many years have passed. After a person has been killed, the guilt or responsibility for the death may follow the killer for years. Thus, although an action is quickly completed, the force of that action continues. In a similar way, actions may have long-term legal or economic consequences, but for Buddhists it is the moral force of the action that is called karma. Buddhists were particularly interested in the further analysis of this type of karma.

The Origins of the Theory of Karma

The theory that good and bad actions affect a person in the future appears in the early *Upaniṣads.* In the *Bṛhadāraṇyaka Upaniṣad* (III.2.13), a man is said to "become a good man through good action and a bad man through bad action." In the *Chāndogya Upaniṣad* (V.10.7) a person is said to be reborn through a good womb through good conduct *(caraṇa)* and a bad womb through bad conduct. Both of these statements are representative of theories that accept the karmic effects of actions. However, theories of karma in India were still in a state of flux during the period when the Buddha appeared, and many other explanations of karma were being advanced.

A variety of theories of karma is found in the *Āgamas.* The Buddha is said to have been a proponent of karma. According to the *Aṅguttara Nikāya* (vol. 1, p. 287), "The Buddha is an advocate of karma *(kammvādin),* an advocate of the position that actions have effects *(kiriyavādin),* and an advocate of concerted action *(viriyavādin).*" The acknowledgment of karma is directly related to spiritual endeavor, since religious endeavor is usually based on the recognition of free will. The view that a person receives the fruits of his actions is possible only if he has a free will. Beliefs that man's destiny is determined by the gods or by fate or is a matter of chance leave no room for free will. A person cannot be held responsible for his actions according to such theories.

If karma is interpreted in a very mechanical manner, it, too, can be seen as a fatalistic teaching. Fatalistic interpretations of karma were advocated by a number of non-Buddhist groups. Buddhists, by interpreting karma through the teaching of Dependent Origination, affirmed free will and the value of religious practice. If the Self is considered to be a permanent and substantial entity, then it cannot change and cannot be affected by the fruits of a person's actions. If the causal relations that affect a person are not acknowledged, then the causal laws governing karma also cannot be recognized. Consequently, Buddhists applied the Middle Way between annihilationist and eternalist positions and their teachings concerning Dependent Origination to karma and thereby refuted fatalistic theories of karma.

During the time of the Buddha, most of the Six Heretical Teachers denied the efficacy of karma. Although the Jaina teacher Mahāvīra recognized the efficacy of karma, he emphasized its results by focusing on the three punishments *(daṇḍa)* for physical, verbal, and mental bad actions. In contrast, the Buddha emphasized the motive behind an action in his theory of karma. Instead of the three punishments, he discussed the three types of karma (physical, verbal, and mental) and emphasized mental karma in particular. A large number of teachings concerning karma is found in the *Āgamas.* Many of these stress the inevitable repercussions of a person's actions, as is illustrated by the following passage from the *Fa-chü ching* (*T* 4:565a, *Dharmapada*): "There is no place where one can flee from bad karma."

Only a few passages concerning karma are found in the *Suttanipāta,* but the following is significant for its use of the term *"vipāka":* "The wise who perceive dependent origination correctly understand action and its differently maturing *(vipāka)* fruit" (v. 653). The term *"vipāka"* may be translated "fruitional" or "maturing." However, since the term has the prefix *"vi,"* meaning "different," it came to mean "differently maturing" and was thus translated *i-shu* in Chinese. While karma (the action or cause) is good or bad, its result is pleasure or suffering. The results of karma are neutral in the sense that they are neither good nor bad. The results of karma are thus said to mature in a way that makes them qualitatively different from their karmic causes. Later, during the period when *abhidharma* treatises were being compiled, the relationship between good and bad causes and morally neutral results was codified through rules concerning "differently maturing cause and effect" *(vipāka-hetu, vipāka-phala).* The term *vipāka* is found frequently in the *Āgamas.*

In addition, early in Buddhism good karma was said to bring a good result and bad karma to bring a bad result. In *abhidharma* treatises this relationship was described as homogeneous cause *(sabhāga-hetu)* and concordant effect *(niṣyanda-phala).* Early texts also stated that good actions led to fortune while bad actions led to misfortune. Pleasure and suffering are the psychological equivalent of fortune and misfortune. Terms such as "meritorious *(puṇya)* karma" and "merit" appear frequently in the *Āgamas.* The terms "white karma" *(śuklakarman)* and "black karma" *(kṛṣṇakarman)* were sometimes used in the *Āgamas* to refer to good and bad actions.

The Nature of Karma

Theravāda teachings on karma are organized and explained in Buddhaghosa's *Atthasālinī* (chap. 3, ll. 92–136). Sarvāstivādin theories of karma are presented in detail in the chapter on karma of the *Abhidharmakośa.*

In Buddhism, actions are generally divided into three categories: physical, verbal, and mental. Of these three, mental actions consist solely of mental constituents. In contrast, physical and verbal actions consist of a mixture of mental constituents, such as the motive and decision to do something, and verbal or physical constituents, such as calling out with the voice or movements of the body. Because both physical and mental constituents play roles in karma, *abhidharma* scholars devoted considerable energy to determining whether the essential nature of karma was mental or physical.

According to the Theravāda School, the essence of all three types of action is volition *(cetanā). Cetanā* is explained as the power to create a type of consciousness. The Theravāda School thus stresses the mental aspect of action.

The Sautrāntika School also maintained that volition was the essence of karma. Actions were considered to be the functioning of volition. To demonstrate their relation to volition, actions were analyzed into three stages: consideration of the appropriateness of the action (Ch. *shen-lü ssu*), arrival at a decision (Ch. *chüeh-ting ssu*), and direction of the body or mouth to perform the action (Ch. *tung-fa sheng-ssu*).[2] Physical and verbal actions were manifested in the last stage.

In the Theravāda School, the actions of the body are called *kāyaviññati* (physical expressions) and fall under the category of physical karma. In other words, physical actions are expressions of the volition that is the essence of karma. In a similar manner, inflections and changes of the voice are called verbal expressions. Volition is thus expressed through verbal acts such as cursing or indistinct prattling. The essence of any action is volition. Physical and verbal actions have no good or bad qualities in and of themselves. The moral quality of actions is determined by the mind through intention.

In contrast, the Sarvāstivādins did not consider the essence of physical and verbal karma to be volition. Without bodily actions and speech, physical and verbal karma cannot exist. Consequently, the essence of physical karma is said to be the configuration of the body *(saṃsthāna)* at the instant when a physical act is completed. In a similar manner, the essence of verbal karma is the last sound when a verbal act, such as lying or swearing, is completed. According to a classification found in the *Āgamas,* karma could be divided into two major categories: karma limited to mental processes *(cetanā karma)* and karma in which the mental processes are expressed through physical or verbal actions *(cetayitvā karma).* Sarvāstivādins argued that physical and verbal karma should be classified in the latter category and not the former.

Manifested and Unmanifested Activity

As was explained earlier, actions can be divided into two categories: those that can be perceived or heard and those that cannot be perceived. These two categories are called manifested activity *(vijñapti-karman)* and unmanifested activity *(avijñapti-karman)* by Sarvāstivādin thinkers. Since mental activity is never manifested outside one's mind, these categories are not applied to mental activity. But they are applied to physical and verbal actions. Physical actions can be perceived by the eye and verbal actions by the ear. These aspects of man's actions are consequently called manifested actions. Such actions end in an instant, yet they still retain the potency to produce a karmic effect. Since that potential cannot be perceived, it is called unmanifested activity. Manifested activities have a physical existence in the sense that they can be perceived by the eyes or ears, but such manifested activity can then produce unmanifested *(avijñapti)* karma. Because unmanifested karma has a physical aspect, often originating in manifested karma, it is called *avijñapti-rūpa* (unmanifested matter). *Avijñapti-karman* can be thought of as manifested action that has ended but has produced a force or potential that continues to exist. When conditions are suitable, that potential will produce an effect. *Avijñapti-karman* thus serves as an intermediary between cause and effect.

The Sarvāstivādins argued that *avijñapti-karman* has a physical existence. Since it cannot be seen, they did not classify it as a visual object, but as a mental object, one that was not composed of atoms. The other schools of Nikāya Buddhism disagreed with the Sarvāstivādin position.

The Sautrāntikas, maintaining that the essence of physical, verbal, and mental karma was volition, did not recognize the distinction between manifested and unmanifested karma. However, since the mental faculty of volition lasted only an instant, they had to recognize that some intermediary between an action and its karmic result must exist. For the Sautrāntikas, the seeds *(bīja)* of volition serve this function. Seeds rise and cease in a continuous stream *(saṃtati)* that gradually changes *(pariṇāma)* until at last the seeds have sufficient power to produce a result *(viśeṣa)*. This type of intermediary force between an action and its karmic result was called "accumulation" *(upacaya)* by the Mahāsaṅghikas and "indestructible" *(avipraṇāśa)* by the Sammatīyas. The term *"avijñapti,"* translated into Chinese in several ways, is also discussed in the *Ch'eng-shih lun* (*T* 32:290b, *Tattvasiddhiśāstra*?) and the *She-li-fu a-p'i-t'an lun* (*T* 28:526c, 581a, *Śāriputrābhidharmaśāstra*?). The schools of Nikāya Buddhism generally recognized some imperceptible force that served as an intermediary between karmic cause and effect, although the name they gave this force varied.

The Essence of the Precepts: A Special Type of Unmanifested Activity

One of the major reasons for the Sarvāstivādin insistence that unmanifested matter existed was their interest in a type of *avijñapti-rūpa* called the "essence of the precepts."[3] The essence of the precepts resembles unmanifested activity or karma as the force that joins actions with their karmic results, but is different in certain ways. These differences can probably be attributed to developments within Sarvāstivādin doctrine.

Sarvāstivādin thinkers argued that when a person is ordained with the precepts, he is physically endowed with a force that helps him refrain from doing wrong. This power is called the "essence of the precepts." For example, when a layman accepts the five lay precepts, he vows not to take life. This vow helps him regulate his actions after the ordination and leads him to refrain from wrongdoing that might result in killing. In the same manner, a person who vows not to drink alcoholic beverages may be able to refrain from partaking of them even though he wants to drink them. Such resolve is due to the power of his vow. This power that discourages wrongdoing is instilled within a person at the time of his ordination. It continues to exist in a physical sense even when the persons forgets about the precepts, is asleep, or is thinking about wrongdoing. However, if a person does not perform all the proper actions of the ceremony or if he neglects to recite some of the words of his vows at his ordination, then the essence of the precepts is not instilled in him. The essence of the precepts is thus thought of as a power created by physical actions but invisible to the eye. It is therefore classified as *avijñapti-rūpa* (unmanifested matter).

The essence of the precepts provided a concept that was used to classify Buddhist adherents. A Buddhist layman or woman was distinguished from a non-Buddhist by his or her possession of the essence of the five lay precepts. A monk would have a different type of essence of the precepts, which distinguished him from a Buddhist layman. Thus a person was not a monk simply because he wore robes *(kaṣāya)* or lived an austere life, but because he had been instilled with the essence of a particular set of precepts. Similarly he did not cease to be a monk if he broke (minor) precepts; he still possessed the essence of the precepts.

Theories on the essence of the precepts were an important concern of monks. The schools of Nikāya Buddhism maintained a number of doctrinal positions on the concept. The Sarvāstivādin School considered the essence of the precepts to have a physical existence and classified it as unmanifested matter *(avijñapti-rūpa).* The Sautrāntikas categorized it as seeds *(bīja).* The Theravāda School considered the essence of the precepts to lie in volition *(cetanā),* an explanation found in Buddhaghosa's *Visuddhimagga* (chap. 1, sec. 17, Path of Purification). The term "essence of the precepts" (Ch. *chieh-t'i*) does not appear in the Chinese translation of the *Abhidharmakośa,* but the phrase "the unmanifested (aspect) of discipline" (Ch. *lü-i wu-piao*) is found.

With some exceptions, the essence of the precepts is instilled in a person at the time of ordination and continues to exist until death. Eight types of essences are enumerated; these correspond to the precepts for laymen, laywomen, male novices, female novices, probationary nuns *(śikṣamāṇā),* monks, nuns, and the special set of eight precepts maintained by some lay Buddhists on *uposatha* days. This list of eight is sometimes reclassified into four types: the five precepts for the laity, the ten precepts for novices (which include the six precepts of the *śikṣamāṇā*), the full precepts for monks and nuns, and the eight precepts for lay believers on *uposatha* days. Of these, the essence of the eight precepts lasts only one day and night, ending at daybreak the day after the precepts are taken. The other essences of the precepts last until one's death but may be terminated by announcing that one no longer has the will to observe the precepts or that one abandons the precepts. At that time, one loses the essence of the precepts.

The Three Types of Restraints

Unmanifested matter or karma is classified into three categories: that which restrains from evil *(saṃvara),* that which does not restrain from evil *(asaṃvara),* and that which neither restrains nor does not restrain from evil *(naivasaṃvara-nāsaṃvara).* "That which does not restrain" refers to evil precepts such as vowing that one will make butchering animals his profession. "That which neither restrains nor does not restrain" refers to the possibilities that are not solely good or evil precepts; it may be called a neutral type of unmanifested karma. Without vowing to do either good or bad, a good mind arises in a person for a time, and then an evil mind. Or a person may do good for a time and then evil. In such a case, either good or evil unmanifested karma could be produced.

"That which restrains from evil" is classified into three subcategories: the restraints of the formal precepts of the *vinaya (prātimokṣa-saṃvara),* the restraints arising out of meditation *(dhyānajasaṃvara),* and the restraints arising through the attainment of a particular stage on the path to enlightenment *(anāsrava-saṃvara). Prātimokṣa-saṃvara* refers to the restraints against doing wrong that a person feels because he has been ordained with the precepts. *Dhyānajasaṃvara* refers to the power of meditation to prevent evil. In the East Asian Buddhist tradition, it is also translated as the "restraints of quiet contemplation" or the "precepts accompanying meditation." This type of restraint ends when the practitioner emerges from meditation. *Anāsvara-saṃvara* refers to the power that prevents wrongdoing that is obtained by a practitioner who has realized enlightenment. In the East Asian Buddhist tradition, it is called "the restraints arising from the path" (Ch. *tao-chü-chieh*) or the "untainted restraints" (Ch. *wu-lou lü-i*). These restraints are lost if the practitioner backslides. The last two types of restraints are called "precepts that arise out of the practitioner's state of mind" *(citta-anuvartin).*

Classification of Karma

One of the most fundamental ways of classifying karma is by referring to the part of the body that performs the action. The result is a threefold classification of physical, verbal, and mental karma. Other systems of classification were also developed. Of these, the most important is based on moral standards. A threefold classification of good, bad, or morally neutral karma is used often in Buddhist texts. According to the *Abhidharmakośa,* good karma leads to tranquility. Good karma is divided into two categories: actions leading to a differently maturing result that is desired and actions leading to *nirvāṇa.* Karma is thus judged on whether a welcomed result is obtained through an action or not. Since pleasure is the result of differently maturing effects that lead to desirable results, karma that produces pleasure is called "good." The monastic rules of the *prātimokṣa* are useful guides to practices, which will lead to the realization of *nirvāṇa* and thus are also called "good."

Karma that leads to a pleasurable result is "good." But because this good karma belongs to the realm of birth and death, it is called "impure good" (in contrast to the "pure" good, which leads toward *nirvāṇa*). A concrete example of such impure good is the path of the ten good acts *(daśa kuśala-karma-pathāḥ).*

1. Abstention from killing living things
2. Abstention from stealing
3. Abstention from unchaste activities
4. Abstention from lying
5. Abstention from malicious speech
6. Abstention from harsh speech
7. Abstention from indistinct chatter
8. Abstention from covetousness
9. Abstention from anger
10. Abstention from wrong views

The opposite actions are called "the path of the ten bad acts." These lists have been used as guides for good and bad actions since the time of the *Āgamas.* Bad karma leads to the differently maturing effect of suffering. Neutral karma is an action that leads to neither pleasure nor suffering.

Nirvāṇa is a pure good *(anāsrava-kuśala),* but it is not a type of karma. Rather, *nirvāṇa* transcends karma. In contrast, the path to *nirvāṇa*—the wisdom of enlightenment—is considered to be both pure good and pure karma *(anāsravaṃ-karman).* It is absolute good *(paramārtha-śubha),* which does not lead to a differently maturing effect.

In the Theravāda School, pure karma performed by someone who is still practicing *(sekha)* leads to a differently maturing effect. It may result in either the attainment of the stage where no further practice is necessary *(asekha-phala* or *arahant)* or one of the lower stages where religious practice is still necessary before becoming an *arahant.* Pure karma performed by someone at the final stage produces no effect.

Good was classified into four categories by the Sarvāstivādins: (1) absolute good, namely, *nirvāṇa;* (2) intrinsic good, namely, the five qualities of mind that are intrinsically good (shame, embarrassment, refraining from hatred, refraining from craving, and the absence of ignorance); (3) concomitant good, namely, those qualities that are not intrinsically good but that function concomitantly with the five intrinsically good qualities; (4) responsive good *(samutthānena kuśalāḥ),* namely, good that arises in response to intrinsic or concomitant good. Among the varieties of good included in this last category are karma from verbal or physical actions, unmanifested karma, and certain of the *dharmas* that do not arise concomitantly with the mind. The four categories of good are used to explain how the ten general functions of good act.

Several other classifications of karma are found in the *Abhidharmakośa.* Karma is categorized as meritorious *(puṇya),* which is good performed in the desire realm; unmeritorious, which is evil performed in the desire realm; and immovable. Good actions (such as certain meditations or trances) pertaining to the form and formless realms are called immovable karma.

Karma is also categorized as actions that result in a pleasant birth somewhere between the desire realm and the Third Meditation Heaven of the form realm *(sukha-vedanīya-karma),* actions resulting in an unpleasant rebirth in the desire realm *(duḥkha-vedanīya-karma),* and actions resulting in a birth that is neither pleasant nor suffering in the Fourth Meditation Heaven of the form realm or above *(aduḥkha-asukha-vedanīya-karma).*

Karma may also be categorized by comparing it with colors such as black (evil), black and white (good but impure actions of the desire realm), white (good), and neither black nor white (pure or *anāsrava*). The time at which recompense occurs provides another standard for classifying karma. Actions may entail recompense in this life *(dṛṣṭa-dharma-vedanīyaṃ karma),* in the next life *(upapadya-vedanīyaṃ karma),* in a future life after but not in the next birth *(aparaparyāya-vedanīyaṃ karma),* or at an indeterminate time *(aniyatā-vedanīyaṃ karma).*

The Existence of the Past and Future

Because the Sarvāstivādins used the term "unmanifested matter" to refer to the "essence of the precepts," unmanifested matter gradually lost its significance as the factor tying karmic cause and effect together. This development was probably related to the Sarvāstivādin insistence that conditioned *dharmas* exist in the past, present, and future. The *dharmas* that function instantaneously in the present arise from the future through the power of "origination," one of the four characteristics found in the list of *dharmas* not concomitant with the mind. Each *dharma* has these four characteristics (origination, subsistence, decay, and extinction) concomitant with it. Through these characteristics (or forces), *dharmas* exist in the future until they arise in the present. There they subsist for an instant and then fall into the past. The present consists of those *dharmas* that are functioning at a particular instant. The *dharmas* that have fallen into the past are said actually to exist there by the Sarvāstivādins. Karmic forces, too, exist in the past until the time comes for them to produce a result. Conditioned *dharmas* function only in the present, but the essence of the *dharmas* exists at all times. The Sarvāstivādin position was summarized by East Asian Buddhists as the affirmation of the eternal existence of the essence of all *dharmas* that exist in the past, present, or future (Ch. *san-shih shih-yu fa-t'i heng-yu*).

Other schools, such as the Mahāsaṅghikas and the Sautrāntikas opposed the Sarvāstivādin position by arguing that karmic forces existed as seeds in the present. They denied that *dharmas* existed in the past. Their position is summarized by East Asian Buddhists as the affirmation of the existence of *dharmas* in the present, but not in the past and the future (Ch. *hsien-tsai yu-t'i kuo-wei wu-t'i*).

CHAPTER 13

The Elimination of Defilements and the Path to Enlightenment

The Meaning of Defilement

ACCORDING TO the Sarvāstivādin text *Ju a-p'i-ta-mo lun* (*T* 28:984a, *Abhidharmāvatāraśāstra#*), "Defilements are so named because they cause both the body and mind to be afflicted and suffer. They are also called proclivities *(anuśaya).*" The term "defilement" is further explained as referring to that which disturbs the mind and body and prevents tranquility. According to the *Visuddhimagga* (Harvard Oriental Series, vol. 41, p. 586), "The defilements are so named because they themselves are defiled *(saṅkiliṭṭha)* and because they defile *(saṅkilesika)* the *dhammas* associated with them." According to this explanation, the Pāli term *"kilesa"* is derived from the same root as *saṅkilissati* (to stain or defile). The definition of the Sanskrit term *"kleśa"* in the *Ju a-p'i-ta-mo lun* is based on the Sanskrit root *kliś* (to afflict). However, the Sanskrit term *"kliṣṭamanas"* (often translated into English as "afflicted consciousness") was derived from the meaning "stained." The term "defilement" *(kleśa)* does not appear very often in the *Āgamas,* but it occurs frequently in *abhidharma* literature.

In the Pāli *Vibhaṅga* (chap. 17, sec. 9, par. 952) or Book of Analysis, a list of eight defilements *(aṭṭha kilesavatthūni)* is presented: greed, hatred, delusion, pride, wrong views, doubts, sloth, and distraction. Two more are added in the *Dhammasaṅgaṇi* (no. 1229) to make a total of ten defilements *(dasa kilesavatthūni):* absence of embarrassment before others over one's wrongdoings and absence of shame for one's wrongdoings. This list of ten defilements was used frequently in Theravādin discussions of the defilements. A later noncanonical *abhidhamma* text, the *Abhidhammatthasaṅgaha* (p. 32) mentions several other lists in its systematization of the various sets of defilements used since the *Āgamas*. Included are the four (impure) outflows *(āsava),* four violent outflows *(ogha),* four yokes *(yoga),* four bonds *(kāyagantha),* four graspings *(upādāna),* six hindrances *(nīvaraṇa),* seven proclivities *(anusaya),* ten fetters *(saṃyojana),* and ten defilements. Most of these ways of classifying the defilements had appeared in the *Āgamas*.

Āsrava (P. *āsava*) is the oldest of these terms. It appears in both the *Suttanipāta* and the *Dhammapada,* where it is used to define one of the qualifications of an enlightened person: he has exhausted all his outflows (P. *āsavā khīṇā*). In Buddhist texts this term is used in the sense of outflow because the mind's defilements move outward and affect other things. In Jainism, the term is used with the sense of inflow because defilements are said to flow from the external world into the body, where they adhere to the *ātman.* The use of the term in both Buddhist and Jaina texts indicates that its origins are very early. Buddhist texts list four major types of *āsrava:* sensual desire *(kāma-āsrava),* desire for existence *(bhāva-āsrava),* wrong views *(dṛṣṭi-āsrava),* and ignorance *(avidyā-āsrava).* The terms *"ogha"* (violent outflow of defilements) and *"yoga"* (yoke) are also early. The contents of the four violent outflows of defilements and the four yokes are identical to the four outflows.

Six hindrances *(nīvaraṇa)* are mentioned in the *Abhidhammatthasaṅgaha,* although usually only five are listed in the *Āgamas.* The seven proclivities are also discussed in various places in the *Āgamas.* The ten fetters are usually divided into two groups in the *Āgamas*—five that bind sentient beings to the form and formless realms and five that bind beings to the desire realm. By cutting off such defilements, the practitioner is able to escape from the cycles of repeated births and deaths. Two lists of ten fetters are included in the *Abhidhammatthasaṅgaha*—ten fetters found in the *suttas* and a slightly different list of ten fetters according to *abhidhamma* texts. By rearranging the first list of ten fetters, two additional fetters were included: jealousy and parsimony. The revised list is also found in sources such as the *Dhammasaṅgaṇi* (no. 1113). The ten fetters from the *abhidhamma* texts and the ten defilements listed above were both developed during the period when the Pāli *abhidhamma* texts were being compiled.

The proliferation of terms for the defilements is due, in part, to disagreements about whether the defilements are viewed as actually staining the mind or as merely obscuring its true nature. Those monks who maintained that the basic nature of the mind was pure adhered to the position that the defilements obscured or covered the true, untainted essence of the mind. The mind itself could not be tainted or stained.

A variety of ways of classifying the defilements developed within Buddhism. Many of the same elements are found in the various lists; thus, most of the important varieties of defilements are included in the longer lists such as the ten fetters or ten defilements. The following elements found in the ten defilements are particularly important: craving *(lobha),* hatred *(dveṣa),* delusion *(moha),* pride *(māna),* wrong views *(dṛṣṭi),* doubt *(vicikitsā),* torpor *(styāna),* and distraction *(auddhatya).* Cravings are subdivided into cravings for desirable objects and cravings for continued existence. The latter is further classified into cravings for continued existence in the form realm and for continued existence in the formless realm. Wrong views may be divided into five types as is demonstrated in the following discussion.

According to the Sarvāstivādin work *Abhidharmāvatāraśāstra* (*T* 1554), defilements may also be called proclivities. A list of seven proclivities also found in Pāli sources is included in the text: craving for sensual pleasures, craving for continued existence, hatred, pride, ignorance, wrong views, and doubts. This list dates back to the *Āgamas;* but usually the cravings for sensual pleasures and cravings for continued existence were combined into the single category of craving or lust, yielding a list of six proclivities. Most *abhidharma* texts adopted this list of six proclivities, called the basic proclivities *(mūla-anuśaya)* in the *Abhidharmakośa.* The proclivity of wrong views is sometimes expanded into five types: belief in a Self, clinging to the extremes of eternalism or annihilationism, disbelief in causation, clinging to wrong views, and the belief that rituals lead to salvation. When these are added to the remaining five proclivities (craving, anger, pride, ignorance, and doubt), a list of ten is produced. This list is the basis for the discussion on proclivities in the *Abhidharmakośa.* When the ten proclivities are considered in terms of the realms in which they exist, the types of mind in which they function, and the manner in which they can be eliminated, a list of ninety-eight proclivities is produced.

While the Sarvāstivādin School considered defilements *(kleśa)* and proclivities to be identical, the Sautrāntika and Mahāsaṅghika traditions distinguished between the two. According to Sautrāntika teachings (*Abhidharmakośa,* p. 278, l. 19), "When the defilements are in a latent state [lit., sleeping], they are called proclivities. When they are active [lit., awake], they are called bonds *(paryavasthāna).*" This definition is based on deriving the meaning of the word *anuśaya* from the root *śī* 'to sleep'. In an ordinary person (or worldling), defilements such as greed and hatred are obviously not cut off, but neither are they constantly active. Rather, they are always present in a latent state and become active only when circumstances are suitable for their appearance.

Some Buddhists argued that defilements were stored in the unconscious as seeds until they functioned actively. The Yogācāra doctrine of a store-consciousness *(ālaya-vijñāna)* arose out of a need to explain how such seeds were stored and how memory functioned. The Sarvāstivādins, however, maintained that all *dharmas* ceased functioning after an instant. Instead of being stored in a consciousness, potential defilements existed in a time period, the future. They were connected to the continuous stream *(saṃtāna)* of a person's *dharmas* by the force of the *dharma* of possession *(prāpti)*. Because the defilements were present in a latent form through the power of possession, they could not be said to have been eliminated in a worldling even though they were not being manifested at a particular time.

The Ninety-eight Proclivities

One of the major ways of classifying defilements or proclivities is by the type of knowledge that can destroy them. Using this method, many proclivities can be divided into four groups *(catuṣ-prakāra)* on the basis of which of the Four Noble Truths are used to eliminate them. These proclivities can thus be eliminated by knowledge of suffering, its cause, *nirvāṇa,* or the path. Such proclivities or defilements are conceptual errors *(darśana-heya-kleśa)* concerning religious truths that can be destroyed through the path of insight *(darśana-mārga)*. Although these defilements can be eliminated through an understanding of the Four Noble Truths, other defilements cannot be destroyed so readily. These other defilements *(bhāvanā-heya-kleśa)* must be eliminated through the practices of the path of meditation *(bhāvanā-mārga)* because they have become so habitual and ingrained that knowledge is not sufficient to cut them off. Only through constant religious practice can such defilements as craving, hatred, ignorance, and pride be eliminated. In contrast, the five wrong views and doubt are all conceptual defilements and can be completely eliminated through a knowledge of the Four Noble Truths and Dependent Origination. To a certain extent, craving, hatred, ignorance, and pride can also be eliminated through knowledge of the Four Noble Truths since these four defilements exist as both conceptual errors and as defilements that must be eliminated through practice. In contrast, the five wrong views and doubt exist only as defilements that can be destroyed through knowledge. A list of five types *(pañca-prakārāḥ)* of defilements is produced when the defilements destroyed by practice are added to the conceptual defilements destroyed by the Four Noble Truths.

Defilements may also be classified according to which of the three realms (desire, form, formless) they belong. For example, since the desire realm is characterized by much suffering, eliminating the craving for sensual pleasure in this realm is not too difficult. However, because the form and formless realms are characterized by subtle types of bliss, eliminating the craving for existence in those realms is more difficult. Thus, the craving for existence in both of the higher (the form and formless) realms can be eliminated only after the craving for sensual pleasures has been cut off. (The cravings for existences in the two upper realms are destroyed at the same time, not consecutively.) By classifying defilements according to the realm to which they pertain and how they are eliminated, a list of ninety-eight is produced.

Thirty-six types of defilements are found in the desire realm. Ten are cut off by an understanding of the noble truth of suffering. Only seven (craving, hatred, ignorance, pride, doubt, disbelief in causation, and clinging to wrong views) are eliminated by the noble truths of the cause of suffering and *nirvāṇa.* The three proclivities of belief in a Self, belief in extremist views, and belief that rituals lead to salvation are not affected by knowledge of the noble truths of the cause of suffering and *nirvāṇa.* Eight proclivities are eliminated by the truth of the path (the same seven as for the previous two truths and the belief that rituals result in salvation). Thus thirty-two proclivities of the desire realm are eliminated through the Four Noble Truths. Four more are cut off through meditation, making a total of thirty-six.

The defilement of hatred is not found in the form and formless realms. Since the desires for food and sex do not arise in these two realms, no object of hatred is present in them. Otherwise, the same distribution of defilements specified for the desire realm prevails. The result is that nine proclivities are cut off by the truth of suffering, six each by the truths of the cause of suffering and *nirvāṇa,* seven by the truth of the path, and three by meditation. Thirty-one proclivities are found in each of the two higher realms. Thus a total of ninety-eight proclivities is listed for the three realms.

Of the ninety-eight proclivities, eleven are said to be particularly strong. From among the proclivities cut off by the truth of suffering, they are (1–5) the five wrong views, (6) doubt, and (7) ignorance. From among the proclivities cut off by the truth of the cause of suffering are (8) disbelief in causation, (9) clinging to wrong views, (10) doubt, and (11) ignorance. Their influence extends throughout the particular realm *(dhātu)* and land *(bhūmi)* in which a person acts. (The three realms are further divided into nine lands: desire realm, the Four Meditation Heavens of the form realm, and the Four Formless Heavens.) Universal causes even call forth those defilements that can only be cut off by contemplations on the truths of *nirvāṇa* and the path or by meditation. Consequently, these eleven are called "universal proclivities." In the Sarvāstivādin enumeration of the six causes, their activity is described as "universal cause" *(sarvatragahetu)* because of their influence on other defilements.

Nine of the universal proclivities (all except the belief in a Self and belief in extreme views) are called the "defilements that bind a person to the upper realms."

Ignorance may be further classified into two types: concomitant ignorance and special ignorance *(avidyā-āveṇikī)*. The first type always functions concomitantly with other defilements. However, ignorance also functions in other ways. It lies at the base of all incorrect thoughts and thus is the foundation of all mental functions. In other words, ignorance functions as the basis of defiled and evil states of mind as well as neutral and good states. "Special ignorance" refers to these aspects of ignorance (its activity independent of any other defilements and its influence on all other mental faculties). When ignorance is described as one of the twelve links of Dependent Origination, it is ignorance in this special sense.

Further pondering on the nature of ignorance eventually led to the Yogācāra notion of an afflicted consciousness *(kliṣṭa-manas* or *manas)*. The concept of primordial ignorance (Ch. *ken-pen wu-ming* or *wu-shih wu-ming*) expounded in the *Ta-sheng ch'i-hsin lun* (*T* nos. 1666–1667, Awakening of Faith) probably was an extension of the idea of special ignorance. Thus the Sarvāstivādin distinction between concomitant and special ignorance had major significance for later Buddhism.

The 108 Defilements

Besides the ninety-eight proclivities, the Sarvāstivādins had a list of 108 defilements (the result of adding ten bonds [*paryavasthāna*] to the ninety-eight proclivities). The ten bonds (also called secondary defilements or *upakleśa*) are absence of shame, absence of embarrassment, jealousy, parsimony, remorse, drowsiness, distraction, torpor, anger, and concealment of wrongdoing.

As was explained earlier in this chapter, lists such as this were derived from a basic set of six (which is sometimes expanded to ten) proclivities.

By analyzing the basic list in various ways, additional lists were generated, such as the nine fetters *(saṃyojana),* the five fetters binding a person to the upper realms, the five fetters binding a person to the desire realm, and the three bonds (*bandhana:* craving, hatred, delusion).

According to the "Chapter on Proclivities" of the *Abhidharmakośa,* all defilements are encompassed by the lists of proclivities and secondary defilements. However, the list of seventy-five *dharmas* contained in the "Chapter on Faculties" *(indriya)* of the *Abhidharmakośa* does not agree in many respects with the views presented in the "Chapter on Proclivities." For example, forty-six of the seventy-five *dharmas* are mental faculties. Many of these concern defilements such as the six general functions of defilement (delusion, negligence, indolence, disbelief, torpor, and distraction), the two general functions of evil (absence of shame, absence of embarrassment), and the ten minor functions of defilement (anger, concealment of wrongdoing, parsimony, jealousy, rejection of criticism, causing injury, resentment, deceit, flattery, and conceit). However, some of the most important categories discussed in the "Chapter on Proclivities" are not mentioned in the above lists of *dharmas.* Among them are craving, hatred, pride, and doubt. The category of indeterminate *dharmas* in the "Chapter on Faculties" is described as consisting of "remorse, drowsiness, investigation, scrutiny, and so forth." If the phrase "and so forth" is interpreted as meaning craving, hatred, pride, and doubt, the result would be a list of eight indeterminate *dharmas* and a total of forty-six mental faculties. In fact, these are the usual numbers of *dharmas* included in these two categories.

Vasubandhu probably did not clearly define the place of craving and other important proclivities in the lists of *dharmas* because he was concerned with different sets of problems when he wrote the "Chapter on Faculties" and the "Chapter on Proclivities." Moreover, such discrepancies may indicate that Vasubandhu was drawing on a variety of scholastic traditions when he wrote the *Abhidharmakośa* and did not always reconcile the differences between them.

Stages of Practice

In the *Āgamas* the levels of attainment of the Buddha's disciples are judged according to a fourfold hierarchy: (1) stream-entrant *(srotāpatti;* P. *sotāpatti),* (2) once-returner *(sakṛdāgāmin;* P. *sakadāgāmin),* (3) nonreturner (S. and P. *anāgāmin*), and (4) *arhat* (P. *arahant*). Each of these stages is divided further into two parts: a path leading to the stage (hereafter translated as candidate) and the actual stage or fruit itself.

The first stage, stream-entrant, refers to a person who has entered the stream of Buddhism. Originally the term was used to refer to anyone who had a pure and indestructible faith in Buddhism. However, in the *Āgamas* (*SN,* vol. 5, pp. 356–357; *Shih-sung lü* [*T* 23:129a, *Sarvāstivadavinaya*]), the standard explanation is that it refers to one who has cut off the three fetters: the belief in a substantial Self, the belief that the performance of rituals will lead to salvation, and doubts about Buddhist doctrine. A stream-entrant will not fall into a bad rebirth (such as a denizen of hell, hungry ghost, animal, or *asura* [demigod]). He is destined to attain enlightenment and will do so within seven rebirths in this world.

A person who has attained the second stage, once-returner, has cut off the three fetters and weakened the hold of the three poisons (*tridoṣāpaha:* craving, hatred, and delusion). A once-returner will return to this world one more time and then attain salvation. A person who has reached the third stage, nonreturner, does not return to this world in any future birth; rather, he repeatedly is born and dies in heaven until he enters *nirvāṇa.* He has cut off the five lower fetters (the previously mentioned three fetters, along with hatred and the belief that a person has a substantial Self) that tie him to existence in the desire realm *(kāmadhātu).* The fourth and final stage is the *arhat,* a person who has cut off all his defilements. He has obtained the wisdom that is salvation and his mind is freed from defilements.[1]

The most important early list of stages consists of eight steps, beginning with candidate for stream-entrant and culminating with the actual stage of *arhat.* Other more detailed explanations of the stages of the *śrāvaka* are occasionally found in the *Āgamas.* For example, in the *Fu-t'ien ching* (*T* 1:616a, *Dakkhiṇeyyā*) of the *Chung a-han ching (Madhyamāgama),* eighteen stages of training *(śaikṣa)* and nine stages beyond training *(aśaikṣa)* are mentioned. This was a further elaboration of the traditional eight stages. The stages of practice described in the *abhidharma* literature are based on such teachings from the *Āgamas.*

The Stages of Practice According to the Theravāda School

In the Theravāda School, the levels of practice are classified into seven stages of purification:

1. Morals *(sīla-visuddhi)*
2. Mind *(citta-visuddhi)*
3. Views *(diṭṭhi-visuddhi)*

4. Transcending doubts *(kaṅkhāvitaraṇa-visuddhi)*
5. Knowledge and vision of what constitutes the path *(maggāmagga-ñāṇadassana-visuddhi)*
6. Knowledge and vision of the method of salvation *(paṭipadāñāṇa-dassana-visuddhi)*
7. Wisdom *(ñāṇadassana-vissuddhi)*

The seven purifications are mentioned in the *Āgamas,* as well as in such works as the *Ch'eng-shih lun* (*T* 1646, *Tattvasiddhiśāstra?*) and the *Yü-ch'ieh lun* (*T* 1579, *Yogācārabhūmiśāstra#*). They are also described in detail in Buddhaghosa's *Visuddhimagga.*

The first level of practice, purification of morals, concerns the observance of the precepts. The second, purification of the mind, involves the development of pure meditations and the realization of eight attainments *(samāpatti).* These two purifications provide the foundation necessary for the realization of wisdom (*Visuddhimagga,* Harvard Oriental Series, vol. 41, p. 375).

The remaining five purifications are concerned with wisdom itself. According to the *Visuddhimagga,* discernment *(jānana)* is analyzed into three components: perception *(saññā),* consciousness *(viññāṇa),* and wisdom *(paññāṇa). Saññā* may be translated as sense perception, while *viññāṇa* refers to analytical understanding based on sense perceptions. *Paññāṇa* or wisdom refers to a more profound and complete form of insight or understanding (*Visuddhimagga,* p. 369). Wisdom is said to exist as right views *(diṭṭhi),* knowledge *(ñāṇa),* and vision *(dassana).* Wisdom is also often equated with the combination of knowledge and vision *(ñāṇadassana).*

The last five purifications are discussed in chap. 18–22 of the *Visuddhimagga.* The discussion of the purification of knowledge and vision (wisdom) in chap. 22 is particularly important since it concerns the levels of enlightenment. From purification of views to purification of the knowledge and vision of the method of salvation, the practitioner has not realized enlightenment and is still involved with mundane knowledge. In the last purification, that of wisdom, he is concerned with the wisdom that comes with enlightenment, with pure, untainted knowledge.

The first two purifications consist of preliminary practices. Theravāda practice begins with morality and then progresses with meditation. When these have been mastered, practices leading to wisdom begin. These consist of meditations designed to develop wisdom. Among the subjects used are the impermanence, nonsubstantiality, and suffering that characterize the five aggregates. The twelve bases, eighteen elements, twenty-two faculties *(indriya),* Four Noble Truths, and twelve links of Dependent Origination are also subjects of meditation.

The third of the seven purifications concerns views. In this purification, the various *dhammas* of name and form *(nāma-rūpa)* are seen as they actually are through meditations on the four primary elements *(mahābhūta),* eighteen elements *(dhātu),* twelve bases, and five aggregates.

The fourth purification, on transcending doubts, focuses on the origination, change, and cessation of name and form. Doubts and misconceptions concerning causation during the past, present, and future are eradicated. Among these misconceptions are the views that causes do not exist, that all is created and controlled by a god, that man has an eternal soul, and that a person completely ceases to exist with death. Through this purification, the practitioner obtains knowledge based on the Dhamma, knowledge of things as they actually are, and correct views.

The fifth purification, knowledge and vision concerning the path, concerns discrimination between the correct path to salvation and wrong practices or theories of salvation.

The sixth purification, knowledge and vision concerning the method of salvation, concerns knowledge of the correct path to salvation. By following the path, the practitioner gradually obtains the nine knowledges based on contemplation of origination and cessation, contemplation of dissolution, contemplation of appearance as terror, contemplation of appearance as danger, contemplation of dispassion, desire for deliverance, contemplation of reflection, equanimity about formations, and conformity with truth. Through these knowledges, the practitioner discerns the correct path.

The above four purifications leading to wisdom (third through sixth) are all stages of worldlings *(puthujjana)* still bound by fetters. Even though knowledge and vision are purified, true knowledge and vision have not yet arisen. However, the ninth knowledge of the sixth purification (conformity with the truth [*saccānulomikaṃ ñāṇaṃ*]) is wisdom concerning the Four Noble Truths. From it arises knowledge of the change of lineage *(gotrabhūñāṇa),* which leads to purification of wisdom, the seventh and last purification. The seventh purification is divided into four stages: the knowledges of the path of stream-entrant, once-returner, nonreturner, and *arahant.* Although the knowledge of change of lineage lies between the sixth and seventh purifications, it belongs to neither of them. Between the sixth and seventh purifications, the practitioner ceases to be a worldling and obtains the knowledge that he now belongs to the lineage of sages *(āriya).*

In terms of Sarvāstivādin doctrine (explained below), this stage would correspond to that of acquiescence *(kṣānti)* in the degrees of favorable roots. In the Sarvāstivādin path, the stages of the worldling *(pṛthagjana)* are divided into the three degrees of the wise and the four degrees of favorable roots (warmth, summit, acquiescence, and pinnacle of worldly truth). The third through the sixth of the Theravāda purifications would correspond to the three degrees of the wise and to the stages of warmth, summit, and acquiescence in the Sarvāstivādin path. However, there are points on which the two versions of the path do not agree.[2]

From knowledge in conformity with truth, the practitioner progresses to the knowledge of change of lineage and from there to the purification of wisdom, the seventh purification. The purification of wisdom is the path of sages. In the Sarvāstivādin path, it would correspond to the paths of insight, meditation, and no further training (discussed later in this chapter). According to the *Visuddhimagga,* three ways of entering this sagely path exist: faith, wisdom, and meditation. A person who enters through the first gate, faith, and has become a candidate for stream-entrant is called a *saddhānusārin* (one whose practice is based on faith). From the time he becomes a stream-entrant until he becomes an *arahant,* he is called a *saddhāvimutta* (one liberated by faith).[3]

A person who uses the second gate, wisdom, and has become a candidate for stream-entrant is called a *dhammānusārin* (one whose practice is based on Dharma). From the time he becomes a stream-entrant until he becomes a candidate for *arahant*hood, he is a *diṭṭhippatta* (one who has realized correct views). When he has become an *arahant,* he is called a *paññāvimutta* (one liberated by wisdom).

A person who uses the third gate, meditation, and is anywhere between being a candidate for stream-entrant and a candidate for *arahant* is called a *kāyasakkhin* (bodily witness). When he becomes an *arahant* and attains the trances of the formless realm, he is called an *ubhatobhāgavimutta* (twice liberated one); in other words, he is liberated by way of the trances and by way of the supermundane path based on insight (*Visuddhimagga,* p. 565).

Thus, there are three gates to the sagely path according to Theravādin doctrine: faith, wisdom, and meditation. When the practitioner is a candidate for stream-entrant, he may be called one whose practice is based on faith, one whose practice is based on Dharma, or a bodily witness, depending on the gate through which he enters. Between the stages of stream-entrant and candidate for *arahant*hood, he may be called one liberated by faith, one who has realized correct views, or bodily witness (as he was above). After he has become an *arahant,* he may be called one liberated by faith (as he was above), one liberated through wisdom, or twice liberated. These seven ranks in the three gates are sometimes collectively called the "seven sages." In Sarvāstivādin doctrine, only the gates of faith and wisdom are discussed. The relations of the seven ranks in the three gates are illustrated in Figure 5.

The *Visuddhimagga* relies primarily on discussions from the *Āgamas* for its treatment of the defilements cut off in practice, but it goes into more detail. Among the defilements to be cut off are the ten fetters *(saṃyojana),* ten defilements *(kilesa),* ten wrongnesses *(micchatta),* eight worldly states *(lokadhamma),* five types of parsimony *(macchariya),* three perversions *(vipallāsa),* four ties *(gantha),* four bad ways *(agati),* four impure influxes *(āsava),* four violent outflows *(ogha),* four yokes *(yoga),* five hindrances *(nīvaraṇa),* adherence *(parāmāsa),* four types of grasping *(upādāna),* seven proclivities *(anusaya),* three stains *(mala),* ten wrong actions, and twelve unwholesome arousals of thought *(cittupāda).* Many elements are repeated in these lists, but they are all destroyed by the knowledges of the four paths (stream-entrant and so forth). The explanations of how the various defilements are destroyed is primarily based on the *Āgamas.*

Knowledge of the change of lineages *(gotrabhūñāṇa)* does not arise only during the transition from the sixth purification (knowledge and vision of the method of salvation) to the seventh purification (purification of wisdom). It also arises when the practitioner progresses to the path of the once-returner, nonreturner, or *arahant.* Each of the four stages of candidate is considered to belong to a different lineage *(gotra).*

The Three Degrees of the Wise and the Four Degrees of Favorable Roots

The Sarvāstivādin system of the stages of practice is described in detail in works such as the *Jñānaprasthānaśāstra* (*T* 1544) and the *Mahāvibhāṣā* (*T* 1545). These explanations were presented in a systematic manner in the chapter on the wise and the sages of the *Abhidharmakośa* (*T* 1558–1559). The first seven stages—those of a worldling *(pṛthagjana)*—are divided into the three degrees of the wise and the four degrees of favorable roots. Next, the practitioner enters into the degrees of being a saint, which are classified as three paths: the path of insight into the truth *(satyadarśanamārga),* the path of meditation *(bhāvanāmārga),* and the path in which nothing remains to be learned *(aśaikṣa).* In the paths both of insight and of meditation, the practitioner is a *śaikṣa,* a person who still must study and practice even though he is a sage. When he has nothing more to learn *(aśaikṣa)* or accomplish in religious terms, he becomes an *arhat.*

According to the Sarvāstivādin view of the path, before a person enters the three degrees of the worthy, he must undergo preliminary

Figure 5. The Seven Sages of the Theravada Path

Sarvāstivādin Equivalent	Path of Insight	Path of Meditation	Path of No Further Training
Gate of Faith	*Saddhānusārin*	——— *Saddhāvimutta* ———	
Gate of Wisdom	*Dhammānusārin*	*Diṭṭhippatta*	*Paññāvimutta*
Gate of Meditation	——— *Kāyasakkhin* ———		*Ubhatobhāgavimutta*
Four Candidates and Four Fruits	Candidate for Stream-entrant	Six Stages from Stream-entrant to Candidate for *Arahant*	*Arahant*

practices to purify his body. These practices correspond to the first two stages in the Theravāda path of purification through observance of the precepts and purification through meditation. (However, the Theravāda purification through meditation also corresponds in part to the three degrees of the wise.)

Three sets of practices contribute to the preliminary purification of the body. First, the practitioner must observe the precepts and rectify his conduct. He should live in a tranquil setting where he can quiet his mind. Second, he must reduce his desires and learn to be satisfied with whatever he possesses. Third, he should learn to be satisfied with whatever clothing, food, or shelter he possesses; he should also vow to cut off his defilements and to follow the religious path. By cultivating these practices and attitudes, he develops a healthy body and tranquil mind. He finds a quiet place to practice and fosters the willpower necessary for leading a religious life. He is ready to begin the practice of meditation.

After passing through these preliminary stages, the practitioner performs religious austerities to attain the three degrees of the worthy: the fivefold view for quieting the mind, particular states of mindfulness, and a general state of mindfulness. The fivefold view for quieting the mind consists of five types of yogic practices that calm the mind and correspond to calm abiding *(śamatha)*. The five are meditations on impurity, compassion, Dependent Origination, classifications of the elements, and counting the breaths. The meditations on impurity and counting the breaths are particularly important.

Once the practitioner is firmly established in calm abiding, he begins to practice insight meditation *(vipaśyanā)*, which consists of the cultivation of particular and general states of mindfulness. Four types of mindfulness *(catvāri smṛty-upasthānāni)* are stressed: mindfulness of the impurity of the body, mindfulness that all sensations are ill *(duḥkha),* mindfulness that the mind is impermanent, and mindfulness that all phenomena *(dharma)* are nonsubstantial. If a practitioner meditates on these subjects individually, he is cultivating particular states of mindfulness. Cultivation of these states of mindfulness destroys four types of wrong views *(viparyāsa-catuṣka),* namely, wrongly perceiving phenomena as pure, blissful, eternal, or substantial. Next is the cultivation of a general state of mindfulness. While he is performing his meditation on the *dharmas,* the practitioner turns his attention to the body, sensations, mind, and the *dharmas* together and realizes that all have the characteristics in common of being impure, impermanent, ill, and nonsubstantial.

After the practitioner has completed the three degrees of the wise (sometimes called the "external degrees of the worldling"), he advances through the four degrees of favorable roots (also called the "internal degrees of the worldling"). The three degrees of the wise and the four degrees of favorable roots are preparatory steps *(prayoga)* for the path of insight and are thus stages of the worldling. The four degrees of favorable roots are warmth *(uṣmagata),* peak *(mūrdhan),* acquiescence *(kṣānti),* and the pinnacle of worldly truth *(laukikāgratā).*

The practices for these stages consist primarily of meditations on sixteen aspects of the Four Noble Truths. In regard to the truth of suffering, the practitioner contemplates how phenomena are (1) impermanent *(anitya),* (2) suffering *(duḥkha),* (3) nonsubstantial *(śūnya),* and (4) Selfless *(anātmaka).* In regard to the truth of the cause of suffering, he considers (5) how defiled causes *(hetu)* result in suffering, (6) how suffering originates *(samudaya)* and increases, (7) how suffering is caused by a series of causes *(prabhava),* and (8) how conditions *(pratyaya)* act as contributing causes to suffering. When contemplating the truth of *nirvāṇa,* the practitioner considers (9) how the defilements all cease *(nirodha),* (10) how *nirvāṇa* is peaceful *(śānta)* because it is free of confusion brought about by the defilements, (11) how *nirvāṇa* is excellent *(pranīṭa)* because it is free of all ills, and (12) how *nirvāṇa* constitutes an escape *(niḥsaraṇa)* from all misfortunes. In regard to the truth of the path, he considers (13) how the path *(mārga)* is sagely, (14) how it is reasonable *(nyāya)* because it accords with the truth, (15) how it leads to the attainment *(pratipatti)* of *nirvāṇa,* and (16) how it results in liberation *(nairyāṇika)* from *saṃsāra.*

Up to this point, religious practice for the Sarvāstivādin consists of observing the precepts, reducing desires, and learning to be satisfied with whatever is possessed, as well as meditations based on impurity, the counting of breaths, the Four Noble Truths, and the four states of mindfulness. Meditations on the Four Noble Truths are particularly central to these practices. After the practitioner advances from the stages of the worldling to the stages of the saint, in which he follows the paths of insight and meditation, he continues his meditations on the Four Noble Truths. As the practitioner's knowledge of the Four Noble Truths becomes more profound, he is able to cut off the defilements through the power of his deepening wisdom. Since the four degrees of favorable roots are realized through practices based on the Four Noble Truths, these degrees represent differences in the profundity of the practitioner's understanding of the Truths.

The first degree is called "heat" *(uṣmagata)* because it is a sign of the "flames" of the religious path that will rise in the practitioner. The second degree is called "summit" *(mūrdhan)* because the practitioner has advanced to the highest point of his religious life up to this time. It is the last stage from which a bad rebirth is still possible. The practitioner also realizes that if he continues, still higher levels of understanding can be reached. In a similar way, when a mountain climber has climbed a peak, he sees still higher peaks ahead to conquer.

The third stage is called "acquiescence" *(kṣānti)* because the practitioner acquiesces to the Four Noble Truths. It is a form of enlightenment in regard to mundane wisdom. A person will not backslide beyond this stage once he has reached it. The practitioner's religious "family" *(gotra)* and the ultimate goal he has the potential to realize is determined while he is in the stage of acquiescence. People with three types of potential are found practicing in the four stages of favorable roots: those with the potential to become *arhats* (*śrāvaka-gotra* or *śiṣya-gotra; Abhidharmakośa,* p. 348), those with the potential to become *pratyekabuddhas,* and those with the potential to become Buddhas. When a person of the *śrāvaka-gotra* is at the stages of heat *(uṣmagata)* or peak *(mūrdhan),* his *gotra* may change to either of the other two; but once he has realized the stage of acquiescence *(kṣānti)* as a person of the *śrāvaka-gotra* his *gotra* will never change. Those people who belong to either the *pratyekabuddha* or the Buddha *gotra* do not change their *gotra* and are limited to the goals of their particular "family." Thus, the practitioner's *gotra* is permanently determined when he reaches the stage of acquiescence (*T* 29:120c).

A person must spend a long time practicing in the stage of acquiescence. Once he passes through it, he attains the pinnacle of worldly truth *(laukikāgratā),* the highest *dharma* of the mundane. It is the highest form of enlightenment based on mundane knowledge and is produced through frequent meditation on the sixteen aspects of the Four Noble Truths. Since it is the highest point on this part of the path, it lasts only an instant. Afterward, the sagely paths appear and the practitioner enters the path of insight.

Advanced Stages of Practice According to the *Abhidharmakośa*

In the path of insight *(darśana-mārga),* pure *(anāsrava)* knowledge, the wisdom of enlightenment, emerges and develops. In contrast, the previous stages of the three wise degrees and four degrees of favorable roots are based on impure *(āsrava)* and conventional knowledge *(saṃvṛti-jñāna).* According to the Sarvāstivādins, practices based on impure knowledge could lead to pure knowledge even though, strictly speaking, such a relationship ran counter to the standard law of cause and effect. With this pure knowledge, the practitioner realizes cessation through analysis *(pratisaṅkhyā-nirodha),* an unconditioned *dharma.* This type of causal relation is called the separative effect *(visaṃyoga-phala);* no general or active cause *(kāraka-hetu)* is found in this relation.

Other schools suggested another approach to the problem of explaining how pure enlightenment could arise from a mind seemingly defiled. According to them, everyone intrinsically possessed the qualities that would enable him to realize enlightenment. The Mahāsaṅghikas, Discriminators, and others maintained that the original nature of the mind was pure. Later, this type of doctrine developed into the Mahāyāna Tathāgatagarbha (Buddha-nature) tradition, which held that every person possessed pure, unconditioned *dharmas* from the beginning.

The full form of the term "the path of insight" is "the path of insight into truth" *(satyadarśanamārga).* The practitioner is enlightened by the profundity of the Four Noble Truths. This enlightenment has two aspects: acquiescence *(kṣānti)* and knowledge *(jñāna).* Through acquiescence, the defilements are cut off; and by knowledge, cessation through analysis *(pratisaṅkhyā-nirodha)* is obtained. The path of insight consists of fifteen instants. The first instant is devoted to acquiescence to the First Noble Truth (that existence is suffering) in the desire realm. From the time of this realization, the practitioner is a sage *(ārya-sattva).* During the second instant, knowledge of the truth of suffering in the desire realm is realized. In the third instant, the practitioner acquiesces to the truth of suffering in the form and formless realms; and in the fourth instant, he obtains knowledge of the truth of suffering in the form and formless realms. This pattern is repeated for the three truths of the cause of suffering, its extinction, and the path. However, in the fifteenth instant (acquiescence of the truth of the path for the two higher realms) knowledge of the truth of the path for the two higher realms—in fact, knowledge of all Four Noble Truths—is clearly seen with the wisdom of enlightenment. Consequently, these fifteen instants constitute the path of insight. It is not the case, however, that the sixteenth instant (knowledge of the truth of the path in the two higher realms) is not experienced at all. Rather, it is repeated over and over just as the validity of the Four Noble Truths may be repeatedly perceived. What would have corresponded to the sixteenth instant is the beginning of the path of meditation.

The path of insight into the Four Noble Truths is also called entering into "the sagely path of pure wisdom and cutting off the defilements that bind one to life" *(niyāmāvakrānti)*. Through it, the eighty-eight defilements that may be cut off through an understanding of the Four Noble Truths are destroyed.

A distinction is drawn between two types of practitioners who enter the path of insight. The first, the *śraddhānusārin* (the person whose practice is based on faith), is someone with dull faculties. He enters the path of insight through faith. The second, the *dharmānusārin* (the person whose practice is based on his understanding of the Dharma), is someone with sharp faculties. He enters the path of insight through his meditations on the Dharma. In terms of the stages of the four candidates and four fruits, entry to the path of insight corresponds to the stage of being a candidate for stream-entrant.

In the sixteenth instant of realization of the Four Noble Truths, the practitioner enters the path of meditation *(bhāvanā-mārga)*. There he repeats his religious practices until they have become ingrained. Since the sixteenth instant of the path of insight is a repetition of the experience of the fifteenth instant, the path of meditation may be said to begin at the sixteenth instant, a point that corresponds to the fruit of stream-entrant. Because the sixteen instants follow each other in a necessary progression, once the practitioner has entered the path of insight, he is assured of realizing the fruit of stream-entrant.

When a person who practices in accord with faith *(śraddhānusārin)* enters the path of meditation, he is said to be "one who has realized pure knowledge through faith" *(śraddhādimukta)*. The person who practices in accord with his understanding of the Dharma *(dharmānusārin)* is said to be "one who has attained correct views" *(dṛṣṭiprāpta)* when he enters the path of meditation. The following six stages are included in the path of meditation: (1) the fruit of stream-entrant, (2) the candidate and (3) the fruit of once-returner, (4) the candidate and (5) the fruit of nonreturner, and (6) the candidate of *arhat*. A nonreturner who has realized the absorption of cessation *(nirodha-samāpatti)* is called a "bodily witness" *(kāyasākṣin)*. When the practitioner finally cuts off all defilements, he is called "one who no longer needs to practice" *(aśaikṣa)*. The person whose practice is based on faith must still guard himself against retrogression after he has become an *arhat* even though his mind is freed of defilements *(sāmayaikī kāntā cetovimuktiḥ)*. He must also wait for the appropriate time to enter meditations. In contrast, the person whose practice has been based upon an understanding of the Dharma will not be subject to retrogression after he becomes an *arhat (asamayavimukta)*. He is able to enter meditation whenever he chooses and realizes emancipation through wisdom *(prajñāvimukta)*, which destroys ignorance. If he can also enter the absorption of cessation he is said to have realized emancipation through both wisdom and meditation *(ubhayatobhāgavimukta)*.

The seven stages on the sagely path—*śraddhānusārin, dharmānusārin, śraddhādhimukta, dṛṣṭiprāpta, kāyasākṣin, prajñāvimukta, ubhayatobhāgavimukta*—are collectively known as the "seven sages." Although a list of seven sages is also found in Theravāda sources, the Theravāda list differs from that of the *Abhidharmakośa*. Various other stages are also described in the *Abhidharmakośa*. For example, a person who will be reborn only several more times *(kulaṅkula)* before becoming an *arhat* is included as a subdivision of those who are candidates for once-returner. Five (or sometimes seven) subdivisions of nonreturner are specified, including the nonreturner who realizes *parinirvāṇa* while he is between lives in the *antarābhava (antarā-parinirvāyin)*. Six (or sometimes nine) types of *arhats* are distinguished on the basis of such criteria as whether or not they backslide and the circumstances under which they might backslide. When all of these categories were collected the result was a list of eighteen categories of those in training *(śaikṣa)* and nine categories of those who had completed their training, a total of twenty-seven types of wise men and sages.

A schematic list of the Sarvāstivādin path is outlined below.

The Stages of the Sarvāstivādin Path

I. Preliminary practices
II. Seven stages of the wise
    A. Three degrees of the wise
        1. Fivefold meditation for quieting the mind
        2. Particular states of mindfulness
        3. General state of mindfulness
    B. Four degrees of favorable roots (internal degrees of the worldling)
        1. Warmth *(uṣmagata)*
        2. Peak *(mūrdhan)*
        3. Acquiescence *(kṣānti)*
        4. Pinnacle of worldly truth *(laukikāgratā)*
III. Seven degrees of the sage

- A. The paths of training
  - 1. The path of insight *(darśana-mārga;* candidate for stream-entrant)
    - a. The practitioner who is in accord with faith *(śraddhānusārin)*, progresses to 2a
    - b. The practitioner who is in accord with the Dharma *(dharmānusārin),* progresses to 2b
  - 2. The path of meditation *(bhāvanā-mārga;* stream-entrant to candidate for *arhat*)
    - a. He who has realized pure knowledge through faith *(śraddhādhimukta)*
    - b. He who has attained correct views *(dṛṣṭiprāpta)*
- B. The path of no further training *(aśaikṣa; arhat)*

The Ten Types of Knowledge

Enlightenment is based on pure *(anāsrava)* knowledge. According to Sarvāstivādin doctrine, wisdom *(prajñā)* is the mental faculty with the broadest range of functions concerning knowledge. Wisdom enables people to understand, a function that is also called investigation *(pravicaya).* Wisdom is analyzed by dividing it into three aspects: *kṣānti, jñāna,* and *dṛṣṭi. Kṣānti* (acquiescence) eliminates doubts. *Jñāna* (knowledge) has the function of firmly establishing the understanding. *Dṛṣṭi* usually means "views" in Buddhism, as in the list of five wrong views or the correct views mentioned in the eightfold path. In this instance, it might be translated as "looking," since it refers to inferring and searching for the truth. In the sixteen instants of the path of insight, *dṛṣṭi* would be included with the eight instants of acquiescence, since an element of seeking exists in acquiescence. Because the defilements are not completely cut off by acquiescence, the practitioner must seek further to eliminate them completely.

Wisdom is sometimes classified according to the method by which it is attained, as in a list of three types of knowledge gained as the practitioner travels the path to salvation: wisdom gained through hearing, through thought, and through religious practice. The first type is wisdom resulting from hearing the Dharma preached or from reading books. This type of wisdom is also said to be innate, whereas the next two types are developed through practice. The second type, wisdom through thought, is the result of contemplation, especially contemplation of correct doctrines. The third type, wisdom through religious practice, arises by putting the first two types of wisdom into practice through meditation. In other words, it is equivalent to appropriating the wisdom for oneself and making it an integral part of oneself. Usually discussions of wisdom in *abhidharma* literature refer to this last type (*Abhidharmakośa*, *T* 29:116c).

The most basic classification of wisdom is twofold: impure *(anāsrava)* and pure *(āsrava)* wisdom. Since knowledge is the most important aspect of wisdom, the same division into pure and impure is used for knowledge. These two classifications, in turn, are expanded into the following ten types of knowledge *(daśa-jñānāni)* (a brief description of the object or function of each knowledge is included).

1. Conventional knowledge *(saṃvṛti-jñāna)*—knowledge in the everyday sense of the word; both conditioned and unconditioned *dharmas* may also be objects of this type of knowledge
2. Knowledge of *dharmas (dharma-jñāna)*—the true aspects of *dharmas* and the Four Noble Truths relative to the desire realm
3. Subsequent knowledge *(anvaya-jñāna)*—the Four Noble Truths relative to the form and formless realms
4. Knowledge of suffering *(duḥkha-jñāna)*—defilements subject to the First Noble Truth eliminated
5. Knowledge of origination *(samudaya-jñāna)*—defilements subject to the Second Noble Truth eliminated
6. Knowledge of cessation *(nirodha-jñāna)*—defilements subject to the Third Noble Truth eliminated
7. Knowledge of path *(mārga-jñāna)*—defilements subject to the Fourth Noble Truth eliminated
8. Knowledge of the minds of others *(paracitta-jñāna)*
9. Knowledge of extinction *(kṣaya-jñāna)*—the knowledge that the defilements have been extinguished, suffering understood, the cause of suffering eliminated, *nirvāṇa* realized, and the path completed
10. Knowledge of nonproduction *(anutpāda-jñāna)*—the knowledge that the conditions that would allow any further suffering or rebirths to occur are absent

Except for conventional knowledge and some forms of the knowledge of other minds, all of these types of knowledge are "pure" in the sense that they are free from the bonds of the defilements and have their basis in truth and *nirvāṇa*. The last two types of knowledge, the knowledges of extinction and nonproduction, lack the aspect of "seeking" or "looking" *(dṛṣṭi)*. The knowledge of extinction refers to understanding that all the defilements have been extinguished and that everything that should be accomplished has in fact been accomplished. The knowledge of non-production is the understanding that the circumstances that would lead to further practice will not arise again. Because both of these are knowledges of a state of completion, they have no element of seeking in them, but they do have the quality of knowledge. The second through the seventh types of knowledges involve the elimination of both doubts and conjecture and therefore have both the aspects of looking *(dṛṣṭi)* and knowledge *(jñāna)*.

Knowledge of other minds may be either a pure or an impure knowledge. Advanced practitioners of both Buddhism and heterodox religions were thought to be able to acquire five superhuman abilities (clairvoyance, clairaudience, knowledge of the minds of others, the ability to go wherever one wished, and the ability to remember past lives). Buddhist practitioners were thought to naturally obtain the knowledge of the minds of others when they became sages. In such a case, this knowledge was pure. But when it was obtained by a non-Buddhist, it was impure.

Other than the above nine types of pure knowledge (nos. 2–10), all types of knowledge acquired through hearing, thought, and religious practice are conventional types of knowledge.

Meditation

The cultivation of wisdom must be based on a foundation of meditation. Thus, the practice of meditation precedes the acquisition of wisdom. The Sanskrit term used for meditation here is *samādhi,* which may be translated as "concentration." In *samādhi,* the mind is not agitated; even if one's attention moves or changes, the mind will not be agitated. *Samādhi* may be contrasted with the term *"yoga,"* which comes from a root meaning "to join together." The mind is focused and joined to the object. *Yoga* is thus a quiescent form of mental concentration. In Early Buddhism, the term *"samādhi"* is often used. The term *"dhyāna"* was used to refer to the meditative stages that resulted in *samādhi.*

The term *"yoga"* is not used very often in Buddhist texts, but examples of it can be found in the *Āgamas* and *abhidharma* texts. In *abhidharma* texts, *samādhi* is defined as the state in which the mind is concentrated on one object *(citta-eka-agratā)* and thus has approximately the same content as *"yoga."*

The *dhyāna* (trances) are divided into four classes: first, second, third, and fourth. This classification occurs in the *Āgamas.* The best type of *samādhi* occurs when two types of meditation, calm abiding *(śamatha)* and insight *(vipaśyanā),* are in equilibrium. As the practitioner progresses through the four *dhyānas,* his power of concentration intensifies. In the first *dhyāna* he applies investigation *(vitarka)* and scrutiny *(vicāra)* to the outside world. From the second *dhyāna* onward his perception of the outside world has been cut off, and investigation and scrutiny are no longer applied. In the first through the third *dhyāna* he still experiences a physical bliss. But in the fourth *dhyāna* this bliss has disappeared. The mind is pure and established in equanimity. The essence of the four *dhyānas* is the concentration on a single object. Since wisdom functions along with meditation, the functioning of wisdom becomes stronger as the practitioner progresses in his meditation.

Meditation exists in the desire realm, but it is always incomplete. Consequently, the desire realm is a place where the everyday scattered or unfocused mind predominates. It is not a place of meditation *(dhyāna-bhūmi)* as are the form and formless realms. Between the desire realm and the first *dhyāna* is a preparatory stage of meditation *(anāgamya).* In both this stage and the first *dhyāna,* investigation and scrutiny are applied. In the intermediate stage *(dhyāna antara)* between the first and second *dhyāna,* only scrutiny is present; investigation has ceased. Both scrutiny and investigation are functions of thought, but investigation ceases first because it is a coarser form of mental activity. From the second *dhyāna* onward neither investigation nor scrutiny is present.

Within the fourth *dhyāna* is a concentration without perception *(asaṃjñi samāpatti)* in which all perception has completely ceased. Non-Buddhists are said to be particularly fond of entering this trance and often to mistake it for *nirvāṇa.* If a person dies while he is in this trance, he will be reborn in the realm without perception, which is a part of the Fourth Meditation Heaven. *Nirodha-samāpatti* (cessation absorption) resembles concentration without perception. But in *nirodha-samāpatti,* the mental functions down to sensation cease. Only Buddhists enter this form of meditation. If a person dies while he is in it, he will be reborn in the realm of neither perception nor nonperception *(naiva-samjñā-nasamjñā-āyatana)* in the formless realm.

While the practitioner is in the fourth *dhyāna,* he is never completely free of some sense of his body. Higher forms of meditation, however, consist of consciousness only, devoid of any sense of the physical body. These higher meditations are called the four formless absorptions. The term "form" in this case refers to the physical body. In the four trances the practitioner was aware of his body while he meditated. If he died while he was in one of the *dhyānas,* he was reborn in the corresponding heaven in the form realm. Those who die while in the formless absorptions are similarly reborn in the formless realm. Since the formless realm is devoid of matter, it cannot be said to exist as a physical place.

However, birth and death occur within the formless realm, and time must therefore exist in it. The four formless absorptions are the infinity of space, the infinity of consciousness, nothingness, and neither perception nor nonperception.

Nirvāṇa and the Three Realms

The three realms (desire, form, and formless) correspond to meditative and mental states. The three realms compose the conditioned *(saṃskṛta)* world in which sentient beings go through cycles of birth and death. According to *abhidharma* texts, *nirvāṇa* lies outside the conditioned world. It is a realm beyond space and time. Although it is eternal, it seems devoid of content, a realm of nothingness. An *arhat* cuts off all his defilements, extinguishes his karma, and abandons both body and mind when he enters final *nirvāṇa.* Because even the wisdom gained in enlightenment is conditioned, it, too, must be abandoned. Thus, nothing remains when he enters *nirvāṇa.* This view of *nirvāṇa* was criticized by Mahāyāna Buddhists as being the extinction of body and mind. One of the major reasons for the rise of Mahāyāna was the dissatisfaction with this view of *nirvāṇa.* Consequently, Mahāyāna Buddhists sought to find their goal within this conditioned world so that they might view both their goal and the world in a more positive manner.

PART THREE

EARLY MAHĀYĀNA BUDDHISM

CHAPTER 14

The Evolution of the Order after Aśoka

India after Aśoka

THE MAURYAN EMPIRE declined rapidly after the death of King Aśoka (r. c. 268–232 B.C.E.) and was finally destroyed by the general Puṣyamitra in approximately 180 B.C.E.[1] Puṣyamitra founded the Śuṅga dynasty; however, his power never extended beyond the Gangetic plain. Also at this time, a succession of Greek kings invaded northwestern India and established several dynasties. In southern India the Śātavāhana dynasty, an Āndhran dynasty, was established on the Deccan plain and remained in power from 200 B.C.E. until the third century C.E. During the four centuries in which this dynasty ruled, a flourishing culture developed in politically stable South India. Finally, along the east coast in the former lands of Kaliṅga, the Ceti dynasty was founded. Its third king, Khāravela (fl. first century B.C.E.), was particularly famous. Inscriptions describing his accomplishments have been discovered, but the later history of the dynasty is unknown.

Śuṅga Dynasty

The Śuṅga dynasty, founded by Puṣyamitra, lasted for 112 years. Although Puṣyamitra supported Brahmanism and persecuted Buddhism, most later kings in this dynasty favored Buddhism. Inscriptions record that King Dhānabhuti-Vāchiputa contributed a gate *(toraṇa)* and stone building *(silākaṃmaṃta)* to the Buddhist *stūpa* at Bhārhut. His son,

Prince Vādhapāla, made contributions for the erection of the railing *(vedika)* that surrounds the *stūpa*. In addition, Queen Nāgarakhitā gave donations for the construction of the railing. Inscriptions found at Mathurā reveal that Vādhapāla also helped with the building of the railing there.

Bhārhut and Sāñcī

Bhārhut is situated in the southwestern part of central India on the main road from the west coast inland to Magadha. Because of its location, the Buddhist complex at Bhārhut was completely destroyed by non-Buddhists who invaded India. In 1873 A. Cunningham, a British general who conducted an archeological survey of India, discovered the ruins. The east gate and those parts of the railing that had suffered the least damage were subsequently taken to the Calcutta Museum, restored, and exhibited. They indicate that Bhārhut was a magnificent site. An inscription concerning King Dhānabhuti was found on a pillar of the east gate. The *stūpa* dates from the middle of the second century B.C.E., the height of the Śuṅga dynasty.

Pāṭaliputra and Vidiśā were the political centers of the Śuṅga dynasty. Because King Aśoka's son Mahinda was a native of Vidiśā, the town became a major center of Buddhism; there were many *stūpas* in its environs. More than sixty of these *stūpas,* known collectively as the "Bhīlsa Topes," have been discovered. Although most of them are in ruins, the ones at Sāñcī—approximately twenty, both large and small—are still in good condition. The famous great *stūpa* at Sāñcī is well preserved. It is an imposing structure, 16.4 meters high and with a diameter of 37 meters. Research has revealed that it began as a small tiled *stūpa* built during Aśoka's time and that subsequently it was covered with stone and expanded to its present proportions during the Śuṅga dynasty. Railings were later built around it and four gates pointing in the cardinal directions were constructed. Of the four gates, the southern one is the oldest. An inscription states that it was constructed during the early period of the Andhran dynasty. Thus the *stūpa* was gradually built and expanded during the Mauryan, Śuṅgan, and Āndhran dynasties. The four gates are covered with delicate relief carvings that have made Sāñcī famous among art historians.

Since most of the kings of the Śuṅga dynasty favored Buddhism, the religion made substantial advances during this period. Many of the railings of Bhārhut were carved at this time. The inscriptions on them indicate that the biography of the Buddha and the *jātaka* tales were the favorite subjects for carving. Fifteen scenes from the biography of the Buddha and thirty-two from the *Jātakas* have been identified. In the scenes from the biography of the Buddha, the figure of the Buddha is not represented as a human being but is instead symbolized by the *bodhi*-tree with an adamantine seat before it. Animals and people are depicting paying homage to the seat. Because the Buddha had entered *nirvāṇa,* many felt that he could not be represented in human form. In addition, the appearance of *bodhi*-trees representing the seven past Buddhas (Śākyamuni was the seventh) in the carvings suggests that people believed in the seven Buddhas during this period.

The names of those people who contributed to the construction of the railings and other structures at Bhārhut were recorded in inscriptions at the site. An examination of the surviving 209 inscriptions yields valuable information about those who supported the construction of Bharhut. Names of individual monks and nuns are included in the inscriptions. Some of them had titles such as *peṭakin* (one who upholds a *piṭaka*) or *pacanekāyika* (one who is well versed in the five *Nikāyas*). Such titles indicate that the canon was already divided into at least the *Sutta-piṭaka* and *Vinaya-piṭaka* at this time. An *Abhidhamma-piṭaka* may also have been established by this time. The term "five *Nikāyas*" suggests that the *Sutta-piṭaka* was already divided into five parts, probably in the same manner as was done in Pāli Buddhism. The title *suttantika* (*sutta*-master) is also found.

Six examples occur of people called *bhāṇaka* (chanters of scripture). Pāli sources, such as the *Visuddhimagga,* include the terms *Dīgha-bhāṇaka* (one who chants the *Dīgha-nikāya)* and *Majjhima-bhāṇaka* (one who chants the *Majjhima-nikāya*), indicating that some people specialized in certain *Nikāyas.* The term *"Dharma-bhāṇaka"* (chanters of the Dharma) appears in Mahāyāna sources. Since the inscriptions at Bharhut use only the term *"bhāṇaka,"* the contents of the chanting remain unclear. One of the six chanters in these inscriptions is called *ārya* (sage) and three are called *bhadanta* (venerable). These four chanters were monks; however, the other two chanters have no appellation indicating that they were monks. The previously mentioned *peṭakin* was called the "sage *(aya)* Jāta" and was thus clearly a monk. "The master of the five *Nikāyas,*" however, was only called "Budharakhita," leaving his status unclear. The "*sutta*-master" was called the "sage *(aya)* Cula" and was therefore a monk.

Sāñcī is southwest of Bhārhut, near the border between central and western India. The inscriptions collected from Sāñcī number 904, many more than were found at Bhārhut. Included among these are inscriptions on the lids and bases of five funerary urns discovered at *stūpa* number 2. The contents of two of the urns are identified as the "remains of the sage of the Kāsapagota family who taught in the Himalayan area" and "the remains of the sage Majhima." In such works as the *Samantapāsādikā* (*T* 24:685a), these two men are said to have spread Buddhism to the Himalayan regions during Aśoka's reign. Another urn is identified as containing the remains of "Mogaliputa" and may have contained the relics of Moggaliputta Tissa, King Aśoka's teacher. Four urns were discovered in *stūpa* number 3. One of these has an inscription identifying the contents as the remains of "Sāriputa." The inscription on another states that it contains the remains of "Mahā-mogalāna." These may have some relation to two of the Buddha's chief disciples, Śāriputra and Mahā-moggallāna (S. Mahāmaudgalyāyana); however, the urns appear to date only from the second century B.C.E.

The four gates and the railings at Sāñcī were built in the first century B.C.E. The gates are decorated with delicate relief carvings portraying deities who guard Buddhism, as well as twenty-eight scenes from the Buddha's life and six from *jātaka* tales. The names of a very large number of donors are also found on the gates and railings. Included are monks, nuns, and lay believers. The names of many more nuns than monks are recorded. The large number of inscriptions such as "a donation of the nun Yakhī who is a resident of Vāḷīvahana" indicate that many of the donors did not live at Sāñcī. Many of the monks and nuns were from Vidiśā. The residences of some donors are not recorded.

In inscriptions concerning lay believers, the appellations *upasāka* (layman) and *upāsikā* (laywoman) rarely appear; usually only their names are recorded. The reason for this omission remains unclear. There are also five examples in which the donors are called "householder" *(gahapati)* and seventeen in which they are called "head of the guild" *(seṭṭhi)*. The greater frequency of the term "head of the guild" is an indication of the large numbers of believers from the merchant class. In addition, there are two or three examples of contributions by villages and several by Buddhist organizations *(Bodha-goṭhī, Bauddha-goṣṭhī)*. One Greek donor is also mentioned.

In one inscription the donor is described as a monk who had "mastered the five collections *(nikāyas)*." According to another inscription, a laywoman named Avisinā of Maḍalachikaṭa who was well versed in the *sūtras (sūtātikinī)* made a contribution. (This inscription appears twice.) One example of a layman versed in the *sūtras (suttantika)* is also recorded. Two inscriptions describe the donors (one layman, one monk) as reciters *(bhāṇaka)*. Although the schools of Nikāya Buddhism must have existed at the time when Sāñcī and Bhārhut were being established, it is noteworthy that not a single reference to any of these schools appears in the inscriptions from the two sites.

Near Sāñcī are two sets of *stūpas,* the Andher and Bhojpur *stūpas,* which are usually grouped together with the Bhīlsa Topes. Reliquaries and inscriptions have been discovered at the three Andher *stūpas,* located in a small village to the southwest of Bhīlsa. The names "Mogaliputa" and "Hāritīputa" appear in the inscriptions.

Besides Sāñcī and Bhārhut, another important site in central India is found at Buddhagayā, the place where Śākyamuni Buddha attained enlightenment. A *caitya* (memorial mound) was constructed at this site at an early date. During the Śuṅga dynasty, a magnificent balustrade was built around the site of the Buddha's enlightenment, but only remains of it survive today. The center of this sacred site is the "adamantine throne" at the foot of the *bodhi*-tree where Śākyamuni was seated at the time of his enlightenment. During the Gupta dynasty the great *stūpa* of Buddhagayā was erected. (The great *stūpa* found there today is a restoration done at a later date.) The oldest surviving structure at the site today is a part of its balustrade. Traditional accounts maintained that it dated back to the time of Aśoka, but recent research has revealed that it was built after Bhārhut had been constructed. Among the carvings on the balustrade are five that probably concern the biography of the Buddha and two that are related to the *Jātakas.*

Several other important sites exist in central India. Part of an old balustrade was unearthed at Pāṭaliputra, suggesting the magnificence of the temples established by Aśoka at the Aśokārāma. Many other temples and *stūpas* must have existed in central India, but little remains to be seen today. However, a stone pillar erected at the order of King Aśoka and inscriptions in Brāhmī script dating from the second century B.C.E. were discovered at Sārnāth, the site of the Buddha's first sermon. The inscription on the capstone for a balustrade notes that it was contributed by the nun Saṃvahikā. A *stūpa* must also have existed at the Aśokārāma. Discovery of a Buddhist site from the Śuṅga dynasty was also made at Lauṛiyā Nandangaṛh in Bihar. Apparently a large *stūpa* existed there, but no inscriptions have been found.

The Kāṇva Dynasty

The ninth king of the Śuṅga dynasty, Devabhūti, ruled ten years until approximately 70 B.C.E., when he was assassinated at the instigation of his minister Vasudeva. The Kāṇva dynasty, founded by Vasudeva, lasted forty-five years and ruled the Ganges River basin. It was a weak dynasty, however, and during the rule of its fourth king was conquered by the Āndhran dynasty from the south. The Magadha region subsequently fell under the rule of the Andhra dynasty for a long period.

The Macedonian Kings of Northwestern India

From approximately 180 B.C.E., when the strength of the Mauryan Empire was already on the wane, a series of foreign peoples began invading northwestern India, which was thereafter dominated by foreign armies for a long time. The first of these foreign invaders were the Greeks, called *"yavana"* in Sanskrit and *"yona"* in Pāli, both terms that were probably based on the place name "Ionia."

Alexander the Great invaded India in 327 B.C.E., spreading Greek culture and customs, but had been repulsed by Candragupta (r. ca. 321–297 B.C.E.), the founder of the Mauryan dynasty. After Alexander's death, only western India continued under Macedonian rule. Seleucus I, founder of the Seleucid dynasty, dispatched a Greek named Megasthenes to serve as his envoy in Candragupta's court at Pāṭaliputra in central India. Megasthenes was stationed in Pāṭaliputra from ca. 303 to 292 B.C.E. and wrote a record of his experiences there that became famous. By about the middle of the third century B.C.E., Bactria (modern Balkh, the area between the Oxus and Indus rivers in northern Afghanistan) and Parthia had gained their independence from Seleucid rule. From the third century B.C.E. to the middle of the second century B.C.E., another Seleucid king, Antiochus III of Syria, and the fourth king of Bactria, Demetrios, invaded India. They occupied northern India and advanced into central India. In the first century B.C.E. King Maues of the Śaka people invaded India and ended the rule of Macedonian kings in northwestern India.

Of the Macedonian kings recorded in Indian history, Menandros (known in Indian languages as Milinda) is particularly important. Menandros invaded India and ruled an area extending from central India to Afghanistan from approximately 160 to 140 B.C.E. The capital of his empire was Śākala.

Menandros is thought to have held a number of debates with a Buddhist monk, Nāgasena, and to have been converted to Buddhism. The contents of their talks were collected and compiled into the *Milindapañha* or *Questions of King Milinda.* The Pāli text of this work includes a number of additions by later authors; however, the earliest part of the text can be determined by comparing the Pāli text with the Chinese translation, the *Na-hsien pi-ch'iu ching* (*T* 1670a). Those parts found in both versions constitute the oldest elements of the work and offer a fascinating view of certain aspects of Indian Buddhism during the first and second centuries B.C.E. No elements of Mahāyāna Buddhism are included in the work, which shows Buddhist doctrine in the transitional period between the *Āgamas* and the development of *abhidharma* literature.

In 1937 a reliquary was discovered at Shinkot in the Swat River Valley in the upper reaches of the Indus River. According to the inscription on it, the remains were enshrined in the reliquary during the reign of King Milinda (or Minadra, according to the inscription), providing additional evidence that Buddhism was followed in northern India during the time of Milinda.

During Aśoka's reign, Majjhantika was sent as an emissary to northwestern India to establish a Buddhist order there. Although much of the early history of this area is not known, it is clear that the Sarvāstivādin School became the dominant Buddhist school in Kashmir and Gandhāra. The remains of many Buddhist *stūpas* have been discovered in northwestern India, indicating that Buddhism was flourishing in this area by the second century B.C.E. One of the most important of these finds is the Dharmarājikā *stūpa* discovered at Taxila. The oldest part of the *stūpa* dates from the time of King Aśoka. The ruins in the area reveal that the Dharmarājikā *stūpa* was huge, surrounded by lodgings for believers, and undoubtedly one of the major Buddhist centers in North India for a long time. A roll of thin silver plate was discovered in one of the old halls near the *stūpa* in 1914. According to the inscription on it, a Bactrian named Urasaka had enshrined a relic of the Buddha in a hall he had built that was dedicated to a bodhisattva. The inscription is late, dating from the middle of the first century C.E., but many Buddhist antiquities excavated at Sirkap in Taxila are much older; the oldest dates from the second century B.C.E.

Inscriptions have been found indicating that a number of Greeks had converted to Buddhism by the first century B.C.E. According to an inscription on a reliquary urn found in the Swat Valley, the urn contained a relic of Śākyamuni Buddha and had been installed there by a Greek governor *(meridarkh)* named Theodoros. A copper plate found at the same site records that the *stūpa* was built by the *meridarkh* and his wife. The term "*meridarkh*" refers to an office in the Greek administrative system. Although it may be translated as "governor," the *meridarkh* probably did not govern a very large territory. The significant fact, however, is that Buddhist believers devout enough to commission *stūpas* could be found among this class of officials.

Greek Buddhists were found even in Aśoka's time. Among the Buddhist missionaries dispatched by Aśoka was a Greek named Dhammarakkhita, who went to Aparāntaka to spread Buddhism. Greek donors are also mentioned in the inscriptions at Sāñcī, suggesting that some Greeks must have converted to Buddhism soon after their arrival in India.

Buddhism was a rational and moral religion, easily adopted by foreign peoples. Greeks could readily respond to the Buddha's teachings and worship at Buddhist *stūpas.* In contrast, Brahmanism and Hinduism included much folk religion. They were based on a caste system that, according to the *Laws of Manu,* regarded foreigners as *mleccha* (impure barbarians). Consequently, few foreigners adopted Hinduism. Buddhism, with its emphasis on doctrine and reason, was much more attractive to foreigners. Moreover, according to Buddhist teachings, all castes were fundamentally equal, and foreigners were not discriminated against. Not only the Greeks, but the foreign invaders of India who followed them, including the Śakas, Parthians, and Kuṣāṇas, often became supporters of Buddhism.

The Śaka Invasion

The Śaka people are referred to as the *sai-chung* in the Chinese dynastic history, the *Han shu.* At one time they had lived near the Ili River in Central Asia, but around 180 B.C.E. they were forced by the Uighurs to move west. The Śakas eventually destroyed the Macedonian state in Bactria and made that their base. However, the Hsiung-nu later pushed the Uighurs further west, and the Uighurs in turn conquered Bactria (Ch. Ta-hsia). The Śaka, forced to move south, invaded India. Around 100 B.C.E. Maues became the first Śaka king. He conquered northern India and was on an expedition to conquer Mathurā when he died. Maues had called himself "the king of kings," but after his death the Śaka people broke apart into smaller groups. The various areas they had conquered were each ruled in a semiautonomous fashion by governor-generals called *kṣatrapa* or *mahākṣatrapa.* Particularly important were Kusuluka and his son Patika, who ruled in North India, and Rajula, who ruled in Mathurā.

The Śaka rulers patronized Buddhism. According to a copper plate found at the *stūpa* at Taxila, which dates from the first century B.C.E., Patika built *stūpas* in areas where none had existed and installed the relics of Śākyamuni Buddha in them. He is also credited with the establishment of monasteries. According to the inscription on a pillar topped by lions found at Mathurā, Ayasia Kamuïa, the wife of the *mahākṣatrapa*

Rajula, along with her relatives and the women in the palace, commissioned the building of a *stūpa* with a relic of Śākyamuni Buddha. They also built monasteries and gave alms to the Sarvāstivādin School. Rajula's son, Śuḍasa, gave land for the support of cave-temples to two monks of the Sarvāstivādin School, Buddhadeva and Budhila. This inscription, which dates from about 10 B.C.E., includes the earliest mention of the name of a school of Nikāya Buddhism.

Parthia

Parthia was originally located southeast of the Caspian Sea. In the third century B.C.E. Arsakes rebelled against the king of Syria and established the Parthian kingdom. The Chinese have traditionally called the Parthians *"an-hsi,"* a transliteration of Arsakes. The Parthians extended their borders at the expense of the Greeks, and later during the reign of King Azes invaded India. The next king, Gondopharnes, lived around the beginning of the common era and ruled in northwestern India. By the end of the first century C.E., the Parthians had replaced the Śakas as rulers of northwestern India; shortly afterward, the Kuṣāṇa dynasty replaced the Parthians as the conquerors of northwestern India.

The Parthians were Buddhist. A number of Parthian monks played important roles in carrying Buddhism to China. For example, An Shih-kao (the character *"an"* was taken from the term *"an-hsi"* or Parthia and was used as an ethnikon indicating the monk's Parthian nationality) was a prince from Parthia. He became a Buddhist monk, studied *abhidharma,* and mastered a number of meditation techniques. After he arrived in China during the reign of Emperor Huan (r. 146–167) of the Later Han, he translated many works from the *Āgamas* and *abhidharma* literature. Several decades later, during the reign of Emperor Ling (r. 168–189), another Parthian, An Hsüan, traveled to China. In the middle of the third century a Parthian named T'an-ti is reported in China.

Kuṣāṇa Dynasty

The Kuṣāṇas, known to the Chinese as the "Ta-yüeh-chih" or Uighurs, were originally in Central Asia between Tun-huang and Ch'i-lian; they moved west after they were defeated by the Hsiung-nu in the second century B.C.E. For a time they settled to the north of the Oxus River, but then moved on to defeat the Ta-hsia. By around 129 B.C.E. they had advanced into the former kingdom of Bactria. At that time there were five tribes of Uighurs, the strongest being the Kuṣāṇas. They added to their power when they brought the other four tribes under their control. In the last half of the first century C.E., they conquered Parthia and invaded India under their leader, Kujūla Kadphises. He was succeeded by Wema Kadphises. In the first half of the second century C.E., he was followed by the famous King Kaniṣka, who had seized power from the Kadphises' lineage. Kaniṣka created an empire that stretched from Central Asia into Afghanistan and included the northwestern and northern parts of India.

Kaniṣka's empire was the largest in South Asia since Aśoka's time. It encompassed peoples of many races including Indians, Greeks, Śakas, and Parthians. Moreover, the Kuṣāṇa Empire occupied a key position on the trade routes between the Roman Empire, India, and China. The cultures of the various peoples living under Kuṣāṇa rule combined with the stimulus provided by East-West trade produced a dynamic new society and culture in North India. A new movement in Buddhism, the Mahāyāna tradition, developed impressively under Kuṣāṇa rule. In addition, Buddhism was stimulated by Greek and Greco-Roman culture to produce new forms of architecture and carving. The art of Gandhāra, for example, was noticeably influenced by the Greeks. Buddhist temples began to appear with Corinthian columns and capitals, as well as Greek decorative patterns. Greek influence eventually even reached Japan by way of Central Asia and China. The architecture of the Horyūji Temple in Nara, Japan, clearly reflects Greek influence.

During this period, Buddhist carving advanced. Sculptures were strongly influenced by Greek sculpture, as is evident from the Greek style of the facial expressions and clothing, particularly the folds of the cloth, portrayed in the carvings. The influence of Greco-Roman art on Buddhist architecture and sculpture of human figures was already evident in the Parthian period. Images of the Buddha himself, however, were not produced at this time. They first appeared in Gandhāra (in the northern part of modern Pakistan) and in Mathurā in central India during the last half of the first century C.E., the early part of the Kuṣāṇa dynasty. During the second century C.E. Buddhist sculpture proliferated.

The Buddha was first portrayed in sculpture in the context of reliefs depicting his biography and earlier lives. These reliefs were used to ornament Buddhist *stūpas* and Buddhist architecture at such sites as Bharhut and Sāñcī in central India. In these early reliefs, however, the Buddha was only symbolized, not represented with a human figure. Only with the emergence of Gandhāran art was the Buddha portrayed in human form. At first, he was depicted as being approximately the same size as the other figures in the reliefs even though he was the central figure. Later, however, the figure of the Buddha was made larger than the other figures. Finally, he was removed from the biographical scenes, and independent images of the Buddha were sculpted.

Independent images of the Buddha served as objects of worship and consequently had a different function from the Buddha portrayed in reliefs depicting his biography. Such objects of worship may have been developed by those who were carving reliefs depicting the Buddha's biography in response to the *stūpa* worship cults. Buddhist biographical literature also may have played a role in these developments. Whether the portrayal of the Buddha in human form was due to the influence of Greek sculptors or whether it was the result of inevitable developments in Buddhist doctrine remains a question. If it were due to developments in Buddhist doctrine, then it probably had its roots in *stūpa* worship and lay beliefs in the Buddha's power to save people. According to Nikāya Buddhist doctrine, which was formulated by monks, when the Buddha died he entered into "*nirvāṇa* without remainder" and thus abandoned his physical body. Since he could no longer be seen, he could not be portrayed with any form, human or otherwise.

The beliefs of Kujūla Kadphises and Wema Kadphises are not clearly known; but during their reigns, Buddhism appears to have flourished in northern India, where many Buddhist ruins have been found, including the Dharmarajikā *stūpa* at Taxila, the Kuṇāla *stūpa,* and the ruins at Kalawān. Many discoveries at these sites date from the Kuṣāṇa period. The ruins at Kalawān include the largest monastery found in northern India. An inscription from a *caitya* hall from the site includes the date "the 134th year of Azes," which corresponds to 77 C.E. The inscription records the enshrinement of relics in the *caitya* hall and their presentation to the Sarvāstivādin School, the earliest mention in northern India of a school of Nikāya Buddhism.

Among the later inscriptions, which date from the second century C.E. on, is one found near Peshawar in northern Pakistan. There King Kaniṣka established the famous great *stūpa* of Kaniṣka, the ruins of which were excavated at Shāh-jī-kī Ḍherī. An urn for relics was discovered that had been enshrined at the Kaniṣka-vihāra (monastery). The inscription on the urn clearly states that the Kaniṣka-vihāra belonged to the Sarvāstivādin School. An inscription dated 148 C.E. on a small copper *stūpa* from Kurram near Peshawar records the enshrinement of the Buddha's relics and their donation to the Sarvāstivādin School.

Among the other inscriptions from northern India that include the names of schools is one mentioning the construction of a water supply and another recording the excavation of a well, both for the Sarvāstivādins. According to other inscriptions, a copper ladle was given to Kāśyapīya School and earthen jars to the Bahuśrutīya and Kāśyapīya schools. These inscriptions date from approximately the second century C.E.

The Sarvāstivādin School was particularly strong in northern India. But many inscriptions concerning the building of *stūpas* in northern India do not mention the name of any of the schools of Nikāya Buddhism. For example, an inscription records the enshrinement of relics by two Greek *meridarkhs* (governors). The Śaka governor Patika had relics enshrined and *stūpas* built at various sites including Kshema at Taxila, but these *stūpas* apparently were not given to any particular school. These inscriptions were dated approximately the first century C.E. Most of the inscriptions concerning *stūpas* were similar to these and did not include the name of any of the schools of Nikāya Buddhism.[2]

Buddhist sites have also been found in Afghanistan. The discovery of Aśokan inscriptions at Lampāka and Kandahār proved that Buddhism was being spread in these areas by the time of King Aśoka. The subsequent history of Buddhist proselytization in these areas is not known in detail, but by the beginning of the common era Buddhism was flourishing. In modern times many Buddhist archeological sites have been excavated in Afghanistan, including the remains of the castle town of Bergrām, the *stūpas* at Bīmarān, and the ruins from Haḍḍa and Shotorak. Further to the west are the cave-temples of Bāmiyān, within which are two very large stone Buddhas and some murals. Bergrām has been identified as the ancient site of Kāpiśī. Illustrations of the Buddha's biography and other antiquities have been found at this site. A reliquary was discovered in an ancient *stūpa* at Bīmarān. According to an inscription on it, a man named Śīvarakṣita built a *stūpa* to enshrine the relics of the Buddha during the Śaka period.

Many artifacts have also been found at Haḍḍa. According to an inscription on a water vase, it had been placed in a *stūpa* for the Buddha's relics during the Kuṣāṇa dynasty. A bronze reliquary was found at Wardak, to the west of Kabul. On it was an inscription stating that the Buddha's relics had been enshrined within the Vagramarega Monastery and that they had been given to the Mahāsaṅghika School. A wish for King Huviṣka's good fortune was also expressed in the inscription, which was dated the fifty-first year of the era, a date corresponding to 179 C.E. during the Kuṣāṇa period. Although many inscriptions have been discovered in both northern India and Afghanistan, only a few include the names of the schools of Nikāya Buddhism.

Kaniṣka's support for the Sarvāstivādin School is clearly manifested in the inscription found at the great *stūpa* of Kaniṣka. His support is also the subject of a number of legends. For example, according to the *Ma-ming p'u-sa chuan* (*T* 2046), a biography of Aśvaghoṣa, when Kaniṣka attacked central India, he demanded the Buddha's begging bowl and Aśvaghoṣa as compensation. In response to the king's request, Aśvaghoṣa went to northwestern India and spread Buddhism there. Kaniṣka also paid homage to Pārśva of the Sarvāstivādin School, and at Pārśva's recommendation assembled five hundred *arhats* and convened a council. This council is commonly called the Fourth Council. The huge two-hundred-fascicle *Mahāvibhāṣā* (*T* 1545) is said to have been compiled as a result of this council.

Kaniṣka was succeeded by Vāṣiska, Huviṣka, and Vāsudeva. The strength of the dynasty gradually waned, and by the end of the third century, it occupied only a small part of northern India. Buddhism continued to flourish in northern India during this period. Earlier in Mathurā, a governor *(kṣatrapa)* named Śuḍasa had established the Guha-vihāra (monastery). Later during the Kuṣāṇa dynasty, in the forty-seventh year of the epoch that began with Kaniṣka, King Huviṣka had the Huviṣka-vihāra constructed at Jamālpur on the outskirts of Mathurā. It was decorated with beautiful carvings. These were destroyed by non-Buddhists, however, and today the monastery is in ruins. Many fragments of fences, pillars, and Buddhist images have been found in the ruins. Many other temples also were located at Mathurā. Inscriptions found around Mathurā indicate that a number of the schools of Nikāya Buddhism had monasteries there, including the Mahāsaṅghika (mentioned in six inscriptions), Sarvāstivāda (two inscriptions), Sammatīya (one inscription), and Dharmaguptaka (one inscription). Many other inscriptions that do not include the names of any of the schools have also been found. Mathurā's status as a major Buddhist center is confirmed by passages in the travel diaries of Fa-hsien and Hsüan-tsang.

Mathurā and Gandhāra are famous as the two sites where the Buddha was first portrayed in human form in sculpture. The first images were made at Mathurā at approximately the same time they first appeared at Gandhāra. However, the images from Mathurā, which had long been an advanced center of plastic arts, are not copies of those from Gandhāra and are done in a different style, indicating that the images at the two sites were probably created independently.[3] Perhaps the artists of Mathurā were stimulated by the appearance of the Gandhāran images of the Buddha to sculpt images in their own style. Few examples of Mathurān treatments of the Buddha's biography have been found, but many portrayals of people honoring the Buddha have been found among the Mathurān artifacts. In early examples, the object of worship is the *bodhi*-tree or a *stūpa*. Later these objects were replaced with a human figure of the Buddha, and finally, figures of various bodhisattvas and Buddhas were made. In the dedicatory inscriptions on the Mathurān statues of the Buddha, the carvings themselves are sometimes referred to simply as "images" *(pratimā)* rather than as "images of the Buddha." Identical images are referred to in some inscriptions as "a seated image of a bodhisattva" but in others as "a seated image of the Buddha." The variety in terms used to refer to the carvings probably indicates differences in their use. However, the doctrinal reasons underlying such distinctions in terminology remain unclear.

The Āndhran Dynasties

The Āndhran dynasties are divided into two periods. During the first, the Śātavāhana royal house ruled the Deccan peninsula. The second period consists of the decline of the Śātavāhana royal house and the emergence of a number of local kings, each of whom defended his own territory.

With the decline of Mauryan power around 200 B.C.E., the Śātavāhana family, which came from the western part of the Deccan, increased their influence. Their power, which lasted until the third century C.E., was based on an area with Paithan (Prastiṣṭhāna), the southern terminus of the Southern Route, at its center; but they seem to have come from an area that included Nāsik and Akolā to the north. By the second century C.E., the Śātavāhana dynasty was at its height; it extended to a large area to the south of the Vindhya Mountains and the Narmadā River, which served as the natural boundaries between central and southern India. For a time, the Śātavāhanas even extended their rule north of the Narmadā River. The capital of their kingdom was at Dhānyakaṭaka, on the eastern seacoast near the banks of the Kṛṣṇā River.

Traditionally, the Śātavāhana royal family is said to have ruled for 460 years and to have produced thirty kings. A number of these "kings," however, were the heads of branches of the family. It is probably more accurate to say that the Śātavāhana family ruled for approximately 300 years with seventeen to nineteen kings reigning during this period. By the third century C.E. the Śātavāhana family had lost its power and the Deccan was ruled by a number of different families, each controlling a small area. During this period the Ikṣvāku royal family established itself in the region around the lower reaches of the Godāvarī River. It was a strong supporter of Buddhism. By the fourth century the Gupta dynasty had united India.

Cave-temples

One of the major distinguishing features of Buddhism in the Deccan is the cave-temples found in the area, especially in the Ghats, the mountain range along the west coast. Approximately twelve hundred cave-temples have been found in India; seventy-five percent of them are Buddhist, with the oldest dating from the first or second century B.C.E. The excavation of cave-temples reached its peak during the next several centuries.

Rocky mountains, barren of trees, are found throughout the Deccan. Since there was not enough wood to build monasteries, they were carved out of rock. In these mountainous areas, monasteries and *stūpas* were constructed in large caves instead of on level ground as in other parts of India. Cave-temples, because they were constructed out of long-lasting material, provide significant information about monastery life in ancient India. The most famous cave-temples are found at Ajantā, Bhājā, Nāsik, Kārlī, and Ellora. Two types of caves are found at these sites: caves used for worship, which contained a *stūpa,* and caves used as quarters for monks.

The caves used for worship are called *cetiyaghara.* The *stūpas* found in them are made of stone and are much smaller than those found above the ground. A complex of cells for monks *(vihāra)* usually encircled a large rectangular chamber. The entrance to the complex was on one wall. Entryways to a number of cells *(layana),* each serving as the residence of one or two monks, were found on the other three walls of the central chamber. One particularly large *vihāra* at Ellora consists of three stories with a total of more than a hundred cells for monks. The large central chamber was used for events such as the fortnightly assembly *(uposatha),* at which the precepts were recited. The entryways and the pillars in the *cetiyagharas* were often elaborately carved, while the *vihāras* were usually plain. However, the *vihāras* at Ajantā and Ellora are carved. The wall paintings at Ajantā are particularly famous.

Nāsik is a city to the west of Ajantā and Ellora. The cave-temples in this area are midway up the slope of mountains outside the city. There are a total of twenty-three cave-temples with the oldest dating from the second century B.C.E. An inscription in the fourteenth cave records that it was commissioned by a high official who lived in Nāsik during the reign of King Kaṇha. This king has been identified as King Kṛṣṇa, who was the second ruler of the Āndhran dynasties and the younger brother of Simuka, the first king of the Śātavāhana dynasty. If this is correct, the cave would have been excavated during the first half of the second century B.C.E. The style of the letters of the inscriptions in the *stūpa* hall of the thirteenth cave indicates that they date from the second century B.C.E. According to this inscription, the village of Dhaṃbika raised the funds for the cave.

Despite all of this Buddhist activity, the Āndhran dynasties generally supported Brahmanism, probably because the performance of horse sacrifices and other rituals resulted in great prestige for the rulers. In the first or second century C.E., Nāsik was occupied by the Kṣaharāta family of the Śakas. According to two inscriptions in the eighth cave, the Kṣaharāta governor *(kṣatrapa)* Uṣavadāta contributed both money and land to Buddhists. Uṣavadāta's name also appears in a cave at Kārlī. Other records of Śaka contributions are found in the eighth and seventeenth caves.

At the beginning of the third century, Nāsik was recaptured by the Śātavāhanas. According to an inscription in the third cave, Gotamīputra Śrī Śātakaruṇi crushed the Kṣaharātas and defeated the Greeks, Śakas, and Pallavas while conquering a large area. In the third cave at Nāsik his name appears twice as a donor of land and caves. Śrī Pulumāyi, also of the Śātavāhanas, is listed as a contributor to the cave-temples in another inscription from the third cave. A further inscription in this third cave reports that the cave was given to the order of monks of the "Bhadāvaniya" (Bhadrayānika or Bhadrayānīya) School by the empress dowager of Gotamīputra, and an additional inscription states that Śrī Pulumāyi, the direct successor of Gotamīputra, gave land to the monks of the Bhadrayānīya School. A number of other caves, including the sixth, tenth, and fifteenth, were given to the universal *saṅgha.* The recipients of many of the other caves are unknown. A Mahāyāna image, which was added later, is found in the seventeenth cave.

The Bhadrayānīya School is also mentioned in the cave-temple complex of Kaṇheri near Bombay, which consists of 109 large and small cave-temples. One of the larger caves at the center of the complex serves as the *caitya* hall. This central *caitya* was donated to the masters of the Bhadrayānīya School during the reign of the illustrious King Yajñaśrī in the latter part of the Śātavāhana dynasty (near the end of the second century C.E.). The other caves at Kaṇheri were excavated during the period between the end of the second century C.E. and the eighth century. The seventieth cave also was given to the Bhadrayānīya School, while the twelfth, forty-eighth, seventy-seventh, and eighty-first were donated to the universal order.

The cave-temples at Kārlī are in the sides of mountains on the road between Bombay and Poona. These caves are as old as those at Nāsik. The center of the complex is a large cave with a *caitya* in it 13.87 meters wide and 37.87 meters long, making it the largest *stūpa* hall in India.

This splendid example of Indian cave-temple architecture was excavated within a century of the beginning of the common era. According to an inscription, it was the gift of a guild *(seṭhi)*. However, the names of individual donors are carved on eleven pillars within the cave. One pillar containing relics was given by a chanter *(bhāṇaka)* of the "Dhammutariya" (Dharmottarīya) School named Sātimita. Nine of the pillars were donated by Greeks. The cave was thus the result of contributions from a variety of sources. According to one inscription in the cave, a governor *(kṣatrapa)* named Usabhadāta of the Kṣaharāta family of the Śakas donated the village of Karajika for the support of all those in the universal order who had gone forth from their homes and were staying at the cave-temple *(pavajitānam cātudisasa sagha)*. The *caitya* cave, consequently, did not belong to any particular school of Nikāya Buddhism.

Later this area was controlled by the Śātavāhana dynasty. Inscriptions from this later period are also found in the *caitya* cave. According to one, the village of Karajika was eventually given to the monks and novices of the Mahāsaṅghika School who were residing in the cave-temples *(pavajitāna bhikhuna nikāyasa Mahāsaghiyāna)*, indicating that the cave-temples were later controlled by the Mahāsaṅghika School. To the north of the *caitya* hall in the quarters for monks is an inscription concerning the donation of a meeting hall *(maṭapo)* with nine rooms to the Mahāsaṅghika School in the twenty-fourth year of the reign of King Śrī Pulumāyi.

The caves at Bhājā are near Kārlī. At their center is a cave that served as a *caitya* hall. It is flanked by caves on either side with cells for monks. None of the caves, including the central one, is very large. The caves date from the first century B.C.E. or earlier and are thus older than those at Kārlī; the seventeenth is the oldest. Eight inscriptions have been found at the caves. Four of these record the names of donors. The remaining four are found on small *stūpas* at the edges of the caves and record the names of the elders whose remains are contained in the *stūpas*. The residents of the caves at Bhājā do not seem to have belonged to any one particular school of Nikāya Buddhism.

Junnār is a town forty-six miles north of Poona. Near the town are five sets of cave-temples with a total of more than 150 large and small cave-temples that were carved between the first century B.C.E. and the second century C.E. Approximately thirty inscriptions have been collected from these caves that concern donations of *stūpa* halls *(cetiyaghara)*, cave-temples *(leṇa)*, water tanks, mango trees, land, and so forth. The majority of the donors were local inhabitants. The *stūpa* hall of the fifty-first cave at Mount Sivanerī in Junnār was contributed by a rich and influential merchant. Three Greek donors and one Śaka are also mentioned in other inscriptions. A large meeting-hall was donated by a minister for the Śaka governor Nahapāna (Uṣavadāta's father-in-law), indicating that the Kṣaharāta family of the Śakas controlled a wide area. An inscription at Junnār records the donation of a cave and water tank to the order of nuns of the "Dhammutariya" School. This is the only example of an inscription concerning nuns from the cave-temples, probably because nuns usually lived in towns rather than in caves.

Twenty-eight caves are found at Ajantā. The *stūpa* halls of the ninth and tenth caves and the nearby quarters for monks in the twelfth and thirteenth caves are the oldest, dating from the beginning of the common era. Inscriptions in the *stūpa* hall of the tenth cave and in the quarters for monks of the twelfth cave concern donors. The former was given by relatives of King Pulumāyi and the latter by merchants. The eleventh, fourteenth, and fifteenth caves, all with quarters for monks, were opened next. The rest of the caves were developed after the Gupta period. These later caves, especially the first and second, are famous for their exquisite carvings and beautiful wall paintings.

Ellora, containing thirty-four caves, is near Ajantā. The oldest caves, the first through the twelfth, are Buddhist. The tenth cave is a *stūpa* hall, while the others contain quarters for monks. All were developed during the Gupta period. They are elaborately carved and contain Mahāyāna images, just as the later caves at Ajantā. The thirteenth through the twenty-ninth caves are Hindu; included among them is the Kailāsa temple, famed for the high quality of its carving. The remaining five temples are Jaina.

Stūpas

The ruins of large *stūpas* exist at Amarāvatī and Nāgārjunakoṇḍa in the eastern part of the Deccan. Amarāvatī is on the southern bank of the Kistna (Kṛṣṇā) River about sixty miles from the mouth, just to the east of the old city of Dharanikoṭ (Dhānyakaṭaka). The great *stūpa* at Amarāvatī, with a fifty-meter diameter at its base, was mostly intact when it was discovered in 1797. However, the preceding year, the local ruler had established his new capital at Amarāvatī. The great *stūpa* was subsequently destroyed and used as building materials for the new city. The carved marble panels and fence around the *stūpa* were removed, and the ruins of the *stūpa* were eventually converted into a pond. Some of the marble carvings, however, were saved; today they are in the collections of the British Museum in London and museums in Madras and Calcutta. They suggest the former splendor of Amarāvatī. Tall portals faced each of the four cardinal directions. The structure was surrounded by a walk for circumambulation with a balustrade on the outside. This magnificent structure was worthy of its name, Mahācetiya (great shrine). The *stūpa* dates back to before the beginning of the common era. In the middle of the second century C.E., it was remodeled to make the imposing structure described above.

Many of the 160 inscriptions from Amarāvatī date from the second and third centuries C.E., but eleven of them are even older. According to one inscription dating from the reign of King Pulumāyi of the Śātavāhana dynasty, the children of the merchant Puri commissioned a sculpture of the wheel of the Dharma to present to the large *stūpa* of the Buddha, which was the property of the "Cetiya" (Caitika) School, indicating that the great *stūpa* belonged to the Cetiya School in the second century C.E. In other inscriptions from Amarāvatī, the "Cetika" or "Cetiyavadaka" School is mentioned.

In inscriptions recording gifts from laymen, the term "householder" *(gahapati)* was often used to describe the donor. If the donor was a member of the Buddhist order, then he or she was often called a monk or a nun; but in some inscriptions the donor was called "one who has gone forth from home" *(pavajita)* or a male or female religious mendicant *(samaṇa* or *samaṇika)*. Phrases were also used such as "(donated) by a nun together with her daughters" or "(given) by a woman who has gone forth from her home together with her daughter who has also gone forth." In the last two cases, the inscription probably referred to a daughter born before the woman had entered the order. If such were not the case, then the woman would have given birth while she was a nun. Similar passages are not found in the inscriptions from northern India.

The remains of many Buddhist *stūpas* have been found in the area around the lower reaches of the Kistna River. Particularly important are two very large *stūpas* at Bhaṭṭiprolu and Ghaṇṭaśālā, which have diameters at their bases of 45 and 37 meters, respectively. The large *stūpa* at Bhaṭṭiprolu is very old. The style of the lettering on an inscription on a small box for relics found inside it dates from the third century B.C.E., indicating that the *stūpa* was probably constructed during the reign of Aśoka. Altogether eleven inscriptions, mostly records of donors, have been found at the *stūpa* at Bhaṭṭiprolu.

Five inscriptions have been discovered at Ghaṇṭaśālā. They date from the third century C.E. and record the names of donors. Among them is an inscription containing a term that seems to indicate that the "Aparaseliya" (Aparaśaila) School was active in the area at this time.

A stone pillar with an inscription has been found at Dhānyakaṭaka

(Dharanikoṭ), the capital of the Śātavāhana dynasty. According to the inscription, a minister gave the pillar, which had a wheel of the Dharma on it, to the order of monks of the "Pubbaseliya" (Pūrvaśaila) School. The pillar was then set up at the eastern gate of a large monastery *(mahāvihāra),* indicating that the monastery belonged to the Pubbaseliya School at one time.

Nāgārjunakoṇḍa (also known as Nāgārjunikoṇḍa), situated on a plateau on the south bank of the middle reaches of the Kistna River, was the capital for the Ikṣvāku state. Although the name of the site seems to indicate that it had some connection with the great Mahāyāna Buddhist thinker Nāgārjuna (ca. 150–250), the inscriptions found at this site contain no mention of Nāgārjuna. The Ikṣvāku family's power was at its height along the Kistna River during the second and third centuries C.E. Fifty-six inscriptions, many of them long, have been found from among the ruins of the large and small *stūpas,* monasteries, and mortuary temples of Nāgārjunakoṇḍa. One inscription records the gift of a pillar to a large *stūpa (mahācetiya)* by a queen of the Ikṣvāku family named Mahātalavari Cātisiri in the sixth year of the reign of King Siri Virapurisadata. The name of an eminent king of the Ikṣvākus, Vātsiṭhiputa Siri Cātamūla, also appears in the above inscription. Altogether ten inscriptions relating the gifts of Queen Mahātalavari Cātisiri have been found at Nāgārjunakoṇḍa. According to one of them the great *stūpa* belonged to the "Aparamahāvinaseliya" School, which may be identical with the Aparaśaila School. Six inscriptions concerning the contributions of other queens have also been discovered. A number of inscriptions record gifts to the Aparamahāvinaseliya School. According to one, Queen Mahātalavari Cātisiri gave a *cetiyaghara* (worship hall) to the school.

Śrīparvata, a mountain on which Nāgārjuna is said to have lived, is at Nāgārjunakoṇḍa and was the site of the Culadhammagiri monastery. An inscription from a worship hall at the monastery records the gift of the hall by elder monks from "Tambapaṃnaka" (Sri Lanka). Because Nāgārjunakoṇḍa had been a port in the middle reaches of the Kistna River, relations had been maintained with Sri Lanka through visits of Sri Lankan monks to the city. An inscription records the presence of a Sri Lankan monastery ("Sīhaḷavihāra") in the area and the gift of a water tank to the Pūrvaśaila School.

An inscription recording the gift of a monastery to monks of the Bahuśrutīya School was found approximately four hundred meters from the great *stūpa* at Nāgārjunakoṇḍa. Inscriptions were found in another area recording the construction of a monastery and the erection of pillars for the universal order on land belonging to the Mahīśāsaka School. According to another inscription, a stone carved with the footprints of the Buddha was enshrined at a monastery belonging to the Mahāvihāravāsin sect (a Sri Lankan order) of the Vibhajyavāda. The frequent appearance of the names of these schools at Nāgārjunakoṇḍa indicates that as time passed, monasteries increasingly were controlled by individual schools.

The names of donors outside the Ikṣvāku family appear in the dedicatory inscriptions from Nāgārjunakoṇḍa, but the major donors were clearly the queens of the Ikṣvāku family. The great *stūpa* was probably built through their efforts. The ruins at Nāgārjunakoṇḍa were discovered in 1926 and subsequently yielded many inscriptions and fragments of carvings. In recent years, however, the Kistna River has been dammed below Nāgārjunakoṇḍa to produce hydroelectric power, submerging the ruins beneath the waters of the man-made Nāgārjuna Lake. The discovery of a container said to hold the remains of Nāgārjuna's disciple Āryadeva was reported from Naṇḍūra, near Nāgārjunakoṇḍa, but doubts remain about the correct interpretation of the inscription.

The Mahāyāna Order and Archeological Evidence

The archeological evidence concerning the development of the Buddhist order after the Mauryan Empire has been surveyed in the preceding pages. Modern scholars have been puzzled, however, by the absence of any inscriptions regarding the Early Mahāyāna order. Even though many inscriptions referring to donations to the schools of Nikāya Buddhism have been found, no similar inscriptions about the Early Mahāyāna orders have been discovered. Some scholars have argued that the absence of such archeological evidence indicates that Mahāyāna orders did not exist yet. Other scholars have suggested that Mahāyāna Buddhists were probably considered to be heretics and that Mahāyāna Buddhism most likely began as an underground movement suppressed by the more established forms of Buddhism. Consequently, open expression of support for Mahāyāna Buddhism, such as inscriptions, did not appear until later.

The term "Mahāyāna" does not appear in an inscription until the second or third century C.E., yet the dates at which Mahāyāna texts were translated into Chinese prove that Mahāyāna texts existed in North India during the Kuṣāṇa dynasty. (These early texts are discussed in the next chapter.) Clearly, the absence of Mahāyāna inscriptions does not prove that Mahāyāna Buddhism did not exist during the first few centuries of the common era.

The Chinese pilgrim Fa-hsien, who left Ch'ang-an for India in 399, described three types of temples that he found on his journey: Hīnayāna temples, Mahāyāna temples, and temples in which both Hīnayāna and Mahāyāna Buddhism were practiced. Later, Hsüan-tsang, who left China for India in 629, described Indian Buddhism in more detail, mentioning the same three types of monasteries.[4] Of the temples Hsüan-tsang visited, sixty percent were Hīnayāna, twenty-four percent were Mahāyāna, and fifteen percent were temples where both Hīnayāna and Mahāyāna were practiced. Even if Hsüan-tsang's figures for both Mahāyāna and mixed (Hīnayāna and Mahāyāna) monasteries are combined, they total only forty percent. Although the Mahāyāna tradition was not the dominant form of Buddhism in India at this time, then, it was clearly present. Since the descriptions of Indian Buddhism by both Fa-hsien and Hsüan-tsang generally agree, these accounts probably accurately portray the state of Indian Buddhism for their respective periods. If a significant number of Mahāyāna temples existed by 400 C.E., when Fa-hsien visited India, it is likely that at least a few existed one or two centuries earlier. Thus, the absence of inscriptions concerning Mahāyāna orders from the second and third centuries is not sufficient evidence to argue that no Mahāyāna order existed at that time. Moreover, the doctrinal development of the Chinese translations of early Mahāyāna texts from the second century C.E. discussed in the next chapter indicates the existence of a Mahāyāna order.

The state of Mahāyāna orders during the first few centuries of the common era can be investigated from other perspectives. First, the names of the schools of Nikāya Buddhism are not found in stone inscriptions until the schools had already existed for a long time. For example, the schools are not mentioned in inscriptions dating from the first or second century B.C.E., such as those from Sāñcī and Bhārhut. Nor are the schools mentioned in inscriptions from cave-temples that were opened before the beginning of the common era, such as those at Nāsik, Kārlī, and Bhājā. The earliest mention of a school is found on the inscription of a pillar with a lion-capital that was discovered at Mathurā. This inscription records the contribution of a *stūpa* and monastery to the entire Sarvāstivādin order. (In other words, the gift was not limited to the monks of a particular Sarvāstivādin monastery.) The Mahāsaṅghika School is also mentioned. The name of Governor-general Rajula in the inscription has enabled scholars to date it to approximately 10 B.C.E.

Mathurā was opened to Buddhism only after Buddhism had spread throughout central India. Later, the Sarvāstivādins were active in Mathurā for a considerable period. Mathurā was the birthplace of Upagupta, a teacher of Aśoka and an important figure in the lineages recorded in sources from the Northern tradition. Consequently, the discovery of inscriptions concerning the Sarvāstivādin School at Mathurā is not surprising. The date of the inscription, the earliest one mentioning a school of Nikāya Buddhism, seems late, however, particularly when it is considered in light of the schisms that had already occurred in Buddhism. If the Buddha died in 484 B.C.E., as is commonly held by Western scholars, then some of the later schisms of Nikāya Buddhism would have occurred during the reign of Aśoka, and the Sarvāstivādin School would have existed since the third century B.C.E. If Ui Hakuju's date of 386 B.C.E. for the Buddha's death is accepted, then the Sarvāstivādin School would have existed since the second century B.C.E. Whichever date is correct, 10 C.E. is surprisingly late for the first reference of a school of Nikāya Buddhism in an inscription.

The situation is similar when inscriptions from northern India are considered. An inscription from Shinkot dating from the time of King Milinda records only the enshrinement of relics. Similar passages from a *stūpa* at Dharmarājika and from an inscription recording the establishment of a *stūpa* by a *meridarkh* (governor) also include no mention of schools. The earliest inscription from a *stūpa* mentioning the name of a school was found on a copper plaque at Kalawān and is dated 77 C.E. It records the presentation of a building to house a *stūpa* to the Sarvāstivādin School. The next earliest inscriptions mentioning the names of schools of Nikāya Buddhism date from the second century C.E. Particularly famous are an inscription on a reliquary discovered at the great *stūpa* of Kaniṣka and another inscription on a *stūpa*-shaped copper reliquary found at Kurram. Both inscriptions date from the second century and concern donations to the Sarvāstivādin School. A second-century inscription on a reliquary found at Wardak records the gift of a temple to the Mahāsaṅghika School. Many other inscriptions from such places as Mathurā, Nāsik, Kārlī, Amarāvatī, and Nāgārjunakoṇḍa record contributions to the schools of Nikāya Buddhism.[5] These inscriptions date from the second and third centuries C.E. However, *stūpas* existed at sites such as Nāsik, Kārlī, and Bhaṭṭiprolu as early as the second century B.C.E. Many inscriptions exist that record contributions to these *stūpas,* but they include no mention of schools. In fact, the names of Nikāya schools are mentioned in only a small proportion of all the inscriptions.

As has been argued elsewhere in this study, Buddhist *stūpas* originally were not affiliated with the Nikāya Buddhist orders. In approximately the first century C.E. *stūpas* belonging to these schools began to appear. However, their numbers were far fewer than those *stūpas* not affiliated with Nikāya schools. Early Mahāyānists might well have used the *stūpas* that were not affiliated with the Nikāya schools as bases for proselytizing. The doctrinal reasons for this state of affairs are explained in chapter sixteen.

CHAPTER 15

Mahāyāna Texts Composed during the Kuṣāṇa Dynasty

THE EXAMINATION of inscriptions in the previous chapter did not provide sufficient evidence to prove that a Mahāyāna order existed before the third century of the common era. However, the inscriptions did indicate that many *stūpas* were not affiliated with any particular Hīnayāna school. In the next chapter, the people who lived and practiced their religion around these *stūpas* will be discussed. In this chapter, the existence of Mahāyāna texts in northern India at the beginning of the common era will be established.[1] Through an investigation of the contents of those texts, the nature of Mahāyāna Buddhism at the beginning of the common era will be determined. Since Mahāyāna *sūtras* claim to be the words of the Buddha, the date and circumstances of their emergence cannot be determined directly from statements in the *sūtras* themselves. However, this problem can be examined by working backward from dated Chinese translations of early Mahāyāna texts.

The Translations of Lokakṣema

According to a famous legend, the first transmission of Buddhism to China occurred when Emperor Ming (r. 57–75) of the Later Han dreamed about a golden man. When he subsequently sent emissaries to the Uighurs to inquire about the dream in 67 C.E., they returned to Loyang with two missionaries, Chia-she-mo-t'eng (Kāśyapa Mātaṅga?) and Chu Fa-lan (Dharmaratna?). These two men are said to have translated a text into Chinese under the title of *Ssu-shih-erh chang ching*

(*Sūtra in Forty-two Sections, T* 784). An examination of this work, however, reveals that it is composed of excerpts from *sūtras* that were translated at a later date. Consequently, the legend of Emperor Ming's dream cannot be recognized as fact.

Although the first transmissions of Buddhism to China probably did occur around the beginning of the common era, Buddhist works were not translated into Chinese until approximately one century later. During the reigns of Emperors Huan (r. 146–167) and Ling (r. 167–189), the Parthian monk An Shih-kao came to China and translated thirty-four Hīnayāna works in forty fascicles including the *An-pan shou-i ching* (*T* 602). Shortly afterward, Chih Lou-chia-ch'an (Lokakṣema?), a monk of Kuṣāṇa, came to China and translated fourteen works in twenty-seven fascicles, including the *Tao-hsing pan-jo ching* (*T* 224, *Aṣṭasāhasrikā-PP**). Although several scholarly problems exist concerning the works he translated, modern scholars agree that twelve of the fourteen works Lokakṣema is said to have translated are authentic.[2] Lokakṣema was actively engaged in translation during the Kuang-ho (178–183) and Chung-p'ing (184-198) eras. Since he arrived in China earlier, the original texts on which his translations were based can be traced to the Kuṣāṇa empire sometime before 150 C.E. Determining how far before 150 C.E. the texts can be dated remains a difficult problem.

Among the works translated by Lokakṣema are the *Tao-hsing pan-jo ching* (*T* 224, 10 fasc., *Aṣṭasāhasrikā-PP**), *Pan-chou san-mei ching* (*T* 418?, 1 fasc., *Bhadrapālasūtra*), *Shou-leng-yen san-mei ching* (not extant, 2 fasc., *Śūraṅgamasamādhisūtra*), *Tun-chen-t'o-lo ching* (*T* 624, 3 fasc., *Drumakinnararājaparipṛcchā#*), *A-she-shih-wang ching* (*T* 626, 2 fasc., *Ajātaśatrukaukṛtyavinodana#*), and *A-ch'u-fo-kuo ching* (*T* 313, 2 fasc., *Akṣobhyatathāgatasyavyūha#*).

The *Tao-hsing pan-jo ching* is a translation of the *Aṣṭasāhasrikā-PP (Perfection of Wisdom in 8,000 Lines).* The contents of Lokakṣema's translation are almost identical to the contents of Kumārajīva's translation of the *Perfection of Wisdom in 8,000 Lines* (*T* 227), completed in 408. Thus by Lokakṣema's time the *Perfection of Wisdom in 8,000 Lines* had already assumed its final form. The *Tao-hsing ching*'s length of ten fascicles and its organization into thirty chapters suggest that the Indian text had a long history before it reached the length and format found in Lokakṣema's translation. The final three chapters (on the bodhisattva Sadāprarudita and other topics) were the last to be compiled. They include passages concerning the making of Buddha images and thus must have been composed sometime during or after the last half of the first century C.E., when images of the Buddha first appeared. The first twenty-seven chapters are older, but these chapters were not all composed at the same time, since earlier and later portions of the text can be distinguished. The twenty-fifth chapter concerns the transmission of the text to later generations and probably marked the end of the text at one time. The twenty-sixth and twenty-seventh chapters were added to the text later; they concern such topics as the appearance of Akṣobhya Buddha and his Buddha-field. Of the first twenty-five chapters, the first, "The Practice of the Way" (Tao-hsing), is the oldest. The compilation of the text was obviously a complicated process that occurred in a series of stages. The earliest version of it was probably composed sometime between 100 B.C.E. and 50 C.E.

The sixteenth chapter of the *Tao-hsing ching* includes teachings from the bodhisattva Maitreya and a discussion of Akṣobhya's Buddha-field. In the twenty-fourth chapter, Akṣobhya Buddha's performance of bodhisattva practices in past lives is discussed. These topics are also found in the *A-ch'u-fo-kuo ching* (*T* 313, *Akṣobhyatathāgatasyavyūha#*), translated by Lokakṣema. Consequently, the earliest version of the *Akṣobhyatathāgatasyavyūha* was probably composed earlier than 50 C.E., before the sixteenth and twenty-fourth chapters of the *Tao-hsing ching* were composed.

Lokakṣema's translation of the *Śūraṅgamasamādhisūtra* is not extant. However, its contents can be deduced from Kumārajīva's translation of the *sūtra* (*T* 642). This *sūtra* concerns the power of an intense meditation that forms the basis of a bodhisattva's practices. With the help of this meditation, a practitioner can make substantial progress in his cultivation of the six perfections. The important role of the six perfections in the *sūtra* indicates that the text is closely related to the perfection of wisdom *sūtras*. The concern with the progression of the stages of practice suggests a connection with the *Daśabhūmikasūtra,* a text that relates the stages of practice on the bodhisattva path. In fact, the term "*shih-ti*" (ten stages or *daśabhūmi*) appears in Kumārajīva's translation of the *Śūraṅgamasamādhisūtra.* The descriptions of the power of the *śūraṅgama* concentration probably arose from reflections on the willpower and self-awareness required of the men who performed bodhisattva practices. The bodhisattva Mañjuśrī was a personification of the ideal figure who had mastered such religious practices. Consequently, the practices performed by Mañjuśrī in times past are described in the *sūtra.* The *Śūraṅgamasamādhisūtra* reveals that the Mahāyāna bodhisattva viewed his practice as being distinct from that of the Hīnayāna practitioners. The *Śūraṅgamasamādhisūtra* is one of the most fundamental early Mahāyāna *sūtras.* Lokakṣema's translation indicates that it existed in northern India in the first century C.E.

The *Tou-sha ching* (*T* 280) is related to the *Avataṃsakasūtra.* Since the

Daśabhūmikasūtra, another text closely connected to the *Avataṃsakasūtra,* is quoted in the *Śūraṅgamasamādhisūtra,* early versions of a number of *sūtras* related to the *Avataṃsakasūtra* must have existed before the first century C.E.

The *Bhadrapālasūtra* (*T* 418, *Pan-chou san-mei ching*), translated by Lokakṣema, concerns meditations leading to visualizations of the Buddha. These meditations were closely related to belief in the Buddha Amitābha. Although Lokakṣema did not translate the "Smaller" *Sukhāvatīvyūha,* his translation of the *Bhadrapālasūtra* indicates that beliefs concerning Amitābha Buddha were already present in India during the Kuṣāṇa dynasty. Consequently, the earliest versions of the *sūtras* concerning Amitābha probably existed before the first century C.E. However, the extant versions of the "Larger" and "Smaller" *Sukhāvatīvyūhas* were compiled later. A visualization exercise using an image of the Buddha is described in Lokakṣema's translation of the *Bhadrapālasūtra,* indicating that the version of the *sūtra* Lokakṣema translated was probably compiled after the last half of the first century C.E., when images of the Buddha first appeared. However, an image of the Buddha is not an indispensable requirement for visualizations of the Buddha. In fact, visualizations of the Buddha might have developed first, with early sculptures of the Buddha developing afterward on the basis of those visualizations. The earliest version of the *Bhadrapālasūtra* might have antedated the appearance of images of the Buddha.

The *Drumakinnararājaparipṛcchā* (*T* 624, *Tun-chen-t'o-lo ching*), translated by Lokakṣema, contains a detailed thirty-two-part explanation of the six perfections. According to the *sūtra,* the practitioner can realize many of the more advanced stages on the path to enlightenment through the six perfections. Among the benefits that may accrue to the diligent practitioner are the realization of the stage of acquiescence to the truth that *dharmas* are unproduced *(anutpattika-dharma-kṣānti),* the attainment of the stage from which no backsliding occurs *(avivartika),* progression through the ten stages *(daśabhūmi),* and nearing enlightenment. The concept of expedient teachings *(upāya)* is also explained. This *sūtra* is closely related to such works as the perfection of wisdom *sūtras,* the *Daśabhūmikasūtra,* and the *Śūraṅgamasamādhisūtra.*

Lokakṣema's translation of the *Ajātaśatrukaukṛtyavinodana* (*T* 626, *A-she-shih-wang ching*) contains a sermon the Buddha is said to have preached to King Ajātaśatru when the king was feeling deeply remorseful because he had killed his father. The Buddha explains that everything arises from the mind. The mind, however, is not a substantial entity that can be grasped; it is empty. Nevertheless, the basic nature of the mind is purity; it cannot be tainted by defilements. Thus, the major theme of this *sūtra* is that the basic nature of the mind is originally pure, a teaching that would later develop into Tathāgatagarbha doctrine and form an important type of Mahāyāna thought. In connection with this teaching, the *sūtra* includes an account of how Mañjuśrī had practiced religious austerities in past ages, completing all the practices necessary to attain Buddhahood long ago. All Buddhas and bodhisattvas have practiced under Mañjuśrī's guidance. Even Śākyamuni Buddha, when he was a bodhisattva, practiced under Mañjuśrī. In fact, according to a famous passage in the *Fang-po ching* (*T* 629), a partial translation of the *Ajātaśatrukaukṛtyavinodana,* Mañjuśrī was the original teacher of Śākyamuni. Thus Mañjuśrī is called "the mother and father of those on the Buddha's path" (*T* 15:451a). Mañjuśrī is a personification of the wisdom produced through enlightenment, wisdom that is based on the original pure nature of the mind. Mañjuśrī and Maitreya are two of the earliest bodhisattvas to appear in Mahāyāna Buddhism, and the *Ajātaśatrukaukṛtyavinodana* is an important text for investigating the origins of these bodhisattvas.

The *Kāśyapaparivarta** (*T* 350, *I jih-mo-ni-pao ching*), translated by Lokakṣema, describes the practices of bodhisattvas by arranging them into groups, each composed of four *dharmas.* This exposition is followed by a list of thirty-two qualities a bodhisattva must possess. The *sūtra* is thus primarily concerned with bodhisattva practices and includes an early example of bodhisattva precepts. The *sūtra* is one of the oldest included in the *Mahāratnakūṭa* collections of *sūtras.* Consequently, early versions of the *Ratnakūṭa* must have existed by the first century C.E.

In conclusion, a survey of the works translated by Lokakṣema reveals that by the first century C.E. scriptures concerning the following Mahāyāna topics existed in northern India: perfection of wisdom, Akṣobhya Buddha, the doctrines of the *Avataṃsakasūtra,* Amitābha Buddha, the *śūraṅgama-samādhi,* visualizations of the Buddha such as the *pratyutpanna-samādhi,* teachings concerning Mañjuśrī, the doctrine that the original nature of the mind is pure, and the teachings that typify the *Mahāratnakūṭa* collection of *sūtras.* Lokakṣema did not translate any works related to the *Lotus sūtra (Saddharmapuṇḍarīka);* but surveys of Lokakṣema's translations reveal that representative works of the other significant varieties of Mahāyāna literature were found in northern India by the first century C.E.

During the reign of Emperor Ling (168–189), at the same time that Lokakṣema was active, Yen Fo-t'iao and An Hsüan were translating the *Ugradattaparipṛcchā* (*T* 322, *Fa-ching ching*), a *sūtra* belonging to the

Mahāratnakūṭa group. Chih Yao, K'ang Meng-hsiang, and Wei-chi-nan were also translating works at this time. Later, between approximately 222 and 253, Chih Ch'ien translated works such as the *Vimalakīrtinirdeśa.* He is credited with the translation of thirty-six works totaling forty-eight fascicles. The works translated by Chih Ch'ien probably were not all compiled in India between Lokakṣema's time and his; some of them probably existed before Lokakṣema's time. Thus by the end of the first century C.E., Mahāyāna Buddhist thought in northern India existed in many varieties. The first versions of the perfection of wisdom *sūtras* and texts concerning Akṣobhya Buddha were probably compiled even earlier and date back to before the common era.

The Earliest Mahāyāna Scriptures

Although Lokakṣema's translations include the earliest extant Mahāyāna scriptures, texts antedating those translations must have existed. Such texts are quoted in Lokakṣema's translation the *I jih-mo-ni-pao ching* (*T* 350, *Kāśyapaparivarta**), in which a bodhisattva is advised to study both the *Liu po-lo-mi ching* (*Ṣaṭpāramitā, Sūtra* on the Six Perfections) and the *P'u-sa-tsang ching (Bodhisattvapiṭaka).* Since these last two *sūtras* are cited in the *I jih-mo-ni-pao ching,* they must have been compiled before it. In addition, in the *Fa-ching ching* (*T* 322, *Ugradattaparipṛcchā*), translated by Yen Fo-t'iao and An Hsüan in 181, practitioners are advised to chant the *San-p'in ching (Triskandhaka)* six times every twenty-four-hour period. Since the *Triskandhaka* is cited in the *Fa-ching ching* it must antedate the *Fa-ching ching.* Since the *I jih-mo-ni-pao ching* and the *Fa-ching ching* were compiled by the end of the first century C.E., the three Mahāyāna texts cited in them probably date back to sometime before the beginning of the common era.[3]

Among the *sūtras* translated by Chih Ch'ien is the *Ta a-mi-t'o ching* (*T* 362, *Sukhāvatīvyūha**), completed sometime between 223 and 252. Two of the earliest Mahāyāna *sūtras,* the *Tao-chih ta-ching* and the *Liu po-lo-mi ching,* are cited in the *Ta a-mi-t'o ching.* The *Liu po-lo-mi ching (Ṣaṭpāramitā)* cited in the *Ta a-mi-t'o ching* is probably the same work referred to in the *I jih-mo-ni-pao ching.* Unfortunately, nothing is known about the *Tao-chih ta-ching.*

In conclusion, the *sūtras* translated by Lokakṣema and Chih Ch'ien were not the first Mahāyāna *sūtras.* Rather, these translations clearly reveal the existence of an even earlier group of Mahāyāna scriptures. The emergence of the very first Mahāyāna scriptures can thus be placed in the first century B.C.E.

The Origins of the *Prajñāpāramitāsūtras* in South India

According to the following passage from the *Tao-hsing pan-jo ching* (*T* 224), the perfection of wisdom *sūtras* first arose in South India. "After the Buddha's death, the perfection of wisdom spread in the south. From the south it spread to the west, and from the west to the north" (*T* 8:446a–b). Similar passages indicating that the perfection of wisdom literature had its origins in the south are found in the *Ta-p'in pan-jo ching* (*T* 8:317b) and the *Hsiao-p'in pan-jo ching* (*T* 8:555a).

Such passages by themselves do not provide conclusive evidence that the perfection of wisdom literature came from the south; but other evidence does suggest that Mahāyāna Buddhism flourished in South India at an early date. After the *prajñāpāramitā* literature had appeared, Nāgārjuna is said to have lived at Śrīparvata or Brāhmaragiri in South India and to have received the patronage of the Śātavāhana royal family. An inscription has been found indicating that Śrīparvata was at Nāgārjunakoṇḍa. Among the disputes discussed in the Theravāda work *Kathāvatthu* are several identified by Buddhaghosa in his commentary involving positions maintained by a Vetulyaka School, which he called the Mahāsuññatavādin School (*The Debates Commentary*, bk. 17, chap. 6–10). The adherents of this school may have been advocates of *prajñāpāramitā* positions. The *Kathāvatthu* contains detailed information about Buddhism in the south, but it is much less complete in its presentation of the doctrines of the northern schools, such as the Sarvāstivādins. Consequently, the inclusion of Mahāsuññatavādin positions in this text may indicate that the Mahāsuññatavādin School was from South India. According to the Sri Lankan chronicles, King Goṭhābaya expelled the Vetulyaka monks from Sri Lanka in the third century C.E.

According to the *Ju fa-chieh p'in (Gaṇḍavyūha)* chapter of the *Hua-yen ching* (*T* 9:687c; 10:332c, 677a, *Avataṃsakasūtra*), when Mañjuśrī left the Buddha at Śrāvastī, he traveled to the south. There he lived at a large *caitya* to the east of Dhanyākara (Chüeh-ch'eng), a place that may correspond to Dhānyakaṭaka. Among Mañjuśrī's many believers was a youth named Sudhana. According to the *Gaṇḍavyūha*, Sudhana went on a long journey to hear the Dharma and visited Avalokiteśvara, who was staying on Mount Kuang-ming (Potalaka?) in South India (*T* 9:717c). The *Gaṇḍavyūha* is thus closely related to Buddhism in South India. In addition, many of the stories about Mañjuśrī concern South India.

The above evidence suggests that many Early Mahāyāna scriptures originated in South India. An investigation of inscriptions from South India reveals that the schools of Nikāya Buddhism in the Mahāsaṅghika lineage were also prominent in South India. Although these inscriptions date from the second century C.E. and later, these schools must certainly have been present in South India before the second century C.E. On the basis of such evidence, some scholars have argued that Mahāyāna Buddhism might have developed out of the Mahāsaṅghika School. In fact, some connection seems to have existed between the two forms of Buddhism. However, since the doctrines of the Mahāsaṅghika School and the schools that split off from it (such as the Pūrvaśaila, Uttaraśaila, and Caitika) are not clearly known, the similarities between Mahāyāna Buddhism and the schools in the Mahāsaṅghika lineage cannot be determined with precision.

The Significance of Predictions about the Rise of Mahāyāna during the "Latter Five Hundred Years"

The thousand years following the Buddha's death are often divided into two five-hundred-year periods in Buddhist texts. Statements about the decline of the true teaching during the latter five hundred years occur frequently in Mahāyāna texts. The phrase "latter five hundred years" is contrasted with the "former five hundred years," the first five hundred years after the Buddha's death. According to the stories in the *Vinaya* about the founding of the order of nuns, when Śākyamuni Buddha first admitted women to the Buddhist order, he stated that his teaching should last a thousand years; the admission of nuns to the order, however, would shorten the period to five hundred years. Consequently, the true teaching was expected to flourish during the former five hundred years, but to decline during the latter five hundred years. Mahāyāna texts stress that the true teaching had to be carefully guarded and maintained during the latter five hundred years. The presence of such words in Mahāyāna texts suggests that these texts were composed sometime later than five hundred years after the Buddha's death.

Early Mahāyāna texts date from the first century B.C.E. If the Buddha died in 484 B.C.E., then "the former five hundred years" would have elapsed in the first century C.E. If the Buddha died in 386 B.C.E., then the "former five hundred years" would have elapsed in the second century C.E. These dates must be reconciled with the evidence suggesting that Mahāyāna texts began appearing in the first century B.C.E.

The Mahāyāna texts that include statements about the latter five hundred years are usually later texts or late recensions of early texts. For example, studies of perfection of wisdom literature reveal examples of such statements in Kumārajīva's translation of the *Aṣṭasāhasrikā-PP* (*T* 4:555c), which was completed in 408, but not in the earlier translation of this *sūtra* by Lokakṣema dated 179 (*T* 224). Of the translations of *Pañcaviṃśatisāhasrikā-PP* these statements appear in Hsüan-tsang's translation (*T* 7:594b, 809a), dated between 659 and 653, but not in the translations by Mokṣala (*T* 221), completed in 291, or by Kumārajīva (*T* 223), completed in 404. Consequently, statements concerning the latter five hundred years were probably not included in the earliest versions of Mahāyāna *sūtras* but were added later. The figure of five hundred years after the Buddha's death cannot be used to determine the date of the first appearance of Mahāyāna scriptures.[4]

Studies concerning the history of the translation of Buddhist scriptures into Chinese reveal that a variety of Mahāyāna scriptures was circulating in India during the Kuṣāṇa dynasty in the first century C.E. If scriptures existed at this time, then authors and believers must also have been present. These early believers must have put Mahāyāna teachings into practice and cultivated the six perfections and the *śūraṅgama-samādhi*. Places for practice must have been established. Because teachings were transmitted from teacher to disciple, orders must have formed. The existence of such institutions can easily be imagined in first-century India.

CHAPTER 16

The Origins of Mahāyāna

Mahāyāna and Hīnayāna

THE TERM "Mahāyāna" is usually translated as "Great Vehicle" and the term "Hīnayāna" as "Small Vehicle." The original meaning of the element *hīna* in the term "Hīnayāna" is "discarded"; it also denotes "inferior" or "base." The appellation "Hīnayāna" thus was a deprecatory term used by Mahāyāna practitioners to refer to Nikāya (Sectarian) Buddhism. No Buddhist groups ever referred to themselves as Hīnayānists.

It is unclear whether Mahāyānists referred to the whole of Nikāya Buddhism as Hīnayāna or only to a specific group. The arguments of the *Ta-chih-tu lun* (*T* 1509, *Mahāprajñāpāramitopadeśa*) are primarily directed against the Vaibhāṣikas of the Sarvāstivādin School. The Sarvāstivādins were viewed as Hīnayānists in this and many other Mahāyāna texts. Unfortunately, it is not known whether the term "Hīnayāna" in Mahāyāna scriptures also referred to the Theravādins and Mahāsaṅghikas.

In his travel diary, the Chinese Buddhist pilgrim Fa-hsien (d. 423?) divided the areas where Indian Buddhism was practiced into three categories *(Fo-kuo chi, T* 2085, *Record of Buddhist Lands):* Mahāyana, Hīnayāna, and mixed (Hīnayāna and Mahāyāna practiced together in the same area). A comparison of Fa-hsien's travel diary to that of another Chinese pilgrim, Hsüan-tsang (600–664), *Hsi-yu chi* (*T* 2087, *A Record of Travels to Western Regions*), clearly indicates that Fa-hsien used the term "Hīnayāna" to refer to all of the schools of Nikāya Buddhism. Hsüan-tsang understood Indian Buddhism in approximately the same manner. Hsüan-tsang placed the epithet "Hīnayāna" in front of the names of certain schools, such as the Sarvāstivādin, Sammatīya, and Lokottaravādin. In other cases, he noted that the people of an area were Hīnayāna Buddhists or that they followed Hīnayāna teachings, but he did not designate the name of their school. When he discussed the two areas where he found Theravādins and the three places where he found Mahāsaṅghikas, he used only the name of the school without the epithet "Hīnayāna."[1] This difference is probably not significant. However, when he discussed the five areas where he found groups associated with the Sri Lankan Theravāda School, he referred to them as "Mahāyāna Theravādins."[2] The Abhayagiri sect of the Theravāda School that was influential in Sri Lanka at this time seems to have adopted many Mahāyāna teachings. Later, it was expelled from Sri Lanka by the Mahāvihāra sect, which dominates Sri Lankan Buddhism today. The surviving commentaries *(Aṭṭhakathā)* of the Mahāvihāra sect, when closely examined, include a number of positions that agree with Mahāyāna teachings. Consequently, Hsüan-tsang referred to the Sri Lankan Theravāda School as "the Mahāyāna Theravāda School." Thus, Hsüan-tsang did not regard all sects of Nikāya Buddhism as Hīnayāna. However, he regarded the Lokottaravādin sect, which is of Mahāsaṅghika lineage, as Hīnayāna despite the many Mahāyāna elements found in the Lokottaravādin biography of the Buddha, the *Mahāvastu.*

Hīnayāna and Mahāyāna Buddhism are not so clearly distinguished in I-ching's (635–713) travel diary, the *Nan-hai chi-kuei nei-fa chuan* (*T* 2125, *A Record of Buddhism in India and the Malay Archipelago).* I-ching observed no significant differences in the life styles of Hīnayāna and Mahāyāna monks. Both followed the *vinaya,* were expected to use three robes and a begging bowl, and based their practice on the Four Noble Truths. I-ching noted that "those who paid homage to bodhisattvas and read Mahāyāna *sūtras*" were Mahāyāna practitioners, while those who did not do so were Hīnayāna. Only the Mādhyamika and Yogācāra schools were consistently referred to as Mahāyāna.[3] I-ching spent most of his time at the large monastery at Nālandā in central India. His use of the terms "Hīnayāna" and "Mahāyāna" may indicate that the divisions between the two types of Buddhism were not very clearly observed at Nālandā in the seventh century.

Hsüan-tsang and I-ching traveled in India when Mahāyāna Buddhism was in its middle period. Their writings, consequently, do not describe Early Mahāyāna Buddhism. However, in general, the term "Hīnayāna" was most often applied to the Sarvāstivādin School.

The terms "Śrāvakayāna" (vehicle of the listener) and "Bodhisattvayāna" (vehicle of the bodhisattva) are even older than the terms "Hīnayāna" and "Mahāyāna." Hīnayāna was eventually substituted for Śrāvakayāna and Mahāyāna for Bodhisattvayāna. Śrāvakayāna was probably used to refer to Nikāya Buddhism in general.

The Meaning of Hīnayāna and Mahāyāna

The element *yāna* in the terms "Hīnayāna" and "Mahāyāna" literally means "vehicle," and it refers to Buddhist doctrine. By practicing in accordance with doctrine, a person could cross the river of cyclic existence, traveling from the shore that represented the realm of delusion to the other shore, which represented the realm of enlightenment. Doctrine was compared to a vehicle that would take the practitioner to salvation.

The differences between Hīnayāna and Mahāyāna doctrine are many. But the major difference, at least according to the Mahāyāna tradition, lies in the attitudes of each toward the salvation of others. The Mahāyāna tradition maintains that a person must save himself by saving others. The Mahāyāna descriptions of religious practice as the six perfections *(pāramitā)* illustrate how a person could benefit himself only by helping others. These doctrines reflected a view of the world based on the teaching of Dependent Origination.

In contrast, according to Sarvāstivādin and Theravādin doctrine, the goal of practice was to attain salvation for oneself by cutting off all defilements. Once salvation had been attained, the practitioner had accomplished all that was to be done and entered *nirvāṇa.* Saving others was not a necessary requirement for the completion of practice. Even after enlightenment had been attained, helping others was not required. Śrāvakayāna Buddhism was sometimes called "Buddhism for disciples" because it could be mastered by practicing under qualified teachers. The practitioner was not required to progress from being student to teacher. The term *"śrāvaka,"* which means "listener" or "one who studies," also reflects these qualities. This lack of social concern is probably related to the understanding of the doctrine of Dependent Origination professed by many of the schools of Nikāya Buddhism. For them, Dependent Origination referred to the interaction of discrete entities, each with its own nature.

Within the Śrāvakayāna tradition, teachings were transmitted from teacher to disciple. Preaching the Dharma and teaching were practices performed by monks. Because Śrāvakayāna doctrines did not require monks to help others as an integral part of their practice, however, these doctrines were considered "Hīnayāna" by Mahāyāna advocates. While Mahāyānists called the Hīnayāna tradition "Buddhism for disciples," they conceived of the Mahāyāna tradition as a form of Buddhism that would allow them to become teachers. It was a teaching that would enable them to become Buddhas, to become equal to the Buddha, the teacher of the *śrāvakas*. Mahāyāna Buddhism encouraged the practitioner to teach even while he was studying, an attitude based on the premise that the practitioner already possessed the potential necessary to realize Buddhahood. A person who knew that he had this potential was called a bodhisattva. The Mahāyāna conception of the bodhisattva was modeled on the accounts of Śākyamuni Buddha's former lives, which were related in Buddhist literature. Thus, Mahāyāna Buddhism was a teaching or vehicle for bodhisattvas, a *bodhisattvayāna*. Some Mahāyāna practitioners believed that all people, not only themselves, possessed the potential to become Buddhas. These practitioners wished to help all other people realize that they too had this potential and consequently stressed the importance of helping others. Their beliefs eventually developed into the doctrine that all sentient beings possess the Buddha-nature. Thus, Mahāyāna Buddhism was concerned with lay people and this world while Hīnayāna Buddhism was a monastic form of Buddhism characterized by withdrawal from the everyday world.

These differences in attitudes between Hīnayāna and Mahāyāna Buddhism resulted in a variety of divergent doctrines. For Hīnayāna Buddhists, *nirvāṇa* was the final goal, characterized by some Mahāyānists as the extinction of body and mind. In contrast, Mahāyāna Buddhists argued that the practitioner was to attain "active *nirvāṇa*" *(apratiṣṭhita-nirvāṇa)* in which he did not remain quiescent. Bodhisattvas such as Mañjuśrī, Samantabhadra, and Avalokiteśvara had more powers than Buddhas, but continued to devote themselves to saving sentient beings instead of attaining Buddhahood. Buddhas such as Amitābha or Śākyamuni (as an eternal Buddha) never entered extinction *(parinirvāṇa)*. They continued to help sentient beings. Entering *nirvāṇa* was seen as nothing more than an expedient means to help save sentient beings. Nobody actually entered *nirvāṇa* as an ultimate state, according to this Mahāyāna view.

The emergence of these teachings was made possible by the development of the doctrine of nonsubstantiality *(śūnyatā)* and new interpretations of the concepts of the Middle Way and Dependent Origination that diverged from the views of Nikāya Buddhism. Mahāyāna views of the Buddha also differed from those of Nikāya Buddhism. Mahāyāna Buddhism distinguished three bodies of the Buddha: *dharmakāya* (*dharma* body), *saṃbhogakāya* (body of bliss), and *nirmāṇakāya* (manifested body). The stages of practice for the Mahāyānists led to the attainment of Buddhahood. Consequently, Mahāyāna paths to enlightenment such as the ten stages *(daśabhūmi)* or forty-two stages had little in common with the Hīnayāna list of four candidates and four fruits or with the Hīnayāna goal of becoming an *arhat.* Some Mahāyānists conceived of the Buddha as a savior of helpless beings and developed doctrines concerning easier paths to salvation or the Buddha's use of his own power to save men. Such doctrines were found only in Mahāyāna Buddhism.

Still other differences between Hīnayāna and Mahāyāna Buddhism could be indicated, but the basic distinction lies in the Mahāyāna insistence that helping others is a necessary part of any effort to save oneself while Hīnayāna doctrine stresses the salvation of oneself.

The Three Sources of Mahāyāna Buddhism

The origins of Mahāyāna Buddhism are still not completely understood. Three sources appear to have made significant contributions to the rise of Mahāyāna Buddhism. These sources are stated briefly here and then explained in more detail in the following sections of this chapter. The first source is Nikāya (Sectarian) Buddhism. Many modern scholars have maintained the view that Mahāyāna Buddhism developed out of the Mahāsaṅghika School. But since the Mahāsaṅghika School continued to exist long after Mahāyāna Buddhism arose, the rise of Mahāyāna cannot be explained simply as the transformation of the Mahāsaṅghikas into Mahāyānists. While it is true that the many similarities between Mahāsaṅghika and Mahāyāna doctrines prove that the Mahāsaṅghika School did influence Mahāyāna Buddhism, teachings from the Sarvāstivādin, Mahīśāsaka, Dharmaguptaka, and Theravāda schools were also incorporated into Mahāyāna Buddhism. The doctrines of the Sarvāstivāda School in particular were often mentioned in Mahāyāna texts, and Sammatīya teachings also were influential. The relation between Nikāya Buddhism and Mahāyāna Buddhism clearly is not a simple one.

The second source is the biographical literature of the Buddha composed by people sometimes said to have belonged to the "vehicle that praised the Buddha" (Ch. *tsan-fo sheng*).[4] Although this literature may have had its origins in Nikāya Buddhism, it eventually developed in ways that transcended sectarian lines and contributed to the rise of Mahāyāna Buddhism.

The third source is *stūpa* worship. After the Buddha's death, his remains were divided and placed in eight *stūpas* built in central India. These became centers where pious Buddhists congregated. Later, King Aśoka had *stūpas* built in other parts of India, further contributing to the spread of *stūpa* worship. These cults appear to have contributed significantly to the rise of Mahāyāna Buddhism.

Since Mahāyāna texts do not describe the circumstances that gave rise to Mahāyāna Buddhism, any investigation must be partially based on speculation. In the following pages, the three sources of Mahāyāna Buddhism introduced above are discussed in more detail.

Nikāya Buddhism and Mahāyāna

As was noted earlier, Nikāya Buddhism was often referred to by the deprecatory epithet "Hīnayāna" (inferior vehicle) by Mahāyāna Buddhists. Nikāya Buddhism, however, contributed much to Mahāyāna Buddhism. For example, Mahāyāna texts such as the *Ta-chih-tu lun* (*T* 1509, *Mahāprajñāpāramitopadeśa,* attributed to Nāgārjuna) and the *Ta-pin pan-jo ching* (*T* 223, *Pañcaviṃśatisāhasrikā-PP**) often included references to Sarvāstivādin teachings. Mahāyāna works also adopted the twelvefold classification of the Buddhist scriptures used by the Sarvāstivādin, Mahīśāsaka, and Dharmaguptaka schools. The Vātsīputrīya fivefold classification of *dharmas* (Ch. *wu fa-tsang*) was cited in the perfection of wisdom *sūtras.* Thus it is apparent that authors of many of the Mahāyāna scriptures had studied Hīnayāna doctrines.[5]

Doctrinal similarities between Hīnayāna and Mahāyāna works do not prove that the authors of Mahāyāna texts were current or former members of the schools of Nikāya Buddhism. Although Sarvāstivādin doctrine is far removed from Mahāyāna thought, Sarvāstivādin teachings were often mentioned or incorporated into Mahāyāna texts. In terms of content, however, Mahāsaṅghika doctrine is much closer to Mahāyāna thought than is Sarvāstivādin doctrine. The best summary of Mahāsaṅghika doctrine is found in Vasumitra's *Samayabhedoparacanacakra* (*T* 2031).[6] Although Vasumitra was a member of the Sarvāstivādin School, he seems to have been an unbiased scholar and to have accurately collected and summarized the teachings of other schools. In one of the sections of his work, Vasumitra grouped together the doctrines of four schools (the Mahāsaṅghika, Lokottaravādin, Ekavyavahārika, and Kaukuṭika) of Mahāsaṅghika lineage and noted that the four taught that "the Buddhas, the World-honored Ones, are all supermundane. All the Tathāgatas are without impure *(sāsrava) dharmas*" (*T* 49:15b). This position differs from that of the Sarvāstivādin School, but is close to Mahāyāna teachings. The four schools also upheld the doctrine that "the Buddha can expound all the teachings with a single utterance" (*T* 49:15b). According to the *Mahāvibhāṣā* (*T* 27:410a–b), this doctrine was also maintained by the Vibhajyavādins. It is also referred to in a well-known passage in the *Vimalakīrtinirdeśa* (*T* 14:538a). Vasumitra also noted that these schools upheld the positions that "the *rūpakāya* (form-body) of the Tathāgata is limitless. The divine power of the Tathāgata is also limitless. The lifetimes of the Buddhas are limitless. The Buddha never tires of teaching sentient beings and awakening pure faith within them" (*T* 49:15b–c). These teachings are close to Mahāyāna ideas about the *saṃbhogakāya* (body of bliss) of the Buddha and are evidence of the close relationship of these schools to Mahāyāna Buddhism.

Vasumitra also described the doctrines concerning bodhisattvas maintained by the schools of the Mahāsaṅghika lineage. "No bodhisattvas have any thoughts of greed, anger, or doing harm to others. In order to benefit sentient beings, bodhisattvas are born into inferior states through their own wishes" (*T* 49:15c). The position that bodhisattvas can consciously choose where they will be born is similar to Mahāyāna teachings and differs significantly from the Sarvāstivādin position that birth is determined only by karma.

The Mahāsaṅghikas maintained that "the original nature of the mind is pure; it becomes impure when it is affected by adventitious defilements" (*T* 49:15c). This teaching is also important in Mahāyāna Buddhism. It was maintained by other groups within Nikāya Buddhism. For example, it is found in the *Śāriputrābhidharmaśāstra* (*T* 28:697b). It was also advocated by the Discriminators and appears in the Pāli *suttas*. Although this doctrine was not unique to the Mahāsaṅghika School, Mahāsaṅghika views of the Buddha were certainly close to those found in Mahāyāna Buddhism and provide evidence of a deep tie between the thought of the two groups. The exact nature of the relationship between the Mahāsaṅghika order and Mahāyāna adherents unfortunately is still unclear. Since the Sarvāstivādins also made doctrinal contributions to Mahāyāna Buddhism, the most significant and difficult problem that remains to be solved is determining what institutional ties might have existed between the Mahāsaṅghika order and Mahāyāna Buddhists.

Biographies of the Buddha

The *Mahāvastu* is a biography of the Buddha produced by the Lokottaravādins, adherents of a school related to the Mahāsaṅghika School. The

Mahāvastu[7] describes ten grounds *(bhūmi)* or stages a future Buddha would pass through on his way to Buddhahood. Mahāyāna texts such as the *Shih-ti ching (T* 287, *Daśabhūmikasūtra)* contain similar teachings on the ten stages that have often been cited as evidence indicating that Mahāyāna Buddhism arose from the Mahāsaṅghika School. However, the *Mahāvastu* and similar literature concerning the Buddha's life transcend sectarian lines. For example, at the end of the *Fo pen-hsing chi ching* (*T* 190, *Abhiniṣkramaṇasūtra*?), a Dharmaguptaka text, it is noted that the very same biography is called the *Ta-shih (Mahāvastu)* by the Mahāsaṅghika School and various other names by the Sarvāstivādin, Kāśyapīya, and Mahīśāsaka schools, thus indicating that these schools shared a common biography of the Buddha (*T* 3:932a).

Differences do exist between the biographies of the Buddha extant today. The Mahāsaṅghika *Mahāvastu,* the Dharmaguptaka *Fo pen-hsing chi ching,* and the Sarvāstivādin School's *Lalitavistara*[8] are not identical. The *Mahāvastu* in particular diverges from the others. But earlier, the schools do seem to have shared the same biography. Perhaps the story's literary qualities enabled it to transcend sectarian differences. For example, Aśvaghoṣa, author of the *Buddhacarita,* had close connections with the Sarvāstivādin School, but he has also been connected with the Bahuśrutīya, Kaukuṭika, Sautrāntika, and Yogācāra traditions,[9] and thus cannot be said to belong to any single school. Rather, he and other poets, such as Mātṛceta, may be said to belong to the "vehicle of those who praise the Buddha" (Ch. *tsan-fo sheng*).

Mātṛceta lived in the second or third century and ranks next to Aśvaghoṣa as a Buddhist poet. His poems, exemplified by such works as the *Śatapañcāśatka-stotra* (One-hundred-fifty strophes) and the *Varnāharvarṇa-stotra* (Four-hundred strophes), were well loved throughout India.[10] In his poems, Mātṛceta praises the Buddha. Because the Buddha is portrayed in a very human way, Mātṛceta seems to have been influenced by Sarvāstivādin doctrines. However, Mātṛceta also praises the Buddha's virtues as innumerable, the Buddha's wisdom as thorough, and his mind as limitless, descriptions close to Mahāyāna views of the Buddha's character. Some of the verses praise the Great Vehicle (Mahāyāna). Others explain the six perfections and the doctrine of nonsubstantiality, both Mahāyāna teachings, leading some modern scholars to believe that Mātṛceta belonged to the Mādhyamika School.

To stress the importance of faith in the Buddha, poets fervently praised him and used literary expressions that transcended sectarian doctrinal considerations. Buddhist poets wrote their works with purposes different from those of scholars who were concerned with doctrinal issues. The term "vehicle of those who praise the Buddha" appears in Kumārajīva's translation of the *Saddharmapuṇḍarīkasūtra* (*T* 9:9c); but a corresponding term does not appear in the Sanskrit versions of the *sūtra.* In the *Mahāvibhāṣā,* the teaching of the Discriminators who argued that the Buddha expounded all his teachings in a single sound is criticized: "Those (who compose) hymns of praise for the Buddha are too verbose and exceed the truth" (*T* 27:410a–b). This passage evidently refers to the poets who were composing hymns of praise for the Buddha.

The biographers of the Buddha were probably identical to those people who belonged to the "vehicle of those who praise the Buddha." In the following discussion, the relationship between Mahāyāna Buddhism and the early authors of these biographies (those who preceded Aśvaghoṣa) is considered.

Biographies of the Buddha probably developed out of *vinaya* literature. In the beginning of the *Mahāvastu* is a statement that the *Mahāvastu* was originally included in the Lokottaravādin *vinaya.* The title of the biography, *Mahāvastu,* corresponds to the first chapter *(Mahākhandhaka)* of the *Mahāvagga* portion of the Pāli *Vinaya.* The terms *"vastu," "vagga,"* and *"khandhaka"* all were used with the meaning of "chapter" or "division." The title *"Mahāvastu"* could thus be translated as "The Great Chapter." Moreover, a biography of the Buddha is found at the beginning of the Pāli *Mahākhandhaka,* and E. Windisch has demonstrated that, in fact, parts of the *Mahāvastu* correspond to sections of the *Mahākhandhaka.* As the biography of the Buddha was expanded, it was separated from the *vinaya* and assumed the form of the *Mahāvastu.* The title of the Mahīśāsaka equivalent of the *Mahāvastu, P'i-ni-tsang ken-pen* or "basis of the *vinaya-piṭaka,*" indicates that the biography's origins were in the *vinaya.*

As the *nidāna* (stories illustrating the origins of the precepts) and the *avadāna* (cautionary tales warning against infringements of the precepts) in the *vinaya* developed, the biography of the Buddha was enlarged and eventually separated from the *vinaya.* The people who compiled the Buddha's biography had motives different from those who had studied the *nidāna* and *avadāna* in the *vinaya.* Their interest in the Buddha developed out of a desire to understand the causes of the Buddha's enlightenment and the practices that led to enlightenment. Narratives of the Buddha's life were compiled and expanded with these issues in mind, resulting in literature that had much in common with the *jātakas,* the tales of the Buddha's previous lives. The biographies of the Buddha did not have a necessary relationship to the *vinaya.* Rather, the compilers of biographies of the Buddha were searching for the causes of enlightenment and by chance chose the biographical material in the *vinaya* as the basis for their works.

Among the extant biographies of the Buddha are the *Mahāvastu,* produced by the Lokottaravādin branch of the Mahāsaṅghika School; the *Fo pen-hsing chi ching* (*T* 190, *Abhiniṣkramaṇasūtra*?) of the Dharmaguptaka School; and the *Lalitavistara* (Sanskrit, Tibetan, and two Chinese versions, *T* 186 and 187, exist) of the Sarvāstivādin School. Although the last work is Sarvāstivādin, some of the extant versions, the Sanskrit and *T* 187, were altered so much in later times that they are completely Mahāyāna in character and contain terms such as *ju-lai-tsang (tathāgatagarbha)* and *ch'ing-ching fa-chieh* (pure *dharma*-realm). The above-named texts are Sectarian works; but much of their content does not reflect any Sectarian affiliation.

A number of other biographies that do not have any clear doctrinal affiliation are also extant. Among them are *Kuo-ch'ü hsien-tsai yin-kuo ching* (*T* 189), *T'ai-tzu jui-ying pen-ch'i ching* (*T* 185, possibly of Mahīśāsaka origins), *Hsiu-hsing pen-ch'i ching* (*T* 184), *Chung pen-ch'i ching* (*T* 196), *I-ch'u p'u-sa pen-ch'i ching* (*T* 188, *Abhiniṣkramaṇasūtra*?), *Fo pen-hsing ching* (*T* 193), and *Fo-so-hsing tsan* (*T* 192, *Buddhacarita**). The terms *"pen-ch'i"* (original arising), *"pen-hsing"* (primordial practices), and *"so-hsing"* (practices) in the titles reflect the compilers' concern with the origins and basic activities that led to enlightenment. The biographers focused their attention primarily on the events leading up to enlightenment, often abbreviating or ignoring events that followed the Buddha's enlightenment.

The biographies all include a number of the same type of events. The first is the prediction *(vyākaraṇa)* by Dīpaṅkara Buddha that the future Śākyamuni would in fact be successful in his quest for Buddhahood. The stories begin by noting that the future Śākyamuni was a young Brahman at that time. Texts differ about his name, but among those given are Sumati, Sumedha, and Megha. Regardless of the name, later biographies all begin with a former Buddha predicting the future Śākyamuni's eventual attainment of Buddhahood. The stories behind the prediction also varied. According to some versions, the prediction occurred when the young Brahman offered five flowers that he had bought from a woman to Dīpaṅkara Buddha. According to other versions, the young man was watching Dīpaṅkara approach in a religious procession when he realized that a mud puddle lay in Dīpaṅkara's path. The young man quickly unfastened his long hair and spread it over the mud puddle so that Dīpaṅkara's feet would not be soiled. Dīpaṅkara then predicted that the young man would eventually attain enlightenment and the future Śākyamuni responded by vowing that he indeed would attain it. Apparently, these stories of Dīpaṅkara's prediction circulated widely among the biographers of the Buddha.

Predictions of Buddhahood are an important element in Mahāyāna thought. Dīpaṅkara's prediction of Śākyamuni's Buddhahood is mentioned often in Mahāyāna scriptures. Eventually questions were asked about the religious practices the future Śākyamuni Buddha had performed before he had received Dīpaṅkara's prediction. The Buddha's biography was consequently extended further back in time until it covered his practices for three incalculable eons.

According to these scriptures, after he received Dīpaṅkara's prediction, the future Buddha practiced the six perfections. The people who were so vitally concerned with the events and practices that led to enlightenment naturally supposed that a future Buddha performed practices different from those who aspired to become an *arhat* or *pratyekabuddha.* Expositions of the six perfections were first developed by the authors of biographies of the Buddha to characterize the special practices of a future Buddha. The list of ten perfections in the introduction *(nidāna-kathā)* of the Pāli *Jātaka* is probably a later expansion of the six perfections. According to the *Mahāvibhāṣā* (*T* 27:892b–c), doctrines of both four perfections and six perfections were maintained by Sarvāstivādin thinkers, with the doctrine of the four perfections eventually being declared orthodox within the Sarvāstivādin School. The biographies of the Buddha, without exception, all list six perfections, and this list of six perfections was incorporated into Mahāyāna scriptures. The authors of the biographies of the Buddha thus devised the six perfections to describe the unique practices that would lead to Buddhahood, practices that differed considerably from those followed by the Buddha's disciples.

These thinkers were also concerned with the stages of practice through which a bodhisattva passed on his way to Buddhahood. In some biographies, the following fixed phrase appears: "He had attained the tenth stage. Only one more life remained before he attained Buddhahood. He was nearing omniscience." (For example, see *Kuo-ch'ü hsien-tsai yin-kuo ching, T* 3:623a.) The ten stages are explained in detail only in the *Mahāvastu.* However, other biographies often contain the phrase "He had attained the tenth stage." Even though other biographies do not contain detailed explanations of the ten stages, the authors of the biographies obviously knew about the ten stages. The authors thus widely believed that a bodhisattva passed through ten stages and finally reached a position from which he would be reborn and attain Buddhahood in his next life. These doctrines concerning the ten stages were later utilized in Mahāyāna scriptures. The concept that a bodhisattva might attain a stage from which only one more birth would be required before he attained Buddhahood *(eka-jāti-pratibaddha)* was also applied to Maitreya. Determining whether this idea arose first in relation to Śākyamuni or to Maitreya has proved to be surprisingly difficult.

Additional important points concerning biographies of the Buddha could be raised, but the above discussion should demonstrate the special characteristics of this genre of Buddhist literature. Many of the doctrines found in this literature later appeared in Mahāyāna scriptures. For example, the story of how the future Śākyamuni Buddha descended from Tuṣita heaven, assumed the form of a white elephant, and entered the womb of Māyā probably was developed by these biographers, as was the list of the eight key events in a Buddha's life (descent from Tuṣita heaven, entering his mother's womb, birth, leaving lay life, defeating the demons that represent the defilements, attaining enlightenment, preaching, and death).

Many similarities between biographies of the Buddha and Mahāyāna scriptures can be indicated. However, the fundamental differences between the two types of literature must not be overlooked. Biographies of the Buddha investigated the background of an individual who was already recognized as a Buddha. The bodhisattva discussed in these biographies had already received a prediction *(vyākaraṇa)* of his eventual Buddhahood and was therefore assured of success in his religious quest. In biographies such as the *Mahāvastu,* the possibility of many Buddhas appearing in the world at the same time was recognized. Consequently, many bodhisattvas, all of whom were assured of their eventual Buddhahood, had to exist.

In contrast, the bodhisattva portrayed in many Mahāyāna scriptures was only an individual who aspired to attain enlightenment. His eventual enlightenment was not assured. He had not received a prediction that he would eventually attain enlightenment and he even backslid in his practice. He was the ordinary man as bodhisattva. Of course, great bodhisattvas (who were not subject to backsliding and other ills) such as Samantabhadra, Mañjuśrī, Avalokiteśvara, and Maitreya were also mentioned in Mahāyāna scriptures along with the obscure, ordinary practitioner of Mahāyāna Buddhism who considered himself a bodhisattva. The question of what caused ordinary Buddhist practitioners to consider themselves bodhisattvas still remains to be answered. Since the lavish praise given the Buddha in biographies does not explain this development, another explanation must be sought. Thus, although similarities between the biographies of the Buddha and Mahāyāna scriptures exist, fundamental differences are also present.

Jātakas and *Avadānas*

Closely related to the biographies of the Buddha are the *jātakas* (stories of the Buddha's former lives) and the *avadānas* (P. *apadāna,* 'edifying tales concerning the Buddha'). The full title of the *Mahāvastu* is, in fact, the *Mahāvastu-avadāna.* The difference between the terms "*jātaka*" and "*avadāna*" is difficult to distinguish, partly because the meaning of the word "*avadāna*" changed over the long period during which the genre of stories was recited. Both the *jātakas* and *avadānas* are mentioned in the twelvefold classification of Buddhist literature, indicating that they were considered literary genres early in Buddhist history. Among the *Nikāyas* are texts, such as the *Mahāpadānasuttanta,* that incorporate the word *apadāna* into their titles. In the context of the twelvefold division of Buddhist literary genres, the term "*avadāna*" can usually be explained as meaning a parable or edifying fable.[11] Sometime after the contents of the *Āgamas* had been fixed, the *avadānas* were compiled independently. The Pāli *Apadāna,* a work in the *Khuddaka-nikāya,* is representative of this development. Later, many *avadāna* tales were compiled and the genre flourished. However, many details of the process of compilation are still unclear.

Today numerous works classified as *avadāna* literature are extant. Many of these texts date from approximately the beginning of the common era. Besides the *Mahāvastu,* the Sanskrit texts of the *Avadānaśataka* (cf. *T* 200), the *Divyāvadāna,* and the *Sumāgadhāvadāna* (cf. *T* 128–129) and others have been published. In addition, many later *avadāna* works are extant, but have not yet been published.[12] These unpublished texts were compiled over a period of several centuries and are mainly mythological. They differ from earlier *avadāna* literature in this respect.

Jātaka tales are listed in both the ninefold and twelvefold classifications of Buddhist literature, indicating that they were established as an independent genre of Buddhist literature early in Buddhist history. *Jātaka* tales are among the subjects found in the carvings at Bhārhut, with twelve such tales identified in the Bhārhut inscriptions.[13] Thus, by the second century B.C.E. a number of tales had already been composed. During the subsequent centuries, many more were produced. *Jātaka* tales are presented as the former lives of the Buddha, but the material for the tales is frequently taken from Indian folk tales and fables. The content is often close to that found in the *avadāna* literature. The Pāli work, the *Jātaka,* contains 547 tales and was named after the genre it epitomizes. A five-fascicle Chinese translation (*T* 154) of the text exists. In addition, many works composed primarily of *jātaka* tales are extant, including the *Ta chuang-yen lun ching* (*T* 201, *Kalpanāmaṇḍitikā**), *Avadānaśataka, Divyāvadāna, Wu-pai ti-tzu tzu-shuo pen-ch'i ching* (*T* 199), *P'u-sa pen-hsing ching (T* 155, *Bodhisattvapūrvacarya?),* and *Seng-ch'ieh-lo-ch'a so-chi ching* (*T* 194). The *Liu-tu chi-ching* (*T* 152, *Ṣaṭpāramitāsaṅgraha*?) and the *P'u-sa pen-yüan ching* (*T* 153, *Bodhisattvāvadāna*?) include *jātaka* tales reworked to illustrate Mahāyāna themes. The *jātaka* tales cited in the *Ta-chih-tu lun (T* 1509, *Mahāprajñāpāramitopadeśa)* exhibit prominent Mahāyāna characteristics. Consequently, some scholars have argued that the *jātaka* tales contributed significantly to the development of Mahāyāna thought. However, the *Liu-tu chi-ching* (*T* 152, *Ṣaṭpāramitāsaṅgraha*?) contains sections composed after the perfection of wisdom *sūtras*. Extreme care must be exercised in determining whether the "Mahāyāna *jātaka* tales" were composed before or after the earlier Mahāyāna texts.

Drawing clear distinctions between the genres of biographical literature on the Buddha, such as the *jātakas* and *avadānas,* is very difficult. The authors of this literature must have played a significant role in the early development of Mahāyana thought. It would be revealing to know how these people made their living, what type of place they lived in, and what type of people they associated with. Answers to these problems would contribute greatly to our understanding of the rise of Mahāyāna Buddhism. Unfortunately, the available literature does not shed light on the answers to these questions.

Some of these parables and metaphors were called *upamā.* They are found in such works as the *Po-yü ching* (*T* 209) and the *Hsien-yü ching (T* 202, *Damamūkanidānasūtra).* Buddhists have used parables and metaphors to explain their teachings since the time of the Buddha. The tales used by the Dārṣṭāntikas (those who explain by using metaphors and parables) probably belong to this tradition. Many of the doctrines taught by the Dārṣṭāntikas are cited or introduced in the *Mahāvibhāṣā* (*T* 1545). The Dārṣṭāntikas are said to have been forerunners of the Sautrāntikas, but the validity of this claim is questionable.[14] One of the most famous Dārṣṭāntikas was Kumāralāta, the author of several works. Although he is said to have been a contemporary of Nāgārjuna, he is not mentioned in the *Mahāvibhāṣā.* Rather, his poems are cited in the *Ch'eng-shih lun* (*T* 1646, *Tattvasiddhiśāstra*?).[15] Consequently, he probably lived sometime between the compilation of the *Mahāvibhāṣā* and the *Tattvasiddhiśāstra.* A Sanskrit fragment of a work said to have been written by him, the *Kalpanāmaṇḍitikā,* was discovered in Central Asia. However, a Chinese translation of this work (*T* 201) that is close to the Sanskrit fragment is said to be by Aśvaghoṣa. Modern scholars still disagree about the authorship of the text.[16]

Stūpa Worship and Mahāyāna Buddhism

The role of *stūpa* worship in the rise of Mahāyāna Buddhism cannot be ignored. It is important in many Mahāyāna *sūtras,* including the *Saddharmapuṇḍarīkasūtra* (*T* 262) and the *A-mi-t'o ching (T* 366, "Smaller" *Sukhāvatīvyūha).*[17] In addition, the Mahāyāna concern with a savior Buddha can be traced to worship at *stūpas.*

In Nikāya Buddhism, the Buddha was thought of as a teacher of the Dharma. The Dharma he preached was particularly emphasized because if a person followed that Dharma, it would lead him to salvation. No matter how much the Buddha was viewed as a superhuman being, he was not considered to be capable of acting as a savior. Rather, he was praised because he had successfully accomplished that which was difficult to accomplish. Nikāya Buddhism focused on the Dharma rather than on the Buddha and consequently emphasized monasticism and rigid adherence to the precepts. In contrast, Mahāyāna Buddhism was originally concerned with laymen. Doctrines for lay bodhisattvas play a prominent role in the oldest Mahāyāna *sūtras.* Only later did Mahāyāna Buddhism increasingly develop into a religion in which monks assumed prominent positions.

Laymen were unable to strictly observe the precepts or to devote much time to meditation and thus could not put the Buddha's teachings into practice in the traditional ways. Instead, they had to depend on the Buddha's compassion for their salvation. While monastic Buddhism emphasized the Buddha's teaching, lay Buddhism emphasized the role of the Buddha in salvation. Teachings concerning the saving power of the Buddha appeared in response to the religious needs of laymen. Beliefs in the Buddhas Amitābha and Akṣobhya reflected the layman's desire to depend on someone greater than himself. This need is reflected in the following statement by Śākyamuni Buddha in the *Saddharmapuṇḍarīkasūtra* (*T* 9:14c): "The three realms are completely insecure. They are like a burning house, full of suffering. Yet the three realms are all mine and the sentient beings within them are my children."

For lay Buddhism to develop doctrinally, centers were necessary where teachers could meet students and thereby transmit doctrines to the next generation. If the lay organizations had been subordinate to the monastic orders, they would have been compelled to receive and follow the instructions of monks. Any independent development of lay doctrine under such circumstances would have been difficult. Thus, centers independent of monastic control must have existed, where people could practice, develop teachings emphasizing the Buddha, and pass these traditions on to younger generations. *Stūpas* served as such centers.

Stūpas were predominantly for laymen. According to the Pāli *Mahāparinibbānasūtta,* when the Buddha was about to die, he told Ānanda that the monks and nuns were not to conduct a funeral service over his remains. Rather the monks were "to strive for the highest good" (P. *sadattha*). As for his remains, the Buddha stated that "Brahmans with deep faith and worthy householders would pay reverence to the remains (P. *sarīra-pūjā*) of the Tathāgata."[18] After the Buddha's death, the Mallas of Kuśinagara performed the funeral. His remains were then divided and eight *stūpas* erected by laymen. Thus from the very beginning, *stūpas* were protected and maintained by laymen, and laymen did homage at them. According to another passage in the *Mahāparinibbānasūtta,* four places were considered sacred to the Buddha after his death. Worship halls and memorial mounds *(cetiya)* were erected at all of them: his birthplace at Lumbinī, the site of his enlightenment at Buddhagayā, the site of his first sermon at the Deer Park, and the site of his death at Kuśinagara. Pilgrims soon began visiting these places. Thus was *stūpa* worship begun by laymen and later transmitted and maintained primarily by laymen. Even today, *stūpas (pagodas)* in Burma are administered by committees of pious laymen; monks may not participate in the administration of these *stūpas*.

King Aśoka commissioned many *stūpas*. Archeological investigations of the ruins of many of the older surviving *stūpas* have revealed that their oldest strata probably date back to Aśoka's time. The cores of the *stūpas* of central India at Bhārhut and Sāñcī and the Dharmarājikā *stūpa* at Taxila are all very early, with their oldest layers dating back to the second or third century B.C.E. Many more *stūpas* were built around the beginning of the common era. Almost all the old inscriptions excavated in recent times bear some relation to *stūpas*. Although *stūpas* were constructed and maintained by laymen, and although the majority of the donors were laymen and laywomen, they were not the only people who worshipped at them. Inscriptions on the pillars, railings, and finials at Bharhut and Sāñcī record the names of a number of monks and nuns who made donations to the *stūpas*. Since monks and nuns had few possessions, their presentation of goods suggests the profundity of their devotion.

By the beginning of the common era, *stūpas* were being built within the confines of temples. Alongside these *stūpas,* quarters for monks were constructed, making it easy for monks to present their offerings to the *stūpas*. The monasteries probably had the *stūpas* built on their grounds in response to the growing popularity of *stūpa* worship outside the monasteries. Proof of this change of attitude appears in a number of sources. For example, the Theravāda *Vinaya* does not mention *stūpas* even though *stūpas* have been built within the confines of Theravāda monasteries for centuries. Apparently, Theravāda monks began making offerings at *stūpas* only after the *Vinaya* had been compiled. In contrast, the Sarvāstivādin and Mahāsaṅghika *vinayas* (*T* 1435 and 1425) mention Buddha images, indicating that the compilation of these two *vinayas* was probably completed later than the Pāli *Vinaya*. Thus some *vinayas* compiled after monks had already begun worshipping at *stūpas* include discussions of *stūpa* worship. The Sarvāstivādin and Mahāsaṅghika *vinayas* state that a strict distinction must be maintained between properties and objects that belong to the monastic order and those that belong to the *stūpa* (*T* 22:498a; 23:352b). They could not be used interchangeably. If a monk used *stūpa* property to benefit the order, he was to be charged with a *pārājika* offense for stealing. According to the Dharmaguptaka and Mahīśāsaka *vinayas* (*T* 1421 and 1428), the *stūpa* represented "the Buddha in the order."[19] Although *stūpas* might be built within the monastery, items belonging to the Buddha were to be distinguished from those belonging to the order. Thus the *vinayas,* the legal codes for the orders, indicate that the *stūpas* were independent of the monastic orders.

Sources such as Vasumitra's *Samayabhedoparacanacakra* suggest that the Dharmaguptaka School encouraged contributions to *stūpas* by maintaining that "offerings to *stūpas* produced great merit" (*T* 49:17a). In contrast, orders of the Mahāsaṅghika lineage such as the Caitika, Aparaśaila, Uttaraśaila, and Mahīśāsaka schools maintained that "offerings made to *stūpas* would result in only a small amount of merit" (*T* 49:16a). At least four inscriptions concerning the Caitika School have been found at Amarāvatī in southern India. These inscriptions are probably connected with the great *stūpa (mahācetiya)* at Amarāvatī, an important site in the third and fourth centuries. Although the Caitika School maintained that the merit earned by making offerings at *stūpas* was minimal, large *stūpas* were still associated with the school.

Later sources, such as the *Mahāvibhāṣā* (*T* 1545) and the *Abhidharmakośa* (*T* 1558), also maintained that contributions to the monastic order produced much more merit than those made to *stūpas* (*T* 27:678b). Thus, although *stūpa* worship was practiced within Nikāya Buddhism, the monastic orders did not always coexist harmoniously with the *stūpa* cults. Buddhist believers were often discouraged from making offerings at the *stūpas,* suggesting that *stūpa* worship was introduced into the monastic orders after the orders had been established for a period of time and that the monks did not want to see *stūpa* worship grow in influence. In addition to *stūpas* within monasteries, there were other *stūpas* that were not affiliated with any of the schools of Nikāya Buddhism and that were managed by laymen. This division is clear from the many inscriptions that have been discovered by archeologists in recent times. The vast majority of the inscriptions concerning *stūpas* do not mention the name of a school.[20]

Flowers, incense, banners, flags, music, and dance were used in the ceremonies accompanying *stūpa* worship. Even at the Buddha's funeral, the Mallas of Kuśinagara employed music, dance, flowers, and incense to honor, revere, and respect the corpse of the Buddha before it was cremated, as is described in detail in the *Mahāparinibbānasutta* (*DN,* vol. 2, p. 159). The use of music and dance in such a ceremony was clearly forbidden to those living a monastic life. In the precepts for novices, monks, and nuns, the enjoyment of such entertainments was clearly prohibited. Music, dance, theater, architecture, and other arts conflicted with the standards of monastic life, which aimed at transcending worldly concerns. Such arts could not have flourished in Buddhist monasteries. But they did develop around *stūpa* worship and were later adopted into Mahāyāna Buddhism, where they were elaborated further. These traditions of music and dance were later transmitted to China along with Mahāyāna Buddhism, and then to Japan as *gigaku.*

Stūpa worship had a social as well as a religious dimension. It began immediately after the Buddha's death, and through the support of its adherents, *stūpa* worship gradually began to flourish. The *stūpas* erected in various areas were thronged with worshippers and pilgrims. To erect a *stūpa,* land had to be contributed by individuals. Since the land was given for a religious purpose, it was no longer owned by any particular individual. Besides the *stūpa* itself, lodging for pilgrims, wells, and pools for bathing were built on the land. These facilities were the property of the *stūpa.* A walkway around the *stūpa* was constructed so that pilgrims could worship as they circumambulated the *stūpa.* A fence with gates enclosed the area. Carvings on the fence and on the gates to the *stūpa* illustrated incidents from the Buddha's biography and the good deeds and selfless acts he had performed in his past lives. Religious specialists who explained the *jātaka* tales and the biography of the Buddha to the worshippers probably resided at the *stūpa,* as did people who managed the lodgings for the pilgrims. A religious order began to take shape.[21]

Since the *stūpas* had property, people must have been present to manage it. Gold, silver, flowers, incense, and food must have been given to the *stūpa* by believers and pilgrims. Although such alms were presented to the Buddha, they were undoubtedly accepted and used by those people who cared for the *stūpa.* These people were very different from ordinary lay believers, but also were probably not members of a monastic order. They were religious specialists who were neither laymen nor monks. As these religious specialists repeatedly explained the illustrations of the *jātakas* and the biography of Śākyamuni Buddha, they extolled Śākyamuni's religious practices in his past lives as the practices of a bodhisattva and praised his greatness and deep compassion. Gradually they must have advanced doctrines to explain the Buddha's power to save others. In this way they attracted more followers to the *stūpas*.

Worship at *stūpas* might well have led to meditations in which the Buddha was visualized. Even today Tibetan pilgrims at Buddhagayā can be seen prostrating themselves hundreds of times in front of *stūpas*. Long ago as people repeatedly performed such practices while intently thinking of the Buddha, they might have entered a concentration *(samādhi)* in which the Buddha appeared before them. This concentration would correspond to the *pratyutpanna-samādhi* described in some Mahāyāna texts. Thus Mahāyāna meditations in which the Buddha is visualized may have originated in the religious experiences of people worshipping the Buddha at *stūpas*. Such religious experiences might have resulted in people coming to the belief that they were bodhisattvas.

In conclusion, the establishment of *stūpas* and the accumulation of property around them enabled groups of religious specialists to live near the *stūpas*. These people formed orders and began developing doctrines concerning the Buddha's powers to save. The references in many Mahāyāna texts to *stūpa* worship indicate the central role of these orders in the emergence of Mahāyāna Buddhism. In some Mahāyāna texts, a bodhisattva group *(bodhisattvagaṇa)* is mentioned as existing separately from the order of monks of the Nikāya schools *(śrāvakasaṅgha)*.[22] The *bodhisattvagaṇa* probably had its origins in the groups of people who practiced at *stūpas*. However, the origins of the advocates of the perfection of wisdom literature must be sought in different areas.

CHAPTER 17

The Contents of Early Mahāyāna Scriptures

The Earliest Mahāyāna Scriptures

THE EARLIEST KNOWN Mahāyāna scriptures are the *Liu po-lo-mi ching (Ṣaṭpāramitā), P'u-sa tsang-ching (Bodhisattvapiṭaka), San-p'in ching (Triskandhakadharmaparyāya),* and the *Tao-chih ta-ching.*[1] These texts are thought to be very early because they are cited in some of the first Mahāyāna scriptures to be translated. The *Liu po-lo-mi ching (Ṣaṭpāramitā)* is quoted in such texts as Lokakṣema's 179 C.E. translation of the *Kāśyapaparivarta* (*T* 350) and Chih Ch'ien's (fl. 223–253) translation of the Larger *Sukhāvatīvyūhasūtra* (*T* 362). The bodhisattva is urged to chant the *Ṣaṭpāramitā* in these early texts.

The *P'u-sa tsang-ching (Bodhisattvapiṭaka)* is cited in texts such as Lokakṣema's translation of the *Kāśyapaparivarta* (*T* 350) and Dharmarakṣa's translation of the *Vimaladattāparipṛcchā* (*T* 338). The *San-p'in ching (Triskandhakadharmaparyāya)* is cited in such texts as the translation of the *Ugradattaparipṛcchā* by An Hsüan and Yen Fo-t'iao (*T* 322), the *Vimaladattāparipṛcchā* translated by Dharmarakṣa in 289 (*T* 338), the *Ssu-ho-mei ching* translated by Chih Ch'ien (*T* 532), and the *Śikṣāsamuccaya.* The *Tao-chih ta-ching* is cited in Chih Ch'ien's translation of the Larger *Sukhāvatīvyūha* (*T* 362). Since the translations by Lokakṣema, An Hsüan, and Yen Fo-t'iao were done during the reign of Emperor Ling (168–189), the Mahāyāna texts they translated are clearly early. The *Ṣaṭpāramitā, Bodhisattvapiṭaka,* and *Triskandhakadharmaparyāya* are even older, since they are quoted in these early translations.

The very earliest Mahāyāna scriptures such as the *Ṣaṭpāramitā* are no longer extant. Consequently, the date of their composition cannot be determined from the texts themselves. However, approximate dates can be determined indirectly. Early versions of texts such as the *Kāśyapa-parivarta* (translated into Chinese by Lokakṣema as the *I jih-mo-ni-pao ching, T* 350) were probably compiled in the first century of the common era. Since the *Ṣaṭpāramita* was quoted in these texts, the *Ṣaṭpāramitā* and the other earliest Mahāyāna texts were probably compiled in the first century B.C.E. The *Ṣaṭpāramitā* is treated as a typical Mahāyāna *sūtra* in the *Ta-chih-tu lun (T* 1509, 25:308a and 349b, *Mahāprajñāpāramitopadeśa).* The *Ṣaṭpāramitā* apparently was an influential text. As its title implies, it probably consisted of a description of the practice of the six perfections. In the course of treating each of the six perfections equally, early Mahāyānists eventually realized that the perfection of wisdom was particularly important. Perfection of wisdom *sūtras* probably first appeared after the *Ṣaṭpāramitā* was compiled.

Although the *Bodhisattvapiṭaka* is mentioned in several early texts, its contents are not clearly known. However, the *Fu-lou-na hui* (*Pūrṇaparipṛcchā#*) in the *Ta-pao chi-ching (T* 310.17, *Mahāratnakūṭa),* translated by Kumārajīva, was originally called the *P'u-sa tsang-ching (Bodhisattvapiṭaka).* In Kumārajīva's translation of this text, *sūtras* called the *P'u-sa tsang-ching* and the *Ying liu po-lo-mi ching* are cited, suggesting that the text Kumārajīva used was compiled later than the earliest version of the *P'u-sa tsang-ching.* In addition, several other texts bear the title of *P'u-sa tsang-ching,* including translations by Seng-chia-p'o-lo (Saṅghabhara?) and Hsüan-tsang (*T* 1491 and 310.12). Hsüan-tsang's translation is twenty fascicles long; the middle thirteen fascicles contain an explanation of the six perfections. These translations were completed long after Mahāyāna Buddhism had arisen and thus cannot be used to determine the contents of the earliest version of the *P'u-sa tsang-ching.* At the same time, these later works are probably related to the early version of the *P'u-sa tsang-ching.*

A general idea of the contents of the *San-p'in ching (Triskandhakadharmaparyāya)* can be gained from passages in such texts as the *Fa-ching ching (T* 322, *Ugradattaparipṛcchā).* Confession ceremonies were a major topic of the *San-p'in ching.* According to the *Yu-chia chang-che ching (T* 323, *Ugradattaparipṛcchā),* the following subjects were discussed in the *San-p'in ching:* worship at the *stūpa,* confession before the Buddha of one's past wrongdoing, the cultivation of joy at another's accomplishments, the transference of one's merits to help others, and the invitation to the Buddha to the place of practice. The procedures for ceremonies to worship the Buddha six times during each twenty-four-hour day were also included.[2] Dharmarakṣa is credited with translating a one-fascicle work entitled *San-p'in hui-kuo ching* (not extant), which may have been related to the *San-p'in ching.* Among extant texts, the *She-li-fu hui-kuo ching* (*T* 1492, *Triskandhaka*?) and the *Ta-sheng san-chü ch'an-hui ching* (*T* 1493, *Karmāvaraṇapratiprasrabdhisūtra#*) are probably part of the tradition that produced the *San-p'in ching (Triskandhakadharmaparyāya).* Further research on this group of texts is needed.

Perfection of Wisdom *(Prajñāpāramitā) Sūtras*

The largest perfection of wisdom text is the *Ta pan-jo po-lo-mi-to ching* (*T* 220, *Mahāprajñāpāramitāsūtra)* translated into Chinese by Hsüan-tsang. It is six hundred fascicles long and divided into sixteen assemblies (or parts). Perfection of wisdom *sūtras* were not always such large works. At first a number of separate texts circulated independently. Later they were collected together to make larger works such as the one mentioned above.

The oldest *sūtra* in this group is the *Tao-hsing pan-jo ching* (*T* 224) translated by Lokakṣema. Since the translation was completed around 179, the original text probably dates back to the first century C.E. It belongs to the same group of texts as the *Hsiao-p'in pan-jo ching* (*T* 227) translated by Kumārajīva and the Sanskrit *Perfection of Wisdom in 8,000 Lines (Aṣṭasāhasrikā-PP).* It corresponds to the fourth and fifth assemblies in *Ta pan-jo ching* (*T* 220). The *Kuang-tsan pan-jo ching* translated by Dharmarakṣa (*T* 222) corresponds to the *Fang-kuang pan-jo ching* (*T* 221) translated by Mokṣala, the *Ta-p'in pan-jo ching* (*T* 223) translated by Kumārajīva, the Sanskrit *Perfection of Wisdom in 25,000 Lines (Pañcaviṃśatisāhasrikā-PP),* and the second assembly in *Ta pan-jo ching* (*T* 220). Other well-known perfection of wisdom *sūtras* are the *Perfection of Wisdom in 100,000 Lines* (*Śatasāhasrikā-PP, T* 220.1), *Suvikrāntavikrāmiparipṛcchā* (*T* 220.16), *Vajracchedikā* (*T* 220.9, 235–239), and *Adhyardhaśatikā* (*T* 220.10, 240–244). Among smaller, shorter works expounding perfection of wisdom doctrines, the *Heart sūtra* (*Prajñāpāramitāhṛdayasūtra, T* 249–256) is particularly well known. Sanskrit versions of all of these *sūtras* exist.[3] They have also been completely translated into Tibetan although their organization differs on certain points from the Chinese translations.

The term *"prajñāpāramitā"* means "perfection of wisdom." In the *Ta-chih-tu lun (T* 1509, *Mahāprajñāpāramitopadeśa),* the term was explained as referring to crossing the sea of *saṃsāra* (life and death) to the far shore of *nirvāṇa* or enlightenment. Consequently, *prajñāpāramitā* was sometimes translated as *"chih-tu"* in Chinese (literally "crossing by means of wisdom") as in the title of the *Ta-chih-tu lun*. The wisdom specified in *prajñāpāramitā* is the wisdom of emptiness or nonsubstantiality, through which the practitioner clings to nothing and is bound by nothing. Thus although the term "perfection" is used, it is a perfection that does not aim at completion. It is wisdom based on practice through which one is always progressing toward the ideal.

The fierce determination and power required to practice the perfection of wisdom is obtained through mental concentrations *(samādhi)*. A variety of concentrations is described in Mahāyāna texts, but the most important one is the *śūraṅgama-samādhi,* a dauntless and powerful concentration that destroys all defilements. In the chapter on the Great Vehicle *(Ta-sheng p'in)* of *Ta-p'in pan-jo ching* (*T* 8:251a, *Pañcaviṃśatisāhasrikā-PP**) a list of 108 concentrations is given with the *śūraṅgama-samādhi* mentioned first. The *śūraṅgama-samādhi* was thus thought to provide the Mahāyānist with the strength to progress in his practice. This concentration is described in the *Śūraṅgamasamādhisūtra.* Although Lokakṣema's translation of this text has not survived, a later translation by Kumārajīva (*T* 642) is extant. According to that text, the *śūraṅgama* concentration is first obtained in the *dharmameghābhūmi,* the tenth of the ten stages of the bodhisattva path. The text was thus associated with the *Daśabhūmikasūtra.* Elsewhere in the *Śūraṅgamasamādhisūtra,* perfection of wisdom teachings, the importance of the aspiration for enlightenment, and a stage beyond which the practitioner will not backslide are explained. The *sūtra* was compiled early in the history of Mahāyāna Buddhism and is closely related to both the *Avataṃsakasūtra* (through the *Daśabhūmikasūtra*) and the perfection of wisdom literature.

The *A-ch'u fo-kuo ching* (*T* 313, *Akṣobhyatathāgatasyavyūha#*) is also closely connected to the perfection of wisdom *sūtras.* Akṣobhya Tathāgata long ago made a number of vows, including one that he would become omniscient and never become angry at any sentient being while he practiced to attain enlightenment. Because he never allowed himself to be moved by anger he was called the Immovable (Akṣobhya) Buddha. A similar story concerning Akṣobhya Buddha is also found in the *Tao-hsing pan-jo ching* (*T* 224, *Aṣṭasāhasrikā-PP,* translated by Lokakṣema), indicating that the earliest version of the *Akṣobhyatathāgatasyavyūha* is probably earlier than the *Tao-hsing pan-jo ching.* Adherents of the perfection of wisdom *sūtras* sometimes vowed to be reborn in Akṣobhya's Buddha-land, which was called Abhirati (Land of Joy). Amitābha worship does not appear in the perfection of wisdom *sūtras* and consequently must have originated elsewhere or under different circumstances.

In the chapter on seeing Akṣobhya Buddha's land in the *Wei-mo ching* (*T* 474–476, *Vimalakīrtinirdeśa),* Vimalakīrti is said to have originally been from Abhirati, Akṣobhya's land. The explanation of nonsubstantiality in this *sūtra* is famous, as is the discussion of nonduality, which culminates in Vimalakīrti's eloquent silence. Although the *Vimalakīrtinirdeśa* was not translated into Chinese by Lokakṣema, it was translated by Chih Ch'ien soon afterward. The work was thus probably compiled later than the early perfection of wisdom *sūtras* or the *A-ch'u fo-kuo ching* (*T* 313, *Akṣobhyatathāgatasyavyūha#*). No Sanskrit version of the *Vimalakīrtinirdeśa* is extant, but it is quoted in such Sanskrit texts as the *Śikṣāsamuccaya, Prasannapadā,* and *Bhāvanākrama.*[4]

The *Avataṃsakasūtra*

The full name of the *Avataṃsakasūtra* in Sanskrit is the *Buddhāvataṃsaka mahāvaipulyasūtra* (Ch. *Ta-fang-kuang fo-hua-yen ching, T* nos. 278, 279, 293). The term *"vaipulya"* (P. *vedalla*) is a title given to a *sūtra* said to include profound doctrines. It is included as a category in both the ninefold and twelvefold divisions of the Buddhist scriptures. According to some Mahāyāna texts, Mahāyāna *sūtras* should be identified with the *vaipulya* category in the ninefold or twelvefold divisions of the Buddha's teachings. The central element in the title of this *sūtra* is *"Buddhāvataṃsaka."* The term *"avataṃsaka"* means "a garland of flowers," indicating that all the virtues that the Buddha has accumulated by the time he attains enlightenment are like a beautiful garland of flowers that adorns him. Another title of the *sūtra, Gaṇḍavyūha,* probably is unconnected to the title *Buddhāvataṃsaka. "Vyūha"* means "ornament." The meaning of *"gaṇḍa"* is not clear, but it may mean "stem" or "stalk." According to other explanations, it may mean "miscellaneous flowers." Thus *Gaṇḍavyūha* might mean "ornament of miscellaneous or various flowers," but this interpretation is not certain. Generally, *Gaṇḍavyūha* is considered to be the original name of the "Chapter on Entering the *Dharmadhātu*" (*Ju fa-chieh p'in,* see *T* 295 for an example) that is included in the *Avataṃsaka.*

The *Avataṃsaka* was translated into Chinese by Buddhabhadra in 421 C.E. (*T* 278). This translation, consisting of sixty fascicles and divided into thirty-four chapters, was based on a Sanskrit text that had been brought to China from Khotan by Chih Fa-ling. Thus the Sanskrit text of the *Avataṃsaka* was compiled before 400, probably by 350. Later, in 699, it was translated into Chinese again by Śikṣānanda (*T* 279). This version was eighty fascicles long and divided into thirty-nine chapters. Still later a Tibetan translation divided into forty-five chapters was made. Because the Sanskrit text used in Buddhabhadra's Chinese translation had been brought from Khotan, some modern scholars have argued that additions and revisions to the *sūtra* were done in Central Asia. However, the Sanskrit text upon which the Tibetan translation was based was probably brought from India, not Central Asia. The possibility of Central Asian additions to the text requires further investigation.

The *Avataṃsaka* originally was not as lengthy a text as it is today. In the *Ta-chih-tu lun (T* 1509, *Mahāprajñāpāramitopadeśa),* the *Daśabhūmika* and *Gaṇḍavyūha* are quoted. Thus, before they were incorporated into the *Avataṃsaka,* these two works must have circulated independently. Even earlier is Lokakṣema's translation, the *Tou-sha ching* (*T* 280), which is an early version of the *Avataṃsaka*'s chapters on the "Names of the Tathāgata" *(Ming-hao p'in)* and on "Enlightenment" *(Kuang-ming-chüeh p'in).* Chih Ch'ien's translation, the *P'u-sa pen-yeh ching* (*T* 281), primarily corresponds to the "Chapter on Pure Practices" *(Ching-hsing p'in)* of the *Avataṃsaka.* The early compilation of the *Daśabhumikasūtra* is demonstrated by the descriptions of the ten stages *(daśabhūmi)* in the *Shou-leng-yen san-mei ching (T* 642, *Śūraṅgamasamādhisūtra)* and other early Mahāyāna works. The *Daśabhūmikasūtra* itself was translated into Chinese by Dharmarakṣa around 297 (*T* 285). Consequently, the *Avataṃsaka* is clearly composed of a number of individual *sūtras* that circulated independently and were later compiled into a large work. Among the earliest parts of the *Avataṃsaka* are the *Daśabhūmikasūtra, P'u-sa pen-yeh ching,* and *Tou-sha ching.*

The *Avataṃsaka* is said to reveal the Buddha's enlightenment just as it is, that is, without shaping the contents to fit the needs of the audience. The Buddha preaches the *sūtra* while he is in the ocean-seal concentration *(sāgaramudrā-samādhi)* in which everything is clearly manifested in his mind. Because the teaching was extremely difficult to understand, *śrāvakas* such as Śāriputra and Maudgalyāyana are said to have not understood the *sūtra* at all and to have acted as if they were deaf and dumb.

The realm of enlightenment described in the *sūtra* is the world of Vairocana, the Buddha of Pervasive Light. (The Buddha mentioned in later Esoteric Buddhist texts is called Mahāvairocana.) He has attained unlimited virtues, paid homage to all Buddhas, taught myriads of sentient beings, and realized supreme enlightenment. A cloud of manifested Buddhas issues from the hair follicles of Vairocana's body. He is a majestic Buddha who opens the Buddhist path to sentient beings. His wisdom is compared to the ocean (mind), which reflects light (objects) everywhere without limit.

The Buddha's enlightenment is complete in and of itself; words cannot accurately describe it. Consequently, the Buddha's enlightenment must be explained by describing its causes, the bodhisattva practices that result in enlightenment and Buddhahood. The *Avataṃsaka* thus consists of a description of the austerities of the bodhisattva as he strives to realize enlightenment. The stages on the path to enlightenment and the wisdom realized in various stages are systematically discussed. Among the stages described are the ten abodes (*avastha*? or *vihāra*?), the ten practices to benefit others (*caryā*?), the ten stages at which the practitioner's merits are given to other sentient beings (*pariṇāmanā*?), and the ten grounds *(daśabhūmi).* The ten grounds, explained in detail in the section of the *Avataṃsaka* entitled the *Daśabhūmika,* were particularly important in demonstrating the unique qualities of the bodhisattva's practices. In this text, the last of the six perfections, the perfection of wisdom, was expanded by adding four new aspects to it—skill in means *(upāya),* vows *(praṇidhāna),* strength *(bala),* and knowledge *(jñāna)*—making a new total of ten perfections. By practicing the ten perfections in order over ten stages, a person can realize supreme enlightenment. The *Shih-chu p'i-p'o-sha lun* (*T* 1521), a commentary on the *Daśabhūmika* attributed to Nāgārjuna, exists in Chinese. Its discussion of how faith in Amitābha Buddha can lead to Buddhahood, a path of easy practice, has been particularly influential in East Asia.

In the sixth ground, Facing Wisdom *(abhimukhī),* the bodhisattva cultivates the perfection of wisdom and gains insight into Dependent Origination. Because true wisdom appears before him, this stage is called "facing wisdom." Included in this section of the text are the famous words "The three realms are empty and false. They are simply the products of the one-mind. The elements of the twelve links of Dependent Origination all depend on the mind" (cf. *T* 10:194a). According to this view, all man's experiences are formed and shaped by his cognitive faculties; and man's experiences and cognitions are all attributable to the "one-mind." The "one-mind" mentioned in this passage may be interpreted as the Tathāgatagarbha, the innately pure nature of the mind referred to in many Buddhist scriptures. Consequently, according to the *Avataṃsaka* "the mind, the Buddha, and sentient beings—these three are not different" (*T* 9:465c).

The teaching that the original nature of the mind is pure constitutes one of the major traditions in Mahāyāna thought. It is found in the perfection of wisdom literature as well as in such *sūtras* as the *Wei-mo ching (T* 474–476, *Vimalakīrtinirdeśa), Ta-chi ching* (*T* 397, *Mahāsaṃnipāta*?), *A-she-shih-wang ching* (*T* 626–629, *Ajātaśatrukaukṛtyavinodana#*), and *Wen-shu-shih-li ching-lü ching (T* 460, *Paramārthasaṃvṛtisatyanirdeśa).* If the original nature of the mind of even an ordinary person is pure, then everyone has the potential to realize Buddhahood. The importance of developing the aspiration to enlightenment is emphasized in the *Avataṃsaka,* since this beginning step sets off the process that will result in supreme enlightenment. According to the *Avataṃsaka,* "At the time of the first aspiration to enlightenment, supreme enlightenment is realized" (*T* 9:449c). The teaching by some Hua-yen masters that Buddhahood is realized when the practitioner has completed the ten stages of faith (Ch. *hsin-man ch'eng-fo*), the beginning stages of the Hua-yen path, is based on such passages.

The *P'u-sa pen-yeh ching* (*T* 281,), a text that consists primarily of the "Chapter on Pure Practices" *(Ching-hsing p'in)* of the *Avataṃsaka* with material added to the beginning and end, circulated as an independent text. Detailed descriptions of the practices of both lay and monastic bodhisattvas are included in it. Particularly famous is the interpretation of the formula for taking refuge in the Three Jewels. It begins "When I put my faith in the Buddha, I also vow that I shall awaken the supreme aspiration in sentient beings and help them realize the path" (*T* 10:447c).

In the *Ju fa-chieh p'in (Gaṇḍavyūha),* the indescribable realm of the Buddha's enlightenment and the practices and vows of the bodhisattva Samantabhadra, which enable people to enter that fabulous realm, are discussed. These subjects are related through the story of the youth Sudhana and his travels in search of the Dharma. When Sudhana heard Mañjuśrī preach, the aspiration to realize enlightenment arose within him. To put the teachings of Samantabhadra into practice, Sudhana traveled and visited fifty-three teachers. Finally, he received Samantabhadra's teachings and realized enlightenment and the *dharmadhātu.*

Sanskrit texts of several sections of the *Avataṃsaka* are extant. The *Daśabhūmika* (or *Daśabhūmiśvara*) and the *Gaṇḍavyūha* have been published. The *Gaṇḍavyūha* concludes with verses, which circulated independently at one time, concerning Samantabhadra's practices and vows. The Sanskrit text of the verses has been published as the *Bhadracārī-praṇidhāna-rāja.* Several sections of the chapters on the bodhisattvas Bhadraśrī and Vajradhvaja are found in the *Śikṣāsamuccaya* and thus are preserved in Sanskrit. The latter chapter is cited under the title *Vajradhvajasūtra,* suggesting that it circulated independently for a time.[5]

The *Lotus Sūtra*

The Sanskrit title of the *Lotus Sūtra* is *Saddharmapuṇḍarīkasūtra.* A ten-fascicle Chinese translation of the *sūtra* was completed in 286 by Dharmarakṣa (*T* 263). Chih Ch'ien is said to have translated the chapter on "Parables" as the *Fo i san-ch'e-huan ching,* but the historicity of this tradition is questionable. The *Sa-t'an fen-lo-t'i ching* (*T* 265, translator unknown) is a one-fascicle Chinese translation of the chapters on "Devadatta" and the "Apparition of the Jeweled *Stūpa,*" which was completed around the time of Dharmarakṣa. The translation by Dharmarakṣa is a complete text with twenty-seven chapters. However, at an earlier date many of the chapters seem to have circulated independently. The earliest part of the text, the chapter on "Skill in Means" *(upāyakauśalya),* dates from before the second century C.E. Since images of the Buddha are mentioned in the verses of this chapter, it can probably be dated no earlier than the latter half of the first century C.E.

The standard Chinese translation of the text is the *Miao-fa lien-hua ching* (*T* 262) by Kumārajīva, which was finished in 405 or 406. Kumārajīva's translation was not quite complete because it did not include the "Chapter on Devadatta," the verses from the "Chapter on Avalokiteśvara," and half of the "Chapter on Bhaiṣajyarāja (Medicine King) Bodhisattva." Around 490 Fa-hsien obtained the Sanskrit text of the "Chapter on Devadatta" in Kao-ch'ang (in Turfan) and brought it back to China, where he translated it together with Fa-i. However, their translation was not used in the commentaries on the *Lotus Sūtra* by Fa-yün (476–529, *T* 1715) or by Shōtoku Taishi (574–622, *T* 2187). Thus, the translation of the "Chapter on Devadatta" must have been added to the *Lotus Sūtra* after their time. Chih-i (538–597) commented on the "Chapter on Devadatta" in his *Fa-hua wen-chü* (*T* 34:114c), but explained that the chapter was not included in the Kumārajīva translation. In 601 the missing sections of the Kumārajīva translation were translated by Jñānagupta and others to produce a more complete text entitled *T'ien-p'in miao-fa lien-hua ching* (*T* 264). The modern version of Kumārajīva's translation includes the "Chapter on Devadatta" and many, but not all, of the missing parts translated later and thus differs from Kumārajīva's original translation.

People over a wide area of Asia believed in the *Lotus Sūtra.* A complete Tibetan translation of the text exists, and Sanskrit manuscripts of it have been discovered in various places in Asia. Particularly important are the Sanskrit manuscripts from Nepal, Gilgit in northern India, and Kashgar and Khādalik in Central Asia. The Nepalese manuscript was published by H. Kern and B. Nanjio. Since then, other manuscripts of the *Lotus Sūtra* have also been published. Modern translations into English and Japanese have also appeared.[6] Passages in the *Lotus* and *Prajñāpāramitā sūtras* stated that copying, preserving, reading, preaching, and honoring these texts would result in great merit. Thus, many of the copies of these texts that were made to produce merit have survived and been discovered in recent times.

The term *"saddharma"* in the title of the *Lotus Sūtra (Saddharmapuṇḍarīkasūtra)* means "true teaching." The true teaching is compared to a white lotus *(puṇḍarīka),* which grows in mud but is not defiled by impurities. The *sūtra* was composed to explain the true teaching (namely, the pure nature of the mind).

Passages in the "Introduction" and in the *sūtra* from the chapter on "Parables" (chap. 3) onward often refer to the *Lotus Sūtra.* Such mentions of the *Lotus Sūtra* within the text of the *sūtra* itself refer to the chapter on "Expedient Devices" (chap. 2), the oldest part of the text. This chapter concerns the teaching of the One Buddha-vehicle, a doctrine that leads even *śrāvakas* and *pratyekabuddhas* to develop the knowledge and insight of a Buddha. *Śrāvakas* and *pratyekabuddhas* gain confidence that they can attain Buddhahood when they discover that they have the Buddha-nature. Although no term exactly corresponding to Buddha-nature appears in the *Lotus Sūtra,* the basic concept is contained in this passage: "The original nature *(prakṛti)* of *dharmas* is forever pure *(prabhāsvara)*" (v. 102 from the Sanskrit of the chapter on "Expedient Devices"). This teaching has the same meaning as the doctrine found in the perfection of wisdom literature that the mind is innately pure. This doctrine later developed into Tathāgatagarbha teachings and the view that all sentient beings possessed the Buddha-nature.

The term *"saddharma"* in the *sūtra*'s title refers to the teachings that explain the three vehicles in such a way that the One-vehicle is revealed as the ultimate message of Buddhism (Ch. *k'ai-san hsien-i*). In terms of principles, this teaching is based on the true aspect of all *dharmas (dharmatā),* that all *dharmas* are innately pure, even though the purity of *dharmas* (or of the mind) is obscured in the ordinary person by defilements. In subjective terms, the *sūtra* is based on the practicing bodhisattva's awareness of his own Buddha-nature. In the *sūtra,* this original purity is compared to a white lotus growing in a muddy pond.

In the chapters following "Parables," to prove that even *śrāvakas* possess the true Dharma, the Buddha makes predictions *(vyākaraṇa)* that *śrāvakas* such as Śāriputra will realize Buddhahood in the future. Although the followers of each of the three vehicles—*śrāvakas, pratyekabuddhas,* and bodhisattvas—all perform the different practices of their respective vehicle, they make equal progress on the path to Buddhahood. According to the "Expedient Devices" chapter, "There is only one vehicle, not two or three" (*T* 9:8a). (In contrast, according to the *Vimalakīrtinirdeśa,* the followers of the *śrāvaka*-vehicle are disparaged as having "rotten" or inferior seeds and are said to have no possibility of realizing Buddhahood. However, if *śrāvakas* and *pratyekabuddhas* cannot realize ultimate salvation, then the teaching of the *Vimalakīrtinirdeśa* cannot be called a complete version of Mahāyāna, since some beings are not included within the scope of the Buddha's compassion.)

The One-vehicle teaching of the *Lotus Sūtra* probably arose out of the need to formulate a teaching that would account for the salvation of Hīnayāna practitioners. In historical terms, after a period of emphasizing the opposition of and differences between the Hīnayāna and Mahāyāna traditions, Mahāyāna thinkers formulated new teachings such as those of the *Lotus Sūtra,* which would encompass the two traditions. The appeal of such teachings was based on the popularity of *stūpa* worship, as is clear in the chapter on the "Apparition of the Jeweled *Stūpa*" *(stūpasaṃdarśana).*

In East Asia the *Lotus Sūtra* has often been interpreted by dividing it into two major parts. The first half of the *sūtra,* particularly the chapter on "Expedient Devices," is called the "section on manifestation" (Ch. *chi-men*). The second half of the *sūtra,* particularly the chapter on "The Lifespan of the Thus Gone One" *(tathāgatayuṣpramāṇa),* is called the "fundamental section" (Ch. *pen-men*). The chapter on "The Lifespan of the Thus Gone One" is said to contain teachings that "explain the manifestations and reveal the original Buddha" (Ch. *k'ai-chi hsien-pen*). The revelation that Śākyamuni actually realized enlightenment eons ago is said to corroborate the teaching in the chapter on "Expedient Devices" that the Buddha-nature is eternal (Ch. *Fo-hsing chang-chu*). The figure of Śākyamuni as a man who realized enlightenment at Buddhagayā and died at eighty years of age is revealed to be nothing more than an expedient device to encourage sentient beings to practice Buddhism. He is merely a manifestation of the eternal Buddha.

The *Lotus Sūtra* is divided into twenty-eight chapters. The twenty chapters preceding the chapter on "The Supernatural Powers of the Thus Gone One" *(tathāgatarddhyabhisaṃkāra)* constitute the earlier part of the text. These twenty chapters can also be divided into earlier and later strata, suggesting that the text we have today is the result of a complex process of compilation. All but the last six of the twenty-eight chapters include verses that repeat the contents of the prose portions of the text. The verses are written in Prakrit and appear to be earlier than the prose. In the last six chapters, the chapter on "The Universal Gate of Avalokiteśvara" *(samantamukhaparivarto namāvalokiteśvaravikurvaṇanirdeśaḥ)* is noteworthy because it describes the multitudinous ways Avalokiteśvara saves sentient beings.

A number of scriptures associated with the *Lotus Sūtra* exist. The *Wu-liang-i ching* (*T* 276) is called the "opening *sūtra*" (Ch. *k'ai-ching*) for the

Lotus Sūtra in East Asia because lectures on the *Lotus Sūtra* were often preceded by a talk on the *Wu-liang-i ching*. The text contains the famous statement by the Buddha that in more than forty years of preaching, he had not yet revealed the ultimate teaching (which was to be explained in the *Lotus Sūtra*, *T* 9:386b).

The *Kuan p'u-hsien p'u-sa hsing-fa ching* (*T* 277) is regarded as the "capping *sūtra*" (Ch. *chieh-ching*) for the *Lotus Sūtra* in East Asia because the bodhisattva Samantabhadra plays a key role in both it and the last chapter of the *Lotus*. Lectures on the *Lotus Sūtra* were often concluded with a talk on that *sūtra*. A confession ceremony included in the *Kuan p'u-hsien p'u-sa hsing-fa ching* has been influential in East Asia.

The *Ta fa-ku ching* (*T* 270, *Mahābherīhārakaparivarta#*) was influenced by the theme of the harmonization of the three vehicles presented in the *Lotus Sūtra*. This work further develops a number of topics presented in the *Lotus Sūtra*, especially the Tathāgatagarbha doctrine. Discussions of the One-vehicle and the universality of the Buddha-nature are also included.

The Pure Land *Sūtras*

In the East Asian Pure Land tradition, the following three *sūtras* are particularly important: *Wu-liang-shou ching* (*T* 360, "Larger" *Sukhāvatīvyūha**), *A-mi-t'o ching* (*T* 366, "Smaller" *Sukhāvatī[amṛta]vyūha*), and *Kuan wu-liang-shou-fo ching* (*T* 365). Modern scholars believe that the *Kuan wu-liang-shou-fo ching* was composed in either China or Central Asia. However, even though the *sūtra* may not have been composed in India, the contents reflect Indian views.

The earliest extant Chinese translation of the "Larger" *Sukhāvatīvyūha* is the *Ta a-mi-t'o ching* (*T* 362) translated by Chih Ch'ien sometime between 223 and 253. Later, the *sūtra* was repeatedly translated. East Asian Buddhists traditionally have claimed that it was translated into Chinese a total of twelve times; however only five of these translations have survived (*T* nos. 310.5, 360–363). In addition, a Tibetan translation of the *sūtra* exists and Sanskrit versions have been published.[7]

According to one of the Chinese translations, the *Wu-liang-shou ching*, the bodhisattva Dharmākara made forty-eight vows that were fulfilled when he later attained Buddhahood and became Amitābha Buddha. However, in other translations of the *sūtra* (*T* 361 and *T* 362) the number of vows is only twenty-four. Additional variations in the contents and number of vows can be found in the latest Chinese translation (*T* 363), the Tibetan translation, and the Sanskrit version of the *sūtra*. A comparison of the various translations of the text reveals how the contents of the vows changed from the earliest versions to the later ones. A survey of changes in the numbers and contents of the vows indicates that the "Smaller" *Sukhāvatīvyūha* was not compiled very long before the version of the "Larger" *Sukhāvatīvyūha* that Chih Ch'ien used for his translation.

Besides the "Larger" *Sukhāvatīvyūha,* Lokakṣema translated the *Bhadrapālasūtra* (also known as the *Pratyutpannasamādhisūtra, Pan-chou san-mei ching, T* 418). This *sūtra* contains a description of a meditation through which a person can visualize Amitābha Buddha in front of him. Thus, belief in Amitābha must have been established before the *Bhadrapālasūtra* was composed. In addition, many of the *sūtras* translated by Chih Ch'ien (*T* nos. 532, 533, 559, 632, and 1011) contain passages on Amitābha. The frequent mention of Amitābha in a variety of *sūtras* and the numbers of bodhisattvas who are identified with the past lives of Amitābha (some fifteen,[8] including monks, princes, and world-ruling kings) indicate that belief in Amitābha did not originate with the composition of the *Sukhāvatīvyūha.*

From among the many stories concerning the past lives of Amitābha Buddha, the story of the bodhisattva Dharmākara is the most important. However, Dharmākara and Amitābha do not seem to have been identified with each other at first. Moreover, the stories of Amitābha's past lives as various bodhisattvas do not seem to be related to each other according to recent research by the Japanese scholar Fujita Kōtatsu. Since the names of many of these bodhisattvas appear in the early translations by Chih Ch'ien and Dharmarakṣa, the stories of these bodhisattvas are probably as early as those about Dharmākara. Consequently, Dharmākara and Amitābha do not appear to have been closely linked to each other at first. In fact, legends about Amitābha antedate the appearance of the stories of Dharmākara. The names Amitābha (Unlimited Light) and Amitāyus (Unlimited Life) by themselves originally do not seem to have had any clear Buddhist content. But once the story of Dharmākara's vows was added to the story of Amitābha, then belief in Amitābha was influenced by Mahāyāna ideals of the Buddha's compassion. Moreover, the element *"ākara"* (treasury) in the name Dharmākara is used in Tathāgatagarbha thought and thus helps locate belief in Amitābha within the Mahāyāna tradition.[9]

The *Pan-chou san-mei ching (T* 416–419, *Bhadrapālasūtra)* also concerns Amitābha Buddha, but in the context of the meditative exercises in which the practitioner visualized the Buddha. It thus has no direct connection with Dharmākara's vows. In this *sūtra* Amitābha Buddha is significant as a Buddha of Unlimited Light or Life who is taken as the object of a visualization exercise. The two conceptions of Amitābha—Amitābha as an object of a visualization meditation (in the *Bhadrapālasūtra*) and Amitābha as the embodiment of compassion (in the "Larger" *Sukhāvatīvyūha*)—were finally combined in the *Kuan wu-liang-shou-fo ching* (*T* 365). Most modern scholars believe that this *sūtra* was compiled in either China or Central Asia.[10] However, the story of King Ajātaśatru and his mother Vaidehi appears in early sources such as the *Wei-sheng-yüan ching* (*T* 507), translated by Chih Ch'ien. Moreover, meditations on a special land where a person may be reborn through pure actions (Ch. *ch'ing-ching yeh-ch'u*) has its roots in early Buddhist traditions.[11]

The *A-mi-t'o ching (T* 366, "Smaller" *Sukhāvatīvyūha*) is composed of descriptions of the adornments of the Western Paradise and praises for Amitābha's achievements by the Buddhas of the six directions. Its contents are simpler than the descriptions of visualizations of the Buddhas or the vows of Dharmākara. But it is tied to the "Larger" *Sukhāvatīvyūha* by the statement that ten eons have passed since Amitābha became a Buddha. The statement from the "Smaller" *Sukhāvatīvyūha* may have been incorporated into the "Larger" *Sukhāvatīvyūha*. Although this statement by itself does not provide sufficient evidence to determine the order in which the two *sūtras* were composed, the evidence strongly suggests that the "Smaller" *Sukhāvatīvyūha* is the older text.

The most important *sūtras* concerning Amitābha have been surveyed above, but many other Mahāyāna scriptures contain references to Amitābha. Since Amitābha is mentioned in the *Pan-chou san-mei ching (T* 418, *Bhadrapālasūtra),* translated by Lokakṣema in 179, belief in Amitābha was undoubtedly evident in northern India in the first century C.E. It is unclear, however, whether the compilation of the oldest extant version of the "Larger" *Sukhāvatīvyūha* (*T* 362) can be dated as early as this.

Both the names "Amitābha" (Unlimited Light) and "Amitāyus" (Unlimited Life) are used to refer to the Buddha who presides over the Western Paradise. The light emanating from Amitābha Buddha is described in detail in two of the Chinese translations of the *Sukhāvatīvyūha,* the *Ta a-mi-t'o ching* (*T* 362, 12:302b–303b, 309a) and the *P'ing-teng-chüeh ching* (*T* 361, 12:281c–286b). According to the *Ta a-mi-t'o ching,* the lifespan of Amitābha is, in fact, limited. After Amitābha enters *nirvāṇa,* he will be succeeded by the bodhisattva Avalokiteśvara (Ch. Kai-lou-hsuang p'u-sa). In addition, many other aspects of the *Ta a-mi-t'o ching* have not been systematized, indicating that this text is a very early version of the "Larger" *Sukhāvatīvyūha.* In contrast, according to the *P'ing-teng-chüeh ching,* Amitābha will not enter *nirvāṇa* (*T* 12:290b). In the vows of the *Wu-liang-shou ching* translation (*T* 360),

Amitābha's unlimited life is emphasized much more than his unlimited light.

According to the *Wu-liang-shou ching,* the bodhisattva Dharmākara made his primordial vows *(pūrva praṇidhāna)* after five eons of contemplation. (The vows are called "primordial" in the sense that they were made in the past before Amitābha had attained Buddhahood.) After eons of practice, his vows were fulfilled and he became Amitābha Buddha and established the Western Paradise. He welcomes all who wish to be reborn in his Pure Land and thereby saves them. Rigorous practice is not required of those who wish to be reborn in the Pure Land. They need only have faith *(śraddhā)* in Amitābha's primordial vows and recite his name *(nāmadheya).* Even a bodhisattva with inferior faculties and without the strength to observe the precepts or meditate can quickly attain a stage of spiritual progress from which he will not backslide by relying upon Amitābha's vows. Consequently, belief in Amitābha was called a path of easy practice (Ch. *i-hsing-tao*).

The path of easy practice is based on the teaching that salvation can be attained through faith (P. *saddhā-vimutti*).[12] Faith and doubt are opposed to each other. As faith deepens, doubts about the validity of the teachings is vanquished. Even if a practitioner with deep faith wished to doubt Buddhist teachings, he would be unable to do so. Thus even at the beginning of practice, the mind can be freed of doubts and an elementary form of salvation realized through the functioning of faith. And since neither the vigorous practice of religious austerities nor the understanding of difficult doctrines is required to attain salvation through faith, even a person of dull intellect or a person who is submissive and sincere can attain salvation through faith. Of course, salvation through faith is not complete salvation. Later, the practitioner is expected to realize such stages as salvation through wisdom (P. *paññā-vimutti*), salvation through both wisdom and meditation (P. *ubhatobhāga-vimutti*), and salvation of the mind (P. *cetovimutti*).

The term "salvation through faith" is used in this sense in the *Āgamas.* The term also has a long history in Theravāda Buddhism and appears in such works as Buddhaghosa's *Visuddhimagga* (Path of Purification). The term *"saddhā-vimutti"* is not found in Sarvāstivādin works, but similar terms such as *"śraddhā-adhimukti"* were used in the Sarvāstivādin School. In Mahāyāna Buddhism terms such as "salvation through faith" do not seem to have been used. According to some Mahāyāna texts, while faith will not lead to salvation, it will lead to the stage of nonretrogression *(avivartika, avaivartika).* According to the *Shih-chu p'i-p'o-sha lun* (*T* 26:41b, *Daśabhūmikavibhāṣā*?) attributed to Nāgārjuna, "Some people practice with strict austerities; others use the expedient of faith as an easy practice to progress rapidly to the stage of nonretrogression." Thus the importance of faith is noted in a number of Mahāyāna texts. According to the *Hua-yen ching (T* 9:433a, *Avataṃsaka),* "Faith is the foundation of the path and the mother of merits. All good *dharmas* are increased through it." The *Ta-chih-tu lun (T* 25:63a, *Mahāprajñāpāramitopadeśa)* states that "the great ocean of the Buddha's teaching may be entered through faith and crossed by wisdom."

Faith in Amitābha Buddha drew upon older teachings that were an established part of Buddhism. Some modern scholars have argued that faith in Amitābha Buddha was established in response to the *Bhagavadgītā*'s concept of *bhakti* (devotion). Although faith in Amitābha has elements in common with devotion to Kṛṣṇa, the term *"bhakti"* does not appear in the *Sukhāvatīvyūha.*

Indian scriptures concerning Amitābha seem to have been composed by people different from those who compiled the perfection of wisdom literature. Belief in Amitābha was widespread among Mahāyāna Buddhists. References to Amitābha and his Pure Land (Sukhāvatī) are found in many Mahāyāna scriptures, and rebirth in Pure Land is recommended as goal in many of these works. According to the Japanese scholar Fujita Kōtatsu, Amitābha Buddha is referred to in more than one-third of the translations of Indian Mahāyāna scriptures in the Chinese canon, a total of more than 270 *sūtras* and *śāstras.* Many of Amitābha's vows are cited in the *Pei hua ching* (*T* 157, *Karunāpuṇḍarīkasūtra**), indicating that this text was closely connected to the *Sukhāvatīvyūha.* The Sanskrit text of the *Karunāpuṇḍarīkasūtra* has been published.[13]

Several other figures besides Amitābha should be mentioned in connection with Pure Land thought. As was discussed earlier, Akṣobhya Buddha and his Pure Land, Abhirati, are described in the perfection of wisdom *sūtras.* Belief in Akṣobhya, however, was never as popular as faith in Amitābha.

Maitreya's Tuṣita Heaven was sometimes regarded as a Pure Land. Maitreya is mentioned as the future Buddha in the *Āgamas,* where he is considered to be a bodhisattva who will attain Buddhahood in his next life *(eka-jāti-pratibaddha).* Having already completed the austerities necessary to attain Buddhahood, he waits in Tuṣita Heaven for the appropriate time for his rebirth in this world where he will attain enlightenment under a *puṃnāga* tree and preach three times in order to save sentient beings. Later belief in Maitreya changed dramatically. In the *Kuan mi-le p'u-sa shang-sheng tou-shuai-t'ien ching* (*T* 452), the adornments of Tuṣita Heaven and the way in which a person can be reborn there are described. The belief in rebirth in Tuṣita Heaven was particularly influential in China and Japan. The Sanskrit text of the *Maitreyavyākaraṇa* has been published.[14]

Scriptures Concerning Mañjuśrī

Along with Maitreya, Mañjuśrī Kumārabhūta was a very important and honored bodhisattva. Both figures appear in very early Mahāyāna texts. For example, Maitreya and Mañjuśrī are both mentioned in Lokakṣema's Chinese translation of the *Aṣṭasāhasrikā-PP,* completed in 179 C.E. (*T* 224), indicating that Mañjuśrī was clearly known by the first century C.E.

Mañjuśrī is generally thought of as manifesting the wisdom that results from enlightenment and is therefore closely associated with perfection of wisdom *(prajñāpāramitā)* literature. Since, however, he does not appear in either the *Ta pan-jo ching* (*T* 223, *Pañcaviṃśatisāhasrikā-PP**) or the *Chin-kang pan-jo ching* (*T* 235, *Vajracchedikā**), it appears that originally he was not closely tied to *prajñāpāramitā* literature; rather, literature about him may have initially been composed by people who were not concerned with *prajñāpāramitā* teachings. (*Prajñāpāramitā* texts in which Mañjuśrī plays a central role, such as *T* 232–233, the *Saptaśatikā-PP**, were compiled later.) Mañjuśrī also does not appear in such early Mahāyāna *sūtras* as the *A-ch'u fo-kuo ching* (*T* 313, *Akṣobhyatathāgatasya-vyūha#*), *Pan-chou san-mei ching (T* 417–418, *Bhadrapālasūtra),* and *Ta a-mi-t'o ching* (*T* 362, *Sukhāvatīvyūha**). Eight great lay bodhisattvas led by Bhadrapāla are central figures in the *Pan-chou san-mei ching.*

Mañjuśrī plays a key role in the *Shou-leng-yen san-mei ching (T* 642, *Śūraṅgamasamādhisūtra).* According to this text, from time immemorial Mañjuśrī has practiced under countless Buddhas and has already completed the practices necessary to attain Buddhahood. In the past, he was known as the Buddha Lung-chung-shang (Sanskrit unknown). Passages in the first chapter of the *Lotus Sūtra* (*T* 262) and in Lokakṣema's Chinese translation of the *Ajātaśatrukaukṛtyavinodana* (*T* 626) state that Mañjuśrī has been a great bodhisattva since long ago. Such passages indicate that Mañjuśrī was a noteworthy figure from early in Mahāyāna Buddhism. According to the *Fang-po ching* (*T* 629), a partial translation of the *Ajātaśatrukaukṛtyavinodana,* Mañjuśrī has been practicing from long ago. When Śākyamuni was a child in one of his past lives, he was introduced by Mañjuśrī to a Buddha and then went on to attain enlightenment. Thus Śākyamuni's attainment of Buddhahood is due to Mañjuśrī's help. Moreover, Mañjuśrī has helped not only Śākyamuni, but all Buddhas, and is therefore said to be "the father and mother of those on the path to Buddhahood" (*T* 15:451a).

Mañjuśrī is an advanced bodhisattva who realized the stage of nonretrogression many eons ago. He is also the personification of wisdom. Since Mañjuśrī is often associated with teachings concerning the innate wisdom that all people possess, he can also be viewed as a personification of the practices that will lead to the development and realization of that wisdom. The *A-she-shih-wang ching* (*T* 626, *Ajātaśatrukaukṛtyavinodana#*) contains a detailed presentation of the teaching that the mind is originally pure. Mañjuśrī is called a "chaste youth" *(kumārabhūta)* and a "Prince of the Dharma." Yet he has the power to guide Buddhas. He has not yet realized Buddhahood, suggesting that he is forever advancing in his practice. Mañjuśrī's activities can be understood as representing the process of uncovering the originally pure nature of the mind, which has been obscured by adventitious defilements.

According to the *A-she-shih-wang ching* (*T* 15:389a), Mañjuśrī and twenty-five other bodhisattvas lived and practiced on a mountain. In the *Gaṇḍavyūha* chapter of the *Avataṃsaka,* Mañjuśrī is said to have left Śākyamuni at Śrāvastī and traveled south to the city of Dhanyākara, where he lived in a large *stūpa* hall *(mahācaitya)* in a grove of *sāla* trees *(mahādhvaja-vyūha-sāla-vanaṣaṇḍa).* There he gathered many believers around him. Such passages suggest the probable existence of an order of monastic bodhisattvas that honored and believed in Mañjuśrī. In addition, according to the *Ta-chih-tu lun* (*T* 25:756b, *Mahāprajñāpāramitopadeśa),* Maitreya and Mañjuśrī led Ānanda to the outside ring of iron mountains surrounding the world, where they convened a council on Mahāyāna scriptures. Passages like this one indicate that Mañjuśrī and Maitreya were considered to be particularly important bodhisattvas. In the *Wen-shu-shih-li fo-t'u yen-ching ching* (*T* 318, *Mañjuśrībuddhakṣetraguṇavyūhasūtra#*), translated by Dharmarakṣa in 290, ten great vows made by Mañjuśrī are described. Through these ten vows Mañjuśrī purified and adorned a Buddha-land. Mañjuśrī's vows are reflected in the practices of the bodhisattva Samantabhadra. According to the *Gaṇḍavyūha,* the youth Sudhana was urged by Mañjuśrī to go on a journey in search of the Dharma. Through the practices recommended by Samantabhadra, Sudhana finally realized enlightenment. Thus the religious practices associated with Samantabhadra are said to be based upon the wisdom of Mañjuśrī.

Dharmarakṣa's translation of the *Ajātaśatrukaukṛtyavinodana* is entitled *Wen-shu-shih-li p'u-ch'ao san-mei ching* (*T* 627) and thus includes Mañjuśrī's name (Wen-shu-shih-li) in the title. Mañjuśrī's name appears in the titles of many other *sūtras* translated into Chinese by a variety of people including Lokakṣema, Dharmarakṣa, Kumārajīva, and Nieh Tao-chen (see *T* nos. 318, 458–461, 463–464). In addition, Mañjuśrī plays a major role in many *sūtras* even if his name does not appear in the title. For example, in the *Vimalakīrtinirdeśa,* Mañjuśrī leads the group of bodhisattvas and *śrāvakas* that visit Vimalakīrti, who is lying ill in bed. In the *sūtra,* Mañjuśrī is clearly the head of the bodhisattvas and superior to Maitreya.

In conclusion, the perfection of wisdom *sūtras* and Amitābha worship were important types of early Mahāyāna Buddhism. However, teachings concerning Mañjuśrī also represented an important tradition within Mahāyāna. Further investigation into the significance of Mañjuśrī would contribute significantly to our understanding of the origins of Mahāyāna Buddhism.

Miscellaneous Other Mahāyāna Scriptures

Many Mahāyāna scriptures were composed before Nāgārjuna's time. Besides those texts discussed above, a number of early works belonging to the *Pao-chi ching (T* 310, *Ratnakūṭa)* and the *Ta-fang-teng ta-chi-ching* (*T* 397, *Mahāsaṃnipātasūtra*?) date from this time. Bodhiruci's Chinese translation of the *Ratnakūṭa* is 120 fascicles in length and divided into forty-nine assemblies. The Tibetan translation is organized in a similar manner. The Tibetan translation does not represent a direct transmission from India, however, but has been influenced and supplemented by referring to the Chinese translation.

The individual works within the *Ratnakūṭa* originally circulated as independent texts and were later collected into the *Ratnakūṭa* in India or Central Asia. A Sanskrit version of the collection must have existed at one time, since the Chinese pilgrim Hsüan-tsang is said to have brought it to China. After translating the huge 600-fascicle *Ta pan-jo po-lo-mi-to ching* (*T* 220, *Mahāprajñāpāramitāsūtra*?), Hsüan-tsang was able to translate only one part of the *Ratnakūṭa,* the 20-fascicle *Ta p'u-sa tsang-ching* (*T* no. 310.12, *Bodhisattvapiṭaka#*), before he died. Bodhiruci translated the rest of the Sanskrit text later, between 707 and 713. His translation constitutes the text of the extant *Ratnakūṭa.* In compiling the translation, Bodhiruci incorporated previous Chinese translations of sections of the *Ratnakūṭa* that apparently were based on the same text as the Sanskrit manuscripts he was using. When the Sanskrit text seemed to be more complete than the Chinese, he would supplement the older Chinese translation (*K'ai-yüan shih-chiao lu, T* 55:570b).

The *Ratnakūṭa* includes a variety of materials without any clear principle of organization. For example, the forty-sixth assembly, in which Mañjuśrī preaches perfection of wisdom (*T* 310.46, *Saptaśatikā-PP#*), was also included in the *Ta pan-jo po-lo-mi-to ching* (see *T* no. 220.7, *Mahāprajñāpāramitāsūtra*?). The forty-seventh assembly, *Pao-chi p'u-sa hui* (*T* no. 310.47, *Ratnacūḍaparipṛcchā#*), is also found in the *Mahāsaṃnipātasūtra* (*T* no. 397.11). The existence of a Sanskrit text of the *Ratnakūṭa* at one time is indicated by citations of it in the *Prasannapadā* and the *Śikṣāsamuccaya.* It is not clear, however, whether the Sanskrit text was of the same size as the Chinese translation. A large number of Sanskrit texts connected with the *Ratnakūṭa* have been discovered and published, among them the *Kāśyapaparivarta.*[15]

The Chinese translation of the *Mahāsaṃnipātasūtra,* the *Ta-fang-teng ta-chi-ching* (*T* 397), was done by Dharmakṣema and others. Later, translations by Narendrayaśas were added; it was edited into its present form by the Sui dynasty monk Seng-chiu (fl. 586–594). It is a sixty-fascicle work divided into seventeen chapters (*K'ai-yüan shih-chiao lu, T* 55: 588b). Older versions of the Chinese translation apparently were only about thirty fascicles long. At least one of the works in the Tibetan canon has the term "great collection" (Tib. *ḥdus-pa-chen-po*) preceding its title, suggesting a possible connection with the *Ta-fang-teng ta-chi-ching,* but further investigation reveals little in common. The *Ta-fang-teng ta-chi-ching* includes lists of *dharmas,* discussions of the characteristics of *dharmas,* and expositions of the doctrine that the mind is innately pure. In addition, many Esoteric Buddhist elements are found in it including *dhāraṇī* and astrology. Only a few Sanskrit fragments of *sūtras* in this collection have been found. However, the discovery at Gilgit of a manuscript of the *Mahāsaṃnipāta ratnaketu dhāraṇī sūtra* should be noted. The manuscript has since been published by Nalinaksha Dutt.[16]

Many other early Mahāyāna *sūtras* exist besides those mentioned above. Among those with extant Sanskrit versions are the *Śālistambasūtra* (*T* 278–279, 710–711), which concerns Dependent Origination; *Samādhirājasūtra* (*T* 639–641); *Bhaiṣajyagurusūtra;* and *Suvarṇaprabhāsottamasūtra* (*T* 663–665).[17]

Sanskrit Texts

Because of the disappearance of Buddhism from India, a complete Mahāyāna canon in Sanskrit does not exist. However, Sanskrit Mahāyāna texts have been found in a number of areas and are gradually being published. More have been discovered in Nepal than anywhere else. Particularly famous as Sanskrit Mahāyāna texts from Nepal are the following group known as the "Nine Dharma Jewels": *Lalitavistara, Aṣṭasāhasrikāprajñāpāramitā, Daśabhūmika, Gaṇḍavyūha, Laṅkāvatāra, Suvarṇaprabhāsa, Samādhirāja, Saddharmapuṇḍarīka,* and *Tathāgataguhyaka.* Many Esoteric Buddhist texts in Sanskrit have also been found. Today Nepalese manuscripts are preserved in England, France, Japan, and Calcutta.

Around the end of the nineteenth century, a number of expeditions to Central Asia discovered many Sanskrit manuscripts in the desert. The expeditions of such men as Aurel Stein, Paul Pelliot, Albert von Le Coq, and the Ōtani expedition brought Sanskrit texts back to Europe and Japan. The German expedition carried a great many manuscripts back to Berlin. The study of the manuscripts began in this century and gradually some have been published. Publishing information can be found in Yamada Ryūjō's *Bongo Butten no shobunken.*[18]

In 1931 a large number of Buddhist texts were discovered in an old *stūpa* at Gilgit in Kashmir. Among them was an almost complete version of the Mūlasarvāstivādin *Vinaya,* as well as many Mahāyāna texts. Some of these have been published by Nalinaksha Dutt in *Gilgit Manuscripts.* Raghu Vira and his successor, Lokesh Chandra, have also published part of the *Śata-piṭaka.*

During the 1930s Rāhula Sānkṛtyāyana traveled to Tibet, where he found many Sanskrit manuscripts of Buddhist texts in monasteries. Photographs of the texts are preserved at the Jayaswal Research Institute in Patna. The texts are gradually being published in the Tibetan Sanskrit Works Series. The contents of most of these manuscripts have not yet been sufficiently studied; however, a large proportion of the Mahāyāna texts appear to be concerned with Esoteric Buddhism. Also included are treatises on *abhidharma* and Mahāyāna Buddhism, as well as works on Buddhist logic.

The largest set of Sanskrit Mahāyāna texts is the series entitled Buddhist Sanskrit Texts published by the Mithila Institute. Almost all of the Sanskrit texts of Mahāyāna works discovered in Nepal, Tibet, Gilgit, and other areas are included in it. Important Sanskrit texts have also been published by the Italian scholar Giuseppe Tucci in the Series Orientale Roma.

CHAPTER 18

Theory and Practice in Early Mahāyāna Buddhism

The Practitioner's Awareness That He Is a Bodhisattva and That His Mind Is Pure in Nature

THE FULL FORM of the term "bodhisattva" is *bodhisattva mahāsattva.* "Bodhisattva" means "a being *(sattva)* who seeks enlightenment *(bodhi).*" *"Mahāsattva"* means "a great person" and refers to a person who makes the great vow to become a Buddha and undertakes the strenuous practice required to attain that goal. A bodhisattva must believe that he has the character or nature necessary to become a Buddha. In this respect, the Mahāyāna practitioner's position differs from that of both the Hīnayānist and those people who praised the Buddha (Ch. *tsan-fo sheng*).

Hīnayāna or Nikāya Buddhist doctrine was formulated with the intention of enabling the practitioner to become an *arhat.* The Hīnayānist could not conceive of himself as attaining the same degree of enlightenment as the Buddha and consequently did not recognize in himself the qualities that would enable him to become a Buddha. Only as great a man as Śākyamuni could become a Buddha. This difference in the ways in which the practitioner viewed himself and his potential constitutes the basic distinction between Hīnayāna and Mahāyāna Buddhism.

People who praised the Buddha were vitally interested in the practices that led to the attainment of Buddhahood. In their biographies of the Buddha, they extolled his superior practices. Insofar as they preached a bodhisattva teaching, they were close to Mahāyāna Buddhist ideals. However, for those who praised the Buddha, the figure of the bodhisattva was someone whose eventual Buddhahood was already determined, someone who had already received a prediction *(vyākaraṇa)* that guaranteed his Buddhahood. In most cases the bodhisattva referred to was Śākyamuni as a bodhisattva. In one of his previous lives, the future Śākyamuni had received a prediction from Dīpaṅkara Buddha concerning his eventual attainment of Buddhahood. Through that prediction, the future Śākyamuni had become confident of his position as a bodhisattva.

Because the average Mahāyāna practitioner had not received a prediction from a Buddha concerning his eventual attainment of Buddhahood, he had to look elsewhere for assurance that he would attain enlightenment. He did so by looking within himself for the presence of elements that would lead to Buddhahood. Although both Mahāyānists and the people who praised the Buddha were vitally interested in the figure of the bodhisattva, their views of him were fundamentally different. For those who extolled the Buddha, the bodhisattva was a chosen man; for the Mahāyānist, a bodhisattva could be an ordinary person; indeed, the Mahāyāna practitioner sometimes referred to himself as a bodhisattva.

The earliest extant example of the Mahāyāna usage of the term "bodhisattva" occurs in the *Tao-hsing pan-jo ching* (*T* 224, *Aṣṭasāhasrikā-PP**). The term is used in this *sūtra* in a way that suggests that it had already been in use with its Mahāyāna sense for a considerable time before the text was compiled. Thus the advocates of perfection of wisdom built upon the theories of the bodhisattva and his six perfections developed by the people who praised the Buddha, but then broadened the term "bodhisattva." Consequently, Mahāyāna was at first called *"bodhisattvayāna"* (*T* 8:247b). Later, this usage was extended further and applied to the Three Vehicles as *śrāvakayāna, pratyekabuddhayāna,* and *bodhisattvayāna* (or *Buddhayāna*).

In Early Mahāyāna texts, no mention is made of a Buddha-element or nature *(Buddha-dhātu),* that is, the potential to become a Buddha. The statement that all sentient beings have the Buddha-element first appears in the Mahāyāna version of the *Mahāparinirvāṇasūtra.* The origins of this doctrine can be sought, however, in the statements in Early Mahāyāna texts, such as the *Aṣṭasāhasrikā-PP* (p. 5), that the original nature of the mind is pure *(prakṛtiś cittasya prabhāsvarā).*[1] This doctrine first appeared in the *A-she-shih-wang ching* (*T* 626, *Ajātaśatrukaukṛtyavinodana#*) and later in many other Mahāyāna texts.

If the original nature of the mind is pure, then the manifestation of that original nature is equivalent to the attainment of Buddhahood. The Mahāyānist's vow to attain Buddhahood was based on the belief that the mind is innately pure. The people who cultivated the aspiration to attain enlightenment *(bodhicitta),* who vowed to realize Buddhahood, were called bodhisattvas. A related teaching is found in many Mahāyāna *sūtras:* all *dharmas* are innately pure (*sarvadharmāḥ prakṛti pariśuddhāḥ,* Conze, *Aṣṭadaśasāhasrikā-PP,* [p. 42]). This teaching appears in such Mahāyāna *sūtras* as the *Prajñāpāramitā, Ta-chi ching (T* 397, *Mahāsaṃnipātasūtra),* and *Saddharmapuṇḍarīkasūtra* (v. 102 of the "Chapter on Expedient Teachings" in the Sanskrit text). This doctrine implies that the mind is not different from all *dharmas.*

Besides the ordinary practitioner as bodhisattva, major or celestial bodhisattvas whose names are well known—Mañjuśrī, Maitreya, Samantabhadra, and Avalokiteśvara—are discussed in Mahāyāna texts. The origin and significance of these important bodhisattvas is different from that of the ordinary practitioner as bodhisattva. Maitreya Bodhisattva developed out of Maitreya the future Buddha, a bodhisattva who was destined to become a Buddha in his next life. The figures of both Maitreya Bodhisattva and Śākyamuni Bodhisattva are closely related to the concept of the bodhisattva who is destined to become a Buddha in his very next life *(eka-jāti-pratibaddha).* Śākyamuni Bodhisattva is a figure developed by those people who praised the Buddha in poems and biographies. In contrast, Mañjuśrī and Samantabhadra are figures found only in Mahāyāna Buddhism. Mañjuśrī is mentioned often in connection with the doctrine that the mind is originally pure in nature. Avalokiteśvara was probably introduced into Buddhism from an outside source.

The recognition by Mahāyāna Buddhists that more than one Buddha could appear in the world at the same time entailed the existence of many bodhisattvas who would attain enlightenment in their next lifetime. It is clear that Mahāyānists recognized the existence of multitudes of powerful bodhisattvas. Moreover, the force of these bodhisattvas' vows to save other sentient beings led to the recognition of bodhisattvas who had completed the practices necessary to realize Buddhahood but had decided not to enter Buddhahood. Thus, such bodhisattvas as Mañjuśrī and Avalokiteśvara had powers that exceeded even those of Buddhas. As Mahāyāna Buddhist doctrine developed, stories about the powerful attributes of many bodhisattvas were narrated, but the characteristic Mahāyāna bodhisattva was, in fact, the ordinary person as bodhisattva.

The Cultivation of the Perfections and the Armor of the Vows

The Mahāyāna Buddhist's realization that he was in fact a bodhisattva meant that his religious practices were intended for the benefit of both himself and others. (The *arhat,* in contrast, performed religious practices primarily for his own benefit.) The Buddha himself had striven to help sentient beings and had displayed great compassion *(mahākaruṇā)* and friendliness *(mahāmaitrī)* toward others. A bodhisattva who had vowed to become a Buddha consequently had to help others first. Only by becoming involved in aiding others could the bodhisattva complete his own religious practices.

Bodhisattva practices are characterized as the six perfections *(pāramitā),* a categorization of practices originally developed to describe Śākyamuni Buddha's practices that were then extensively incorporated into Mahāyāna scriptures.[2] Stories about the six perfections are collected in the *Liu-tu chi-ching* (*T* 152, *Ṣaṭpāramitāsaṅgraha*?). They are also described in the *jātakas.* At first, the number of perfections was not set at six. The Sarvāstivādins of Kashmir had a list of four: giving *(dāna),* morality *(śīla),* vigor *(vīrya),* and wisdom *(prajñā).* The other two elements of the six perfections, patience *(kṣānti)* and meditation *(dhyāna),* were included in the four perfections as components of morality and wisdom (*Mahāvibhāṣāśāstra, T* 27:892b). Biographies of the Buddha generally adopted the six perfections. The Sarvāstivādin biography *P'u-yao ching* (*T* 186, *Lalitavistara**) follows the six perfections and sometimes adds a seventh, skill in means *(upāyakauśalya)* (*T* 3:483a, 484a, 540a; Lefmann, *Lalitavistara,* p. 8).

Ten perfections appear in Pāli sources (*Jātaka,* ed. V. Fausböll, vol. 1, pp. 45–47). The ten consist of five of the six perfections (giving, morality, wisdom, vigor, and patience) and five other perfections: renunciation *(nekkhamma),* truth *(sacca),* resolve *(adhiṭṭhāna),* friendliness *(mettā),* and equanimity *(upekhā).* The Theravāda list differs from the list of ten perfections found in several Mahāyāna works such as the *Shih-ti ching* (*T* 287, *Daśabhūmikasūtra**). Mahāyāna works generally adopted the six perfections used by the authors of biographies of the Buddha. However, since ten perfections were needed to correspond to the ten stages of the *Daśabhūmikasūtra,* four additional perfections were sometimes added to the standard six, making ten (*T* 10:517c; *Daśabhūmika,* ed. J. Rahder, p. 57). The four additional perfections were skill in means, vows *(praṇidhāna),* strength *(bala),* and knowledge *(jñāna).*

The term *"pāramitā"* is derived from the word *"parama,"* meaning "highest" or "most excellent." In the Pāli *Jātakas* the term *"pāramī,"* derived from *"parama,"* is used in the same sense as *pāramitā.* Modern scholars usually translate *pāramitā* as "perfection," as in the term "perfection of wisdom" *(prajñāpāramitā).* However, one of the most important early translators of Indian texts into Chinese, Kumārajīva (d. 409?), interpreted the word as meaning "crossing over to the other shore" *(pāram-ita)* and translated *prajñāpāramitā* as "crossing by wisdom (to the shore of enlightenment)."

Although *pāramitā* can be translated as "perfection," the word "perfection" implies a static state in which nothing more need be done. However, according to the *Prajñāpāramitāsūtras,* the correct practitioner of perfection of wisdom is someone who does not recognize perfection of wisdom as he practices it, someone who does not even recognize the bodhisattvas. Although he practices giving, he does not boast of his good actions, nor does he cling to the concept of good. The donor, the recipient, and the act of giving are all nonsubstantial. These attitudes are called the three spheres of purity *(trimaṇḍala-pariśuddhi)* and constitute the perfection of giving. As the practitioner gives, he does not cling to the idea or act of giving. Even as he tries to perfect his giving, he does not cling to the idea of perfecting his actions. In this way, the practice of the perfections is never completed. The perfections are based on nonsubstantiality.

Prajñāpāramitā is wisdom in regard to nonsubstantiality, wisdom without obstacles, wisdom that is direct intuition into the essence of all. In contrast, wisdom that discriminates among objects is called "skill in means." According to the *Vimalakīrtinirdeśa,* "The perfection of wisdom is the bodhisattva's mother; skill in means is his father" (*T* 14:549c). Both wisdom and skill in means are essential for bodhisattva practices.

A bodhisattva's practice is not performed for his own benefit. He must always help others without thinking of his own Buddhahood. His practice is therefore endless, and he must have uncommon resolve to embark on such a path. His resolve is compared to that of a warrior wearing armor who is going to the battleground. The bodhisattva is thus said to wear the armor of his vows *(mahāsaṃnāha-saṃnaddha).* Even as he is leading countless sentient beings to *nirvāṇa,* he knows that no substantial beings exist who are to be led, that not even he exists as a substantial being. The bodhisattva's spiritual aspiration and determination are the basis for all his practice.

Dhāraṇī and *Samādhi*

Descriptions of bodhisattvas using *dhāraṇī* (spoken formulae) and practicing a variety of *samādhi* (concentrations) are found in many Mahāyāna scriptures. *Dhāraṇī* played little or no role in the *Āgamas* or in the literature of Nikāya Buddhism, but became important with the rise of Mahāyāna Buddhism.[3] According to the *Ta-chih-tu lun (T* 25:95c, *Mahāprajñāpāramitopadeśa), dhāraṇī* enabled a person "to assemble various good *dharmas* and maintain them without losing them." In other words, *dhāraṇī* were said to have the power to preserve good and prevent evil. They were particularly useful in memorizing teachings and preventing loss of memory. Other formulae aided the analytical faculties or enabled a person to remain unmoved no matter what he heard, helping practitioners understand doctrine and expound it eloquently. In an age when teachings were preserved and transmitted primarily through memorization, the power of such formulae was highly regarded. In later times *dhāraṇī* were primarily used as magical incantations, as well as in the performance of *samādhis* (concentrations) in Mahāyāna Buddhism.

The term *"samādhi"* refers to the maintenance of a tranquil mind or to the spiritual power that results from focusing the mind on one object. Three concentrations described in the *Āgamas*—on nonsubstantiality *(śūnyatā),* signlessness *(animitta),* and wishlessness *(apraṇihita)*—later were highly praised in the perfection of wisdom *sūtras.* A variety of new *samādhi* were developed and described in Early Mahāyāna texts. The two basic types expounded were still *śamatha* (calm abiding) and *vipaśyanā* (insight meditation). When the mind is tranquil and is focused on one object, then correct insight can occur.

The religious practices of Mahāyāna Buddhism differed from those of Hīnayāna Buddhism. Many new concentrations reflecting these differences were developed in the Mahāyāna tradition. In the "Chapter on the Great Vehicle" in the *Ta-p'in pan-jo ching* (*T* 8:251a–b, *Pañcaviṃśatisāhasrikā-PP**), 108 concentrations are listed. The first is the *śūraṅgama-samādhi,* which was produced through the power of the strict practices by which the perfection of wisdom was advanced. (See chapter 15.)

Another Mahāyāna concentration, the *pratyutpanna-samādhi,* is not included among the 108 concentrations listed in the perfection of wisdom literature, but it is described in the *Pan-chou san-mei ching (T* 417–418, *Bhadrapālasūtra).* A famous concentration, it consists of entering into the *samādhi* through focusing one's attention on the Buddha. Once the practitioner has entered the *samādhi,* the Buddha appears before him. The *pratyutpanna-samādhi* probably arose in connection with the worship at the Buddha's *stūpa* and with the confession of wrongdoing that sometimes accompanied worship of the Buddha. In the *San-p'in ching (Triskandhakadharmaparyāya),* one of the very oldest Mahāyāna *sūtras,* the practices of confession, feeling joy at the accomplishments of others, and inviting the Buddhas and bodhisattvas to the place of practice are described. These practices were performed in front of the Buddha. However, at the time the *sūtra* was compiled, images of the Buddha did not exist. Consequently, these practices must have been performed in front of *stūpas* honoring the Buddha. Other texts describe additional *samādhi.* The ocean-seal concentration *(sāgaramudrā-samādhi)* is described in the *Hua-yen ching (T* 278–279, *Avataṃsakasūtra).* The Buddha enters the Concentration of the Abode of Immeasurable Doctrine *(ananta-nirdeśa-pratiṣṭhānaṃ nāma samādhiḥ)* when he preaches the *Fa-hua ching* (*T* 262, *Saddharmapuṇḍarīkasūtra**). The name of each concentration describes the mode of the insight gained; but through all of them, the practitioner gains insight into the fundamental nature of phenomena by entering into such profound concentrations.

Bodhisattva Practices

Both lay and monastic bodhisattvas are mentioned in Mahāyāna literature. In the *Tao-hsing pan-jo ching* (*T* 224, *Aṣṭasāhasrikā-PP**), a very early Mahāyāna text translated into Chinese in 179 C.E., the bodhisattvas described are laymen. The existence of monastic bodhisattvas is not yet clearly evident in the text. In the *Ta-p'in pan-jo ching* (*T* 223, *Pañcaviṃśatisāhasrikā-PP**), translated in 404, both types of bodhisattvas are mentioned; however, no special set of precepts for monastic bodhisattvas is included. Monastic bodhisattvas are expected to guard their chastity and are called *kumārabhūta* (chaste youths), but little more is stated. In the description of the six perfections, the giving or teaching of the Dharma is included in the discussion of the perfection of almsgiving, but the gift of material wealth receives more attention. The "ten good acts (or precepts)," part of the perfection of morality, are divided into three categories: physical, verbal, and mental. The ten good precepts consist of the three physical prohibitions against killing, stealing, and sexual misconduct; the four verbal prohibitions against false speech, slander, deceitful speech to disrupt relations between people, and frivolous talk; and the three mental prohibitions against lust, anger, and wrong views. The ten good precepts appear not only in the perfection of wisdom *sūtras,* but in other Mahāyāna scriptures whenever the perfection of morality is explained. The third of the ten good precepts, no sexual misconduct, is a lay precept. For a monk, complete chastity would be required, as in the case of the chaste youth who would have to be free of any sensual desire. In addition, in some early Mahāyāna *sūtras* the five lay precepts or the eight precepts for laymen to observe on *uposatha* days were presented as the basis of morality for lay bodhisattvas.[4]

In the exposition of the ten stages of the bodhisattva in the *Daśabhūmikasūtra* (*T* 287), the precepts are explained in the discussion of the second stage, *vimalā-bhūmi* (the immaculate), with emphasis on the ten good precepts. Thus the ten good precepts are repeatedly presented as typical precepts for the bodhisattva in early Mahāyāna literature suggesting that Early Mahāyāna Buddhism was primarily a religious movement of laymen. Later the monastic precepts of Nikāya Buddhism were adopted by Mahāyāna practitioners, and the monastic bodhisattva became a full-fledged Buddhist monk who underwent a full monastic ordination *(upasaṃpadā)* and observed the rules of the *prātimokṣa.*

Examples of the practices of bodhisattvas can be found in a number of Early Mahāyāna *sūtras.* Typical practices are the six perfections described in the perfection of wisdom and other *sūtras. Stūpa* worship is portrayed in the "Chapter on Pure Practices" *(Ching-hsing p'in)* of the *Hua-yen ching (T* 278–279, *Avataṃsakasūtra)* and in the *Yu-ch'ieh chang-che ching (T* 310.19, 322–323, *Ugradattaparipṛcchā).* Visualizations of the Buddha are described in the *Pan-chou san-mei ching (T* 416–419, *Bhadrapālasūtra).* A form of Buddhism based on faith, a development peculiar to Mahāyāna, is depicted in the Pure Land *sūtras.* Faith also plays the central role in the *Saddharmapuṇḍarīka.* In the chapter on expedient teachings in the *Saddharmapuṇḍarīka, stūpa* worship is encouraged; and throughout the work, people are encouraged to copy the *sūtra.* In the oldest parts of the text, a list of three practices focusing on the *sūtra* is given: memorization, recitation, and explanation. In later parts of the text two more practices, copying and honoring the *sūtra,* are added, making a total of five practices. Even more practices are added to these in the Sanskrit text. Memorization, recitation, and explanation all concern the teaching *(dharmaparyāya).* These practices as well as copying and honoring *(pūjā)* the *sūtra* could also focus on the physical book *(pustaka)* itself. *Pūjā* consisted of installing the text as the jewel of the Teaching (*Dharmaratna* of the Three Jewels) and offering it flowers, incense, banners, and canopies. Music was played at such ceremonies, which had originally been performed at *stūpas* and were later adopted for use in *pūjā* honoring sacred texts. *Pūjā* for books is repeatedly encouraged in the perfection of wisdom *sūtras* and other Mahāyāna texts.

Since monks were prohibited by the *vinaya* from viewing or listening to music, dance, and theater, they probably would not have participated in the performance of these activities. Consequently, these ceremonies must have been performed by (and probably originated among) laymen. They were both an expression of faith and an opportunity for socializing.

The Stages of a Bodhisattva's Progress

In the oldest Mahāyāna *sūtras,* a bodhisattva's progress toward enlightenment was described with the same stages used to characterize a *śrāvaka*'s practice. For example, in the *Tao-hsing pan-jo ching* (*T* 224, Lokakṣema's 179 C.E. translation of the *Aṣṭasāhasrikā-PP**), a bodhisattva is said to hear the perfection of wisdom and then progress through such stages as stream-entrant, once-returner, nonreturner, and *arhat*.

In the *Ta-p'in pan-jo ching* (*T* 223, Kumārajīva's 404 C.E. translation of the *Pañcaviṃśatisāhasrikā-PP**) and the *(Shih-ti ching* (*T* 287, *Daśabhūmikasūtra**), the stages of enlightenment are discussed in terms unique to Mahāyāna. A Mahāyāna explanation of enlightenment is included in the *Tao-hsing pan-jo ching*. Among the stages described that are not found in Nikāya Buddhist sources are the arising of the aspiration to attain enlightenment *(bodhicitta-utpāda)*, the stage of nonretrogression *(avaivartika)*, acquiescence to the truth that *dharmas* have no origination *(anutpattika-dharma-kṣānti)*, becoming a prince or chaste youth *(kumāra-bhūmi)*, consecration *(abhiṣeka)*, and the assurance of Buddhahood in the next life *(eka-jāti-pratibaddha)*. These stages are not yet systematized in the *Hsiao-p'in pan-jo ching* (*T* 227, Kumārajīva's translation of *Aṣṭasāhasrikā-PP**). The stages of consecration and the assurance of Buddhahood in the next life were adopted from biographies of the Buddha by Mahāyāna thinkers. Advanced bodhisattvas who are close to attaining Buddhahood are believed to have reached these stages.

The stages of nonretrogression and acquiescence to the truth that *dharmas* have no origination appear in many Mahāyāna *sūtras* and are important levels of practice. *Anutpattika-dharma-kṣānti* refers to the degree of enlightenment that results in the assurance that *dharmas* are not originated. It is an acquiescence obtained through enlightenment concerning nonsubstantiality, and according to some sources results in entering the stage of nonretrogression. These stages of enlightenment are typically Mahāyānist; however, modern scholars are still undecided about whether their origins are to be found among Early Mahāyāna thinkers or among groups that praised the Buddha (Ch. *tsan-fo sheng*). The stage of the chaste youth *(kumāra-bhūmi)* appears frequently in the *Ta-p'in pan-jo ching* (*T* 223, *Pañcaviṃśatisāhasrikā-PP**); it is also included in the ten abodes (Ch. *shih-chu*) (see below). In the *Ta-p'in pan-jo ching*, it is explained as referring to a bodhisattva who is leading a chaste and ascetic life.[5] In this stage the bodhisattva is compared to a youth or prince because he has practiced and realized the stages of acquiescence to the nonorigination of *dharmas* and nonretrogression. He is like a young man who has become prince of the Dharma and will soon rise to the position of Buddha. The bodhisattva Mañjuśrī is called "Mañjuśrī-kumarabhūta" and is often viewed as having attained this stage. (In the case of Mañjuśrī, the term seems to refer to his celibacy and asceticism.)

These stages received scattered consideration in Early Mahāyāna texts. More systematic formulations are also found in which the stages were organized into four, five, or ten stages *(bhūmi)* or into ten abodes. In biographies of the Buddha such as the *Mahāvastu* or *Fo pen-hsing chi-ching* (*T* 190, *Abhiniṣkramaṇasūtra*?), the following four basic practices of the bodhisattva were treated as stages: sincerely practicing good such as the ten good precepts, vowing to attain Buddhahood, mastering the six perfections, and attaining the stage of nonretrogression.[6] The ten stages were also mentioned in biographies of the Buddha. The following description of the bodhisattva is typical: "He served the various Buddhas and accumulated unlimited merits. For eons, he strove and performed the practices of the ten stages; in his next life he will attain Buddhahood" (*Fo pen-hsing chi-ching, T* 3:463a). Among the extant biographies, the ten stages are fully enumerated only in the *Mahāvastu.*[7]

The simplest list of the stages of the bodhisattva's practice is found in the *Hsiao p'in pan-jo ching* (*T* 227, *Aṣṭasāhasrikā-PP**).[8] The following four types of bodhisattva are listed: the bodhisattva who has just developed the aspiration to attain enlightenment *(prathamayāna samprasthitha),* the bodhisattva who is practicing the six perfections (Ch. *hsing liu po-lo-mi*), the bodhisattva who has attained the stage of nonretrogression *(avinivartanīya),* and the bodhisattva who will attain Buddhahood in his next life *(eka-jāti-pratibaddha).* Although it is a simple list, it is different from the stages of progress for the *śrāvakas.* The list of four types of bodhisattvas later appeared in many other Mahāyāna scriptures including the *Ta-p'in pan-jo ching* (*T* 223, *Pañcaviṃśatisāhasrikā-PP**).

Later, other stages, such as that of the *śrāvaka,* were incorporated into these lists. Thus a typical list of four stages would be worldling *(pṛthagjana), śrāvaka, pratyekabuddha,* and Buddha. Sometimes the stage of bodhisattva was added before the Buddha, making a total of five stages.[9] An early version of this list is found in the *Hsiao-p'in pan-jo ching.* It was later adopted for use in the *Ta-p'in pan-jo ching,* where a highly developed version of the four types of bodhisattvas was presented. The four stages were expanded to make ten stages, seven or eight of which may be attained by both Hīnayāna and Mahāyāna practitioners. Consequently, this list was called "the ten stages held by both Hīnayānists and Mahāyānists." The relationship of these ten stages to the original five is shown in Figure 6.

Kumārajīva translated the first stage (*śuklavidarśanā-bhūmi* or pure insight) as *kan-hui* (dry wisdom). According to the *Ta-chih-tu lun (T* 25:586a, *Mahāprajñāpāramitopadeśa),* wisdom at this stage is not yet nourished by the "water" of meditation and enlightenment cannot be realized. In the second stage, *gotra-bhūmi* (family), the path of the practitioner is determined; he performs the practices of the *śrāvaka, pratyekabuddha,* or bodhisattva path, and thus enters a particular "family" of

Figure 6. Two Sets of Stages Inclusive of Both Hīnayānists and Mahāyānists

Five stages	Ten stages of the *Ta-p'in pan-jo ching*
1. Worldling	1. Pure insight *(śuklavidarśanā-bhūmi)*
	2. Family *(gotra-bhūmi)*
	3. Eighth man *(aṣṭamaka-bhūmi)*
	4. Insight *(darśana-bhūmi)*
2. *Śrāvaka*	5. Weakening *(tanu-bhūmi)*
	6. Separation from desire *(vītarāga-bhūmi)*
	7. Accomplishment *(kṛtāvī-bhūmi)*
3. *Pratyekabuddha*	8. *Pratyekabuddha-bhūmi*
4. Bodhisattva	9. *Bodhisattva-bhūmi*
5. Buddha	10. *Buddha-bhūmi*

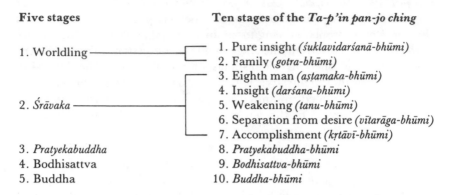

practitioners. In the third stage the *śrāvaka* as "eighth man" enters the path of insight *(darśana-mārga)* and becomes a candidate for stream-entrant (the eighth and lowest stage of the four paths and their four fruits that culminated in *arhat*hood). He thus enters the stages of the sage *(ārya)*. For the bodhisattva, entering the path of insight is equivalent to seeing the true nature of phenomena and attaining the stage of acquiescence to the truth of the nonorigination of *dharmas*. The fourth stage, *darśana-bhūmi* (insight), corresponds to the fruit of stream-entrant for the *śrāvaka*. For the bodhisattva, it is the stage of nonretrogression following acquiescence to the truth of the nonorigination of *dharmas*. The fifth stage, *tanu-bhūmi* (weakening), corresponds to the fruit of once-returner for the *śrāvaka*. In it, the three poisons are weakened. For the bodhisattva, it refers to the stage where he has passed beyond the stage of nonretrogression but has not yet realized Buddhahood. The sixth stage, *vītarāga-bhūmi* (separation from desire), corresponds to the fruit of nonreturner for the *śrāvaka*. For the bodhisattva, it signifies the acquisition of the five superhuman powers. The seventh stage, *kṛtāvī-bhūmi* (accomplishment), for the *śrāvaka* is the accomplishment of all that must be done to become an *arhat*. The *śrāvaka*'s practices are completed, since he does not aspire to attain higher goals. For the bodhisattva, the attainment of this stage is assurance that he will attain Buddhahood. The eighth stage, *pratyekabuddha-bhūmi,* is the last stage for those who follow *pratyekabuddha* practices and is marked by the attainment of the enlightenment of the *pratyekabuddha*. In the ninth stage, *bodhisattva-bhūmi,* the Mahāyānist cultivates bodhisattva practices, particularly the six perfections. In later texts these perfections are described in greater detail, in terms of the ten stages attained only by bodhisattvas. However, the ten stages attained by both Hīnayānists and Mahāyānists do not contain detailed instructions on these practices. In the tenth stage, *Buddha-bhūmi,* the practitioner has attained Buddhahood.

The ten stages described above illustrate practices for all three vehicles and thus are called "the ten stages held in common." Another set of ten stages describes the degrees of practice and attainments unique to bodhisattvas. The concept of stages exclusively for bodhisattvas is found in the biographies of the Buddha as part of the description of Śākyamuni Buddha's practices and his progress toward enlightenment. Although ten stages are actually listed only in the *Mahāvastu,* the Lokottaravādin biography, the concept of a set of ten stages is alluded to in all of the other biographies of the Buddha. Descriptions of the ten stages were developed primarily by followers of the *Avataṃsakasūtra.* In the *P'u-sa pen-yeh ching* (*T* 281), an early version of this system, the ten abodes (*daśavihāra*?) was expounded. The description of the ten stages *(daśabhūmayaḥ)* reached its final form in the *Shih-ti ching* (*T* 285–287, *Daśabhūmikasūtra**). Because these stages are only for bodhisattvas, the system may be considered an elaboration of the four types of bodhisattva described in the *Hsiao-p'in pan-jo ching* (*T* 227, *Aṣṭasāhasrikā-PP**).

The ten stages found in the *Daśabhūmikasūtra* are described below. In the first stage, *pramudhitā-bhūmi* (the joyous), the practitioner is joyful because he has obtained correct knowledge of Mahāyāna practice. In the second stage, *vimalā-bhūmi* (the immaculate), through observing the precepts he removes many of the defilements from his mind. The ten good precepts are listed in this section. As he progresses, he masters *dhāraṇī* and his wisdom becomes clearer; he thus reaches the third stage, *prabhākarī-bhūmi* (the radiant). The fourth stage is called *arciṣmatī-bhūmi* (the blazing) because the defilements are burned by the fires of wisdom. Since the more subtle defilements are difficult to subdue, the fifth stage is called *sudurjayā-bhūmi* (extremely difficult to conquer). As he progresses in his practice, he realizes wisdom about Dependent Origination; this sixth stage is called *abhimukhī-bhūmi* (facing wisdom). In the seventh stage *dūraṅgamā-bhūmi* (the far-going), the practitioner has cut off the defilements of the three realms and thus is far removed from the three realms. Next, he meditates on nonsubstantiality *(śūnyatā);* but because his meditation is profound, he has difficulty in freeing himself from the negative aspects of nonsubstantiality. He finally frees himself only when the Buddhas encourage and admonish him by touching him on the top of his head. In this stage he has surpassed the *arhats* and *pratyekabuddhas.* From the eighth stage onward, practice is a natural part of his actions and progress is effortless. In the eighth stage, nondiscriminating knowledge operates freely and undisturbed by any defilements. This stage is consequently called *acalā-bhūmi* (the immovable). In the ninth stage, *sādhumatī-bhūmi* (good intelligence), the practitioner is able to preach eloquently and convert others with perfect ease. The tenth stage marks the completion of the *dharmakāya* (body of the Dharma). Like space, this "body" has no limits. Because its wisdom is like a cloud, the tenth stage is called *dharmameghā-bhūmi* (cloud of the Dharma).

The term *"bhūmi"* literally means "ground," but it is used in these lists to mean "stage." When a person performs religious practices, he progresses through a continuum; but at times he arrives at a seeming impasse. Then he will break through and progress rapidly. Those stages of rapid progress are called *bhūmi.* A *bhūmi* functions like soil or the earth insofar as it has the power to promote growth to other stages. A *bhūmi* thus provides the basis for practice and preparation to reach the stage above it. Figure 7 is a comparative chart showing the ten stages listed in various *sūtras.*

The Bodhisattva Orders

Two types of Mahāyāna bodhisattva are distinguished in Mahāyāna literature: lay and monastic. The monastic bodhisattva model was the youth *(kumāra)* who practiced religious austerities and lived a celibate life. No precepts specifically for the monastic bodhisattva seem to have existed. In the older Mahāyāna texts the precepts mentioned are all lay precepts. The ten good precepts are cited most often, but they are sometimes combined with the five lay precepts or the eight lay precepts observed on *uposatha* days. In addition, the terms "son of a good family" *(kulaputra)* and "daughter of a good family" *(kuladuhitṛ),* which appear frequently in Mahāyāna texts, both refer to lay believers.

According to some texts, female bodhisattvas could miraculously change themselves into men through religious practice. Since a male body was believed to be necessary for the realization of Buddhahood, this belief suggested that women too could realize the supreme goal, though not as females. Such teachings indicate that early Mahāyānists appealed to female devotees and practitioners. The people who preached Mahāyāna Buddhism were called "preachers of the Dharma" *(dharmabhāṇaka).* Many were lay bodhisattvas, and according to inscriptions, some were women.

Monastic bodhisattvas practiced at *stūpas* or at rude dwellings in the forest *(āraṇyāyatana),* sites described in the *Yu-chia chang-che lun (T* 322–323, *Ugradattaparipṛcchā).* Religious practice at *stūpas* honoring the Bud-

Figure 7. Comparison of the Different Systems of the Ten Stages

Daśabhūmika Ten Stages	*P'u-sa pen-yeh ching* (*T* 281) Ten Abodes	*Mahāvastu* Ten Stages	*Perfection of Wisdom* Ten Stages
1. *Pramuditā* (joyful)	*Fa-i* (aspiration to enlightenment)	*Durārohā* (difficult to enter)	*Śuklavidarśanā* (pure insight)
2. *Vimalā* (immaculate)	*Chih-ti* (well-regulated abode)	*Baddhamālā* (fastening)	*Gotra* (family)
3. *Prabhākarī* (radiant)	*Ying-hsing* (religious practice)	*Puṣpamaṇḍitā* (adorned with flowers)	*Aṣṭamaka* (eighth man)
4. *Arciṣmatī* (blazing)	*Sheng-kuei* (noble rebirth)	*Rucirā* (beautiful)	*Darśana* (insight)
5. *Sudurjayā* (difficult to conquer)	*Hsiu-ch'eng* (completion of practice)	*Cittavistarā* (expansion of the mind)	*Tanu* (weakening)
6. *Abhimukhī* (facing wisdom)	*Hsing-teng* (ascending)	*Rūpavatī* ((lovely)	*Vītarāga* (separation from desire)
7. *Dūraṅgamā* (far-going)	*Pu-t'ui* (nonretrogression)	*Durjayā* (difficult to conquer)	*Kṛtāvī* (accomplishment)
8. *Acalā* (immovable)	*T'ung-chen* (chaste youth)	*Jamanideśa* (ascertainment of birth)	*Pratyekabuddha*
9. *Sādhumatī* (good intelligence)	*Liang-sheng* (crown prince)	*Yauvarājya* (installation as crown prince)	Bodhisattva
10. *Dharmameghā* (cloud of the Dharma)	*P'u-ch'u* (last birth before Buddhahood)	*Abhiṣekatā* (consecration and coronation)	Buddha

dha focused on worship, as is described in the "Chapter on Pure Practices" in the *Hua-yen ching (T* 278–279, *Avataṃsakasūtra).*[11] These *stūpas,* generally situated in villages, were visited by lay bodhisattvas who would give alms, worship at the *stūpa,* and receive instructions from monastic bodhisattvas. The forest centers *(āraṇyāyatana)* were situated away from the distractions of the villages and were mainly centers of meditation. Younger monastic bodhisattvas would receive instruction in the practice of religious austerities and guidance from a more experienced member of the group who would act as preceptor *(upādhyāya).* In this respect, the monastic bodhisattvas were organized in a fashion similar to that of the orders of Nikāya Buddhism. According to passages in the *Yu-chia chang-che ching (T* 322–323, *Ugradattaparipṛcchā)* and the *Shih-chu p'i-p'o-sha lun* (*T* 1521, *Daśabhūmikavibhāṣā*?, attributed to Nāgārjuna), monastic bodhisattvas led ascetic lives.

The lay bodhisattvas in Mahāyāna Buddhism played an influential role. In the *Vimalakīrtinirdeśa,* the layman Vimalakīrti preached the Dharma. In the *Yu-chia chang-che ching,* the names of ten merchant leaders such as Ugradatta are listed, and in the *Pan-chou san-mei ching (T* 416–419, *Bhadrapālasūtra),* a group of five hundred merchant leaders, including Bhadrapāla, is noted. Although the merchants mentioned in these *sūtras* were probably not all historical figures, the major role of such figures in Mahāyāna scriptures reveals that some lay bodhisattvas must have attained profound levels of enlightenment.

Because Mahāyāna doctrine would have made it difficult for bodhisattvas to participate in orders with Hīnayāna monks and lay believers, the bodhisattvas formed their own orders. Passages frequently appear in Mahāyāna texts strongly cautioning against allowing *śrāvakayāna* attitudes to arise. The *Shih-chu p'i-p'o-sha lun* (*T* 26:93a) warns that "falling to the stage of *śrāvaka-bhūmi* or *pratyekabuddha-bhūmi* is called the death of the bodhisattva. It is called the loss of everything." The very fact that Mahāyāna Buddhists referred to Nikāya Buddhism by the derogatory epithet "Hīnayāna" (inferior vehicle) would have made communal living and practice very difficult. Moreover, since Early Mahāyāna Buddhism was primarily lay in character, it did not have to depend upon the monastic orders of Nikāya Buddhism to survive.

In the opening passages of Mahāyāna *sūtras,* the audience that has assembled to hear the Buddha's teaching is always described. Monks are mentioned first, followed by the nuns, pious laymen, and pious laywomen. The names of the bodhisattvas in the audience are listed last. When monastic bodhisattvas are mentioned, they are never listed together with the Hīnayāna monks. Without exception, the orders of Mahāyāna bodhisattvas and Hīnayāna monks are always treated separately in Mahāyāna *sūtras*. This fact indicates that the two orders must have been separate. In some Mahāyāna texts both a *bodhisattva-gaṇa* (bodhisattva group) and a *bhikṣu-saṅgha* (order of monks) are mentioned, indicating that the Mahāyāna organizations at this time were called *gaṇa*. The term *"bodhisattva-saṅgha"* also occurs in some texts.[12] The terms *"gaṇa"* and *"saṅgha"* were both used at this time to refer to religious organizations and had similar meanings.

The existence and details of the *bodhisattva-gaṇa* must be deduced from scanty evidence. No concrete descriptions of the organization of these groups are found in Mahāyāna *sūtras* or *śāstras*. Only in the *Shih-chu p'i-p'o-sha lun* (*T* 1521, *Daśabhūmikavibhāṣā*?, attributed to Nāgārjuna) is there even a small amount of information. The early Mahāyāna organizations seem to have functioned with an incomplete or small set of rules. Consequently, they later adopted the rules used by the Hīnayāna monastic orders.

NOTES

Chapter 2

1. *Sarvadarśanasaṅgraha,* sec. 2. "Bauddhadarśanam."
2. Matsunami, "Seisen no goroku"; Nakamura, "Sāriputta ni daihyō sareru saishoki no Bukkyō," pp. 455–466.
3. *Sarvadarśanasaṅgraha,* sec. 3. "Ārhatadarśanam."
4. Matsunami, *"Dasavēyāriya sutta"; Jaina Sūtras.*
5. *Mahāvaṃsa,* pp. ix–lxiii.
6. Jacobi, "Buddhas und Mahāviras Nirvāṇa," pp. 322–332.
7. Kanakura, *Indo kodai seishinshi,* p. 338f.
8. Ibid., p. 347; Fei Ch'ang-fang, *Li-tai san-pao chi, T* 49:95b.
9. Ui, "Butsumetsu nendairon," p. 5f.
10. Nakamura, "Mauriya ōchō no nendai ni tsuite." For research on the royal families of ancient India, see Nakamura, *Indo kodaishi,* vol. 5, p. 243f.; Tsukamoto, *Shoki Bukkyō kyōdanshi no kenkyū,* p. 62f. For the materials on the date of the death of the Buddha, see ibid., p. 27f.; Lamotte, *Histoire du Bouddhisme Indien,* pp. 13–15.
11. Ui, "Agon no seiritsu ni kansuru kōsatsu," p. 394f.
12. Miyamoto, "Gedatsu to nehan no kenkyū."
13. Yamaguchi, *Bukkyō shisō nyūmon,* p. 128f.
14. Fujita, "Sanjō no seiritsu ni tsuite: byakushibutsu kigenkō," pp. 91–100; Sakurabe, "Engaku kō," pp. 40–51.

Chapter 3

1. According to Ui Hakuju, the most basic elements of the Buddha's thought were that all *saṃskāras* were impermanent, that all was suffering, and that all

phenomena were nonsubstantial ("Genshi Bukkyō shiryōron," p. 224). Watsuji Tetsurō has argued that the Buddha's thought cannot be distinguished from that of his disciples (*Genshi Bukkyō no jissen tetsugaku,* p. 36f.).

2. For *nirvāṇa,* see Miyamoto, "Gedatsu to nehan no kenkyū."

3. For the Middle Path, see Miyamoto, *Konponchū to kū,* p. 265f.

4. For Śākyamuni's views on caste, see Fujita, "Genshi Bukkyō ni okeru shisei byōdōron," pp. 55–61.

5. For the teaching of no-Self, see Hirakawa, "Muga to shutai," pp. 381–421; and idem, "Shoki Bukkyō no rinri," pp. 45–74.

6. For *dharma,* see Hirakawa, "Shohō muga no hō," pp. 396–411; and idem, "Genshi Bukkyō ni okeru 'hō' no imi," pp. 1–25.

7. For the teaching that the mind is originally pure, see Hirakawa, *Shoki Daijō Bukkyō no kenkyū,* pp. 200–217.

8. For the stream-entrant, see Funahashi Issai, *Genshi Bukkyō shisō no kenkyū,* pp. 184–203; and Hirakawa, "Shingedatsu yori shingedatsu e no tenkai," p. 57f.

9. Ui, "Genshi Bukkyō shiryōron," p. 235.

Chapter 4

1. For the harmonious *saṅgha,* see Hirakawa, *Genshi Bukkyō no kenkyū,* pp. 295–300.

2. For the *saṅgha,* see ibid., pp. 1–92. For the *bodhisattva gaṇa,* see Hirakawa, *Shoki Daijō Bukkyō no kenkyū,* pp. 777–811.

3. For the eight weighty rules, see Hirakawa, *Genshi Bukkyō no kenkyū,* pp. 520–525.

4. For the numbers of precepts in the various *vinayas,* see Hirakawa, *Ritsuzō no kenkyū,* pp. 430–478.

5. Hirakawa, *Genshi Bukkyō no kenkyū,* pp. 454–504.

Chapter 5

1. For the First Council, see Akanuma, *Bukkyō kyōten shiron,* p. 2f.; Kanakura, *Indo chūsei seishinshi,* vol. 2, p. 196f.; Tsukamoto, *Shoki Bukkyō kyōdanshi no kenkyū,* p. 175f.; Przyluski, *Le Concile de Rājagṛha.*

2. For discussions of the oldest strata of the *Āgamas* and the *Vinaya,* see Ui, "Genshi Bukkyō shiryōron," pp. 112–260; Watsuji, *Genshi Bukkyō no jissen tetsugaku,* "Introduction"; Hirakawa, *Ritsuzō no kenkyū,* pp. 1–113; Oldenberg, *The Vinayapiṭaka,* pp. ix–lvi; Rhys Davids, *Buddhist India,* p. 176f.

3. For the organization of the *Vinayapiṭaka,* see Hirakawa, *Ritsuzō no kenkyū,* pp. 417–509, 591–669.

4. For literature on the *Vinaya,* see ibid., pp. 58–113.

5. For the problems in determining the school to which the *Tseng-i a-han ching* belongs, see Hirakawa, *Shoki Daijō Bukkyō no kenkyū,* pp. 29–46.

6. For the organization of the *sūtra-piṭaka,* see Maeda Egaku, *Genshi Bukkyō seiten no seiritsushi kenkyū,* p. 619f.

7. For a study of Pāli Buddhist literature, see Geiger, *Pāli Literatur und Sprache.*

8. For Sanskrit texts of the *Āgamas,* see Yamada, *Bongo Butten no shobunken,* pp. 32–55.

9. Hoernle, *Manuscript Remains of Buddhist Literature Found in Eastern Turkestan.* For publishing information on the manuscripts discovered by the German expedition, see Waldschmidt, *Sanskrithandschriften aus den Turfanfunden,* vol. 1, pp. xxvi–xxxii.

10. Maeda Egaku, *Genshi Bukkyō seiten no seiritsushi no kenkyū,* p. 482f.

Chapter 6

1. Miyamoto, *Konponchū to kū,* p. 370.

2. For Buddhism after the death of the Buddha, see Maeda Egaku, *Genshi Bukkyō seiten no seiritsushi kenkyū,* part 1.

3. For political history, see Kanakura, *Indo kodai seishinshi,* p. 338f.; Nakamura, *Indo kodaishi,* vol. 5, pp. 243f. and 277f.; Tsukamoto, *Shoki Bukkyō kyōdanshi no kenkyū,* p. 62f.

4. For the Second Council, see Tsukamoto, *Shoki Bukkyō kyōdanshi no kenkyū,* p. 208f.; Akanuma, *Bukkyō kyōten shiron,* p. 84f.; Hirakawa, *Ritsuzō no kenkyū,* pp. 671–733; Kanakura, *Indo chūsei seishinshi,* vol. 2, p. 216f.; Hofinger, *Étude sur le concile de Vaiśālī.*

5. For the "ten points" of the *Vinaya,* see Kanakura, "Jūji hihō ni taisuru shobuha kaishaku no idō."

6. Akanuma, *Indo Bukkyō koyū meishi jiten,* pp. 25–28.

Chapter 8

1. The use of the term *"nikāya"* to mean "school" is found in I-ching's *Record of the Buddhist Religion as Practiced in India and the Malay Archipelago* (*T* 54:205a), I-ching's *Mahāvyutpatti,* and Vasumitra's *Samayabhedoparacanacakra.* It does not seem to be a common usage in the Theravāda tradition, however.

2. Ui, "Butsumetsu nendairon," pp. 2–111; Nakamura, *Indo kodaishi, Nakamura Hajime senshū,* vol. 6, pp. 409–437.

3. Bareau, *Les Sectes bouddhiques du Petit Véhicule,* pp. 309–310.

4. I-ching, *Mahāvyutpatti,* ed. Ogihara Unrai as *Bonkan taiyaku Bukkyō jiten,* p. 234; I-ching, *Nan-hai chi-kuei nei-fa chuan, T* 54:204c–206b; English translation: *A Record of the Buddhist Religion as Practiced in India and the Malay Archipelago,* pp. 1–20.

Chapter 9

1. In Buddhaghosa's *Visuddhimagga,* chap. 3, v. 96, p. 87, and chap. 14, v. 71, p. 381, the terms "Pāḷi" and "Aṭṭhakathā" (commentary) are mentioned together, indicating that Pāḷi was used to refer to the *Tipiṭaka.* The word "Pāḷi" thus has the meanings of both the Pāli language (Pālibhāsā) and scripture.

2. In the introduction of the *Mahāvibhāṣā,* the position that the *abhidharma* is the Buddha's teaching is forcefully argued (*T* 1545, 27:1a–c).

3. For the *Kṣudraka-piṭaka* see Lamotte, *Histoire du Bouddhisme Indien,* pp. 174–176; Maeda Egaku, *Genshi Bukkyō seiten no seiritsushi kenkyū,* p. 681f.

4. Mizuno, "Pāri seiten seiritsushijō ni okeru *Mugegedō* oyobi gishaku no chii."

5. *Milindapañha (The Questions of Milinda)* was published by V. Trenkner. A Siamese edition also can be used. The text has also been translated into Japanese. See Mizuno, "Mirinda monkyō-rui ni tsuite," pp. 17–55; and Nakamura's detailed study, *Indo to Girisha to no shisō kōryū.* The *Peṭakopadesa,* translated by Ñyāṇamoli as *The Piṭaka-disclosure,* and the *Nettipakaraṇa,* translated by Ñyāṇamoli as *The Guide,* have both been published by the Pāli Text Society. Also see Mizuno, "*Peṭakopadesa* ni tsuite," pp. 52–68; Ogihara, *Ogihara Unrai bunshū,* p. 206f.; Satō Ryōjun, "*Nettipakarana* ni tsuite," pp. 124–126.

6. Some of the manuscripts discovered by the German expedition to Turfan were published in Waldschmidt, *Sanskrithandschriften aus den Turfanfunden.* Recently, Sanskrit fragments of the *Saṅgītiparyāya* have been published in *Das Saṅgītisūtra und sein Kommentar Saṅgītiparyāya;* and in *Das Pañcavastukam und die Pañcavastukavibhāṣā.*

7. Takasaki, "Remarks on the Sanskrit Fragments of the *Abhidharma-dharmaskandhapādaśāstra,*" pp. 33–41 (left); and *Dharmaskandha,* edited by Siglinde Deitz as *Fragmente des Dharmaskandha: ein Abhidharma-Text in Sanskrit aus Gilgit.*

8. Bareau, "Les Origines du *Śāriputrābhidharmaśāstra,*" pp. 69–95; Mizuno, "*Sharihotsu abidonron* ni tsuite," pp. 109–134.

9. Hirakawa, ed., *San'yaku taishō Kusharon sakuin,* vol. 3, pp. ii–x.

10. See note 6 of this chapter.

11. Yamaguchi, *Seshin no Jōgōron;* Vasubandhu, *Karmasiddhi-prakaraṇa,* trans. E. Lamotte, pp. 151–171; Vasubandhu's *Pañcaskandhaprakaraṇa of Vasubandhu,* ed. Shanti Bhikṣu Sastri. Also see Yamaguchi, "Seshin no *Shakukiron* ni tsuite," pp. 35–68; idem, "Daijō hi-Butsusetsu ni taisuru Seshin no ronpa: *Shakukikiron* daiyonshō ni taisuru ichi kaidai," p. 269f. The above two studies by Yamaguchi are included in *Yamaguchi Susumu Bukkyōgaku bunshū.*

Chapter 10

1. Sakurabe, *Kusharon no kenkyū,* p. 23f.

2. For *mātṛkā,* see ibid., p. 23f.; Akanuma, *Bukkyō kyōten shiron,* p. 113f.; and Miyamoto, *Daijō to shōjō,* p. 728f.

3. For *dharmas,* see Watsuji, "Bukkyō ni okeru hō no gainen to kū benshōhō," p. 461f.; Kanakura, "Bukkyō ni okeru hō no go no gen'i to hensen" and "Bukkyō ni okeru hō no imi," p. 83f.; and Hirakawa, "Genshi Bukkyō ni okeru 'hō' no imi," pp. 1–25.

4. For a discussion of absolute and conventional existence, see Hirakawa, "Setsu issai ubu no ninshikiron," pp. 3–19.

5. For theories about unconditioned *dharmas* presented by the various schools, see Mizuno, "Muihō ni tsuite," pp. 1–11.

6. For a discussion of the mental faculties, see Katsumata, *Bukkyō ni okeru shinshikisetsu no kenkyū,* pp. 319–461; and Mizuno, *Pāri Bukkyō wo chūsin to shita Bukkyō no shinshikiron,* chap. 3.

7. For a full discussion of concepts in Nikāya Buddhism .that may have served as forerunners to *ālaya-vijñāna,* see Katsumata, *Bukkyō ni okeru shinshikisetsu no kenkyū,* pp. 513–559. Katsumata discusses Early and Nikāya views that the mind is innately pure on pp. 463–485.

8. For a discussion of the instantaneous existence of *dharmas,* see Hirakawa, "Usetsuna to setsunametsu," pp. 159–178.

Chapter 11

1. The discussions of cosmology, rebirth, and the twelve links of Dependent Origination in this chapter are based on the "Chapter on Cosmology" of the *Abhidharmakośa.* The presentation of the six causes, four conditions, and five effects is based on the end of the "Chapter on Faculties" of Vasubandhu's *Abhidharmakośa* (translated by L. M. Pruden as *Abhidharmakośabhaṣyam,* vol. 1, pp. 254–325). In this chapter, the analysis has been limited to the main points in the *Abhidharmakośa.* For more information, the secondary sources listed in the previous chapter should be consulted. For studies of the twelve links of Dependent Origination, see Watsuji, *Genshi Bukkyō no jissen tetsugaku,* chap. 2; Akanuma, *Genshi Bukkyō no kenkyū,* p. 475f.; and Kimura, *Genshi Bukkyō shisōron, Kimura Taiken zenshū,* vol. 3, pp. 363–448.

Chapter 12

1. For studies of karma, see Kimura, *Shōjō Bukkyō no shisōron, Kimura Taiken zenshū,* vol. 5, pp. 495–657; Akanuma, "Gō no kenkyū," *Bukkyō kyōri no kenkyū;* Mizuno, "Gōsetsu ni tsuite," pp. 463–473; Funahashi Issai, *Gō no kenkyū;* Hirakawa, "Shōjō Bukkyō no rinri shisō."

2. For a discussion of the Sanskrit equivalents of these terms, see Funahashi, *Gō no kenkyū,* pp. 53–61.

3. For a discussion of the essence of the precepts, see Hirakawa, *Genshi Bukkyō no kenkyū,* pp. 165–222.

Chapter 13

1. For a discussion of the four stages, see Hirakawa, *Shoki Daijō Bukkyō no kenkyū,* pp. 408–441.

2. For the seven purifications, see Mizuno, *Pāri Bukkyō wo chūshin to shita Bukkyō no shinshikiron,* p. 929f.

3. Liberation through faith is a teaching peculiar to Theravāda Buddhism; see Hirakawa, "Shingedatsu yori shingedatsu e no tenkai," pp. 51–68.

Chapter 14

1. The description of the political history of this period is based on Kanakura, *Indo chūsei seishinshi,* vol. 2; Nakamura, *Indo kodaishi, Nakamura Hajime senshū,* vol. 6; Takada, *Butsuzō no kigen,* chap. 4. Also see idem, *Indo nankai no Bukkyō bijutsu;* Bareau, *Les Sectes bouddhiques du Petit Véhicule,* pp. 32–51; and Dutt, *Buddhist Monks and Monasteries of India.*

2. For more on this issue, see Hirakawa, *Shoki Daijō Bukkyō no kenkyū,* pp. 661–698.

3. For the emergence of Buddhist carving at Mathurā and Gandhāra, see Takada, *Butsuzō no kigen,* p. 209f.

4. The distribution of Hīnayāna and Mahāyāna Buddhism in India is discussed in Hirakawa, *Shoki Daijō Bukkyō no kenkyū,* pp. 699–728.

5. Inscriptions concerning Hīnayāna schools are not discussed in this study. For discussions of such inscriptions, see Tsukamoto, *Shoki Bukkyō kyōdanshi no kenkyū,* p. 450f.; Lamotte, *Histoire du Bouddhisme Indien,* pp. 578–585. For the primary sources for such a study, see Shizutani, *Indo Bukkyō himei mokuroku.*

Chapter 15

1. This chapter is based on the first chapter of the author's *Shoki Daijō Bukkyō no kenkyū.* The following sources are useful: Shiio, *Bukkyō kyōten gaisetsu;* Akanuma, *Bukkyō kyōten shiron;* Miyamoto, *Daijō to shōjō;* Kajiyoshi Kōun, *Genshi hannyagyō no kenkyū;* Ui, *Bukkyō kyōtenshi;* Higata, *Suvikrāntavikrāmiparipṛcchā Prajñāpāramitāsūtra.*

2. See Hirakawa, *Shoki Daijō Bukkyō no kenkyū,* pp. 72–98.

3. For a discussion of the oldest Mahāyāna scriptures, see ibid., pp. 98–133.

4. For a discussion of "the latter five hundred years," see ibid., pp. 65–72.

Chapter 16

1. For the use of the term "Hīnayāna" by Fa-hsien and Hsüan-tsang, see Hirakawa, *Shoki Daijō Bukkyō no kenkyū,* pp. 700–718.

2. Ibid., p. 713.

3. Ibid., pp. 718–721.

4. Hirakawa surveys the use of the term *tsan-fo sheng* in ibid., pp. 169–170.

5. Ibid., pp. 746–775.

6. For the *Samayabhedoparacanacakra,* see Higata and Kimura, "Ketsujūshi bunpashi kō." A Japanese translation of the Tibetan version of the text can be found in Teramoto, *Chibettogo bunpō.*

7. The *Mahāvastu* was published by É. Senart from 1882 to 1897. J. J. Jones published an English translation from 1949 to 1956. Since 1963, R. Basak has issued three volumes of the text *(Mahāvastu Avadāna).* For further information about research, publications, and translations of this work, see Yamada, *Bongo Butten no shobunken,* p. 66.

8. For information on the publication of the *Lalitavistara,* see Yamada, *Bongo Butten no shobunken,* p. 67. Published too late to be included in Yamada's work is *Lalitavistara,* ed. P. L. Vaidya.

9. On Aśvaghoṣa, see Kanakura, *Memyō no kenkyū;* Yamada, *Bongo Butten no shobunken,* p. 69; Tsuji, *Sansukuritto bungakushi,* pp. 11–17. Sanskrit texts of Aśvaghoṣa's *Buddhacarita, Saundarananda,* and the *Śāriputraprakaraṇa* have been published. The relation between the *Kalpanāmaṇḍitikā* discovered by Luders and Kumāralāta's *Dṛṣṭāntapaṅkti* should be noted.

10. A review of D. R. S. Bailey's publication of Mātṛceta's *Śatapañcaśatkastotra* by Tsuji Naoshirō can be found in *Tōyō gakuhō* 33, nos. 3–4 (1951). Also see Nara, "Bukkyō shijin," p. 135; Kanakura, *Memyō no kenkyū,* p. 92f.; and Tsuji, *Sansukuritto bungakushi,* pp. 17–20.

11. On *avadāna,* see Hirakawa, *Ritsuzō no kenkyū,* pp. 329–415.

12. Ogihara has noted seventy-nine Sanskrit texts of *avadāna* and *jātaka* tales, the majority of them being *avadānas* (*Ogihara Unrai bunshū,* p. 451f.). For the *Sumāgadhāvadāna,* see Iwamoto, *Bukkyo setsuwa kenkyū josetsu* and *Sumāgadāvadāna.* The latter includes the text and studies on it. For information on the publication of *avadāna* texts, see Yamada, *Bongo Butten no shobunken,* pp. 61–66. Too late to be included in Yamada's bibliography are P. L. Vaidya's publications of the *Avadānaśataka, Divyāvadāna, Jātakamālā* of Aryaśūra, and the *Avadānakalpalatā* of Kṣemendra.

13. Higata, *Honshōkyōrui no shisōshiteki kenkyū,* p. 22.

14. Miyamoto, "Hiyūsha, Daitoku Hokku, Tōju, Yumanron no kenkyū," pp. 117–192.

15. Miyamoto, *Daijō to shōjō,* p. 164.

16. Yamada, *Bongo Butten no shobunken,* p. 72.

17. For the relation between Mahāyāna Buddhism and *stūpas,* see Hirakawa, *Shoki Daijō Bukkyō no kenkyū,* pp. 549–601; Nakamura, "Gokuraku jōdo no kannen no Indogakuteki kaimei to Chibettoteki hen'yō," pp. 131–153; and Fujita, *Genshi jōdo shisō no kenkyū,* pp. 250–253.

18. Hirakawa, *Shoki Daijō Bukkyō no kenkyū,* pp. 618–627.

19. Hirakawa, *Genshi Bukkyō no kenkyū,* pp. 355–360.

20. For the relation between *stūpas* and Nikāya Buddhism, see Hirakawa, *Shoki Daijō Bukkyō no kenkyū,* pp. 603–657.

21. On the organizations around Buddhist *stūpas,* see ibid., pp. 788–796.

22. On the *bodhisattvagaṇa,* see ibid., pp. 797–811.

Chapter 17

1. Hirakawa, *Shoki Daijō Bukkyō no kenkyū,* p. 98–133.

2. Shizutani, "*Konkōmyōkyō* 'Gōshōmetsubon' no seiritsu ni tsuite"; Tokiya, "Chibetto-yaku no *Bosatsuzōkyō* no yakuchū," p. 122f.

3. For Sanskrit texts of the *Prajñāpāramitāsūtras,* see Yamada, *Bongo Butten no shobunken,* pp. 83–90. Among the works published too late to be mentioned in Yamada's work are the *Aṣṭasāhasrikā-PP,* ed. P. L. Vaidya; *Suvikrāntavikrāmi-*

pariprcchā, Vajracchedikā, Adhyardhaśatikā, Svalpākṣarā, Kauśika-PP, Prajñāpāramitāhṛdaya, Saptaśatikā, all in *Mahāyāna-sūtra-saṅgraha,* Buddhist Sanskrit Texts vol. 17; *Aṣṭādaśasāhasrikā-PP,* ed. E. Conze, chap. 55–70.

4. Mochizuki Ryōkō, "*Daijōshū bosatsugakuron* ni in'yō sareta *Yuimakyō* Bonbun danpen ni tsuite," p. 112f.; Yuyama, "Kamalaśīla no *Bhāvanākrama* ni in'yō sareta *Yuimakyō,*" pp. 105–125.

5. For the Sanskrit texts of the *Avataṃsaka* and its translations, see Yamada, *Bongo Butten no shobunken,* pp. 90–92. The *Daśabhūmika* and the *Gaṇḍavyūha* have been published by the Mithila Institute in Buddhist Sanskrit Texts.

6. For the Sanskrit texts of the *Lotus Sūtra,* see Yamada, *Bongo Butten no shobunken,* pp. 92–95. A Sanskrit text has also been published by Mithila Institute in Buddhist Sanskrit Texts vol. 6.

7. For the Sanskrit texts, see Yamada, *Bongo Butten no shobunken,* p. 96f.; *Sukhāvatīvyūhasūtra,* ed. A. Ashikaga; *Mahāyāna-sūtra-saṁgraha,* Buddhist Sanskrit Texts vol. 17, pp. 221–253.

8. Fujita, *Genshi jōdo shisō no kenkyū,* pp. 339–345; Yabuki, *Amida Butsu no kenkyū,* p. 82f.

9. Hirakawa, "Nyoraizō to shite no Hōzō bosatsu," pp. 1287–1306; idem, "Amida butsu to Hōzō bosatsu," pp. 163–178.

10. Tsukinowa, *Butten no hihanteki kenkyū,* p. 144f.; Nakamura, *Jōdo sanbukyō* 2:207; Fujita, *Genshi jōdo shisō no kenkyū,* pp. 121–136.

11. Hirakawa, "Daijō kyōten no hattatsu to Ajaseō no setsuwa," p. 7f.; Hayashima, "Jōdokyō no shōjōgōshokan ni tsuite," pp. 231–248.

12. For salvation through faith, see Hirakawa, "Shingedatsu yori shingedatsu e no tenkai," pp. 51–68.

13. *Karuṇāpuṇḍarīkasūtra,* ed. I. Yamada.

14. *Maitreyavyākaraṇa,* ed. S. Levi, pp. 381–422; *Gilgit Manuscripts,* vol. 4, pp. 187–214; Ishikami, "Miroku juki wayaku," pp. 35–48.

15. For Sanskrit texts of the *Ratnakūṭa,* see Yamada, *Bongo Butten no shobunken,* pp. 96–100.

16. For Sanskrit fragments of the *Mahāsaṃnipātasūtra,* see ibid., pp. 100–101. For the Sanskrit texts of *T* 310.47 and 397.11, see *Mahāsaṃnipāta-ratnaketu-dhāraṇī-sūtra,* vol. 4, *Gilgit Maniscripts,* ed. N. Dutt, pp. 1–141.

17. Among the Early Mahāyāna Sanskrit texts included in *Mahāyāna-sūtra-saṅgraha,* Buddhist Sanskrit Texts, vol. 17 are part 8, *Śālistambasūtra;* part 9, *Madhyamakaśālistambasūtra;* and part 13, *Bhaiṣajyaguruvaiḍūryaprabharājasūtra.* The Sanskrit text of the *Samādhirājasūtra* is included as vol. 2 of Buddhist Sanskrit Texts. The Sanskrit text of the *Bhaiṣajyagurusūtra* was published by Dutt in *Gilgit Manuscripts,* vol. 1, pp. 1–32. For additional information on Sanskrit texts discussed in this section, see Yamada, *Bongo Butten no shobunken,* pp. 101–109.

18. Yamada, *Bongo Butten no shobunken.*

Chapter 18

1. For the doctrine that the nature of the mind is originally pure, see Hirakawa, *Shoki Daijō Bukkyō no kenkyū,* pp. 196–217.

2. See Hirakawa, "Roku-haramitsu no tenkai," pp. 23–35.
3. For *dhāraṇī,* see Hirakawa, *Shoki Daijō Bukkyō no kenkyū,* pp. 218–227.
4. For the ten good actions, see ibid., pp. 426–474, and Hirakawa, "Shoki Daijō Bukkyō no kaigaku to shite no jūzendō," pp. 167–203.
5. For *kumāra,* see Hirakawa, *Shoki Daijō Bukkyō no kenkyū,* pp. 334–336.
6. See ibid., p. 185.
7. For the ten stages in the *Mahāvastu,* see ibid., pp. 187–191. The second stage in the text of the *Mahāvastu* is *baddhamānā.* This reading has been changed in accordance with Edgerton's dictionary.
8. For the four types of bodhisattvas, see Hirakawa, *Shoki Daijō Bukkyō no kenkyū,* pp. 286–330.
9. See ibid., pp. 336–340.
10. For the significance of the ten stages common to Hīnayānists and Mahāyānists, see ibid., pp. 354–358.
11. The *Ugradattaparipṛcchā* and the "Chapter on Pure Practices" of the *Avataṃsakasūtra* are discussed in ibid., pp. 483–548.
12. For the bodhisattva order, see ibid., pp. 777–811.

BIBLIOGRAPHICAL ESSAY

Introduction

A number of surveys of Indian Buddhism have been published in Western languages during this century. By far the most authoritative of these is Étienne Lamotte's *Histoire du Bouddhisme Indien des origines à l'ère Śaka,* a work that covers Early and Sectarian Buddhism. An authoritative English translation, *History of Indian Buddhism,* has been published. Edward Conze's *Buddhism: Its Essence and Development* and Hans Wolfgang Schumann's *Buddhism: An Outline of Its Teachings and Schools* are clearly written and suitable as introductory texts. On a more advanced level, Edward Conze's *Buddhist Thought in India: Three Phases of Buddhist Philosophy* is a good source for Buddhist thought but is often so terse that it can be confusing. Anthony Kennedy Warder's *Indian Buddhism* is a comprehensive survey discussing both history and doctrine, although the quality of its coverage is uneven, particularly in the later phases of Buddhist thought. E. J. Thomas' *The History of Buddhist Thought* is dated but still contains lucid explanations of Buddhism from a Theravāda perspective. Kanakura Yenshō's *Hindu-Buddhist Thought in India* is one of the few surveys that discusses the relationship between Hinduism and Buddhism in more than a perfunctory manner. David Kalupahana's *Buddhist Philosophy: A Historical Analysis* and A. L. Herman's *An Introduction to Buddhist Thought: A Philosophic History of Indian Buddhism* stress philosophical issues within Buddhism. Bu-ston's *History of Buddhism* and Tāranātha's *History of Buddhism in India* are valuable primary sources written from a traditional perspective. Diaries by the Chinese pilgrims Fa-hsien, Hsüan-tsang, and I-ching have been translated into English; they are invaluable first-hand accounts of the condition of Indian Buddhism. Their contents are also described in K. L. Hazra's *Buddhism as Described by the Chinese Pilgrims.*

The recently published *Encyclopedia of Religion* contains several lucid and insightful discussions of Indian Buddhism in general. Among the most noteworthy entries are Luis Gómez's "Buddhism: Buddhism in India" (2:351–385) and "Buddhist Literature: Exegesis and Hermeneutics" (2:529–541), André Bareau's "Buddhism, Schools of: Hīnayāna Buddhism" (2:444–457), Nakamura Hajime's "Buddhism, Schools of: Mahāyāna Buddhism" (2:457–472), and Hirakawa's "Buddhist Literature: Survey of Texts" (2:509–529). Many of the entries and their bibliographical annotations are major sources for the student of Buddhism and should be consulted. The *Encyclopedia of Religion*'s predecessor, Hastings' *Encyclopedia of Religion and Ethics,* also includes some very informative entries.

Several valuable reference tools for the study of Buddhism have been published. Volume 2 of *L'Inde classique,* edited by Louis Renou and Jean Filliozat, presents much valuable information on Indology and Buddhism in the form of an encyclopedia. Paul Demiéville's *Hōbōgirin,* an encyclopedia of Buddhism in French, has a number of very important long articles on Buddhist topics. These topics are listed in alphabetical order under the Japanese translation of the term being discussed, but only a few of the possible topics that could have been listed are actually investigated. *The Encyclopedia of Buddhism,* being published in English in Sri Lanka, is complete through the letter "B." This may not seem very helpful, but many Sanskrit and Pāli Buddhist names and technical terms begin with the first two letters of the alphabet. Although the quality of the *Encyclopedia of Buddhism* is uneven, some of its entries are excellent. Erik Zürcher's *Buddhism: Its Origins and Spread in Words, Maps and Pictures* includes maps that illustrate the propagation of Buddhism. Ñyāṇatiloka's *Buddhist Dictionary* is the best dictionary in English for Buddhist terms used in early Indian Buddhism.

For further bibliographical information, several major works are available including *Guide to the Buddhist Religion* by Frank Reynolds et al. and Reynolds' bibliographical essay "Buddhism" in the second edition of Charles Adams' *Reader's Guide to the Great Religions* (pp. 156–222). The *Guide to the Buddhist Religion* is an excellent reference for a student planning a paper since it contains detailed descriptions of primary and secondary sources available on a variety of topics. Nakamura Hajime's *Indian Buddhism: A Survey with Bibliographical Notes* includes numerous references to research by both Western and Japanese scholars. De Jong's extensive articles "A Brief History of Buddhist Studies in Europe and America" and "Recent Buddhist Studies in Europe and America, 1973–1983" published in *Eastern Buddhist* n.s. 7 and 17, respectively, are a critical review of the development of Buddhist studies in the West from its beginnings until recently. Other more specialized bibliographies or essays on sources are mentioned in the appropriate chapters.

Translations of individual Buddhist texts will be mentioned in the bibliographical notes for separate chapters, but the existence of useful anthologies of Buddhist texts should be noted. The collections of texts edited by Edward Conze, W. T. De Bary, and Stephan Beyer all contain both Hīnayāna and Mahāyāna texts.

Chapter 1. Indian Religion at the Time of the Buddha

One of the best surveys of classical Indian civilization is A. L. Basham's *The Wonder that Was India.* For historical surveys of India during the periods covered by this book, see volumes 1 through 5 of the *History and Culture of the Indian People* edited by R. C. Majumdar. Majumdar's *An Advanced History of India* serves as a good survey of Indian history. Romila Thapar has written a number of historical studies of these periods including *A History of India,* vol. 1. Indian society at the time of the Buddha is discussed in Uma Chaudhury's *The Social Dimensions of Early Buddhism.* For further sources on Indian culture and history, see Maureen Patterson's *South Asian Civilizations: A Bibliography.*

For Vedic religion, Arthur Keith's *The Religion and Philosophy of the Vedas and Upanishads* and Maurice Bloomfield's *The Religion of the Veda* are reliable sources.

Although little is known about most of the systems of thought that existed around the time of the Buddha, rich sources exist for Jainism. Padmanabh Jaini's *The Jaina Path of Purification* is a clearly written and authoritative survey of Jaina thought in English. Walter Schubring's *The Doctrine of the Jainas, Described after Old Sources* is a reliable study of early Jaina thought. A. L. Basham's *History and Doctrine of the Ājīvikas: A Vanished Indian Religion* is the definitive work on another tradition at the time of the Buddha. Other useful sources are S. B. Dasgupta's *A History of Indian Philosophy,* D. D. Kosambi's *The Culture and Civilization of Ancient India in Historical Outline,* B. M. Barua's *The History of Pre-Buddhist Philosophy,* and A. L. Basham's "The Background to the Rise of Buddhism" in *Studies in the History of Buddhism,* pp. 13–32. The *Brahmajāla-suttanta,* translated as *The Sacred Net, Dialogues of the Buddha,* vol. 2, and as *The Discourse on the All-Embracing Net of Views: The Brahmajāla Sutta and Its Commentarial Exegesis* by Bhikkhu Bodhi, contains information on other non-Buddhist theories of karma and rebirth with a critique from a traditional Buddhist perspective.

Chapter 2. The Life of the Buddha

Hirakawa notes that only fragments of information on the Buddha's biography are found in most early sources. Listed below are some of the longer passages on the Buddha's life from early sources in the Pāli tradition.

Vinaya, "Mahāvagga I"; English translation: *The Book of Discipline,* Sacred Books of the Buddhists, vol. 14, pp. 1–129.

Sutta-nipāta, chap. 3, part 1, etc., *Pabbajasutta;* English translation: *Woven Cadences,* Sacred Books of the Buddhists, vol. 15, pp. 61–114; and *The Group of Discourses,* Pāli Text Society Translation Series, no. 44, pp. 69–128.

Mahāpadānasuttanta, Dīgha-nikāya 14; English translation: *Dialogues of the Buddha,* vol. 3, pp. 1–41.

Mahāparinibbāna suttanta, Dīgha-nikāya 16; English translation: *Dialogues of the Buddha,* vol. 2, pp. 71–191.

Ariyapariyesanasutta, Majjhima-nikāya 26; *Middle Length Sayings,* vol. 1, pp. 203–219.

Mahāsaccakasutta, Majjhima-nikāya 36; *Middle Length Sayings,* vol. 1.

Jātaka, vol. 1, (Nidānakathā); *Jātaka,* vol. 2, *Avidūrenidāna* ff.; English translation: T. W. Rhys Davids, *Buddhist Birth Stories;* excerpts in H. C. Warren, *Buddhism in Translations,* pp. 5–83.

Most of these sources have been translated and arranged into chronological order by Bhikkhu Ñāṇamoli in *The Life of the Buddha as It Appears in the Pāli Canon, The Oldest Authentic Record.* Many of these Pāli texts on the Buddha's biography have corresponding passages in the Chinese canon.

Michael Carrithers' *The Buddha* and Mizuno Kōgen's *The Beginnings of Buddhism* are good popular introductions to the biography of the Buddha. Surveys of the term "Buddha" and its interpretations can be found in both the *Encyclopedia of Religion* (2:319–332) and *Encyclopedia of Buddhism* (3:357–380). The most exhaustive study of the biography of the historical Buddha is found in André Bareau's three-volume *Recherches sur la biographie du Buddha dans les Sūtrapiṭaka et les Vinayapiṭaka anciens.* This authoritative work can be supplemented with his article "La Jeunesse du Bouddha dans les *Sūtrapiṭaka* et les *Vinayapiṭaka* anciens," *Bulletin de l'École française d'Extrême-Orient* 61 (1974): 199–274. In English, E. J. Thomas' *The Life of the Buddha as Legend and History* is dated and focuses on Pāli sources but is still extremely valuable. Alfred Foucher's *The Life of the Buddha According to the Ancient Texts and Monuments of India* serves as a good supplement for Thomas. Nakamura Hajime's *Gotama Buddha* is an English translation and condensation of a very thorough study in Japanese of Śākyamuni Buddha and is thus based on a broader range of sources than Thomas' volume. Frank Reynolds has traced some of the development of Śākyamuni's biography in the article "The Many Lives of the Buddha" in *The Biographical Process,* pp. 37–61. A number of traditional biographies of the Buddha have been translated including the *Jātaka, Mahāvastu, Lalitavistara,* and Aśvaghoṣa's *Buddhacarita.*

Some of the Buddha's disciples have also been the subject of studies. Malalesekera's *Dictionary of Pāli Proper Names* and Nalinaksha Dutt's *Early Monastic Buddhism* are valuable tools for learning about the figures mentioned in the Buddha's biography. Among the significant studies of the Buddha's disciples are John Strong's "The Legend of the Lion-Roarer: A Study of the Buddhist Arhat Piṇḍola Bhāradvāja," *Numen* 26 (1979): 50–88, Witanachi's "Ānanda," *Encyclopedia of Buddhism* 1:529–536, and Tsukamoto Keishō's "Mahākāśyapa's Precedence to Ānanda at the Rājagṛha Council," *Journal of Indian and Buddhist Studies* 11, no. 2: 824–817.

The enigmatic figure of the *pratyekabuddha* is the subject of Ria Kloppenborg's *The Paccekabuddha: A Buddhist Ascetic,* K. R. Norman's "The Pratyekabuddha in Buddhism and Jainism," *Buddhist Studies: Ancient and Modern,* pp. 92–106, and Fujita Kōtatsu's "One Vehicle or Three?" *Journal of Indian Philosophy* 3 (1975): 79–166.

Chapter 3. Early Buddhist Doctrine

The translations of the Pāli canon described in chapter 5 provide the student with abundant primary source material for the study of this stage of Buddhist thought. Reynolds' *Guide to the Buddhist Religion* and the bibliographies at the end of the chapters in David Kalupahana's *Buddhist Philosophy* also provide the student with a useful guide to sources in the *Nikāyas* on topics in Early Buddhist doctrine.

H. C. Warren's *Buddhism in Translations* is a superb collection of translations from Pāli sources arranged according to subject. One of the best introductions to Early Buddhist doctrine is Walpola Rahula's immensely popular *What the Buddha Taught,* which is arranged in accordance with the Four Noble Truths. Mizuno Kōgen's *Primitive Buddhism* is typical of Japanese descriptions of the earliest Buddhist teachings. Nalinaksha Dutt's *Early Monastic Buddhism* contains detailed studies of a number of topics, often with interpretations from *abhidharma* sources. Govind Chandra Pande's *Studies in the Origins of Buddhism* is a technical study of Early Buddhism from a variety of perspectives that includes an attempt to distinguish earlier and later passages in the texts. In addition, all of the basic surveys mentioned in the bibliographical notes for the introduction include good discussions of this period of Buddhist thought.

Specialized studies on a variety of topics exist. For example, the topics of *nirvāṇa* and enlightenment, the ultimate goals of Buddhist practice, have long fascinated a number of scholars. Tom Kasulis provides a good introduction to many issues of interpretation in "Nirvāṇa," *Encyclopedia of Religion* 10:448–456. Earlier in this century, La Vallée Poussin and Stcherbatsky argued over the correct interpretation of *nirvāṇa;* their views and those of other early Western scholars are described in Guy Welbon's book *Buddhist Nirvāna and Its Western Interpreters.* More recently Rune Johansson has investigated the topic from a psychological perspective in *The Psychology of Nirvana.* Jan Ergardt *(Faith and Knowledge in Early Buddhism* and *Man and His Destiny: The Release of the Human Mind)* and Lambert Schmithausen ("On Some Aspects of Descriptions of Theories of 'Liberating Insight' and 'Enlightenment' in Early Buddhism," *Studien zum Jainismus und Buddhismus: Gedenkschrift für Ludwig Alsdorf,* pp. 199–250) have contributed impressive studies of the presentation of these topics in early texts. The *arhat* has been discussed in many of the above-mentioned studies as well as in I. B. Horner's *Early Buddhist Theory of Man Perfected* and Karel Werner's "Bodhi and Arahataphala: From Early Buddhism to Early Mahāyāna" in *Buddhist Studies: Ancient and Modern,* pp. 167–181. Padmanabh Jaini compares the Jaina and Early Buddhist views on omniscience in "On the Sarvajñātva of Mahāvīra and the Buddha" in *Buddhist Studies in Honor of I. B. Horner,* pp. 71–90.

Dependent Origination has been discussed by a number of scholars. Among the recent significant studies are Johansson's *The Dynamic Psychology of Early Buddhism,* David Kalupahana's *Causality: The Central Philosophy of Buddhism,* and Alex Wayman's "Buddhist Dependent Origination," *History of Religion* 10 (1971): 185–203. For an exploration of the philosophical significance of no-Self teachings, see Steven Collins' *Selfless Persons: Imagery and Thought in Theravāda Buddhism,* G. P. Malalesekera's article "Anattā," *Encyclopedia of Buddhism* 1: 567–576, and Nakamura Hajime's "The Problem of Self in Buddhist Philosophy" in *Revelation in Indian Thought,* pp. 99–118.

Few early texts contain teachings for lay believers, but the translations at the end of Walpola Rahula's *What the Buddha Taught* include three selections. Teachings for lay Buddhists are discussed in D. K. Barua's *An Analytical Study of the Four Nikāyas* and Joseph Masson's *La Religion populaire dans le canon bouddhique Pāli.*

Chapter 4. The Organization of the Order

The full Theravāda *Vinaya* has been translated into English by I. B. Horner as *The Book of the Discipline.* Buddhaghosa's commentary on the *Vinaya,* the *Samantapāsādikā,* has been partially translated from Pāli by N. A. Jayawickrama, and a complete translation from Chinese has been done by Hirakawa and Bapat. Lists of rules for several other schools are found in Charles Prebish's *Buddhist Monastic Discipline: The Sanskrit Prātimokṣa Sūtras of the Mahāsaṃghika and Mūlasarvāstivādins.*

One of the fullest discussions of the order is found in John Holt's *Discipline: The Canonical Buddhism of the Vinayapiṭaka.* For a briefer survey, see Charles Prebish's "Vinaya and Prātimokṣa: The Foundation of Buddhist Ethics" in *Studies in the History of Buddhism,* pp. 189–208. Hirakawa has written two major books on the *Vinaya* and monastic discipline in Japanese, but little of his work on this topic is available in English except for an article, "The Twofold Structure of the Buddhist Saṃgha," *Journal of the Oriental Institute* 15, no. 2 (1966): 131–137, and a summary of his book *Ritsuzō no kenkyū* [A study of the *Vinayapiṭaka*], pp. 1–26 (left). Other useful works on monastic life are Sukumar Dutt's *Early Buddhist Monachism* and *Buddhist Monks and Monasteries of India,* Gokuldas De's *Democracy in Early Buddhist Saṃgha,* Nalinaksha Dutt's *Early Monastic Buddhism,* Nagao Gadjin's "The Architectural Tradition in Buddhist Monasticism" in *Studies in the History of Buddhism,* pp. 189–208, and N. Tatia's "The Interaction of Jainism and Buddhism and Its Impact on the History of Buddhist Monasticism" in *Studies in the History of Buddhism,* pp. 321–338. The *Hōbōgirin* includes two major articles on specific types of rules: theft or *chūtō* (3:551–558) and attempted offenses or *chūranja* (3:507–522).

Since a number of versions of the *Vinaya* exist in Chinese translation, the texts can be compared to elucidate the development of the canon. This approach has been followed in studies such as Pachow's *A Comparative Study of the Prātimokṣa on the Basis of Its Chinese, Tibetan, Sanskrit, and Pāli Versions,* Erich Frauwallner's *The Earliest Vinaya and the Beginnings of Buddhist Literature,* Prebish's "The Prātimokṣa Puzzle: Facts Versus Fantasy," *Journal of the American Oriental Society* 94 (April–June 1974): 168–176, and Kun Chang's *Comparative Study of the Kaṭhinavastu.* C. S. Upasak's *Dictionary of Early Buddhist Monastic Terms* is a valuable source for defining the extensive technical nomenclature used to discuss Buddhist monastic life.

The role of women in Buddhism has attracted attention in recent years. The classic study on this topic in Early Buddhism is I. B. Horner's *Women under Primitive Buddhism.* Her work has been extended in studies such as Meena Talim's *Women in Early Buddhist Literature,* Diana Paul's *Women in Buddhism,* Kabilsingh's *A Comparative Study of Bhikkhuṇī Pātimokkha,* Nancy Falk's "The Case of the Vanishing Nuns" in *Unspoken Worlds,* pp. 207–224, Jan Willis' "Nuns and Benefactresses: The Role of Women in the Development of Buddhism" in *Women, Religion and Social Change,* pp. 59–86, Kajiyama Yūichi's "Women in Buddhism," *Eastern Buddhist* 15 (1982): 53–70, and André Bareau's "Un Personnage bien mysterieux: L'Espouse du Bouddha" in *Indological and Buddhist Studies,* pp. 31–59.

Modern Theravāda orders in Sri Lanka and Southeast Asia have been the subject of a number of valuable studies by anthropologists, sociologists, and historians. Among the more important works are the trilogy by S. J. Tambiah (*Buddhism and the Spirit Cults in North-east Thailand, World Conqueror and World Renouncer,* and *The Buddhist Saints of the Forest and the Cult of Amulets*), Michael Carrithers' *Forest Monks of Sri Lanka: An Anthropological and Historical Study,* and Michael Mendelson's *Sangha and State in Burma.* Extensive bibliographies of these fascinating studies can be found in Reynolds' *Guide to the Buddhist Religion* and in two bibliographical essays by Reynolds: "From Philology to Anthropology: A Bibliographical Essay on Works Related to Early, Theravāda and Sinhalese Buddhism" in *The Two Wheels of the Dhamma,* pp. 107–121, and "Tradition and Change in Theravāda Buddhism," *Contributions to Asian Studies* 4 (1973): 94–104. The third volume of Bechert's *Buddhismus, Staat und Geselleschaft in den Ländern des Theravāda-Buddhismus* includes a bibliography of close to two thousand items on Theravāda.

Chapter 5. The Establishment of the Early Buddhist Canon

The compilation of the early canon has been discussed in two articles in the *Encyclopedia of Religion,* "Buddhist Literature: Survey of Texts" by Hirakawa (2: 509–529) and "Buddhist Literature: Canonization" by Lewis Lancaster (2: 504–509). In addition, reliable discussions can be found in many of the surveys mentioned in the introduction. Gregory Schopen questions a number of assumptions about the early canon in "Two Problems in the History of Indian Buddhism: The Layman/Monk Distinction and the Doctrines of Transfer of Merit," *Studien zur Indologie und Iranstik* 10 (1985): 9–47.

Erich Frauwallner's *The Earliest Vinaya and the Beginnings of Buddhist Literature* is an important study of the early *Vinaya.* For information on the *sūtrapiṭakas,* see D. K. Barua's *An Analytical Study of the Four Nikāyas,* which contains comparative charts of the Chinese *Āgamas* and Pāli *Nikāyas* on pp. 8–30; Thich Minh Chau's *Chinese Āgamas and the Pāli Majjhima Nikāya;* Mizuno Kōgen's *Buddhist Sūtras: Origin, Development, Transmission;* Mayeda Egaku's "Japanese Studies on the Schools of the Chinese Āgamas" in *Zur Schulzugehövigkeit von Werken der Hinayana-Literatur,* pp. 94–103; and J. W. de Jong's "Les Sūtrapiṭaka des Sarvāstivādin et des Mūlasarvāstivādin" in *Mélanges d'Indianisme à la memoire de Louis*

Renou, pp. 395–402. For thoughtful discussions of the comparative value of Sanskrit texts and Chinese translations and other issues in Buddhist literature, see Lewis Lancaster's articles "Editing of Buddhist Texts" in *Buddhist Thought and Asian Civilization,* pp. 145–151 and "Buddhist Literature: Its Canons, Scribes and Editors" in *The Critical Study of Sacred Texts,* pp. 215–229.

A bibliography of both editions of the canon and secondary literature on the Buddhist canon can be found in Günter Grönbold's *Der buddhistiche Kanon: Eine Bibliographie. Vinaya* literature is surveyed in Yuyama Akira's bibliography, *Vinaya-Texte.* Heinz Bechert has edited a volume on the language of Early Buddhism, *The Language of the Earliest Buddhist Tradition.*

Most of the Pāli canon has been translated into English. Many of the translations are listed in the bibliography at the end of this book under the Pāli titles or the author's name when it is known. For an introduction to the Pāli canon, see Wilhelm Geiger's *Pāli Literature and Language,* vol. 1, pp. 8–58. Full and detailed discussions of Pāli literature are found in two classic surveys, B. C. Law's *A History of Pāli Literature* and Malalesekera's *The Pāli Literature of Ceylon.* More recent surveys are K. R. Norman's very thorough *Pāli Literature* and Russell Webb's *An Analysis of the Pāli Canon.*

Sanskrit Buddhist literature is surveyed in several sources. For Hīnayāna texts in Sanskrit and Prakrit, see K. R. Norman's *Pāli Literature.* Yamada Ryūjō's *Bongo Butten no shobunken* [Sanskrit Buddhist literature] is a survey of Sanskrit Mahāyāna texts. Other sources are the second volume of Moriz Winternitz's *A History of Indian Literature* and J. K. Nariman's *A Literary History of Sanskrit Buddhism.* Renou and Fillizoat's *L'Inde classique* contains bibliographical information.

Chapter 6. The Development of the Buddhist Order

Many of the primary sources on schisms and councils have been translated into Western languages. For more information on them, see the section on chapter 8 of the bibliographic essay. Nalinaksha Dutt has discussed the spread of Buddhism in *Early History of the Spread of Buddhism and the Early Buddhist Schools.* Other information can be found in the many regional studies of the development of Indian Buddhism by such authors as Nalinaksha Dutt, Jean Naudou, Gayatri Sen Majumdar, and B. G. Gokhale.

Hirakawa's dating of the historical Buddha is not followed by most Western scholars but is used by a number of prominent Japanese scholars. For discussions of this issue in Western languages, see Heinz Bechert's "The Date of the Buddha Reconsidered," *Indologica Taurinensia* 10 (1982): 29–36, which advocates a position close to that of Hirakawa. It may be contrasted with André Bareau's "La Date du Nirvāṇa," *Journal Asiatique* 241 (1953): 27–62, and M. M. Singh's "The Date of the Buddha-Nirvāṇa," *Journal of Indian History* 39, no. 3 (1961): 359–363. Additional sources for the date of the Buddha are discussed in the bibliographical listings of studies of the Buddha's life in chapter 2.

Chapter 7. The Buddhism of King Aśoka

Many of the primary sources necessary for the study of Aśoka have been translated into English, including John Strong's *The Legend of King Aśoka: A Study and Translation of the Aśokāvadāna,* Wilhelm Geiger's *Mahāvaṃsa, or the Great Chronicle of Ceylon,* and Eugen Hultzsch's *The Inscriptions of Aśoka.* Aśoka's inscriptions are also available in a paperback edition, *The Edicts of Aśoka,* by N. A. Nikam and Richard McKeon. Extensive selections can be found in most of the studies in the following paragraph.

The reign of King Aśoka has been studied extensively by modern scholars. Among the better surveys are Romila Thapar's *Aśoka and the Decline of the Mauryas,* a study that stresses Aśoka's political motives. It can be compared with B. G. Gokhale's *Buddhism and Asoka* and R. Mookerjee's *Asoka.* Pierre Herman Leonard Eggermont's *The Chronology of the Reign of Asoka Moriya* suggests a time table for Aśoka's reign. Heinz Bechert's "The Importance of Aśoka's So-called Schism Edict" in *Indological and Buddhological Studies,* pp. 61–68, defines Aśoka's place in the history of Buddhist sectarianism in a manner that agrees with Hirakawa's chronology. A. L. Basham's article, "Aśoka and Buddhism: A Reexamination," *Journal of the International Association of Buddhist Studies* 5 (1982): 131–143, is a critical review of modern scholarship on the subject. John Strong examines legends about Aśoka's teacher Upagupta in "The Buddhist Avadānis.s and the Elder Upagupta," *Mélanges chinois et bouddhiques* 22 (1985): 863–881. Finally, S. J. Tambiah's *World Conqueror and World Renouncer* includes discussions of Aśoka and the influence of the universal ruler ideal on subsequent Buddhist history.

Chapter 8. The Development of Nikāya Buddhism

The primary and secondary sources listed in this chapter are also important in the study of the issues presented in chapters 6 and 9–13. Many of the vital primary sources on the rise of the Hīnayāna schools have been translated into English, including such Theravāda sources as the *Dīpavaṃsa, Mahāvaṃsa, Kathāvatthu,* Buddhaghosa's *Kathāvatthu-aṭṭhakathā* (commentary on the *Kathāvatthu*), the *Vinaya,* and Buddhaghosa's *Samantapāsādikā* (commentary on the *Vinaya*). Among the sources from the Northern tradition, Masuda Jiryo's "Origin and Doctrines of Early Indian Buddhist Schools," *Asia Major* 2 (1925): 1–78, an annotated English translation of Hsüan-tsang's Chinese rendering of the *Samayabhedoparacanacakra,* is very useful. In addition, the histories of Buddhism by both Tāranātha and Bu-ston, as well as the travel diaries of Fa-hsien, Hsüan-tsang, and I-ching, have been translated into English.

Paul Demiéville has translated the historical section of Chi-tsang's *San-lun hsüan-i* and surviving fragments of Paramārtha's comments on the *Samayabhedoparacanacakra* into French in "L'Origine des sectes bouddhiques d'après Paramārtha," *Mélanges chinois et bouddhiques* 1 (1931): 15–64. Bhavya's *Nikāyabhedavibhaṅga-vyākhyāna* and Vinītadeva's *Samayabhedoparacanacakre nikāyabhedopa-*

deśana-saṅgraha have been translated into French in Bareau's article "Trois traités sur les sectes bouddhiques," *Journal Asiatique* 242 (1954): 229–266; 244 (1956): 167–200.

Only a few of the primary sources for this chapter are not available in English or French. Among them are the *A-yü-wang ching (Aśokarājasūtra),* Tzu-en's commentary on the *Samayabhedoparacanacakra* (*Zokuzōkyō* 1.83.3), *Divyāvadāna* (no. 26, "Pāmśupradānāvadāna"; no. 27, "Kuṇalāvadāna"), and inscriptions described in such works as Shizutani Masao's *Indo Bukkyō himei mokuroku* [Catalog of Indian Buddhist inscriptions]. However, the *A-yü-wang ching* is an abbreviated version (with some differences) of the *Aśokāvadāna* translated by John Strong in *The Legend of King Aśoka.* Tzu-en's comments are summarized in Masuda's translation of the *Samayabhedoparacanacakra.*

André Bareau's *Les Sectes bouddhiques du Petit Véhicule* is the best secondary study of the schools of Nikāya Buddhism in a Western language. For those who do not read French, Nalinaksha Dutt's *Buddhist Sects in India* and S. N. Dube's *Cross Currents in Early Buddhism* (based primarily on the *Kathāvatthu*) should be consulted. Several articles in the *Encyclopedia of Religion* include good bibliographies and summaries of the positions of the schools: Bareau's article on Hīnayāna schools (2:444–457), Reynolds and Clifford on Theravāda (14:469–479), Gómez on Mahāsāṃghika (9:120–122) and Sarvāstivāda (13:75–80), and Skorupski on Sautrāntika (13:86–88). These studies also contain information about the doctrinal positions of many of the lesser-known schools. Although the articles "Sarvāstivādins," "Sautrāntikas," and "Sects (Buddhist)" in Hastings' *Encyclopedia of Religion and Ethics* are dated, they are still worth consulting.

Among the primary sources for the councils that have been translated are the *Dīpavaṃsa, Mahāvaṃsa, Vinaya* ("Chapter on the Five Hundred" and "Chapter on the Seven Hundred"), and the *Samantapāsādikā.* The best study of the Buddhist councils is André Bareau's *Les Premiers Conciles bouddhiques.* The Second Council has also been discussed by Paul Demiéville ("À propos du concile de Vaiśālī," *T'oung pao* 40 [1951]: 239–296), Marcel Hofinger *(Étude sur la concile de Vaiśālī),* and Nalinaksha Dutt *(Buddhist Sects in India).* The results of their studies have been summarized and critically examined in Charles Prebish's "A Review of Scholarship on the Buddhist Councils," *Journal of Asian Studies* 33 (February 1974): 239–254, and "Mahāsāṅghika Origins: The Beginnings of Buddhist Sectarianism" (co-authored with Jan Nattier), *History of Religions* 16 (1977): 237–272.

The history of the Sri Lankan Theravāda tradition is investigated in Walpola Rahula's *The History of Buddhism in Ceylon: The Anuradhapura Period, 3rd Century B.C.–19th Century A.D.,* E. W. Adikaram's *Early History of Buddhism in Ceylon,* K. L. Hazra's *History of Theravāda Buddhism in Southeast Asia, with Special Reference to India and Ceylon,* and Heinz Bechert's three-volume *Buddhismus, Staat und Geselleschaft in den Ländern des Theravāda-Buddhismus.* (The last volume of Bechert's work contains an extensive bibliography.) The Theravāda exegete Buddhaghosa is discussed by B. C. Law in his monograph *Buddhaghosa.* Among the studies on Mahāyāna influences in Sri Lanka are Bechert's "Mahāyāna Literature in Sri Lanka: The Early Phase" in *Prajñāpāramitā and Related Systems,* pp.

361–368, and Senarat Paranavitana's "Mahāyānism in Ceylon," *Ceylon Journal of Science, Section G: Archeology, Ethnography, etc.* 2, no. 1 (December 1928): 35–71.

Chapter 9. *Abhidharma* Literature

Most of the Theravāda *abhidhamma-piṭaka,* some of the later works on it, and the *Abhidhammattha-saṅgaha,* an important compendium of *abhidhamma,* have been translated into English; these works are listed in the bibliography of related readings under their Pāli titles. This literature is also discussed in surveys of Pāli texts such as K. R. Norman's *Pāli Literature.* The Sarvāstivādin tradition has not been studied as thoroughly by Westerners, but Louis de La Vallée Poussin's French annotated translation of Vasubandhu's systematization of *abhidharma* thought, *L'Abhidharmakośa de Vasubandhu,* is an invaluable source. An English translation of La Vallée Poussin's work is being published by Asian Humanities Press. Translations of parts of the *Abhidharmakośa* into English have been done by Stcherbatsky, Dowling, and Hall; these are discussed in the sections on chapters 10 and 12 of the bibliographic essay. La Vallée Poussin also translated and discussed important passages from such works as the *Mahāvibhāṣā* in "Documents d'Abhidharma," *Mélanges chinois et bouddhiques* 1 and 5. Dharmaśrī's *Abhidharmahṛdayaśāstra* has been translated into French by I. Armelin and into English by Charles Willemen. Skandhila's *Abhidharmāvatāraśāstra* has been translated into French by Marcel Van Weltem, and Ghoṣaka's *Amṛtarasa* has been translated into French by Van den Broeck. Collett Cox's *Controversies in Dharma Theory* includes a partial translation of Saṅghabhadra's *Abhidharma-nyānānusāraśāstra,* a Sarvāstivāda critique of Vasubandhu's *Abhidharmakośa.*

Among the secondary studies of Sarvāstivāda *abhidharma* literature are Anukul Chandra Banerjee's *Sarvāstivāda Literature,* Takakusu Junjirō's "On the Abhidharma Literature of the Sarvāstivādins," *Journal of the Pāli Text Society* 14 (1904–1905): 67–146, and Mizuno Kōgen's essay on "Abhidharma Literature" in *Encyclopedia of Buddhism* 1:64–80. Separate articles on *abhidharma* texts such as the *Abhidharmakośa* and *Abhidharma-mahāvibhāṣā* are also found in the *Encyclopedia of Buddhism.* Erich Frauwallner's valuable series of articles in German, "Abhidharma Studien," explore a variety of textual issues such as the dating of texts.

Only a few *abhidharma* texts from other traditions survive. For discussions, see Bareau's "Les Origines du *Śāriputrābhidharmaśāstra,*" *Le Muséon* 63 (1950): 69–95, and Thich Thein Chau's "The Literature of the Pudgalavādins," *Journal of the International Association of Buddhist Studies* 7, no. 1 (1984): 7–40, and "Les Réponses des Pudgalavādins aux critiques des écoles bouddhiques," *Journal of the International Association of Buddhist Studies* 10, no. 1 (1987): 33–53. K. Venkataramanan has translated a Sammitīya text into English, "Sammitīya-nikāya-śāstra," *Visva-Bharati Annals* 5 (1953): 155–242. The *Ch'eng-shih lun (Satyasiddhiśāstra)* is briefly discussed in Takakusu's *The Essentials of Buddhist Philosophy,* pp. 74–79. For a more thorough examination of this text, see Katsura Shōryū's doctoral dissertation "A Study of Harivarman's 'Tattvasiddhi'."

The transitional phase between the *Nikāyas* and *abhidharma* has been discussed in Watanabe Fumimaro's *Philosophy and Its Development in the Nikāyas and Abhidharma,* Étienne Lamotte's article "Khuddakanikāya and Kṣudrakapiṭaka," *East and West* 8 (1957):341-348, Lance Cousins' "The *Paṭṭhāna* and the Development of the Theravādin Abhidhamma," *Centenary Volume of the Journal of the Pāli Text Society* (1981): 22-46, Johannes Bronkhorst's "Dharma and Abhidharma," *Bulletin of the School of Oriental and African Studies* 48, no. 2 (1985): 305-319, Przyluski's *Le Concile de Rājagṛha,* Bareau's "Les Sectes bouddhiques du Petit Véhicule et leurs Abhidharmapiṭaka," *Bulletin de l'École française d'Extrême-Orient* 50 (1952): 1-11, and André Migot's "Un Grand disciple du Bouddha: Śāriputra," *Bulletin de l'École française d'Extrême-Orient* 46 (1954): 405-554.

Chapter 10. The Organization of the *Dharmas* in the *Abhidharma*

Among the most critical primary sources for the theory of *dharmas* are Vasubandhu's *Abhidharmakośa* for the Sarvāstivāda and Sautrāntika perspectives and the *Dhammasaṅgaṇi* and the *Abhidhammattha-saṅgaha* for Theravāda theory.

Several articles in the *Encyclopedia of Religion* may be consulted for a basic survey of *dharma* theory: "Dharma, Buddhist Dharma and Dharmas" (4:332-338), "Sarvāstivāda" (13:75-80), and "Sautrāntika" (13:86-88). The classic study of Sarvāstivāda *dharma* theory in English is Fedor Ippolitovich Stcherbatsky's *The Central Conception of Buddhism and the Meaning of the Word "Dharma."* Although it was first published over sixty years ago, it still contains valuable information. More recently, a number of other works have appeared. Sukomal Chaudhury's *Analytical Study of the Abhidharmakośa* and the introduction to Hirakawa's index of the *Abhidharmakośa (San'yaku taishō Kusharon sakuin)* provide good summaries of the contents of Vasubandhu's seminal systematic treatment of Buddhist doctrine. Alexander Piatigorski's *The Buddhist Philosophy of Thought* is an interpretative study of *abhidharma.* Bruce Cameron Hall's doctoral dissertation, "Vasubandhu on 'Aggregates, Spheres, and Components': Being Chapter One of the *Abhidharmakośa*" includes a translation of the first chapter of the *Abhidharmakośa.* Herbert Guenther's *Philosophy and Psychology in the Abhidharma* compares Sarvāstivāda, Theravāda, and Yogācāra scholastic theories. Among the better scholarly articles on the meaning of the term *dharma* and the theories concerning it are Hirakawa's "The Meaning of 'Dharma' and 'Abhidharma,' " in *Indianisme et bouddhisme,* pp. 159-175; A. K. Warder's "Dharmas and Data," *Journal of Indian Philosophy* 1 (1971): 272-295; Paul Williams' "On the Abhidharma Ontology," *Journal of Indian Philosophy* 9 (1981): 227-257; and Kajiyama Yūichi's "Realism of the Sarvāstivāda" in *Buddhist Thought and Asian Civilization,* pp. 114-131.

Theravāda views on *dhammas* are described in Ñyāṇatiloka's authoritative *Guide through the Abhidhamma-piṭaka.* John Ross Carter's *Dhamma: Western Academic and Sinhalese Buddhist Interpretations* includes an extensive discussion of the term *dhamma.* In Karunadasa's *Buddhist Analysis of Matter* material *dharmas* are examined from the Theravāda perspective. Rune Johansson's "Citta, Mano, Viññāna," *University of Ceylon Review* 23, nos. 1-2 (1965): 165-212, analyzes terms concerned with consciousness from a psychological perspective. Among the other works that discuss *abhidhamma* are Jayasuriya's *The Psychology and Philosophy of Buddhism,* Kashyap's *Abhidhamma Philosophy,* Ñyāṇaponika's *Abhidhamma Studies,* and E. R. Saratchandra's *Buddhist Psychology of Perception.*

Several specialized issues in *dharma* theory have been the topic of detailed articles and books by a number of scholars. One of the most basic problems for *abhidharma* thinkers was the explanation of the continuity and integration of the personality. The Pudgalavādin position is refuted in the ninth chapter of Vasubandhu's *Abhidharmakośa,* translated by Stcherbatsky as *The Soul Theory of the Buddhists,* and in the Theravāda *abhidhamma* text, the *Kathāvatthu.* Another explanation for the continuity of the mind, the Sautrāntika theory of seeds, is discussed by P. S. Jaini in "The Sautrāntika Theory of *Bīja,*" *Bulletin of the School of Oriental and African Studies* 22 (1959): 236–249. Karunaratna's article on *bhavaṅga* in *Encyclopedia of Buddhism* 3:17–20, and Wijesekera's "Canonical References to the Bhavaṅga" in *Malalesekera Commemoration Volume,* pp. 348–352, present a Theravāda approach. The *abhidharma* interpretation of time is discussed by Braj Sinha in *Time and Temporality in Sāṁkhya-Yoga and Abhidharma Buddhism* and by La Vallée Poussin in "La Controverse du temps et du pudgala dans le *Vijñānakāya,*" *Études Asiatiques* 1 (1925): 343-376, and "Documents d'Abhidharma," *Mélanges chinois et bouddhiques* 5 (1937): 7–187.

P. S. Jaini examines several of the *dharmas* that are neither material nor mental in "The Vaibhāṣika Theory of Words and Meanings," *Bulletin of the School of Oriental and African Studies* 22 (1959): 95–107, and "Origin and Development of the Theory of *Viprayukta Saṃskāras,*" *Bulletin of the School of Oriental and African Studies* 22, no. 3 (1959): 531-547. Issues of language and interpretation are discussed in George Bond's *Word of the Buddha: The Tipiṭaka and Its Interpretation in Early Buddhism* and Ñāṇananda's *Concept and Reality in Early Buddhist Thought.* Bareau surveys unconditioned *dharmas* in *L'Absolu en philosophie bouddhique: Évolution de la notion d'asaṃskṛta.*

Chapter 11. Buddhist Cosmology and the Theory of Karma

Hirakawa's discussion of Sarvāstivāda cosmology, rebirth, and the twelve links of Dependent Origination is based on the "Chapter on Cosmology" of the *Abhidharmakośa* (fasc. 8–12 of the Chinese translation). The theory of the six causes, four conditions, and five fruits is found in the "Chapter on Faculties" of the *Abhidharmakośa* (fasc. 6–7). Since the *Abhidharmakośa* account includes many details not mentioned in this chapter, interested readers should consult La Vallée Poussin's French translation.

La Vallée Poussin's articles "Cosmology and Cosmogony, Buddhist" (4:129–138) and "Ages of the World (Buddhist)" (1:187–190) in Hastings' *Encyclopedia of Religion and Ethics* are excellent introductory surveys primarily based on the *Abhidharmakośa.* The same author has written a book-length article on cosmology in French entitled, "Bouddhisme: Études et materiaux," *Mémoires de l'Academie royale du Belgique* 6 (1919). The most recent study of Buddhist cosmology is Randolph Kloetzli's *Buddhist Cosmology: From Single World System to Pure Land: Science and Theology in the Image of Motion and Light.* The first volume, *Cosmology,* of

William McGovern's *A Manual of Buddhist Philosophy* contains much useful information. B. C. Law's *Buddhist Conception of Spirits* includes stories about hungry ghosts based on Pāli sources. His *Heaven and Hell in Buddhist Perspective* is also based only on Pāli sources but can be supplemented by Daigan and Alicia Matsunaga's *The Buddhist Concept of Hell,* which contains Mahāyāna materials. J. R. Haldar's *Early Buddhist Mythology* includes legends about the realm of the gods. For a survey of Buddhist attitudes toward animals, see the *Hōbōgirin* article "Chikushō." H. G. A. Van Zeyst's "Arupa loka," in *Encyclopedia of Buddhism* 2:103–104, is a brief description of the realm without form. Alex Wayman examines the status of the *gandharva* in "The Intermediate State Dispute in Buddhism," in *Buddhist Insight,* pp. 251–267. A later Pāli cosmological text, the *Lokapaññati,* has been translated into French by E. Denis. A late Thai text on cosmology, the *Traibhūmikathā,* has been translated into English by Frank and Mani Reynolds as *Three Worlds according to King Ruang.*

For discussions of causation, see Kalupahana's *Causality: The Central Philosophy of Buddhism* and Ken Tanaka's "Simultaneous Relation *(Sahabhū-hetu)*: A Study in Buddhist Theory of Causation," *Journal of the International Association of Buddhist Studies* 8, no. 1 (1985): 91–111.

Chapter 12. Karma and *Avijñapti-rūpa*

In addition to the surveys of Indian Buddhism noted in the section on the introduction of the bibliographical essay, Mizuno Kōgen's article "Karman: Buddhist Concepts," *Encyclopedia of Religion* 8:266–268, and John Strong's "Merit: Buddhist Concepts," *Encyclopedia of Religion* 9:383–386, are basic presentations of the subject. Also worth consulting are Fujita Kōtatsu's "The Doctrinal Characteristics of *Karman* in Early Buddhism" in *Indological and Buddhological Studies,* pp. 149–160, and Sasaki Genjun's "The Concept of Kamma in Buddhist Philosophy," *Oriens Extremus* 3 (1956): 185–204.

Buddhist ethics are discussed in Tachibana Shundō's *The Ethics of Buddhism,* H. Saddhatissa's *Buddhist Ethics: Essence of Buddhism,* and G. S. Misra's *Development of Buddhist Ethics.* Because morality is the foundation for Buddhist practice, ethics and karma are examined in many other sources. For a comprehensive bibliography of Buddhist ethics, see Frank Reynolds' "Buddhist Ethics: A Bibliographical Essay," *Religious Studies Review* 5, no. 1 (January 1979): 40–48. Since the world was ordered in accordance with the ethical qualities of beings, many of the sources in chapter 11 are useful.

Morality in the contemporary Theravāda tradition is investigated in a number of articles in a special issue of the *Journal of Religious Ethics* 7 (Spring 1979) and in Winston King's *In the Hope of Nibbāna: An Essay on Theravāda Buddhist Ethics.*

Some of the disputes between the Hīnayāna schools concerning karma are discussed in James McDermott's article "The Kathāvatthu Kamma Debates," *Journal of the American Oriental Society* 95, no. 3 (1975): 424–433. Several issues in the Theravāda interpretation of karma are discussed in McDermott's "Is There Group Karma in Theravāda Buddhism?" *Numen* 23 (1976): 67–80, Jean-

Michel Agasse's "Le Transfert de mérite dans le Bouddhisme Pāli classique," *Journal Asiatique* 226 (1978): 311–332, and John Holt's "Assist the Dead by Venerating the Living: Merit Transfer in the Early Buddhist Tradition," *Numen* 28, no. 1 (1981): 1–28.

The reconciliation of karma with impermanence was a recurring theme in the work of La Vallée Poussin; see, for example, his "La Négation de l'âme et la doctrine de l'acte," *Journal Asiatique* 9, no. 20 (1902): 237–306 and 10, no. 2 (1903): 357–449. The evolution of his position is traced in Maryla Falk's "Nairatmya and Karman: The Life-long Problem of Louis de La Vallée Poussin's Thought" (*Louis de La Vallée Poussin Memorial Volume,* pp. 429–464). Falk includes her own views on the problem of reconciling the no-Self teaching and karma. Vasubandhu's discussion of the imperishability of karma, the *Karmasiddhi-prakaraṇa,* has been translated into English by Stefan Anacker and into French by Étienne Lamotte.

For a short explanation of unmanifested matter, see S. K. Nanayakkara's article "Avijñapti" in *Encyclopedia of Buddhism* 2:460–461, or Sasaki Genjun's "Avijñapti—A Buddhist Moral Concept" in *Inde Ancienne,* vol. 1, pp. 89–98. This topic is discussed at much greater length in Thomas Dowling's unpublished doctoral dissertation "Vasubandhu on the *Avijñapti-rūpa:* A Study in Fifth-Century *Abhidharma* Philosophy," which includes a partial translation of chapter four of the *Abhidharmakośa.*

Chapter 13. The Elimination of Defilements and the Path to Enlightenment

Vasubandhu's *Abhidharmakośa* and Buddhaghosa's *Visuddhimagga* are the basic primary sources for this chapter.

Useful discussions of the defilements can be found in the entries "Anusaya" (1:775–777) and Āśrava" (2:204–214) in the *Encyclopedia of Buddhism* and "Bonnō" (2:121–133) in *Hōbōgirin.* Among the specialized studies on the subject are Lamotte's "The Passions and Impregnations of the Passions in Buddhism," in *Buddhist Studies in Honor of I. B. Horner,* pp. 91–104; P. V. Bapat's "Kleśa (Kilesa) in Buddhism: With Special Reference to Theravāda Buddhism," in *Bonnō no kenkyū;* and Padmanabh S. Jaini's "*Prajñā* and *Dṛṣṭi* in the Vaibhaṣika Abhidharma," in *Prajñāpāramitā and Related Systems,* pp. 403–417.

Sarvāstivāda versions of the path are described by Leon Hurvitz in "Path to Salvation in the *Jñāna-prasthāna,*" *Studies in Indo-Asian Art and Culture* 5 (1977): 77–102, and "The Road to Buddhist Salvation as Described by Vasubhadra," *Journal of the American Oriental Society* 87 (1967): 434–486. The role of the Four Noble Truths in the path is examined by Alfonso Verdu in *Early Buddhist Philosophy in the Light of the Four Noble Truths* and by Alex Wayman in "The Sixteen Aspects of the Four Noble Truths and Their Opposites," *Journal of the International Association of Buddhist Studies* 3, no. 2 (1980): 67–76. Several early alternative versions of the path are investigated in Rod Buckwell's "The Buddhist Path to Liberation," *Journal of the International Association of Buddhist Studies* 7, no. 2 (1984): 7–40.

Meditation has been the subject of a number of important studies in recent years. For Early Buddhism, see Tillman Vetter's *The Ideas and Meditative Practices of Early Buddhism.* General surveys of Theravāda meditation include Winston King's *Theravāda Meditation;* Ñyāṇaponika's *The Heart of Buddhist Meditation,* which focuses on *vipassanā;* and Vajirañāṇa's *Buddhist Meditation in Theory and practice.* Conze's "The Meditation on Death" in *Thirty Years of Buddhist Studies,* pp. 87–104, and George Bond's "Theravāda Buddhism's Meditation on Death and the Symbolism of Initiatory Death," *History of Religions* 19, no. 3 (1980): 237–258, focus on one of the more spectacular forms of early meditation. The trances *(jhāna)* are considered from the Theravāda perspective in Lance Cousins' "Buddhist Jhāna: Its Nature and Attainment according to Pāli Sources," *Religion* 3 (1973): 115–131, and Henepola Gunaratna's *The Path of Serenity and Insight: An Explanation of the Buddhist Jhānas.* The meditations on love, sympathy, and equanimity are investigated in Harvey Aronson's *Love and Sympathy in Theravāda Buddhism* and Nagao Gadjin's "Tranquil Flow of Mind: An Interpretation of *Upekṣā*" in *Indianisme et Bouddhisme,* pp. 245–258. Jack Kornfield's *Living Buddhist Masters* surveys meditation in the contemporary Theravāda tradition.

Few studies of meditation in Hīnayāna schools other than the Theravāda have been written, but among them are Alex Wayman's "Meditation in Theravāda and Mahīśāsaka," *Studia Missionalia* 25 (1976): 1–28, and several studies by Leon Hurvitz on Sarvāstivāda sources in Chinese. Paul Griffiths' *On Being Mindless* compares the trance of cessation in the Theravāda, Vaibhāṣika, and Vijñānavāda traditions. Walpola Rahula contrasts trances in "A Comparative Study of Dhyānas according to Theravāda, Sarvāstivāda, and Mahāyāna" in *Zen and the Taming of the Bull,* pp. 101–109.

For discussions on the goal of the path, see Donald Swearer's "Arhat" in *Encyclopedia of Religion* 1:403–405, André Bareau's "Les Controverses rélatives à la nature de l'arhant dans le Bouddhisme anciens," *Indo-Iranian Journal* 1 (1957): 240–251; La Vallée Poussin's "Le Corps de l'arhat est-il pur?" *Mélanges chinois et bouddhiques* 1 (1932): 5–125; Leon Hurvitz's "The Eight Deliverances" in *Studies in Pāli and Buddhism,* pp. 121–169; and Karel Werner's "Bodhi and Arahataphala: From Early Buddhism to Early Mahāyāna" in *Buddhist Studies: Ancient and Modern,* pp. 167–181. Other sources are included in the discussion of *nirvāṇa* in the section on chapter 3 of the bibliographical essay.

Chapter 14. The Evolution of the Order after Aśoka

For the political history of this period, see the histories in chapter 1, Nalinaksha Dutt's *Mahāyāna Buddhism,* or K. L. Hazra's *Royal Patronage of Buddhism in Ancient India.* Among the general surveys on Buddhist sites are Vidya Dehejia's *Early Buddhist Rock Temples,* Debala Mitra's *Buddhist Monuments,* H. Sarkar's *Studies in Early Buddhist Architecture of India,* Sukumar Dutt's *Buddhist Monks and Monasteries of India,* and James Fergusson's *History of Indian and Eastern Architecture.* Specialized volumes on many of the sites discussed in this chapter have been published. Some of the better studies are Alexander Cunningham's *The*

Stūpa of Bhārhut, John Marshall's *Taxila* and *Guide to Sāñcī,* and James Burgess' *The Buddhist Stūpas of Amarāvatī and Jaggayyapeṭa.*

The Greeks and Buddhism are discussed by Étienne Lamotte in "Alexandre et le Bouddhism," *Bulletin de l'École française d'Extrême-Orient* 44 (1947–1950): 147–162, and George Woodcock's *The Greeks in India.*

Chapter 15. Mahāyāna Texts Composed during the Kuṣāṇa Dynasty

A number of the Buddhist scriptures mentioned in this chapter have been translated into English, but in most cases the translation is based on a later Chinese or Tibetan translation and cannot be considered a reflection of the earliest stage of Mahāyāna scriptures. When used judiciously, however, they can be employed in the investigation of Early Mahāyāna themes. Among the texts that have been translated are the *Bhadrapālasūtra* (also known as the *Pratyutpanna-Buddha-Sammukhāvasthita-samādhi-sūtra*), *Śūraṅgamasamādhisūtra, Vimalakīrtinirdeśa, Lotus Sūtra (Saddharmapuṇḍarīka), Aṣṭasāhasrikā-prajñāpāramitā, Avataṃsaka, Daśabhūmika,* and parts of the *Mahāratnakūṭa, Gaṇḍavyūha,* and *Bodhisattvapiṭaka.*

For a complete listing of translations of Mahāyāna texts into English, French, and German, see the revised edition of Peter Pfandt's *Mahāyāna Texts Translated into Western Languages: A Bibliographical Guide.* The Chinese Buddhist bibliographies that Hirakawa consulted while tracing the translations of early scriptures are surveyed in Okabe Kazuo's "The Chinese Catalogues of Buddhist Scriptures," *Komazawa Daigaku Bukkyōgakubu kenkyū kiyō* 38 (1980): 1–13 (left).

Secondary studies of many of these Buddhist scriptures are listed in the sections on chapters 17 and 18 of the bibliographical essay. However, the following textual studies of the composition of the *Aṣṭasāhasrikā-prajñāpāramitā* should be mentioned here. Lewis Lancaster has extensively studied this text; some of his research is incorporated into his articles "The Chinese Translation of the *Aṣṭasāhasrikā-prajñāpāramitāsūtra* Attributed to Chih Ch'ien," *Monumenta Serica* 28 (1968): 246–257, and "The Oldest Mahāyāna Sūtra: Its Significance for the Study of Buddhist Development," *Eastern Buddhist* 8, no. 1 (1975): 30–41. Other studies on the text are Andrew Rawlinson's "The Position of the *Aṣṭasāhasrikā Prajñāpāramitā* in the Development of Early Mahāyāna" in *Prajñāpāramitā and Related Systems,* pp. 3–34, and Edward Conze's "The Composition of the *Aṣṭasāhasrikā Prajñāpāramitā,*" *Bulletin of the School of Oriental and African Studies* 14 (1952): 251–262.

Chapter 16. The Origins of Mahāyāna

For a detailed presentation of Hirakawa's views on *stūpa* worship during the rise of Mahāyāna, see his article in English, "The Rise of Mahāyāna Buddhism and Its Relationship to the Worship of Stūpas," *Memoirs of the Research Department of the Tōyō Bunko* 22 (1963): 57–106. Other works on the *stūpas* and the cult surrounding them are André Bareau's "La Construction et le culte des stūpa d'apres le *Vinayapiṭaka,*" *Bulletin de l'École française d'Extrême-Orient* 50 (1962): 229–274; Mireille Bénisti's "Étude sur la stūpa dans l'Inde ancienne," *Bulletin de l'École française d'Extrême-Orient* 50 (1960): 37–116; P. C. Bagchi's "The Eight Great Caityas and Their Cult," *Indian Historical Quarterly* 17 (1941): 223–235; Kajiyama Yūichi's "Stūpas, the Mother of Buddhas and Dharma-body" in *New Paths in Buddhist Research,* pp. 9–16; the volume edited by Anna Libera Dallapiccola, *The Stūpa: Its Religious, Historical and Architectural Significance;* and Adrian Snodgrass' *The Symbolism of the Stūpa.* Although Hirakawa's views have gained recognition in recent years, they have also been criticized and refined. Shizutani Masao has argued that a proto-Mahāyāna period when the term "Mahāyāna" was not yet used must be postulated, but his arguments have not yet been presented in English. Richard Robinson has criticized arguments for the importance of lay believers in "The Ethic of the Householder Bodhisattva," *Bharati* (1966): 31–55. Paul Harrison also stresses the role of monastic bodhisattvas in "Who Gets to Ride in the Great Vehicle? Self-Image and Identity Among the Followers of the Early Mahāyāna," *Journal of the International Association of Buddhist Studies* 10, no. 1 (1987): 67–89. Hirakawa himself admits that *stūpa* worship does not explain the origins of the perfection of wisdom tradition. Gregory Schopen has argued for the importance of the "Cult of the Book" and has discussed a number of religious themes in the rise of Mahāyāna in several technical articles including "Mahāyāna in Indian Inscriptions," *Indo-Iranian Journal* 21 (1979): 1–19, and "The Phrase 'sa pṛthivīpradeśaś caityabhūto bhavet' in the *Vajracchedikā:* Notes on the Cult of the Book in Mahāyāna," *Indo-Iranian Journal* 17 (1975): 147–181.

The gradual transformation of the biography of the Buddha and its possible influence on Mahāyāna thought and practice are discussed in David Snellgrove's "Śākyamuni's Final Nirvāṇa," *Bulletin of the School of Oriental and African Studies* 36 (1973): 399–411; Jaini's "Buddha's Prolongation of Life," *Bulletin of the School of Oriental and African Studies* 21 (1958): 546–552; Bareau's "The Superhuman Personality of the Buddha and Its Symbolism in the *Mahāparinirvāṇasūtra* of the Dharmaguptaka" in *Myths and Symbols,* pp. 9–22; and Telwatte Rahula's *A Critical Study of the Mahāvastu.* Translations of biographies of the Buddha and other primary source material are described in chapter 2.

Borrowing between Hīnayāna schools and Mahāyāna is indicated in Nalinaksha Dutt's *Aspects of Mahāyāna Buddhism and Its Relation to Hīnayāna* (revised as *Mahāyāna Buddhism*) and Heinz Bechert's article "Notes on the Formation of the Buddhist Sects and the Origins of Mahāyāna" in *German Scholars on India,* vol. 1, pp. 6–18. Luis Gómez explores one aspect of this process in "Proto-Mādhyamika in the Pāli Canon," *Philosophy East and West* 26 (1976): 137–165. Alex Wayman discusses the relationship between a Hīnayāna school and Mahāyāna theories of an intrinsically pure mind in "The Mahāsāṅghika and the *Tathāgatagarbha,*" *Journal of the International Association of Buddhist Studies* 1 (1978): 35–50. Lamotte presents the arguments for Northern (Sarvāstivāda) influence in his article "Sur la formation du Mahāyāna" in *Asiatica: Festchrift Friedrich Weller,* pp. 377–396. Graeme MacQueen has argued that ecstatic inspirations may have played a role in the compilation of Mahāyāna *sūtras* in "Inspired Speech in Early Mahāyāna Buddhism," *Religion* 11 (1981): 303-319 and 12 (1982): 49-65. André Bareau summarizes some of these issues in the third appendix of his *Les Sectes bouddhiques du Petit Véhicule,* pp. 296-305.

Chapter 17. The Contents of Early Mahāyāna Scriptures

Since a list of primary sources for Early Mahāyāna Buddhism is included in the section on chapter 15 of the bibliographical essay, secondary literature on early Mahāyāna texts is reviewed below.

Perfection of wisdom texts are surveyed in Edward Conze's *The Prajñāpāramitā Literature* and R. Hikata's *Suvikrāntavikrāmiparipṛcchā Prajñāpāramitāsūtra: An Introductory Essay on Prajñāpāramitā-Literature.* Kao Kuan-ju discusses the *Avataṃsaka* in *Encyclopedia of Buddhism* 2:435-446. Fujita Kōtatsu's article "One Vehicle or Three?" *Journal of Indian Philosophy* 3 (1975): 79-166, is an excellent survey of one of the main themes of the *Lotus Sūtra,* the *ekayāna.* Fujita is also the author of "Pure Land Buddhism and the *Lotus Sūtra*" in *Indianisme et bouddhisme,* pp. 117-130. Lamotte discusses the eternal Buddha portrayed in the *Lotus* in "Lotus et Bouddha supramondain," *Bulletin de l'École française d'Extrême-Orient* 69 (1981): 31-44. Because the *Lotus Sūtra* played a major role in East Asian Buddhism, it has been extensively studied by Japanese scholars. Nakamura Hajime summarizes the work of many of these scholars in English in "A Critical Survey of Studies of the Lotus Sūtra" in *Dengyō Daishi kenkyū,* pp. 1-12 (left).

Indian Pure Land texts are discussed in the articles "Akṣobhya" (1:363-368) and "Amita" (1:434-463) in the *Encyclopedia of Buddhism* and "Amitābha" (1: 235-237) and "Pure and Impure Lands" (12:90-91) in the *Encyclopedia of Religion.* Étienne Lamotte's translation of the *Vimalakīrtinirdeśa* includes an excellent discussion of Buddha-lands. Henri de Lubac discusses Amitābha extensively in his *Aspects du Bouddhisme.* In "Sukhāvatī as a Generalized Religious Goal in Sanskrit Mahāyāna Sūtra Literature," *Indo-Iranian Journal* 19 (1977): 177-210, Gregory Schopen analyzes the use of Pure Land in the many Mahāyāna texts that cite it as a goal but do not give it a central place in their doctrinal presentations. Schopen analyzes the earliest inscription mentioning Amitābha in "The Inscription on the Kuṣān Image of Amitābha and the Character of the Early Mahāyāna in India," *Journal of the International Association of Buddhist Studies* 10, no. 2 (1987): 99-137.

For an introduction to some of the bodhisattvas who became important in the Mahāyāna tradition, see the following articles in the *Encyclopedia of Religion:* "Celestial Buddhas and Bodhisattvas" (3:133-143), "Bhaiṣajyaguru" (2:128-129), "Maitreya" (9:136-141), and "Mañjuśrī" (9:174-175). Mañjuśrī and Maitreya are discussed in Hirakawa's article "Mañjuśrī and the Rise of Mahāyāna Buddhism," *Journal of Asian Studies* [Madras, India] 1, no. 1 (Sept. 1983): 12-33. Lamotte's "Mañjuśrī," *T'oung Pao* 48 (1960): 1-96, traces the development of this bodhisattva beyond Early Buddhism. P. S. Jaini surveys the development of Maitreya in "Stages in the Bodhisattva Career of the

Tathāgata Maitreya," in *Maitreya, The Future Buddha,* pp. 54–90. Baiṣajyaguru is discussed by Leonard Zwilling in "Bhaiṣajyaguru and His Cult" in *Studies in the History of Buddhism,* pp. 413–421.

Chapter 18. Theory and Practice in Early Mahāyāna Buddhism

Several surveys of Mahāyāna thought serve as introductions to the themes of this chapter. Among the older surveys are D. T. Suzuki's *Outlines of Mahāyāna Buddhism* and *On Indian Buddhism,* La Vallée Poussin's "Mahāyāna" in *Encyclopedia of Religion and Ethics* 8:330–336, and Edward Conze's "Mahāyāna Buddhism" in *Thirty Years of Buddhist Studies,* pp. 48–86. Nalinaksha Dutt's *Aspects of Mahāyāna Buddhism and Its Relation to Hīnayāna* and *Mahāyāna Buddhism* are more technical studies but well worth the effort. For a more recent view of Mahāyāna, see Nakamura Hajime's "Buddhism, Schools of: Mahāyāna Buddhism" in *Encyclopedia of Religion* 2:457–472. Doctrinal aspects of Early Mahāyāna are examined in Paul Williams' *Mahāyāna Buddhism.*

La Vallée Poussin's article "Bodhisattva (In Sanskrit Literature)" in *Encyclopedia of Religion and Ethics* 2:739–753 provides a good survey of bodhisattvas. In recent years, a number of good studies have been published on the development of Early Mahāyāna conceptions of the bodhisattva. Among them are A. L. Basham's "The Evolution of the Concept of Bodhisattva" in *The Bodhisattva Doctrine in Buddhism,* pp. 19–59, and Kajiyama Yūichi's "On the Meaning of the Words Bodhisattva and Mahāsattva" in *Indological and Buddhist Studies,* pp. 253–270. The *arhat* and the bodhisattva are compared in Nathan Katz' *Buddhist Images of Human Perfection* and Walpola Rahula's "The Bodhisattva Ideal in Theravāda and Mahāyāna" in *Zen and the Taming of the Bull,* pp. 71–77. For studies of the bodhisattvas portrayed in specific early texts, see Nancy Schuster's "The Bodhisattva Figure in the *Ugraparipṛcchā*" in *New Paths in Buddhist Research,* pp. 26–56, and Nancy Lethcoe's "The Bodhisattva Ideal in the *Aṣṭa* and *Pañca Prajñāpāramitā Sūtras*" in *Prajñāpāramitā and Related Systems,* pp. 263–280. Nancy Schuster's study of texts in which women are changed into men ("Changing the Female Body," *Journal of the International Association of Buddhist Studies* 4, no. 1 [1980]: 24–69) is significant for clarifying the social context of Early Mahāyāna. Luis Gómez's study "The Bodhisattva as Wonder-worker" in *Prajñāpāramitā and Related Systems,* pp. 221–261, presents the more miraculous side of the activity of the bodhisattva. The articles on specific bodhisattvas mentioned in the last chapter should also be consulted.

An Early Mahāyāna meditation on the Buddha is discussed by Paul Harrison in "Buddhānusmṛti in the *Pratyutpanna-Buddha-Sammukhāvasthita-samādhi-sūtra,*" *Journal of Indian Philosophy* 6 (1978): 35–57. For additional information on other Early Mahāyāna meditations, see Priscilla Pedersen's "The Dhyāna Chapter of the *Bodhisattvapiṭaka-sūtra.*" The *Hōbōgirin* includes a survey of precepts for the bodhisattva under "Bosatsukai" (2:133–142). Some of the issues that arise when ethical action is considered in the light of nonsubstantiality and other Mahāyāna teachings are discussed by Luis Gómez in "Emptiness and Moral Perfection," *Philosophy East and West* 23 (1973): 361–373, and Yūki Reimon in

"The Construction of Fundamental Evil in Mahāyāna," *Proceedings of the IXth International Congress for the History of Religions: Tokyo and Kyoto, 1958.*

Mahāyāna versions of the path are succinctly presented in Nakamura Hajime's article "Bodhisattva Path" in *Encyclopedia of Religion* (2:265–269). Two articles in the *Encyclopedia of Religion,* Charles Hallisey's "Pāramitās" (11:196–198) and Tadeusz Skorupski's "Prajñā" (11:477–481), emphasize the early roots of Mahāyāna thought. For a more extensive treatment of the path and perfections, see Har Dayal's classic study *The Bodhisattva Doctrine in Buddhist Sanskrit Literature* or Nalinaksha Dutt's *Mahāyāna Buddhism.* Étienne Lamotte's annotated translation of the *Mahāprajñāpāramitāśāstra* attributed to Nāgārjuna provides extensive information on all of the perfections; his annotations serve as a guide to further sources. Finally, Brian Galloway has collected passages from Indian texts that suggest some Indian groups may have argued for the possibility of sudden advances on the path; see his "Sudden Enlightenment in Indian Buddhism" and "Once Again on the Indian Sudden-Enlightenment Doctrine," *Wiener Zeitschrift für die Kunde Süd- und Ostasiens und Archiv für Indische Philosophie* 25 (1981): 205–211 and 29 (1985): 207–210.

BIBLIOGRAPHY

The bibliography is divided into two sections. The first lists Japanese writings cited by the author in the Japanese-language edition. The second is a list, compiled by the editor-translator, of works in other languages on Indian Buddhism.

Japanese Sources Cited

Akanuma Chizen. *Bigandei-shi Biruma-butsu den* (Japanese translation of the Burmese biography of the Buddha by Bishop Bigandet). Tokyo: Kōshisha shobō, 1915.

———. *Bukkyō kyōri no kenkyū* (Studies in Buddhist doctrine). Nagoya: Hajinkaku shobō, 1939.

———. *Bukkyō kyōten shiron* (A history of the Buddhist canon). Nagoya: Hajinkaku shobō, 1939.

———. *Genshi Bukkyō no kenkyū* (Studies in Early Buddhism). Nagoya: Hajinkaku shobō, 1939.

———. *Indo Bukkyō koyū meishi jiten* (Dictionary of Indian Buddhist proper nouns). Nagoya: Hajinkaku shobō, 1931.

———. *Kanpa shibu Agon goshōroku* (A comparative study of the four *Āgamas* in Chinese and Pāli). Nagoya: Hajinkaku shobō, 1929.

———. *Shakuson* (Biography of Śākyamuni). Kyoto: Hōzōkan, 1934.

Anesaki Masaharu. *Konpon Bukkyō* (Early Buddhism). Tokyo: Hakubunkan, 1910.

Dainihon Bukkyō zensho (Collection of works by Japanese Buddhists). Edited by Bussho kankōkai. 157 vols. Tokyo: Dainihon Bukkyō zensho kankōkai, 1912–1922.

Fujita Kōtatsu. "Genshi Bukkyō ni okeru shisei byōdōron" (The equality of the four castes in Early Buddhism). *Indogaku Bukkyōgaku kenkyū* 2, no. 1 (1953): 55–61.

———. *Genshi jōdo shisō no kenkyū* (Studies in early Pure Land thought). Tokyo: Iwanami shoten, 1970.

———. "Sanjō no seiritsu ni tsuite: byakushibutsu kigenkō" (On the establishment of the Three Vehicles: The origin of the *pratyekabuddha*). *Indogaku Bukkyōgaku kenkyū* 5, no. 2 (1957): 91–100.

Fukuhara Ryōgon. *Jōjitsuron no kenkyū* (A study of the *Satyasiddhiśāstra*). Kyoto: Nagata bushōdō, 1969.

———. *Shitairon no kenkyū* (A study of the Four Noble Truths). Kyoto: Nagata bunshōdō, 1972.

———. *Ubu abidatsumaronsho no hattatsu* (The development of the Sarvāstivāda *abhidharma* treatises). Kyoto: Nagata bunshōdō, 1965.

Funahashi Issai. *Genshi Bukkyō shisō no kenkyū* (Studies in Early Buddhist thought). Kyoto: Hōzōkan, 1952.

———. *Gō no kenkyū* (A study of karma). Kyoto: Hōzōkan, 1954.

Funahashi Suisai. *Kusha no kyōgi oyobi rekishi* (The doctrine and history of the *Abhidharmakośa*). Kyoto: Hōzōkan, 1940.

Hayashima Kyōshō. "Jōdokyō no shōjōgōshokan ni tsuite" (On meditations on a land of purity). In *Higata Hakushi koki kinen ronbunshū,* edited by Higata hakushi koki kinenkai, pp. 231–248. Fukuoka: Kyūshū Daigaku bungakubu, 1964.

———. *Shoki Bukkyō to shakai seikatsu* (Early Buddhism and life in Indian society). Tokyo: Iwanami shoten, 1964.

Higata Ryūshō. *Honshōkyōrui no shisōshiteki kenkyū* (Studies in the history of thought within *jātaka* literature). Tokyo: Tōyō bunko, 1954.

Higata Ryūshō and Kimura Taiken. "Ketsujūshi bunpashi kō" (A history of councils and schisms). In *Kokuyaku daizōkyō: Ronbu,* vol. 13, appendix. Tokyo: Kokuminsha bunko, 1921.

Hirakawa Akira. "Amida butsu to Hōzō bosatsu" (Amitābha Buddha and the bodhisattva Dharmākara). In *Indo shisō to Bukkyō,* edited by Nakamura Hajime Hakushi kanreki kinenkai, pp. 163–178. Tokyo: Shunjūsha, 1973.

———. "Daijō kyōten no hattatsu to Ajaseō no setsuwa" (The development of Mahāyāna Buddhist literature and the legends of King Ajātaśatru). *Indogaku Bukkyōgaku kenkyū* 20, no. 1 (1971): 1–12.

———. "Genshi Bukkyō ni okeru 'hō' no imi" (The meaning of "*dharma*" in Early Buddhism). *Waseda daigaku daigakuin bungaku kenkyūka kiyō* 14 (1968): 1–25.

———. *Genshi Bukkyō no kenkyū* (A study of Early Buddhism). Tokyo: Shunjūsha, 1964.

———. "Muga to shutai" (Selflessness and the subject). In *Muga to jiga* (Selflessness and self), edited by Nakamura Hajime, pp. 381–421. Kyoto: Heirakuji shoten, 1974.

———. "Nyoraizō to shite no Hōzō bosatsu" (The bodhisattva Dharmākara as

Buddha-nature). In *Jōdokyō no shisō to bunka,* edited by Etani Ryūkai Sensei koki kinenkai, pp. 1287–1306. Kyoto: Bukkyō Daigaku, 1972.

———. *Ritsuzō no kenkyū* (A study of the *Vinaya-piṭaka*). Tokyo: Sankibō Busshorin, 1960.

———. "Roku-haramitsu no tenkai" (The development of the six perfections). *Indogaku Bukkyōgaku kenkyū* 21, no. 2 (1973): 23–35.

———. *San'yaku taishō Kusharon sakuin* (Index and concordance to the *Abhidharmakośa*). 3 vols. Tokyo: Daizō shuppansha, 1978.

———. "Setsu issai ubu no ninshikiron" (Sarvāstivāda views on cognition). *Hokkaidō daigaku bungakubu kiyō* 2 (1953): 3–19.

———. "Shingedatsu yori shingedatsu e no tenkai" (The development from liberation through faith to liberation of the mind). *Nihon Bukkyō gakkai nenpō* 31 (1965): 51–68.

———. "Shohō muga no hō" (The meaning of the term *"dharma"* in the phrase "*dharmas* are nonsubstantial"). *Indogaku Bukkyōgaku kenkyū* 16, no. 2 (1968): 396–411.

———. "Shōjō Bukkyō no rinri shisō—gō no rinri: Abidaruma Bukkyō taikei yori" (Ethical thought in Hīnayāna Buddhism: The ethics of karma from the *abhidharma* system). In *Sekai rinri shisōshi sōsho: Indo-hen* (Library on the history of world ethics: Indian volume), pp. 209–239. Tokyo: Gakugei shobō, 1959.

———. "Shoki Bukkyō no rinri" (Ethics in Early Buddhism). In *Kōza Tōyō shisō* (Lectures on Oriental thought), vol. 5, edited by Nakamura Hajime et al., pp. 45–74. Tokyo: Tōkyō Daigaku shuppankai, 1967.

———. "Shoki Daijō Bukkyō no kaigaku to shite no jūzendō" (The path of the ten virtues as Early Mahāyāna precepts). In *Bukkyō kyōdan no kenkyū* (Studies in Buddhist orders), edited by Yoshimura Shuki, pp. 167–203. Kyoto: Hyakkaen, 1968.

———. *Shoki Daijō Bukkyō no kenkyū* (Studies in Early Mahāyāna Buddhism). Tokyo: Shunjūsha, 1968.

———. "Usetsuna to setsunametsu" (Transience). In *Indo Bukkyōgaku ronshū,* edited by Kanakura hakushi koki kinen ronbunshū kankōkai, pp. 159–178. Kyoto: Heirakuji shoten, 1966.

Inoue Tetsujirō and Hori Kentoku. *Shakamuniden* (Biography of Śākyamuni). 1911.

Ishikami Zennō. "Miroku juki wayaku" (Japanese translation of Maitreya's predictions of Buddhahood). *Suzuki gakujutsu zaidan kenkyū kiyō* 4 (1967): 35–48.

———. "Shoki Bukkyō ni okeru dokkyō no imi to dokuju kyōten ni tsuite" (On the meaning of chanting and chanting scriptures in Early Buddhism). *Sankō bunka kenkyūjo nenpō* 2 (1968): 45–90.

Iwamoto Yutaka. *Bukkyō setsuwa kenkyū josetsu* (An introduction to research on Buddhist tales). Kyoto: Hōzōkan, 1967.

———. *Indoshi* (History of India). 1956. Reprint. Tokyo: Sankibō Busshorin, 1982.

———. *Sumāgadāvadāna*. 1968. Reprinted as vol. 5 of *Bukkyō setsuwa kenkyū* (Studies in Buddhist tales). Tokyo: Kaimei shoin, 1978.

Kajiyoshi Kōun. *Genshi hannyagyō no kenkyū* (Studies in early perfection of wisdom literature). Tokyo: Sankibō Busshorin, 1944.

Kanakura Enshō. "Bukkyō ni okeru hō no go no gen'i to hensen" (The original meaning of the term *"dharma"* and its later development). In *Indo tetsugaku Bukkyōgaku kenkyū*. Vol. 1, *Bukkyōgaku-hen* (Studies in Indian philosophy and Buddhist studies. Vol. 1, Buddhist studies). Tokyo: Shunjūsha, 1973.

———. "Bukkyō ni okeru hō no imi" (The meaning of *dharma*). In *Indo tetsugaku Bukkyōgaku kenkyū*. Vol. 1, *Bukkyōgaku-hen* (Studies in Indian philosophy and Buddhist studies. Vol. 1, Buddhist studies), p. 83f. Tokyo: Shunjūsha, 1973.

———. *Indo chūsei seishinshi* (A history of medieval Indian spirituality). 2 vols. Tokyo: Iwanami shoten, 1949, 1962.

———. *Indo kodai seishinshi* (A history of ancient Indian spirituality). Tokyo: Iwanami shoten, 1939.

———. *Indo seishin bunka no kenkyū: toku ni Jaina wo chūshin to shite* (Studies in Indian spiritual culture: With special reference to Jainism). Tokyo: Baifūkan, 1944.

———. *Indo tetsugaku Bukkyōgaku kenkyū*. Vol. 1. *Bukkyōgaku-hen* (Studies in Indian philosophy and Buddhist studies. Vol. 1, Buddhist studies). Tokyo: Shunjūsha, 1973.

———. *Indo tetsugakushi* (The history of Indian philosophy). Kyoto: Heirakuji shoten, 1962.

———. *Indo tetsugaku shiyō* (The essentials of the history of Indian philosophy). Tokyo: Kōbundō, 1948.

———. "Jūji hihō ni taisuru shobuha kaishaku no idō" (A comparison of the explanations of the ten violations of the *Vinaya* as reported by the various schools). In *Indo tetsugaku Bukkyōgaku kenkyū*. Vol. 1, *Bukkyōgaku-hen* (Studies in Indian philosophy and Buddhist studies. Vol. 1, Buddhist studies). Tokyo: Shunjūsha, 1973.

———. *Memyō no kenkyū* (A study of Aśvaghoṣa). Kyoto: Heirakuji shoten, 1966.

Katsumata Shunkyō. *Bukkyō ni okeru shinshikisetsu no kenkyū* (Buddhist theories of mind and consciousness). Tokyo: Sankibō Busshorin, 1961.

Kimura Taiken. *Abidatsumaron no kenkyū* (A study of *abhidharma* treatises). Tokyo: Heigo shuppansha, 1922. Reprinted in *Kimura Taiken zenshū,* vol. 4. Tokyo: Daihōrinkaku, 1968.

———. *Daijō Bukkyō shisōron* (A discourse on Mahāyāna thought). Tokyo: Meiji shoin, 1940. Reprinted in *Kimura Taiken zenshū,* vol. 6. Tokyo: Daihōrinkaku, 1968.

———. *Genshi Bukkyō shisōron* (A discourse on Early Buddhist thought). Tokyo Meiji shoin, 1936. Reprinted in *Kimura Taiken zenshū,* vol. 3. Tokyo: Daihōrinkaku, 1968.

———. *Shōjō Bukkyō shisōron* (A discourse on Hīnayāna Buddhist thought).

Tokyo: Meiji shoin, 1935. Reprinted in *Kimura Taiken zenshū,* vol. 5. Tokyo: Daihōrinkaku, 1968.

Kokuyaku issaikyō (Japanese annotated translations of selected scriptures from the Buddhist canon). Edited by Iwano Masao. New edition. 257 vols. Tokyo: Daitō shuppansha, 1978–present.

Kumoi Shōzen. *Bukkyō kōki jidai no shisō kenkyū* (Studies in [Indian] thought at the time of the rise of Buddhism). Kyoto: Heirakuji shoten, 1967.

Maeda Egaku. *Genshi Bukkyō seiten no seiritsushi kenkyū* (Studies in the history of the formation of the Early Buddhist canon). Tokyo: Sankibō Busshorin, 1964.

———. *Shakuson* (Śākyamuni). Tokyo: Sankibō Busshorin, 1972.

Maeda Eun. *Daijō Bukkyōshiron* (A discourse on the history of Mahāyāna Buddhism). Tokyo: Morie shoten, 1903.

Masunaga Reihō. *Konpon Bukkyō no kenkyū* (Studies in Early Buddhism). Chiba: Kazama shobō, 1948.

Masutani Fumio. *Āgama shiryō ni yoru Butsuden kenkyū* (Research on materials for the biography of the Buddha found in the *Āgamas*). Tokyo: Zaike Bukkyō kyōkai, 1962.

Matsunami Seiren. "*Dasavēyāriya sutta* no wayaku" (Japanese translation of the *Dasavēyāriya sutta*). *Taishō daigaku kenkyū kiyō* 53 (1968): 150–100 (left).

———. "Rokushi gedō no shisō seishin" (The thought and spirituality of the Six Heterodox Teachers). In *Sekai seishinshi kōza.* Vol. 3, *Indo seishin,* pp. 101–118. Tokyo: Risōsha, 1940.

———. "Seisen no goroku: Jainakyō no seiten *Isibhāsiyāiṃ* wayaku" (Records of the sages: A Japanese translation of the Jaina scripture, the *Isibhāsiyāiṃ*). In *Kyūshū daigaku bungakubu sōritsu yonjū shūnen kinen ronbushū* (Festschrift for the fortieth anniversary of the establishment of the humanities division of Kyushu University), pp. 57–140 (left). Fukuoka: Kyūshū Daigaku bungakubu, 1966.

Miyamoto Shōson. *Chūdō shisō oyobi sono hattatsu* (The Middle Way and its development). Kyoto: Hōzōkan, 1944.

———. *Daijō to shōjō* (Mahāyāna and Hīnayāna). Tokyo: Yakumo shoten, 1944.

———. "Gedatsu to nehan no kenkyū" (A study of liberation and *nirvāṇa*). *Waseda daigaku daigakuin bungaku kenkyūka kiyō* 6 (1960).

———. "Hiyūsha, Daitoku Hokku, Tōju, Yumanron no kenkyū" (The Dārṣṭāntikas, Dharmatrāta, Kumāralāta, and the *Dṛṣṭāntapankti*). *Nihon Bukkyōgaku kyōkai nenpō* 1 (1928): 117–192.

———. *Konponchū to kū* (The basis [of Buddhism]: the Middle Way and nonsubstantiality). Tokyo: Daiichi shobō, 1943.

———, ed. *Bukkyō no konpon shinri* (The fundamental truths of Buddhism). Tokyo: Sanseidō, 1956.

Miyasaka Yūshō. *Bukkyō no kigen* (The beginnings of Buddhism). Tokyo: Sankibō Busshorin, 1972.

Mizuno Kōgen. *Bukkyō to wa nanika* (What is Buddhism?). Tokyo: Kyōiku shinchōsha, 1965.

———. *Genshi Bukkyō* (Early Buddhism). Kyoto: Heirakuji shoten, 1956.

———. "Gōsetsu ni tsuite" (On theories of karma). *Indogaku Bukkyōgaku kenkyū* 2, no. 2 (1954): 463–473.

———. "Jūroku daikoku no kenkyū" (A study of the sixteen countries of [central India]). *Bukkyō kenkyū* 4, no. 6 (1940).

———. "Mirinda monkyō-rui ni tsuite" (Concerning the versions of the Questions of King Milinda). *Komazawa Daigaku kenkyū kiyō* 17 (1959): 17–55.

———. "Muihō ni tsuite" (Unconditioned *dharmas*). *Indogaku Bukkyōgaku kenkyū* 10, no. 1 (1962): 1–11.

———. *Pāri Bukkyō wo chūshin to shita no shinshikiron* (Theory of mind and consciousness focusing on Pāli Buddhism). Tokyo: Sankibō Busshorin, 1964.

———. "Pāri seiten no seiritsushijō ni okeru *Mugegedō* oyobi gishaku no chii" (The place of the *Paṭisambhidāmagga* and its commentary in the history of the Pāli canon). *Bukkyō kenkyū* 4, nos. 3–6 (1940–1941).

———. "*Peṭakopadesa* ni tsuite" (On the *Peṭakopadesa*). *Indogaku Bukkyōgaku kenkyū* 7, no. 2 (1959): 52–68.

———. *Shakuson no shōgai* (Biography of Śākyamuni Buddha). Tokyo: Shunjūsha, 1960.

———. "*Sharihotsu abidonron* ni tsuite" (On the *Śāriputrābhidharmaśāstra*). In *Indogaku Bukkyōgaku ronshū,* edited by Kanakura Enshō koki kinen ronbunshū kankōkai, pp. 109–134. Kyoto: Heirakuji shoten, 1966.

Mochizuki Ryōkō. "*Daijōshū bosatsugakuron* ni in'yō sareta *Yuimakyō* Bonbun danpen ni tsuite" (Sanskrit fragments of the *Vimalakīrti-nirdeśa* quoted in the *Śikṣāsamuccaya*). In *Yuimakyō gisho ronshū,* edited by Nihon Bukkyō genryū kenkyūkai, p. 112f. Kyoto: Heirakuji shoten, 1962.

Mochizuki Shinkō. *Bukkyō kyōten seiritsushi ron* (Study of the history of the formation of the Buddhist canon). Kyoto: Hōzōkan, 1946.

Nagai Makoto. *Nanpō shoden Butten no kenkyū* (Studies of Theravāda scriptures). Tokyo: Chūbunkan shoten, 1936.

Nagai Makoto, Ueda Tenzui, and Ono Seiichirō. *Bukkyō no hōritsu shisō* (Buddhist legal thought). Tokyo: Daitō shuppansha, 1936.

Nakamura Hajime. *Genshi Bukkyō no seikatsu rinri* (Early Buddhism and the ethics of livelihood). *Nakamura Hajime senshū,* vol. 15. Tokyo: Shunjūsha, 1972.

———. *Genshi Bukkyō no seiritsu* (The formation of Early Buddhism). *Nakamura Hajime senshū,* vol. 12. Tokyo: Shunjūsha, 1969.

———. *Genshi Bukkyō no shisō* (Early Buddhist thought). *Nakamura Hajime senshū,* vols. 13–14. Tokyo: Shunjūsha, 1970–1971.

———. "Genshi Bukkyō seiten seiritsushi kenkyū no kijun ni tsuite" (On the criteria for research on the history of the formation of the Early Buddhist scripture). In *Nakamura Hajime senshū,* vol. 14, pp. 259–479. Tokyo: Shunjūsha, 1971.

———. "Gokuraku jōdo no kannen no Indogakuteki kaimei to Chibettoteki hen'yō" (The Indological explanation of the concept of a pure land and

its Tibetan development). *Indogaku Bukkyōgaku kenkyū* 11, no. 2 (1963): 131–153.
———. *Gotama Budda: Shakusonden* (Biography of Śākyamuni Buddha). Kyoto: Hōzōkan, 1958.
———. *Indo kodaishi* (History of ancient India). *Nakamura Hajime senshū,* vols. 5–6. Tokyo: Shunjūsha, 1963, 1969.
———. *Indo shisō no shomondai* (Problems in Indian thought). *Nakamura Hajime senshū,* vol. 10. Tokyo: Shunjūsha, 1967.
———. *Indo to Girisha to no shisō kōryū* (The interchange between Indian and Greek thought). *Nakamura Hajime senshū,* vol. 16. Tokyo: Shunjūsha, 1968.
———. *Jōdo sanbukyō* (Japanese translation of the three major Pure Land scriptures). 2 vols. Tokyo: Iwanami shoten, 1963.
———. "Mauriya ōchō no nendai ni tsuite." *Tōhōgaku* 10 (1955).
———. "Sāriputta ni daihyō sareru saishoki no Bukkyō" (The earliest Buddhism as typified by Sāriputta). *Indogaku Bukkyōgaku kenkyū* 14, no. 2 (1966): 455–466.
———. *Shūkyō to shakai rinri* (Religion and social ethics). Tokyo: Iwanami shoten, 1959.
Nanden daizōkyō (Japanese translation of the Pāli canon). Edited by Takakusu Junjirō. 65 vols. Tokyo: Daizōkyō shuppansha, 1935–1941.
Nara Yasuaki. "Bukkyō shijin Mātorichēta no shisōteki tachiba" (The intellectual stance of the Buddhist poet Mātṛceṭa). *Indogaku Bukkyōgaku kenkyū* 2, no. 1 (1953): 135–136.
Nishi Giyū. *Genshi Bukkyō ni okeru hannya no kenkyū* (Studies on the place of wisdom in Early Buddhism). Yokoyama: Ōkurayama bunka kagaku kenkyūjo, 1953.
———. *Shoki Daijō Bukkyō no kenkyū* (Studies in Early Mahāyāna Buddhism). Tokyo: Daitō shuppansha, 1945.
Ogihara Unrai. *Kan'yaku taishō Bonwa daijiten* (Sanskrit-Japanese dictionary with reference to Chinese translations). Taipei: Hsin-wen-feng ch'u-pan kung-ssu, 1988.
———. *Ogihara Unrai bunshū* (Collected essays). Tokyo: Taishō Daigaku Bukkyōgaku Ogihara Unrai kinen kenkyūkai, 1938.
Ōyama Ken'ei. *Ibushūrinron-jukki hotsujin* (Introduction to Tzu-en's *I-bu-tsung-lun-lun shu-chi*). Kyoto: Nagata bunshōdō, 1891.
Saigusa Mitsuyoshi. "Sōōbu no kyō no kazu ni tsuite" (On the number of texts in the *Saṃyutta-nikāya*). *Shūkyō kenkyū* 192 (1967): 1–32.
Sakaino Kōyō. *Kairitsu kenkyū* (Studies on the precepts). 2 vols. in *Kokuyaku daizōkyō.* Tokyo: Daitō shuppansha, 1928.
Sakamoto Yukio. *Kegon kyōgaku no kenkyū* (Studies in the doctrines of the *Avataṃsaka*). 2d ed. Kyoto: Heirakuji shoten, 1964.
Sakurabe Ken. "Engaku kō" (The *pratyekabuddha*). *Ōtani gakuhō* 36, no. 3 (1956): 40–51.
———. *Kusharon no kenkyū: kai konpon* (Studies in *Abhidharmakośa:* The chapters on elements and faculties). Kyoto: Hōzōkan, 1969.

Sasaki Genjun. *Abidatsuma shisō kenkyū* (Studies in *abhidharma* thought). Tokyo: Kōbundō, 1958.

———. *Bukkyō shinrigaku no kenkyū* (Studies in Buddhist psychology). Tokyo: Nihon gakujutsukai, 1960.

Satō Mitsuo. *Genshi Bukkyō kyōdan no kenkyū* (A study of the Early Buddhist order). Tokyo: Sankibō Busshorin, 1963.

Satō Mitsuo and Satō Ryōchi. *Ronji fu Kakuon chū* (The Kāthavatthu and Buddhaghosa's commentary). Tokyo: Daitō shuppansha, 1933.

Satō Ryōjun. "*Nettipakaraṇa* ni tsuite" (On the *Nettipakaraṇa*). *Indogaku Bukkyōgaku kenkyū* 12, no. 2 (1966): 124–126.

Shiio Benkyō. *Bukkyō kyōten gaisetsu* (Outline of the Buddhist canon). Tokyo: Kōshisha, 1933.

Shizutani Masao. *Indo Bukkyō himei mokuroku* (Catalog of Indian Buddhist inscriptions). Kyoto: Heirakuji shoten, 1979.

———. "*Konkōmyōkyō* 'Gōshōmetsubon' no seiritsu ni tsuite" (On the composition of the chapter on eliminating obstacles in the Sūtra on Golden Light). *Ryūkoku daigaku ronshū* 328 (1940).

Tachibana Shundō. *Kōshō Shakusonden* (A critical biography of the Buddha). Tokyo: Fuzanbō, 1940.

Taishō shinshū daizōkyō (Newly edited Buddhist canon of the Taishō era). Edited by Takakusu Junjirō et al. 100 vols. Tokyo: Daizō shuppansha, 1924–1934.

Takada Osamu. *Butsuzō no kigen* (The origins of Buddhist images). Tokyo: Iwanami shoten, 1967.

———. *Indo nankai no Bukkyō bijutsu* (Buddhist art in India and Southeast Asia). Tokyo: Sōgeisha, 1943.

Takagi Shun'ichi. *Kusha kyōgi* (*Abhidharmakośa* doctrine). 1919.

Tatsuyama Shōshin. *Indo Bukkyōshi* (History of Indian Buddhism). Kyoto: Hōzōkan, 1944.

———. *Nanpō Bukkyō no yōtai* (The condition of Southern [Theravāda] Buddhism). Tokyo: Kōbundō, 1964.

Teramoto Enga. *Chibettogo bunpō* (Tibetan grammar). Kyoto: Heirakuji shoten, 1940.

———. *Chibetto shoden Jōbukutenten-zō ibusetsushū* (The Tibetan version of Vinītadeva's *Nikāya-bhedopadeśana-saṅgraha*). 1935.

———. *Tāranāta Indo Bukkyōshi* (Tāranātha's history of Indian Buddhism). Tokyo: Heigo shuppansha, 1928.

———. *Zōkanwa-san'yaku taikō Ibushūrinron* (Comparison of the Tibetan, Chinese, and Japanese translations of the *Samayabhedoparacanacakra*). Reprint. Tokyo: Kokusho kankōkai, 1967.

Tokiwa Daijō. *Butsuden shūsei* (Compilation of the biography of the Buddha). Tokyo: Heigo shuppansha, 1924.

Tokiya Kōki. "Chibetto-yaku no *Bosatsuzōkyō* no yakuchū" (Annotated Japanese translation of the Tibetan translation of the *Bodhisattva-piṭaka*). *Ryūkoku daigaku ronshū* 397 (1971): 122f.

Tomomatsu Entai. *Bukkyō ni okeru bunpai no risō to jissai* (Distribution [of wealth] in Buddhism: The ideal and the actual situation). 2 vols. Tokyo: Shunjūsha, 1965, 1970.

———. *Bukkyō keizai shisō kenkyū* (Studies in Buddhist economic thought). Tokyo: Tōhō shoin, 1932.

Tsuji Naoshirō. *Indo* (India). Tokyo: Meicho fukyūkai, 1943.

———. *Indo bunmei no akebono* (The dawn of Indian civilization). Tokyo: Iwanami shoten, 1967.

———. *Rigu weda sanka* (Hymns of the Ṛg-veda). Tokyo: Iwanami shoten, 1970.

———. *Sansukuritto bungakushi* (A history of Sanskrit literature). Tokyo: Iwanami shoten, 1973.

———. *Wēda to Upanishadō* (The *Vedas* and *Upaniṣads*). *Tsuji Naoshirō chosakushū*, vol. 1. Kyoto: Hōzōkan, 1981.

Tsukamoto Keishō. *Ashōka Ō* (King Aśoka). Kyoto: Heirakuji shoten, 1973.

———. "Kandahār shutsudo no Aśoka hōchoku" (The Aśokan edict discovered at Kandahār). In *Indogaku Bukkyōgaku ronshū,* edited by Kanakura Enshō koki kinen ronbunshū kankōkai, pp. 153–166. Kyoto: Heirakuji shoten, 1966.

———. *Shoki Bukkyō kyōdanshi no kenkyū* (Studies on the Early Buddhist order). Kyoto: Heirakuji shoten, 1966.

Tsukinowa Kenryū. *Butten no hihanteki kenkyū* (Critical studies in Buddhist scriptures). Kyoto: Hyakkaen, 1971.

Ui Hakuju. "Agon ni arawareta Butsuda-kan" (The view of the Buddha in the *Āgamas*). In *Indo tetsugaku kenkyū,* vol. 4, pp. 69–245. Tokyo: Kōshisha, 1924–1930. Reprint. Tokyo: Iwanami shoten, 1965.

———. "Agon no seiritsu ni kansuru kōsatsu" (A study on the formation of the *Āgamas*). In *Indo tetsugaku kenkyū,* vol. 3, pp. 303–418. Tokyo: Kōshisha, 1924–1930. Reprint. Tokyo: Iwanami shoten, 1970.

———. "Aiku-Ō kokubun" (The inscriptions of King Aśoka). In *Indo tetsugaku kenkyū,* vol. 4, p. 337. Tokyo: Kōshisha, 1924–1930. Reprint. Tokyo: Iwanami shoten, 1965.

———. *Bukkyō hanron* (A summary of Buddhism). Tokyo: Iwanami shoten, 1947–1948.

———. *Bukkyō kyōtenshi* (History of the Buddhist canon). Tokyo: Tōsei shuppansha, 1957.

———. *Bukkyō shisō kenkyū* (Studies in Buddhist thought). Tokyo: Iwanami shoten, 1940.

———. "Butsumetsu nendairon" (Theories about the death of the Buddha). In *Indo tetsugaku kenkyū,* vol. 2, pp. 2–111. Tokyo: Kōshisha, 1924–1930. Reprint. Tokyo: Iwanami shoten, 1970.

———. "Genshi Bukkyō shiryōron" (Concerning the sources for Early Buddhism). In *Indo tetsugaku kenkyū,* vol. 2, pp. 112–260. Tokyo: Kōshisha, 1924. Reprint. Tokyo: Iwanami shoten, 1970.

———. "Hasshōdō no gen'i to sono hensen" (The original meaning of the

Eightfold Path and its later developments). In *Indo tetsugaku kenkyū,* vol. 3, pp. 3–61. Tokyo: Kōshisha, 1924–1930. Reprint. Tokyo: Iwanami shoten, 1970.

———. *Indo tetsugakushi* (History of Indian Buddhism). Tokyo: Iwanami shoten, 1932.

———. "Jūni innen no kaishaku: engisetsu no igi" (The explanation of the twelve causal links: The significance of Dependent Origination). In *Indo tetsugaku kenkyū,* vol. 2, pp. 261–343. Tokyo: Kōshisha, 1924–1930. Reprint. Tokyo: Iwanami shoten, 1970.

———. "Rokujūni kenron" (The sixty-two [heterodox] views). In *Indo tetsugaku kenkyū,* vol. 3, pp. 203–302. Tokyo: Kōshisha, 1924–1930. Reprint. Tokyo: Iwanami shoten, 1970.

———. "Rokushi gedō kenkyū" (A study of the Six Heterodox Teachers). In *Indo tetsugaku kenkyū,* vol. 2, pp. 345–423. Tokyo: Kōshisha, 1924–1930. Reprint. Tokyo: Iwanami shoten, 1970.

Watanabe Baiyū. *Abidatsumaron no kenkyū* (Studies of *abhidharma* treatises). Tokyo: Heibonsha, 1954.

Watanabe Kaigyoku. *Ōbei no Bukkyō* (Buddhism in America and Europe). In *Watanabe Kaigyoku ibunshū: Kogetsu zenshū,* vol. 1, p. 1f. Tokyo: Daitō shuppansha, 1933.

Watanabe Shōkō. *Bukkyō no ayumi* (The course of Buddhism). Tokyo: Daihōrinkaku, 1957.

———. *Okyō no hanashi* (Talks on the *sūtras*). Tokyo: Iwanami shoten, 1967.

———. *Shin Shakusonden* (A new biography of the Buddha). Tokyo: Daihōrinkaku, 1966.

Watsuji Tetsurō. "Bukkyō ni okeru hō no gainen to kū no benshōhō" (The concept of *dharma* and the dialectics of nonsubstantiality within Buddhism). In *Watsuji Tetsurō zenshū,* vol. 9, p. 461f. Tokyo: Iwanami shoten, 1961–1963.

———. *Bukkyō rinri shisōshi* (The history of Buddhist ethics). *Watsuji Tetsurō zenshū,* vol. 19. Tokyo: Iwanami shoten, 1961–1963.

———. "Bukkyō tetsugaku no saisho no tenkai" (The first developments of Buddhist philosophy). In *Watsuji Tetsurō zenshū,* vol. 5. Tokyo: Iwanami shoten, 1961–1963.

———. *Genshi Bukkyō no jissen tetsugaku* (The practical philosophy of Early Buddhism). Tokyo: Iwanami shoten, 1927.

———. "Jinkaku to jinruisei" (Personality and human nature). In *Watsuji Tetsurō zenshū,* vol. 9. Tokyo: Iwanami shoten, 1961–1963.

Yabuki Keiki. *Amida Butsu no kenkyū* (Studies on Amitābha Buddha). Tokyo: Meiji shoin, 1911.

Yamada Ryūjō. *Bongo Butten no shobunken* (Sanskrit Buddhist literature). Kyoto: Heirakuji shoten, 1959.

———. *Daijō Bukkyō seiritsuron josetsu* (Preliminary studies for a theory of the formation of Mahāyāna Buddhism). Kyoto: Heirakuji shoten, 1959.

Yamaguchi Susumu. *Bukkyō shisō nyūmon* (Introduction to Buddhist thought). Tokyo: Risōsha, 1968.

———. "Daijō hi-Butsusetsu ni taisuru Seshin no ronpa: *Shakukiron* no daiyonshō ni taisuru ichi kaidai" (Vasubandhu's refutation of the position that Mahāyāna is not the teaching of the Buddha: A bibliographical introduction to chapter four of the *Vyākhyā-yukti*). In *Tōhō gakkai sōritsu daijūgoshūnen: Tōhōgaku ronshū,* p. 269f. Tokyo: Tōhō gakkai, 1962.

———. "Indo Bukkyō haseki no ichi in'en" (A reason for the analysis of Indian Buddhism). In *Yamaguchi Susumu Bukkyōgaku bunshū* (Collected essays in Buddhist studies by Yamaguchi Susumu), vol. 1. Tokyo: Shunjūsha, 1972.

———. *Seshin no Jōgōron* (Vasubandhu's *Karmasiddhi-prakaraṇa*). Kyoto: Hōzōkan, 1951.

———. "Seshin no *Shakukiron* ni tsuite" (Vasubandhu's *Vyākhyā-yukti*). *Nihon Bukkyō gakkai nenpō* 25 (1960): 35–68.

———. *Yamaguchi Susumu Bukkyōgaku bunshū* (Collected essays in Buddhist studies by Yamaguchi Susumu), vol. 1. Tokyo: Shunjūsha, 1972.

Yamaguchi Susumu and Funahashi Issai. *Kusharon no genten kaimei: Sekenbon* (A textual study of the *Abhidharmakośa:* Chapter on cosmology). Kyoto: Hōzōkan, 1955.

Yamaguchi Susumu, Ōchō Enichi, Andō Toshio, and Funahashi Issai. *Bukkyōgaku josetsu* (An introduction to Buddhist studies). Kyoto: Heirakuji shoten, 1961.

Yamamoto Tatsurō, ed. *Indoshi* (History of India). Tokyo: Yamakawa shuppansha, 1977.

Yuyama Akira. "Kamalaśīla no *Bhāvanākrama* ni in'yō sareta *Yuimakyō*" (Quotations of the *Vimalakīrtinirdeśa* in Kamalaśīla's *Bhāvanākrama*). *Tōhōgaku* 38 (1969): 105–125.

Related Readings

Abhidhammattha-saṅgaha. Translated by Shwe Zan Aung and C. A. F. Rhys Davids as *Compendium of Philosophy.* London: Luzac, 1910. Reprint. 1956.

Adikaram, E. W. *Early History of Buddhism in Ceylon.* Migoda: Puswella, 1946.

Agasse, Jean-Michel. "Le Transfert de mérite dans le Bouddhisme Pāli classique." *Journal Asiatique* 226 (1978): 311–332.

Ahir, D. C. *Buddhist Shrines in India.* Delhi: B. R. Publishing, 1986.

Alexander, P. C. *Buddhism in Kerala.* Annamalainagar: Annamalai University, 1949.

Aṅguttara Nikāya. Translated by F. L. Woodward and E. M. Hare as *The Book of Gradual Sayings.* Pāli Text Society Translation Series, vols. 22, 24–27. London: Luzac, 1951–1955. (Originally published by Oxford University Press, London, 1932–1936.)

Aronson, Harvey. *Love and Sympathy in Theravāda Buddhism.* Delhi: Motilal Banarsidass, 1980.

Āryaśūra. *Jātaka-mālā.* Edited by P. L. Vaidya. Buddhist Sanskrit Texts, vol. 21. Darbhanga: Mithila Institute, 1959.

———. Translated by J. S. Speyer as *The Jātakamālā: Garland of Birth-stories of Āryaśūra.* Delhi: Motilal Banarsidass, 1971. (Originally published in 1895.)

———. Translated by Peter Khoroche as *Once the Buddha Was a Monkey.* Chicago: University of Chicago Press, 1989.

Aśoka. *The Edicts of Aśoka.* Edited and translated by N. A. Nikam and Richard P. McKeon. Chicago: University of Chicago Press, 1958.

Aṣṭasāhasrikāprajñāpāramitā. Edited by Edward Conze. Calcutta: Asiatic Society, 1958.

———. Edited by Edward Conze as *The Gilgit Manuscript of the Aṣṭādaśasāhasrikāprajñāpāramitā: Chapters 55 to 70, corresponding to the 5th Abhisamaya.* Rome: Istituto Italiano per il Medio ed Estremo Oriente, 1962.

———. Edited by Edward Conze as *The Gilgit Manuscript of the Aṣṭādaśasāhasrikāprajñāpāramitā: Chapters 70 to 82 corresponding to the 6th, 7th and 8th Abhisamayas.* Rome: Istituto Italiano per il Medio ed Estremo Oriente, 1974.

———. Edited by P. L. Vaidya. Buddhist Sanskrit Texts, vol. 4. Darbhanga: Mithila Institute, 1960.

———. Translated by Edward Conze as *The Perfection of Wisdom in Eight Thousand Lines and Its Verse Summary.* Bolinas: Four Seasons Foundation, 1973.

Aśvaghoṣa. *Buddhacarita.* Translated by Edward H. Johnston as *The Acts of the Buddha.* Calcutta: Baptist University Press, 1936; *Acta Orientalia* 15 (1937): 1–128. Reprint. Delhi: Munshiram Manoharlal, 1972.

Avadānaśataka. Edited by P. L. Vaidya. Buddhist Sanskrit Texts, vol. 19. Darbhanga: Mithila Institute, 1959.

Avataṃsakasūtra. Translated by Thomas Cleary as *The Flower Ornament Scripture.* Boulder, Colo.: Shambala, 1984.

Bagchi, Prabodh Chandra. "The Eight Great Caityas and Their Cult." *Indian Historical Quarterly* 17 (1941): 223–235.

Banerjee, Anukul Chandra. *Sarvāstivāda Literature.* Calcutta: Mukhopadyaya, 1957.

Bapat, P. V. "Kleśa (Kilesa) in Buddhism: With Special Reference to Theravāda Buddhism." In *Bonnō no kenkyū,* edited by Sasaki Genjun, pp. 119–128. Tokyo: Shimizu Kōbundō, 1975.

———, ed. *2500 Years of Buddhism.* Delhi: Ministry of Information and Broadcasting, 1959.

Bareau, André. *L'Absolu en philosophie bouddhique: Évolution de la notion d'asaṃskṛta.* Paris: Centre de Documentation universitaire, 1951.

———. "Buddhism, Schools of: Hīnayāna Buddhism." *Encyclopedia of Religion* 2:444–457.

———. "La Construction et le culte des stūpa d'après le *Vinayapiṭaka.*" *Bulletin de l'École française d'Extrême-Orient* 50 (1962): 229–274.

———. "Les Controverses rélatives à la nature de l'arhant dans le bouddhisme anciens." *Indo-Iranian Journal* 1 (1957): 240–251.

———. "La Date du Nirvāṇa." *Journal Asiatique* 241 (1953): 27–62.

———. "La Jeunesse du Bouddha dans les *Sūtrapiṭaka* et les *Vinayapiṭaka* anciens." *Bulletin de l'École française d'Extrême-Orient* 61 (1974): 199–274.

———. "Les Origines du *Śāriputrābhidharmaśāstra.*" *Le Muséon* 63 (1950): 69–95.

———. "Le Parinirvāṇa du Bouddha et la naissance de la religion bouddhique." *Bulletin de l'École française d'Extrême-Orient* 61 (1974): 275–299.

———. "Un Personnage bien mysterieux: L'Espouse du Bouddha." In *Indological and Buddhist Studies: Volume in Honor of Professor J. W. de Jong on His Sixtieth Birthday,* edited by L. Hercus et al., pp. 31–59. Canberra: Australian National University Press, Faculty of Asian Studies, 1982.

———. "The Place of the Buddha Gautama in the Buddhist Religion during the Reign of Aśoka." In *Buddhist Studies in Honor of Walpola Rahula,* edited by Somaratna Balasooriya et al., pp. 1–9. London: Fraser, 1980.

———. *Les Premiers Conciles bouddhiques.* Paris: Presses universitaires de France, 1958.

———. *Recherches sur la biographie du Buddha dans les Sūtrapiṭaka et les Vinayapiṭaka anciens.* 3 vols. Paris: Publications de l'École française d'Extrême-Orient, 1970–1983.

———. *Les Religiones de l'Inde.* Vol. 3, *Bouddhisme, Jaïnisme religiones archaïques,* pp. 1–246. Paris: Payot, 1966.

———. *Les Sectes bouddhiques du Petit Véhicule.* Saigon: École française d'Extrême-Orient, 1955.

———. "Les Sectes bouddhiques du Petit Véhicule et leurs *Abhidharmapiṭaka.*" *Bulletin de l'École française d'Extrême-Orient* 50 (1952): 1–11.

———. "The Superhuman Personality of the Buddha and Its Symbolism in the *Mahāparinirvāṇasūtra* of the Dharmaguptaka." In *Myths and Symbols: Studies in Honor of Mircea Eliade,* edited by Joseph Kitagawa et al., pp. 9–22. Chicago: University of Chicago Press, 1969.

———. "Trois traités sur les sectes bouddhiques attibués à Vasumitra, Bhavya et Vinitadeva." *Journal Asiatique* 242 (1954): 229–266; 244 (1956): 167–200.

Barua, Benimadhab. *The History of Pre-Buddhist Indian Philosophy.* Delhi: Motilal Banarsidass, 1970. (Originally published by University of Calcutta, Calcutta, 1921.)

———. "Pratītya-samutapāda as Basic Concept of Buddhist Thought." In *B[imala]. C[hurn]. Law Volume,* vol. 1, edited by D. R. Bhandarkar, pp. 574–589. Calcutta: Indian Research Institute, 1945.

Barua, Dipak Kumar. *An Analytical Study of the Four Nikāyas.* Calcutta: Rabindra Bharati University, 1971.

———. *Vihāras in Ancient India: A Survey of Buddhist Monasteries.* Calcutta: Indian Publications, 1969.

Basham, A. L. "Aśoka." *Encyclopedia of Religion* 1:466–469.

———. "Aśoka and Buddhism: A Reexamination." *Journal of the International Association of Buddhist Studies* 5 (1982): 131–143.

———. "The Background to the Rise of Buddhism." In *Studies in the History of Buddhism,* edited by A. K. Narain, pp. 13–32. Delhi: B. R. Publishing, 1980.

———. "The Evolution of the Concept of Bodhisattva." In *The Bodhisattva Doctrine in Buddhism,* edited by Leslie Kawamura, pp. 19–59. Waterloo, Ont.: Wilfred Laurier University Press, 1981.

———. *History and Doctrine of the Ājīvikas: A Vanished Indian Religion.* London: Luzac, 1951.

———. *The Wonder that Was India: A Survey of the Culture of the Indian Sub-continent before the Coming of the Muslims.* New York: Grove Press, 1959.

Bechert, Heinz. "The Beginnings of Buddhist Historiography." In *Religion and Legitimation of Power in Sri Lanka,* edited by Bardwell Smith, pp. 1–12. Chambersburg, Pa.: Anima Publications, 1978.

———. *Buddhismus, Staat und Geselleschaft in den Ländern des Theravāda-Buddhismus.* 3 vols. Frankfurt: Metzner, 1967; Wiesbaden: Harrassowitz, 1967, 1973.

———. "The Date of the Buddha Reconsidered." *Indologica Taurinensia* 10 (1982): 29–36.

———. "The Importance of Aśoka's So-called Schism Edict." In *Indological and Buddhological Studies: Volume in Honor of Professor J. W. de Jong on His Sixtieth Birthday,* edited by L. Hercus et al., pp. 61–68. Canberra: Australian National University, Faculty of Asian Studies, 1982.

———. "Mahāyāna Literature in Sri Lanka: The Early Phase." In *Prajñāpāramitā and Related Systems: Studies in Honor of Edward Conze,* edited by Lewis Lancaster, pp. 361–368. Berkeley Buddhist Studies Series, no. 1. Berkeley: University of California, 1977.

———. "Notes on the Formation of the Buddhist Sects and the Origins of Mahāyāna." In *German Scholars on India,* edited by Cultural Department of the Embassy of the Federal Republic of Germany in New Delhi, vol. 1, pp. 6–18. Varanasi: Chowkamba Sanskrit Series Office, 1973.

———. "Saṃgha." *Encyclopedia of Religion* 13:36–40.

———. *Die Sprache der ältesten buddhistischen Überlieferung/The Language of the Earliest Buddhist Tradition.* Göttingen: Vandenhoeck & Ruprecht, 1980.

———. "Theravāda Buddhist Saṅgha: Some General Observations on Historical and Political Factors in Its Development." *Journal of Asian Studies* 24, no. 4 (1970): 761–778.

Bechert, Heinz, and Richard Gombrich. *The World of Buddhism.* New York: Facts on File, 1984.

Bénisti, Mireille. "Étude sur la stūpa dans l'Inde ancienne." *Bulletin de l'École française d'Extrême-Orient* 50 (1960): 37–116.

Beyer, Stephan. *The Buddhist Experience: Sources and Interpretations.* Encino, Calif.: Dickenson Publishing, 1974.

Bhaiṣajyaguru-sūtra. Translated by Gregory Schopen in "The *Bhaiṣajyguru-sūtra* and the Buddhism of Gilgit." Ph.D. diss., Australian National University, 1978.

Bhattacharya, Narendra Nath. *History of Researchers on Indian Buddhism.* New Delhi: Munshiram Manoharlal, 1981.

Bloch, J. *Les Inscriptions d'Aśoka.* Paris: Société d'Edition les Belles Lettres, 1950.

Bloomfield, Maurice. *The Religion of the Veda.* New York: G. P. Putnam's Sons, 1908.

Bond, George D. "Theravāda Buddhism's Meditation on Death and the Symbolism of Initiatory Death." *History of Religions* 19, no. 3 (1980): 237–258.

———. *Word of the Buddha: The Tipiṭaka and Its Interpretation in Early Buddhism.* Colombo: Gunasena, 1982.

Brahmajāla-suttanta. Translated by Bhikkhu Bodhi as *The Discourse on the All-Embracing Net of Views: The Brahmajāla Sutta and Its Commentarial Exegesis.* Kandy: Buddhist Publications Society, 1978.

———. Translated by T. W. Rhys Davids and C. A. F. Rhys Davids as *The Sacred Net,* in *Dialogues of the Buddha,* vol. 2. Sacred Books of the Buddhists, no. 3. London: Luzac, 1959.

Bronkhorst, Johannes. "Dharma and Abhidharma." *Bulletin of the School of Oriental and African Studies* 48, no. 2 (1985): 305–319.

Brough, John. *The Gāndhārī Dharmapada.* London: Oxford University Press, 1962.

Buckwell, Rod. "The Buddhist Path to Liberation." *Journal of the International Association of Buddhist Studies* 7, no. 2 (1984): 7–40.

Buddhaghosa. *Atthasālinī.* Translated by Pe Maung Tin and C. A. F. Rhys Davids as *The Expositor.* Pāli Text Society Translation Series, no. 8. London: Pāli Text Society, 1920–1921. Reprint. London: Luzac, 1958.

———. *Kathāvatthu-aṭṭhakathā.* Translated by B. C. Law as *The Debates Commentary.* Pāli Text Society Translation Series, no. 28. London: Luzac, 1969. (Originally published by Oxford University Press, London, 1940.)

———. *Samantapāsādikā.* 7 vols. Edited by J. Takakusu and M. Nagai. London: Pāli Text Society, 1924–1947.

———. *Samantapāsādikā.* Introductory chapter translated by N. A. Jayawickrama as *The Inception of Discipline and the Vinayanidāna.* Sacred Books of the Buddhists, vol. 21. London: Luzac, 1962.

———. *Samantapāsādikā.* Translated by B. V. Bapat and Hirakawa Akira as *Shan-chien-p'i-p'o-sha: A Chinese Version by Saṅghabhadra of Samantapāsādikā.* Poona: Bhandarkar Oriental Research Institute, 1970.

———. *Sammohavinodanī.* Translated by Ñāṇamoli as *The Dispeller of Illusion.* Pāli Text Society Translation Series. London: Luzac, 1983.

———. *Visuddhimagga.* Edited by H. C. Warren and D. Kosambi. Harvard Oriental Series, no. 41. Cambridge: Harvard University Press, 1950.

———. *Visuddhimagga.* 2d ed. Translated by Ñāṇamoli as *The Path of Purification.* Berkeley: Shambala, 1976. (Originally published by A. Semage, Colombo, 1964.)

———. *Visuddhimagga.* Translated by Pe Maung Tin as *The Path of Purity.* 3 vols. London: Pāli Text Society, 1923–1931.

Buddhavaṃsa. Translated by I. B. Horner as *Chronicle of Buddhas.* Sacred Books of the Buddhists, vol. 58. London: Luzac, 1975.

Burgess, James. *The Buddhist Stūpas of Amarāvatī and Jaggayyapeṭa.* Varanasi: Indological Book House, 1970.

Bu-ston. *History of Buddhism*. Translated by E. Obermiller. Tokyo: Suzuki Research Foundation, 1964. (Originally published by Institut für Buddhismus-Kunde, Heidelberg, 1931–1932.)

Cariyāpiṭaka. Translated by I. B. Horner as *The Basket of Conduct*. Sacred Books of the Buddhists, vol. 58. London: Luzac, 1975.

Carratelli, G. Pugliese, and G. Garbini. *A Bilingual Graeco-Aramaic Edict by Aśoka: The First Greek Inscription Discovered in Afghanistan*. Serie Orientale Roma, vol. 29. Rome: Istituto Italiano per il Medio ed Estremo Oriente, 1954.

Carrithers, Michael. *The Buddha*. New York: Oxford University Press, 1983.

———. *Forest Monks of Sri Lanka: An Anthropological and Historical Study*. Delhi: Oxford University Press, 1983.

Carter, John Ross. *Dhamma: Western Academic and Sinhalese Buddhist Interpretations*. Tokyo: Hokuseidō Press, 1978.

Carter, John Ross, et al. *The Threefold Refuge in the Theravāda Buddhist Tradition*. Chambersburg, Pa.: Anima Publications, 1982.

Chang, Kun. *Comparative Study of the Kaṭhinavastu*. Indo-Iranian Monographs, no. 1. The Hague: Mouton, 1957.

Chau, Thich Minh. *Chinese Āgamas and the Pāli Majjhima Nikāya*. Saigon: Institute of Higher Buddhist Studies, 1964.

———. *Milindapañha and the Nāgasenabhikṣuśāstra: A Comparative Study through Pāli and Chinese Sources*. Calcutta: K. L. Mukhopadyaya, 1964.

Chau, Thich Thein. "The Literature of the Pudgalavādins." *Journal of the International Association of Buddhist Studies* 7, no. 1 (1984): 7–40.

———. "Les Réponses des Pudgalavādins aux critiques des écoles bouddhiques." *Journal of the International Association of Buddhist Studies* 10, no. 1 (1987): 33–53.

Chaudhury, B. N. *Buddhist Centres in Ancient India*. Calcutta: Sanskrit College, 1969.

Chaudhury, Sukomal. *Analytical Study of the Abhidharmakośa*. Calcutta: Firma KLM, 1983.

Chaudhury, Uma. *The Social Dimensions of Early Buddhism*. Delhi: Oxford University Press, 1987.

Collcutt, Martin. "Monasticism: Buddhist Monasticism." *Encyclopedia of Religion* 10:41–44.

Collins, Steven. "Kalyāṇmitta and Kalyāṇamittatā." *Journal of the Pāli Text Society* 1986: 51–72.

———. *Selfless Persons: Imagery and Thought in Theravāda Buddhism*. Cambridge: Cambridge University Press, 1982.

———. "Soul: Buddhist Concepts." *Encyclopedia of Religion* 13:443–447.

Conze, Edward. *Buddhism: Its Essence and Development*. New York: Harper Torchbooks, 1959.

———. *Buddhist Meditation*. London: Allen & Unwin, 1956.

———, trans. *Buddhist Scriptures*. Baltimore: Penguin, 1959.

———. *Buddhist Thought in India: Three Phases of Buddhist Philosophy*. Ann Arbor, Mich.: University of Michigan Press, 1967.

———, trans. *Buddhist Wisdom Books.* New York: Harper & Row, 1958.
———. "The Composition of the *Aṣṭasāhasrikā Prajñāpāramitā.*" *Bulletin of the School of Oriental and African Studies* 14 (1952): 251–262.
———. "The Development of Prajñāpāramitā Thought." In Edward Conze, *Thirty Years of Buddhist Studies: Selected Essays,* pp. 123–147. Columbia, S.C.: University of South Carolina Press, 1968.
———, trans. *The Large Sūtra on Perfect Wisdom.* Berkeley: University of California Press, 1975.
———. "Mahāyāna Buddhism." In Edward Conze, *Thirty Years of Buddhist Studies: Selected Essays,* pp. 48–86. Columbia, S.C.: University of South Carolina Press, 1968.
———. "The Meditation on Death." In Edward Conze, *Thirty Years of Buddhist Studies: Selected Essays,* pp. 87–104. Columbia, S.C.: University of South Carolina Press, 1968.
———. *The Prajñāpāramitā Literature.* The Hague: Mouton, 1960.
———, ed. *Buddhist Texts through the Ages.* New York: Philosophical Library, 1954.
Cousins, Lance S. "Buddhist Jhāna: Its Nature and Attainment according to Pāli Sources." *Religion* 3 (1973): 115–131.
———. "The *Paṭṭhāna* and the Development of the Theravādin Abhidhamma." *Centenary Volume of the Journal of the Pāli Text Society* (1981): 22–46.
Cox, Collett Davis. "Controversies in Dharma Theory: Sectarian Dialogues on the Nature of Enduring Reality." Ph.D. diss., Columbia University, 1983.
Cunningham, Alexander. *The Stūpa of Bhārhut.* Varanasi: Indological Book House, 1962.
Dallapiccola, Anna Libera, ed. *The Stūpa: Its Religious, Historical and Architectural Significance.* Wiesbaden: Steiner, 1980.
Daśabhūmika. Edited by J. Rahder in *Daśabhūmikasūtra et Bodhisattva-bhūmi: chapitres Vihāra et Bhūmi.* Paris: Paul Geunther, 1926.
———. *Daśabhūmikasūtram.* Edited by P. L. Vaidya. Buddhist Sanskrit Texts, vol. 7. Darbhanga: Mithila Institute, 1967.
———. Translated by Honda Megumu in "Annotated Translation of the *Daśabhūmika-sūtra.*" In *Studies in South, East and Central Asia,* edited by Dennis Sinor, pp. 115–276. Śata-piṭaka Series, no. 74. Delhi: International Academy of Indian Culture, 1968.
Dasgupta, S. *A History of Indian Philosophy.* 5 vols. Cambridge: Cambridge University Press, 1922–1955.
Dayal, Har. *The Bodhisattva Doctrine in Buddhist Sanskrit Literature.* London: Routledge, 1931.
De, Gokuldas. *Democracy in Early Buddhist Saṃgha.* Calcutta: Calcutta University, 1962.
De Bary, William Theodore, ed. *The Buddhist Tradition in India, China, and Japan.* New York: Modern Library, 1969.
Dehejia, Vidya. *Early Buddhist Rock Temples.* Ithaca, N.Y.: Cornell University Press, 1972.

Demiéville, Paul. "L'Origine des sectes bouddhiques d'après Paramārtha." *Mélanges chinois et bouddhiques* 1 (1931): 15–64.

———. "À propos du concile de Vaiśālī." *T'oung pao* 40 (1951): 239–296.

Denis, E., ed. and trans. *La Lokapaññati et les idées cosmologiques du bouddhisme ancien.* 2 vols. Lille: Atelier, Reproduction des thèses, Université de Lille, 1977.

Deo, S. B. *History of Jaina Monasticism, From Inscriptions and Literature.* Poona: Ceccam College Postgraduate and Research Institute, 1956.

Dhammasaṅgaṇi. Edited by Edward Müller. London: Pāli Text Society, 1885. Reprint. London: Routledge & Kegan Paul, 1978.

———. Translated by C. A. F. Rhys Davids as *A Buddhist Manual of Psychological Ethics of the Fourth Century B.C.* 3d ed. Pāli Text Society Translation Series, no. 41. London: Luzac, 1974.

Dharmaskandha. Edited by Siglinde Dietz as *Fragmente des Dharmaskandha: ein Abhidharma-Text in Sanskrit aus Gilgit.* Göttingen: Vanderhoeck & Ruprecht, 1984.

Dharmaśrī. *Abhidharmahṛdayaśāstra.* Translated by Charles Willemen as *The Essence of Metaphysics: Abhidharmahṛdaya.* Brussels: Publications de l'Institut belge des Hautes Études bouddhiques, 1975.

———. *Abhidharmahṛdayaśāstra.* Translated by Indumati Armelin as *Le Coeur de la loi supreme: Traité de Fa-cheng.* Paris: Geunther, 1978.

Dhātukathā. Translated by U Nārada and Thein Nyun as *Discourse on Elements.* Pāli Text Society Translation Series, no. 34. London: Luzac, 1962.

Dīgha Nikāya. Translated by T. W. Rhys Davids and C. A. F. Rhys Davids as *Dialogues of the Buddha.* Sacred Books of the Buddhists, vols. 2–4. London: Luzac, 1971–1973. (Originally published by Oxford University Press, London, 1899–1921.)

Dīpavaṃsa. Edited and translated by B. C. Law as *Chronicle of the Island of Ceylon, or the Dīpavaṃsa, a Historical Poem of the 4th Century A.D.* Ceylon: Saman Press, 1959.

Divyāvadāna. Edited by P. L. Vaidya. Buddhist Sanskrit Texts, vol. 20. Darbhanga: Mithila Institute, 1959.

Dowling, Thomas. "Vasubandhu on the *Avijñapti-rūpa:* A Study in Fifth-Century *Abhidharma* Philosophy." Ph.D. diss., Columbia University, 1976.

Dube, S. N. *Cross Currents in Early Buddhism.* Delhi: Manohar, 1980.

Durt, Hubert. "The Counting Stick *(Śalākā)* and the Majority/Minority Rule in the Buddhist Community." *Journal of Indian and Buddhist Studies* 23 (1974): 470–464.

Dutt, Nalinaksha. *Aspects of Mahāyāna Buddhism and Its Relation to Hīnayāna.* London: Luzac, 1930. (Revised and reprinted as *Mahāyāna Buddhism* by Motilal Banarsidass, Delhi, 1978.)

———. *Buddhist Sects in India.* Calcutta: Mukhopadhyaya, 1970.

———. *Early History of the Spread of Buddhism and the Early Buddhist Schools.* Calcutta Oriental Series, no. 14. London: Luzac, 1925.

———. *Early Monastic Buddhism.* Calcutta: Calcutta Oriental Book Agency, 1960.

Dutt, Nalinaksha, and Krishna Datta Bajpai. *Development of Buddhism in Uttar*

Pradesh. Lucknow: Publication Bureau of the Government of Uttar Pradesh, 1956.

Dutt, Sukumar. *The Buddha and Five After-Centuries*. London: Luzac, 1957.

———. *Buddhist Monks and Monasteries of India: Their History and Their Contribution to Indian Culture*. London: Allen & Unwin, 1962.

———. *Early Buddhist Monachism*. London: Paul, Trench & Trübner, 1924.

Eggermont, Pierre Herman Leonard. *The Chronology of the Reign of Asoka Moriya*. Leiden: Brill, 1956.

———. "New Notes on Asoka and His Successors," *Persica* 1, no. 2 (1965–1966): 27–71.

Eliot, Charles, *Hinduism and Buddhism*. 3 vols. London: Arnold, 1921. Reprint. New York: Barnes & Noble, 1971.

Ergardt, Jan T. *Faith and Knowledge in Early Buddhism: An Analysis of the Contextual Structure of an Arahant-formula in the Majjhima-Nikāya*. Leiden: Brill, 1977.

———. *Man and His Destiny: The Release of the Human Mind: A Study of Citta in Relation to Dhamma in Some Ancient Indian Texts*. Leiden: Brill, 1986.

Fa-hsien. *A Record of Buddhistic Kingdoms: Being an Account by the Chinese Monk Fa-hsien of His Travels in India and Ceylon (A.D. 399–414) in Search of the Buddhist Books of Discipline*. Translated by James Legge. New York: Dover, 1965. (Originally published by Clarendon Press, Oxford, 1886.)

Falk, Maryla. "Nairatmya and Karman: The Life-long Problem of Louis de La Vallée Poussin's Thought." In *Louis de La Vallée Poussin Memorial Volume*, edited by Navendra Nath Law, pp. 429–464. Calcutta: Calcutta Oriental Press, 1940.

Falk, Nancy. "The Case of the Vanishing Nuns: The Fruits of Ambivalence in Ancient Indian Buddhism." In *Unspoken Worlds: Women's Religious Lives in Non-Western Cultures*, edited by Rita Gross, pp. 207–224. San Francisco: Harper & Row, 1980.

Fergusson, James. *History of Indian and Eastern Architecture*. Rev. ed. by James Burgess. 2 vols. Delhi: Munshiram Manoharlal, 1967. (Originally published by John Murray, London, 1910.)

Foucher, Alfred. *L'Art gréco-bouddhique du Gandhāra*. 2 vols. Paris: Leroux, 1922.

———. *The Beginnings of Buddhist Art and Other Essays in Indian and Central Asian Archaeology*. Varanasi: Indological Book House, 1972. (Originally published by Humphrey Milford, London, 1917.)

———. *The Life of the Buddha According to the Ancient Texts and Monuments of India*. Translated by Simone B. Boas. Middletown, Conn.: Wesleyan University Press, 1963. (An abbreviated translation of the author's *La Vie du Bouddha d'après les textes et les monuments de l'Inde*. Reprint. Paris: Payot, 1969.)

Frauwallner, Erich. "Abhidharma Studien." *Wiener Zeitschrift für die Kunde Süd- und Ostasiens und Archiv für Indische Philosophie* 7 (1963): 20–36; 8 (1964): 59–99; 15 (1971): 69–121; 16 (1972): 95–152; 17 (1973): 97–121.

———. *The Earliest Vinaya and the Beginnings of Buddhist Literature*. Serie Orientale Roma, vol. 8. Rome: Istituto Italiano per il Medio ed Estremo Oriente, 1956.

———. *Die Philosophie des Buddhismus.* Berlin: Akademie-Verlag, 1958.

Fujita, Kōtatsu. "The Doctrinal Characteristics of *Karman* in Early Buddhism." In *Indological and Buddhological Studies: Volume in Honor of Professor J. W. de Jong on His Sixtieth Birthday,* edited by L. Hercus et al., pp. 149–160. Canberra: Australian National University, Faculty of Asian Studies, 1982.

———. "One Vehicle or Three?" Translated by Leon Hurvitz. *Journal of Indian Philosophy* 3 (1975): 79–166.

———. "Pure and Impure Lands." *Encyclopedia of Religion* 12:90–91.

———. "Pure Land Buddhism and the *Lotus Sūtra.*" In *Indianisme et bouddhisme: Mélanges offerts à Mgr. Étienne Lamotte,* pp. 117–130. Louvain: Université catholique, Institut Orientaliste, 1980.

Galloway, Brian. "Once Again on the Indian Sudden-Enlightenment Doctrine." *Wiener Zeitschrift für die Kunde Süd- und Ostasiens und Archiv für Indische Philosophie* 29 (1985): 207–210.

———. "Sudden Enlightenment in Indian Buddhism." *Wiener Zeitschrift für die Kunde Süd- und Ostasiens und Archiv für Indische Philosophie* 25 (1981): 205–211.

Gaṇḍavyūhasūtra. Edited by P. L. Vaidya. Buddhist Sanskrit Texts, vol. 5. Darbhanga: Mithila Institute, 1960.

———. Partially translated by Luis Gómez in "Selected Verses from the *Gaṇḍavyūha:* Text, Critical Apparatus, and Translation." Ph.D. diss., Yale University, 1967.

Ganhar, J. N., and P. N. Ganhar. *Buddhism in Kashmir and Ladakh.* Delhi: Privately published by the authors, 1956.

Geiger, Magdalena, and Wilhelm Geiger. *Pāli Dhamma: Vornemlich in der kanonischen Literatur.* Munich: Bavarian Academy of Sciences, 1920.

Geiger, Wilhelm. *Pāli Literatur und Sprache.* Strassburg: Trübner, 1916. Translated by B. Ghosh as *Pāli Literature and Language.* 2nd ed. Delhi: Oriental Books Reprint, 1968.

Gilgit Manuscripts. Edited by Nalinaksha Dutt et al. 4 vols. Vol. 1, Srinagar, 1939; vols. 2–4, Calcutta: J. C. Sarkhel, 1939–1959.

Glassenapp, H. von. *Der Jainismus: Eine Indische Erlösungsreligion.* Hildesheim: Olms, 1969. (Originally published by Alf Häger Verlag, Berlin, 1925.)

Gokhale, Balkrishna Govind. *Buddhism and Asoka.* Baroda: Padmaja Publications, 1948.

———. *Buddhism in Maharashtra: A History.* Bombay: Popular Prakashan, 1976.

———. "Early Buddhism and the Brāhmaṇas." In *Studies in the History of Buddhism,* edited by A. K. Narain, pp. 67–80. Delhi: B. R. Publishing, 1980.

———. "The Early Buddhist Elite." *Journal of Indian History* 43 (1965): 391–402.

———. "Early Buddhist View of the State." *Journal of the American Oriental Society* 89 (1969): 731–738.

Gómez, Luis O. "The Bodhisattva as Wonder-worker." In *Prajñāpāramitā and*

Related Systems: Studies in Honor of Edward Conze, edited by Lewis Lancaster, pp. 221–261. Berkeley Buddhist Studies Series, no. 1. Berkeley: University of California, 1977.

———. "Buddhism: Buddhism in India." *Encyclopedia of Religion* 2:351–385.

———. "Buddhist Literature: Exegesis and Hermeneutics." *Encyclopedia of Religion* 2:529–541.

———. "Emptiness and Moral Perfection." *Philosophy East and West* 23 (1973): 361–373.

———. "Language: Buddhist Views of Language." *Encyclopedia of Religion* 8:446–451.

———. "Mahāsāṃghika." *Encyclopedia of Religion* 9:120–122.

———. "Proto-Mādhyamika in the Pāli Canon." *Philosophy East and West* 26 (1976): 137–165.

———. "Sarvāstivāda." *Encyclopedia of Religion* 13:75–80.

Gómez, Luis O., and Johnathon Silk, eds. *Studies in the Literature of the Great Vehicle: Three Mahāyāna Buddhist Texts.* Ann Arbor: Center for South and Southeast Asian Studies, University of Michigan, 1989.

Griffiths, Paul. *On Being Mindless: Buddhist Meditation and the Mind-body Problem.* La Salle, Ill.: Open Court Press, 1986.

Grönbold, Günter. *Der buddhistische Kanon: Eine Bibliographie.* Wiesbaden: Harrassowitz, 1984.

Guenther, Herbert V. *Philosophy and Psychology in the Abhidharma.* Baltimore: Penguin, 1971.

Gunaratna, Henepola. *The Path of Serenity and Insight: An Explanation of the Buddhist Jhānas.* Delhi: Motilal Banarsidass, 1985.

Haldar, Aruna. *Some Psychological Aspects of Early Buddhist Philosophy Based on the Abhidharmakośa of Vasubandhu.* Calcutta: Asia Society, 1981.

Haldar, J. R. *Early Buddhist Mythology.* Delhi: Manohar, 1977.

Hall, Bruce Cameron. "Vasubandhu on 'Aggregates, Spheres, and Components': Being Chapter One of the *Abhidharmakośa.*" Ph.D. diss., Harvard University, 1983.

Hallisey, Charles. "Pāramitās." *Encyclopedia of Religion* 11:196–198.

Hanayama Shinshō. *Bibliography on Buddhism.* Tokyo: Hokuseido Press, 1961.

Harrison, Paul M. "Buddhānusmṛti in the *Pratyutpanna-Buddha-Sammukhāvasthita-samādhi-sūtra.*" *Journal of Indian Philosophy* 6 (1978): 35–57.

———. "Who Gets to Ride in the Great Vehicle? Self-Image and Identity Among the Followers of the Early Mahāyāna." *Journal of the International Association of Buddhist Studies* 10, no. 1 (1987): 67–89.

Hastings, James. *Encyclopedia of Religion and Ethics.* 13 vols. New York: Charles Scribner's Sons, 1908–1927. Reprint. 1955.

Hazra, Kanai Lal. *Buddhism as Described by the Chinese Pilgrims.* Delhi: Munshiram Manoharlal, 1983.

———. *History of Theravāda Buddhism in Southeast Asia, with Special Reference to India and Ceylon.* Delhi: Munshiram Manoharlal, 1982.

———. *Royal Patronage of Buddhism in Ancient India.* Delhi: D. K. Publications, 1984.

Henning, W. B. "The Aramaic Inscription of Aśoka Found in Lampāka." *Bulletin of the School of African and Oriental Studies* 13 (1949): 80–88.

Herman, A. L. *An Introduction to Buddhist Thought: A Philosophic History of Indian Buddhism.* New York: University Press of America, 1983.

Hikata, R. *Suvikrāntavikrāmiparipṛcchā Prajñāpāramitāsūtra: An Introductory Essay on Prajñāpāramitā-Literature.* Fukuoka: Kyushu University, 1958.

Hirakawa, Akira. "Buddhist Literature: Survey of Texts." *Encyclopedia of Religion* 2:509–529.

———. "Introduction." In *San'yaku taishō Kusharon sakuin.* Edited by A. Hirakawa. 3 vols. Vol. 3, pp. i–xliv. Tokyo: Daizō shuppansha, 1978.

———. "Mañjuśrī and the Rise of Mahāyāna Buddhism." *Journal of Asian Studies* (Madras, India) 1, no. 1 (Sept. 1983): 12–33.

———. "The Meaning of 'Dharma' and 'Abhidharma'." In *Indianisme et bouddhisme: Mélanges offerts à Mgr. Étienne Lamotte,* pp. 159–175. Louvain: Université catholique, Institut Orientaliste, 1980.

———. "The Rise of Mahāyāna Buddhism and Its Relationship to the Worship of Stūpas." *Memoirs of the Research Department of the Tōyō Bunko* 22 (1963): 57–106.

———. *Ritsuzō no kenkyū* (A study of the *Vinayapiṭaka*). English summary, pp. 1–26 (left). Tokyo: Sankibō Busshorin, 1960.

———. "Stūpa Worship." *Encyclopedia of Religion* 14:92–96.

———. "The Twofold Structure of the Buddhist Saṃgha." *Journal of the Oriental Institute* 15, no. 2 (1966): 131–137.

Hōbōgirin: Dictionnaire encyclopédique du Bouddhisme d'après les sources chinoises et japonaises. Edited by Paul Demiéville. Tokyo: Maison franco-japonaise, 1929–present.

Hoernle, A. F. Rudolph, ed. and trans. *Manuscript Remains of Buddhist Literature Found in Eastern Turkestan.* Oxford: Clarendon Press, 1916.

Hofinger, Marcel. *Étude sur la concile de Vaiśālī.* Louvain: Bureaux du Muséon, 1946.

Holt, John. "Assist the Dead by Venerating the Living: Merit Transfer in the Early Buddhist Tradition." *Numen* 28, no. 1 (1981): 1–28.

———. *Discipline: The Canonical Buddhism of the Vinayapiṭaka.* Delhi: Motilal Banarsidass, 1981.

Horner, I. B. *Early Buddhist Theory of Man Perfected.* London: Williams & Norgate, 1936.

———. *Women under Primitive Buddhism.* Delhi: Motilal Banarsidass, 1975. (Originally published by Routledge, New York, 1930.)

Hosaka, Gyokusen. "Āśrava." *Encyclopedia of Buddhism* 2:202–214.

Hsüan-tsang. *Hsi-yu chi.* Translated by Samuel Beal as *Si-yu-ki: Buddhist Records of the Western World.* London: Trübner, 1884. Reprint. Delhi: Munshiram Manoharlal, 1969.

Hultzsch, Eugen, trans. *The Inscriptions of Aśoka.* Vol. 1, *Corpus Inscriptionum Indicarum.* Delhi: Indological Book House, 1969. (Originally published by Clarendon Press, Oxford, 1925.)

Hurvitz, Leon. "The Abhidharma on the 'Four Aids to Penetration'." In *Bud-*

dhist Thought and Asian Civilization, edited by Leslie Kawamura and Keith Scott, pp. 59–74. Emeryville, Calif.: Dharma Publishing, 1978.

———. "Dharmaśrī and the Sixteen Degrees of Mindfulness." *Journal of the International Association of Buddhist Studies* 2, no. 2: 7–30.

———. "The Eight Deliverances." In *Studies in Pāli and Buddhism,* edited by A. K. Narain, pp. 121–169. Delhi: B. R. Publishing, 1979.

———. "Fa-sheng's Observations on the Four Stations of Mindfulness." In *Mahāyāna Buddhist Meditation: Theory and Practice,* edited by Minoru Kiyota, pp. 207–248. Honolulu: University Press of Hawaii, 1978.

———. "Path to Salvation in the *Jñāna-prasthāna.*" *Studies in Indo-Asian Art and Culture* 5 (1977): 77–102.

———. "The Road to Buddhist Salvation as Described by Vasubhadra." *Journal of the American Oriental Society* 87 (1967): 434–486.

I-ching. *Mahāvyutpatti* (*T* 2133). Edited by Ogihara Unrai as *Bonkan taiyaku Bukkyō jiten* (Sanskrit Chinese Buddhist dictionary). Tokyo: Heigo shuppansha, 1915. Reprint. Tokyo: Sankibō Busshorin, 1959.

———. *A Record of the Buddhist Religion as Practised in India and the Malay Archipelago (A.D. 671–695).* Translated by J. Takakusu. Delhi: Munshiram Manoharlal, 1966. (Originally published by Clarendon Press, Oxford, 1896.)

Itivuttaka. Translated by F. L. Woodard as "*Itivuttaka:* As It Was Said." In *Minor Anthologies of the Pāli Canon, Part 2,* pp. 115–199. Sacred Books of the Buddhists, vol. 8. London: Oxford University Press, 1948.

Jacobi, Hermann. "Buddhas und Mahāviras Nirvāṇa und die politische Entwicklung Magadhas zu jener Zeit." *Sitzungberichte der Preussichen Akademie der Wissenschaften* 1930, pp. 322–332.

Jaina Sūtras. Translated by Hermann Jacobi in Sacred Books of the East, vols. 22, 45. Oxford: Clarendon Press, 1884, 1895. Reprint. New York: Dover, 1968.

Jaini, Padmanabh S. *Abhidharmadīpa.* Introduction contains information on Sarvāstivāda. Tibetan-Sanskrit Works Series, no. 4. Patna: Kashi Prasad Jayaswal Institute, 1959.

———. "Buddha's Prolongation of Life." *Bulletin of the School of Oriental and African Studies* 21 (1958): 546–552.

———. *The Jaina Path of Purification.* Berkeley: University of California Press, 1979.

———. "The Jina as a Tathāgata: Amṛtacandra's Critique of Buddhist Doctrine." In *Malalesekera Commemoration Volume,* edited by O. H. de A. Wijesekera, pp. 148–156. Colombo: Malalesekera Commemoration Volume Editorial Committee, 1976.

———. "On the Sarvajñātva of Mahāvīra and the Buddha." In *Buddhist Studies in Honor of I. B. Horner,* edited by L. Cousins, pp. 71–90. Dordrecht: Reidel, 1974.

———. "Origin and Development of the Theory of *Viprayukta Saṃskāras.*" *Bulletin of the School of Oriental and African Studies* 22, no. 3 (1959): 531–547.

———. "*Prajñā* and *Dṛṣṭi* in the Vaibhāṣika Abhidharma." In *Prajñāpāramitā and*

Related Systems: Studies in Honor of Edward Conze, edited by Lewis Lancaster, pp. 403–417. Berkeley Buddhist Studies Series, no. 1. Berkeley: University of California, 1977.

———. "The Sautrāntika Theory of *Bīja.*" *Bulletin of the School of Oriental and African Studies* 22 (1959): 236–249.

———. "Stages in the Bodhisattva Career of the Tathāgata Maitreya." In *Maitreya, The Future Buddha,* edited by Allen Sponberg and Helen Hardacre, pp. 54–90. New York: Cambridge University Press, 1988.

———. "The Vaibhāṣika Theory of Words and Meanings." *Bulletin of the School of Oriental and African Studies* 22 (1959): 95–107.

Jātaka. Edited by V. Fausböll. 6 vols. London: Luzac, 1877–1896. Reprint. London: Pāli Text Society, 1962.

———. Translated by E. B. Cowell as *The Jātaka or Stories of the Buddha's Former Births.* 3 vols. London: Luzac, 1969. (Originally published by Cambridge University Press, Cambridge, 1895–1913.)

———. Translated by T. W. Rhys Davids, *Buddhist Birth-Stories (Jātaka Tales): The Commentarial Introduction Entitled Nidāna-kathā, The Story of the Lineage.* Revised by Mrs. Rhys Davids. London: George Routledge & Sons, 1925.

Jayasuriya, W. F. *The Psychology and Philosophy of Buddhism, An Introduction to the Abhidhamma.* Colombo: Buddhist Missionary Society, 1976.

Jayatilleke, Kulatissa Nanda. *Early Buddhist Theory of Knowledge.* London: Allen & Unwin, 1963.

Johansson, Rune E. A. "Citta, Mano, Viññāṇa." *University of Ceylon Review* 23, nos. 1–2 (1965): 165–212.

———. *The Dynamic Psychology of Early Buddhism.* London: Curzon Press, 1979.

———. *The Psychology of Nirvana.* London: Allen & Unwin, 1969.

Jones, John Garrett. *Tales and Teachings of the Buddha: The Jātaka Stories in Relation to the Pāli Canon.* London: Allen & Unwin, 1979.

Jong, J. W. de. "A Brief History of Buddhist Studies in Europe and America." *Eastern Buddhist,* n.s. 7 (May 1974): 56–106; (October 1974): 49–82.

———. "Recent Buddhist Studies in Europe and America, 1973–1983." *Eastern Buddhist,* n.s. 17 (Spring 1984): 79–107.

———. "Les Sūtrapiṭaka des Sarvāstivādin et des Mūlasarvāstivādin." In *Mélanges d'indianisme à la memoire de Louis Renou,* pp. 395–402. Paris: De Boccard, 1968.

Joshi, Lal Mani. *Studies in the Buddhistic Culture of India.* Delhi: Motilal Banarsidass, 1967.

Kabilsingh, Chatsumarn. *A Comparative Study of Bhikkhuṇī Pātimokkha.* Varanasi: Chaukamba Orientalia, 1984.

Kajiyama, Yūichi. "On the Meaning of the Words Bodhisattva and Mahāsattva." In *Indological and Buddhist Studies: Articles in Honor of Professor J. W. de Jong on His Sixtieth Birthday,* edited by L. Hercus et al., pp. 253–270. Canberra: Australian National University, Faculty of Asian Studies, 1982.

———. "Realism of the Sarvāstivāda." In *Buddhist Thought and Asian Civiliza-*

tion, edited by Leslie Kawamura and Keith Scott, pp. 114–131. Emeryville, Calif.: Dharma Publishing, 1977.

———. "Stūpas, the Mother of Buddhas and Dharma-body." In *New Paths in Buddhist Research,* edited by A. K. Warder, pp. 9–16. Durham, N.C.: Acorn Press, 1985.

———. "Women in Buddhism." *Eastern Buddhist* 15 (1982): 53–70.

Kalupahana, David. *Buddhist Philosophy: A Historical Analysis.* Honolulu: University Press of Hawaii, 1976.

———. *Causality: The Central Philosophy of Buddhism.* Honolulu: University Press of Hawaii, 1975.

Kanakura, Yenshō. *Hindu-Buddhist Thought in India.* Translated by Shōtarō Iida and Neal Donner. Yokohama: Hokke Journal, 1980.

Kao, Kuan-ju. "Avataṃsaka Sūtra." *Encyclopedia of Buddhism* 2:435–446.

Karunadasa, Y. *Buddhist Analysis of Matter.* Colombo: Government Press, 1967.

Karuṇapuṇḍarīkasūtra. Edited by I. Yamada. London: Luzac, 1968.

Karunaratna, Upali. "Anusaya." *Encyclopedia of Buddhism* 1:775–777.

———. "Bhavaṅga." *Encyclopedia of Buddhism* 3:17–20.

Kashyap, Jagdish. *Abhidhamma Philosophy, or The Psycho-ethical Philosophy of Early Buddhism.* Delhi: Bharatiya Vidya Prakasha, 1982.

Kasulis, Thomas P. "Nirvāṇa." *Encyclopedia of Religion* 10:448–456.

Kāśyapaparivarta. Translated by Bhikkhu Pāsādika in *Linh Son: Publication d'études bouddhologiques* 1–9 (Nov. 1977–Nov. 1979).

Kathāvatthu. Translated by Schwe Zan Aung and C. A. F. Rhys Davids as *Points of Controversy.* London: Luzac, 1969. (Originally published by Humphrey Milford, London, 1915.)

Katsura, Shōryū. "A Study of Harivarman's 'Tattvasiddhi'." Ph.D. diss., University of Toronto, 1976.

Katz, Nathan. *Buddhist Images of Human Perfection: The Arahant of the Suttapiṭaka Compared to the Bodhisattva and the Mahāsiddha.* Delhi: Motilal Banarsidass, 1982.

Keith, Arthur Berridale. *The Religion and Philosophy of the Vedas and Upanishads.* Harvard Oriental Series, nos. 31–32. Cambridge: Harvard University Press, 1925.

Khosla, Sarla. *History of Buddhism in Kashmir.* Delhi: Sagar Publications, 1972.

Khuddaka-pāṭha. Translated by Bhikkhu Ñāṇamoli as *The Minor Readings, Khuddakapāṭha, and the Illustrator of Ultimate Meaning, Paramatthajotikā.* Pāli Text Society Translation Series, no. 32. London: Luzac, 1960.

King, Winston L. *In the Hope of Nibbāna: An Essay on Theravāda Buddhist Ethics.* La Salle, Ill.: Open Court Press, 1964.

———. "Meditation: Buddhist Meditation." *Encyclopedia of Religion* 9:331–336.

———. *Theravāda Meditation: The Buddhist Transformation of Yoga.* University Park, Pa.: Pennsylvania State University Press, 1980.

Kloetzli, W. Randolph. *Buddhist Cosmology: From Single World System to Pure Land: Science and Theology in the Image of Motion and Light.* Delhi: Motilal Banarsidass, 1983.

———. "Cosmology: Buddhist Cosmology." *Encyclopedia of Religion* 4:113–119.

Kloppenborg, Ria. *The Paccekabuddha: A Buddhist Ascetic.* Leiden: Brill, 1974.

———. *The Sūtra on the Foundation of the Buddhist Order.* Leiden: Brill, 1973.

Konow, Sten, ed. *Kharoṣṭhī Inscriptions.* Corpus Inscriptionum Indicarum, vol. 2, part 1. Calcutta, 1929.

Kornfield, Jack. *Living Buddhist Masters.* Santa Cruz, Calif.: Unity Press, 1977.

Kosambi, D. D. *The Culture and Civilization of Ancient India in Historical Outline.* London: Vikas Publications, 1965.

Kṣemendra. *Avadānakalpalatā.* 2 vols. Edited by P. L. Vaidya. Buddhist Sanskrit Texts, vols. 22–23. Darbhanga: Mithila Institute, 1959.

Lalitavistara. Edited by Salomon Lefmann in *Lalitavistara: Leben und Lehre des Śākya-Buddha.* 2 vols. Halle: Buchhandlung des Waisenhauses, 1902–1908. Reprint. Tokyo: Meicho fukyūkai, 1977.

———. Edited by P. L. Vaidya. Buddhist Sanskrit Texts, vol. 1. Darbhanga: Mithila Institute, 1958.

———. Translated by Phillipe Focaux as *Le Lalita Vistara.* 2 vols. Paris: Leroux, 1884, 1892.

Lamotte, Étienne. "Alexandre et le Bouddhisme." *Bulletin de l'École française d'Extrême-Orient* 44 (1947–1950): 147–162.

———. *Histoire du Bouddhisme Indien des origines à l'ère Śaka.* Bibliothèque du Muséon, no. 43. Louvain: Publications universitaires, 1958. English translation by Sara Boin-Webb as *History of Indian Buddhism, from the Origins to the Śaka Era.* Louvain: Peeters Press, 1988.

———. "Khuddakanikāya and Kṣudrakapiṭaka." *East and West* 8 (1957): 341–348.

———. "Lotus et Bouddha supramondain." *Bulletin de l'École française d'Extrême-Orient* 69 (1981): 31–44.

———. "Mañjuśrī." *T'oung-pao* 48 (1960): 1–96.

———. "The Passions and Impregnations of the Passions in Buddhism." In *Buddhist Studies in Honor of I. B. Horner,* edited by Lance Cousins, pp. 91–104. Dordrecht: Reidel, 1974.

———. "Sur la formation du Mahāyāna." In *Asiatica: Festschrift Friedrich Weller,* pp. 377–396. Leipzig: Harrassowitz, 1954.

Lancaster, Lewis. "Buddhist Literature: Canonization." *Encyclopedia of Religion* 2:504–509.

———. "Buddhist Literature: Its Canons, Scribes and Editors." In *The Critical Study of Sacred Texts,* vol. 2, edited by Wendy O'Flaherty, pp. 215–229. Berkeley Religious Studies Series, no. 2. Berkeley: Graduate Theological Union, 1978.

———. "The Chinese Translation of the *Aṣṭasāhasrikā-prajñāpāramitāsūtra* Attributed to Chih Ch'ien." *Monumenta Serica* 28 (1968): 246–257.

———. "Editing of Buddhist Texts." In *Buddhist Thought and Asian Civilization,* edited by Leslie Kawamura and Keith Scott, pp. 145–151. Emeryville, Calif.: Dharma Publishing, 1977.

———. "The Oldest Mahāyāna Sūtra: Its Significance for the Study of Buddhist Development." *Eastern Buddhist* 8, no. 1 (1975): 30–41.

La Vallée Poussin, Louis de. "Ages of the World (Buddhist)." *Encyclopedia of Religion and Ethics* 1:187–190.

———. "Bodhisattva (in Sanskrit Literature)." *Encyclopedia of Religion and Ethics* 2:739–753.

———. "Bouddhisme: Études et materiaux. Cosmologie: Le Monde des êtres et le monde receptacle." *Mémoires de l'Academie royale de Belgique, classe des lettres et des sciences morales* 6 (1919).

———. *Bouddhisme: Études et materiaux. Théorie des douze causes.* Gand: Université de Gand, 1913.

———. "La Controverse du temps et du pudgala dans le *Vijñānakāya*." *Études Asiatiques* 1 (1925): 343–376.

———. "Cosmology and Cosmogony (Buddhist)." *Encyclopedia of Religion and Ethics* 4:129–138.

———. "Councils and Synods (Buddhist)." *Encyclopedia of Religion and Ethics* 7:179–185.

———. "Death and Disposal of the Dead (Buddhist)." *Encyclopedia of Religion and Ethics* 4:446–449.

———. "Documents d'Abhidharma: Textes relatifs au Nirvāṇa et aux Asaṃskṛtas en géncral." *Bulletin de l'École française d'Extrême-Orient* 30 (1930): 1–28, 247–298.

———. "Documents d'Abhidharma: I. La Doctrine des Refuges; II. Le Corps de l'arhat est-il pur?" *Mélanges chinois et bouddhiques* 1 (1932): 5–125.

———. "Documents d'Abhidharma: I. La Controverse du temps; II. Les Deux, les Quatres, les Trois Vérités." *Mélanges chinois et bouddhiques* 5 (1937): 7–187.

———. "The Five Points of Mahādeva and the *Kathāvatthu*." *Journal of the Royal Asiatic Society* (1910): 413–423.

———. "Mahāyāna." *Encyclopedia of Religion and Ethics* 8:330–336.

———. "La Négation de l'âme et la doctrine de l'acte." *Journal Asiatique* 9, no. 20 (1902): 237–306; 10, no. 2 (1903): 357–449.

———. *The Way to Nirvāṇa: Six Lectures on Ancient Buddhism as a Discipline of Salvation.* Cambridge: Cambridge University Press, 1917.

Law, Bimala Churn. *Buddhaghosa.* Bombay: Bombay Branch, Royal Asiatic Society, 1940.

———. "Buddhaghosa." *Encyclopedia of Buddhism* 3:404–417.

———. *Buddhist Conception of Spirits.* London: Luzac, 1936.

———. *Heaven and Hell in Buddhist Perspective.* Calcutta: Thacker & Spink, 1925.

———. *A History of Pāli Literature.* London: Paul, Trench & Trübner, 1933.

———. *Women in Buddhist Literature.* Varanasi: Indological Book House, 1927.

———, ed. *Buddhistic Studies.* Calcutta: Thacker & Spink, 1931.

Lethcoe, Nancy. "The Bodhisattva Ideal in the *Aṣṭa* and *Pañca Prajñāpāramitā Sūtras.*" In *Prajñāpāramitā and Related Systems: Studies in Honor of Edward Conze,* edited by Lewis Lancaster, pp. 263–280. Berkeley Buddhist Studies Series, no. 1. Berkeley: University of California, 1977.

Lubac, Henri de. *Aspects du Bouddhisme.* 2 vols. Paris: Editions de Seuil, 1951–1955.

McDermott, James P. "Is There Group Karma in Theravāda Buddhism?" *Numen* 23 (1976): 67–80.

———. "The *Kāthavatthu* Kamma Debates." *Journal of the American Oriental Society* 95, no. 3 (1975): 424–433.

McGovern, William. *A Manual of Buddhist Philosophy.* London: Paul, Trench & Trübner, 1923.

MacQueen, Graeme. "Inspired Speech in Early Mahāyāna Buddhism." *Religion* 11 (1981): 303–319; 12 (1982): 49–65.

Mahāparinibbāna suttanta. Translated by T. W. Rhys Davids in *Dialogues of the Buddha* 2:71–191. Sacred Books of the Buddhists, no. 3. London: Luzac, 1959.

Mahāratnakūṭa. Translated by C. C. Chang et al. as *A Treasury of Mahāyāna Sūtras: Selections from the Mahāratnakūṭa Sūtra.* University Park, Pa.: Pennsylvania State University Press, 1983.

Mahāvaṃsa, or the Great Chronicle of Ceylon. Translated by Wilhelm Geiger. London: Luzac, 1964.

Mahāvastu. Edited by É. Senart. 2 vols. Paris: Impr. nationale, 1882–1897.

———. Translated by J. J. Jones. Sacred Books of the Buddhists, vols. 16, 18, 19. London: Luzac, 1949–1956.

Mahāvastu Avadāna. Edited by R. Basak. 3 vols. Calcutta Sanskrit College Research Series. Calcutta: Calcutta Sanskrit College, 1963–1968.

Mahāyāna-sūtra-saṅgraha. Edited by P. L. Vaidya. Buddhist Sanskrit Texts, vols. 17 and 18. Darbhanga: Mithila Institute, 1961–1964.

Maitreya-vyākaraṇa. Edited and translated by Sylvain Lévi as "Maitreya le Consolateur," in *Études d'Orientalisme publiées par le Musée Guimet à la mémoire de Raymond Linoissier,* vol. 2, pp. 381–422. Paris: 1932.

Majjhima Nikāya. Translated by I. B. Horner as *The Middle Length Sayings.* Pali Text Society Translation Series, nos. 29–31. London: Luzac, 1954–1959.

Majumdar, Gayatri Sen. *Buddhism in Ancient Bengal.* Calcutta: Navana, 1983.

Majumdar, R. C. *History and Culture of the Indian People.* 11 vols. London: Allen & Unwin, 1951.

Majumdar, R. C., et al. *An Advanced History of India.* 3d ed. London: Macmillan, 1965.

Malalesekera, G. P. "Akṣobhya." *Encyclopedia of Buddhism* 1:363–368.

———. "Anattā." *Encyclopedia of Buddhism* 1:567–576.

———. *The Pāli Literature of Ceylon.* London: Royal Asiatic Society of Great Britain and Ireland, 1928.

Malalesekera, G. P., ed. *Dictionary of Pāli Proper Names.* 2 vols. London: Luzac, 1960.

Malalesekera, G. P., et al. "Amita." *Encyclopedia of Buddhism* 1:434–463.

———. "Buddha." *Encyclopedia of Buddhism* 3:357–380.

Marshall, John. *Guide to Sāñcī.* Delhi: Manager of Publications, 1955.

———. *Taxila.* 3 vols. Cambridge: Cambridge University Press, 1951.

Masefield, Peter. "The Nibbāna-Parinibbāna Controversy." *Religion* 9 (1979): 215–230.

Masson, Joseph. *La Religion populaire dans le canon bouddhique Pāli*. Louvain: Bureaux du Muséon, 1942.

Matsunaga, Daigan, and Alicia Matsunaga. *The Buddhist Concept of Hell*. New York: Philosophical Library, 1972.

Mayeda, Egaku. "Japanese Studies on the Schools of the Chinese Āgamas." In *Zur Schulzugehövigkeit von Werken der Hīnayāna-Literatur,* edited by Heinz Bechert, pp. 94–103. Göttingen: Vandenhoeck & Ruprecht, 1985.

Meister, Michael, and Nancy Shatzman Steinhardt. "Temple: Buddhist Temple Compounds." *Encyclopedia of Religion* 14:373–380.

Mendelson, E. Michael. *Sangha and State in Burma: A Study of Monastic Sectarianism and Leadership*. Ithaca, N.Y.: Cornell University Press, 1975.

Migot, André. "Un Grand disciple du Bouddha: Śāriputra." *Bulletin de l'École française d'Extrême-Orient* 46 (1954): 405–554.

Milindapañha. Edited by V. Trenckner. 2d ed. London: Royal Asiatic Society, 1928.

———. Translated by I. B. Horner as *Milinda's Questions*. Sacred Books of the Buddhists, vols. 22-23. London: Luzac, 1963-1964.

———. Translated by C. A. F. Rhys Davids as *The Questions of King Milinda*. Sacred Books of the East, vols. 35–36. Oxford: Clarendon Press, 1890, 1894.

Misra, G. S. P. *Development of Buddhist Ethics*. Delhi: Munshiram Manoharlal, 1984.

Mitra, Debala. *Buddhist Monuments*. Calcutta: Sahitya Samsad, 1971.

Miyamoto, Shōson. "Time and Eternity in Buddhism." *Journal of Indian and Buddhist Studies* 7, no. 2 (1958): 3–18.

Mizuno, Kōgen. *The Beginnings of Buddhism*. Tokyo: Kōsei Publishing, 1980.

———. *Buddhist Sūtras: Origin, Development, Transmission*. Tokyo: Kōsei Publishing, 1982.

———. "Karman: Buddhist Concepts." *Encyclopedia of Religion* 8:266–268.

———. *Primitive Buddhism*. Translated by Kōshō Yamamoto. Ube: Karin bunko, 1969.

Mizuno, Kōgen, et al. "Abhidharma Literature." *Encyclopedia of Buddhism* 1:64–80.

Mookerjee, Radhakumud. *Asoka*. 3d ed. Delhi: Motilal Banarsidass, 1962.

Moray, M. S. *History of Buddhism in Gujarat*. Ahmedebad: Saraswati Pustak Bhandar, 1985.

Nagao, Gadjin. "The Architectural Tradition in Buddhist Monasticism." In *Studies in the History of Buddhism,* edited by A. K. Narain, pp. 189-208. Delhi: B. R. Publishing, 1980.

———. "Tranquil Flow of Mind: An Interpretation of *Upekṣā*." In *Indianisme et Bouddhisme: Mélanges offerts à Mgr. Étienne Lamotte,* pp. 245–258. Louvain: Université Catholique, Institut Orientaliste, 1980.

Nāgārjuna. *Le Traité de la Grande Vertu du Sagesse (Mahāprajñāpāramitāśāstra)*. 5 vols. Translated by Étienne Lamotte. Louvain: Bureaux de Muséon, 1944–1980.

Nakamura, Hajime. "Bodhisattva Path." *Encyclopedia of Religion* 2:265–269.

———. "Buddhism, Schools of: Mahāyāna Buddhism." *Encyclopedia of Religion* 2:457–472.

———. "A Critical Survey of Studies of the Lotus Sūtra." In *Dengyō Daishi kenkyū,* edited by Tendai gakkai, pp. 1–12 (left). Tokyo: Waseda Daigaku shuppanbu, 1973.

———. *Gotama Buddha.* Los Angeles: Buddhist Books International, 1977.

———. *Indian Buddhism: A Survey with Bibliographical Notes.* Osaka: KUFS Publication, 1980.

———. "The Problem of Self in Buddhist Philosophy." In *Revelation in Indian Thought,* edited by Harold Coward and Krishna Sivaraman, pp. 99–118. Emeryville, Calif.: Dharma Publishing, 1977.

Ñāṇamoli, Bhikkhu. *The Life of the Buddha as It Appears in the Pāli Canon, The Oldest Authentic Record.* Kandy: Buddhist Publication Society, 1972.

Ñāṇānanda, Bhikkhu. *Concept and Reality in Early Buddhist Thought.* Kandy: Buddhist Publication Society, 1971.

Nanayakkara, S. K. "Avijñapti." *Encyclopedia of Buddhism* 2:460–461.

———. "Bodhicitta." *Encyclopedia of Buddhism* 3:184–189.

Nariman, J. K. *A Literary History of Sanskrit Buddhism.* Delhi: Motilal Banarsidass, 1972.

Naudou, Jean. *Buddhists of Kashmir.* Delhi: Agam Kala Prakasham, 1980. Translated by Brereton and Picrons from *Les Bouddhistes kashmiriens au Moyen Âge.* Paris: Annales du Musée, Bibliothèque d'études, 1968.

Nettipakaraṇa. Translated by Bhikkhu Ñāṇamoli as *The Guide.* Pāli Text Society Translation Series, no. 33. London: Luzac, 1962.

Niyogi, Puspa. *Buddhism in Ancient Bengal.* Calcutta: Jijnasa, 1980.

Norman, K. R. "Devas and Adidevas in Buddhism." *Journal of the Pāli Text Society* (1981): 145–155.

———. *Pāli Literature, Including the Canonical Literature in Prakrit and Sanskrit of All the Hīnayāna Schools of Buddhism.* History of Indian Literature, edited by Jan Gonda, vol. 7, fasc. 2. Wiesbaden: Harrassowitz, 1983.

———. "The Pratyekabuddha in Buddhism and Jainism." In *Buddhist Studies: Ancient and Modern,* edited by Phillip Denwood and Alexander Piatigorsky, pp. 92–106. Totowa, N.J.: Barnes & Noble, 1983.

Ñyāṇaponika, Thera. *Abhidhamma Studies.* 4th ed. Kandy: Buddhist Publication Society, 1984.

———. *The Heart of Buddhist Meditation.* New York: Citadel Press, 1975.

Ñyāṇatiloka, Mahāthera. *Buddhist Dictionary.* 4th ed. Colombo: Buddhist Publication Society, n.d.

———. *Guide through the Abhidhamma-piṭaka.* 3d ed., rev. and enl. by Thera Ñyāṇaponika. Kandy: Buddhist Publication Society, 1957.

Okabe, Kazuo. "The Chinese Catalogues of Buddhist Scriptures." *Komazawa Daigaku Bukkyōgakubu kenkyū kiyō* 38 (1980): 1–13 (left).

Oldenberg, H. *The Buddha: His Life, His Order, His Doctrine.* Varanasi: Indological Book House, 1971. (Originally published as *Buddha sein Leben, seine Lehre, seine Gemeinde* by Hertz, Berlin, 1881.)

———. *The Vinayapiṭaka.* Vol. 1, "Introduction," pp. ix–lvi. London: Williams & Norgate, 1879.

Pachow, W. *A Comparative Study of the Prātimokṣa on the Basis of Its Chinese, Tibetan, Sanskrit, and Pāli Versions.* Sino-India Studies, no. 4. Shantiniketan, India: Sino-Indian Cultural Society, 1955.

Das Pañcavastukam und die Pañcavastukavibhāṣā. Edited by J. Imanishi. Göttingen: Vandenhoeck & Ruprecht, 1966.

Pande, Govind Chandra. *Studies in the Origins of Buddhism.* 2d ed. Delhi: Motilal Banarsidass, 1974.

Paranavitana, Senarat. "Mahāyānism in Ceylon." *Ceylon Journal of Science, Section G: Archeology, Ethnography, etc.* 2, no. 1 (December 1928): 35–71.

Paṭisambhidāmagga. Translated by Ñāṇamoli as *The Path of Discrimination.* Pāli Text Society Translation Series, no. 43. London: Routledge Kegan Paul, 1982.

Patterson, Maureen. *South Asian Civilizations: A Bibliography.* Chicago: University of Chicago Press, 1981.

Paṭṭhāna. Translated by U Nārada as *Conditional Relations.* Pāli Text Society Translation Series, no. 37. London: Luzac, 1969.

Paul, Diana. *Women in Buddhism.* Berkeley: Asian-Humanities Press, 1979.

Pedersen, Kusumita Priscilla. "The 'Dhyāna Chapter' of the *Bodhisattvapiṭakasūtra.*" Ph.D. diss., Columbia University, 1983.

Pérez-Remón, Joaquin. *Self and Non-self in Early Buddhism.* The Hague: Mouton, 1980.

Peṭakopadesa. Translated by Bhikkhu Ñāṇamoli as *The Piṭaka Disclosure.* Pāli Text Society Translation Series, no. 35. London: Luzac, 1964.

Petavatthu. Translated by H. S. Gehman as "Peta vatthu, Stories of the Departed." In *Minor Anthologies of the Pāli Canon, Part 4.* Edited by I. B. Horner. 2d ed. Sacred Books of the Buddhists, no. 30. London: Luzac, 1974.

Pfandt, Peter. *Mahāyāna Texts Translated into Western Languages: A Bibliographical Guide.* Rev. ed. with suppl. Cologne: Brill, 1986.

Piatigorski, Alexander. *The Buddhist Philosophy of Thought: An Essay in Interpretation.* Totowa, N.J.: Barnes & Noble, 1984.

Potter, Karl H., comp. *Bibliography of Indian Philosophies.* Delhi: Motilal Banarsidass, 1970.

Pratyutpanna-Buddha-Sammukhāvasthita-samādhi-sūtra. Translated by Paul Harrison. Ph.D. diss., Australian National University, 1979.

Prebish, Charles. *Buddhist Monastic Discipline: The Sanskrit Prātimokṣa Sūtras of the Mahāsaṃghikas and Mūlasarvāstivādins.* University Park, Pa.: Pennsylvania State University Press, 1975.

———. "Councils: Buddhist Councils." *Encyclopedia of Religion* 4:119–124.

———. "The Prātimokṣa Puzzle: Facts Versus Fantasy." *Journal of the American Oriental Society* 94 (April–June 1974): 168–176.

———. "A Review of Scholarship on the Buddhist Councils." *Journal of Asian Studies* 33 (February 1974): 239–254.

———. "Theories Concerning the Skandhaka." *Journal of Asian Studies* 32 (1973): 669–678.

———. "Vinaya and Prātimokṣa: The Foundation of Buddhist Ethics." In *Studies in the History of Buddhism,* edited by A. K. Narain, pp. 189–208. Delhi: B. R. Publishing, 1980.

Prebish, Charles, and Janice J. Nattier. "Mahāsāṅghika Origins: The Beginnings of Buddhist Sectarianism." *History of Religions* 16 (1977): 237–272.

Przyluski, Jean. *Le Concile de Rājagṛha: Introduction à l'histoire des canons et des sectes bouddhiques*. Paris: Geunther, 1926–1928.

———. *The Legend of King Aśoka.* Translated by Dilip Kumar Biswas. Delhi: Firma KLM, 1967. (Originally published as *Légende de l'empereur Aśoka* [*Aśoka-avadāna*] by Paul Geunther, Paris, 1923.)

Puggalapaññati. Translated by B. C. Law as *Designation of Human Types.* Pāli Text Society Translation Series, no. 12. London: Luzac, 1969. (Originally published by Oxford University Press, London, 1924.)

Rahula, Bhikkhu Telwatte. *A Critical Study of the Mahāvastu.* Delhi: Motilal Banarsidass, 1978.

Rahula, Walpola. "The Bodhisattva Ideal in Theravāda and Mahāyāna." In Walpola Rahula, *Zen and the Taming of the Bull,* pp. 71–77. London: Fraser, 1978.

———. "A Comparative Study of Dhyānas according to Theravāda, Sarvāstivāda, and Mahāyāna." In Walpola Rahula, *Zen and the Taming of the Bull,* pp. 101–109. London: Fraser, 1978.

———. *The History of Buddhism in Ceylon: The Anuradhapura Period, 3rd Century B.C.–19th Century A.D.* 2d ed. Colombo: Gunasena, 1966.

———. *What the Buddha Taught.* Rev. ed. Bedford, England: Fraser, 1959.

Rāṣṭraparipṛcchā. Translated by Jacob Ensink as *The Questions of Rāṣṭrapāla.* Zwolle: J. J. Tijl, 1952.

Rawlinson, Andrew. "The Position of the *Aṣṭasāhasrikā Prajñāpāramitā* in the Development of Early Mahāyāna." In *Prajñāpāramitā and Related Systems: Studies in Honor of Edward Conze,* edited by Lewis Lancaster, pp. 3–34. Berkeley Buddhist Studies Series, no. 1. Berkeley: University of California, 1977.

Regamey, Constantin. "Le Problème du Bouddhisme primitif et les derniers travaux de Stanislaw Schayer." *Rocznik Orientalistyczny* 21 (1957): 37–58.

Renou, L., and J. Fillizoat. *L'Inde classique,* vol. 2, pp. 315–608. Paris: Imprimerie Nationale, 1953.

Reynolds, Frank. "Buddhism." In *A Reader's Guide to the Great Religions,* edited by Charles Adams, pp. 156–222. 2d ed. New York: Free Press, 1977.

———. "Buddhist Ethics: A Bibliographical Essay." *Religious Studies Review* 5, no. 1 (January 1979): 40–48.

———. "From Philology to Anthropology: A Bibliographical Essay on Works Related to Early, Theravāda and Sinhalese Buddhism." In *The Two Wheels of the Dhamma,* edited by Bardwell Smith, pp. 107–121. Chambersburg, Pa.: American Academy of Religion, 1972.

———. "The Many Lives of the Buddha." In *The Biographical Process: Studies in the History and Psychology of Religion,* edited by Frank Reynolds and Donald Capps, pp. 37–61. The Hague: Mouton, 1976.

———. "Tradition and Change in Theravāda Buddhism: A Bibliographical Essay on Works Related to Early, Theravāda, and Sinhalese Buddhism." *Contributions to Asian Studies* 4 (1973): 94–104.

Reynolds, Frank, and Robert Campany. "Buddhist Ethics." *Encyclopedia of Religion* 2:498–504.
Reynolds, Frank, and Regina T. Clifford. "Theravāda." *Encyclopedia of Religion* 14:469–479.
Reynolds, Frank, and Charles Hallisey. "Buddha." *Encyclopedia of Religion* 2:319–322.
Reynolds, Frank, and Mani Reynolds, trans. *Three Worlds According to King Ruang*. Berkeley Buddhist Series, no. 4. Berkeley: University of California, 1982.
Reynolds, Frank, et al. *Guide to the Buddhist Religion*. Boston: Hall, 1981.
Rhys Davids, T. W. *Buddhism*. London: Macmillan, 1920.
———. *Buddhist India*. 3d ed. Calcutta: Susil Gupta, 1957. (Originally published by G. P. Putnam's Sons, New York, 1903.)
Robinson, Richard H. "The Ethic of the Householder Bodhisattva." *Bharati* (1966): 31–55.
Robinson, Richard H., and Willard Johnson. *The Buddhist Religion*. 3d ed. Belmont, Calif.: Wadsworth, 1982.
Rockhill, William. *The Life of the Buddha and the Early History of His Order*. London: Trübner, 1884.
Rosenberg, O. *Die Probleme der buddhistischen Philosophie*. Heidelberg: Harrassowitz, 1924.
Ruegg, Seyfort. "The Uses of the Four Positions of the *Catuṣkoṭi* and the Problem of Description of Reality in Mahāyāna Buddhism." *Journal of Indian Philosophy* 5 (1977): 1–71.
Saddharmapuṇḍarīka sūtra. Translated by Leon Hurvitz as *Scripture of the Lotus Blossom of the Fine Dharma*. New York: Columbia University Press, 1976.
Saddhatissa, H. *Buddhist Ethics: Essence of Buddhism*. London: Allen & Unwin, 1970.
Samādhirājasūtra. Edited by P. L. Vaidya. Buddhist Sanskrit Texts, vol. 2. Darbhanga: Mithila Institute, 1961.
Saṃyutta Nikāya. Translated by C. A. F. Rhys Davids and F. L. Woodward as *The Book of Kindred Sayings or Grouped Suttas*. Pāli Text Society Translation Series, nos. 7, 10, 13, 14, 16. London: Luzac, 1950–1956. (Originally published by Oxford University Press, London, 1917–1930.)
Das Saṅgītisūtra und sein Kommentar Saṅgītiparyāya. Edited by Valentina Stache-Rosen. Sanskrittexte aus den Turfanfund, vol. 9. Berlin, 1968.
Saratchandra, E. R. *Buddhist Psychology of Perception*. Colombo: Ceylon University Press, 1958.
Sarkar, H. *Studies in Early Buddhist Architecture of India*. Delhi: Munshiram Manoharlal, 1966.
Sasaki, Genjun. "Avijñapti—A Buddhist Moral Concept." In *Inde ancienne,* vol. 1, edited by International Association of Orientalists, pp. 89–98. Paris: L'Asiatique, 1976.
———. "The Concept of Kamma in Buddhist Philosophy." *Oriens Extremus* 3 (1956): 185–204.
Schayer, Stanislaw. *Mahāyāna Doctrines of Salvation*. London: Probsthain, 1923.

———. "New Contributions to the Problem of Pre-Hinayanistic Buddhism." *Polski Biuletyn Orientalistyczny* 1 (1937): 8–17.

———. "Precanonical Buddhism." *Archív Orientální* 7 (1935): 121–132.

Schlingroff, D. *Die Religion des Buddhismus.* 2 vols. Sammlung Göschen, vol. 174. Berlin: De Gruyter, 1962.

Schlumberger, Daniel, et al. "Une Bilingue grêco-araméenne d'Asoka." *Journal Asiatique* 246 (1958): 1–48.

Schmithausen, Lambert. "On Some Aspects of Descriptions of Theories of 'Liberating Insight' and 'Enlightenment' in Early Buddhism." In *Studien zum Jainismus und Buddhismus: Gedenkschrift für Ludwig Alsdorf,* edited by Klaus Bruhn and Albrecht Wezler, pp. 199–250. Wiesbaden: Steiner, 1981.

———. "On the Problem of the Relation of Spiritual Practice and Philosophical Theory of Buddhism." In *German Scholars on India,* edited by Cultural Department of the Embassy of the Federal Republic of Germany in New Delhi, vol. 2, pp. 235–250. Bombay: Nachiketa Publications, 1977.

Schopen, Gregory. "The Inscription on the Kuṣān Image of Amitābha and the Character of the Early Mahāyāna in India." *Journal of the International Association of Buddhist Studies* 10, no. 2 (1987): 99–137.

———. "Mahāyāna in Indian Inscriptions." *Indo-Iranian Journal* 21 (1979): 1–19.

———. "The Phrase 'sa pṛthivīpradeśaś caityabhūto bhavet' in the *Vajracchedikā:* Notes on the Cult of the Book in Mahāyāna." *Indo-Iranian Journal* 17 (1975): 147–181.

———. "Sukhāvatī as a Generalized Religious Goal in Sanskrit Mahāyāna Sūtra Literature." *Indo-Iranian Journal* 19 (1977): 177–210.

———. "Two Problems in the History of Indian Buddhism: The Layman/Monk Distinction and the Doctrines of Transfer of Merit." *Studien zur Indologie und Iranstik* 10 (1985): 9–47.

Schubring, W. *Die Lehre der Jainas.* Berlin: De Gruyter, 1935. English translation by W. Beurlen, *The Doctrine of the Jainas, Described after Old Sources.* Delhi: Motilal Banarsidass, 1962.

Schumann, Hans Wolfgang. *Buddhism: An Outline of Its Teachings and Schools.* Wheaton, Ill.: Theosophical Publishing House, 1973.

Schuster, Nancy. "The Bodhisattva Figure in the *Ugraparipṛcchā.*" In *New Paths in Buddhist Research,* edited by A. K. Warder, pp. 26–56. Durham, N.C.: Acorn Press, 1985.

———. "Changing the Female Body: Wise Women and the Bodhisattva Career in Some *Mahāratnakūṭasūtras.*" *Journal of the International Association of Buddhist Studies* 4, no. 1 (1981): 24–69.

Sharma, Sharmistha. *Buddhist Avadānas (Socio-Political Economic and Cultural Study).* Delhi: Eastern Book Linkers, 1986.

Singh, Madan Mohan. "The Date of the Buddha-Nirvāṇa." *Journal of Indian History* 39, no. 3 (1961): 359–363.

Sinha, Braj M. *Time and Temporality in Sāṁkhya-Yoga and Abhidharma Buddhism.* Delhi: Munshiram Manoharlal, 1983.

Sircar, Dinesh Chandra. *Select Inscriptions Bearing on Indian History and Civilization.* Vol. 1, *From the Sixth Century B.C. to the Sixth Century A.D.* 2d ed. Calcutta: University of Calcutta, 1965.

Skandhila. *Abhidharmāvatāraśāstra.* Translated by Marcel Van Veltem as *Le Traité de la descente dans la profonde loi (Abhidharmāvatāraśāstra) de l'Arhat Skandhila.* Louvain: Université catholique, Institut Orientaliste, 1977.

Skorupski, Tadeusz. "Dharma: Buddhist Dharma and Dharmas." *Encyclopedia of Religion* 4:332–338.

———. "Prajñā." *Encyclopedia of Religion* 11:477–481.

———. "Sautrāntika." *Encyclopedia of Religion* 13:86–88.

Snellgrove, David. *The Image of the Buddha.* Tokyo: Kodansha, 1978.

———. *Indo-Tibetan Buddhism: Indian Buddhists and Their Tibetan Successors.* 2 vols. Boston: Shambala, 1987.

———. "Śākyamuni's Final Nirvāṇa." *Bulletin of the School of Oriental and African Studies* 36 (1973): 399–411.

———. "In Search of the Historical Buddha." *South Asian Review* 7 (1974): 151–157.

Snodgrass, Adrian. *The Symbolism of the Stūpa.* Ithaca, N.Y.: Southeast Asia Program, Cornell University, 1985.

Stcherbatsky, Fedor Ippolitovich. *The Conception of Buddhist Nirvaṇa.* The Hague: Mouton, 1965. (Originally published by Academy of Sciences of U.S.S.R., Leningrad, 1927.)

———. *The Central Conception of Buddhism and the Meaning of the Word "Dharma."* Delhi: Indological Book House, 1970. (Originally published by Royal Asiatic Society, London, 1923.)

Strong, John. "The Buddhist Avadānists and the Elder Upagupta." *Mélanges chinois et bouddhiques* 22 (1985): 863–881.

———. *The Legend of King Aśoka: A Study and Translation of the Aśokāvadāna.* Princeton: Princeton University Press, 1983.

———. "The Legend of the Lion-Roarer: A Study of the Buddhist Arhat Piṇḍola Bhāradvāja." *Numen* 26 (1979): 50–88.

———. "Merit: Buddhist Concepts." *Encyclopedia of Religion* 9:383–386.

Subramanian, K. R. *Buddhist Remains in Āndhra.* Madras: Diocesan Press, 1932.

Sukhāvatīvyūhasūtra. Edited by Atsuji Ashikaga. Kyoto: Hōzōkan, 1965.

———. Edited by P. L. Vaidya. In *Mahāyāna-sūtra-saṅgraha.* Buddhist Sanskrit Texts, vol. 17, pp. 221–253. Darbhanga: Mithila Institute, 1961.

———. Translated by Max Müller in *Buddhist Mahāyāna Texts.* Sacred Books of the East, vol. 49. Oxford: Oxford University Press, 1894.

Śūraṅgamasamādhisūtra. Translated by Étienne Lamotte as *La Concentration de la marche héroïque. Mélanges chinois et bouddhiques* 13 (1965): 1–308.

———. Translated by R. E. Emmerick as *The Khotanese Śūraṅgamasamādhisūtra.* London: Oxford University Press, 1967.

Sutta-nipata. Translated by Robert Chalmers as *Buddha's Teachings*. Harvard Oriental Series, no. 37. Cambridge: Harvard University Press, 1932.

———. Translated by E. M. Hare as *Woven Cadences of Early Buddhists*. Sacred Books of the Buddhists, vol. 15. London: Oxford University Press, 1945.

———. Translated by K. R. Norman as *The Group of Discourses* with alternative translations by I. B. Horner and Walpola Rahula. Pāli Text Society Translation Series, no. 44. London: Routledge & Kegan Paul, 1984.

Suvarṇaprabhāsottamasūtra. Translated by R. E. Emmerick as *The Sūtra of Golden Light*. London: Luzac, 1970.

Suzuki, D. T. *On Indian Buddhism*. New York: Harper & Row, 1968.

———. *Outlines of Mahāyāna Buddhism*. New York: Schocken, 1963. (Originally published by Luzac, London, 1907.)

Swearer, Donald. "Arhat." *Encyclopedia of Religion* 1:403–405.

Tachibana, Shundō. *The Ethics of Buddhism*. London: Oxford University Press, 1926.

Takakusu, Junjirō. *The Essentials of Buddhist Philosophy*. 3d ed. Edited by Wing-tsit Chan and Charles Moore. Westport, Conn.: Greenwood Press, 1973. (Originally published by Office Appliance Co., Honolulu, 1956.)

———. "On the Abhidharma Literature of the Sarvāstivādins." *Journal of the Pāli Text Society* (1904–1905): 67–146.

Takasaki, Jikidō. *An Introduction to Buddhism*. Tokyo: Tōhō gakkai, 1987.

———. "Remarks on the Sanskrit Fragments of the *Abhidharma-dharmaskandhapādaśāstra*." *Indogaku Bukkyōgaku kenkyū* 13, no. 1 (1965), pp. 33–41 (left).

Talim, Meena. *Woman in Early Buddhist Literature*. Bombay: University of Bombay, 1972.

Tambiah, S. J. *Buddhism and the Spirit Cults in North-east Thailand*. Cambridge: Cambridge University Press, 1970.

———. *The Buddhist Saints of the Forest and the Cult of Amulets*. Cambridge: Cambridge University Press, 1984.

———. *World Conqueror and World Renouncer*. Cambridge: Cambridge University Press, 1976.

Tanaka, Kenneth. "Simultaneous Relation *(Sahabhū-hetu)*: A Study in Buddhist Theory of Causation." *Journal of the International Association of Buddhist Studies* 8, no. 1 (1985): 91–111.

Tāranātha. *History of Buddhism in India*. Translated by Lama Chimpa and Alaka Chattopadyaya. Simla: Indian Institute of Advanced Study, 1970.

Tatia, N. "The Interaction of Jainism and Buddhism and Its Impact on the History of Buddhist Monasticism." In *Studies in the History of Buddhism*, edited by A. K. Narain, pp. 321–338. Delhi: B. R. Publishing, 1980.

Thapar, Romila. *Aśoka and the Decline of the Mauryas*. 2d ed. Delhi: Oxford University Press, 1973.

———. *A History of India*, vol. 1. Baltimore: Penguin, 1966.

Theragāthā. Translated by K. R. Norman as *Elder's Verses 1*. Pāli Text Society Translation Series, no. 38. London: Luzac, 1969.

Therīgāthā. Translated by K. R. Norman as *Elder's Verses 2.* Pāli Text Society Translation Series, no. 40. London: Luzac, 1971.

Thomas, Edward Joseph. *The History of Buddhist Thought.* 3d ed. New York: Barnes & Noble, 1963. (Originally published by Routledge & Kegan Paul, London, 1927.)

———. *The Life of the Buddha as Legend and History.* 3d ed. London: Routledge & Kegan Paul, 1949.

Tsukamoto, Keishō. "Mahākāśyapa's Precedence to Ānanda at the Rājagṛha Council." *Journal of Indian and Buddhist Studies* 11, no. 2 (1963): 824–817.

Udāna. Translated by F. L. Woodward as "Udāna: Verses of Uplift" in *Minor Anthologies of the Pali Canon.* Sacred Books of the Buddhists, vol. 8, pp. 1–114. London: Oxford University Press, 1948. (Originally published 1935.)

Ugraparipṛcchā. Translated by Nancy Schuster in "The *Ugraparipṛcchā,* the *Mahāratnakūṭasūtra* and Early Mahāyāna Buddhism." Ph.D. diss., University of Toronto, 1976.

Upasak, C. S. *Dictionary of Early Buddhist Monastic Terms.* Varanasi: Bharati Prakashan, 1975.

Upatissa. *Vimuttimagga.* Translated by N. R. M. Ehara et al. as *The Path of Freedom.* Colombo: Deerasuriya, 1961.

Vajirañāṇa Parahavahera, Mahāthera. *Buddhist Meditation in Theory and Practice: A General Exposition According to the Pāli Canon of the Theravāda School.* Colombo: Gunasena, 1962.

Vajracchedikā Prajñāpāramitā. Translated and explained by Edward Conze as "The Diamond Sutra" in *Buddhist Wisdom Books,* pp. 21–107. London: Allen & Unwin, 1958.

Van den Broeck, José. *La Saveur de l'immortel (A-p'i-t'an Kan Lu Wei Lun): La Version chinoise de l'Amṛtarasa de Ghoṣaka.* Louvain: Université catholique, Institut Orientaliste, 1977.

Van Zeyst, H. G. A. "Arūpa loka." *Encyclopedia of Buddhism* 2:103–104.

Vasubandhu. *Abhidharmakośa.* Translated by Louis de La Vallée Poussin as *L'Abhidharmakośa de Vasubandhu.* 6 vols. Paris: Geunther, 1923–1931. Translated by Leo M. Pruden as *Abhidharmakośabhāṣyam.* 5 vols. Berkeley: Asian Humanities Press, 1988–.

———. *Karmasiddhi-prakaraṇa.* Translated by Étienne Lamotte as "Traité de la demonstration de l'acte." *Mélanges chinois et bouddhiques* 4 (1935–1936): 207–263.

———. *Karmasiddhi-prakaraṇa.* Translated by Stefan Anacker in *Seven Works of Vasubandhu: The Buddhist Psychological Doctor,* pp. 92–120. Delhi: Motilal Banarsidass, 1984.

———. *Karmasiddhi-prakaraṇa.* Translated by Leo Pruden as *Karmasiddhi-prakaraṇa.* Berkeley: Asian Humanities Press, 1988.

———. *Pañcaskandha-prakaraṇa of Vasubandhu.* Edited by Shanti Bhiksu Sastri. Kelaniya, 1969.

———. *Pañcaskandha-prakaraṇa.* Translated by Stefan Anacker in *Seven Works of Vasubandhu: The Buddhist Psychological Doctor,* pp. 65–76. Delhi: Motilal Banarsidass, 1984.

———. *The Soul Theory of the Buddhists.* Translated by Fedor Ippolitovich Stcherbatsky. Varanasi: Bharatiya Vidya Prakasan, 1976. (Originally published as *Bulletin de l'Academie des Sciences de Russie* 1920:823–854 and 937–958, St. Petersburg.)

Vasumitra. *Samayabhedoparacanacakra* (*T* 2031). Translated by Masuda Jiryō as "Origin and Doctrines of Early Indian Buddhist Schools." *Asia Major* 2 (1925): 1–78.

Venkataramanan, K. *Nāgārjuna's Philosophy as Presented in the Mahāprajñāpāramitā-śāstra.* Tokyo: Tuttle, 1966.

———. Trans. "Sāṃmitīya-nikāya-śāstra." *Visva-Bharati Annals* 5 (1953): 155–242.

Verdu, Alfonso. *Early Buddhist Philosophy in the Light of the Four Noble Truths.* Washington, D.C.: University Press of America, 1979.

Vetter, Tillman. *The Ideas and Meditative Practices of Early Buddhism.* Leiden: Brill, 1988.

Vibhaṅga. Translated by U Thittila as *The Book of Analysis.* Pāli Text Society Translation Series, no. 39. London: Luzac, 1969.

Vimalakīrtinirdeśa. Translated by Sara Boin from Étienne Lamotte's French version as *The Teaching of Vimalakīrti (Vimalakīrtinirdeśa).* London: Pāli Text Society, 1976.

Vimana vatthu. Translated by Jean W. Kennedy as "Vimana vatthu: Stories of the Mansions" in *Minor Anthologies of the Pāli Canon, part 4,* edited by Jean W. Kennedy. Sacred Books of the Buddhists, vol. 30. London: Luzac, 1942.

Vinaya. Translated by I. B. Horner as *The Book of the Discipline.* Sacred Books of the Buddhists, vols. 10, 11, 13, 14, 20, 25. London: Luzac, 1938–1966.

Vinaya-viniścaya-upalī-paripṛcchā. Translated by Pierre Python as *Vinaya-viniścaya-upalī-paripṛcchā: Enquête d'Upāli pour une exégèse de la discipline.* Paris: Maisonneuve, 1973.

Waldschmidt, Ernst. *Sanskrithandschriften aus den Turfanfunden.* 5 vols. Wiesbadsen: Steiner, 1965.

Warder, Anthony Kennedy. "Dharmas and Data." *Journal of Indian Philosophy* 1 (1971): 272–295.

———. *Indian Buddhism.* Delhi: Motilal Banarsidass, 1970.

Warren, Henry Clarke. *Buddhism in Translations.* Cambridge: Harvard University Press, 1922.

Watanabe, Baiyū. *Thoughts, Literature, and Monasteries in Early Buddhism.* Tokyo: Minshukai honbu, 1948.

Watanabe, Fumimaro. *Philosophy and Its Development in the Nikāyas and Abhidharma.* Delhi: Motilal Banarsidass, 1983.

———. "A Study of the First Chapter in the *Abhidharmasāraśāstra.*" In *New Paths in Buddhist Research,* edited by A. K. Warder, pp. 119–134. Durham, N.C.: Acorn Press, 1985.

Watters, Thomas. *On Yuan Chwang's Travels in India.* Edited by T. W. Rhys Davids and S. W. Bushell. New York: AMS, 1971. (Originally published by Royal Asiatic Society, London, 1904–1905.)

Wayman, Alex. "Buddhism." In *Historia Religionum, Handbook for the History of Religions,* vol. 2, edited by C. Jouco Bleeker and George Widengren, pp. 372–464. Leiden: Brill, 1971.

———. "Buddhist Dependent Origination." *History of Religion* 10 (1971): 185–203.

———. "The Intermediate State Dispute in Buddhism." In Alex Wayman, *Buddhist Insight,* pp. 251–267. Delhi: Motilal Banarsidass, 1983.

———. "The Mahāsāṅghika and the *Tathāgatagarbha.*" *Journal of the International Association of Buddhist Studies* 1 (1978): 35–50.

———. "Meditation in Theravāda and Mahīśāsaka." *Studia Missionalia* 25 (1976): 1–28.

———. "The Sixteen Aspects of the Four Noble Truths and Their Opposites." *Journal of the International Association of Buddhist Studies* 3, no. 2 (1980): 67–76.

———. "Two Traditions of India—Truth and Silence." *Philosophy East and West* (October 1974): 389–403.

Webb, Russell. *An Analysis of the Pāli Canon.* Kandy: Buddhist Publications Society, 1980.

Welbon, Guy. *Buddhist Nirvāṇa and Its Western Interpreters.* Chicago: University of Chicago Press, 1968.

Werner, Karel. "Bodhi and Arahataphala: From Early Buddhism to Early Mahāyāna." In *Buddhist Studies: Ancient and Modern,* edited by Phillip Denwood and Alexander Piatigorsky, pp. 167–181. Totowa, N.J.: Barnes & Noble, 1983.

Wijajayaratna, Mohan. *Le Moine bouddhique selon les textes du Theravāda.* Paris: Editions du Cerf, 1983.

Wijesekera, Oliver Hector de Alwis. "Canonical References to the Bhavaṅga." In *Malalesekera Commemoration Volume,* edited by O. H. de A. Wijesekera, pp. 348–352. Colombo: Malalesekera Commemoration Volume Editorial Committee, 1976.

Williams, Paul. "On the Abhidharma Ontology." *Journal of Indian Philosophy* 9 (1981): 227–257.

———. *Mahāyāna Buddhism.* London: Routledge, Chapman & Hall, 1989.

Willis, Janice D. "Nuns and Benefactresses: The Role of Women in the Development of Buddhism." In *Women, Religion and Social Change,* edited by Yvonne Haddad and Ellison Findly, pp. 59–86. Albany, N.Y.: State University of New York Press, 1985.

Winternitz, Moriz. *A History of Indian Literature.* Calcutta: University of Calcutta Press, 1933.

Witanachi, C. "Ānanda." *Encyclopedia of Buddhism* 1:529–536.

Woodcock, George. *The Greeks in India.* Tokyo: Tuttle, 1966.

Yamaguchi, Susumu. *Dynamic Buddha and Static Buddha.* Tokyo: Risōsha, 1958.

———. *The Mahāyāna Way to Buddhahood: Theology of Enlightenment.* Los Angeles: Buddhist Books International, 1982.

Yūki, Reimon. "The Construction of Fundamental Evil in Mahāyāna." In *Proceedings of the IXth International Congress for the History of Religions: Tokyo and Kyoto, 1958.* Tokyo: Maruzen, 1960.

Yuyama, Akira. Systematische Übericht über die buddhistische *Sanskrit-Literatur.* Erster Teil: *Vinaya-Texte.* Wiesbaden: Steiner, 1979.
Zürcher, Erik. "Amitābha." *Encyclopedia of Buddhism* 1:235–237.
———. *Buddhism: Its Origins and Spread in Words, Maps and Pictures.* New York: Routledge & Kegan Paul, 1962.
———. "Missions: Buddhist Missions." *Encyclopedia of Religion* 9:570–573.
Zwilling, Leonard. "Bhaiṣajyaguru and His Cult." In *Studies in the History of Buddhism,* edited by A. K. Narain, pp. 413–421. Delhi: B. R. Publishing, 1980.

INDEX

Abhayagiri-vihāra sect, 91, 115, 124-125, 133, 257
Abhidhammatthasaṅgaha, 135, 156, 161, 169, 198, 333-334
Abhidhammāvatāra, 161
Abhidharma (abhidhamma), 107, 139-169, 295, 333-338; as absolute and conventional truth, 146; commentarial literature on, 130, 133-138; meaning of, 127, 139, 142; selection of topics for, 139-142
Abhidharmadīpa, 137-138
Abhidharma-kathā (discussions of *abhidharma*), 139
Abhidharmakośa (*T* 1558-1559), 136-138, 141, 143-146, 149-150, 154-159, 170-184, 199-203, 208-217, 272, 333-337
Abhidharmakośaśāstrakārikāvibhāṣya, 137
Abhidharmāmṛtarasaśāstra (*T* 1553), 136, 333
Abhidharma-piṭaka, 127-133, 140, 142, 161, 334; of Sarvāstivāda, 131-132, 135, 333; of Theravāda, 129-131, 333, 334
Abhidharmāvatāraśāstra (*T* 1554), 197, 199, 333
Abhimukhī-bhūmi (facing wisdom), 281, 307, 309
Abhirati, 278-279, 290
Absorption of cessation *(nirodhasamāpatti),* 166, 213, 218
Absorption without perception *(asaṃjñisamāpatti),* 166, 218
Acalā-bhūmi (immovable), 308-309
Adaptability of mental faculties *(kāyakammaññatā),* 162
Adbhūtadharma (abbhūtadhamma), 75
Adhyardhaśatikā (*T* 220.10, 240-244), 277
Afghanistan, 228, 232, 234
Āgama, 38, 71-75, 147, 153, 161, 329; compared with Pāli texts, 74, 329
Agghikhandupamasutta, 87
Aggregates *(skandha),* 31, 43-44, 48, 53, 56, 140, 150, 152, 169, 176, 205-206, 334; existence of subtle *(ekarasa-skandha),* 164
Ahogaṅga, Mount, 81, 83, 90
Ajantā, 237, 240
Ajātaśatru, King, 35-36, 78, 250, 288
Ajātaśatrukaukṛtyavinodana (*T* 626-629), 248, 250-251, 281, 291-292, 297
Ajita, 35
Ajita Keśakambala, 16-17
Ājīvikas, 17, 35, 100, 325
Ājñātakauṇḍinya, 31
Akanuma Chizen, 74
Akolā, 236
Akṣobhya Buddha, 249, 251-252, 270, 278-279, 290, 341
Akṣobhyatathāgatasyavyūha (*T* 310.6, 313), 248-249, 278-279, 291
Alakadeva, 88
Āḷavī, 33
Alexander the Great, 78, 228
Aliyavasāṇi, 101
Amarapura Fraternity, 126
Amarāvatī, 241, 245, 332
Amitābha (Amitāyus), 4, 250, 259, 270, 278, 287-290, 341
Amoghavajra, 126
Āmrapālī, 36
Anāgata-bhayāni, 101
Analytical cessation *(pratisaṅkhyā-nirodha),* 145, 147-148, 169, 181, 212
Anamattagiyasutta, 87
Ānanda, 23, 33-34, 36, 83-87, 89, 93, 106, 111, 123, 292, 326; and rivalry with Mahākāśyapa, 85, 326
Andhaka schools, 114-116, 175
Andhakaṭṭhakathā, 133
Andher, 227

ABOUT THE AUTHOR

Hirakawa Akira is professor emeritus of Indian philosophy at Tokyo University. In 1983 he was elected president of the Japanese Association of Indian and Buddhist Studies, the most important academic organization for Buddhist studies in Japan. Hirakawa is the author or editor of over 20 books and 240 scholarly articles and reviews on Buddhism. He is currently directing the compilation of a Chinese-Sanskrit dictionary of Buddhist terms.

ABOUT THE TRANSLATOR

Paul Groner holds a doctorate in Buddhist studies from Yale University. He studied under Hirakawa Akira for several years in Japan and has worked with him on a number of projects. Professor Groner is on the faculty of the Department of Religious Studies at the University of Virginia. Among his publications is *Saichō: The Establishment of the Japanese Tendai School.*

ASIAN STUDIES AT HAWAII

No. 1 *Bibliography of English Language Sources on Human Ecology, Eastern Malaysia and Brunei.* Compiled by Conrad P. Cotter with the assistance of Shiro Saito. 1965. Two Parts. (Available only from Paragon Book Gallery, New York.)

No. 2 *Economic Factors in Southeast Asian Social Change.* Edited by Robert Van Niel. 1968. Out of print.

No. 3 *East Asian Occasional Papers (1).* Edited by Harry J. Lamley. 1969. Out of print.

No. 4 *East Asian Occasional Papers (2).* Edited by Harry J. Lamley. 1970.

No. 5 *A Survey of Historical Source Materials in Java and Manila.* Robert Van Niel. 1971.

No. 6 *Educational Theory in the People's Republic of China: The Report of Ch'ien Chung-Jui.* Translated by John N. Hawkins. 1971. Out of print.

No. 7 *Hai Jui Dismissed from Office.* Wu Han. Translated by C. C. Huang. 1972. Out of print.

No. 8 *Aspects of Vietnamese History.* Edited by Walter F. Vella. 1973. Out of print.

No. 9 *Southeast Asian Literatures in Translation: A Preliminary Bibliography.* Philip N. Jenner. 1973. Out of print.

No. 10 *Textiles of the Indonesian Archipelago.* Garrett and Bronwen Solyom. 1973. Out of print.

No. 11 *British Policy and the Nationalist Movement in Burma, 1917–1937.* Albert D. Moscotti, 1974. Out of print.

No. 12 *Aspects of Bengali History and Society.* Edited by Rachel Van M. Baumer. 1975.

No. 13 *Nanyang Perspective: Chinese Students in Multiracial Singapore.* Andrew W. Lind. 1974.

No. 14 *Political Change in the Philippines: Studies of Local Politics preceding Martial Law.* Edited by Benedict J. Kerkvliet. 1974. Out of print.

No. 15 *Essays on South India.* Edited by Burton Stein. 1976.

No. 16 *The* Caurāsī Pad *of Śrī Hit Harivaṁś.* Charles S. J. White. 1977.

No. 17 *An American Teacher in Early Meiji Japan.* Edward R. Beauchamp. 1976. Out of print.

No. 18 *Buddhist and Taoist Studies I.* Edited by Michael Saso and David W. Chappell. 1977.

No. 19 *Sumatran Contributions of the Development of Indonesian Literature, 1920–1942.* Alberta Joy Freidus. 1977.

No. 20 *Insulinde: Selected Translations from Dutch Writers of Three Centuries on the Indonesian Archipelago.* Edited by Cornelia N. Moore. 1978.

No. 21 *Regents, Reformers, and Revolutionaries: Indonesian Voices of Colonial Days, Selected Historical Readings, 1899–1949.* Translated, edited, and annotated by Greta O. Wilson. 1978.

No. 22 *The Politics of Inequality: Competition and Control in an Indian Village.* Miriam Sharma. 1978.

No. 23 *Brokers of Morality: Thai Ethnic Adaptation in a Rural Malaysian Setting.* Louis Golomb. 1979. Out of print.

No. 24 *Tales of Japanese Justice.* Ihara Saikaku. Translated by Thomas M. Kondo and Alfred H. Marks. 1980. Out of print.

No. 25 *Mandarins, Gunboats, and Power Politics: Owen Nickerson Denny and the International Rivalries in Korea.* Robert R. Swartout, Jr. 1980.

No. 26 *Nichiren: Selected Writings.* Laurel Rasplica Rodd. 1980. Out of print.

No. 27 *Ethnic Groups and Social Change in a Chinese Market Town.* C. Fred Blake. 1980.

No. 28 *The Evolution of Hindu Ethical Ideals.* S. Cromwell Crawford. 1982. Out of print.

No. 29 *Experimental Essays on Chuang-tzu.* Edited by Victor H. Mair. 1983.

No. 30 *Songs of Nepal.* Siegfried Lienhard. 1984.

No. 31 *The Origins of Japan's Modern Forests: The Case of Akita.* Conrad Totman. 1985.

No. 32 *Thailand in Transition: The Role of Oppositional Forces.* Ross Prizzia. 1985.

No. 33 *Law and the State in Traditional East Asia: Six Studies on the Sources of East Asian Law.* Edited by Brian E. McKnight. 1987.

No. 34 *Buddhist and Taoist Practice in Medieval Chinese Society: Buddhist and Taoist Studies II.* Edited by David W. Chappell. 1987.

No. 35 *An American Scientist in Early Meiji Japan: The Autobiographical Notes of Thomas C. Mendenhall.* Edited by Richard Rubinger. 1989.

No. 36 *A History of Indian Buddhism: From Śākyamuni to Early Mahāyāna.* Hirakawa Akira. Translated and edited by Paul Groner. 1990.

No. 37 *Ilocano Irrigation: The Corporate Resolution.* Henry T. Lewis. 1991.

No. 38 *The Cavern-Mystery Transmission: A Taoist Ordination Rite of A.D. 711.* Charles D. Benn. 1991.

No. 39 *The Shanghai Taotai: Linkage Man in a Changing Society, 1843–90.* Leung Yuen-sang. 1990.

Orders for Asian Studies at Hawaii publications should be directed to the University of Hawaii Press, Order Department, 2840 Kolowalu Street, Honolulu, Hawaii 96822. Present standing orders will continue to be filled without special notification.